Torrance at his desk, reading E.H. Hutten, *The Ideas of Physics*

H.R.H. the Duke of Edinburgh presenting the Templeton Prize
to T.F. Torrance on 21st March 1978 at Buckingham Palace

ATONEMENT

The Person and Work of Christ

Thomas F. Torrance

Edited by

Robert T. Walker

Paternoster:
thinking faith

Milton Keynes • Colorado Springs • Hyderabad

IVP Academic

An imprint of InterVarsity Press
Downers Grove, Illinois

First published 2009 by Paternoster in the UK
First published 2009 by InterVarsity Press in the USA

Paternoster is an imprint of Authentic Media
9 Holdom Avenue, Bletchley, Milton Keynes, Bucks, MK1 1QR, UK
1820 Jet Stream Drive, Colorado Springs, CO 80921, USA
Medchal Road, Jeedimetla Village, Secunderabad 500 055, A.P., India
www.loveauthentic.com

Authentic Media is a division of Biblica UK, previously IBS-STL UK,
Biblica UK is limited by guarantee, with its registered office at
Kingstown Broadway, Carlisle, Cumbria CA3 0HA. Registered
in England & Wales No. 1216232. Registered charity in
England & Wales No. 270162 and Scotland No. SCO40064.

InterVarsity Press, PO Box 1400, Downers Grove, IL 60515, USA

World Wide Web: www.ivpress.com
E-mail: mail@ivpress.com

British Library Cataloguing in Publication Data
A catalogue record for this book is available from the British Library
UK ISBN: 978-1-84227-668-6

Library of Congress Cataloging-in-Publication Data
A catalog record for this book is available from the US Library of Congress
US ISBN: 978-0-8308-2892-0

Scripture quotations are taken from the King James Version or the Revised
Standard Version of the Bible, or are the author's own translation.

U.K. Cover Design by J.G. Tordai / Panos Pictures
U.S. Cover Design by Cindy Kiple

Indexed and Typeset in 11pt Palatino by the
HANDSEL PRESS
EDINBURGH

Printed in the United States of America

CONTENTS

The help of the Hope Trust, 32 Moray Place, Edinburgh, and
the Drummond Trust, 3 Pitt Terrace, Stirling
is gratefully acknowledged

Thanks are expressed also to the Templeton Foundation,
to Life and Work, and to Dr Thomas S. Torrance for
permission to reproduce the photos at the front of
this volume 2, and to the Revd Alex Slorach for
one of the photos used in volume 1

PREFACE by Thomas S. Torrance

This book on Atonement is a companion volume to that on Incarnation published in the autumn of 2008. As was the case with the earlier volume, my late father Thomas Forsyth Torrance had planned to publish this work earlier in the present decade but had been prevented from completing the necessary editing work by the stroke he suffered in January 2003. And as with the former volume, the task of preparing the underlying material for publication has been expertly undertaken by my cousin Robert Torrance Walker. The final outcome, I feel sure, corresponds exactly with what my father had initially intended to offer for publication. A good part of the content of this volume originated in ideas presented in lectures my father delivered, in evolving form, up to his retirement from New College, University of Edinburgh, at the end of the 1978-79 Academic Session. I am delighted that the theological discussions in the present volume can now be available more widely, and extremely grateful to Robert for his unwavering dedication over a long period to securing this end.

Department of Economics
Heriot-Watt University
Edinburgh, May 2009

SYNOPSIS

(iii) The person of Christ is the key to understanding the relation of the Word to the written word
  (1) The parallels between the hypostatic union of God and man and of the Word with the written word
  (2) The differences between God in Christ and the Word in the written word
    Torrance's doctrine of scripture is deeply Christological
    The significance of Jesus Christ as Word of God to man become obedient human word
    A doctrine of scripture must be patterned on and reflect the uniqueness of the person of Christ

(e) Reconciliation is objective and subjective

Atonement must be worked into the mind and heart of man, defeating sin from within

God's personal forgiveness and creation of joint knowing between man and himself

The reconciliation achieved in the person of Christ is at once objective and subjective

(i) The restoration of the human mind to truth with God

The breach between humanity's idea of God and the truth of God - the grasping of a lie

The renewal of the human mind from within and below through the incarnation

(ii) Reconciliation involves subjective as well as objective union with God – *'noetic'* and *'ontic'* union

The 'noetic' relation between God and man in Christ was twofold

The realising of oneness of mind and heart between man and God in the life of Jesus

The hypostatic union brought to fulfilment in the final oneness on the cross

(iii) A comparison with Socrates: Jesus died to achieve union between truth and being

The establishment of the human mind on the truth of God and the humanising of man

(f) Reconciliation means 'Immanuel', God with us

(i) Reconciliation is not automatic but always personal in its encounter with us

(ii) God with us means we with God, our adoption into the communion of the divine life

The assurance of God with us – the dawning already of the kingdom and its fellowship

(g) Reconciliation is cosmic

(i) The whole creation is involved in reconciliation – a cosmic peace

(ii) Reconciliation is identical with the living person of Christ

The cross and its reconciliation are the ultimate secret of human history

Chapter Six

(b) The church lives in two times, the time of this passing world and the time of the new creation
> The church is sent as a servant to live the life of the new creation within the old

(i) The language of apocalyptic, the new seen through the language of the old
> As the old man perishes day by day, so the new man is renewed day by day

(ii) The millennium time of the already inaugurated kingdom
> Millennium time is hidden from sight, but seen by faith and present in the eucharist

(iii) The need to think christologically, to hold together the two times
> The concept of a 1000 year earthly reign fails to recognise the majesty of the risen Christ

(c) The church lives 'between the times' – between resurrection and final advent

(d) As in the days of his earthly life Jesus waits for the 'hour' of final consummation
> The church is commanded to lift up its head in joy, for its 'redemption is drawing near'

(a) 'Spiritual body' means more body and not less body

(b) The reality of Christ's resurrection body can only be discerned through the Spirit
> The sacraments are the pledges of participation in Christ's risen humanity

Chapter Ten

(a) The apostolic tradition is given permanent form in the New Testament

  Apostolic scripture is so conjoined to the divine Word as to be the written word of God to man

  The New Testament acknowledged as the authentic apostolic tradition

(b) The relation between the Word made flesh and the written word

 (i) The relation of the written word to the living Word is like that of the flesh to the incarnate Word

 (ii) The relation of the written word to the living Word is unlike that of the flesh to the incarnate Word

  The sacramental and eschatological relation between the written and the incarnate Word – election and judgement

  The sacramental participation of scripture in the whole divine-human Word of Christ

 (iii) The communication of properties between the written and the incarnate Word

  The guiding analogy of the relation between the divine and human natures of Christ

 (iv) The basic text is the obedient humanity of Jesus Christ

  The New Testament is the inspired secondary text

Chapter Eleven

  The church is grounded and rooted in the eternal purpose of God in Christ

  The three forms of the church: preparatory, new in Christ and eternal in the new creation

  The mission of the church to proclaim by word and life the reconciling love of God

  The earthly beginning of the church in Adam

  The calling of the church with Abraham and its establishment at Sinai

  Israel constituted as prophet of God bearing his oracles and the promise of the Messiah

  Israel the preparatory form of the church waiting for fulfilment

(a) Israel the chosen people of God

(b) Israel the servant of the Lord

(c) Israel the bearer of the Messiah

  The transition to the new covenant only through the death and resurrection of the Messiah

  The Christian church now grafted on to Israel and part of the race of Abraham

EDITOR'S INTRODUCTION

In these very readable and accessible lectures T.F. Torrance continues from the point he had reached in *Incarnation* at the approach to the cross. In *Atonement* he begins with the meaning of the cross and with thorough biblical-theological interpretation takes us through the great New Testament themes: atonement, reconciliation, redemption, resurrection, ascension, sending of the Spirit, apostolic foundation of the church, high-priesthood and heavenly reign of Christ, doctrine of the church and its mission, the final coming of Christ. At every point Torrance sees the inter-connectedness of all Christian doctrine and brings out the full significance of the great events of Jesus' life from the cross to Pentecost. These lectures demonstrate the full impact and importance for the church of the doctrine of the person of Jesus Christ portrayed in *Incarnation*. Rich in biblical depth and theological penetration the lectures are moving, challenging and indeed thrilling in the freshness of their approach and overriding sense of the fullness of the love of God in Christ that reaches out through the Spirit to the final redemption of all creation.

The purpose of the introduction

The purpose is:

(a) to explain the relation of *Atonement* to *Incarnation* and of the work and person of Jesus Christ

(b) to summarise the theology of these lectures on atonement and outline their leading themes

(c) to select and outline major points of challenge and fruitfulness in Torrance's theology.

Readers are referred to the introduction to *Incarnation* for an account of the nature and purpose of the Torrance dogmatics lectures, the leading features of their theology in general, and an explanation of the text of the lectures and the process of editing them.

Since this introduction as a summary of Torrance's theology of Christ's person and work is rather full, there are two ways in which readers may wish to use it. They can read through it for a general overview, and they can also read each section before reading the relevant chapter(s) in the lectures.

A The relation between *Incarnation* and *Atonement*: Christology and Soteriology

Atonement is the sequel to *Incarnation*, where the theme is *the person and life of Jesus Christ*, with the emphasis falling upon *who* Jesus is and the way that determines the significance of his life. In *Atonement* the theme is *the person and work of Jesus Christ*, with the emphasis falling upon his *work* of salvation understood in the light of who he is. Together the two books comprise T.F. Torrance's lectures at New College, Edinburgh on the doctrine of Jesus Christ.

The concept of the person of Christ and of salvation in his person

The concept of the person of Christ is central to Christian theology, just as the phrase 'in Christ' is to the New Testament. The person of Christ is the whole reality of his person, the fact that in his person he is the eternal Son of God and yet also son of man. His person as son of man, as a human person, is not different from his person as the Son of God. The reality of his human person as Jesus is therefore not to be understood as a second person, in addition to his person as eternal Son. As human person his reality is not to be found *apart from*, but *in* his reality as the person of the Son. It is *in* the person of the Son that he is also a fully individual human person.

This is the New Testament 'mystery of Christ' explored in *Incarnation*, the reality of the whole Christ known to faith, the miracle of the incarnation, that the Son of God is now man. In his person he is true God and true man, bearing in his person all the riches of God for us and at the same time all the riches of true humanity. In him are hid all the treasures of wisdom and knowledge and he is our righteousness, sanctification and redemption, to use biblical language. His humanity, his flesh and blood to use the language of John 6, is the bread of life. In his person, in his one person, there are contained all the treasures of salvation – in him, inside his person and never outside it. Jesus Christ is and contains our salvation in himself, in his person, but as Calvin argued this is no use to us as long he remains outside of us, in a manner distant from us until we are united to him through faith, incorporated into him by the Spirit. Our salvation is and remains 'in Christ', to use the oft-repeated and pivotal Pauline phrase, and becomes accessible to us only through union with him through the Spirit.

Our salvation is in the person of Christ, but the person of Christ includes in itself all that he has done for us and worked out in his life, death, resurrection and ascension. Hence the person of Christ properly understood includes within itself what he has done and the whole

Christ is his person and everything which he has achieved for our salvation in the human nature which he wears for us.

Christology and Soteriology, person and work not to be separated

In Christian theology the doctrine of Christ has traditionally been thought of in terms of his person and his work, with the doctrine of the person of Christ, who he is, being known as 'Christology' and the doctrine of the work of Christ, what he did, being known as 'Soteriology'. Together Christology and Soteriology make up the doctrine of Jesus Christ and in the nature of the case the two belong together and are not to be understood apart from each other. Christology may be thought of as the doctrine of *the person of Christ in his work* and Soteriology as the doctrine of *the work of Christ in his person.*

One whole Christ from birth to ascension and a contrast of emphases in Christology and Soteriology

There is another difference between the two. Although Jesus Christ is one whole Christ comprising person and work from birth to ascension, the emphasis in Christology falls on the incarnation since that was the event in which the eternal Son became the man Jesus and lived out his life on earth. The nature of the becoming man and the nature and significance of the person of Jesus in his life and work are central. In Soteriology the emphasis falls more on the death, resurrection and ascension of Jesus and his sending of the Spirit, since those are the climactic events in which he achieved salvation for humankind.

A further point of contrast between Christology and Soteriology is that in Christology the focus falls naturally on the incarnation as the *beginning* of salvation, while in Soteriology the focus falls on the events at the end of Jesus' life as its *completion.* In both person and work are involved, for the incarnation as God becoming man is already God in the person of Christ acting for our salvation. It is the eternal Son assuming human nature into unity with his own person and this is already the beginning of the sanctification of man and the elevation of humanity in Jesus into fellowship with God.

The hypostatic union is the heart of both Christology and Soteriology

For Torrance, the 'hypostatic union', the union of God and man in the *hypostasis* or person of the Son, is the heart of salvation and its unbreakable linchpin. He who is the eternal Son of God, of one being with the Father, is he who is now also man and the fact that the same person who is fully and truly God is now fully and truly man, means that his person is and constitutes in itself (or in himself) the union of God and humanity. The same person stands on the side of God and on the side of humanity. The same person is at once God and man. In his one person, therefore, God and man, God and all humanity, are now irrevocably and eternally united. God and man can now no more be separated from one another in Christ than the person of Christ can be undone, or the incarnation, crucifixion and resurrection be reversed.

The hypostatic union is one dynamic event from incarnation to ascension

For Torrance it is also important that the hypostatic union can only be understood dynamically. The union of God and man in the person of Jesus Christ, while magnificently and truly articulated as 'two natures in one person' at the Council of Chalcedon of 451 AD, is not to be interpreted statically. It is event, a becoming, the action of God in beginning and continuing to be a human being. The action of God in becoming man begins with seedless conception and slow embryonic growth in the womb of Mary. It continues with birth at Bethlehem and the gradual growth of Jesus in wisdom and stature to adulthood. Then throughout the life of Jesus the union of God and man in him is maintained and worked out in the teeth of temptation and all the assaults of evil which attempt to tear it apart, to divide Jesus' humanity from his deity, tempting him to use his power as God to escape from being man. Holding firm in Jesus' life, the hypostatic union is steadfastly carried forward to the cross and maintained under the full judgement of God on our sin and the final assault of evil on his person, and so it emerges triumphant, unscathed and complete in the resurrection and ascension of Jesus.

The hypostatic union is ongoing event worked out through death into new creation

The hypostatic union is thus to be understood as an ongoing event, which had its beginning in Mary and at Bethlehem, but had to grow and be worked out and maintained throughout the life of Jesus. It had to achieve its end of gathering sinners into solidarity with himself and then of bearing their sin and dying for them in lonely substitution and representation on the cross. Under the judgement of God, in which he the judge took his own divine judgement into his human heart and bore it, he maintained faith in God and kept his hypostatic union firm, so that it emerged as enduring reality in the new creation on the other side of death.

Soteriology as Christology worked out, person and work as one whole Christ

It can thus be seen that Soteriology is Christology worked out in the life of Jesus. The Son of God became son of man in order as God and as man to achieve salvation for us in his own person and humanity. A person is living person, acting person, living event in history, and therefore person is not simply bare person but action and work also, person in work and in action. As living person, Jesus in his life is the working out of our salvation in his own person and human life. Person is the person doing the work and the work becomes and is part of his person. The person is the union of God and man, and the work is the working out and living out of that union down into death and up into resurrection where it becomes eternally living event. In the nature of the case, therefore Christology and Soteriology, the person and the work of Christ cannot be separated. Christology issues in Soteriology and the hypostatic union is not the union of two static natures in one person, but living person who is God acting and man acting, one person performing the work of salvation. Together, person and work make up the one whole Jesus Christ. Christology becomes clothed with Soteriology, just as 'Jesus is clothed with his gospel' (to use the language quoted by Torrance from Calvin), and Soteriology has its meaning and dynamic in the person of its agent. The argument of *Atonement* flows uninterruptedly out of the argument of *Incarnation*.

B The leading themes of Torrance's Soteriology

Since the leading features of Torrance's theology have already been summarised in the introduction to *Incarnation*, the purpose here will be to focus on the themes which are more specific to Soteriology and to outline the central structure of the argument as a guide to understanding the whole.

The approach to the atonement

The mystery of atonement – we can only start from the decisive new act of God in Christ

As he approaches the atonement and the cross as presented in the New Testament, Torrance is aware from the outset that the meaning of the cross of Jesus Christ is one that we cannot penetrate by human reason or by any theories of atonement as such. There is no logical relation between the death of Jesus at Calvary and the forgiveness of our sins. The infinite and holy mystery of the cross is one in which in the passion and death of Christ on the cross God has intervened decisively on our behalf to establish our lives on an entirely new basis. We can only begin from the new basis, from the fact that it has come about in the death and resurrection of Jesus and we can only follow him in what he has accomplished for us. For Torrance we cannot think our way *into* the cross of Christ but only *out from* it. We may understand it only from the resurrection side of it, by *metanoia*, by repentance and change of mind, by following Christ and thinking our way *from* it. The infinite mystery of atonement is something which he has accomplished within his own person and act and which transcends any merely rational explanation and outstrips any Old Testament prefiguration.

The Old Testament the essential preparation to understanding the atonement in Jesus

Even though the person and act of Jesus far transcends it, the Old Testament prefiguration is the indispensable preparation to understanding what happened in him. Without the long training by God of Israel in the necessary concepts and categories of thought, we could not even begin to understand the mystery of atonement in his person. New Testament images, metaphors, ways of thinking and language are all based in and drawn from the Old Testament and therefore Torrance begins his account with tracing the roots of New Testament language and thought in the Old. The death of Jesus as a ransom and sacrifice is the fulfilment of the covenant and of Old Testament sacrifice, at once of the day of atonement and of the passover in a new covenant and covenant meal. The eternal priesthood of Jesus, for which he was consecrated on earth and continues in heaven, is the fulfilment of the full Old Testament concept of priesthood, of the priesthood of Moses and the priesthood of Aaron, the priesthood of the word and the priesthood of obedient witness, the act of God and the act of man.

The atonement is ultimately inconceivable outside the person and act of Jesus

What Jesus accomplished within his own person could not have been foreseen or imagined in advance. It was inconceivable that here in this living self-offering made once for all Jesus should do what all the Old Testament acts of sacrifice were unable to accomplish, let alone that it should be God himself making atonement, God acting from the side of God and from the side of man, as Judge and judged, priest and sacrifice in one. The person of Jesus Christ the mediator holds together in a living synthesis in himself all the Old Testament images and prefigurings of atonement. In the unity of his person and work atonement is something which Jesus Christ has done and which cannot be imagined outside his person and act. Obedient Christian theology therefore can only follow Christ in his word and act, in his word and deed, knowing him to be the reality we seek to understand, a reality which was not there until he did it, which was inconceivable until he did it and which no-one but he could have done.

Concepts of atonement transformed and held together in Christ

Torrance's approach to the doctrine of the atonement is one in which he begins each chapter with careful biblical interpretation and spends time examining the meaning and context of biblical words, particularly of New Testament words and concepts in the light of their Old Testament foundation and background. Critical though the Old Testament is for understanding atonement in the New, it is the person and work of Jesus which are all-determinative for establishing its meaning, since what he said and did gives new meaning to the Old Testament concepts. Torrance takes two sayings of Jesus, 'This is the new covenant in my blood' and 'The son of man came not to be served but to serve and to give his life as a ransom for many' and uses them to structure his opening account. From his six chapters on the atonement, the following points may be highlighted as central and outlining the heart of his teaching.

1 The theology of the atonement

(a) Atonement is the fulfilment of the covenant: the significance of Christ as God and man

Throughout his theology Torrance emphasises the significance of Jesus Christ as God and man in one person. In everything he does, Jesus is the act of God and the act of man, the act of God as man in the one person of Christ. In him therefore and his atonement, the covenant with Israel (and in and through them with all peoples) comes to fruition in ultimate and final fulfilment, both from the side of God and of the people. In him God establishes himself as the God of his people, dwelling literally in their midst, taking them to himself by taking their sin on himself and atoning for it, while at the same time he acts from their side, in obedient amen to the covenant, in obedient acceptance of the judgement and discipline of the covenant and in obediently fulfilling the covenant in his own life and heart on behalf of the people. It is only through atonement that the fulfilment of the covenant and its universalisation can take place, for only through the ultimate judging of sin and the putting of it away through the agony and passion of Jesus in his life and death, can the people and all peoples be cleansed of their sin and made the people of God.

The place of the sacraments in expressing better than words the meaning of atonement

For Torrance, the sacraments are given to us to express more fully than words ever can the mystery of the atonement and of our incorporation into Christ. In baptism, we are incorporated into Christ's baptism completed on the cross, baptised into his death and united with him in his resurrection. In holy communion, we are given the sacrament of his passion so that in its celebration we may show forth his death until he comes again and as we eat the bread and drink the cup have communion with him through his body and blood shed on the cross. As Torrance says, 'That is the meaning of the atonement which the sacrament expresses better than words.' The importance of the sacraments for the nourishment of faith and for the eschatological perspective embedded in them is seen in the number of times Torrance refers to them.

(b) The life of Christ a ransom, poured out on the cross for the redemption of the many

In giving his life as a ransom in redemption of the many, Jesus fulfils in himself the Old Testament concepts of redemption. Torrance examines the New Testament words for redemption, paying particular attention to which Hebrew words are translated by which Greek words in the Greek Old Testament and which therefore lie behind and inform their meaning in the New Testament. Behind redemption in the New Testament Torrance finds the threefold Hebrew root *padah*, *kipper* and *gaal*, three verbs each describing a different aspect of redemption but overlapping in meaning:

(i) *padah*, redeem, ransom, refers to a mighty act of God in deliverance of his people out of bondage and oppression into liberty, as in the redemption of Israel out of Egypt.

(ii) *kipper*, redeem, ransom, refers to God's covering of sin through the provision of an equivalent and is the word regularly used in the Old Testament for atoning for sin.

(iii) *gaal*, redeem, refers to redemption out of slavery or bankruptcy by someone with a kinship in blood or a sharing in common property. The noun *go'el* refers to the person of the redeemer, the 'kinsman-redeemer' as they are known in translation.

The distinction in meaning is not always maintained in the Old Testament and sometimes the words can be used more or less interchangeably, but together they help constitute the rich concept of redemption in the New Testament where all three are interwoven in the person and life of Jesus. Atonement and redemption in the New Testament is the mighty act of deliverance out of sin, guilt and the powers of evil into the liberty of the kingdom through the covering of sin in sacrifice by someone sharing kinship in flesh and blood with those redeemed. In Jesus it is God himself who redeems his people, not only as God but in virtue of his being *go'el*, their kinsman through incarnation.

(c) The priesthood of Jesus Christ and the letter to the Hebrews

In his chapter on the priesthood of Christ Torrance focuses on the letter to the Hebrews, pointing out the close parallels between the teaching of Hebrews and that of Paul on law and justification. Torrance's analysis of the nature of priesthood in the Old Testament and of Jesus' priesthood in the New is one of his most distinctive and important doctrines. There are at least four major points:

(i) all priesthood in the bible is from God, is his initiative and is by his appointment. Although the priest represents the people, the priest is appointed by God to represent them and not by the people themselves. The whole initiative and movement comes from God. There is no concept of man acting on God, let alone of man trying to appease God by sacrifice. It is God who forgives, who wills to forgive and who takes the initiative in forgiveness.

(ii) although again and again in the bible the priesthood forsake their true function, the priest is primarily to be thought of as mediator of the word of God, teacher of it and witness to it. The basic concept of priesthood is represented by Moses and Aaron together and in that sense may be said to be a double priesthood, with Moses as the 'logos' priest, or priest of the word, and Aaron as the liturgical priest, the one who witnesses to the word of God and acts only on its basis and in obedience to it. Moses' priesthood is primary: his function is to mediate the word of God to the people, he receives the word of God and takes it to the people. In obedience to it he ordains Aaron as the liturgical priest, to act in witness to the word and at God's appointment to act in liturgical witness to God's will to forgive through the provision of sacrifice. While the priest in the Old Testament is said to 'make atonement', that is by way of obedience to the provision of God for forgiveness within the covenant and is not to be thought of as an acting on God.

(iii) just as the high priest on the day of atonement represented all Israel, symbolised by his wearing the names of the 12 tribes on his shoulders and breastplate, so Christ in his life, death, and resurrection represents all humanity, the one for the many. Just as Christ assumed the human nature of all humanity in the incarnation, so in his death he died for all – 'one died for all; therefore all have died' (2 Cor 5.14). For Torrance, the range of representation is the same in the incarnation and the atonement - incarnation and atonement are integral to each other and whoever Christ represents in one he represents in both.

(iv) while Jesus' priesthood begins on earth it becomes eternal in the resurrection. He is 'the priest of the resurrection' who by the power of his resurrection life ever lives to intercede for his people. The heavenly priesthood of Christ, much neglected in theology and the church in general, is one of the major emphases of Torrance. It is the continuing priesthood of Christ, his presentation before the Father in heaven of his once and for all self-offering on the cross, which is our only offering to God. We are accepted in his offering, in his prayer and his is the faith we present before the face of the Father as our own. Jesus is not only the God *whom* we worship and the mediator *through whom* we worship, but the one *with whom* we worship, who as man offers perfect faith and worship and who is 'the pioneer and perfecter of our faith' and the leader of our worship.

(d) Atonement as justification, reconciliation and redemption in the teaching of Paul

In successive chapters Torrance looks at the Pauline concept of atonement as justification, as reconciliation and as redemption:

(i) in justification the emphasis is on righteousness in terms of the law and on freedom from the bondage of the law in the complete fulfilment of law and of judgement in the atoning death and resurrection of Christ.

(ii) in reconciliation the emphasis is on the personal element of restoration to fellowship and peace with God through the overcoming of the enmity and obstacle of sin in the wonderful exchange achieved by Christ for us in his humanity.

(iii) in redemption the emphasis is on the mighty act of redemption in Christ, completed in the pouring out of the Spirit and reaching out to the final redemption of the body and of the whole universe in the new creation.

Although Torrance's three chapters deal with different aspects of atonement in Paul, they overlap and share common themes in different ways. The following points are central to Torrance's understanding of Paul and fundamental to his own theology.

(i) Justification, reconciliation and redemption are complete in the person and work of Christ

Throughout his theology, Torrance emphasises that the person and work of Jesus Christ cannot be separated. Salvation is in him, inside his person which cannot be separated from his work. The work of salvation is the act of his person, the decisive act of God in history accomplishing our justification, reconciliation and redemption in his person. This means that justification, for example, or reconciliation, cannot be thought of simply as a work accomplished by Christ, as something which he did to fulfil the law. It is a work, but it is a work which is essentially the work of his person, which is inseparable from his person and is to be found only within his person, in the inseparable unity of his person and work.

(ii) Justification, reconciliation and redemption are the act of God and man in Christ

Again throughout his theology, Torrance emphasises that in Jesus Christ we have the act of God and of man, of God as man in his one person. Justification, reconciliation and redemption therefore must be thought of not simply as the act of God for our salvation, but also as the real act of man, of God as man for us. The importance of this for Torrance's theology and for understanding it cannot be overstated. Justification is not simply the act of God judging sin, atoning for it himself and declaring us righteous in his beloved Son, it is man saying amen to the righteous judgement of God and at the same time fulfilling all righteousness in his own perfect life and humanity. Reconciliation is thus not simply God reconciling the world to himself in Christ, but reconciliation worked out, achieved and realised by Christ as man within his own person, in his own mind, life, heart and soul. Redemption is the mighty act of God in which mankind is liberated from bondage and decay into the new creation through the resurrection of the man Jesus Christ from the dead in the fullness of physical existence.

(iii) Justification, reconciliation and redemption can only take place through the complete assertion of the truth of God and the complete fulfilment of the law

Torrance stresses that atonement can only take place through the complete assertion of the truth and righteousness of God against sin and evil. Justification of the ungodly therefore does not mean that there is any lessening of judgement or overlooking of sin but the contrary. There can only be forgiveness through the naming of sin as sin and its designation as untruth by the truth of God. Any mitigation of judgement would mean that God had not really opposed sin and that sin had not been confronted to the full and dealt with. The very Godness of God, the steadfast love, truth and rightness of God, means his direct opposition to the lie of sin and if God did not judge sin to the full he would 'unGod himself' as Torrance puts it.

The mystery and miracle of atonement in Christ is that there is at once total and utter opposition to sin and at the same time its complete forgiveness, at once the maintenance of the righteousness of God and the justification of the ungodly, without any bypassing or belittling of judgement but the opposite. Forgiveness takes place only in and through total judgement, the judgement of the holy love of God. For Torrance, it is because forgiveness does not take place apart from judgement but only through it, that we know it is real and total. It is because the voice of forgiveness and of judgement are the same, because it is the same voice which judges us which also forgives us, that is what tells us and that is why we know we are really and truly forgiven. On the cross, the voice of judgement and forgiveness are the same voice, the voice of total judgement and the voice of total forgiveness. In the passion of Christ on the cross it is one and the same voice, and one identical with the voice of the Father.

(iv) Justification, reconciliation and redemption are the liberation of humanity from the abstract legal and ethical order into direct personal relation with God

One of the most interesting and significant elements of Torrance's theology is his understanding of the nature of sin, law and the moral order. In its very nature sin is not only rebellion but deception. As alienation from life in God and the truth of God, human sin is a fall into corruption, chaos and decay where man can no longer know or perceive the truth of God as he is. In that situation God gives humanity the law to order human life and restrain chaos from overwhelming it and in order to reveal something of his holy will for them. The law is holy and given by God and yet in the nature of the case it is abstract and can only reinforce the distance between man and God. It is only given in the situation where humanity no longer knows God, where there is a gap between the 'is' and the 'ought', between what people are and what they ought to be. In that situation where human beings are *not* what they ought to be, law can only reinforce the fact that they are not what they should be. No amount of trying to keep the law can bridge the essential gap between the 'is' and the 'ought' and can result only in external conformity to the law, for the human heart and mind remains unchanged in alienation from God in its very roots.

In fact as Paul saw, even though it is holy and given by God the law becomes 'the strength of sin'. It is used by the powers of evil not only to accuse the sinner but as an abstract shield for the sinner to hide behind from the presence of God, yielding only an outward conformity to the law and enabling the sinner to claim a self-righteousness while withholding from God the obedience of the heart. In Jesus Christ, as Torrance sees clearly, God steps out from behind the law and meets us personally and face to face in him. Justification is 'under the law' but 'apart from law' in the language of Paul. While given by God, the whole legal and moral order is only of interim validity, for in justification and reconciliation it is fulfilled but at the same time transcended in direct and personal relations between God and the human person.

(v) Atonement as justification, reconciliation and redemption is completed and actualised in the church through the sending of the Spirit

For Torrance, the sending of the Spirit is the completion of the atonement, for with the coming of the Spirit the atonement is actualised in the disciples. Through the Spirit the atonement which is already complete in the person of Christ is actualised in the church as through union with him it begins to partake of everything that he is for them. The justification, reconciliation and redemption which was worked out in the person of Jesus and finalised for us in his risen humanity now begins to be worked out in us through our incorporation into him.

(vi) Justification, reconciliation and redemption which are essentially corporate in Christ reach out to the whole of creation in a cosmic peace

For Torrance the far reaching effects of atonement in Christ reach out in two ways. They reach backwards through the undoing of sin and guilt to re-establish contact with creation, making the past to serve the purpose of redemption, and they reach forward through the Spirit to the unveiling of the full reality of Christ and the establishment of a vast cosmic peace. Redemption in Christ, which is essentially corporate in him involving solidarity with the whole body of humanity for which he died, means reconciliation with the very fabric of the universe and a reconciliation which must reach out through the gospel to the whole of creation and the ends of the universe.

2 The resurrection and ascension of Jesus and his sending of the Spirit

The resurrection of Jesus from the dead and his ascension into heaven are two of the mighty events of his life and an integral part of his whole salvation. His resurrection and ascension mean the justification and forgiveness of humanity and the lifting up of man into participation in the life and love of the holy Trinity.

(a) *The resurrection of Jesus Christ*

(i) *The resurrection is the mighty act of God in the person of Christ defeating death*

The resurrection of Jesus Christ is not simply the raising of someone from the dead but the mighty act of God in his person undoing death itself in a new creation. In his risen humanity, Jesus is 'the firstborn from the dead' and the 'first fruits' of the new creation. In his incarnation Jesus became a human being of flesh and blood. In his resurrection he rises in the same body, but one which is no longer subject to the disintegrating processes of death and which has been transformed into 'glorious body', freed from corruption and decay. That is an almighty creative act, comparable in significance to creation itself, and one in which the whole of creation will follow and for which it is waiting and groaning in expectation and hope.

(ii) *The resurrection is the fulfilment of the incarnation and atonement*

The resurrection of Jesus in the body shows that when God became man in him that was not a temporary episode, merely for the time he lived on earth. It also shows that Jesus had realised in the body, in the actual physical and space-time existence of human life, the salvation he had come to accomplish for humanity. The resurrection demonstrates that the hypostatic union of true God and true man in the person of Christ had held firm through death and hell until it had been fulfilled and established as a permanent reality in the new creation. The resurrection thus demonstrates the fulfilment and permanence of the incarnation.

There is an inseparable relation here between the resurrection, atonement and the incarnation. Just as the incarnation is fulfilled in the atonement, so the atonement is realised in the resurrection. Just as the hypostatic union of God and man in the incarnation is worked out in the life of Jesus and fulfilled in his person in his reconciliation of God and man in atonement, so the resurrection is the fulfilment of justification and the actualisation of the forgiveness of the atonement. The undoing of sin in atonement means the undoing of death which is its natural consequence and therefore forgiveness in the bible means the overcoming of death. If death is not actually overcome then the act of forgiveness has not ultimately touched sin at its very root and undone it. Thus as Paul saw, the bodily resurrection of Jesus is critical to the gospel, 'If Christ has not been raised, your faith is futile and you are still in your sins.'

The resurrection is the fulfilment of justification and without it justification is empty

Similarly, the resurrection is the fulfilment of justification. The resurrection of Jesus in his human nature means that in his person there has been established a positive human righteousness. His risen humanity is our risen life and our risen and permanent righteousness. In his life on earth, in his growth in wisdom and stature and favour with God and man, in his life of service, love, prayer, faith and obedience to the Father, Jesus is our human righteousness. When therefore he rises from the dead, having made atonement for us, having in the midst of bearing the judgement of God fulfilled all human righteousness in obedient amen to it and continued faith and trust in God right down into death, then in his resurrection his righteousness is established as our righteousness. The risen righteousness of Christ is the positive content of our justification.

For Torrance, if we have no doctrine of the risen righteousness of Christ and of our union with him through the Spirit then we have mutilated and gravely emptied the doctrine of justification of much of its content. For him therefore a 'purely legal' or a 'purely forensic' understanding of justification (that our status as sinners is purely one of having righteousness 'reckoned' to us, i.e. that through Christ we are treated as righteous in terms of the law while still sinners in ourselves) overlooks the positive righteousness of the risen Jesus and the fact that we are brought into real union with him through the Spirit. We are still sinners and have no righteousness of our own, but through real union with Christ and his righteousness we do have a real righteousness in him and are made righteous in him, not simply declared to be righteous.

(iii) The resurrection is the beginning of the new creation headed by Jesus

The bodily resurrection of Jesus is literally the beginning of a new creation headed by Jesus. He is the new man, the head of the new race, the firstborn of the dead, the firstfruits of the new creation, the new Adam who breathes life into others and who as such is said to be 'a life-giving spirit'. As Torrance points out in this connection, being a 'spiritual body' as Jesus was after his resurrection does not mean that he is less body but more body. His body is now new and 'glorious body', so alive and full of life that he makes others alive and is said to be 'a life-giving spirit' (Phil 3.21; 1 Cor 15.45). What has happened to Jesus will happen to the whole human race and indeed to the whole of creation. He is the pioneer, the one who is in his person the secret and life-giving renewal of the whole universe. That as Torrance emphasises is the cosmic significance for the New Testament of the incarnation, atonement and resurrection of the Son of God in our humanity.

(iv) A real resurrection is fundamental to the Christian faith

For Torrance, just as for Karl Barth in the modern era and classical theology in general, the real resurrection of Jesus is critical and fundamental to the Christian faith. As Torrance says, a resurrection that is not bodily is not resurrection and if Jesus' death was a real bodily event then so also was his resurrecton. A bodily resurrection, like the incarnation, is the ultimate affirmation of the reality of creation and of creaturely being. Everything for the Christian faith depends on the fact that God actually became incarnate in Jesus, that 'in him the whole fullness of deity dwells bodily' to quote Paul, that in our flesh and blood existence in space and time we have nothing less than God himself meeting us face to face in Jesus Christ. For Torrance, if Jesus is not risen in the body then ultimately the gospel has nothing to say to men and women of flesh and blood and does not actually reach them in their physical existence. The gospel has lost its kernel and nerve centre and been emasculated of its motive power.

(v) The nature of the resurrection event

Torrance devotes a full chapter to the nature of the resurrection and here his theology and his interest in science overlap in his ground breaking discussion of the nature of the incarnation and of the resurrection in relation to space and time. While the resurrection of Jesus is an event which takes place within creation, it is not an event on the same level as other events and is not to be thought of as an interruption of the natural order. It is an almighty creative event. While it is a real event in space and time it is an event of an entirely different order. Just as the creation can be observed once it has come into being but the process of creation out of nothing cannot itself be observed, so the manner of the resurrection event cannot be traced or observed but once Jesus has risen and appears to us in space and time, then he can be seen and touched but not completely apprehended within the old framework or held down within it.

The resurrection is an event in history but one going beyond it into a new creation

For Torrance, the resurrection is an event in history but one going beyond it into a new creation. It means the undoing and redemption of the past into a new order of being, the death of the old creation and its resurrection into new space and time. In his resurrection Jesus is the beginning of a new reality and of new space and time. More real and more bodily than the old creation subject to death and decay, the resurrection reality of Jesus is a creative act of God which until his return can be known only through word and Spirit by faith and cannot be apprehended (or if at all only dimly) within the framework of space and time as we know it at present.

The openness and non-prescriptiveness of the modern concept of scientific law

With his understanding of science Torrance was aware of the way in which the modern concept of scientific law had moved away from the old prescriptive model to a much more open and flexible one. For him many theologians and ministers still operate with a concept of scientific law as rigid prescriptive laws which cannot be broken. When so understood, such a view rules out all possibility of miracle or of real divine intervention in history as an interference in natural processes and a breaking of the laws of nature. In fact, for Torrance, modern science particularly after Einstein is not inherently hostile to the concept of God or divine intervention in the way it is still thought to be especially by non-scientists. Torrance quotes the celebrated American physicist and expert on scientific law Richard Feynman. Not a believer himself, but in order to illustrate his point when lecturing at Princeton on the difference between the modern concept and the Newtonian concept of law which excluded miracles, Feynman said, 'You know, this would not be hostile even to Christian views of incarnation and resurrection.'[1]

(b) The ascension of Jesus Christ

Often sadly neglected and bypassed the ascension is for Torrance one of the most important of all theological doctrines. The interconnectedness of all Christian doctrine in the one person of Christ from his incarnation to his final coming again means that if any one doctrine is neglected or not given its proper place then every other doctrine is weakened and impoverished. So it is with the doctrine of the ascension. It is a vital part of Christian faith and an essential link in

---

[1] 'Interview with Professor Thomas F. Torrance', in *Different Gospels*, ed. by Dr Andrew Walker, Hodder & Stoughton, London 1988, p. 44.

the chain of doctrine. Take it out of the picture and other doctrines suffer a loss of significance and coherence and can find themselves hanging in the air and similarly downplayed.

(i) The ascension creates a pause in the parousia, creating time for the gospel before the final coming of Jesus

For Torrance there is strictly only one *parousia* or coming-and-presence of Christ in the New Testament but the effect of the ascension is to create a pause in it and to delay or hold back the final coming of Jesus in order to give time for the preaching of the gospel and repentance. If Jesus had not ascended, says Torrance, then the last judgement would have been upon us with no time for the preaching of the gospel or for repentance. By withdrawing his physical presence Jesus has created time for the gospel without lessening its eschatological urgency and the need stated in his parables to be ready at all times for his coming. Torrance also points out how Jesus' parables of the nobleman going into the far country show that he envisaged a considerable gap between his physical leaving of the disciples and his return. It is the ascension which creates the pause between his 'first coming' and his 'second coming' as they came to be known.

(ii) The ascension is the obverse of the incarnation and marks its fulfilment

The incarnation is the coming of God 'down' to humanity, to assume human flesh and to be one with man in the person of Christ. The ascension is Jesus' taking of our humanity in his person into the presence of God into the union and communion of the love of the Trinity. From the very beginning the goal and purpose of the incarnation was the reconciliation of humanity to God through the atoning union of God and man in Christ. Beginning on earth, the whole movement of the reconciling union of man to God in Christ was completed in heaven, in Christ's taking our humanity into the eternal fellowship of love in the Trinity. If the incarnation, says Torrance, was the meeting of God and man on earth in man's place, then the ascension is the meeting of man and God in heaven in God's place. The ascension can thus be seen to be the obverse of the incarnation and its fulfilment.

(iii) The ascension and the sending of the Spirit are the completion of the atonement

The ascension of Jesus and his sending of the Spirit to realise in the minds and hearts of the disciples the atonement he had won for them marks the completion of the atonement. Through the coming of the Spirit the work of atonement already realised in the person of Christ was realised in the church. The work of the Spirit is to so unite the church to Christ in heaven that all the treasures of salvation in Christ begin to be realised in the church. They are not realised in the church as a possession which it has for itself but only as the church lives in union with Christ. Then through the Spirit the church is given to live by the faith of Christ so that his faith becomes its faith and the prayer of Christ himself on earth, '*Abba*, Father' is put into the lips of the church and it is given to pray '*Abba*, Father'.

(iv) A proper doctrine of the ascension is fundamental to the Christian faith

A proper understanding of the ascension is vital to the church's grasp not only of the risen reality and continuing ministry of Jesus Christ but of the certainty of his return and the unveiling of the new creation. Without the ascension, the church's focus shifts inevitably away from the risen Christ, simply to his ministry on earth and he becomes a spiritualised Jesus, lacking the reality of his continuing humanity. There is a loss of the threefold office of Christ as king, priest and prophet.

(1) The ascension and the continuing ministry of Jesus Christ as king, priest and prophet

The ascension of Christ the king

It is in the ascension of Jesus to the right hand of the Father that he is 'made both Lord and Christ' as Peter saw in his sermon on the day of Pentecost. In his ascension Jesus is enthroned to rule over heaven and earth, for as Paul saw also 'he must reign until he has put all his enemies under his feet'. The ascension is the inauguration of the kingdom of Christ and of his heavenly rule over all the powers in the universe. Without it the church lacks the triumphant New Testament certainty of Jesus' victory over all the powers of death and guilt in his death and resurrection. The reign of Christ however is not one in which he rules by power and earthly might but by the power of the gospel, the power of his word and Spirit.

The ascension of Christ the priest

The ascension is the beginning of the heavenly or continuing priesthood of Christ, a major theme of the letter to the Hebrews. The ministry of Christ, begun on earth as prophet, priest and king is continued in heaven as king, priest and prophet. As high priest, Jesus Christ presents before the Father his once and for all offering of himself on our behalf and 'ever lives to make intercession' for his people. As the eternal leader of our intercession and himself our one true prayer, Jesus is the leader and mediator of the church's worship and prayer, a point central to Torrance's understanding of Christian liturgy and worship.

The ascension of Christ the prophet

As king and priest, Christ reigns through his word, through the power of the word and truth of God, the power of the gospel of his redeeming love and the power of his heavenly intercession. Through the Spirit, he himself is present in the church, continuing his own prophetic ministry in its ministry. In the church's ministry of word and sacrament, it is Christ himself who speaks to people through its word, who incorporates them into his baptism and feeds them with himself the Word of God incarnate in our humanity, the bread of his living word and risen life.

(2) The ascension and the final coming of Jesus

By withdrawing himself from physical and visible presence to us, Jesus creates for Torrance a threefold relation to himself in his ascension. The fact that Jesus is not tangibly present to us focuses attention on his reality in heaven, where he is known to us on earth through his presence in his word and Spirit. At the same time, since the only knowledge we can have of him is through the witness of the apostles in the New Testament, Jesus sends us back to them, to his historical life on earth for knowledge of him in heaven. Together, those two elements, the heavenly reality of Christ known immediately through the Spirit but mediately and historically through the gospel, point inevitably forward to the day when Jesus will come again and no longer be physically absent, but present and we will know him face to face without the need for word and sacrament.

As Torrance puts it, the ascension creates a threefold relation to Christ:

(i) historical relation to the historical Jesus Christ,

(ii) sacramental relation to the crucified and risen Jesus Christ,

(iii) eschatological relation to the ascended and advent Christ.

At its heart, the ascension creates an intense tension between the reality of the new creation in Christ and the old creation of death and decay, an intense awareness of the fact that the new world is already real in Christ and yet absent from us in its full manifestation, a longing for the day when the reality we already know and taste through word and sacrament will be unveiled and fully and visibly present. For Torrance a proper understanding of the ascension is at the heart of understanding the triumphant New Testament sense of the risen reality of Jesus Christ and its certain hope of his final unveiling in the new creation.

(v) The nature of the ascension event

For Torrance, the nature of the ascension event is closely related to the nature of the resurrection event and follows on from it. The death of Jesus was his death as part of our old space-time creation as we know it. His resurrection on the other side of death and beyond old space-time was his resurrection in new space-time, a space-time which he himself had created by his resurrection, by his putting the old space-time to death in his death and raising himself in his new body to create new space-time. (Torrance has here in his chapter on the ascension a helpful if brief discussion, complementing that in *Incarnation*, on the modern scientific and dynamic view of space-time where if we can so summarise it, it is bodies-in-motion that create space-time rather than space and time being separate, prior, static containers into which bodies are placed.)

An event in space and time but going beyond them

The forty days of Jesus' life on earth after the resurrection was a time when Jesus already himself in new space and time through his resurrection was able to appear to the disciples within old space and time – hence the rather baffling nature of his appearances. The ascension was the event in which already himself in new space and time but with one foot as it were (if we can put it like that) in old space and time for the disciples' sake, Jesus departed from old space and time into the presence of God as symbolised by the cloud. The ascension was the withdrawal and separation from our senses of Jesus in new space-time, marking the end of his continuing but intermittent presence in old space-time after his resurrection. For Torrance, the ascension is an event in space-time but going beyond it and which therefore needs to be thought out both in relation to space and time and yet as going beyond them into God.

(c) The coming of the Holy Spirit and the creation of the apostles and apostolic tradition

The ascension of Jesus leads directly to his sending of the Holy Spirit, 'for if I do not go away', said Jesus, 'the Counsellor [Advocate-Spirit] will not come to you; but if I go, I will send him to you.' The sending of the Spirit is one of Jesus' mighty acts of salvation, for in it he completed the atonement in the minds and hearts of his disciples and the church. In the coming of the Holy Spirit, Jesus himself returned to be present in the church and through the Spirit to create the apostolate and found the church as his body on the basis of their witness.

(i) The role of the Spirit is to witness to Christ and open the human mind and heart to his truth

The role of the Spirit is to witness to Christ, to remind the disciples and through them the church of all that Jesus had told them, to declare him to them and to guide them into all his truth. The Spirit does not speak of himself but of Christ and opens the minds and hearts of humanity to receive him. The Spirit of God is God in his ability to be present to the creature and to open up the creaturely mind and heart to know God himself in his revelation in Christ. The Spirit reveals Christ and opens up the creature to know and receive him.

This does not mean however that Christ is not equally present in all that the Spirit does. Just as 'God was in Christ reconciling the world to himself' so Jesus Christ is himself present in the work of the Spirit. In revelation, as in creation, atonement and redemption, Father, Son and Spirit are all inseparably involved.

The Spirit is the 'shaliach' in whom Christ himself is present and active

In order to explain the relation of the Spirit to Christ here Torrance uses the Hebrew concept of '*shaliach*' which lies behind the New Testament concept of the apostles as the special representatives of Christ. A '*shaliach*' is so authorised to represent someone that in their word and act the person they represent is regarded as personally present. Just as Jesus was the unique '*shaliach*' of the Father in word and deed, so the Spirit is the unique '*shaliach*' of Christ and so in turn through the work of the Spirit are the apostles.

(ii) The creation of the apostolate as the definitive and authorised witness to Jesus Christ

Through his sending of the Spirit to complete his revelation of himself to the disciples, to bring them to full understanding of everything they could not understand before the completion of atonement and reconciliation, Jesus made the disciples his apostles, his '*sheluchim*', his specially chosen and commissioned envoys, authorised to represent him in word and deed. The disciples had already been selected and specially trained during the life of Jesus on earth, but now with their minds opened to full comprehension they were made apostles, his definitive and specially inspired witnesses. It is their apostolic testimony and witness which is the foundation of the church and their understanding is the one which Jesus means his church to have of him. The mind of Jesus himself is uniquely enshrined in the apostolic mind and the apostolic gospel is his full and final revelation of himself.

(iii) The creation of apostolic tradition and the New Testament

As the apostles under the inspiration of the Holy Spirit translated Jesus' self-witness into human testimony to him, the tradition they had been given by Jesus became apostolic tradition and was given permanent form in the New Testament. Through the Spirit and through the presence of Christ himself in their word, the tradition of the apostles encapsulated in the Gospels and Epistles of the New Testament became apostolic scripture, so joined to the divine Word as to be the written word of God to man. The New Testament became acknowledged as the authentic apostolic tradition and as the only foundation of the one, holy, catholic and apostolic church.

(iv) The question of the relation between the Word made flesh and the written word

The creation through the Spirit of apostolic word and apostolic scriptures to become the written word of the New Testament through which Christ himself speaks, raises the question of the relation between the Word made flesh and the written word, the relation between the living Word of God who is Christ himself and the written word of God in the Old and New Testaments. Torrance has several guiding principles to outline here, all fundamental to his theology.

(d) The doctrine of scripture: the apostolic (and prophetic) basis of the church

(i) The basic text of the New Testament is the obedient humanity of Jesus Christ

The basic text of the apostles and of the New Testament is Jesus Christ himself. The text they 'read', interpreted and preached was a living text, Jesus Christ in his obedient humanity, in the unity of his word, deeds and life, inseparable in his person. That is the one and only basic text of the apostles, the living, obedient humanity of Jesus Christ.

(ii) The New Testament is the inspired secondary text

The New Testament is the inspired witness through which we read and know the basic text. It is Christ's own creation through the Spirit so that in the apostolic gospel of its pages he may still confront people with the basic text of revelation in his own humanity. The secondary text is also revelation, for it is the inspired text through which the basic text is given objectively to us to be received subjectively through the Spirit. The New Testament is the inspired and indispensable window for knowledge of Jesus Christ.

(iii) The person of Christ is the key to understanding the relation of the Word to the written word

At this point it is the person of Christ and the relation between divine and human nature in his person which supplies the pattern to understanding the nature of the written word. For Torrance, the hypostatic union of God and man in the person of Christ supplies the basic analogy for understanding the relations between divine and human not only in scripture but in theology in general. The way that God and man are united in Christ becomes the guiding analogy for the way that divine Word and human word are united in scripture. For Torrance there are close parallels and a major difference between the hypostatic union and scripture.

(1) The parallels between the hypostatic union of God and man and of the Word with the written word

(i) In both there is the assumption of either human nature or word into union with the divine.

(ii) In both there can be no division or separation between either the divine and human natures of Christ or between the divine Word and the human word. In the case of scripture, the divine Word has assumed the human word into union with himself and can no longer be separated from or known apart from the written word.

(iii) In both there can be no confusion or change between either the divine and human nature of Christ or between the divine and human word in scripture, but each remains what it was and is. In the case of scripture this means that although inseparable from the human word, the divine Word remains divine Word and is not changed into human word or confused with it. Similarly although inseparably united to the divine Word, the human word of scripture is not changed into it or confused with it. The written and human word of scripture remains human word and is not divinised.

(2) The differences between God in Christ and the Word in the written word

(i) While in both there is a union of human and divine, in the hypostatic union the union is *in* the person of Christ whereas in scripture the union is between the person of Christ and the human word of scripture and is therefore *outside* his person. The written word of scripture though used and sanctified in its use by God as his word, is not assumed into one person with the divine Word and is therefore not the same kind of union as the hypostatic union.

(ii) The hypostatic union is a union of divine and human in the person of Christ, whereas with scripture the union is not simply between human word and divine Word but between human word and a Christ who is at once divine Word and true human word. For Torrance there is a sacramental relation between scripture and the divine-human Word of Christ in which scripture as the secondary text partakes of but points to the basic text of the true divine-human Word in Christ.

Torrance's doctrine of scripture is deeply Christological

Torrance's doctrine of scripture is deeply and carefully Christological and thought provoking. It also defies easy classification. For Torrance, the heart of scripture is Jesus Christ. In him the eternal and living Word of God, the eternal Son, has become flesh, human body, human heart, mind and soul. In him the Word of God has become flesh in human speech, language and mind. In him the Word of God is now human thought, human will, human understanding and human word, all in the one person of Christ. In him the Word of God has been translated into human flesh, human knowledge of God, human response and human word, all in the obedient humanity of Jesus Christ.

The significance of Jesus Christ as Word of God to man become obedient human word

Jesus Christ is therefore not only Word of God to man, but that Word become human word and human life, and as such also human response and word of man to God. Jesus is Word of God to man become human word and therefore Word of God to man in human word. In his one indivisible person Jesus Christ is the one divine-human Word of God, divine Word and human word. He for Torrance is pre-eminently the Word of God to man, in man and of man which is found in the holy scriptures. He alone is the one and only true Word of God, who as Word become living human word is, in his obedient humanity, the living text we read in the bible.

A doctrine of scripture must be patterned on and reflect the uniqueness of the person of Christ

Whatever else therefore a doctrine of scripture says, for Torrance it must reflect the fact not only that Jesus in his person is the true Word and content of scripture, but that the pattern the Word took in becoming human flesh, human word and life must be our basic pattern and guide in understanding how the scriptures are at once human, written word and God speaking to us in person through them. If God became man in Christ in such a way that there is no confusion or change between his divinity and humanity, but also in such a way that they cannot be divided or separated, the same must be true of the relation between divine and human word in scripture. At the same time, the scriptures reflect and point to the uniqueness of the hypostatic union in Christ. Though there is no personal union between the Word and the written word in scripture, the scriptures partake of the union in Christ. Through the Spirit and through the living Word who speaks through them, the holy scriptures are the one and only place where we are given to hear and know the Word of life.

3 The one church of God in Jesus Christ

In Torrance's chapter on the church the implications of the Christology of *Incarnation* and the Soteriology of *Atonement* become even more apparent, providing a deeply enriching perspective on the nature of the church and its mission. Torrance's trinitarian theology of the church as the work of Father, Son and Spirit, the body of Christ grounded in the incarnation, atonement and Pentecost, the provisional form of the new creation, commissioned to proclaim and live out the reconciling love of God in world mission, is inspiring and humbling. Just as the completeness of salvation in the person of Jesus Christ became earthed in the disciples at Pentecost, so here for Torrance the theology of the incarnation and atonement is seen to have far reaching implications in its outworking and shaping of the life and worship, doctrine and mission of the church. Only a few of Torrance's major themes here may be selected for brief consideration:

(a) *The church is the work of three divine persons, grounded in their eternal communion*

The church is the work of all three persons of the Trinity, Father, Son and Holy Spirit, and is grounded in their eternal communion of love. As the body of Christ, it is the universal family of God sharing sonship with the Son, it is the community of the reconciled finding its life in union with Jesus Christ, and it is the communion of saints living in communion with God through the Holy Spirit. The church is thus not a human creation but rooted in the eternal purpose of God in Christ.

(b) *The three forms of the one church of God*

There is only one church, one people of God in all ages from the beginning of the creation to its end but there are three forms or phases of its life. While it had its earthly beginning in Adam, it was with its calling with Abraham and its establishment at Sinai that the church took definite form as Israel the chosen people of God, the servant of the Lord and prophet to the nations, the womb of the Messiah bearing the promise of salvation for all. Israel was *the preparatory form of the church before the incarnation* waiting for its fulfilment in the Messiah. With his coming the church is gathered up, reconstructed and given new life and *a new form in Jesus Christ* in two stages. First it is called, gathered around Jesus the Messiah, rooted in his historical ministry and trained in its pattern. At the last supper it is cemented to Jesus in the indissoluble bond of the new covenant in his body and blood. Then in the death and resurrection of the Messiah in lonely substitution and in his sending of the Spirit the church was reborn and transformed into the body of the risen Lord. Sent out into history with the world mission of the gospel, the church receives its *final and eternal form when Christ comes again* to judge and renew his creation.

(c) The church is the body of Christ – the twofold New Testament usage

Torrance points out that the New Testament uses the phrase the 'body of Christ' in two ways, to speak of *the whole Christ who includes the church* within his own fullness and to speak of *the church as the body of which he is the head.* As the one for the many, the new man in whom the new race is concentrated, the vine that includes the branches, Jesus Christ contains the church in his fullness. The New Testament also distinguishes the church from Christ: he is the head and it is the body, the servant of which he is Lord.

(d) The church is the provisional form of the new creation

Torrance describes the church as 'the provisional form of the new creation'. It is in the church that the fullness of Christ, the completeness of salvation in his person, is first realised in creation through the Spirit but that is only the first and provisional form of the new creation in Christ for through the mission of the church in word and Spirit the church is extended throughout the world until with the coming of Jesus it becomes co-extensive with the boundaries of creation itself.

(i) The completeness and finished nature of the work of Christ in his person
One of the defining characteristics of Torrance's theology is the way in which it holds together the twin emphasis of the New Testament on the completeness of salvation in Christ together with the imperatives of faith. In Jesus Christ, in his whole work of reconciling atonement as

God and as man in one person, our salvation has been achieved. In his one person, God has intervened on our behalf and in our place and as man has made our response for us. As the high priest appointed by God, Jesus represents God and man in his person, the eternal Son who as man is the pioneer and perfecter of our faith. All the parts of our salvation to use Calvin's language have been completed in the person of Christ.

(ii) What has been completed intensively in Christ must now be fulfilled extensively in the church and in all creation

For Torrance as he puts it, the same salvation which has already been completed intensively within the person of Christ must be fulfilled extensively in the church. Similarly the salvation which is fulfilled intensively in the church as the beginning of the harvest of humanity, must be extended and fulfilled extensively in creation through the expansion of the church in world mission. As the provisional form of the new creation, the church is commanded to reach out with the gospel, to proclaim by word and life the message of the redeeming love of God until at his coming all creation is renewed and gathered up under the headship of Christ.

The church is the servant and herald whose whole life and essence is to be found in Christ alone

The church is only the provisional form of the new creation of Christ and cannot exist for itself, but only as it fulfils his mission of being a fellowship of reconciliation and takes part in his ministry to reach all humanity with his redeeming love. The church can only be the church through continually dying and rising with Christ, finding its life in him and not in itself, being transformed by the renewal of its thinking so that through the Spirit Christ may himself be at work in its ministry.

(e) The church is part of the creed and an essential part of faith in the gospel

As Torrance points out, the church is included in the Apostle's Creed. In itself it is nothing but it is included within faith in the one God, the one mediator and the one Spirit. It belongs to him as his creation and is therefore inseparably bound up with faith in the Trinity and the saving work of Christ through the Spirit. The doctrine of the church is thus essentially evangelical doctrine, part of the gospel and an object of faith.

(f) The attributes of the church – one, holy, catholic and apostolic church

The attributes of the church are the essential 'notes' and properties which it derives from its foundation in Jesus Christ. They are not independent qualities which the church has in itself but affirmations of its nature as it participates in Jesus Christ. They are therefore strictly discernible only to faith. *Its properties are the attributes of Christ himself, but attributes in which the church shares through its union with him.* In the unity, holiness, catholicity and apostolicity of the church, it is therefore the face of Christ himself which comes to view and is discerned and affirmed by faith.

The attributes of the church derive not from itself but essentially from the nature of God himself and are attributes in which it participates only as it is rooted and grounded in him through union and communion with Christ. Unity, holiness and catholicity or universality derive from the very nature of God, from the triune oneness of God himself, from his own divine holiness, and from the immensity of God and the universality of his love. Apostolicity derives from the Father's sending of Christ and Christ's sending of the apostles (*apostellō*, send). The apostolicity of the church is its continuity with its foundation in Christ, its faithfulness to the apostolic teaching that derives from Christ and goes back to the Father. To cease to be faithful to apostolic doctrine and practice means to be no longer faithful to Christ and no longer the one, holy, catholic and apostolic church. Apostolicity is thus the criterion which determines how far the true church is still one, holy and catholic.

Torrance's high theology of the church and his own passionate concern and love for the church as the body of Christ and the one, holy, catholic and apostolic church of God comes out not only in his teaching, but in his life-long commitment to theological training for the ministry, involvement in ecumenical dialogue and endeavours for the renewal of the church in theology and evangelism.

4 The eschatological perspective of Torrance's theology

Running right through Torrance's theology from very early in his career is a vivid sense of the intense eschatological perspective of the New Testament and its integral place in the gospel. His theology is shot through with the apostolic awareness that in the coming of Jesus 'the last days' had been precipitated into the present and people were face to face with God himself in time. Jesus' death signaled the end of the old creation and in his resurrection the new creation had already begun and was waiting for its final unveiling at his coming again.

Eschatology or the doctrine of 'the last things' is therefore a basic and indispensable element in Torrance's theology. The task here is to introduce the essential concepts of eschatology as used by Torrance and then to outline the essential inner logic of New Testament eschatology as he saw it. Although this will be done by breaking down New Testament eschatology into various elements, it is important that these be understood together and as a whole.

The two dimensions of eschatology, vertical and horizontal

Eschatology as the doctrine of the 'last things' or 'end' of history can be thought of in two main ways, the vertical and the horizontal. In terms of the vertical dimension, the accent in eschatology is on the end coming into time and history from above. In terms of the horizontal, the accent is on the final realisation of the end or 'goal' of history. Although both are forms of eschatology, the vertical and horizontal aspects are commonly distinguished from each other as *eschatology* and *teleology*. The emphasis in *eschatology* (from the Greek, *ta eschata*, the last things) is on the 'last things' with God ushering in the end from above and bringing time and history to a close, while in *teleology* (from the Greek, *telos*, purpose, end) the emphasis is on history reaching forward to its goal at the end of time. In both there is a perfect end, either one that comes down from above or one reached progressively through history until the perfect society is realised. In the bible both are held together, but the emphasis is primarily on the end being realised through the action of God from above.

The concept of eschatological 'tension' – the pressure of the 'end' on and in time and history

In eschatology the pressure of the 'end', whether from above or from the future, is thought of in terms of 'tension', the pressure for change exerted by the proximity of the end on those in time and history. In the vertical dimension of eschatology the tension is from above, the tension caused by the invasion of God into history creating the last events. It is the pressure caused by the presence of God in the midst of human history, the tension between Jesus Christ in his holiness, truth and light and human sin. The vertical tension is also often thought of in terms of the tension between eternity and time, between time as the realm of progressive event, of change and becoming, and the presence of the eternal God in time calling man and all time and history to account, redeeming them and creating them anew. In teleology (or teleological eschatology) the tension is caused by the expectation and proximity of the end – the nearer the looming deadline the greater the pressure both in terms of meeting it prepared and in terms of anticipation. In both eschatology and teleology there is tension between what we are in time and history and what the end would have us be, and in both there is the pressure that the time is limited, that it will be cut short by the arrival of the end.

The twofold nature of eschatological tension, between eternity and time, and present and future

The whole nature of biblical eschatology is dramatically intensified by the coming of God himself into time and history in Christ, but there is also a new factor specific to the New Testament which is the fact that the future is no longer simply in the future but has already arrived. The death and resurrection of Jesus mean the end of the old creation and the birth of the new in him. In him, therefore, we already are what we will be, and in that sense what we will be in the future is already a reality here and now, in his person in the present. The full New Testament eschatology involves therefore, as Torrance makes clear, not only the tension between eternity and time, and between present and future, but between the present and a future which is already present in Christ and waiting to be unveiled.

The various elements in the inner logic of New Testament eschatology

(a) The coming of God into time throws the world into crisis creating 'the last days'

It is the coming of God himself into time which creates eschatological ferment and crisis. As long as God remains distant as it were, even if very near in his universal presence, then time can continue as it always has done. But if God himself comes into time and is personally present in the midst, meeting people face to face in the majesty and authority of Jesus, then there is no hiding place for humanity and people are confronted with the ultimate, here and now. That creates crisis, decision, turning everything upside down and the language of the New Testament here as Torrance used to point out is that of earthquake and volcanic disturbance. People were amazed, astonished, dumbfounded at Jesus. As long as God is distant then judgement is distant but when the truth and light of God in Christ are present, then people are searched and questioned down to their very roots.

It is possible, however, to interpret the New Testament eschatological crisis in a rather different way, as the drawing near and impinging of God upon time, precipitating crisis but in a timeless way without actually entering time himself. Such a timeless eschatology interprets New Testament eschatology as the crisis created by the eternal perpetually impinging or knocking upon the door of time without actually ever coming in.

If it is to be true to the New Testament, the coming of God into time must be interpreted as a decisive, real act of God in time. God has actually entered time, not just knocking tangentially at the door or window but invading time to act and to continue to act decisively within it.

There is a second equally important feature of New Testament eschatology which defines and doubly reinforces the coming of God here as a real coming.

(b) God's entering time to effect salvation as man in Jesus makes it reality in our midst

The fact that God has become man and that the whole life, death and resurrection of Jesus is a real act of man, means that God has not come half way to humanity as it were, leaving humanity to go the other half, but that he has so come to humanity that in time and in human flesh he has actually completed for humanity their whole salvation. In the humanity of Jesus, the word of God has become truth in the heart of man, the covenant has been fulfilled from the side of God and from the side of man, and the kingdom of God has begun on earth. It is his real becoming man that tells us that here in Jesus God is actually present alongside us, in time and space just as we are.

There is a third factor which further defines the real presence of God and makes it even more decisive.

(c) The one person of Jesus is the complete salvation of God fulfilled for all in their place

It is the radically substitutionary nature of salvation in Christ which makes his entry into time even more decisive and eschatological. If Jesus has acted on behalf of all humanity and completed the salvation of all inside his person, then whether they will or not he has made it a *fait accompli* and something they are confronted with in his person. If by contrast salvation is simply on offer in his person, then there is a sense in which people can take it or leave it and pass by on the other side. But if Jesus has actually taken the place of each and every single human being before God, and in their place and on their behalf has achieved salvation for them, then they are inescapably involved. The radically substitutionary and representative nature of Jesus' action for each and every person means that they have been set aside and something has been done in their name. They have been signed up for salvation by the action of God and of man in Christ while they were still enemies. The ground has been taken from under their feet and in the person of Christ they are confronted with their own salvation, inescapably involving them in decision.

It is the fact that Jesus is not only God but God acting as man for humanity, and not only as man but as individual man, achieving salvation for us in the reality and individuality of his person and meeting us individually in personal encounter, that involves us in existential decision and in the eschatological tension between the reality of what-and-who he is for us and what we still are in ourselves. It is the fact that Jesus has done something in our name and in our place for each person individually that means we are inescapably involved in decision as he meets each person individually in personal encounter, in the reality of what he is for us in his love and grace and in his calling us to follow him in faith.

A fourth factor heightens the eschatological tension.

(d) The tension in the encounter with Jesus between old and new creation, death and life

The tension is not only the threefold encounter with God in time, God as man in time, and God as man in our place in time, but the fact that what God is now for us in time is *new* man, *new* humanity, involving us in death and resurrection. We are not only set aside by God's taking our place in Christ, so that in union with him we might live out of him and his righteousness, but we are involved in Christ's death and resurrection. In Pauline language, we died with Christ on the cross and we were raised to life with him in his resurrection, so that he in his risen life is our new life, our risen humanity - 'you have died *with Christ* and your life is hid with Christ in God.'

The tension is therefore not only that between eternity and time, between God become man in time and time, (i.e. between eternity-in-time and time), but that between new time and old time, between eternity-in-new-time and old time, the tension between death and resurrection, old creation and new creation. It is this twofold tension which as Torrance points out lies at the heart of the New Testament eschatological tension. In the encounter with Christ, we are involved not only in the encounter with God in time but the encounter with our new humanity in Christ, with God wearing our new humanity in new time.

The second tension involves death and resurrection and is the outcome of the first, of God as man in time fulfilling our salvation. The second tension is that between old humanity in old time and new humanity in new time meeting us in Christ from the other side of death. Here and now, in old time and in the midst of the ongoing reality of the old creation, we are confronted with the reality of the new humanity and creation in Christ. The way there lies through death and resurrection, a way which has already been trodden for us by Jesus

Christ ('I am the way, the truth and the life') and which is ours through union and participation with and in him.

There are two further factors here defining the nature of the eschatological tension.

(e) The ascension and partial distancing in hope of the eschatological focus of tension

First, the ascension of Jesus means the withdrawal from our midst of the focus point of eschatological tension. Jesus the reality of the new creation is no longer in our midst, no longer confronting us here and now on earth in his physical presence with the life of the world to come. He is our new life, our hope, but he has ascended to heaven and so our life and our hope are now in heaven and Paul can speak of 'Christ who is our life' being 'seated at the right hand of the Father'.

The ascension means that the focus of our hope is no longer on earth, as in the forty days after the resurrection, but in heaven. The double fact of the reality of our new life in Christ and its being distanced from us in heaven creates a new element in the eschatological tension. It adds the element of having and yet not having, of knowing what is ours and yet not fully possessing it, of longing and looking forward in certain expectation to what we are to be, the Christian hope that what we already are in Christ we will become when we see him. It is the tension of waiting and groaning, in certain hope and expectation, for what is imminent to faith but not yet fully unveiled and realised in the old creation.

(f) Pulled upward and forward, through union with Christ by the Spirit and the outreach of the gospel, to the realisation of Christ's kingdom at his coming

Second, although the ascension means the withdrawal of the physical presence of the risen Jesus, it also means his coming to be present to the church through the Spirit. It is his withdrawal in his mode of physical presence in order to be with us in his mode of universal presence through word and Spirit. Though the bodily place of the risen Jesus is the new space-time of heaven, we are united to him through the Spirit so that as Calvin says, things which are separated by distance are united through the Spirit.

We are pulled upward (not spatially) by the Spirit, lifted up by him to partake of Christ by union and communion with him in heaven, but we are also pulled forward by the Spirit to meet the advent Christ since we will only see him when he comes again at the end of old time. In addition therefore to the tension of absence and longing, there is also the tension of being drawn upward to Christ and forward to his advent.

The twofold strand in that tension (the upward and forward) is complemented by a third, the tension of the outreach of the gospel throughout the world in preparation for the final coming of Christ and full realisation of the kingdom on earth. It is the ascension which means the enthronement of Christ in heaven and his coming through the Spirit, but the ascension also means the creation of time for the preaching of the gospel and repentance, time for the mission of the gospel to the ends of the earth. As the New Testament puts it, the gospel must first be preached to all nations and then shall the end come. There is therefore a third strand in the eschatological tension which stretches upwards to Christ and forwards to him at his coming, and that is the outreach of the church in world mission. It is the preaching of the gospel to all peoples and tongues which creates the eschatological ferment in and through which Christ by his word rules the nations and prepares the world for his coming.

The various strands in New Testament eschatology cannot be neatly isolated and can only be understood as a whole

Although the various strands of New Testament eschatology have been singled out and considered one by one here in order to try to present it in its inner logic and rationale, it is important that they cannot be isolated from each other or considered apart. They are all bound up together and must be grasped as a whole in order to understand them aright. Concentration on certain elements to the neglect of others leads to some of the well known but one sided eschatologies which have appeared in the theological debate. Torrance's eschatology sees salvation as already realised in the person of Christ, provisionally in the church and as waiting to be realised in creation. Here on earth but united to Christ through the Spirit, the church glimpses and tastes already the power of the new creation to come. The triumphant certainty of the bodily resurrection of Jesus impels the church forward through the preaching of the gospel until the full redemption which is already in Christ is realised by him in all creation at his coming again. For Torrance that is the essential eschatological expectation of the church.

C The challenge of Torrance's theology

The challenge of Torrance's theology is first one of understanding it as a whole. *Incarnation* and *Atonement* are a major read, if only because of their length. Grasping them as a whole is also a task which takes time and commitment because of their depth and scope. The theology they express is at once profound and yet simple in outline, but the wide-ranging nature of the topics and the inter-connectedness of Torrance's theology mean it takes time to see the connections between its different parts and think them through for oneself until it becomes possible to grasp it as an organic whole. Until that is done and until at the same time Torrance's theology is thought through in the light of the bible and in the light of the history of theology, a full appreciation or proper estimate of what he is saying is not really possible.

There are, however, certain points in Torrance's theology which are worthy of selection as meriting further attention here and which will in any case repay careful consideration and thinking through. There are three major topics: the nature of the incarnation, the nature of Jesus Christ's substitution and representation of humanity, and the nature of the Word of God and his relation to the written word. The three topics cannot be considered in isolation but inextricably involve one another and themselves involve a number of sub-topics. Points which have already been covered adequately in this introduction or in the one to *Incarnation* will either not be mentioned or be so only briefly in order to re-emphasise them and indicate their need to be thought through in the mind of the reader. At the same time the fact that a point is not selected here, such as the doctrine of the Trinity, does not mean that it is not central or does not need careful theological consideration.

1 The nature of the incarnation

(a) The person of Christ

The fundamental importance of Christology goes without saying save to reiterate the significance for Torrance of *anhypostasia* and *enhypostasia*, the fact that Christ in his human nature at once represented all humanity and was an individual man, that he was 'man' and 'a man' in one person. Torrance uses *anhypostasia* and *enhypostasia* very illuminatingly on a number of theological problems, for example by pointing out how together they help us to see that Jesus assumed our fallen nature but was not a sinner.[2] The meaning of *anhypostasia* and *enhypostasia* will be expanded on shortly.

(b) The incarnation is real physical event, the act of God in all his fullness in space and time

For Torrance the incarnation, the healing miracles of Jesus, his death on the cross, bodily resurrection and ascension in his risen humanity

---

[2]   *Incarnation* p. 231-32.

are all real events in space and time. Salvation is not just spiritual, whatever that might mean, but involves the whole reality of our physical and mental life, and if it is not a real act by God in our flesh and blood existence then it is hollow and empty. The reality of God, the reality of creation and the reality of the incarnation are bound up together. The fact that it is God in space and time, God becoming man in Christ, is the ultimate affirmation of the reality of physical existence in space and time, so that if it is God taking creation seriously, real God in space and time then it is also real event in space and time, or as we might say, real God means real event. It is the fullness of the living God acting in space and time which means that the whole life of Jesus is full blooded real event and that Jesus in his risen body is not 'less body' but as Torrance says 'more body'.

(c) The incarnation is dynamic event completed in the atonement and resurrection

As argued in *Incarnation*, the incarnation of Jesus Christ, as with his person and his divine and human natures, needs to be interpreted dynamically. It is not a static event. Although God became man in the womb of Mary and in his birth at Bethlehem, that was only the beginning. The birth of Jesus was the start of an ongoing event which until the resurrection was not established as forever ongoing. For Torrance, the incarnation was also the beginning of atonement. It was the assumption of fallen human nature into union with divine nature in the person of Jesus Christ and at the same time it was the sanctification of human nature in union with the divine.

Both elements are equally crucial for Torrance: if Jesus has not assumed sinful nature he has not reached us as we are and we are not saved, but equally if Jesus did not sanctify our sinful nature in the very act of assuming it we are not saved either since then Jesus has not overcome our sin. The atonement, therefore, begins for Torrance with the incarnation, but it has to be worked out through the whole personal growth of human life, worked through the growth of Jesus from infancy and on into adulthood. Throughout his life of sinless assumption of fallen flesh, at each stage in his life of increasing solidarity with sinners, of taking our 'infirmities' and 'diseases' on himself (Matt 8.17), Jesus sanctifies our fallenness by his holiness, until on the cross in total solidarity with sinful humanity and bearing their sin under the final judgement of God, he completes the sanctification of our sinful flesh in his own holiness and willing self-offering of himself in faith on our behalf. The hypostatic union of God and man in Christ began in the incarnation, but it had to be maintained and carried through death and judgement in order to emerge victorious in the resurrection.

Two of the cardinal principles of Torrance's theology can be reiterated here as summing up his teaching on the topic:

(i) incarnation and atonement are inseparable: the incarnation is the beginning of atonement and the atonement is the incarnation worked out through death into resurrection.

(ii) the assumption and sanctification of fallen flesh are equally inseparable and both can only be understood dynamically: Jesus sanctifies (and throughout his life continues to sanctify) our fallen flesh in his very act of assuming it.

2 The nature of Jesus Christ as substitute and representative for humanity

The question of the nature of Jesus Christ as the substitute and representative for humanity is one of the central points of theology where Torrance is most innovative and fruitful. Deeply rooted in both scripture and the classical tradition of soteriology, Torrance holds together in his theology insights which are held together in scripture but which in the history of theology have been too often overridden or downplayed in the attempt to weld the teaching of the bible into a logical system. Torrance attempts to be faithful to biblical ways of thinking and to the integrated understanding it presents of the person and salvation of Jesus Christ. Through building on the foundations of classical Christology but integrating and seeing the implications of its insights, Torrance is able to use innovative and illuminating christological thinking on theological questions. He uses Christology and the pattern of the person of Christ as the clue to doing justice to holding together the various elements in biblical teaching.

The key concepts of 'two natures in one person' and of 'anhypostasia' and 'enhypostasia'

Torrance uses the Chalcedonian understanding of Christ, 'two natures in one person', together with the concepts of *anhypostasia* and *enhypostasia* as the key christological insights.[3] *Anhypostasia* and

---

[3]   On the Council of Chalcedon see *Incarnation* p. 83 and 197ff. and on *anhypostasia* and *enhypostasia* pp. 228-33.

enhypostasia both refer to the nature of the humanity of Christ. As *hypostasia* (or *hypostasis*)[4] in itself means person, reality or personal reality, their meanings are best remembered by their prefixes *an*, not and *en*, in. *An-hypostasia* (*an-hypostasis*) is 'not-person' with the meaning of '*no* independent *personal reality* or existence', while *en-hypostasia* (*en-hypostasis*) is 'in-person' with the meaning of 'fully real and personal *in-the-person-of-the-eternal-Son*'. Since his main discussion of these topics is to be found in *Incarnation*, the following is a summary of his teaching there and of the way in which it informs the structure of his theology and is used by him in his doctrine of atonement and salvation. Jesus Christ is the full reality of God and the full reality of man in one person, in such a way that his divinity and humanity cannot be divided or separated from one another, but each remain fully what they are without any change or confusion with the other. The key concepts of *anhypostasia* and *enhypostasia* add that apart from the incarnation of the Son the human nature of Jesus has *no* independent *personal existence* (it is *an-hypostatic*), but that in the incarnation the humanity of Jesus is fully real, personal and individual *in* the *person* of the Son (it is *en-hypostatic* in him). The incarnation was wholly the work of God but an act of God in which there was full, real human act. Jesus in his humanity was not just an instrument in the hand of God, but was a full human person, with human body, mind, reason, will and soul. In the incarnation, therefore, the reality of God and the reality of man, divine mind and human mind, divine will and human will are both fully together and inseparable in the person of Jesus Christ. As Torrance often said, 'all of God means all of man'. The action of God does not mean less man but more man, it means that man is a full reality and is completely active.

Thought together in that way and seen in their complementarity, *anhypostasia* and *enhypostasia* are for Torrance the christological clue and pattern to the way in which the action of God and the action of man should be held together in theology. The way in which God and man are united in the person of Christ is the pattern for the way in which the action of God and the response of man are held together in election and faith, in the inseparability of unconditional grace and the need for faith.

---

4   *Hypostasia* is the abstract generic form of *hypostasis* and has the general meaning of 'personhood' or 'the state of having personal existence' as opposed to the more concrete *hypostasis*, 'person'. *An-hypostasia* therefore is 'the state of having no independent personhood' or personal existence, whereas *an-hypostasis* is literally 'not-person'. *En-hypostasia* is the similarly generic 'the state of having real personal existence in . . .' and *en-hypostasis* is literally 'in-person'.

(a) Anhypostasia *and* enhypostasia *in the relation between God and man in Christ himself*

(i) Anhypostasia – *the assumption by Christ of the human nature of all humanity as substitute in their place*

Anhypostasia tells us the incarnation was purely the act of God in which he assumed the human nature of all humanity, the human nature common to every single human person. As Torrance points out, there was no personal human will involved. It was an act of unconditional grace in which human will, as represented by Joseph (see chapter 3 of *Incarnation*), is set aside and in Christ God becomes man in the place of and for all humanity.

(ii) Enhypostasia – *the action of Christ as an individual man representing each human person*

Enhypostasia tells us that when God became man for all humanity he did so as individual man, that in Jesus Christ the eternal Son is not only acting as man on behalf of all humanity but doing so as individual man in acutely personal relation and interaction both with the Father and all mankind. In his person as the Son Jesus Christ is man for all and he is one particular man, fully real and individual in his humanity, with his own body, mind and will. As one particular man, Jesus lives on the one hand in his intimate relation to the Father, in personal obedience, in unblemished holiness, love, prayer, worship and the response of faith, taking before God on his own lips our confession of sin in amen to the Father's judgement, and on the other hand Jesus lives in encounter with every other human person. *Enhypostasia* focuses on the reality and significance of Jesus in his unique, individual humanity, in his own personal knowing of the Father and response to him in faith. For Torrance it is only by taking *anhypostasia* and *enhypostasia* together that we can see the whole Jesus Christ without distortion. As he puts it, Jesus is *'at once man, and a man'*. The significance of this for Torrance will shortly become apparent.

(iii) The completeness of salvation from the side of God and of man in Christ

Put together and interpreted dynamically as they need to be, as with the person of Christ and his divine and human natures, *anhypostasia* and *enhypostasia* mean that Jesus Christ is not only the full act of God for salvation but the full of act of man being reconciled to God. If *anhypostasia* is the full act of God as man saving humanity, *enhypostasia* is the full act of man in Christ receiving salvation and responding in faith. Atonement, reconciliation and redemption are complete and full in the person of Christ, both from the side of God and from the side of humanity in faith.

(b) Anhypostasia *and* enhypostasia *in the relation between Christ and humanity*

The first point to be made here is that together *anhypostasia* and *enhypostasia* reinforce the fact that God in Christ has acted for us in our place, *anhypostasia* that *as man* he has acted for all humanity and *enhypostasia* that *as a man* he has done so personally and individually for each and every human being.

(i) *Radical substitution and radical representation in Torrance's theology*

Therefore far from dismissing the substitutionary element in atonement and in the saving work of Christ, Torrance sees it as being even more radical in its implications. In his dying our death under the judgement of God Jesus Christ does not just take our place in his 'passive obedience' to the consequences of our sin, but in his 'active obedience' also he takes our place before God and represents us in his human righteousness and faith. Jesus Christ thus radically supplants us in his active as well as in his passive obedience, even to the extent of making the response of faith in his own obedient, individual and personal humanity.

The *'vicarious humanity' of Jesus Christ – he takes our place in faith*

The radical substitutionary nature of Christ's work can be summed up in the phrase 'the vicarious humanity of Christ' which Torrance once described as 'the cutting edge' of his 'Trinitarian-Christocentric' theology. For him the whole human life of Jesus on earth is of saving significance. It is his becoming man to live out for us and in our place everything that we should be. His humanity is his standing in our place 'to fulfil all righteousness' for us (Matt 3.15), as in his baptism, and offer up to the Father the confession of sin, the worship, prayer and faith which we owe. **This is radical substitution and far from ruling out the need for individual and personal faith on our part it actually intensifies it**. The fact that Jesus takes our place even in faith radically supplants us, setting us aside and calling in question all our righteousness, even the faith we think we can offer. His is the only true response to the Father, which is precisely part of the reason for his becoming man in the one man Jesus.

The *'vicarious humanity' of Jesus Christ intensifies the need for faith, demanding an even more radical repentance*

The fact that Jesus takes our place in faith so cuts the ground from under our feet, removing all our righteousness and even that of the response we think we can offer, that it demands of us an even more radical repentance. Henceforth, we must live as those who have been entirely crucified with Christ, who have risen with him in his resurrection and who live only out of his faith. Galatians 2.20, '*I have been crucified with Christ . . . and the life I now live in the flesh I live by the faith of the Son of God, who loved me and gave himself for me*'. Torrance insisted on the King James translation, '*I live by the faith of the Son of God*', as the one closest to the Greek. For Torrance the only faith and response we can offer to God is that of Jesus Christ so that his faith is our faith and his response and prayer ours. Our whole salvation, even our faith is in the person of Christ, in the humanity of the one divine-human person of the eternal Son of God.

Torrance therefore emphasises the 'finished work' of Christ, that he has completed all the parts of our salvation from God's side and from our side. His self-offering to the Father and his faith on our behalf are the only offerings we can hold up before the Father. The life we live we live out of and by his faith, and our faith does not add anything to his faith, but by the Spirit his faith is made ours and in faith we live in union with him and his faithfulness.

(ii) The significance of anhypostasia *and* enhypostasia *for the nature of salvation in Christ and its mode of operation in humanity*

For Torrance it is in understanding not only the person of Christ himself but the nature and mode of operation of his salvation that *anhypostasia* and *enhypostasia* must be taken together and it is here that Torrance brings out the full significance of *anhypostasia* and *enhypostasia* in their essential complementarity.[5]

(1) Anhypostasia – *the act of God for the salvation of all*

Anhypostasia tells us that God has assumed the human nature of all humanity and in it has acted for the salvation of all, but taken by itself that could be interpreted in a causal and general way to mean that all humanity was necessarily saved.

(2) Enhypostasia – *salvation for all is inside the one man Jesus Christ*

Enhypostasia tells us that the salvation God has effected for all is in the individual person of Christ, that the salvation of all exists in the shape of one particular man, Jesus Christ. It is therefore not just general but particular in Jesus and to be found only in his individual person.

---

5   *Incarnation* p. 231f.

(3) Salvation is not automatic but received individually and personally in encounter with Jesus Christ

Taken together *anhypostasia* and *enhypostasia* tell us that because the salvation of all is in the individual person of Jesus Christ it is not just automatic, but received individually and personally in encounter with him. Because the corporate salvation for all is already individualised in the person of Christ, if we can put it like that, and remains individualised in his person, it can only become ours individually in Christ's coming to us in personal encounter and asking of us the obedience of faith. Salvation is corporate in Christ (the doctrine of the church – for he died for the many and in him humanity is saved as a whole) but it is necessarily individual also in Christ and is ours in union with him. Torrance thus holds together in his theology the New Testament emphasis on the finished salvation of Christ with the need for repentance and faith.

(c) Anhypostasia *and* enhypostasia *in the relation between Christ and the response of faith*

For Torrance, the key concepts of *anhypostasia* and *enhypostasia* can be used to illuminate not only the person of Christ but by extension and analogy the relation between the salvation of God in Christ and the response of faith. Just as in the incarnation, the humanity of Jesus Christ was entirely an act of God which was also the full act of man, so the salvation of God in Christ for all does not exclude the human response of faith but by grace creates it in personal encounter.

Just as Christ's humanity is fully real and enhypostatic in his person so human faith is fully real and enhypostatic in Christ

Just as the act of God in the person of Christ (*anhypostasia*) was also the full response of man in his person (*enhypostasia*), so by analogy the mighty act of God from the side of God and of man in the finished work of Christ (*anhypostasia*) does not preclude the human act of response in faith (*enhypostasia*) but includes it in such a way that the human response of faith is affirmed, has its reality in the finished work of Christ and is seen to be *enhypostatic* in it. Just as the humanity of Christ had no independent existence of its own but is seen to be fully real and individual in the person of the Son of God, so the human act of faith has no independent validity or existence of its own but is fully real and fully individual in its essential relation to Christ and in his person.

Torrance's early use of an- *and* en-hypostasia *to illuminate other modes of expression*

Torrance's realisation of the significance of *anhypostasia* and *enhypostasia* and of their combined fruitfulness for understanding not only the humanity of Christ but the relation between election and faith, grace and faith, Christ and human response, dates from the very beginning of his career and appears already in his first published theological article in 1941. While at appropriate points in his lectures, Torrance uses the analogy with the person of Christ and the theological concepts of *anhypostasia* and *enhypostasia* to clarify the relation between the finished work of Christ and human faith with greater technical precision, he customarily employed different ways to make the same basic point. Other ways already mentioned here are:

(a) what is fulfilled 'intensively' in Christ must be fulfilled 'extensively' in humanity,

(b) living 'by the faith of Christ' (Galatians 2.20),

(c) incorporation in Christ, or union with Christ, through the Spirit.

Jesus Christ's own faith is realised in us through the Spirit

In all three ways of expressing it, the same basic points hold true:

(i) the salvation which is already in Christ needs to be extended to us (a), or to put it the other way round we need to be brought into union with Christ so that we are in him, participating in his salvation (c), or (b) we live and we need to have faith, but the life we live is Christ living in us and the faith by which we live is the faith by which Christ himself lived, the living faith of Christ himself now in us.

(ii) what happens in us is not something different, is not an extra reality to what is already in Christ and does not add anything to it, but is the same reality, the same salvation. Thus in (a) what is fulfilled in us is no different from what has already been fulfilled in Christ but is the same reality now being realised in us through the Spirit. Similarly in (b) our faith is not a different faith from Christ's own faith but through the Spirit the same faith. In (c) Christ has first incorporated himself into our humanity, making our humanity his, and realised in it our full salvation and for Torrance our incorporation into Christ through the Spirit is not a different event from his incorporation into us, but exactly the same event now fulfilled in us. It is the role of the Spirit to realise in us what is in Christ so that, for example, his faith becomes ours and his prayer 'Abba, Father' is put into our lips, or again to put it the other way round, it is the role of the Spirit to lift us up into union with Christ to participate in him and all his blessings.

The enhypostatic inseparability of our faith from that of Jesus Christ himself

For Torrance, faith is what happens when through the Spirit we are brought to see personally that Christ had and has faith for us, that therefore we do not need to have a new and different faith in addition to his faith for us and when we understand this then we realise that the faith we have is in fact the very faith of Christ himself which is now in our hearts by the Spirit.

In his theology, Torrance attempts to be faithful to the way in which the New Testament holds together its emphatic emphasis on the whole work of Christ as God and man with the need for repentance and faith. For Torrance real theology must be inherently evangelical and real evangelism must be inherently theological. The challenge his theology presents to the church is to think through as he has tried to do, by means of careful biblical interpretation, the New Testament gospel in faithfulness to Christ, so that in its worship and life, theology and evangelism, preaching and ministry, it is better able to preach the unconditional grace of God together with its unconditional demands, holding out to all humanity the finished work of Jesus Christ for all together with the imperatives of repentance and faith. If in the light of Christ the gospel can be thought through to its christological basis in him, then the reality of completed salvation can be preached and held together with the need for and the reality of faith in Christ after the analogy of the *an-* and *en-hypostasia* of his person.

3 Knowledge of God through the Son or Word in God

One of the most important topics of theology for Torrance and one of the major emphases throughout his own theology is that of knowledge of God and here knowledge of God and salvation are inseparable. It is only through being restored to true knowledge of God that we can be reconciled and redeemed and it is only through atonement and reconciliation that we can be restored to true knowledge of God. Knowledge of God and reconciliation are mutually inseparable and both are fulfilled and given to us in Jesus Christ. Throughout his theology, therefore, Torrance stresses that the purpose of the incarnation and atonement is not just the forgiveness of sins and physical redemption of humanity, but the formation of genuine human knowledge of God in the humanity of Jesus. Jesus in his incarnate and risen humanity is the one person who knows God and the one point where we can know God as he is, in his triune being as Father, Son and Holy Spirit.

(a) The trinitarian basis of all knowledge of God through Jesus Christ

For Torrance, the ultimate basis of all knowledge of God, in a nutshell, is that Jesus is God himself within God, who in his becoming man became the man who knows God and who through the Spirit communicates and shares his own knowledge of God with us. There are several elements here:

(i) because Jesus is the eternal Word and Son in the very heart of God, knowledge of him is knowledge of God in his inner being and a sharing with him as Son in his own filial relationship and knowledge of the Father.

(ii) the nature of God as Trinity and the nature of Jesus as the Word and Son within God is such that knowledge of him *is* knowledge of God the Father. Jesus is the very image of the Father and so to know him as the Son *is* to know the Father and to know him as the Word *is* to know the very mind and rationality of the Father.

(iii) in his incarnation and in his *enhypostatic* humanity Jesus is the one true human knower of God.

(iv) Jesus through the Spirit makes himself known to us and at the same time opens us up to know him, to participate in his knowledge and assimilate it and know the Father through him.

The ultimate bedrock of knowledge of God is that the incarnate Word is the Word within God

For Torrance the foundation of all knowledge of God is that Jesus Christ comes from *within* the heart of God. He is the God who comes from within the heart of God and therefore he and he alone is able to make God known as he is. Torrance stresses, therefore, that Jesus is the Word *in* God (John 1), eternally in God, who because he has become man, become human flesh, human person and human speech, he is able to make God known to us as he in his own inner being.

The Word has always been Word and person in God

It is supremely important, for Torrance, that the Word did not begin to be when God spoke in creation, let alone when he spoke to humanity, but that the Word has always existed and inheres eternally in the being of God. It is also supremely important for Torrance that the Word is a person and that therefore all knowledge of the Word is personal knowledge, knowledge of the Word in his person as the second person of the Trinity, the eternal Son. When we know the Word, we know him in his being and person in the heart of God and we cannot separate him from that. To know the Word therefore is to know him *personally* in his being in God and through him to know the Father personally in the Spirit. Knowledge of God is always through his Word and Son and always personal, always through the Son in the inseparability of his Word and person.

That is as true of the Old Testament as it is of the New Testament for God is always known personally in his Word. The Old Testament is the prehistory of the incarnation, as Torrance calls it, the Word beginning to shape the concepts, language and mind of Israel in preparation for his coming. The Word in the bible is also always living Word, dynamic Word, who speaks and it is done, who promises and fulfils his promises. The Word is known in the continuity of the history of Israel, the living 'I am', known always in his person, personally through his mighty acts.

The incarnation means the Word of God is now eternally incarnate in the person of Jesus Christ

When the Word became man, the 'I am' of the Old Testament was revealed as the eternal Word and Son become flesh, the Word in God now dwelling on earth. In his person there was a hypostatic union of divine and human nature, divine Word and human word, which in his risen humanity is now the eternal union of the living divine Word and human word. Divine Word and human word, divine act and human act, divine being and human being, are all now eternally inseparable in his one living person. The Word of God cannot therefore be abstracted from his divine-human person but is identical with it. The Word of God is the living Jesus Christ, divine Word become human word in his person.

(b) A deeper view of scripture focussed on the mediator between God and man

The importance of this for Torrance is that it leads to a deeper view of scripture in which it is not regarded, as it sometimes is, as an abstract or as a copy or deposit of divine truth, but in which the truth of scripture is to be found in the living person of Jesus Christ to whom it points. If when we know the word of God in scripture we do not really know God himself in his person and being but are simply given truths about him in words and statements, then a theory of verbal inspiration of some kind is necessary to connect and identify the truths of scripture with the truth as it is in God. In that case, there are two ultimate foci of knowledge, the truth of scripture and the truth in God held together by a theory of inspiration. But if the word of God we know in scripture is the Word who is in God, who has become man, who in his person is the one hypostatic union of God and man, of the Word who is known and the man who knows the Word, then he in his person is the mediating point of knowledge of God. He is the mediator, the new focus of knowledge, the one who holds God and man together in himself, the eternal Word become living human word. Scripture then becomes the indispensable but intermediary mediator, if we can put it like that, of the real mediator, Jesus Christ, and the inspiration of scripture becomes the fact that it has been specially inspired and shaped by the Spirit to be the written word that leads us to and is itself shaped by, structured around and patterned on Jesus Christ.

(i) The Word and truth of God identical with Jesus Christ who always makes himself known

If Jesus Christ is the mediator of knowledge of God, then at once we are involved in a relation of depth between scripture and God in his being. Jesus Christ stands in the middle, reaching back to and into the eternal depths of God and reaching out and down to us through the Spirit and the written word of scripture. The truth remains identical with Jesus Christ in his divine-human person, identical with the being of God in his incarnate person and his own being in the Father and the Spirit. To know this truth and this Word is to know God himself, in his triune being, in the person of Jesus Christ. This is the Word and truth of God, known in the richness of its depth in God, speaking to us in scripture and communicating *himself* through it.

(ii) A simple identification of scripture with the truth of God bypasses the incarnate mediator

This means that there cannot be any simple identification of the Word and truth of God with the written word of scripture without flattening out the relation of depth which should lie between it and God and without bypassing Jesus Christ in his person as the mediator and so disregarding the incarnation. When God makes himself known, he always makes *himself* known and does not just communicate truths about himself. The Word and truth of God always remain identical with himself and now that the Word and truth of God have become incarnate they remain identical with the person of Jesus Christ. They cannot be torn apart from him and therefore scripture cannot just be regarded in a flat one or two dimensional way, as if it could hold the truth in itself or be a transcription of a truth which has been separated from Christ, but it has to be regarded three or four dimensionally in a relation of depth in which it finds its truth in the person of Jesus Christ.

(iii) A christological understanding of the truth of scripture

That does not mean any lessening of scripture, but quite the contrary, its enhancement as the historical human word specially shaped and inspired by the Word to be the means by which he is known, the cradle as it were in which he lies. Torrance himself grew up in a missionary family in which the bible was regarded as the word of God to mankind and through which God himself was to be heard speaking, a view which he held throughout his life. For him the bible was holy scripture. He continued to read it right through two or three times a year in his daily devotions and his language and thought is steeped in the language and thought of the bible, particularly in the familiar language of the King James Version. Torrance grew up believing in the inspiration of the bible (although without any particular theory of it) and a Christ centred view of scripture in which we know the Word of God in Christ addressing us personally. Both aspects of scripture remained central to him and as his theological views matured and deepened he came to see the way in which (as already outlined above) the two are held together through a doctrine of scripture patterned on the person of Christ.

The challenge of knowing scripture and interpreting it theologically and doxologically in Christ

The challenge of Torrance's doctrine of the Word and of scripture is the challenge of taking scripture as a whole and of interpreting it in terms of its *scopus* or goal in Jesus Christ, thus seeing it in its relation of depth with its truth in his incarnate person. It is the challenge of knowing scripture as intimately and thoroughly as we can and interpreting it faithfully, not only historically with the help of the best insights of modern scholarship, but also theologically. Interpreted theologically, the truth of scripture is the incarnate Word, Jesus Christ known in his eternal being in the Trinity. So interpreted, the scriptures become for Torrance not less but more important, not less holy but more so, and through their pages we are opened up in prayer and worship to a knowledge of God as Father, Son and Spirit where theology becomes doxology and doxology flows into theology, and the two are inextricably enmeshed together.

Acknowledgements

It is a pleasure to thank once more the many people, members of Torrance's own family and others who have contributed so much to the publication of these lectures. It has been a privilege to collaborate with Jock Stein of the Handsel Press and Robin Parry of Paternoster Press. To Jock is due the credit for arranging and initiating the project with T.F. Torrance to publish his lectures and from the outset his publishing expertise has been an invaluable help. The labour of typesetting, compilation of indexes and arrangement of photographs is all his. To Robin fell the task of collaborating with InterVarsity Press in the USA and overseeing the final publication. Both have been unstintingly helpful and a great pleasure to work with.

My brothers James and Donald Walker lent their copies of Torrance's lecture handouts. Dr Dennis Rewt contributed a photograph of his own as well as his skills in the digitalisation of photographs. Dr Nathan McDonald gave help with points relating to the Hebrew of the lectures as did Dr Roy Pinkerton and Dr Joanne Walker with the Greek. Several people, Donald and Judith Walker, Marion Foggin, Clare Parsons and Dr Jennifer Floether have commented on elements of the text and made useful suggestions. Professor David Fergusson of New College has been warmly supportive throughout as has Dr Tom Noble who remembered Torrance's recommendation of his introduction to *The School of Faith* as preparatory reading for his lectures. I should also like to thank Professor Trevor Hart and Dr Stephen Holmes for their support and helping to facilitate work on the Torrance lectures. Particular thanks must go to Dr Elmer Colyer, Professor John Webster and Dr Gary Deddo for their careful reading and balanced comments on the text and its merits.

Points of difficulty in the wording of the text or its precise interpretation were discussed with Torrance's brother, the Rev David Torrance. He and my brother Dr James Walker who heard the lectures himself and who like David Torrance has a thorough understanding of Torrance's theology have both read the edited text carefully and made many helpful and perceptive comments or suggestions. Professor Alan Torrance also assisted on a number of points of difficulty. The help of all three has been invaluable and generous in time and support. Thomas S. Torrance has throughout keenly and ably assisted in the lectures' publication on his father's behalf as well as kindly supplying the preface, historical information and a photograph of his father at work.

I would also like to thank my parents, family and friends for their support and encouragement throughout and likewise my colleagues at the Edinburgh University Outdoor Centre at Firbush Point, Loch Tay, not least for their understanding and patience for the many hours I shut myself away in the evenings and days off to work on the lectures. It has been a privilege to be able to do so much of the work in such an inspirational and beautiful setting. Editing the lectures has afforded a unique opportunity both to learn even more from them than in student days and to repay some of the debt of gratitude for them by helping to make them available to a wider audience.

Robert T. Walker
Edinburgh, August 2009

Chapter One

THE ATONEMENT IN THE NEW TESTAMENT

In our course of study so far we have considered the incarnation as the Word become flesh, the Son become servant (*Incarnation*[1] chapter 2), and then we considered the incarnate life of the Son in his union of divine and human natures and considered it as atonement already in operation in the achieving of reconciliation between the Father and his alienated children (*Incarnation* chapters 3 – 7). Now we go on to consider the *passion* of Christ in which he recapitulated the whole work of his incarnate mission and brought it to its triumphant fulfilment in his atoning and reconciling death on the cross. If all that we have considered so far can be subsumed under the saving work of Christ as *prophet*, that is as Word made flesh, as advocate, then what we are now to consider can be subsumed under the saving work of Christ as *priest*, the Son and Word of God undertaking the awful work of expiation of guilt and the reconciling of sinful man to communion with holy God.

The language which the New Testament uses to set this out is drawn from the long history of God's dealings in revelation and reconciliation with his covenant people Israel. That language is used in the sovereign freedom of the New Testament revelation, in the sovereign freedom of the Son of God who, as he comes into the situation prepared for him in Israel, acts both critically and creatively in fulfilment of the Old Testament patterns of understanding and worship provided within the covenant. We must seek therefore to examine that language, and through it and by means of it, seek to understand what the New Testament teaches us of the death of Christ. And yet we must pass beyond the Old Testament language to the actual person and work of Christ himself and allow his person and work as mediator to remould in our obedient understanding of him, even the language divinely prepared in the old covenant, for here it is with the new covenant in the blood of Christ that we are concerned.

---

[1]   T.F. Torrance, *Incarnation*, Paternoster UK and InterVarsity Press USA, Milton Keynes & Downer's Grove, 2008.

1 The approach to the doctrine of atonement

As we approach the doctrine of the death of Christ we do well to
remember two things of prime significance.

(a) *The mystery of atonement*

We recall that in the Old Testament liturgy of the day of atonement[2]
the most important part of the deed of atonement is done within the
veil beyond human sight. After the sacrifice made on the altar in the
holy place, the high priest took some of the blood shed in sacrifice and
disappeared behind the veil, 'ascending' (as it was put) into the holy
of holies. He entered shrouded with a cloud of incense and at the very
risk of his life he approached the divine mercy seat, sprinkled the
sacrificial blood upon it under the shadow of the golden cherubim[3]
and there held communion with God and made intercession for Israel.
That inner mystery God ordained to be completely veiled from human
eyes: the innermost heart of atonement, its most solemn and awful
part, was hidden from public view.[4] It is ineffable.

That divine ordinance from the old covenant serves to remind us, as
we seek to understand the cross, that though the veil of the earthly
temple was rent from top to bottom,[5] Jesus entered within the veil
'into heaven itself',[6] into the holy of holies of God's immediate presence
and there he acted as our high priest and mediator beyond the view of
humankind – the nature of his work was unutterable. That means that
the innermost mystery of atonement and intercession remains mystery:
it cannot be spelled out, and it cannot be spied out. That is the ultimate
mystery of the blood of Christ, the blood of God incarnate, a holy and
infinite mystery which is more to be adored than expressed. Here we
tread the holy ground of the garden of Gethsemane and Calvary and
here we must clap our hand upon our mouth again and again for we
have no words adequate to match the infinitely holy import of
atonement.

It is precisely (in part at least) for that reason that before he suffered
Jesus gave us the sacrament of the Lord's supper, that the broken bread

---

2   Lev 16.

3   Lev 16.12-14.

4   Lev 16.17.

5   Matt 27.51; Mark 15.38; Luke 23.45.

6   See Hebrews, especially chapter 9.11-12, 24.

and the poured out wine enacted in solemn *anamnesis*[7] might speak and communicate to us ever again what our poor human words are unable to do. As often then as we go to holy communion and see the celebrant take the bread in hand and break it and utter anew the words of Jesus, 'This is my body given for you', and pour out the wine and raise the cup and utter anew, 'This is my blood shed for you', we are directed to the fact that here in the action of the sacrament there is extended to us the inexpressible mystery of atonement through the body and blood of the saviour.[8] That sacrament ordained to communicate Christ to us in action forbids us at any point to think that we can enclose the mystery of the blood of Christ in words or in doctrinal formulations, or to think that we can set forth any fully adequate account of its meaning.

(b) A decisive new deed of divine intervention

Here we must recall that in the death of Jesus Christ we have a deed of divine intervention which sets our life on a wholly new basis. It is a decisive deed which makes the ground of our approach to God an act and word of God that cuts away the ground from all our human religion and establishes a new relation to God so utterly wonderful that we are overwhelmed, and so radical that it entails a complete reversal of our previous attitudes and of all our preconceived ideas. This reversal means that *we cannot think our way into the death of Christ because the continuity of our thinking and striving has been interrupted by it, but we may think our way from it* if we follow the new and living way opened up to us in the crucifixion. Here is a deed of unearthly magnitude before which we can only bow in utter humility – far from being able to fit the death of Jesus into our life and our own preconceptions or notions we face the demand that we should be conformed to his death. We can understand the cross only by *metanoia*, repentance and a change of mind, which is correlative on our part to the 'wonderful exchange' or *mirifica commutatio* on Christ's part when he who was rich was made poor for our sakes that we might become rich,[9] when he the just exchanged his place with our place, with us who are utterly unjust, that we might be made the righteousness of God in him. To that atoning reversal of our status, to the atoning exchange it involves, we must be

---

[7]   Gk, 'remembrance', calling to mind again, re-calling.

[8]   See Matt 26.26-28; Mark 14.22-24; Luke 22.17-19; 1 Cor 11.23-26.

[9]   2 Cor 8.9.

obedient in our understanding and mind if we are even to begin to apprehend its significance.

No mere theory of the atonement is possible

Now these two facts, a) the mystery of atonement and b) God's new initiative, tell us that we cannot have any mere theory of the atonement. No merely theoretical understanding is possible, for abstract theoretic understanding does away with the essential mystery by insisting on the continuity of merely rational explanation. But that is just what we cannot give of the awful fact of the descent of the Son of God into our hell and the bearing by the Son of God of divine judgement on our behalf, for all rational explanation must presuppose a basic continuity here between man and God, but that is just what the atonement reveals to be wanting by the very fact that God himself had to descend into our bottomless pit of evil and guilt in order to construct continuity between us and God. Or to put it otherwise, what logical relation is there between the death of Jesus on Golgotha and the forgiveness of our sins today? There is no logical relation, no formal rational continuity – that is why the preaching of the cross is foolishness, sheer unreason to 'the Greeks' as St Paul put it referring to the Gentiles.[10]

There is of course a mighty continuity between the death of Christ on the cross and the forgiveness of our sins, but it is a continuity that God himself achieves and makes through his atoning *act* and the intervention of his own *being*. And therefore the cross provides a wisdom that 'the Greeks' or humankind in general know nothing of. Thus we cannot begin to understand the atonement by bringing to it principles of formal rational continuity or by adopting an abstract theoretic explanation. In seeking to unfold the meaning of the death of the Son of God, therefore, we must have recourse to putting together conjunctive statements[11] based upon the inherent synthesis to be found in the person of the mediator and not in any logical or rational presuppositions which we bring to interpret what he has done for us. Here above all, then, in seeking to understand the death of Christ, we must *follow* Christ, and think only *a posteriori*,[12] seeking throughout to

---

[10]   1 Cor 1.22-25.

[11]   Statements which need to be taken together in order to give an understanding.

[12]   Lat, literally 'from after', hence 'following on the event', 'according to the fact', ie. obedient to reality.

be conformed in mind to Christ himself as the truth. That is the only way to understand and at the same time to reverence the infinite mystery and majesty of this atoning deed on the cross which by its very nature reaches out beyond all finite comprehension into eternity.

(c) *Atonement in the blood of Christ*

If we are to follow Christ himself in word and action in understanding the atonement, as we follow him solemnly in word and action in celebrating the sacrament of his passion, then we must take the way that he himself provided for our understanding. Let us recall the all important fact, to which the Gospels bear very faithful witness, that Jesus revealed himself throughout his ministry only in such a way that his words and his acts kept pace with one another.

(i) *The gradual unfolding of Jesus' mission in word and act*

This is one of the most remarkable things about the way in which all the Gospels present the words and acts of Jesus, their clear presentation of the restraint exercised by him upon any revealing of his messianic mission apart from the unfolding of that mission in his actual life and work. That applies above all to the secret of his passion which he is to accomplish at Jerusalem. For that passion he was consecrated at his baptism in which he identified himself with sinners in order to fulfil the word of God in judgement and forgiveness, but his whole life as the servant of the Lord, as the Son entering upon a mission of obedience to the righteous will of the Father, was his passion, his 'baptism' and his 'cup'[13] as he put it on more than one occasion. And yet it was only gradually that he began to reveal the secret of his passion and the fact that he 'had to' suffer at Jerusalem. On the one hand (as the evangelists make clear) he exercised a sovereign control over all his *acts*, and bringing even the reactions of people against him under the mastery of his purpose, refused to come to the supreme purpose of his life, 'to give his life a ransom for many', until the hour of God arrived. On the other hand he restrained his *words* revealing this purpose and communicated them only as the pattern of his mission began to unfold in its actual course, making his words and acts proceed *pari passu*[14] in the one mission of revelation and reconciliation.

---

[13] Luke 12.50; Mark 10.38.

[14] Lat, 'with equal step', in line with each other.

Jesus reached a stage in his ministry, however, when he set himself to teach the disciples little by little, as they were able to take it in, the secret of his passion.[15] This was a progressive activity. 'And he began to teach them that the son of man must suffer many things, and be rejected by the elders and the chief priests and the scribes, and be killed, and after three days rise again.'[16] It was after this that there took place the transfiguration[17] in which, as Luke tells us, he discussed with Moses and Elijah his 'exodus (*exodon*)'[18] which he would accomplish at Jerusalem,[19] but all the evangelists relate it to a revelation of his messianic secret as the Son who is to die and rise again. On this occasion Jesus set himself to initiate the disciples further into an understanding of his approaching passion.[20] As James Denney pointed out long ago,[21] Jesus deliberately reiterated what he had to say, for he had something very definite and important to communicate to them, though clearly they shrank from receiving it. Then again, when Jesus and his disciples began their last journey up to Jerusalem, he made it clear that he was going forward to meet 'the hour' of his great mission and passion and set himself again to tell them the things that were to happen to him[22] and spoke again of his 'baptism' and his 'cup'.

(ii) The final unfolding of Jesus' mission in word and act

Thus Jesus unfolded his messianic secret in words *pari passu* with the unfolding of his messianic secret in acts, and hence the nearer he approached his 'hour' as he called it, the more he was ready to reveal the mystery of his passion. That he did in two supreme 'words' about his atoning death, the first as he neared Jerusalem and the second at the last supper itself in order to provide the disciples with the means of grasping the awful fact of the crucifixion. There in a final unfolding of word and act he gave his supreme revelation of the meaning of his death. In the midst of the disciples he enacted the holy supper setting forth his crucifixion in the breaking of the bread and in the pouring

---

15   Mark 8.31; Matt 16.21; Luke 9.22.
16   Mark 8.31.
17   Mark 9.2ff.
18   Translated 'departure', RSV, NIV.
19   Luke 9.31.
20   Mark 9.9f.,30f.
21   James Denney, *The Death of Christ*, Hodder & Stoughton, London 1902, p. 26ff.
22   Mark 10.32f.

out of the cup, but along with those acts he uttered words designed to speak of the mystery of his passion. These all important sayings, in the order in which they are given in Matthew and Mark are *first*, 'the son of man came not to be served but to serve, and to give his life as a ransom for many',[23] and *second*, 'This is my body given for you. This is my blood of the new covenant which is shed for many for the remission of sins.'[24]

These two 'words', taken together with all that he had previously spoken, and understood in the context of what he was actually doing at the last supper and clearly set himself to suffer, must form the basis for our doctrine of atonement and redemption. Our approach to the doctrine of the atonement, therefore, must be one in which we take those words together with the acts which they were meant to accompany and in the light of the sacrament in which words and acts are held together in a unity of significance. From that we must seek to understand them, and then from them advance to the fullness of what the New Testament has to teach us about his atoning and reconciling death on our behalf. We shall examine them by taking the second first, the 'word' of the new covenant, and then afterwards seek to understand the nature of the atoning event upon which the new covenant is grounded.

We have already had to consider the concept of the covenant and the essential part of Christ the servant Son in its fulfilment and transformation into the new covenant. But at this point we do well to recapitulate some of that in order to get the setting of the atonement in the covenant quite clear.

2 *The Old Testament covenant and its fulfilment*

Behind all that we hear in the Gospels lies the fact that in creating man God willed to share his divine glory with humanity and willed them to live in communion with himself. With the fall of man and woman and their estrangement from God, the will of God assumed redemptive form in the covenant of grace. God wills unrelentingly to be our God and Father and wills us to be his people and his children, and it was in that redemptive purpose that he made his ancient covenant in the first place with Abraham and Israel, but with the purpose of universal blessing. It was his universal covenant of grace which he began to set

---

23　Matt 20.28; Mark 10.45.

24　See Matt 26.26-28; Mark 14.22-24. Cf. Luke 22.17-19; 1 Cor 11.23-26.

out in Israel, in the midst of humanity, in order to work out a way to the blessing of all nations in its complete fulfilment. In this covenant God gives himself to humanity and assumes humanity into covenant communion with himself. He affirms himself as God and Father and requires of mankind their love and obedience and reliance.

The covenant of Sinai: 'I will be your God, you shall be my people'

That covenant was given its fullest and clearest manifestation at Sinai.[25] 'I will be your God, and you will be my people. I am holy, be you holy.' The covenant had two sides: God's act of sheer grace in which he took Israel into his paternal favour, and Israel's act in obedient response to God's grace set forth in the covenant. In view of Jesus' deliberate relation of his words and acts at the last supper to the covenant of God with his people, it cannot be denied that an adequate and full understanding of Jesus' teaching here has to take into account that essential pattern of the covenant formed between God and Israel: 'I will be your God and you will be my people. Walk before me and be perfect. Walk in all the way that I command you'.[26] Jesus has come to fulfil the covenant will of God both from the side of God, fulfilling all the promises of God to his people, and from the side of man, walking in all the way that the people were commanded to, and as such to be the servant of the Lord in mediating a new covenant.

But at Sinai God's will for his people is revealed in the law and in the accompanying cult he provided an appointed, or covenanted, way of response. Israel is not left to make its own response, for God in his mercy provides for the adequate response of his people in worship and obedience, and does that in such a way that the covenanted ways of response have the form of witness to God's mercy. At every point they inculcate reliance upon God's provision, and point ahead to the complete fulfilment of the covenant promises in a mediator and saviour.

The covenant fulfilled through the faithfulness of God, in judgement and redemption

All through the history of Israel the covenant remained steadfastly upheld by God in spite of the sin and unfaithfulness of his people, so that the sinner came to find that the hope of redemption lay in the

---

25   Exod 19.1ff.

26   A summary by Torrance of the substance of the covenant – see Exod 19.4-8f., 20.1ff.; Gen 17.1-2; Deut 5.1ff.,32-33.

steadfastness of God in keeping covenant even when the only way in which God could faithfully keep covenant and faith with his rebellious people was in judgement. Whatever way that had to take over against the sinner, it was in the covenant faithfulness of God alone that the whole hope of redemption had its source. Hence although the prophets used the language of the mighty acts of God in the past, in the exodus and in the establishment of the covenant at Sinai, or the language of the cult in which those events were given, as it were, a liturgical extension into the worship of Israel throughout history, they bent that language forward to speak of the 'new things' that God would perform and the 'new covenant' which he would institute with his people in which, as Jeremiah put it, they would all know the Lord 'from the least of them to the greatest of them', 'for I will forgive their iniquity and remember their sin no more'.[27] For the prophets it was in the fulfilment of the covenant and therefore in the faithfulness of God in keeping and fulfilling it that the hope of redemption was seen to lie.

The promises and the commands of the covenant both fulfilled in Christ

That covenant is fulfilled in Jesus Christ, for in him God's faithfulness realises his will for his people. The *promises* of the covenant are fulfilled in him, in the ultimate gift of God's very self to man; the *commands* of the covenant are fulfilled in him, in the obedience of the son of man. This realisation of the covenant will and faithfulness of God in Christ is *atonement* – atonement in its fullest sense embracing the whole incarnate life and work of Christ. It involves the self-giving of God to man and the assuming of man into union with God, thus restoring the broken communion between man and God. It involves the fulfilment of the divine judgement on the sin of humanity and the removal of that obstacle or barrier of sin between God and humanity, but that barrier is removed precisely by the complete fulfilment of the covenant, in which God kept faith and truth with humanity in its sin by its complete judgement – therefore it is in this complete judgement alone that men and women can be justified before God and have a just and true place in the covenant-communion with God. That whole work of atonement, of establishing covenant communion, Christ fulfilled in himself, by incarnation and atonement. He fulfilled it in himself as mediator, God and man in one person, acting from the side of God as God and from the side of man as man.

---

[27] Jer 31.31-34.

Now how precisely does the New Testament think of the covenant with Israel as gathered up in the new covenant inaugurated in the blood of Christ at the last supper and fulfilled in the death of the mediator on the cross? Here we have to look at *three important aspects of the old covenant* and see how they point to and so provide us with our initial understanding of the fulfilment of the new covenant in the blood of Christ.

(a) The signs and seals of the covenant – circumcision and passover

The first aspect concerns the divinely given signs that marked out the covenant and sealed it in the actual lives and homes of the people of the covenant, namely, *circumcision* and *passover*, the two sacraments of the Old Testament, sacraments not concerned primarily with the cult but with the actual life of the people. In both of them, the blood of the covenant sealed the covenant, cutting it into the flesh of Israel in circumcision, and in the passover sealing the promise of redemption in the life of Israel and its seed from generation to generation. As we have already had occasion to see, all that is remarkably fulfilled in the incarnation of Jesus of the seed of Abraham although that circumcision is entirely fulfilled, as Paul puts it, only in the total circumcision, that is the crucifixion of the body of Christ on the cross.[28] There once and for all the blood of the covenant is shed and the covenant is for ever cut into our human flesh and fulfilled in it.

But in the Old Testament the blood of the covenant was also shed in the passover in the slaying of the passover lamb and here the blood of the covenant signified the renewal and establishment of the covenant through a mighty act of redemption. The annual celebration of the passover in the homes of the people was looked on as a renewal of the covenant from year to year in the life and flesh of the people, and the renewal therefore of the promise of final messianic redemption after the pattern of a new exodus leading to a new covenant – a favourite theme of the second Isaiah.[29] The new covenant would thus be inaugurated in a great messianic passover, and it is that passover that Jesus celebrated and inaugurated at the last supper. Now what is the relation of the passover to the cult? The Old Testament distinctly speaks of the passover lamb as a sacrifice, and it is in the conception of sacrifice in the passover that we have the link with the other aspects of the Old

---

[28]   See Col 2.11f.

[29]   Isaiah 40 – 55.

Testament covenant that we must note. However, before we do that, we must ask more precisely what does the Old Testament mean by *covenant sacrifice*?

(i) The derivation of the word 'covenant', berith

The Hebrew word for covenant, *berith*, is of uncertain derivation, but there are three main views.

(1) 'Barah', cut – covenant by cutting or sacrifice

The older view (held for example by Gesenius) is that covenant or *berith* derives from *barah* meaning to cut. There is certainly a great deal of evidence for this both within and without the Old Testament. Thus the ancient desert rite of covenant was one in which a stick or stone was broken in two and each part given to one of the parties of the covenant, while redemption of the pledges (*tessera*) of the covenant could be effected only through a matching of the broken parts of the stick or stone to form a whole. Similarly, covenants were formed in the cutting of the flesh and in the flowing together of the blood from the covenanting parties. But within the Old Testament itself the evidence is strong. Thus, 'Gather to me my faithful ones, those that have cut (*karat*) a covenant with me by sacrifice.'[30] The word 'cut' (*karat*) is used some 86 times in the Old Testament in connection with a covenant. It also seems evident that the same derivation is bound up with the original conception of circumcision as a seal to the covenant cut into the flesh of God's people, and so a seal of initiation into the covenant. The covenant sacrifice is also associated with cutting in another significant way. Thus, 'And the men who transgressed my covenant and did not keep the terms of the covenant which they made (*karat*) before me, I will make like the calf which they cut (*karat*) in two and passed between its parts (*batar*)'.[31] Compare Genesis 15, where a different word for 'cut' (*batar*) is used for the cutting of the animals but the same word *katar* for the making or cutting of the covenant, 'And he (Abraham) brought him all these, cut (*batar*) them in two, and laid each half (*batar*) over against the other; but he did not cut (*batar*) the birds in two . . . When the sun had gone down and it was dark, behold

---

[30] Psalm 50.5 RSV/KJV: both the KJV and RSV translate the Hebrew 'cut' as 'made'. Cf. Psalm 105.9, 'the covenant which he made (cut, *karat*) with Abraham'; Jer 31.32 (Hb, v. 31).

[31] Jer 34.18f. (the Hebrew words in these quotations are given in their verbal root forms).

a smoking fire pot and a flaming torch passed between these pieces. On that day the Lord made (*karat*) a covenant with Abram'.[32] This was the establishment of the covenant and circumcision was its sign and seal cut into the flesh.[33]

(2) 'Barah', eat – the concept of the covenant meal

Another view held by many modern scholars is that *berith* derives from another word *barah* meaning to eat or give to eat. If this derivation is correct, the original sense of covenant would refer to the establishment of a bond through a fellowship meal. Thus we find that to set a meal before someone or to partake of a meal with them is equivalent to entering into a covenant with them.[34] We have a similar use in Psalm 69, one of the psalms most often cited by our Lord or in reference to him, for example by the disciples, 'zeal for thy house has consumed me',[35] or 'They gave me poison for food, and for my thirst they gave me vinegar to drink. Let their own table before them become a snare; let their sacrificial feasts be a trap.'[36] Here the psalmist refers to an act in which the covenant was violated through treacherous use of the symbols of the covenant. The evangelists evidently recalled this verse in reference to what was done in the crucifixion of Jesus – by offering him vinegar and gall the Jews deliberately repudiated covenant relations with Christ.[37]

This relation between a meal and the making of a covenant also appears evident in many important places in the Old Testament, for example in the act of Melchizedek in setting bread and wine before Abraham,[38] in the significance of the meal of showbread[39] in which the priests partook before the face of God in the tabernacle, and of course above all in the covenant meal at Sinai when the covenant was established,[40] and with which the passover meal came to be assimilated in the annual celebration of the renewal of the covenant in the homes of the people.

---

32 Gen 15.10,17-18.

33 See Gen 17, esp. v. 10f.

34 See Gen 26.28-31, 31.44-55; cf. Exod 24.11.

35 Psalm 69.9; John 2.17.

36 Psalm 69.21-22.

37 Matt 27.34,48; cf. Mark 15.23,36.

38 Gen 14.18.

39 Also called the 'bread of the Presence', Exod 25.30; Lev 24.5-9.

40 Exod 24.11.

(3) 'Baru', *bind, bond – the bond of the covenant*

There is still a third view, which holds that *berith* derives ultimately from the Akkadian *baru* which carries the conception of chaining, binding. Compare Ezekiel, 'I will cause you to pass under the rod, and will bring you into the bond of the covenant',[41] a conception found elsewhere, for example in the Roman historian Livy. According to Peterson, *berith* derives from an old Semitic root meaning 'oath', which is a related form of the same view of its derivation. At any rate when the term covenant is found in the Old Testament it always or at least very frequently carries with it conceptions of the oath of the covenant, of a binding bond with its covenant promise.

All three views have thus much to say for them – the actual linguistic origin of the word *berith* we shall have to leave to the linguistic experts, but it must be evident that the ideas involved in these various derivations are not contradictory to one another, and certainly that they all had a part to play in the Old Testament concept of the covenant, if not through derivation at least through association. Take the simplest form of covenant relation, the breaking of a piece of bread and the passing of it to the right and the left for participation. That was regarded as creating a bond of loyalty and kindness, and as involving 'mercy and truth', concepts associated so many times with the covenant between God and Israel. Here the three meanings associated with the three suggested derivations are all present and are brought together into one rite. The root idea may well be to 'cut' a covenant or to break into two parts, but that has just as clear a reference to a meal, to the breaking of bread as the Hebrew idiom puts it, as to the cutting of sacrifice, and both involve the conception of covenant engagement. All these elements are undoubtedly combined in the full conception of the Old Testament notion of covenant by covenant sacrifice. That is, the particular covenant rite is the breaking and dividing of a lamb or calf, the eating of it in covenant fellowship, and the cementing of a lasting bond.

(ii) *The inauguration of the new covenant at the last supper*

All that surely comes out very clearly in the Lord's supper which Jesus speaks of as 'the (new) covenant in my blood',[42] and along with the sharing in the cup he distributes the bread broken in covenant enactment and they eat in fellowship together. Picture the action of

---

[41] Ezek 20.37 KJV.

[42] See Matt 26.28; Mark 14.24 – the word 'new' appears in some ancient versions of both Matthew and Mark.

Jesus carefully. He solemnly took bread and broke it, one half in one hand, the other half in the other hand, and said 'Take, eat; this is my body', and beneath his hands in the middle is the cup filled with the blood of the grape, the 'blood of the covenant, which is poured out for many for the forgiveness of sins'.[43] It is distinctly a covenant sacrifice involving a) the breaking of the bread and the shedding of the blood, b) communion in a covenant meal, and c) commitment and solemn obligation, an aspect especially brought out by the epistle to the Hebrews.

But here the Greek steps in to round out the meaning of the Hebrew. The Hebrew *berith* cannot mean a testament, in the sense of a last will and testament, but the Greek *diathēkē* can mean that as well as covenant. St Paul in the epistle to the Galatians and the writer of the epistle to the Hebrews deliberately combine both, and that is probably a tradition that goes back to the evangelists themselves. Thus the fourth Gospel appears to regard Jesus as delivering his last will and testament to the disciples, but included in that last will and testament is above all the gift of his Holy Spirit. And hence the supper is also celebrated in the church as a communion with Christ in and through which he bestows upon us his Spirit giving us to share in his death and resurrection.

That takes us far beyond the point that concerns us here. What we have to consider here is the fact that the Son of God solemnly inaugurated a new covenant in which he bound his disciples to himself in the most solemn and awful way – no longer through animal sacrifice or simply through the breaking of bread, but through the eating of his own body and the drinking of his own shed blood. It is as Paul calls it 'the body and blood of the Lord',[44] which he gave for his church. God himself steps into the place of the sacrifice required in the making of a covenant, and offers himself in Jesus Christ as the sacrificial lamb. And here the Old Testament images of the lamb of atonement and the lamb of the passover are conflated together into what the fourth Gospel calls 'the lamb of God'.[45] At the last supper, therefore, Jesus offers himself as the pascal[46] lamb for sacrifice, then goes out to be laid upon the altar of the cross bearing the sins of the world, and so becomes the means

---

[43]   Matt 26.26-28.

[44]   1 Cor 11.27, cf. 1 Cor 10.16.

[45]   John 1.29.

[46]   Adjective from *pascha*, Greek for 'passover' (Hebrew *pesach*).

by which the new covenant is forged between God and man, forged in such a way that it is once and for all, never to be repeated, but ever to be remembered in the pascal mystery of the Lord's supper.

(b) The covenant and the cult

Here we are concerned with the second major aspect of the Old Testament covenant, the mighty acts of God in the redemption of Israel out of Egypt and the once and for all establishment of Israel as his covenant people at Sinai upon the basis of the law and the cult. Two mighty acts established the covenant, the passover redemption out of the tyranny of Egypt, and the Sinaitic revelation. Thus the covenant rests upon the solemn proclamation of the divine name and of the divine will to forgive iniquity, transgression and sin. The two pledges of the covenant were the decalogue[47] and the cult established in the tabernacle. They are the pledges of the fact that within the covenant God will reveal himself to his people through his word and that he will continue to extend his forgiving mercy to them.

(i) The establishment of the covenant at Sinai and its liturgical extension in the cult

Look at it like this. Once and for all historically, the covenant was established in the unrepeatable events of Exodus and Sinai, which included Moses' act of mediation on behalf of Israel in the fearful sin that led to the breaking of the tables of the law[48] and the reconstituting of the covenant in the second giving of the tables of the law.[49] That belongs to the once and for all events in Israel's history and to the mighty acts of God intervening in it. But cultically all that is given liturgical extension or continuity in the cultic ordinances. Thus the tabernacle was constructed on such a basis that the inner holy of holies represents cultically Mount Sinai shrouded in thick darkness and smoke into which Moses entered again to make intercession for Israel, and to renew the covenant and receive again the law of God establishing Israel once and for all as a nation in covenant with God. The other main elements that belong to the construction of the tabernacle are likewise by way of cultic representation of the mighty acts. Thus in the temple, the laver or the sea as it was called later,

---

[47] 'Ten words', ie. the ten commandments.

[48] Exod 32.

[49] Exod 34.

represents the washing or baptism of Israel in crossing the Red Sea, and the act of the liturgical priesthood, of the high priest in particular, represents a symbolic or cultic repetition of the act of Moses in ascending to commune with God on Mount Sinai. That is repeated every year on the day of atonement[50] when the high priest ascends into the holy of holies and comes back with the renewal of the covenant and the blessing of peace and forgiveness.

(ii) The difference between covenant sacrifice and daily sacrifice

Before we can understand that fully we have to consider the next major aspect of the Old Testament covenant, namely, the mediator of the covenant, but at this point what must be noted is that there is a radical difference between covenant sacrifice and daily sacrifice in the cult. The covenant sacrifice is that which is concerned with the founding or renewing of the whole covenant, and that was cultically performed once a year only on the great day of atonement. But within the covenant there were very many sacrifices all of them apposite, as Calvin showed with remarkable clarity, to the infringements of the different commandments in the decalogue. These lesser sacrifices and oblations were daily or special, and were all dependent for their worth and propriety upon the renewal of the whole covenant annually, and so were dependent upon the one great sacrifice on the day of atonement when the covenant was renewed for the year.

Now the Old Testament makes a distinction between so called involuntary or unwitting sins, that is, sins done *in error* (*bi-shegagah*) and sins *'with a high hand'* (*be-yad-ramah*)[51] – not a very good way of putting it in English. But what that represents is this – sins with a high hand, usually idolatry, blasphemy, and severe crimes like murder and adultery, were sins which shattered the covenant relation with God, and therefore the appointed sacrifices for the atonement of sins incurred within the framework of the covenant were of no avail. When the covenant is broken, *only God acting directly can forgive* and provide the adequate way of witnessing to his forgiveness and judgement – a very clear instance of that is God's treatment of David in his murder and adultery.[52] But for the ordinary misdeeds and sins of the people of the covenant, appropriate sacrifices were provided which were only valid, so to speak, *within* the covenant relation, within its

---

[50] Lev 16, cf. 23.26-32.

[51] Num 15.22f.,29-30.

[52] 2 Sam 11.2 – 12.13.

commands and promises. But all these sacrifices were of no avail if God refused to confirm and renew his covenant mercies on the day of atonement, so that the sacrifices for sin had only suspended effectiveness until the next day of atonement had taken place – that fact is very clearly recognised by the *Mishna*[53] tractate *YOMA*.

(iii) Christ's fulfilment of the covenant sacrifice

Now when Christ came to fulfil the covenant sacrifice, it was the fulfilment of the ultimate sacrifice upon the basis of which all the divine acts of mercy and forgiveness were based. This covenant sacrifice was the basis upon which everything else rested, and apart from the enactment and validity of the one covenant sacrifice, all the words of divine pardon and forgiveness have no avail – the people are still in their sins. But that brings us now to consider the third aspect of the Old Testament covenant without which we cannot understand the rest.

(c) The mediator of the new covenant

At this point we have to seek to understand the significance of the *priesthood* of Christ.[54]

(i) The Old Testament priest as witness to the word of God

The New Testament word for priest, *hiereus*, rests upon the significance of the Old Testament *kohen*. It seems clear that the primary function of the Old Testament *kohen* had to do with the word of God.[55] The priest was a truthsayer, a seer and so the Levitical priesthood was concerned with the *debir*, the holy place of the word or oracle of God. All the

---

53 The collection of Jewish oral law and teaching, accepted along with the Talmud as authoritative in Judaism and secondary only to the scriptures in influence and importance.

54 See further T.F. Torrance, *Royal Priesthood*, 2nd edition, T & T Clark, Edinburgh 1993, chap.1, 'The royal priest'.

55 See Deut 31.9-11f,24f, 33.8-10; cf. the story of Samuel, esp. 1 Sam 2.18, 3.1, 3.19 – 4.1; 2 Chron 15.3, 17.8-9; Mal 2.1-9, esp. v. 7; Hosea 4.6 (cf. 6.6); Neh 8, 9.3; cf. also Lev 10.11; Ezek 22.26, 44.23; Ezra 7.21,25; 2 Kings 17.27-28; 2 Chron 19.8-10. See further the reference, *Royal Priesthood* p. 1, to the article by G. Schrenk on *hiereus* (priest) in Kittel, *Theological Dictionary of the New Testament*, vol. 3, Eng. trans. Eerdmans, Grand Rapids 1966, p. 257ff.

priest does, all liturgical action, answers to the word given to the priest who bears that word and mediates it to people, and only in relation to that primary function of the priest, does he have the liturgical function of sacrifice and oblation. In the Old Testament, sacrifice was originally not the prerogative of the institutional priest, but with the centralisation of the cultus in Jerusalem it came more and more to be his prerogative. In the passover ceremony the head of the house made the sacrifice, though later the sacrificial act was carried out by the priest in the temple, while the sacrificial lamb at the passover was consumed in the home. Even with the centralisation of all sacrifice and oblation upon the altar in Jerusalem, the liturgical function of the priest is by way of 'answer to God's word'. The whole liturgy of oblation was an ordinance of grace initiated by God and ordained by him. It was not an undertaking on the part of man. It is God himself who appoints the sacrifices, so that cultic action is in the form of a divinely appointed response to his word.[56] The liturgical oblations do not have any efficacy in themselves, but have efficacy in so far as they are liturgical obedience to the divine ordinance detailed in all the cultic commandments. They therefore point beyond themselves to God's will to be gracious, to pardon and to forgive.

It is God who forgives: liturgical sacrifice is only witness to God's forgiveness

These cultic acts took place in the tabernacle which was the place in the midst of Israel where God put his name, and lodged his word.[57] It was called the dwelling place of his testimony. There Israel heard God's word and served him as he appointed.[58] Hence the tabernacle was also called the 'tent of meeting'.[59] All action within it was by way of acknowledgement and witness to God's testimony of himself. It was therefore the tent of testimony (*skēnē tou marturiou*), as the Greek Old Testament, the Septuagint, puts it. We cannot emphasise enough then that the sacrificial and liturgical

---

[56]   Exod 23.14f., 25.8ff.,40ff, 26.30ff., etc; Num 7.89ff.

[57]   The word of God, represented by the ten commandments or 'ten words' as they are known in Hebrew, was lodged in the ark or the 'ark of the testimony' as it was also called, Exod 25.8-21, 40.20-21; Deut 10.1-5.

[58]   Exod 25.22.

[59]   Exod 40.34f.

acts were regarded as *witness* and only witness to God's own action and appointment. The real agent in the Old Testament liturgy is God himself. God is not acted upon by means of liturgical sacrifice. Liturgical sacrifice rests upon God's self-revelation and answers as cultic sign to God's own word and action, which is the thing signified.

That is very clear, as we shall see later, in regard to the Old Testament teaching about cultic atonement. The words for atonement, reconciliation, expiation, etc, are *not* used of action upon God, of placating God or propitiating him. God is not the object of this action. He is always subject. It is God himself who performs the act of forgiveness and atonement or expiation. The sacrifices are liturgical expiations which do not act upon God but answer to God's action in forgiveness and merciful cleansing of sin. Atoning sacrifices were sacrifices expiating sin in *witness* to the act of God. In Israel they are never sacrifices by man in an attempt to placate or propitiate God.[60] Thus the question so often posed, 'Do the Old Testament sacrifices remove sin or are they only concerned with liturgical or cultic uncleanness?' is a false question with a false alternative. They are witness to God's covenant will to remove all iniquity, transgression and sin.[61] It is actually God himself who performs the act of forgiveness, propitiation and atonement, while the priestly cultus is designed to answer to his act and bear testimony to his cleansing of the sinner.

(ii) Moses and Aaron – the mediation of the word and priestly witness

The priesthood of the Old Testament in its double character, as mediation of God's word and priestly witness to God's revealed will, is given very clear interpretation in the account of the relations of Moses and Aaron, brother priests of the tribe of Levi.[62] Moses is represented as the unique mediator, the one who talks with God face to face and mouth to mouth.[63] Because of this Philo used to speak of Moses as 'the high priestly *logos*' or 'the high priest, the

---

[60] Cf. C.H. Dodd, *The Bible and the Greeks*, Hodder & Stoughton, London 1935, p.93.

[61] Exod 34.7; Lev 17.11, cf. 16.21, etc; Neh 9.17f.,31-32; Psalm 32.1,5, 51.1f., 78.38, 85.2, 86.5, 130, etc.

[62] Cf. Psalm 99.6.

[63] Exod 33.9-11, 34.27-35; Num 12.1-8; Deut 34.10-12.

logos'. In this supreme relation to God's word, Moses is the priest *par excellence*, whose mediatorial functions are seen as he pleads with God for Israel's forgiveness, even if it means the blotting out of the name of Moses himself from before God,[64] or again upon Mount Horeb as Moses intercedes for Israel in its battle with Amalek.[65] It is to Moses supremely that God reveals himself in the establishing of the covenant and in the writing of the decalogue and establishing of the cultus. It is with Moses that God communes above the mercy-seat on the ark of testimony.[66]

Over against Moses, and in a secondary status, Aaron is regarded as the liturgical priest who carries out continual cultic witness to the actual mediation that came through Moses. In this way the cult was, as we have noted, a liturgical extension into the history of Israel of the once and for all events of Exodus and Sinai. Those events were given permanent form in the covenant of law and sacrificial witness. Thus the holy of holies represented cultically Mount Sinai, and the ascent into it of the high priest was a liturgical reminder of the covenant founded at Sinai on the ground of atonement and intercession. The supreme act of the high priest therefore was on the great day of atonement when bearing the iniquity of the people he ascended into the holy of holies to make atonement for his people. At the very risk of his life and relying upon the blood of the covenant he entered into the presence of God, to confess the sins of the people, and to receive the divine pardon and renewal of the covenant. Then he returned from within the veil to the waiting people with the blessing 'peace be unto you' and to put the name of God, the three-fold *Yahweh* of the Aaronic benediction[67] upon the people of the covenant.

The priesthood of the word and the priesthood of liturgical witness operate together and point forward to the 'suffering servant'

Those two priestly functions as seen in Moses the prophet-priest and Aaron the liturgical priest provide us with the full biblical conception of priesthood, but it is the priesthood of the word which is primary, and the liturgical priesthood secondary. And yet the combination of the two in the covenant made clear that the whole

---

64   Exod 32.7-14,30-32; Num 14.11-24; Deut 9.6-29, esp. 16-20,25f.

65   Exod 17.8-13.

66   Exod 25.21-22.

67   Num 6.22-27.

intention of God was that the two operate together in the actual life and existence of Israel as a holy people. True worship must be done into the flesh, and so the true worship of Israel looks forward to the day of the Lord when his word will become event and be enacted as truth in the heart of his people. Thus the whole intention of the cult is bent forward to point to a new covenant when the word of God will be inscribed upon the tables of the heart[68] and truth will spring out of the land.[69] It was in that line of development that the cult-prophets, in language drawn from the priestly sacrifices and the great salvation events of the Exodus and Sinai liturgically extended in them, place before Israel the doctrine of the *suffering servant*. As a lamb led to the slaughter the servant embodies in flesh and blood the covenant of God with Israel – he is indeed the supreme mediator of the covenant. Here the two aspects of priesthood are brought together into one, for the conceptions of Moses and Aaron are telescoped together in the vicarious life and mission of the servant of the Lord in order to set forth at once the redeeming action of God for Israel and the sacrifice of obedience enacted in Israel, thus pointing ahead to the union of God and man in messianic redemption and breaking into the gospel.

(iii) Jesus the servant who fulfils the Old Testament priesthood and inaugurates the covenant in his own life and death

This is precisely how Jesus thinks of himself at the last supper, as the servant who inaugurates the new covenant in his body and blood, and in the imagery used, that of the pascal lamb and that of the day of atonement are run together, for here as the lines converge in Christ they are inevitably conflated. The Isaianic servant came to be regarded as the instrument within Israel by which the word would be done into the flesh, and by which the vicarious sacrifice for Israel's sin and iniquity would really be carried out, thus mediating the new covenant and its communion between God and his people. So Jesus acts at the last supper, and as he advances to the cross his acts are in fulfilment of the covenant in two senses: in him the covenant word is translated into his obedient humanity, and in him the symbolic sacrifices are no longer symbolic witness to God's will to forgive, for *he is himself the sacrifice in which God's will for forgiveness and salvation is fully enacted and carried out.*

---

[68]   Jer 31.31-34.

[69]   Psalm 85.11 KJV, RSV 'faithfulness' (Hb *emeth*, truth, faithfulness).

'The blood of the covenant' – *covenant sacrifice and covenant communion*

Thus Christ fulfils the covenant in that he is the embodied communion between God and man, and in that he is himself the instrument whereby the covenant is established. He is himself the law or word of God in the flesh, and he is himself the cult, both the high priest and the victim in one person, fulfilling both functions in his one act of vicarious self-sacrifice on the cross. The Son offers his life and death in a covenant sacrifice for the remission of sins and the establishment of covenant communion between God and humanity. As such he is the mediator of the new covenant in his body and blood – and that is precisely what he declares at the supper. 'This is my body for you. This is my blood of the new covenant shed for many for the remission of sins.' Therefore he gave us the sacrament of his passion that in its celebration we may, until he comes again, continue to show forth his death as the inauguration of the new covenant in which, reconciled through the body and blood of Christ shed on the cross, we have communion with the heavenly Father as his dear children. That is the meaning of the atonement which the sacrament expresses better than words.

'A ransom for many' – *the integration of the person and work, life and death of Jesus*

But what of the meaning of the actual event of atoning action whereby all this comes about? That is where we have to turn back for our instruction to the other words of Jesus shortly before his passion. 'The Son of Man came not to be served but to serve, and to give his life as a ransom for many'.[70] Now let us notice right away that in these words Jesus does not regard the work he has to fulfil in his death as divorced from his life. It is his *life* which he has come to give in redemption, or in ransom for the many, and that concerns his whole course of obedience as the incarnate servant-Son. His life as the servant comes to its completion in his sacrifice on the cross, but the significance of that sacrifice reposes also upon the fact that he has lived out a life of perfect obedience to the Father's will in the midst of our estranged humanity. It is his whole life, and above all that life poured out in the supreme sacrifice of death on the cross, that makes atonement for sin, provides the ground and basis for forgiveness, and means the redemption of those whose lives have been forfeit before God because of sin and guilt and death. *Christ himself is our propitiation*, as St John puts it.[71]

---

[70]   Mark 10.45; Matt 20.28.

[71]   1 John 2.2; 4.10 KJV, RSV 'expiation'.

And yet the whole direction of Jesus' life as the servant, and of his obedience as the Son is directed ultimately to 'this hour' in the establishment of the new covenant in the giving of his body and the shedding of his blood. This integration of atonement and incarnation, of the work and person of Christ, is of the most fundamental significance and must not be lost sight of for a moment. The death of Jesus cannot be isolated from his life, while the whole mission of his life presses toward the final act of obedience to the will of God when through the sacrifice of himself in death on the cross, he made expiation for our sins and mediated a new covenant in which we have communion with God as those who have been redeemed from the power of guilt and death and live in the freedom of his children.

The need to interpret the two sayings of Jesus together

Now so far I have been using, without pausing to justify it, the traditional language describing the atoning action of Christ carried through his life and brought to its consummation on the cross. But how precisely are we to interpret this atoning act of redemption? What is the meaning of the actual event on the cross? Here we must take both the *logia* or sayings of Jesus and consider them together and in the light of each other, for they plant our feet at once upon the right path of understanding. The second 'word', spoken at the last supper speaks specifically of the means of redemption and the mode of atonement in the shedding of the blood of Christ, and relates it directly to the covenant will of God, as we have seen. The first 'word' speaks more specifically about the actual event of redemption, and it is into it that we must probe more deeply. It must obviously be interpreted in the light of the end of Mark 8 ('what can a man give in return for his life')[72] as well as Psalm 49 ('no man can ransom himself, or give to God the price of his life . . .')[73] but we are also very fortunate in having two comments on Christ's saying within the New Testament itself, in Timothy ('the man Christ Jesus, who gave himself as a ransom, *antilutron*, for all')[74] and Titus ('Jesus Christ, who gave himself for us to redeem, *lutrōsētai*, us from all iniquity')[75] which are very revealing.

---

[72] Mark 8.34f.

[73] Psalm 49.7-8.

[74] 1 Tim 2.6.

[75] Titus 2.13-14.

In the light of what these other verses have to say, the general meaning seems quite clear. No one can provide for themselves or for another a means of salvation which will be accepted 'in exchange for their life' (*antallagma tēs psychēs*).[76] But this is just what Jesus declares he has come to do: to give his life as a ransom, thus offering an interpretation of his death in terms of cultic atonement and in terms of the suffering servant.

Jesus claims to be the servant who offers his life in an act of sacrifice which will emancipate the lives of 'many'.[77] In the next chapter, therefore, we will consider what Jesus meant by giving his life as a ransom, a *lutron* in redemption of the many, and we will do that by looking at the Old Testament conception of redemption to see what light that throws upon the New Testament understanding.

---

[76]   Matt 16.26; Mark 8.37 KJV/RSV. KJV 'in exchange for', RSV 'in return for'.

[77]   Cf. J.K. Mozley, *The Doctrine of the Atonement*, Duckworth, London 1915, p. 46f.

Chapter Two

REDEMPTION IN THE LIGHT OF THE OLD TESTAMENT

The constraint of the Old Testament scriptures on the life of Jesus

One of the first things we have to say both about Jesus' teaching that he came 'to give his life as a ransom for many (*lutron anti pollōn*)', as about his teaching on 'the new covenant in his blood', is that it is given in a setting in which Jesus is profoundly conscious of the constraint of the will of God upon him. That is not simply a constraint that arises out of his direct consciousness of the Father's will, but a constraint laid upon him by the revelation of the Father's will in the scriptures of the Old Testament. He has come to fulfil the will of God manifested in covenant relation with Israel and therefore he spoke of himself as having to fulfil the Old Testament scriptures. Because his passion is related to the Old Testament and he deliberately laid down his life in such a way as to take upon himself the burden of the servant of which the Old Testament spoke, it is only in the context of the Old Testament revelation that we can rightly appreciate and understand his teaching. Thus we have to take into account not only the teaching of the Old Testament cultus about atoning sacrifice and redemption, but we have to consider very especially certain passages that were undoubtedly in our Lord's own mind as he uttered these words, such as Psalm 49 and Job 33, Exodus 12, Jeremiah 31 and Isaiah 53, to name only some of the most obvious of them. Thus only by careful sifting of the Old Testament background can we reach a true understanding of his words and acts in the New.

The relation of the New Testament to the Old – and of the Greek to the Hebrew

To do this properly, however, we must start not only with the life-setting, the *sitz im leben*,[1] of the New Testament and early Christan writers, but with their intellectual setting, their *sitz im denken*, so to

---

[1]   German, *sitz im leben*, situation in life – *sitz im denken*, situation in thought.

speak, and try to look at the Old Testament inheritance from *their* perspective. It would be false exegesis to alter the New Testament meaning to suit what scholars with a different attitude to the Old Testament might consider, on scholarly grounds, to be the proper meaning of an Old Testament passage. But this means also that from the intellectual setting of the New Testament writers we have to look at the Old Testament in terms of *its own self-interpretation* which it acquired at the hands of its final redactors or transmitters, because it is in that light only that the New Testament and early Christian community regarded it.

On the other hand there has to be combined with this an adequate understanding of the language medium used in the New Testament and early church, and consequently we have to interpret the contribution of Greek to this understanding of the Old Testament inheritance. Thus it is worth noting right away, especially in view of what follows, that the term which the New Testament uses for redemption, *apolutrōsis*, is derived not from the verb but from the noun *lutron* which refers not so much to the act as to the cost of redemption. That should warn us that any account of redemption in the New Testament and early church which does not give central significance to the *lutron*, the price of redemption, is hardly likely to do justice to their understanding. On the other hand, when this word is used to transfer a mode of thought from the Hebraic outlook into the Greek, it cannot even at this point avoid modification in the relation of the price of redemption to the activity and life of the redeemer.

In his 'word' about giving his life as a ransom Jesus makes quite central the concept of redemption and the price of redemption or ransom, *lutron*. What precisely did he mean by that, and what precisely does the rest of the New Testament mean when it speaks of redemption by using the cognate terms *apolutrōsis*, redemption, *lutrousthai*, redeem, etc? To get explicit understanding of these terms we have to turn to the 'theological dictionary' employed by the writers to the New Testament, namely, the Septuagint.[2] There we discover that behind this conception there stand three basic Hebrew terms, *padah*, *kipper* and *go'el* (or *gaal*),[3] each with its cognates speaking of a very different aspect of redemption.

---

[2]   The Greek translation of the Old Testament, also known as the LXX, the Roman numerals for 70 since it was translated by 70 scholars (the actual number was 72).

[3]   *Gaal* is the verbal root of the noun *go'el*, redeemer.

1 The Old Testament terms for redemption

I should like now to examine the understanding of redemption mediated through these terms and draw out their significance for the doctrine of redemption in the New Testament. In doing so we must not forget that the spoken language of Jesus and most of the writers of the New Testament was Aramaic, and that in Aramaic one term tends to displace the others and is usually preferred for two of them, namely *paraq* meaning to tear away, set free, rescue, deliver.[4] That does not mean that we can discount the manifold contribution of these basic Hebrew terms but that they are all regarded as building together one conception of redemption which *paraq* frequently renders in Aramaic and *lutrousthai* and its cognates frequently render in the New Testament.[5] Nor must we forget, on the other hand, that these concepts are radically re-interpreted by the New Testament in its very use of them to speak of the unique sacrifice of Christ, and that ultimately therefore it is from their application to him and not merely from their linguistic history that the terms have doctrinal significance for us.

(a) Padah, pidyon (lutrousthai, lutron), *redeem, ransom*

The term *padah* (with its cognates) is used to speak of redemption with emphasis upon the cost of redemption and the nature of the redeeming act rather than upon the nature of the redeemer. Moreover the object of redemption is always a living thing, and

---

[4] For the use of *paraq* in the Old Testament see Psalms 7.2(3), 136.24; Lam 5.8. For examples of the Aramaic usage see the Targums on Exod 13.13 (for *padah*), on Lev 25.25f (for *goel*). It must be admitted also that even in Hebrew the distinction between the three basic terms mentioned is not always maintained. They overlap in their meanings and can be used sometimes more or less as equivalents. See, for example, Psalm 69.18(19) *gaal, padah*; Hosea 13.14 *padah, gaal*; Jer 31.11(10) *padah, gaal*; Exod 21.30 *kipper, padah*; Psalm 49.7(8) *padah, kipper*; Job 33.24 *padah, kipper*; Jer 31.11 *padah, gaal*. (Root forms only – Hebrew numbering of verses in brackets).

[5] For more on *padah, kipper* and *goel* as background behind the NT *lutron* and *lutrousthai* see further the article by Procksch in Kittel, *Theological Dictionary of the New Testament*, vol. 4, Eng. trans. Eerdmans, Grand Rapids 1967, pp. 328-335.

because the element of substitutionary offering or price is entailed, the idea of a life for a life is involved. A typical use is that which describes the redemption of the first-born[6] while the substitutionary nature of the redemption is clearly seen in the substitution of the tribe of Levi in place of the first-born for priestly service.[7] Another typical use is that which describes *redemption from slavery*.[8] In all these instances the cost of redemption is prescribed by the *law*, so that redemption from slavery is also a redemption in fulfilment of the law.

(i) The redemption of Israel out of Egypt and 'the house of bondage'

But these cultic or liturgical uses appear to be secondary to the primary use of the word to speak of *the redemption of Israel out of Egypt as God's first-born son* which was carried out by God's mighty hand and with the substitutionary sacrifice of the passover lamb. ('By strength of hand the Lord brought us out of Egypt, from the house of bondage.')[9] This is a favourite way of speaking of the redemption of Israel in the Deuteronomic literature.[10] The act of redemption is also pushed back to God's activity with Abraham[11] and can be applied to the personal experience of the individual.[12] Moreover in contrast to redemption as described by *gaal*, redemption as described by *padah* does not appear to involve, or at least involve to the same strong extent, a conception of responsibility or obligation on the part of the redeemer – it is an intervention in sheer grace in which God grants redemption out of oppression, out of anguish or distress, or out of the power of an adversary or alien, and out of the power of death as the last enemy. But it is the redemption of Israel out of Egypt and out of the house of bondage which seems to supply the dominant and exemplary instance of *padah* redemption, and here there lies close to this understanding the concept of redemption not only out of an alien power but out of the bondage of sin and death into a new

---

6   Exod 13.13,15, 34.20; Num 18.15f; cf. Lev 27.27; Num 3.12,46-51.

7   Num 3.12,44ff.

8   Exod 21.8; cf. Lev 25.47ff. where *gaal* is the word used for redemption by a kinsman.

9   Exod 13.14ff.

10   Deut 9.26, 13.5(6), 15.15, 21.8, 24.18.

11   Isaiah 29.22.

12   Psalm 34.22(23).

relationship with God.[13] The exemplary act of divine redemption out of Egypt is made to speak prophetically of a future redemption not only out of Babylon, but into the messianic kingdom of peace and joy.[14]

(ii) Redemption out of divine judgement and alien oppression into the liberty of the kingdom of God

Behind this there lies a point of profound theological significance affecting the biblical meaning of redemption, namely, that redemption is at once out of the judgement of God and out of an alien and repressive power, which for its part is brought under the judgement of God. That is clear in the passover redemption of Israel out of Egypt. The mighty hand of God redeems Israel his son out of the tyrannical oppression of Pharaoh, and redemption is from the avenging angel of death sent by God and is therefore a redemption that involves sacrifice. Somehow redemption out of the power of evil oppression is only possible through redemption from the judgement of God and redemption into a covenant bond with God sealed with the blood of sacrifice. As such it is redemption into joyous victory and freedom.

This is an understanding of redemption of profound theological significance for the New Testament. In the synoptic Gospels, for example, this redemption by the mighty hand of God is related to the breaking in of the kingdom upon those bound in sin, bringing them release and freedom, as for example when Jesus by the finger of God casts out demons and delivers oppressed people from the thraldom of evil into liberty and abundance of life. This aspect is particularly prominent in Luke's Gospel, from the opening chapter, which relates the redemption in Christ to the fulfilment of the messianic hope of Israel, to the twenty-first chapter, which brings the kingdom of God (*basileia tou theou*) and redemption (*apolutrōsis*) into such close relation as really to identify them.[15] It is the mighty act of God's sovereign grace redeeming his people out of their bondage and affliction, but the Gospels reveal how much that act of pure grace cost Jesus himself, for it was his whole life that he poured out in compassion and mercy, giving it in exchange for 'the ransom of many'.

---

[13]   See Psalm 49.15(16), 130.7-8; Hos 13.14; cf. Jer 15.19-21.

[14]   Isaiah 35.10; Jer 31.11f.(10f.)

[15]   Luke 21.28,31.

Redemption through expiation from guilt and the power of sin and darkness[16]

But there is another major point that must be singled out for special attention, that redemption involving sacrificial oblation to God is redemption out of the bondage of guilt and out of the thraldom of sin. It is both deliverance out of oppression and from guilt and punishment at the same time. This is especially evident in St Paul's conception of redemption from the bondage of the law, that is not from the law as such which is God's gift, but from the regime of the law as it is used by sin. The law, which expresses God's will, is holy and exacts from us the judgement of death, and yet this law has become an alien and oppressive tyranny, for the powers of evil use its accusations against the sinner to bind them all the more in the slavery of sin. In this way the law becomes the strength of sin, as St Paul puts it. Redemption that involves the expiation of guilt and the justification of the ungodly[17] renders people not only free from the law but therefore also emancipates them from the alien power of evil.

This is especially important because it brings together the notions of redemption as expiation before God's holy will and redemption out of the powers of darkness. Precisely because the law in its judgement is the strength of sin, and because therefore redemption by the mighty hand of God and redemption by expiation are inseparable, the whole notion of ransom paid to an evil power is impossible on the biblical view. Here evil is revealed as having no right over man, and to have usurped the right of the law of God and through that right to have robbed God of his inheritance in his people and of his people in their inheritance in God. Therefore when someone is justified before God they are free from the power of evil at once.

(iii) Redemption from the wrongful 'exousia' or authority of evil

This is precisely the teaching that is so powerfully expressed on the pages of the gospel in the conception of redemption from the *exousia* or authority of evil. God is the only source of *exousia* (which means both 'might' and 'right'). But God has delegated his *exousia* to others who exercise it rightly only in obedience to God, and who can be known as 'authorities' such as rulers in the state or in the temple. But they become evil 'authorities' when they usurp the *exousia* of God and claim

---

[16]   Cf. T.F. Torrance, *The School of Faith*, James Clarke, London 1959, pp. xcii-xciii.

[17]   Cf. Rom 3.21-25, 4.5.

it as their own, using it for their own ends, thus confounding their own might with the divine right. Typical on the pages of the Gospels is the way in which *exousia* was exercised by the scribes and pharisees. It is in a similar way that the law is regarded, for the law has usurped the *exousia* that belongs to God alone and exercises it as if it were inherent in the law independently of God. On the pages of the Gospels this refers to the way in which the divine law has become entangled with the traditions and commandments of human origin and so has become an oppressive force. That is another way of saying that the law is the strength of sin, for our sin seeks to clothe itself with the *exousia* of the law, to hide behind divine sanctions manifested in the law.

How then is Christ regarded as redeeming us from the oppressive power of evil thus clothed with the law? The Gospels think of the incarnation as the invasion of the mighty Son of God into our domain where evil has come to exercise its sway, in order to break its bonds and to deliver us from its captivity. That is the significance of the whole life of Jesus, particularly from his temptations immediately after his baptism to the agony of Gethsemane and Calvary. In the temptations Jesus was confronted with the *exousia* and glory of the kingdoms of this world and offered them in return for his worship of the devil – that is to say, he was offered the *exousia* and he refused it categorically. He denied the devil any rightful *exousia* and he refused to avoid the way of the cross, the way of the suffering servant into which he had publicly and solemnly entered in his baptismal consecration as the lamb and servant of God. He chose the way of redemption indicated by the suffering servant identified with expiatory sacrifice, and then pressed toward the final act of the servant of the cross, there meeting in full the hour and power of darkness. As he came through the temptations in the wilderness clothed with the power of the Spirit, so he came through the temptation and passion of his self sacrifice on the cross clothed with the power of the resurrection, *Christus victor*, Christ triumphant, endowed with all power in heaven and earth.

(iv) Redemption from sin and evil by the holiness and obedience of Christ

But how did he do it? How did he achieve redemption? The Gospels make it clear that he met and overcame the powers of darkness by his holiness, as the holy one of God. At no point did he evade the demands of the law or the righteousness of God. He came to fulfil all righteousness and to fulfil every jot and tittle of the law, acknowledging to the fullest extent the divine sanction in the law. He submitted himself under the law and was wholly obedient to the Father's will in the life he lived on earth and in Israel. By his very holiness and perfect obedience sin had no power over him, and it was therefore as the holy one in entire fulfilment of the holy will of God that he invaded the domain of evil and redeemed us out of the power of darkness by his holy life and his holy submission to the Father's will even unto the death of the cross. His holiness in our life put us in the right with the holy will of God and so delivered us from the judgement of the law and its *exousia* in which evil seeks to clothe itself. So long as the holy will of God exercises judgement upon sinners through the law, sin and evil embattle themselves behind the law and reduce man to bitter bondage, but in the redemption of Christ by his holiness in which we are justified before God, we are no longer under the judgement or the power of the law. Therefore evil has all its usurped *exousia* stripped away from it and humanity is free from its tyranny.

Redemption that destroys the usurped authority of evil and frees humanity

Thus the redemption envisaged in the New Testament is redemption at infinite cost, but it is such an act of redemption in holiness that it destroys the usurped authority and brings it to naught, denying it any right to which deference should be paid. That, in the New Testament, is the unique sense of *apolutrōsis* as redemption which robs the authorities and powers of darkness and evil of their vaunted right, and by expiation before the holy will of God reveals that they have no inherent right, and no right to the price of ransom. It is through destroying the usurped power of the law and darkness over man that the redeemer 'leads captivity captive'[18] and opens up an entirely new situation in which the old order is annulled and a new order of freedom in the Spirit is ushered in.

To this conception of redemption the Greek language, as we shall see, offers its rich contribution, for *luō* means both to destroy[19] and to loosen, set free or liberate,[20] that is, dissolution and absolution. Thus the Greek tends to strengthen the double significance of redemption as a destruction of the power of evil and also a liberation from evil, a loosing from sin and guilt, and so of forgiveness and cancellation of debt.[21] The term *apolutrōsis* on the other hand emphasises not so much a single deed of atoning redemption as the far-reaching effect of

---

18   See Eph 4.8 KJV.

19   John 2.19; Acts 27.41.

20   John 11.44; Acts 22.30; Matt 21.2; Luke 13.15-16.

21   Cf. 1 John 3.8; Rev 1.5.

atonement. That is to say, the Greek form of the concept in *apolutrōsis* points rather to the state of redemption resulting from the mighty act of grace and power, and so carries a powerful and significant element of eschatological fulfilment still to be revealed in its fullness.

Thus the *padah* concept of redemption lying behind the New Testament language has much to offer in helping us to understand what redemption in Christ is and how he achieved it. Above all, perhaps, it helps us to see the essential unity between dramatic and forensic[22] redemption, that is, redemption by sheer act of grace and by justification. But it is to another word that we must turn to help us see further into the nature of this atoning justification or expiation.

(b) Kipper, kopher (lutrousthai, lutron), *redeem, ransom*

In two of the Old Testament passages which we noted appear to lie behind the 'word' of Jesus in Mark (about giving his life 'as a ransom, *lutron*, for many'), namely Psalm 49 and Job 33,[23] the Hebrew noun *kopher* is used to describe the *price* of the redemption described by the verb *padah*.[24] That brings these aspects into the closest relation and indicates that here we are probing more deeply into the nature of the act, its costly sacrifice, by which the barrier of sin and guilt between God and man is wiped out and man is redeemed. Thus if the term *padah* has to do with redemption from the power of sin, the term *kipper* has to do rather with redemption as the actual wiping out of sin and guilt, and so of effecting propitiation between man and God.

The basic meaning of the root *kpr*, *kipper* (or *kaphar*),[25] seems to mean to cover or to blot out. That is evident from the synonyms that are

---

[22] Legal, in terms of law or the law courts, ie. in terms of righteousness before the law.

[23] Psalm 49.7f (*padah* and *kopher* v. 7(8)); Job 33.22-28 (*padah* and *kopher* v. 24, *padah* v. 28).

[24] See also Exod 21.30 for the use of *kopher* and *pidyon* (*padah*) in the same verse.

[25] There are no vowels in Hebrew and therefore the basic verbal root here is simply the consonants *kpr*. Vowels are added to indicate the pronunciation and take the form of suffixes (dots or other markings) above or below the consonants. *Kaphar* is the basic form of the verb meaning *cover*, and *kipper* is the '*piel*' form of the verb used for *covering sin* or *expiating for sin*..

used along with it, such as *kasah*, to cover, and *machah*, to blot out.[26] The verb *kipper* is very rarely used literally, but is generally used in an extended sense meaning to cover sin or nullify through the offering of a propitiatory gift, and so to conciliate, such as the act of Jacob in 'covering the face' of Esau with a present,[27] or the act of appeasing the wrath of a king by a propitiatory action.[28] In acts of conciliation like this the gift or the offering is called *kopher* which is regarded as an equivalent or compensation, but the term is usually restricted to the gift offered in satisfaction for the shedding of blood, that is of a life for a life,[29] and so it is also applied to the redemption money, the half shekel, paid by every member of Israel at the census.[30] When this concept of atonement or covering is applied to relations with God, however, it is not used to speak of the covering of the face of God and so of conciliating him, but is used to speak of the covering of sin before his face or presence.[31] God is thus not the object of the atonement but the contrary.

The meaning of 'kipper': *God covers sin through the provision of an equivalent*

God is primarily the subject, for it is ultimately God himself who atones, who blots out sin, pardons it, casts it behind his back, invalidates it or annuls it.[32] Even when the priest carries out a liturgical act of atonement, he does what is appointed by God, does it in the presence of God, and what he does liturgically is to cover the sin with the blood of sacrifice, but that is by way of witness to the fact that it is always ultimately God himself and only God who can atone sin and put it away. Moreover, the blood of sacrifice which is used cultically to cover and so atone sin is explained as God's gift and appointment, so that the very use of sacrificial blood in response to the divine requirement points directly to the divine will as the sole reason and source of atonement –

---

[26] Cf. Psalm 32.1, 85.2(3) for *kasah*; Jer 18.23 for *machah* (and *kipper*); Neh 4.5 (Hebrew text 3.37) for the use of both.

[27] Gen 32.20(21).

[28] Prov 16.14.

[29] Exod 21.30; Num 35.31f; Prov 6.35, 13.8.

[30] Exod 30.12-13.

[31] Cf. A.B. Davidson, *The Theology of the Old Testament*, T & T Clark, Edinburgh 1904, p. 321.

[32] Deut 21.8, 'Forgive (*kipper*), O Lord, thy people Israel, whom thou hast redeemed (*padah*)'; Ezek 16.63; Psalm 65.3(4); 2 Chron 30.18.

'the life of the flesh is in the blood; and I have given it for you upon the altar to make atonement for your souls; for it is the blood that makes atonement by reason of the life.'[33] Theologically, then, the term *kipper* carries with it a double significance. As atonement it involves judgement upon the wrong either directly or vicariously through the offering of an equivalent, of life for life, and through this expiation of the wrong, atonement involves reinstatement to favour and restoration to holiness before God.

Perhaps the clearest application of the term can be seen from Psalm 49 where allied terms also help to bring out the meaning of atoning redemption. 'Truly no man can ransom (*padah*) himself (or his brother),[34] or give to God the price (*kopher*) of his life, for the ransom (*pidyon*) of his life is costly, and can never suffice that he should continue to live on for ever and never see the Pit . . . But God will ransom (*padah*) my soul from the power of Sheol, for he will receive me.'[35] Here the term *kopher* is used to describe ransom from the death penalty.[36] The fact that *kopher* is rendered in the LXX[37] not only by *lutron* but has also to be rendered on occasion by *exilasma*, *allagma* and *antallagma*[38] helps to indicate the way in which we are to understand the Hebrew and helps us also to understand the teaching of the New Testament, for example in Mark 10 and Matthew 20[39] about a redemptive expiation for the removal of an objective obstacle between God and man and for the restoration of communion between God and his people.

There are at least four main points that demand attention and fuller discussion here.

(i) The wholeness of redemption

There is a relative difference between the noun *kopher* and the more frequent verb *kipper* which must be noted. *Kopher* belongs more to the sphere of civil law and the verb *kipper* more to the sphere of the cult, but the two are ultimately inseparable from each other for they overlap

---

[33] Lev 17.11.

[34] Another reading here has, 'no man can ransom his brother'.

[35] Psalm 49.7-9 (48.8-10),15 (48.16).

[36] Cf. Job 33.24, 'Deliver (*padah*) him from going down into the Pit, I have found a ransom (*kopher*)...'.

[37] Greek Old Testament.

[38] *Exilasma*, price, equivalent; *allagma*, change, exchange, substitute; *antallagma*, exchange, substitute, equivalent, ransom.

[39] Mark 10.45; Matt 20.28.

in their significance and application. That is to say, here as elsewhere in the Old Testament, the forensic and cultic concepts of redemption have to be held together and not allowed to be separated. As we have seen, there was of course a distinction in the Old Testament teaching between sins done *in error* (*bi-shegagah*) and sins done *with a high hand* (*be-yad-ramah*)[40] but that is not the same thing at all as a distinction between ritual and moral cleansing or between sins consciously committed within the covenant and sins which deliberately infringed the basis of the covenant and so excised the offender from the covenant mercies of God. We shall consider the significance of that later.

It is important to remember that in the Old Testament there was no distinction between what we now call 'moral' and what we now call 'ceremonial'. 'The offences which we call ceremonial were not symbolical, they were real offences to Yahweh, against which his nature reacted . . . what might be called aesthetic or physical unholiness was held offensive to the nature of God in the real sense, in a sense as real as moral offences were offensive to him; and the purifications were true removals of these real causes of offence.'[41] Infringement of these ceremonial requirements was an offence then both because they were appointed by God to bear witness to him, and because they bore witness to the will of God to regard sanctification and redemption as involving the whole life of man.

No dichotomy between law and cult, moral and religious, or physical and spiritual[42]

Because there was no dichotomy between law and cult, between moral and religious things, there is no dichotomy between the realm of ideas and the realm of historical events. And therefore there can be no radical dichotomy between a moral and spiritual conception of redemption on the one hand, and on the other hand a cultic and dramatic conception of redemption, which from the human point of view could be regarded as primitive and mythological. This unity between the physical and the spiritual, the dramatic and the ethical, the cultic and the forensic, is of the utmost importance, for it means that redemption concerns *the whole life of man*. Once a dichotomy begins to be made between dramatic-cultic redemption and moral-ideal redemption, then the wholeness of the conception of redemption in both Old Testament and

---

[40]   Num 15.22f.,27-30.

[41]   A.B. Davidson, *op. cit.* p. 159.

[42]   Cf. T.F. Torrance, *The Mediation of Christ*, revised edition, T & T Clark, Edinburgh 1992, pp. 15-17.

New Testament is not grasped, and it becomes impossible to secure the dramatic conception of redemption from the charge of primitive mythology.

Now that distinction or dichotomy was made by the gnostics and by the rabbis. The distinction between the spiritual and the physical, between the ideal and the historical, is essentially a Hellenistic distinction taken over by later Judaism and is found already in the outlook and ideas of the pharisees, but it was only after the destruction of Jerusalem and the temple and the discrediting of the sadducees that we find this distinction strongly upheld by rabbinic Judaism, apparent even in their criticism of the *Mishnah*[43] and embodied in their radical separation between cult and law, between ritual and moral uncleanness. The same distinction was made by the gnostics,[44] for while they brought together myth and ritual in their worship, this was looked upon as pointing away to what was radically different, a timeless realm of pure idea and spirituality, so that myth and ritual were given a philosophical re-interpretation.

But whether in its rabbinic or gnostic form, the radical dichotomy of which we have been speaking disrupts the whole biblical conception of redemption as the redemption of the whole of human life from sin and corruption, involving the *sanctification of the whole man, body and soul, in the holiness of God*. It is therefore of the utmost importance that we learn from the Old Testament teaching that the dramatic and the ethical, the cultic and the forensic elements in redemption must be held together, for that is basic to all that the New Testament has to say about it.

(ii) The primacy of the covenant in both law and cult

The second point that needs to be emphasised is the primacy of the covenant, both in law and in cult. Indeed, it is primarily in the covenant that these two aspects are held together in unity (the forensic-ethical and cultic-dramatic conceptions of redemption). The covenant is the primary expression of the fact that God has set his love upon Israel and redeemed and sanctified it to be his people. As such the covenant

---

[43]   The *Mishnah* (Hb 'instruction') is the authoritative collection of Jewish Oral Law, traditionally dated in its compilation to the early centuries of the Christian era.

[44]   Gnostics believed in a higher spiritual realm of knowledge or *gnôsis* through the progressive attainment of which man could become closer to God and be liberated from the material realm.

represents not only the will of God for the communion of his people with himself, but it is given to the people to be the very form of their actual existence, not only before God but before all nations. Thus the covenant embraces the whole relation of God to man on the one hand, and on the other it describes the whole existence of Israel as God's people.

A breach in the covenant, therefore, is not only a breach with God but a breach in the actual existence of Israel. It is in this context, in the primacy of the covenant above all, that the Old Testament conception of redemption has its place, so that redemption is not only reconciliation with God, but the re-establishment of Israel's existence as a people before God, as the covenant-partner of God. This covenant relation and existence comes to be described even in the Old Testament in terms of fatherhood and sonship. The covenant means that Israel exists as God's son, his first born, his dear child, and redemption means the restoration of sonship, and of a holy sonship in relation to a holy God. To the whole basis of the covenant belongs the divine word, 'You must be holy, for I am holy'. Breaches of the covenant are therefore opposed by the divine holiness, and also by his mercy and truth, which wills the covenant bond between God and his people and wills to retain it.

Thus the wrath of God is God's holiness and faithfulness directed against breaches in the covenant, and it is wrath precisely because God in his love affirms Israel to be his child and gives himself in covenant mercy to be Israel's God. But because he is Israel's God, who is faithful to his covenant, he takes the side of Israel, defends and protects it as his own people and provides for it in all its need. Because he is Israel's God and Father who has freely gathered Israel into the sphere of his covenant mercies, he provides in his own mercy and initiative, ways and means of reconciliation, of wiping out offences, of cancelling the effects of sin, of re-establishing true relations with himself. Here it cannot be denied that in the Old Testament cult and covenant the expiating of guilt before the wrath of God is the chief element leading to the restoration of true communion with God.

(iii) Atonement lies in God's own will to pardon

We must now remember that the means of atonement and reconciliation with God so elaborately described in the cult are not regarded as having efficacy in themselves as if they worked God's forgiveness or compelled him to bestow his grace upon his people. Such efficacy as they have depends entirely upon the covenant which God of his free grace has established with Israel. Their efficacy is only within the covenant relationship in which they are ways and means appointed by God who thus approaches the sinner as 'covered' with the blood of the covenant and seeks their reconciliation, so that they may be drawn near to God in holiness. That fact distinguishes the Old Testament sacrifices from all heathen notions. And even here within the covenant the sacrifices are not regarded as demanding forgiveness, but as acts of liturgical witness to God's will to pardon, and witness to the fact that God's holiness restores his people to fellowship only on the grounds of the satisfaction of his holy love or the fulfilment of his covenant will. 'The sacrificial system assumes that sin makes a barrier between man and God; and that before the covenant relationship with Yahweh, which the individual normally enjoys as a member of the covenant people, can be restored, the sin must be covered or wiped out. For that Yahweh himself has made provision, and the final act of reparation is the presentation and sprinkling of the blood, the most sacred of all earthly things, as the equivalent of life.'[45]

Sins within the covenant covered by God's provision of the annual covenant sacrifice

As we have seen, it is noteworthy that a distinction is made between the daily and particular sacrifices and oblations, and the great covenant sacrifice made only once a year. The daily oblations and sacrifices are for acts of sanctification and pardon, and concern the daily sins of the people (not including the sins with a high hand), but these sacrifices depend for their efficacy upon the one covenant sacrifice which is offered anew on the great day of atonement, and which explicitly includes all the sins, iniquities and transgressions of Israel, for the covenant embraces the whole life of Israel. This sacrifice represents the cultic renewal of the covenant in the shedding of the blood of the covenant and the sprinkling of it before God.

But it is significant that while it is clearly indicated here that the renewal of the covenant is on the ground of the shedding of blood and in the offering of life for the life of the people, the ultimate nature of the covenant and of the pardon it offers for sin is hidden in the darkness behind the veil and the only explanation really offered is in the word of the Lord, 'I have given it to you upon the altar'.[46] It is an act of pure grace for which no explanation can be given other than the gracious will of God to renew his covenant, to extend his mercy and to have communion with his people. At the same time it is made perfectly

---

[45] J.K. Mozley, *The Doctrine of the Atonement*, Duckworth, London 1915, p. 22-23.

[46] Lev 17.11.

clear that the divine forgiveness can never be taken for granted in the slightest, that the covenant rests upon the pure grace of God alone, upon his active and redeeming intervention in the life and existence of Israel, and that its renewal with a sinful people involves something terrible, something awful and unutterably holy before the face of God.

Sins outside the covenant covered only by God's direct action in judgement and mercy

But what of the sins done 'with a high hand'? Is there no atonement for them? To answer that we have to understand carefully the distinction between these sins and the sins done in error. The latter were not simply involuntary sins or sins done through ignorance, but sins consciously committed through human frailty or passion, that is to say all sins which were not done in deliberate rebellion against the covenant. The sins done with a high hand, in deliberate rebellion, such as idolatry or murder or adultery, were sins that impugned the basis of the covenant relation between God and his people and their committal put the offender outside the covenant relation within which God has promised his pardon and forgiveness. Within the covenant, as we have seen, God has appointed sacrificial acts in cultic atonement for sin, bearing witness to the fact that it is God who pardons within the gracious relation which he has set up in the covenant and that within that relation fellowship with the holy God is only possible on the ground of holiness.

But when people excommunicate themselves from the covenant relationship by sinning with a high hand, for example in idolatrous worship, they thereby cut themselves off from the normal means of grace and can no longer be covered by the blood of the covenant. Then they fall directly under the righteousness and wrath of God and can be pardoned only by the direct action of God in judgement and mercy. If they are to be redeemed they must seek refuge there in the very judgement of God, for only in the execution of his righteous judgement is there to be found his mercy. That is very clear in David's act in throwing himself directly upon the judgement and mercy of God after his sin in the unlawful census of the people.[47]

Now it is highly significant that the Old Testament uses the term *kipper* to speak of atonement for both classes of sins, that is for the atonement of sins committed outwith as well as within the covenant. Behind atonement in both cases lies the recognition that it is always God himself who atones, and that God atones only on the ground of

---

[47]   1 Chron 21 esp. v. 13.

the fulfilment of his righteousness in judgement upon the sin. But whereas within the covenant that judgement is fulfilled in a victim that suffers vicariously, without the covenant no such vicarious provision is made. But it is clearly recognised that if it is God himself who pardons through the covenant sacrifices, the same God can surely pardon apart from the regular sacrifices according to his will and mercy. It is upon that God that in the last resort the Old Testament saints cast themselves for his name's sake.

(iv) The converging lines of thought in the Old Testament

We come now to what is in many respects the most significant element in the whole concept of redemption. This is a point where three lines of thought in the Old Testament converge.

(1) Redemption is grounded in the covenant will of God

It is ultimately God himself and God alone who atones and removes sin and saves. The clear recognition of that fact is found in psalm after psalm in which the psalmist looks past all ritual and sacrificial acts to the divine act of pardon. Some examples may be given.[48] Psalm 65, 'When our transgressions prevail over us, thou dost forgive (*kaphar*) them'. Psalm 78, 'Yet he, being compassionate, forgave (*kaphar*) their iniquity'. Psalm 79, 'Help us, O God of our salvation, for the glory of thy name; deliver us, and forgive (*kaphar*) our sins, for thy name's sake'. The great prophets like Isaiah, Ezekiel and Jeremiah all look behind and beyond the liturgical sacrifices and see the ground of forgiveness in God's mercies alone – and yet it is clearly recognised that the mercy of God belongs to his faithfulness, and belongs therefore to the fulfilment of his righteous judgements in 'mercy and truth'.

In other words, although they look for redemption ultimately to the mercy of God, it is not to any abstract divine mercy, not to any uncovenanted mercy, but precisely to his merciful will to have them as his people. Thus they repose ultimately upon the covenant of God, but the covenant is now seen to belong to the very nature and will of God and to cover all his relations with man, not only with Israel but with all humanity. Ultimately therefore the Old Testament hope for redemption reposes upon the covenant will of God, extended to cover all nations, and it is this exalted understanding of the covenant will of God that leads them to see a new form of the covenant in which God will forgive iniquity and remember sin no more, as Jeremiah put it.[49]

---

[48] Psalm 65.3(4), 78.38, 79.9.

[49] Jer 31.34(33).

(2) God must provide the lamb for judgement – the suffering servant

But if God is to bring redemption directly under a new form of the covenant, who is to bear the righteous judgement upon sin, especially the sin that violated the fundamental basis of the former covenant and excised the sinner from the covenanted means of grace? Nowhere is there any suggestion that God will pardon or redeem apart from judgement. Therefore God himself must 'provide the lamb', as it were. Now it is significant that precisely in the period before, during and after the exile when psalmist and prophet see so clearly that redemption must be sought from God alone, and that the sacrificial cultus in itself and considered as a means of effecting divine propitiation is an abomination, that then far from rejecting the sacrificial cultus it was in fact rehabilitated and reorganised, and we have the great redaction of the pentateuchal[50] literature. That shows very clearly the continued recognition of the fact that God will not pardon apart from judgement and sacrificial expiation, but that if God pardons it is only possible through his own provision of sacrifice, and to that the whole cultus was made to bear witness.

Moses the servant of the Lord as the figure behind the suffering servant

But who, in point of actual fact is to 'stand in the gap', to use Ezekiel's phrase?[51] The answer of second Isaiah is 'the servant of the Lord'.[52] We are thrown back by that expression to consider the figure of Moses as the servant of the Lord. It was because Moses stood in the gap, because he interceded for Israel in its great sin, acting as the representative and mediator of the people before the wrath of God, that God consented to renew the covenant, reissue the warrant of the covenant in the decalogue, and take Israel to be his people in covenant mercy and pardon. Nor can we forget the fact that at last Moses is cut off from entry into the promised land and disappears like a scapegoat into the mountains to be buried by God in an unknown grave, while Israel under Joshua crosses the Jordan to enjoy the promised inheritance.

It is surely the figure of Moses, his intercession and vicarious suffering for Israel, that ultimately lies behind the conception of the

---

50   The 'pentateuch' consists of the so-called five books of Moses (Genesis to Deuteronomy), from the Gk '*pente*', five.

51   Ezek 22.30 KJV.

52   See the 'servant songs' of Isaiah, 42.1-7, 49.1-6, 50.4-10, 52.13 – 53.12 (cf. 61.1-2).

servant in deutero-Isaiah.[53] It was through the mediation of Moses as well as through the exodus redemption that the covenant was established with Israel at Sinai. And it will yet be through a servant of the Lord that the covenant will be mediated in which God will blot out all the sins of his people and cast them behind his back forever, but that servant will mediate such a covenant only through bearing the sins of the people on himself and being cut off out of the land of the living for the sake of God's people, so that they may be forgiven and healed and restored to fellowship with God. The covenant thus mediated will extend far beyond the bounds of Israel for all nations shall come under its light and salvation and share in the fellowship it bestows between God and man.

(3) The covenant must be done into the flesh – the need for a new covenant

There is a third line of Old Testament teaching that converges at this point. We recall the fact that the cult with its means of atonement has its place and efficacy only within the covenant which represents not only the will of God for his people, but their existence before him. In the nature of the case, the cult by its place in the covenant must be enacted into the very existence of Israel, into the obedience of its whole physical and spiritual life before God and before man. Law and cult have no place in God's will merely as such; they have to be kneaded into the very being and understanding and life of Israel; the covenant as God's will must be actualised in the historical existence of Israel, and Israel's covenanted sacrifice in obedience to God's will must be fulfilled in its innermost being and life. The great sign of the covenant which circumscribed the whole sphere of the law and cult was circumcision – it was the sign that the covenant had to be cut into the flesh of God's people. That remained throughout the generations as the sign that the promises of God could be fulfilled only as the covenant will of God could be actualised in the existence of Israel, translated into its whole being, including its very heart, ears, lips etc. It was the sign that at last the covenant would be written into the heart of Israel, into the 'inner man' in the crucifixion of its self-will and in the putting away of 'the enmity of the flesh' (to use Pauline terms).

But once the covenant came to be enacted so deeply into the existence of Israel, its whole form would change – it would become a new covenant. That is precisely the message of the great prophets, deutero-Isaiah, Jeremiah and Ezekiel. But how could this be fulfilled unless redemption were fulfilled, and unless the atoning means of

---

[53] Isaiah 40 – 55, known as 'deutero' or 'second' Isaiah.

redemption through judgement were fulfilled also in the very existence of Israel? That points us again to the twofold conception of the servant of the Lord. Not only must the whole of Israel obediently fulfil the covenant as the servant of the Lord, but the enactment of the principle of atoning redemption through vicarious sacrifice in the midst of Israel means that one servant, gathering up all Israel in himself, will bear the sins of many, fulfilling on behalf of all the covenant will of God from the side of God and from the side of man, and so be the redeemer, the holy one of Israel.

All these lines converge here, at the servant. But who is this servant who fulfils the covenant in himself, who bears the sins of many and brings his people as the servant of the Lord to fulfil his will? Here we have to turn to the third Hebrew root behind the conception of redemption.

(c) Gaal, goel, *redeem, redeemer*

Redemption out of slavery or forfeited rights through a kinship in blood and property

Here we have an important conception of redemption derived out of old Israelite family and family-property law. It is the concept of redemption out of bankruptcy, or bondage or forfeited rights, undertaken by the advocacy of a kinsman who is bound to the person in need not only by blood ties, but by a community in property. Behind this there lies deeply embedded the Old Testament conception of solidarity in blood and property – the basic unit in humanity is essentially a community, which includes a group of people sharing not only in family relationship but in common and inalienable property. And behind that there lies something else, that the real owner of the land was the Lord himself and that it is held in fee or trust by his people.[54] In this context the verb *gaal* means to lay claim to something that has been lost or forfeited or alienated. The noun *goel* describes the claimant who on the ground of a relation of responsibility is the vindicator, the redeemer. In practice the *goel* is the next of kin, so that *goel* generally describes a kinsman-redeemer, for it is primarily they who have the right of redemption or who are primarily responsible for the vindication of an alienated right. That may refer either to some piece of property

---

[54] Lev 25.23; cf. A.R.S. Kennedy, article on *Goel*, in Hastings, *Dictionary of the Bible*, T & T Clark, Edinburgh 1899, vol. II, p. 223.

that has been mortgaged or forfeited,[55] or to some person who has got into difficulties and has sold their self into slavery to a stranger.[56] The *goel* comes to be thought of as an advocate enforcing the claims of the oppressed and downtrodden.[57]

The most familiar image of this whole conception in the Old Testament is that found in the book of Ruth, in which we see Ruth widowed and stateless and poverty-stricken, redeemed out of her lost and helpless condition by Boaz, her kinsman by marriage. It is a redemption which involves not only her property and rights through her dead husband, but one which fulfils the duties which those rights involved, and so results in the restitution of Ruth to a full place and inheritance in the covenant people of Israel.

Goel *redemption is through the person of the goel and the kinship of the redeemer*

The primary characteristic of this root idea, however, is that while in the *padah* type of redemption the main emphasis is laid upon the nature of the act, and in the *kipper* type of redemption the main emphasis is laid upon the nature of the atoning expiation as sacrifice, here in the *gaal* type of redemption the emphasis is laid upon the nature of the *redeemer*, upon the person of the *goel*. The *goel* acts in virtue of their position and relation to the person who is in need through forfeiture of their right or through bondage, and the *goel* redeems them by rightfully claiming the person's cause as their very own, standing in for them by assuming the responsibility for them and taking their burdens upon their own self, since they are unable to do it for themselves. That is conceivable both in a negative and in a positive sense. The *goel* may step in and act as the 'avenger of blood' (*goel ha-dam*),[58] bringing judgement upon the man-slayer, exacting life for life[59] and thus redeeming the blood of the dead, but they may also step into the lost estate of another and restore them to their right, and so *goel* redemption is applicable to redemption out of bankruptcy, or to the deliverance of the oppressed or of orphans from poverty and distress. But in both these applications, the negative and positive, the act of

---

[55] Lev 25.25.

[56] Lev 25.47-49.

[57] Psalm 119.154; Prov 23.11.

[58] Num 35.9-28, esp. 19,21,24-26; Deut 19.6,12.

[59] Cf. Gen 9.5-6.

redemption rests upon or implies a bond of responsible kinship, a property-tie, or a relation of covenant love. And so the *goel* comes to be thought of as advocate and vindicator, and as such as the redeemer, while the noun *geulah*,[60] redemption (or right of redemption), is applied to the general release from debt and the full recovery of rights and inheritance in the year of jubilee.[61]

(i) The Old Testament application of the goel concept to God himself

This remarkable conception of redemption is applied by the Old Testament to God himself. In the book of Job and in the Psalms it is applied to the divine salvation of man in distress and anguish, but it is also applied to the redemption by God of Israel out of the bondage of Egypt and out of the captivity of Babylon, and even applied to messianic and eschatological redemption of God's people at the end of time. In other words, God is conceived as bound up with his people not only through a property relation, but through marriage, for he is husband, as well as Father of his people Israel. Thus the psalmist can pray, 'Remember thy congregation which thou hast purchased of old, which thou hast redeemed (*gaal*) to be the tribe of thy heritage'.[62] And trito-Isaiah[63] can say, 'thou, O Lord, art our Father, our Redeemer (*goel*) from of old is thy name'.[64] Or again the Lord is thought of as having entered into a marriage relation with Israel.[65] It is because God and his people have inheritance in one another that he is claimed as the *goel* redeemer. In this application of the *goel* concept to God, there are three points in particular that should be noted especially.

(1) God alone can be goel in death and judgement

In the Old Testament, for example in Ezekiel, it is clear that while the redemptive efficacy of the *goel* avails between one person and another in daily life, no one is in a position to extend their kinsman-advocacy beyond life, or to the relation that obtains between man and

---

[60] Lev 25.26,29,31,32 (although a noun in the Hebrew, *geulah* is commonly translated here in the KJV and RSV by the verb redeem).

[61] Lev 25.8ff.

[62] Psalm 74.2 KJV/RSV.

[63] 'Third' Isaiah, Isaiah 56 – 66.

[64] Isaiah 63.16.

[65] Jer 3.1ff., 31.32(31); Ezek 16.1ff.; Isaiah 54.1f.,5-8, 61.10, 62.4-5; Hos 2.14,16,19-20.

God.[66] No one can ultimately stand surety for another and make that person's cause their own. No human being can stand in the gap, not even a Noah or a Daniel or a Job, and intercede for them, but God and God alone can act as man's *goel*. In the ultimate things in man's relation with God, in judgement in death, in disaster, no one can be a *goel* for a fellow human being. God alone can step in and deliver us and bestow life upon us in redemption.[67] As this *goel* God enters into the human situation, into the midst of our responsibilities and culpabilities, to stand in for us like a kinsman-advocate and to justify us against judgement, and so to stand surety for us within our frailty, corruption and lostness and so be the life of our life and redeem us. It is not through silver and gold that Israel will be redeemed, but through God himself, as deutero-Isaiah says[68] and therefore it is an act of free grace toward us.

(2) God is the faithful *goel, the holy one who redeems through judgement and sanctification*

When this concept is applied to God, the stress comes to be laid upon his truth or steadfastness, or his holiness. It is as the holy one, as the truth, as the creator, as the Father, as the husband, as the faithful God that he steps in to redeem. But because it is God who acts as *goel*, his redemption is at once judging and saving. Not only does he redeem us out of bondage and death, but he draws us into his holiness and sanctifies us with it, so that in redemption we are given to share in the sanctification of the Lord. Moreover as *goel* he is not only the faithful one who holds on to us in our frailty and death, so that we are redeemed from death and corruption in his abiding possession of us, but as the *goel* he is the creator who bestows life upon us, for we are bound up in the same bundle of life with him and he has taken us for his inheritance.

(3) God is goel *in virtue of the bond of covenant love*

When God is thought of as acting as *goel*, it is in virtue of the bond of love with which he binds himself to his people, in an extended understanding of the covenant relation. It is on the ground of such a covenant relation and because of the blood of the covenant, that God can take our cause as his own, stand in as our kinsman-advocate, justify

---

[66] Ezek 14.14-20; cf. Job 19.25.
[67] Cf. Psalm 49.7(8),15(16); Hos 13.14.
[68] Isaiah 52.3,9.

us against the judgement under which our lives are forfeit, and so redeem us by drawing us out of our bondage into life and communion with himself. This is particularly clear when the *goel* concept is applied to God's redemption of Israel out of Egypt in the passover and the exodus. But when in deutero-Isaiah, Israel is given the promise of a new exodus and redeemer, the holy one of Israel, when God will redeem Israel through his servant as the mediator of his covenant, and when that servant is thought of as bearing upon himself vicariously the sins and the judgements of God's people, it would seem right to identify the servant with the divine *goel*, the Lord himself coming to be Israel's kinsman, and as such to actualise the life of the servant, as himself the covenant actualised in the midst of Israel and himself the covenanted means of its fulfilment in sacrifice and atonement. It seems right to make that identification, yet neither deutero-Isaiah nor trito-Isaiah actually makes it.

That identification hovers upon the lips of their prophecy again and again, but is never actually made, and it could not be made, for to make it would be to assert that God had become incarnate, that God had actually entered into the existence of Israel, had actually taken upon himself the sin of Israel and made expiation for it in atoning sacrifice of himself, in giving his life under judgement in order to redeem the life of Israel. That could not be said until it had actually happened, and yet the amazing thing about the Isaianic prophecies is that they hover on the very brink of saying it. It remained for the New Testament to make that identification and that is what it does do and in so doing gathers up this whole conception of redemption and re-interprets it in terms of what the Son of God actually became and actually did in our humanity.

(ii) *The New Testament application of the* goel *concept to Jesus*

Now let us glance briefly at several ways in which the New Testament does do that.

(1) Kinsman-redeemer

The primary fact that stares us in the face is the incarnation itself, the fact that the Son of God has become bone of our bone and flesh of our flesh, so that we are bone of his bone and flesh of his flesh. As if that were not enough, he has established a new covenant with us, and on the ground of that new covenant, he goes forth to lay down his life in atoning sacrifice and redemption, that is as our kinsman-redeemer, bonded to us by the covenant. But Paul also apples the concept of the marriage relation here, as in Ephesians 5, and it is on that ground that Christ acts as the saviour of the church. It is then on the ground of the kinship between Christ and us that he assumes responsibility for us and stands in for us as our redeemer.

(2) Advocate

Hence secondly we find him spoken of as an advocate who takes our part, vindicates us against judgement and the accusation of our guilt, and sets us free from all our debts. And so even when at the last supper he insisted on calling his disciples not servants but friends, bound so closely with him in a bond of covenant love, and then spoke of leaving them, he promised not to leave them orphaned, that is without an advocate to take their cause upon himself, to stand in for them. He promised therefore to send them his Spirit who would be their advocate (*paraklēton*),[69] and yet in the coming of the advocate Spirit Jesus Christ himself would come and be with them and abide with them. Thus the Johannine writer in his first epistle speaks of Christ as our advocate and as our expiation from sin,[70] and Paul speaks of Christ as he who atones for us in the judgement and vindicates us, justifies us against all the accusations of our sins for he has bound himself to us in a bond of love that nothing in heaven or earth can destroy, not even death itself.[71]

(3) The redeemer of the inheritance

Further, the New Testament thinks of us as having been purchased back by Christ and so claimed as his inheritance. This is particularly clear in the Pauline use of the word *peripoiēsis*, possession, where Christ has made us his inheritance and we are given Christ for our inheritance.[72] Redemption and inheritance are therefore conceptions which in the New Testament cannot be separated out from each other.

---

[69] John 14.16,26, 16.7 (KJV *Comforter*, RSV *Counsellor*).

[70] 1 John 2.1,2.

[71] Rom 8.31-39.

[72] Eph 1.14, 'the guarantee of our inheritance *until we acquire possession of it*', literally 'until the redemption of the possession, *eis apolutrōsin tēs peripoiēseōs*'; cf. Paul in Acts 20.28, 'to feed the church of the Lord which he obtained, *periepoiēsato*, with his own blood'. Cf. 1 Thess 5.9; 2 Thess 2.14. See too Peter, 1 Peter 2.9, 'a people for his possession, *peripoiēsin*'.

(4) Jubilee redemption

Then there is the direct application of the redemption in the year of jubilee[73] to the day of Christ, for it is his coming which achieves for us the cancellation of all debt and the restoration to us of the rights we had forfeited as God's creatures and as members of God's family and household.[74] But that redemption, *geulah*, is applied to the redemptive liberty of the Spirit in an eschatological sense[75] and similarly to the final parousia of Christ as redeemer and consummator.

(5) The avenger of death

Then even the concept of the *goel* as the avenger of death the man-slayer is applied to Christ in the New Testament, for it is as our *goel* that he avenges our death in sin and destroys death itself, so redeeming us from death. In other words, the *Christus victor* (Christ the victor) conception of redemption is linked with the *goel* conception as much as with the *padah* conception of redemption. Not only does he destroy death and the grave in *padah* redemption, but he does so by standing alongside us as our *goel*, for even in the ultimate things he steps in and stands in the gap for us as saviour and redeemer.[76]

2 *Padah, kipper* and *goel* put together[77]

We must now take these three major conceptions of redemption and put them together. It is evident that they are all very closely related in

---

[73] Lev 25.8-55, esp. 10,13,28 etc.

[74] Cf. the 'sabbath rest' of Heb 4.1-10 with Lev 25.1-10 and its linkage of the weekly sabbath with the 'seven weeks (or sabbaths) of years, seven times seven years' (Lev 25.8), making forty-nine years in all with the fiftieth being the year of jubilee.

[75] Cf. Rom 8.21-23; Eph 4.30, 'the day of redemption'.

[76] Cf. Hosea 13.14 (*padah, gaal*) and 1 Cor 15.55. In view of all this one might have expected the New Testament to have applied the term *lutrōtēs*, redeemer, to Christ (cf. LXX Psalms 18.15 [Eng. 19.14], 77.35 [Eng. 78.35]) but it never does. The only time the New Testament uses *lutrōtēs* is found in Stephen's speech where it is applied to Moses (Acts 7.35), which may indicate that Stephen saw the figure of Moses behind that of the servant in the Isaianic prophecies.

[77] For a further outline of *padah, kipper* and *goel* in relation to redemption in Christ and the theology of the early fathers, see T.F. Torrance, *The Trinitarian Faith*, T & T Clark, Edinburgh 1988, p. 168ff.

the teaching of the Old Testament itself, for they overlap in their significance and they converge at two points in their application, in relation to the ultimate act of redemption which God will effect for his people, and in relation to his servant, the mediator of the new covenant who is so closely connected to that redemption. It is when we put these three conceptions together, and think them into each other and see them in their New Testament re-interpretation, that we get the fullness of the biblical conception of atoning redemption through the life and death of Jesus Christ. It is in this light that we are to understand the sayings of Jesus with which we began, spoken as he neared Jerusalem for the last time and as he celebrated the last supper with his disciples. There, he who had already explained to his disciples that he was about to offer his life in atoning expiation and ransom for many, enacted in a sacred meal with them a covenant bond in which he bound his people to himself as their *goel*-redeemer, and then went forth to give his life for them, shedding the blood of the covenant, to justify the ungodly, to deliver sinners from the power of darkness, and to restore lost and forfeited men and women to communion with the Father.

In the later strata of the Old Testament, as we have seen, all three conceptions of redemption are associated with the new exodus and the work of the servant of the Lord. But it is when the New Testament employs the concept of the servant Son in regard to the new covenant established in the blood of Christ, that we see these three aspects of redemption fully brought together and re-interpreted in christology. Nowhere of course is there any schematic use of these concepts, as nowhere in the Old Testament are they side by side and carefully distinguished, but all these three aspects are definitely woven together in the understanding and presentation of redemption in the teaching of the New Testament and in the understanding of the early church. Let us summarise them.

(a) An outline of **padah,** **kipper** *and* **goel** *redemption in the New Testament*

Padah – Redemption by a mighty hand in sheer grace, at once out of the oppression of evil and out of judgement and death. But the mighty hand is the holiness of Christ, his obedience unto the death of the cross. The mighty hand is the blood of Christ, shed freely on our behalf. Here the stress is laid upon the nature of the redeeming act.

Kipper – Redemption by an expiatory sacrifice for sin made in the offering of Christ's life for our life in obedience to the divine will and mercy. He is both the priest and the sacrifice in one, lamb-and-servant of God, shedding his blood in costly ransom or expiation, in order to remove the barrier of guilt and enmity between man and God and God and man, and so effect reconciliation in a holy communion between them. Here the stress is upon the mode of the atoning redemption and on the restoration to fellowship with God that it effects.

Goel – Redemption by a kinsman-advocate, who acting out of a blood tie or covenant bond, or who out of pure love forging such a bond in himself and in the blood of the new covenant, stands in our place, takes our lost cause on himself as his own, makes sure our redemption in himself, and so delivers us out of our bondage into the freedom of our inheritance in God. Here the stress is upon the nature of the redeemer and our kinship with him.

How are these three aspects of redemption to be related to the actual language of the New Testament about the saving work of Christ? That is not easy to state precisely because both the meanings and the various translations criss-cross, but generally we can say that *padah* redemption is described by the term redemption in the New Testament; *kipper* redemption is described by atonement or reconciliation where the notions of expiation and substitutionary sacrifice are involved; *gaal* redemption is described by reconciliation where the notion of restoration to union and communion with God in Christ is uppermost. And yet all these overlap, and defy any such schematism, while the term salvation can cover them all.

(b) An outline of the various aspects of redemption in relation to each other[78]

But there is another way in which we can distinguish them, apart from the actual words employed to convey this manifold redemption, and these three ways correspond remarkably to three main stresses in the understanding of atonement in the history of the church. We may describe that distinction in this way (remembering that they all overlap):

---

[78]   For the following, looked at from the perspective of the threefold office of Christ, cf. T.F. Torrance, *The School of Faith*, pp. lxxxvii-xcv.

(1) Padah *redemption*, by a mighty hand, stresses the *dramatic aspect of atonement* – the active and victorious intervention of God in rescuing and saving us.

(2) Kipper *redemption*, which is expiatory and substitutionary, stresses the *cultic-forensic aspect of atonement.*

(3) Goel *redemption*, with its stress on the nature of the redeemer, stresses the *ontological*[79] *aspect of atonement.*

Now when we look at these aspects in this way, we can see that none of these aspects can stand alone or become the major basis of a doctrine of atonement, without serious dislocation of the biblical understanding and failure to appreciate the fullness of Christ's saving work. Let us then try to assess their significance in relation to one another.

(i) The dramatic element in redemption

Apart from (ii), the expiatory and forensic element, the dramatic concept of redemption cannot avoid an ultimate dualism, for example, that which is crudely expressed in the notion of ransom to the devil. Such a notion easily falls prey to the demand for demythologisation, and once that is carried out, nothing is left but triviality.

Apart from (iii), the ontological element, redemption is dissolved into mere events, into the *beneficia Christi*,[80] or into the timeless repetition of a mystery. Moreover a loss of (ii) and (iii) together so puts the emphasis upon some transcendent act of God, that the actual focus of attention is laid upon human response, and in the end, therefore, a demythologisation of the 'Christus victor' concept of redemption boils down to redemption through existential decision. The lack of ontology[81] is fatal.

(ii) The cultic-forensic element – piacular, expiatory redemption

Apart from (i), the dramatic element, the cultic-forensic degenerates into a pagan notion of placating God. The cultic-forensic aspect does involve an act in which God reconciles himself to man and reconciles man to himself in Jesus Christ. But strike out of it the pure act of God, the sheer intervention in divine grace, and it becomes a Pelagian,[82]

---

[79] Emphasising 'being', stressing who Christ was in his being.

[80] Lat, 'Christ's benefits', ie. the benefits he gives us, what he does for us.

[81] Literally, the science or study of 'being', used here of the being and person of Christ.

[82] Pelagius believed that we co-operate with God for our salvation.

sacerdotalist[83] conception of appeasing an angry God through human mediation. That element lies embedded in Roman Catholic notions of atonement and the mass and its peculiar understanding of merit and satisfaction.

Apart from (iii), the ontological element in atonement, the cultic-forensic degenerates into a legal and cultic fiction with no basis in actual existence and reality and therefore with no relevance to our actual humanity. Thus the doctrine of justification apart from union with Christ cannot avoid the charge of a legal fiction. Moreover to fail to take (iii) seriously would mean a failure to see the saving significance of the humanity of Jesus Christ. Apart from both (i) and (iii) the proper doctrine of Christ as himself the only mediator and our high priest would disappear, and then (ii) would degenerate into ritualistic superstition.

(iii) The ontological element in redemption

Here we have stress on the fact that Christ is himself our redeemer, in the constitution of his person, i.e. stress upon the fact that the work of Christ cannot be divorced from his person. That is the stress upon incarnational redemption.

Apart from (i), the dramatic element, the ontological would degenerate into a Pelagian conception of redemption appropriate to an adoptionist christology,[84] for example as in Socinian[85] heresy or in the so-called 'moral influence' theory of the atonement,[86] Apart from (i) the whole stress of *anhypostasia*[87] in the person and work of Christ would also be lost, with the loss of the concept that salvation is by the pure grace of God alone.

---

[83]   'Priestly', from the Lat *sacerdos*, priest.

[84]   The view that Christ was a man 'adopted' to be the son of God.

[85]   Socinus (1539-64) was unitarian and taught that Christ was not divine but a mortal man begotten through the Holy Spirit (re-begotten in the resurrection to be immortal) and that his death, although not an atoning sacrifice, was accepted as a ground for forgiveness and was important for its revelation of the love of God and its influence on us.

[86]   The theory, associated mostly with Abelard (1079-1142), that emphasises the power of the cross, as a demonstration of the love of God, to evoke the response of repentance and love.

[87]   The fact that the humanity of Christ had no independent existence or reality of its own apart from the Word becoming man – from the Greek *a-hypostasis, no* (independent) *reality*.

Apart from (ii), the cultic-forensic, the ontological would degenerate into a doctrine of deification through union with deity and that would have to be demythologised, or philosophically mythologised (whichever way you prefer), turning it into sheer idealism. Apart from (i) and (ii), stress upon (iii) would result in a conception of redemption through mystic absorption into the divine. For the rationalistic and mystic mind this ontological aspect of redemption, however, is particularly difficult, because when held together with (i) and (ii) it insists on the finality of atonement as inseparably bound up with the particular and contingent with its definite place and date in time, in the historical Jesus. Attempts are made therefore by rationalists and mystics to re-interpret the historical particularity of Jesus symbolically.

(iv) A rough classification of the different church traditions

Now when we see the significance and relevance of these various elements of the full doctrine of atonement, is it possible to see that different churches or traditions have actually laid differing stresses upon them? Could we then assess their importance among the various traditions in the following way?

Lutheran – combines (i) the dramatic and (ii) the cultic-forensic elements.

Anglican – combines (i) the dramatic and (iii) the ontological elements.

Reformed – combines (ii) the cultic and forensic and (iii) the ontological elements (really all three, but this for the sake of discussion).

Greek Orthodox – stresses strongly (iii) the ontological, with a weaker combination of (i) the dramatic.

Roman Catholic – stresses (ii) the cultic-forensic, with a little of (iii) the ontological.

Now of course that is not wholly accurate and very rough, and there are many exceptions, but does it represent in any way the fact that some traditions lay greater stress upon certain aspects of redemption than others? Yet from our study this at least ought to be clear, that we cannot afford to neglect any aspect. All three aspects are to be held together like the three strands of a single rope. We need to recover the wholeness of the biblical understanding of atoning redemption. The greatest dangers today, however, might be said to be in an over stress on the dramatic aspect of atonement and a failure to give the ontological aspect its proper place, resulting in a salvation by pure event stripped of its concrete substance. It is a failure to see that the incarnation insists that the finality of atonement and redemption is inalienably bound up with the particular and contingent in the historical Jesus Christ who is also the very Son of God.

In conclusion, we can now go on to look a little further at the various historical emphases in understanding the doctrine of the atonement.

3 Historical emphases in the doctrine of atonement

(a) Theories of atonement in relation to the three Old Testament aspects of redemption

Historical theories have tended to fall into three main groups, generally known as *moral influence* theory, *ransom* theory,[88] and *penal substitution* theory.[89] This distinction, thrown up by history corresponds in some real measure to the three main aspects in the biblical conception of redemption, yet not entirely: the cultic aspect of the atonement is omitted, for example, but most important of all is the fact that the inter-connections are missing when we look at the atonement in this way, so that the three parts into which atonement is broken up are much narrower and poorer than the three basic aspects or strands of *padah*, *kipper* and *goel* redemption. Let us consider those aspects in the light of the historical theories.

(i) The dramatic aspect of atonement

This has tended to fall into a 'ransom to the devil' theory, or at best a *Christus victor* concept. This theory is mostly patristic and early mediaeval, but it has its modern counterparts in certain Lutheran and Anglo-Catholic circles, not so much in Greek Orthodox or Roman Catholic theology. When the dramatic aspect of the atonement narrows in this way, it has a distinct tendency towards dualism and that provokes 'demythologisation'. It is worth noting that while historians frequently speak of this as patristic and mediaeval, in actual fact it is found only in a small part of patristic

---

[88]   Associated with the *Christus victor* concept, ransom theory saw the death of Christ as a ransom paid to liberate humanity. In the eyes of Origen and many of the Latin Fathers, the ransom was paid to the devil who held humanity captive because of sin.

[89]   The theory that in his death Christ suffered the penalty for our breaking of the law and died as a substitute in our place (*penal*, involving penalty or legal punishment, from the Latin *poena*, punishment, penalty, compensation).

thought, in Origenism and in certain areas of monastic thought where dualism prevailed. It was not held by any of the great fathers (except by Gregory of Nyssa) and we find it again in mediaeval times, in popular and monastic thought, but it is not so evident in the theologians – it was effectively destroyed by Anselm and Bernard of Clairvaux.

(ii) The cultic-forensic aspect of atonement

This has tended to fall apart into two notions:

a) a *cultic* notion of the atonement, without the element of justification, found mostly in liturgical texts and contexts. It tended to be carried forward in the thought of the west mostly in connection with the sacrifice of the mass, without adequate relation to Christ himself in his saving activity. Yet this is by no means exaggerated in the great theologians. For example, of the twenty questions devoted by Thomas Aquinas to the eucharist, only one is devoted to the notion of eucharistic sacrifice. A much better concept is to be found in Anselm's prayers and meditations.

b) a *penal* notion without the priestly aspect – a satisfaction conception of atonement. This derives in the west mostly from the basic thought of Tertullian – and has in it a distinct tendency toward legalism, with little notion of redemption from the law, of salvation 'apart from law'. The development of the penal and satisfaction notions in atonement owes a great deal to the Latin language and highly Latinised concepts as we can see when we compare the western development of these notions, either in Roman or Protestant thought, with the exposition of the penal and satisfaction aspects in the thought of Cyril of Alexandria especially. It was the penal-substitution notion, together with a narrowed understanding of justification, that became dominant in the centuries of so-called Protestant Orthodoxy and today in so-called Evangelical Protestantism.

(iii) The ontological aspect of atonement

This again has tended to fall into two notions:

a) an *incarnational* notion, where the saving element is through knowledge and mystical union with Christ. This is evident very early in the Greek fathers, for example in Clement of Alexandria, and earlier in Ignatius of Antioch – but contrast the Epistle to Diognetus. It became one of the main strands of development throughout the mystical tradition, the stress being laid sometimes more on union with God through mystical vision, sometimes more on union with God through the incarnation.

b) a *subjective* notion of atonement, where the moral influence of the sacrifice of Christ or knowledge of what God has done for us in his love is the saving element – for example in Abelard or in Socinus. Yet this has a profound and moving development in the liturgy, for example in the *Stabat Mater*, or prayer of Mary at the foot of the cross – cf. here Haydn's *Stabat Mater* and the immense power of contemplating the wounds of Jesus.

The unifying effect of the celebration of the eucharist in the church

Behind all those separated strands in the development of the church's understanding of the atonement there has continued the celebration of the *Lord's supper*, the communion in the body and blood of Christ, which enshrines all three major aspects of redemption. Even though different understandings of the eucharist have arisen, owing to differing emphases in the doctrine of the atonement, nevertheless the celebration of the eucharist has tended to give divergent theories some underlying unity in worship. This is a unity in that to which we are directed in holy communion and which is greater and far richer than can be indicated by words or statements, but which bears down upon us in actual communion. On the other hand, the divergence in the understanding of holy communion, not least of the real presence, was exacerbated by different notions of space and time which were taken up into the church's thought at different stages only to split open even wider the divergences in the doctrine of the atonement, making them wide differences held within the unity of common devotion to the self-oblation and sacrifice of Christ for us and our salvation.

There are other important ways in which we have to consider the three main aspects of redemption and the historical divergences in the doctrine of atonement, two further ways which correspond in real measure to *padah*, *kipper* and *goel*.

(b) Christ's threefold office in relation to the three aspects

First we have the *triplex munus*,[90] the threefold office of Christ, as *king*, *priest* and *prophet* which we have been considering in the order, prophet, priest and king. Biblically, the *triplex munus*, the three offices seen side by side, occurs very rarely – in the Old Testament in Micah 3, Jeremiah 18 and Ezekiel 7.[91] Normally the Old Testament and indeed the New Testament speaks only of a *duplex munus*, a

---

[90]   Lat, threefold office; *duplex munus*, twofold office.

[91]   Micah 3.11; cf. Jer 18.18 and Ezek 7.26-27.

twofold office, *king* and *priest* – for example the book of Zechariah[92] or the Apocalypse[93] – this is because the prophetic office, properly and basically regarded, is part of the priestly office. But nevertheless when we consider the rite of *anointing* in the Old Testament we find that prophet, as well as priest and king were anointed, and the notions of prophet, priest and king were thus all drawn into the notion of messianic office.

It was in this way that the *triplex munus* emerged in Christian theology, not so much in the New Testament, as in the early fathers, in Justin Martyr, Hippolytus of Rome and so on. It became much more important in Chrysostom and Cyril of Alexandria and in a whole host of mediaeval theologians including Aquinas, but it was Calvin at the Reformation who made it particularly important, although even he notes that it is the *duplex munus*, the twofold office, that is more basic on the biblical scene. Think then of the correlations here:

(1) **Prophet** – the Word made flesh, the advocate, corresponds to the incarnational or **goel** *aspect of redemption*.

(2) **Priest** – this corresponds to the cultic-forensic or **kipper** *aspect of redemption* – *Christus victima*, Christ the victim.

(3) **King** – this corresponds to the *Christus victor*, Christ the victor, or **padah** *aspect of redemption*, salvation through the mighty act of God, *sola gratia*, by grace alone.

(c) A third method of correlation

But we have to take into account another important threefold strand: *the passive obedience, the active obedience of Christ* and his *incarnational assumption of our fallen humanity*. Taken in the same order we have been considering, the correspondence works out like this:

(1) **Prophet** – **incarnational assumption** of our humanity, the Word made flesh. Christ is more than a prophet, for he *is* the saving Word which he proclaims, that very Word of divine love and pardon enacted in the flesh. As such he is the fulfilment of the Old Testament *goel*.

(2) **Priest** – this corresponds to the **passive obedience** of Christ, his submission to the Father's judgement and his self-offering in sacrifice for our sins – the piacular[94] and cultic side of redemption – *kipper* redemption.

---

[92] Zech 4.14, 6.13.

[93] Rev 1.5-6, 5.10, 20.6, cf. 17.14, 3.21, 1.13.

[94] Making or requiring expiation, from the Latin *piaculum*, expiatory sacrifice.

(3) *King* – this corresponds to the ***active obedience*** of Christ – the way in which Christ broke into our captivity to redeem us and save us, but 'the mighty act' of God here is the holiness of Jesus' life, for it was through his holy life within our alienated humanity that he broke the thraldom of evil and emancipated us from its power.

(d) The correlations summarised

For a full and proper understanding of atonement (and considering them now in the order *padah, kipper* and *goel*), all these three sets of threefold relations have to be put together in the following way:

(1) *Padah redemption – kingly office of Christ – active obedience.*

(2) *Kipper redemption – priestly office of Christ – passive obedience.*

(3) *Goel redemption – prophetic office of Christ – incarnational assumption* of our humanity. Salvation through the Word made flesh – it is this aspect that supplies the inner unity in act and knowledge that underlies the other two and indeed all three.

If we can think these three together then we can think them out in their inner connections. In this way we get a far better and richer apprehension of the doctrine of the atonement than by merely following through the historical theories in the traditional way.

Chapter Three

THE PRIESTHOOD OF CHRIST

1 The threefold office of Christ in atonement

The goel *relation*

Without unduly pressing the three aspects of redemption we have been considering and as outlined in the previous chapter, we can see that the three aspects correspond in a measured degree to the threefold office of Christ as prophet, priest and king. Christ is prophet as the Word become flesh, the Son who declares the Father become man. That corresponds to the *goel* aspect of redemption and provides its ontological ground: it concerns the unity of word and act in the person of the incarnate Son, the mediator. Christ comes as our *goel*-redeemer in word and act, as our advocate who not only gives an account for us to God but stands in for us, taking our cause completely upon himself. It is this *goel* aspect of redemption that we have been considering in the incarnate life and work of the Word and Son of God leading up to the crucifixion, that is, incarnational redemption through the Word and active obedience of Christ. It is on that ground that Jesus went forth to face the cross and in holy obedience to submit to the divine judgement in making an expiatory sacrifice on our behalf; but he did so as the *goel*, so that the *goel* relation lies behind the unity of his person and his sacrificial act. It is through the *goel* relation, so to speak, that he is at once priest and victim.

The kipper *and* padah *relation*

The *kipper* aspect of redemption corresponds to the priestly work of Christ in atonement in which he offered an atoning sacrifice for us and reconciled us to the Father through removing the objective obstacle of guilt between us. That is both a priestly and a forensic[1] act. Here however, this aspect of atonement overlaps with the consideration of the kingly ministry of Christ which corresponds to the *padah* aspect of redemption, the act of the king, 'the mighty arm of the Lord', rescuing us from the alien dominion of sin and evil and taking us into the kingdom of God. As we saw, that is

---

[1]   Involving law or courts of law, fulfilling the requirements of the law.

manifested from the very start of Christ's incarnate life. He was born to be king, redeemer-king, and all through his ministry that kingdom kept breaking in with redemptive power in the healing and liberating of oppressed humanity; but it is supremely in the cross that Christ breaks into the ultimate stronghold of sin, destroying the power of sin and evil and rising again from the dead as the triumphant king enthroned at the right hand of God. It is as the lamb of God that he is enthroned,[2] for his kingly ministry is inseparable from his priestly ministry, but again it is as man that he is exalted to the right hand of God so that the kingdom of Christ is become the kingdom of God with one wearing our humanity on the throne of the divine dominion.[3] All power in heaven and earth is given to the exalted Jesus, so that the kingly ministry is inseparably interwoven with the *goel* ministry of Christ.

The interweaving of the different emphases

Now in the nature of the case, while all these aspects of the ministry of Christ, and all aspects of his redeeming activity, are interwoven and cannot be separated out from each other, the emphasis falls distinctly at certain places. The *goel*-redemption is clearly linked with his life and ministry as the Word made flesh, the Son of God become man, that is with his life and work leading up to the cross. That is continued with the ascension of Christ, for it is as our *goel*-advocate as well as our high priest that he stands in for us and is our eternal surety before the face of God the Father. The *padah*-redemption is clearly evident in his mighty act in breaking the power of sin in death and resurrection and in his triumph over all the principalities and powers of evil, in his ascension to fill all things with his power as lamb of God and so take up his kingdom and reign through the gospel. That stress falls mostly upon what follows the cross, the resurrection, ascension, heavenly intercession and *parousia*, all of which have emphatically to do with the kingly ministry of Christ. But between those two we have the *kipper*-redemption stressed, which corresponds to the work of Christ as priest and judge, but a priest who is a sacrificial victim, and a judge who takes his place among us as the judged. It is then to this central aspect of atoning redemption that we now turn for fuller consideration, to the double emphasis upon the priestly and forensic work of Christ.

---

[2]   Rev 5.12-13, 7.10,17, 17.14 (cf. 19.9-16), 22.1,3.

[3]   Cf. Rev 1.13ff.

2 The final fulfilment of law and cult

As we have seen, our Lord was deeply conscious of acting under the constraint of the Father's will, and that assumed the form not only of fulfilment of the will of God directly revealed but also of the will of God as mediated through the Old Testament revelation, through the divine purpose in the covenant with Israel which took its great expression in the law and the cult. Jesus advanced to the cross in conscious and deliberate fulfilment of that divine will, and in that context, with clear reference to the Old Testament scripture, set himself to fulfil the work of atonement. In order to understand what the New Testament has to say in interpretation of his atoning work we have to look closely at that fulfilment.

(a) The Old Testament tension between prophet and priest, and word and liturgy[4]

We recall that all Old Testament worship had an essentially twofold character so remarkably portrayed in the two functions of Moses and Aaron, in which the priestly function of Aaron was in dependence upon the priestly function of Moses in mediating the word and law of God.[5] The word and law of God were primary, the sacrificial liturgy was secondary, but they were given together. Right away in the Old Testament tradition, we read of a conflict between the two, which emerged into the long tension between prophet and priest, for the priestly element sought to make itself independent of the mediating word given in the law. We see that early on in the incident of the golden calf and the consecration of Aaron to be its priest.[6] That was the occasion of Moses' great intercession which played a significant part in the formal establishment of the covenant at Sinai. But then once again we find Aaron, here supported by Miriam, in revolt from Moses, 'Has the Lord indeed spoken only through Moses?'[7] In that revolt, Miriam is punished by leprosy and the glory or *shekinah*[8] of

---

4   See further T.F. Torrance, *Royal Priesthood*, 2nd edition, T & T Clark, Edinburgh 1993, p. 3ff.

5   Psalm 99.6; see again chap.1, section 2 (c) (i) & (ii).

6   Exod 32.

7   Num 12.2.

8   Num 12.10, the cloud which rested on the tabernacle as a sign of the presence of God. See Exod 40.34-38, 'Then [at the completion and anointing of the tabernacle] the cloud covered the tent of meeting, and the glory of the Lord filled the tabernacle'; cf. 2 Chron 5.13-14, 7.1-3, the appearance of the cloud or glory of God at the dedication of Solomon's temple; cf. also Exod 13.21, 14.19-20, 24.15-18; Matt 17.5 (Mark 9.7; Luke 9.34-35, cf. 32); Acts 1.9.

God leaves Aaron's tabernacle. Once again Moses intervenes in priestly mediation. On both occasions the narrative makes clear that the continual sacrificial priesthood of Aaron depends on the priestly mediation of Moses, that is, upon the word and law of God.

(i) Priestly independence and prophetic protest

The Old Testament tells us, and this is one of its recurring themes, that sin is so deeply ingrained in humanity that it seeks to erect the divine ordinances of worship into liturgy that stands by itself independently of the mediation of the word. That was a persistent sin of Israel. It sought to make the temple and its liturgy independent of God's intervening will as manifested through the law and as continually interpreted and revealed through the ministry of the prophets. They sought to make the temple and its worship a sphere of liturgical action bound up with the natural desires of Israel and to make it operate as action upon God, as manipulation of God's will. In that way it was looked upon as giving Israel security before God, while behind that security Israel sought to go the way of its own desires. But against that independence of the liturgy and priesthood, God sent the prophets, most of them apparently out of the priesthood itself, to protest against the falsification of the cult. However when the priesthood became so very corrupt, God raised up prophets like Amos who had no relation to the priesthood and who came voicing the word of God in criticism of cultic performances. In this prophetic ministry, there was evident an attack upon the independence of the cult, a prophetic and eschatological suspension of liturgy in the demand for obedience to the will of God rather than ceremonial ritual. Hence at last when the prophets were spurned, God promised he would destroy the temple and its liturgy and so overthrow the false security of Israel which rested upon a sinful perversion of the holy liturgy. A chapter in Jeremiah is the outstanding passage here, the chapter which Jesus cited when as the Lord he came suddenly to his temple and cleansed it of its religious and commercial traffic.[9]

(ii) The rehabilitation of torah and cult after the exile

After the exile, there was a rehabilitation of the ancient cult in final liturgical form apparently under Ezra, but under Ezra we also get the rehabilitation of the word of God in the form of *torah*[10] in which the prophetic mediation

---

9 Jer 7; but cf. also Micah 3.11f.; Jer 26.7f.; Mal 2.1-9, 3.1-4.

10 Hb, 'law', or 'instruction in the law'.

of the word of God and the commandments of the word of God tend to be divorced. Two things are to be noticed here therefore.

(1) Liturgised law and legalised liturgy

Here we have the law liturgised, and the liturgy legalised. Along with the resurrected priesthood there emerges the scribe who steps into the place of the old priestly prophets. His business is to keep the law, to write and teach the word of God, to transcribe it and apply it to the life of the people. In this way the law and the priestly liturgy are bound together, but in such a way that together they are made self sufficient and independent – liturgised scripture and legalised liturgy.

(2) No room for the prophet

Here there is no room for the prophet, for the direct intervention of the word in eschatological suspension of the liturgy, for the word of God is made of none effect by the traditions of man. In this situation Ezekiel had already seen the presence of God leave the temple[11] and severe judgement fall on the priesthood. But it is in a psalm that it is put most startlingly, 'We do not see our signs; there is no longer any prophet'.[12] Liturgised scripture and legalised liturgy rule out the charismatic intervention of the living word of God, and Israel is delivered over to God-forsakenness, hardened by sin in the very use of the ordinances of grace. Recall here Daniel who spoke of sealing up sins, sealing up vision and prophet until the coming of the anointed.[13]

(b) The fulfilment of law and cult in the Word made flesh

That is the situation into which Jesus Christ penetrated, the Word become flesh, the law of God become an individual Israelite within Israel, the Son of God born of woman and made under the law. In Christ, the Word tabernacles among mankind, full of grace and truth. The *shekinah*-glory[14] of God now dwells in a man and he is himself the temple of God,[15] so that it is neither in Samaria nor in Jerusalem that people need to go to worship, for the very Word and glory of God are become man in Jesus Christ. As

---

[11] Ezek 9 – 11, esp. 9.3, 10.4ff.,18ff., 11.22f.

[12] Psalm 74.9.

[13] Dan 9.24f., 12.4,9f.

[14] The cloud which rested on the tabernacle (*mishkan*, from the root *shkn*, dwell) in the midst of Israel and symbolised the tabernacling (*shakan*) or dwelling of God among his people is commonly known as the '*skekinah*' or '*skekinah*-glory' of God, Exod 40.34-38.

[15] John 1.14, 2.19-22.

Jesus said to the woman of Samaria, 'I who speak to you am he.'[16] But the coming of the Word made flesh is the breaking in of the kingdom of God into the situation of liturgised scripture and legalised liturgy, an intervention into the situation where people are under the bondage of priest and scribe. The kingdom breaks into that situation with judgement, as was evident in the ministry of John the Baptist, the last in line of the cult-prophets. He was a priest and the son of Zachariah, a ministering priest, who preached that the messiah would come with a threshing flail in his hand and thoroughly cleanse the threshing-floor, the ancient name for the temple which was apparently built upon Araunah's threshing-floor.[17] Therefore Jesus advanced from his baptism, as the fourth Gospel tells us, to cleanse his temple, and spoke the decisive words, 'Destroy this temple, and in three days I will raise it up.'[18]

(i) The primacy of the living Word, calling both scribe and priest to account

Thus into the midst of mankind's estrangement from God where it is at its very worst, into the midst of their religious alienation from God resting on a perversion of both scripture and liturgy, Jesus Christ steps forth as the living Word and calls both scribe and priest to account. He is the Word who has come direct from the Father, the Son come back to the vineyard which has been usurped by those to whom it was given to tend and who had stoned and killed the prophets.[19] He is the one who comes with the manifest *exousia* of God as revealed in his Word of forgiveness and healing of the sick.[20] He has authority over the sabbath and over the temple itself,[21] and even over the law for in face of it he can say, 'But I say unto you'.[22] He is in fact the anointed one,[23] the sent one, the messiah, prophet, priest and king in one, the Lord suddenly come to his temple,[24] the king returned to his dominion, the Word made flesh. It is as that incarnate Word and will and law of God that Jesus presses toward the cross and insists that in his word and act it is God's sovereign kingdom that breaks in. That means Jesus insists

---

16   John 4.26.

17   2 Sam 24.16ff.

18   John 2.19.

19   Matt 21.33-46; Mark 12.1-12; Luke 20.9-19.

20   Mark 2.3-12; Matt 9.2-8; Luke 5.18-26.

21   Matt 12.1-8.

22   Matt 5.22,28,32,34,39,44.

23   Luke 4.18.

24   Mal 3.1.

once again on the subordination of the priesthood and of all priestly functions to God's sovereign initiative, to God's royal grace. And so first of all, as we have seen, he steps into that situation, in the place of the prophet, as the Word made flesh, and goes about proclaiming the word of forgiveness and peace. Only then, in priestly obedience to God's word, does he advance to the living and actual liturgy of atonement.

(ii) Jesus' fulfilment of priestly obedience and liturgical witness

Jesus stepped into the midst of Israel and was made under the law. He was circumcised and had the covenant cut into his flesh. He was redeemed as a first-born son at the age of thirty-one days. At the age of twelve he fulfilled the requirements of the law in taking the yoke of the Torah upon himself[25] and all his life he was obedient to the law, and therefore obedient to the liturgy the law prescribed. He attended the feasts, ate the passover sacrifices and lived fully the life of an Israelite within all its legal and cultic enactments. But in the midst of it all, he lived out the life of the incarnate Word and law of God, insisting on the primacy of the Word of God in forgiveness and worship. That insistence is seen in the fact, for example, that Jesus does not speak of himself in priestly terms nor does he draw upon priestly and liturgical imagery in his parables, and only occasionally in his teaching. It is seen also in the instance when after forgiveness and cleansing he sends a man healed of leprosy back to the priests for a witness to them (*eis martyrion autois*)[26] – so that the priests with the appropriate oblations may bear liturgical witness to the sovereign action of the Word spoken by Christ in cleansing and healing. That is, Jesus forces the priesthood into its proper function of witness to the truth, liturgical acknowledgement of what God has already done and spoken in his grace.

Prophetic ministry in word, and priestly ministry in action, combined in the suffering servant

The significant fact is this, that while in word Jesus exercises his prophetic ministry, in his action he exercises his priestly ministry, and it is as suffering servant of the Lord that he combines both. It is that combination which comes out so strongly in the Johannine Gospel, which is apparently built up on the pattern of the Old Testament liturgy combining at last the passover rite with the act of the high priest on the great day of atonement, when in high priestly intercession Jesus Christ offered himself in sacrifice

---

25 See Luke 2.21,22ff.,42ff.

26 Matt 8.4; Mark 1.44; Luke 5.14, 17.14; cf. Lev 13 – 14.

as the lamb of God and ascended to the throne of the Father, returning with the 'peace be with you'[27] of reconciliation.

Now before we move on to consider the doctrine of priestly atonement in the Epistles of the New Testament, particularly in Paul and Hebrews, let us pause to look at four aspects of Christ's faithful priestly mediation, mediation in which he was not only the prophetic bearer of the Word of God to humanity but as himself that Word, the eternal Word and Son made flesh, acted in priestly atonement, restoring the relation between humanity and God through priestly propitiation, penitence and prayer.

(c) An outline of Christ's faithful priestly mediation

(i) Priestly propitiation – personal healing and reconciliation

We recall the distinction between *kopher* and *kipper* acts of redemption – *kopher* referring to the forensic act of piacular[28] atonement or expiation, *kipper* referring to the cultic or priestly act through which the fellowship between God and man is restored and peace is mediated to mankind. In Latin, propitiation[29] is the term we use to express the fact that the chasm between God and man has been bridged – it is a pontifical[30] act in which the estranged parties have been reconciled, God drawing near to mankind and mankind being brought near to God. The situation in which mankind is involved belongs to the mutual relation between God and humanity, so that a mutual relation needs to be repaired, and restoration needs to be effected in both a manward and in a Godward direction. *Expiation* refers to the piacular act through which reconciliation is effected, but *propitiation* refers to the personal healing and personal reconciliation. The distinctive thing about the biblical notion of propitiation is that it is initiated and carried through by God, but by God both from the side of God toward humanity and from the side of humanity toward God. God *himself* draws near – *he* propitiates himself, provides the ground on which man is brought near to God, and provides the offering or sacrifice with which man appears before God in worship.

That propitiation is wrought out in Jesus Christ himself. He is the God who, in his holy love, judges humanity but who draws near in so doing, for he will not hold himself aloof from men and women; but he is also the man who in our place draws near to God and so submits himself to the

---

27   John 20.19.

28   Piacular, 'making expiation', from the Latin *piaculum*, 'expiatory sacrifice'.

29   *Propitio*, appease, propitiate, render favourable.

30   'Bridge-making', from the Latin *pons* 'bridge', and *facio* 'make'.

divine judgement, offering himself in sacrifice to God. Jesus Christ combines both acts in himself, within the unity of his own incarnate personal life, so that he is himself propitiation acutely personalised in both its Godward and manward aspects. This is the stress in the epistle to the Hebrews and the Johannine writings in which we have emphasised the identity of sacrifice and priest, of work and person, of *pons* and *pontifex*, bridge and bridge-maker. Propitiation is then to be understood as priestly mediation between God and humanity, and humanity and God.

(ii) Priestly penitence – oneness of mind between God and man

This is the aspect of the atonement where we are concerned not so much with the external transaction of juridical or judicial character so much as with the internal *at-one-ment* between God and humanity and humanity and God. This is where we see that oneness of mind between God and man, and man and God is at the heart of atonement, yet it is not a oneness of mind that is detached from the actualisation of it in manward and Godward ways. This is evident in the concept of confession or *homologia*[31] in the epistle to the Hebrews, where confession was not in word or ritual act but in actualised relations between God and man, the divine holiness being brought to bear upon man's innermost being,[32] with men and women in their innermost being opened up and offered to God in such a way that there resulted a cleansed conscience, a holy unity in knowing and living with God.

The repentance into which Christ was baptised

We must consider this also in terms of repentance or penitence. Repentance is not in word or feeling only, but is actualised in the submission of the sinner to the divine judgement and pardon - that was the repentance into which Christ was baptised at the Jordan and into which he stepped in his temptations in the wilderness, where he fasted and prayed while suffering the assaults of evil and chose the way of the cross, laid upon him by the Father for our sakes. We can think of this in two ways:

(a) **the distinction between poena and poenitentia.**[33] Christ bore in his physical existence and in the infliction of death on him the just judgement of God upon our sin. When he in our place submitted himself

---

[31]   Heb 3.1, 4.14, 10.23.

[32]   Heb 4.11-14, 10.15-23.

[33]   *Poena*, penalty; *poenitentia*, repentance, regret. In (a) the distinction between *poena* and *poenitentia*, Torrance's emphasis is on the divine judgement, the *poena* for sin, and on the human acquiescence in that *poena*, the willing acceptance and bearing of the divine judgement in sorrow and agreement with the Father's verdict.

to that, he was fulfilling his baptismal consecration into repentance in the fulfilment of the divine righteousness. But Christ bore all that in his soul, for he took the divine judgement into his mind and innermost being, acquiescing in it, accepting it willingly, and at the same time offering himself willingly to the Father. In this way he entered into the depths of judgement and of sorrow for our sin in a way we can never do. He wrought out in our human nature and in our human soul complete agreement with the Father in his righteous condemnation of our sin, his grief and sorrow over our rebellion and alienation. In vicarious penitence and sorrow for the sin of mankind, Christ met and responded to the judgement and vexation of the Father, absorbing it in his own being.

(b) what we call repentance, **meta-noia,** *change-of-mind.*[34] In his incarnation Christ not only took upon himself our physical existence from God, but in taking it into himself he at the same time healed it, sanctified it, and changed it, bending our will back to agreement with the divine will, and bringing our human mind back into agreement with the divine mind – and so in the innermost being of the incarnate Son, throughout the whole course of his life, Jesus Christ converted the mind and will of estranged humanity back to the Father. That was the great *palingennesia,*[35] the renewing and sanctifying of humanity before God. This was fulfilled in the holiness of Jesus' life, in his perfect obedience to the Father, in the perfecting and offering to God of a human life and spirit in the purity of trust and love and devotion, in the sanctity of prayer and praise and worship. And so we have to consider the whole incarnate life of Christ as the fulfilment of the covenanted communion between God and man in which he himself became our prayer, our oblation, our worship, our faith, our perfect answer to God the Father – henceforth all Christian worship is only in his name, effected through his priestly self-presentation before the Father.[36]

---

[34] In (b) the emphasis is on the positive aspect of repentance, the active conversion of the human mind back into unity and complete fellowship with God. Thus while in (a) *poenitentia* is understood as an aspect of Christ's passive obedience, in (b) Torrance's emphasis is on repentance as active obedience, ie. in terms of the positive healing and restoration of the human mind to communion with God.

[35] Gk, 'rebirth'; cf. Matt 19.28, Titus 3.5, trans. 'regeneration' KJV (Matt 19.28 'new world' RSV).

[36] See further T.F. Torrance, *Theology in Reconciliation*, Geoffrey Chapman, London 1975, chap.3, 'The Paschal Mystery of Christ and the Eucharist, esp. pp. 106f., 109ff., 117ff., 131ff., and chap. 4, 'The Mind of Christ in Worship: The Problem of Apollinarianism in the Liturgy', esp. pp. 139-42, 204-214.

It is at the point of vicarious[37] repentance that we really face up to the radical notion of the priesthood of Christ, priest in our place, in vicarious sorrow and anguish, in vicarious trust and faith, in vicarious worship and thanksgiving.

(iii) Priestly prayer – Christ's self-offering in word and in life
None of these aspects can be separated from one another, far less this from the other aspects we have discussed. But let us now think of this as the self-offering of Christ, in which he prays for us not only with his words but with his life, in which he pleads with his life and life-blood for us sinners – the prayer of priestly self-sacrifice. Here we are concerned with the active obedience as well as the passive obedience of Christ, for it is prayer translated into his physical existence, lived out before the Father in the unspotted existence of a human life and then poured out on the cross. But it remains prayer identical with his personal being in his resurrection and ascension in which he presents himself to the Father in our humanity, and presents us in himself to the Father as those whom he has brothered, redeemed and consecrated in himself, and therefore as sanctified sons and daughters of the heavenly Father. It is towards this that all the redeeming and atoning work of Christ reaches out in fulfilment, in worship at the mercy-seat, in worship at the throne of God.

It is this aspect of the atonement that is particularly evident in the worship and sacramental life of the church – and not least in the eucharist which must be regarded as dramatic prayer in union with the mediation and intercession of our ascended high priest at the right hand of the Father.

(iv) Priesthood and sonship – atonement anchored in the Father-Son relation
The cultic-forensic aspect of the atonement in the Old Testament and New Testament is found to be concerned with the restoration of fellowship between God and man, and man and God who have been

---

[37]   Lat, *vicarius*, 'acting in the place of another'. Christ's vicarious repentance is his repentance in our place. Far from meaning that we do not have to repent, Christ's vicarious repentance demands of us an even more radical repentance, for it demands the total recognition that his is the only true 'baptism into repentance'. We are therefore saved by being baptised into Christ and his baptism. Our repentance, our faith, our worship is a sharing in Christ's. See Gal 2.20 KJV, 'I have been crucified with Christ; nevertheless I live, yet not I, but Christ lives in me, and the life which I now live in the flesh I live *by the faith of* the Son of God (*en pistei tē tou Uiou tou Theou*)'. Cf. T.F. Torrance, *Incarnation*, Paternoster UK & InterVarsity Press USA, Milton Keynes & Downer's Grove, 2008, p. 28 and footnote. See also *Theology in Reconciliation*, p. 141.

alienated from each other – God from humanity through his abhorrence and judgement of sin, that is, in his wrath, and humanity from God in our rejection of the love of God and rebellion against his covenant of grace. In this context, priestly atonement involves the notion of *propitiation* in which God turns away from his wrath to man in forgiveness and man is turned away from rebellion to draw near to God in love. But while in the Old Testament, it is the forensic aspect of this that is dominant, in the New Testament the whole concept of propitiation together with that of wrath, judgement and forgiveness is drawn into the personal Father-Son relationship. That is to say, the notion of priesthood is taken out of its interim-institutional status found in the Levitical priesthood of Israel and anchored deep in the personal and family relationship between God and his people – so that the *goel* notion is pulled over the *kipper* notion of redemption. This is why the New Testament speaks of the penal-substitutionary aspect of atonement, not in the detached forensic categories that have developed in the Latin west, Roman or Protestant, but in terms of the intimacy of the Father-Son relation, in which the Son submits himself to the Father's judgement and is answered through the Father's good pleasure – see here the supreme importance of John McLeod Campbell and his great book *The Nature of the Atonement*,[38] in which he rightly warned us against thinking of atonement in purely penal terms, for we cannot think of Christ being punished by the Father in our place and the New Testament nowhere uses the word *kolazō*, punish, of the relation between the Father and the Son.

3 The doctrine of priestly atonement in the New Testament

Two main emphases corresponding to the Mosaic and Aaronic aspects of priesthood

When we turn to the epistles of the New Testament for the theology of the sacrificial work of Christ, we find two main emphases which very clearly correspond to the two main aspects of priesthood we have been considering – the aspect that concerns the mediation of God's word (as represented by Moses in the Old Testament) and the aspect concerned with sacrificial mediation (as represented by Aaron in the Old Testament). Overarching both of these there is the concept of the messianic kingdom to which we shall return later when we consider again the concept of *padah* redemption in the kingly ministry of Christ.

---

[38]   For an analysis of McLeod Campbell's argument and summary of what he did and did not teach, see T.F. Torrance, *Scottish Theology*, T & T Clark, Edinburgh 1996, chap. 9, 'John McLeod Campbell', pp. 287-315.

This dual aspect of the doctrine of atonement comes out most of all in (i) the epistles of St Paul which are more concerned with atonement in terms of expiation and justification before the word or law of God, and (ii) the epistle to the Hebrews which is more concerned with atonement in terms of Christ's high priestly oblation of himself and his heavenly intercession.

The difference between the Pauline teaching and that of Hebrews is not one of contrariety but one of a different method of approach. Hebrews is addressed to those concerned with the Jewish liturgy. It speaks of Christ's atonement in the language of Old Testament worship and liturgy, and so speaks of those Old Testament actions whose clear fulfilment is seen in Christ, for example the relation of Christ's ascension to the entry of the high priest into the holy of holies. Very little is said here about Christ's resurrection or forty days sojourn on earth afterwards, as there is no analogy or counterpart in the Old Testament liturgy to that. Here too the whole meaning of the act of atonement itself is taken for granted and thought is concentrated on what atonement opens up for the church. St Paul on the other hand speaks a good deal of the resurrection of Christ; it plays a part of primary importance in his thought and casts a light upon the act of atonement which is expounded more fully.

The two emphases supply the twin foundation for the doctrine of atonement

Now both of these two, the Pauline teaching and that of Hebrews, imply one another and a New Testament doctrine of atonement must rest mainly on that twin foundation. In both writers, atonement is the personal intervention of God in Christ reconciling the world and restoring it to oneness with God. In both, the main stress is upon the person of Christ atoning and reconciling, not upon an act of atonement *in abstracto*.[39] There is no attempt anywhere to erect a liturgy of atonement or a sacrament of it in independence of Christ, the living incarnate Word of God. We are not saved by the atoning death of Christ, far less by sacramental liturgical action, but by *Christ himself* who in his own person made atonement for us. *He is* the atonement who ever lives and ever intercedes for us. He is, in the identity of his person and work, priest and sacrifice in one. His *being* mediates his great redeeming work.

(a) The parallels between Hebrews and Paul

It is worth noting the parallels between the teaching of the epistle to the Hebrews and the teaching of Paul in the epistles to the Romans and Galatians.

---

[39]   Lat, 'in the abstract'.

(i) In St Paul's teaching, we have set out the grace of Christ and the gospel of salvation contrasted with law and the works of the law. That is carried further in the contrast between freedom in the Spirit and bondage under the law.

In Hebrews, the contrast is between Christ as sacrificing high priest in his own person and the legal priesthood of the Old Testament, between approach to God in joy and grace in the new covenant and subservience to command in the old covenant.

(ii) In St Paul's teaching, the law in the Old Testament is interpreted in terms of an intermediary between God and man, a sort of buffer holding God's majesty and judgement at a distance from man, suspending the wrath of God, but the gospel works a complete change in our relation to the Mosaic law and therefore to the will of God.

In Hebrews, the liturgical sacrifices are interpreted in terms of intermediate action designed to keep people in remembrance of sin, as well as to point toward forgiveness, suspending full atonement which is yet to come, but the gospel works a complete change in relation to the Aaronic priesthood and all its intermediation.

(iii) In St Paul's teaching, Christian faith looks back behind Moses to Abraham, behind the Mosaic law to the personal covenant of faith.

In Hebrews, Christian faith looks behind Aaron to Abraham's day, to Melchizedek, to a prior and personal priesthood before the institutional priesthood of the Levitical law.

(iv) In St Paul's teaching, faith rests upon the action of Christ who breaks through the bondage of the law and apart from law, and bestows newness of life in his resurrection in full communion with God.

In Hebrews, faith rests upon the priesthood of Christ. With its 'power of an endless life' and eternal Sonship, this is of a different order from the Aaronic priesthood which is legalist and under the power of the 'carnal' commandments. The power and sacrificial virtue of the Aaronic priesthood did not lie in the priesthood itself but in the carnal commandment and external law under which they were subsumed, but here it lies in Christ himself who ever lives and who is our atonement.

In both Paul and Hebrews atonement is grounded on the person of Christ

Thus *both in St Paul and in Hebrews* a legalist doctrine of atonement is false. That is the amazing thing about the Pauline doctrine of justification – it is at once forensic, concerned with law and righteousness in terms of the law, and yet involves the eschatological suspension of law in the freedom of the resurrection. So here in the epistle to the Hebrews, the unity of the priest and the sacrifice in one person once for all ends all legal enactment and temporal repetition of sacrifice under legal ordinances, for Christ breaks a way through the veil into the heavenly kingdom and so opens up for us all real and actual participation in the heavenly life in reconciliation and fellowship with God the Father. It is thus significant in the New Testament record that when Christ was crucified the veil of the temple in Jerusalem was rent from top to bottom.[40]

Thus whether we look at the teaching of Paul or that of Hebrews we find that the theology of atonement is grounded upon the person of Christ as mediator and intercessor, and it is that *work of mediation and intercession in his person* that we must seek to understand.

(b) Mediation from the side of God and from the side of man

We recall here what we found the gospel revealing about human sin as having a twofold character, of rebellion against God, and guilt over against the divine judgement of sin.[41] This sin we saw to belong to man's existence in alienation from God involving the perversion of our whole nature and involving spiritual and physical death.[42] It is in that situation that the eternal Son of God intervenes as our mediator, as true God and true man in one person who acts as judging God and judged man, as loving God and as obedient man. We must think of the work of Christ in terms of a mediation which fully represents both the divine and human side. If sin is qualified as sin by the attitude of God against it, then it is the divine will that must be maintained and justified in the death of Christ. If sin is an act of humanity going down into the roots of human nature and existence bringing death, then the work of Christ from the side of the human creature must be stressed and a human confession before God and obedience to God must be fulfilled.

These two actions are carried out in Christ's mediation and intercession in the unity of God and man in him, and in the unity of his person and work. In the mediation on the cross, that oneness between God and man already wrought out in the incarnation and in the complete oneness between the incarnate Son and the heavenly Father, is fully consummated, and the union between the person of Christ the Son and his work in our flesh is likewise consummated and fulfilled. *It is that oneness which constitutes the inner heart of atonement.* This oneness or at-onement involves oneness of will and mind between man and God. God triumphs not only in defeating and judging sin,

---

[40]   Matt 27.51; Mark 15.38; Luke 23.45.

[41]   T.F. Torrance, *Incarnation*, chap. 7, 'The Kingdom and Christ and Evil', esp. p. 247ff., 251ff.

[42]   *Ibid.*

but in reconciling men and women and in defeating the enmity of their mind[43] to God. There must be restored that perfect communion between God and man which was broken by the rebellion of man and which was necessarily judged by God. This means an atonement which involves the reconciliation of God to humanity and of humanity to God, for it is a reconciliation as real and objective on the side of God as it is to be on the side of humanity.

We are now to think, then, of Christ's mediation between God and man and the atonement he wrought out in achieving that full reconciliation from both sides.

(i) It is *the atoning mediation of Christ as act of God*, of Christ as very God dealing with sinful mankind. In the death of Christ there took place God's supreme act on humanity and for humanity. It is at once the act of God in vindication of himself against sin in judgement, and yet the act of his forgiveness and restoration of humanity to himself.

(ii) It is *the atoning mediation of Christ as act of man*, of Christ as act of man before God. In his death Christ acts as man, bearing our sin and guilt and bringing in himself the perfect submission of man in obedience to God the Father, in confession of the sin of the world and vicarious bearing of it before God. He confesses our sin and submits perfectly to God, restoring mankind to oneness with God, both in regard to life and in regard to mind. In Christ Jesus, men and women are brought into the relation to God of perfect and obedient children and are brought to acquiesce in the divine judgement of sin and to accept the forgiveness offered there.

(c) The oneness and indivisibility of Christ's act as God and as man

It is by combining both acts in himself as true God and true man that Christ works out this atonement, in one indivisible act of the God-man, so that there is reconciliation of God to man and of man to God, but as man Christ does not act independently of God. He does not act as man reconciling God or as man appeasing God. He acts as God who enters into the place of humanity, and brings himself into reconciliation with humanity and brings them into reconciliation with himself, and does that in such a way that the act of humanity's reconciliation with God is not an act just done over their head, but an act that is fully and entirely human act, issuing out the depth of their humanity and directed from humanity toward God the Father. The doctrine of *anhypostasia* and *enhypostasia*[44] is

---

[43]   See Col 1.21; cf. Rom 8.7 (KJV 'enmity', RSV 'hostile').

[44]   *Incarnation*, p. 84.

here of the utmost importance as applied to the atonement, for it means that even as man in atoning action, Christ is act of God, and that atonement is in no sense Pelagian[45] propitiation of God; and it means also that even as God in atoning action, Christ is act of man, and that atonement is man's act of obedient self-offering to God with which he is well pleased. Atonement is the act of God himself, at once from the side of God and from the side of humanity working propitiation and reconciliation, and consummating ultimate and final union and communion or atonement between God and humanity.

It will be recalled that when we were discussing the cultic-forensic aspect of atonement in the Old Testament we noted that there was a relative distinction between the verb *kipper* and the noun *kopher*. While *kopher* belonged mainly to the realm of law and was mainly a forensic category, *kipper* belonged mainly to the realm of the priestly liturgy and was mainly a cultic term. But although the significance of both overlapped as the cultic and the forensic do everywhere else in the Old Testament, there is nevertheless a distinction between them. That distinction belongs in a measure to the distinction between Pauline exposition of atonement and that of the epistle to the Hebrews. While Paul is mostly concerned with *kopher*-atonement, reconciliation through a substitutionary exchange, involving penalty and justification, the epistle to the Hebrews is mainly concerned with *kipper*-atonement, reconciliation through sacrifice involving sanctification and cleansing from sin. Of course the two expositions overlap, but it will be convenient to discuss them separately in order to help us understand atonement first as *reconciliation through sacrifice* and then later, when we consider atonement in the teaching of Paul, as *reconciliation through expiation*.

4 Atonement in the epistle to the Hebrews

Atonement as reconciliation through sacrifice is expounded in this epistle as the work of the mediator in the way we have considered it, so that we shall look first at the priesthood of the incarnate Son and then at the meaning of his atoning act through sacrifice.

(a) *The priesthood of Christ the incarnate Son*

The dual aspect of atonement as act of God and act of man in Christ the mediator is very fully brought out in this epistle. We cannot go into the

---

[45] Human or humanly assisted – Pelagius believed that we co-operate with God for our salvation.

whole exposition, but let us examine a typical passage which gives the meaning clearly, the opening of the third chapter, 'consider the apostle and high priest of our confession, faithful to God who appointed him.'[46] Here we have Christ's twofold function in mediation. He is the apostle or *shaliach* of God, and in Judaism, as W. Manson reminds us, the high priest on the day of atonement was recognised as the *shaliach* of God, not simply of man.[47] He is at once God's apostle and our high priest, made like us in every respect[48] yet without sin. This double function is *God's making*[49] and in this double appointment and function Christ is utterly faithful, *pistos*.

Christ is the faithful apostle. By that the author of the epistle has already explained that he means that Christ is the obedient Son of God, who as such is God's full and final revelation, 'being the brightness of his glory, and the express image of his person, and upholding all things by the word of his power.'[50] In this Christ Jesus, God has spoken his final and complete Word, the Word which *is* the Son of God. God has uttered himself in Jesus Christ, so that the Word which he has always addressed to man in times past now becomes man and becomes as man divine Word and human word. But that Word is the eternal Son of God and now that the Son has become man, the sonship is human as well as divine. Thus the epistle expounds the sonship of Christ as at once that of the eternal Son or Word of God and that of the historical Christ who renders obedient account to God. Nowhere do we get in the New Testament more exalted statements of the deity of Christ or more realistic statements of his humanity and his complete solidarity with mankind. That Christ is God's eternal Son, God's *self*-revelation or Word, is the primary emphasis of this epistle, and it is only when the author has made that clear that he moves on to speak of Christ as our high priest, but in such a way as to show that Christ's high priesthood is part of his Sonship and has no independent status or function.[51] Here then the epistle to the Hebrews finds in Christ the perfect fulfilment of the Old Testament relation of God's prophetic word to priestly oblation. Let us note now several important things that the epistle has to teach us.

---

46   See Heb 3.1-2.

47   W. Manson, *The Epistle to the Hebrews*, Hodder and Stoughton, London 1951, p. 54. The footnote here reads, 'Strack-Billerbeck, III. p. 4 cites *Qid.* 23*b* as authority. See the whole discussion of the term *Shaliach* on pp. 2-4.'

48   Heb 2.17.

49   Heb 3.2.

50   Heb 1.3 KJV.

51   Heb 5.5f.

(i) Priesthood through faithful Sonship in humanity

Christ becomes high priest through maintaining his Sonship faithfully in our existence of sin and weakness. By living out the life of the Son of God within our humanity through his faithfulness,[52] through his suffering obedience[53] and intercession,[54] he becomes our high priest. As such, he is 'made perfect' (*teleiōtheis*),[55] and so perfected and consecrated Son for evermore (*huion eis ton aiōna teteleiōmenon*).[56] What is the meaning of this term *teleioun*, to perfect? It is a) fill, complete, and b) consecrate. Recall here the Old Testament rite of consecration to priesthood. The hands of the priest were 'filled' with the offering and his ordination was regarded as complete when he offered it.[57] It is in the actualisation and realisation of Jesus' Sonship within our human conditions and limitations that he is befitted or consecrated as our high priest, as our representative as well as God's representative.

(ii) Christ's priesthood unique and eternal

The *union of his Sonship with his high priesthood*, his apostleship from God with his priestly function toward God, makes his priesthood *unique and eternal*. This helps us to understand the Old Testament liturgy better, for now we can say a number of things about it.

(1) The Old Testament liturgy as type and shadow

The Old Testament liturgy never reached its *teleiōsis*, its end or completion,[58] never fulfilled its proper function and intention of achieving

---

[52] Heb 3.2,6.

[53] Heb 5.8.

[54] Heb 5.7.

[55] Heb 5.9.

[56] Heb 7.28.

[57] The Old Testament expression 'fill the hands' (*mala yadim*) is translated 'ordain' in English (RSV, cf. KJV 'consecrate'). The Hebrew *mala yadim*, is translated literally in the LXX usually by either *teleioun tas cheiras*, (Exod 29.9,29,33,35; Lev 8.33, 16.32, 21.10; Num 3.3) or *plēroun tas cheiras* (Judges 17.5,12; cf. 1 Chron 29.5 and 2 Chron 13.9, 29.31 where the same expression has reference to self-consecration; cf. also Exod 28.41 where *empiplēnai* is the word used for 'filling' the hands). See further T.F. Torrance, *Royal Priesthood*, p. 79f, and also T.F. Torrance, *Conflict and Agreement*, vol. 2, Lutterworth, London 1960, 'Consecration and Ordination' (repr. from Scottish Journal of Theology, vol. 11.3, 1958, pp. 225ff.), p. 30f., esp. 33ff.

[58] Heb 7.11-19.

atonement.[59] It only pointed to that and is to be understood in this epistle in terms of pattern (*hypodeigma*),[60] shadow (*skia*)[61] and type (*tupos*).[62]

(2) A continual reminder of sin – the way through the veil was not yet open

The very repetition of the Old Testament liturgical sacrifices not only showed their essential imperfection, but was designed to produce *anamnçsis* or remembrance of old sins,[63] designed to keep the wounds of conscience open, so as to point forward to real forgiveness, final and actual atonement, and to the entering in of a better hope (*epeisagōgē de kreittonos elpidos*).[64] This was true of course of the whole Levitical and priestly liturgy. Think of what the epistle to the Hebrews has to say about the *veil*, 'By this the Holy Spirit indicates that the way into the sanctuary is not yet opened as long as the outer tent (or tabernacle) is still standing'.[65] The veil preserved in the midst of Israel the holy mystery of God and cut off entrance into the holy of holies. Only by its removal, that is, only by the destruction of the temple, could the holy presence of God be thrown open to access for all. Thus we are to understand that the whole Levitical liturgy was the means through which a certain access to God was granted, and yet the means whereby real access to God's presence was hindered and deferred until real atonement could be made and the veil would be taken out of the way. The veil therefore served also to protect the people of Israel from the blazing majesty of God, for God is a consuming fire who cannot look upon iniquity, and no one can look upon the face of God and live.[66] The only possible way of access into the presence of such a holy God was symbolised and indicated by the act of the high priest on the day of atonement, when under the thick cloud of incense and bearing the blood of the covenant[67] he entered into the holy place at the risk of his life to ask for pardon and the renewal of God's covenant mercies, and only went in at the command of God who appointed him. When

---

[59]   Heb 10.1-4.

[60]   Heb 8.5, 9.23.

[61]   Heb 8.5, 10.1.

[62]   Heb 8.5; cf. Exod 25.40, LXX *tupos*, pattern, (cf. 25.9, *paradeigma*, pattern).

[63]   Heb 10.3.

[64]   Heb 7.19 – cf. Paul, Rom 8.20.

[65]   Heb 9.8f. – cf. KJV, 'the way into the holiest of all was not yet made manifest while the first tabernacle was yet standing'.

[66]   Exod 33.20.

[67]   Lev 16.12-14 – see also the whole chapter.

atonement in the sacrifice of Christ on the cross was completed, the veil of the temple was rent, and had to be rent.[68]

(3) Christ is both priest and sacrifice

Christ is priest and oblation in one. Atonement is Christ's self-offering.[69] That unity of person and work, of priest and sacrifice in him, means the final end of all ritual sacrificing.[70] This self-offering of Christ is through the eternal Spirit[71] and is therefore eternal. It is once and for all (*hapax* and *ephapax*)[72] – that is, once for all both in the historical sense and in the eternal sense, but it is in the combination of the two senses that the finality of atonement is really consummated.

(4) Christ the priest of the resurrection

Christ then becomes 'priest of the resurrection', as W. Manson expressed it. He who has opened up a way into the very presence of God in heaven itself, is he who by 'the power of an endless life' ever lives as our intercessor, and in him our hope is anchored within the veil.[73] By ascending to the throne of God, Christ as high priest is also our king, and as such in the oneness of his priestly and kingly functions, he is minister or *leitourgos* of the true tabernacle[74] and its heavenly intercession and liturgy. That is regarded as eschatologically, not Platonically,[75] related to the worship of God's children on earth.[76]

(5) Christ the high priest on the day of atonement, representing all Israel

Now in order to gather up this discussion of the priesthood of Jesus the incarnate Son of God let us look at the analogical way in which the writer of the epistle to the Hebrews expounds it. He has in his mind

---

[68] Matt 27.51; Mark 15.38; Luke 23.45.

[69] Heb 7.27, 9.14, cf. 9.28.

[70] Heb 9.12,25-26, 10.12-14.

[71] Heb 9.14.

[72] Heb 7.27, 9.24-28, 10.10, (cf. 10.12,14, 'for all time, *eis to diēnekes'*).

[73] See Heb 7.16,25, 9.24, 6.19 KJV.

[74] Heb 8.2.

[75] That is, in terms of the relation of the kingdom of God and its worship (which has already come in time and presses in on us although it is yet to be manifested fully in the future) to this world and its worship, and not in terms of a timeless, higher, real and ideal world, to which this world is related as shadow and copy.

[76] For further comment on this point, see T.F. Torrance, *Royal Priesthood*, pp. 19-21.

the work of the high priest in Israel on the day of atonement, when as the representative both of his own house and of all Israel, he entered into the holy of holies to sprinkle the atoning blood of the covenant upon the mercy seat and make intercession for Israel and then to return with the divine peace and reconciliation.

In the Old Testament rite, the high priest did that twice, first for himself and for the sons of his own house, and then for Israel.[77] He acted as priest in virtue of his family relation, and as their representative entered into the holy place, not first for Israel, but first for himself and the priesthood. Then on the ground of their renewal in the covenant, their consecration through atonement and their reconciliation with God, the high priest entered the second time into the holy of holies. This time he went as the consecrated representative of *all* Israel and went with the names of all the tribes of Israel inscribed upon his breastplate and shoulders.[78] In their name and bearing their iniquity he entered into the presence of God, so that when he went in all Israel went in with the blood of atoning sacrifice on him. Therefore in that act God renewed the covenant not only with the high priest but with all Israel, and God accepted not only the person of the priest, but of the whole of Israel represented by him.

Atonement takes place in the person of Christ; we are accepted in his self-offering

Now on that basis and on that analogy, the epistle expounds the act of Christ the high priest who not only has our names inscribed on his heart, but was actually made like us in all things,[79] so that he became our very brother, bone of our bone and flesh of our flesh, as Paul put it.[80] Then on the ground of that complete solidarity with us in our humanity, and also in involvement with us in our estrangement from God and bearing our sin and all its contradiction, he entered into the holy presence of God, offering himself as the atoning sacrifice for us and consecrating himself on our behalf. Here the author of the Hebrews runs the two acts of the high priest in entering into the holy place into one, for we are all of the kindred and family of Jesus in virtue of his incarnation into our flesh, and hence when he entered into the holy place and offered himself in sacrifice to God, we entered with him and we are accepted by God in the person of Christ as having suffered and died with him, as if we had offered to God atonement for our own

---

[77] Lev 16.

[78] Exod 28.6-30.

[79] Heb 2.14-18.

[80] Cf. Eph 5.29-32; Gen 2.21-24.

sin. Now under the Old Testament rites the sins of Israel were transferred to the victim by a symbolical rite and it was slain in symbolical substitution for Israel so that it suffered the judgement of God upon sin in Israel's place.[81] Here, however, in the New Testament it is no more with symbolical actions that we are concerned, and that applies not only to cultic symbolism but to legal symbolism – it is not just a cultic or forensic translation that has taken place, in which Jesus has symbolically taken our place, so that cultically and by legal transaction only our sins are taken away and laid on Christ and judged.

Christ is so really one with us in our humanity, that what he did we did in him

The whole teaching of Hebrews pivots upon the profound fact that Jesus Christ *actually* entered into our existence and *actually* shouldered our sin. As such in the fullest solidarity with us he so acted in our humanity that we acted in him, he so acted for us in his own person, that God regards us and accepts us in the person of Christ. Thus when Christ offered himself in sacrifice and consecrated himself, he so did that for us that we were offered to God and we were consecrated in him, for *in his act he who consecrated and we who were consecrated are for ever bound up in one consummated act* – that is the emphatic teaching at the end of the second chapter of Hebrews which the whole epistle then proceeds to unfold and elucidate.

Now note one more thing at this point, again from the second half of the second chapter, how the writer has woven together the notions of the priesthood of Christ with the concept of the *goel*-redeemer and with the concept of *padah*-redemption. It is on the ground of his kinship with us, as our *goel*, that Christ is both our real representative and our true priest, but as such he not only makes priestly atonement before God but slays the man-slayer, death itself and the devil who has the power of death, and so delivers us who through fear of death are all our lives subject to bondage.[82] Here all three concepts of redemption are definitely and inseparably woven together, and it is in that unity that Christ exercises, in our name and in our humanity and person, his priestly functions, so that he actually and really is *our* advocate and *our* surety before God.

(b) Atonement through the mediation of Christ

What then is the atonement in the epistle to the Hebrews? What is accomplished by Christ's self offering and mediation on our behalf? The atonement is the setting of our life on a wholly new basis in relation to God, on the ground of which we have an entirely new approach to God.

---

[81] Lev 16.15.

[82] Heb 2.14-15.

(i) The contrast between the old covenant and the new covenant, Sinai and Calvary

This is described with remarkably vivid language in the twelfth chapter of the epistle in the contrast between the old covenant and the new covenant, between Moses the mediator of the old and Jesus the mediator of the new, between Mount Sinai and Mount Zion. The author of the epistle recalls the founding of the first covenant at Mount Sinai, the mount that burned with fire. There God spoke, and his voice was so terrible to the sinner and so unbearable that even Moses 'feared and quaked exceedingly', and the people entreated that the word of God should not be spoken to them any more.[83] Recall the Old Testament account, when the people in their terror said to Moses, 'You speak to us and we will hear, but let not God speak to us lest we die.'[84] In those circumstances Moses became the mediator of the old covenant. He spoke with God face to face[85] and mediated the word of God to Israel, and Israel responded and bore witness to God liturgically, in obedience to the divine injunctions. Israel was given the law and the sacrificial liturgy in order to stand before God, who is all consuming fire, and yet to stand before him a sinful people in covenant relation with God, pointing to his mercy and pardon. Under that covenant relation with God, approach to God was on the basis of the divine command as epitomised in the ten commandments or decalogue. And so the whole tabernacle was constructed around the decalogue lodged in the holy of holies[86] which represented liturgically the mount that burned with fire shrouded in fire and smoke.

Over against that Old Testament covenant and its liturgy, the epistle to the Hebrews sets in contrast Mount Zion, or as we would call it, Calvary, out of which there comes again the voice of God summoning us to worship, but here the approach to God is not on the basis of God's demand or command, but on the basis of what God in his grace has freely done for us in Jesus Christ. Here we come to Jesus the mediator of the new covenant and to the blood of sprinkling that speaks better things than that of Abel.[87] In the blood of Jesus God has founded a new covenant, a covenant of love in which God has once and for all committed himself to us in pure grace, and so bound himself to us that he will not, cannot, go back upon his Word. How can God go back upon the death of his dear

---

[83]   See Heb 12.18-21 KJV; cf. Exod 19.16-18, 20.18f.

[84]   Exod 20.19.

[85]   Exod 33.11; Num 12.8; Deut 34.10.

[86]   See Exod 34.28-29, 40.1-3,20-21; Deut 10.1-5.

[87]   Heb 12.24 KJV.

Son, upon a covenant sealed with his own blood? On the ground of this covenant, there is an utterly new approach and real access to God, such that we may come boldly to the throne of grace, may receive mercy and find grace to help in time of need.[88]

(ii) The new basis and the new approach

What is the new basis upon which this new approach is grounded? God has not changed. He is still the God of holy love who as such is therefore a consuming fire to the sinner. How can we now approach him in joy and peace and without fear? The answer is to be found in the mystery of the blood of Christ, which tells us that out of the darkness of Calvary there comes not only the unbearable voice of Sinai, the voice of awful judgement, but the voice of pure unmitigated grace, the voice of pardoning love. 'Father forgive them for they know not what they do.'[89]

The voice of judgement is identical with the voice of forgiveness

Look at it like this. When Moses entered into the thick cloud on Mount Sinai to speak to God and intercede for Israel and Israel's forgiveness, he feared and quaked exceedingly.[90] When Jesus approached the hill called Calvary, he said, 'I have a terrible baptism with which to be baptised and how I am constrained until it is accomplished.'[91] 'Now is my soul troubled', he said at the last supper, and went out to pray in desperate anguish in the garden with strong crying and tears shed like drops of his blood, and then at last on the cross, cited the twenty second psalm, 'My God, my God, why hast thou forsaken me?'[92] Jesus Christ is our mediator, who entered into the presence of God who is a consuming fire and we see that judgement and fire upon the cross. But from the cross too there comes the voice of amazing love: the voice of incredible love and mercy and pardon right in the heart of judgement – that is why it is such incredible love.

Or look at it like this. Modern readers of the gospel have been baffled by the paradoxical character of Jesus. On the one hand, they see the Jesus of forked lightning, as he has been called – 'no man ever spoke like this man!'[93] On the other hand, there is the Jesus of the Galilean idyll, the Jesus of idyllic peace and calm and love. People wondered at

---

[88]   Heb 4.16 KJV.

[89]   Luke 23.34.

[90]   Heb 12.21 KJV.

[91]   See Luke 12.50.

[92]   See John 13.21; Mark 14.32-34; cf. Matt 26.36-38; Heb 5.7 KJV; Luke 22.44; Matt 27.46; Mark 15.34; Psalm 22.1.

[93]   John 7.46, cf. KJV 'never man spake like this man.'

the gracious words that fell from his lips.[94] It is the blood on the cross that tells us that those two are the same and out of that oneness there comes the voice of everlasting forgiving love and infinite sympathy and grace. That is the breathtaking mystery of it all, *the mystery of the blood of Christ*, the voice that speaks as all the Old Testament sacrifices could never speak, but it is the very same voice that spoke on Mount Sinai, and it is because of the blood of God that we know it is the same voice.

Only the one who justly condemns us can really forgive us

And look at it like this. Unless the voice of forgiving love is identical with the accusing voice that echoes in your conscience, you cannot trust it. It would be a counterfeit voice, a pure fiction. Only the one who justly condemns us can really forgive us, and only then are we liberated from fear into perfect love and perfect worship of God. That is why the death of Christ speaks so eloquently of the love of God, because of his shed blood which tells us that the God of Sinai and conscience has come himself to forgive our sins in sheer unmitigated love and at cost only to himself. He does not wait for men and women to approach him, but has anticipated them by entering into our human weakness and guilt and by standing on the side of humanity under judgement speaking to us of his forgiveness. Therefore we can come to God not with fear, but on the contrary, with uninhibited joy and peace. Who wants now to listen to the thunder of Sinai when the voice of Christ's blood cries from the ground? Or as St Paul put it, 'who is to condemn? Is it Christ Jesus who died . . . ?'[95] Here in Jesus Christ, in his sacrifice, we are assured that God does not stand apart on the mount of judgement and fire as a mere judge and arbiter of human life, but in Jesus Christ he has entered into our life and stands on the side of our human frailty as God, very God, who bears on his heart the burden of our smitten conscience and guilt and sin. 'There is therefore now no condemnation for those who are in Christ Jesus', to cite Paul again.[96]

The irrevocable nature of atonement and the free grace of God

In order to express the irrevocability and finality of atonement, as well as its character of free or gratuitous grace, the writer to the Hebrews appears to go back to some words of Jesus at the last supper where he spoke of the new covenant in terms of a testament and kingdom that could not be moved. Jesus' words are found in Luke, 'as my Father

---

94   Luke 4.22.

95   Rom 8.34.

96   Rom 8.1.

appointed a kingdom for me, so do I appoint for you (*ka'gō diatithemai humin kathōs dietheto moi ho Patēr mou basileian*) that you may eat and drink at my table in my kingdom . . . '.[97] There we have combined, as we have in Hebrews, the idea of the covenant and kingdom. Here in the epistle to the Hebrews, the Greek *diathēkē* means (as the Hebrew *berith* does not) testament, in the sense of a last will and testament bestowing an inheritance.[98] That combination of testament and covenant in the epistle to the Hebrews expresses the finality of the new covenant and its character as a pure act of free grace. Not only is it a covenant once and for all made and pledged by God in the blood of Christ, but it is a testament to all those who believe in the Son of God through whom they as sons and daughters enter once and for all into his inheritance which he freely bequeaths to them on his death. On the death of the testator the covenant assumes the unconditional form of a pure inheritance. There are no demands attached to this inheritance. God has irreversibly and utterly poured out his love upon us and our relations with him are in the freedom of sons and daughters who enter fully into their inheritance.

Here we see that in the epistle to the Hebrews we have another way of putting Paul's great doctrine, which he expounded in Galatians, of the freedom of the children of God over against the law. Here too the new covenant makes the first one old,[99] and there is a real annulling or displacement (*athetēsis*) of the old ordinance,[100] a change of the law (*nomou metathesis*) and of legal priesthood[101] for another relation and another worship in utter freedom and peace.

(iii) The unique act of atonement

How does the epistle to the Hebrews speak of the act of atonement which brings about this new basis upon which all relations with God are now grounded? It is clear that the liturgical language of atonement is used without stopping to explain to readers what the act of atonement is – that is apparently taken for granted.[102] What the author is concerned

---

[97] Luke 22.29; cf. Matt 19.28.

[98] As seen in chap. 1 above, *diathēkē* can both 'covenant' and 'testament', whereas *berith* can only mean 'covenant'.

[99] Heb 8.13.

[100] Heb 7.18, cf. 10.9.

[101] Heb 7.12.

[102] Cf. Heb 9.5 with its reference to the *hilastērion* or mercy seat on which the atoning blood was sprinkled.

to show is the difference between the Old Testament liturgical witness to it and the reality of New Testament approach. And yet, how far is it actually taken for granted, and how far is it really a recognition of the ultimate mystery of atonement? It is taken for granted that the actual atonement is expiation by the shedding of sacrificial blood, for all things are purged and all sins are expiated by blood.[103] We are reminded of the *locus classicus* or classic passage in Leviticus, 'the life of the flesh is in the blood; and I have given it for you upon the altar to make atonement for your souls; for it is the blood that makes atonement by reason of the life.'[104] Two things are to be said here. Atonement by blood means the substitution of life for life. But why that should constitute an expiation in God's sight is not explicitly said, except that it is God's gracious will. The atonement knows no *why*, no ultimate *why* except God himself. All rests on his ordinance of grace. That means that the ultimate mystery of the atonement recedes into the eternal being of God far beyond our human grasp, to 'the lamb slain before the foundation of the world.'[105] Thus though the writer to the Hebrews appears to take for granted that atonement is through the expiatory shedding of blood, he is intent on respecting its ultimate mystery. In the last analysis it is exactly the same position that is held by St Paul. We can, however, say a few things about the understanding of the act of atonement here in Hebrews.

(1) The oneness of the divine representative and the human representative

The uniqueness of the atoning deed lies in the oneness in Jesus Christ of the divine representative and the human representative. Jesus Christ is at once the apostle of God and by God's appointment, as well as by incarnate qualification, our high priest. In Christ the voice of God the judge and the voice of the intercessor, the voice of condemnation and the voice of pardon, are one and the same. That is expressed remarkably in the term *homologia*, confession.[106] What is the meaning of 'confession'? Compare David's confession in the Psalms, 'For I know my transgressions, and my sin is ever before me. Against thee, thee only, have I sinned, and done that which is

---

[103]   Heb 9.22.

[104]   Lev 17.11.

[105]   See Rev 13.8 – the KJV appears more accurate and closer to the Greek than the RSV at this point.

[106]   Heb 3.1, 4.14, 10.23.

evil in thy sight, so that thou art justified in thy sentence and blameless in thy judgement. Behold, thou desirest truth in the inward being; therefore teach me wisdom in my secret heart.'[107] There we have a confession of a divine righteousness and judgement, and of human sins deserving judgement, confession in which there is no resentment against God's righteousness or against its judgement on us. Confession in holiness is the supreme act of confession in which there is enshrined a perfect oneness between the mind of God and the mind of man.

The 'confession' of Christ, as apostle and high priest, in word and in actual life

In the three instances of *homologia* or 'confession' in the epistle to the Hebrews what is set forth is primarily the confession made by the high priest as he enters within the veil into the holy presence of God. It is the confession of our sin and the confession of God's righteous judgement upon our sin. As apostle Jesus Christ bears witness for God, that God is holy, and brings that holiness to bear directly upon humanity and human sin. As our high priest Jesus Christ acknowledges that God is holy, acknowledges God's holy wrath against our sin and says amen to it. Again as apostle he confesses the mercy and grace of God, his will to pardon and reconcile. As our high priest he intercedes for men and women and confesses them before the face of God as his own flesh and blood.

But Jesus Christ as apostle and high priest offered that twofold confession not in word only but in deed and in life, in action and in concrete reality. That confession was the translation of the Word or truth of God into our flesh and blood in the whole life of Jesus, and the whole life of Jesus was at the same time his answering confession of that divine truth. He was therefore the truth of God, the truth sent from God, incarnated in our humanity. And so from the very beginning to the very end when Jesus stood before Pilate as the truth witnessing a good confession, he was the truth of God done into our flesh, which condemned our sin in the flesh. But he was also the obedient answer of humanity to that truth, and so from beginning to end when he witnessed a good confession before Pontius Pilate he was 'the true and faithful witness, the amen'.[108]

---

[107] Psalm 51.3-4,6.

[108] See Rev 3.14; cf. 1.5. On the concept of witness in the New Testament and on Jesus as the true witness who witnessed a good confession, see T.F. Torrance, *Conflict and Agreement*, vol. 2, pp. 68-70.

*Confession by God in judgement and truth, and by man in the obedient
amen of the cross*

Such a confession by Christ, God and man, in word and in life, is a
confession in ultimate action. As we have seen, sin has objective depth
and involves our whole existence before God, for it involves our death
and judgement as guilty under the divine judgement. No confession
of sin that did not reach down to the depths of our sinful existence,
that did not reach acquiescence in the complete judgement of God
upon our sin in death, would be true confession. Just as God can only
be truth affirming that truth against the lie of sin, so the confession of
that sin can only submit entirely to God's divine assertion of truth
against it, that is in his ultimate repudiation of sin and in final
judgement of it. Christ's confession was an actual submission to the
ultimate judgement of God's truth against our sin, a submission
therefore to the point of death. It is not a matter of mind or word only
but of life, and of final action in the midst of our life and death. Thus
the confession on God's part is the judgement of death, and the
confession on man's part is the confession of its complete righteousness,
a confession actualised in obedient submission to the cross. That is the
complete and perfect confession or *homologia*, and that is why the epistle
to the Hebrews spoke of it in terms of the actual life and obedience of
Jesus in which, both as apostle of God and as high priest, he carried
through his mission and all his relations with sinners to the very end,
to the completion of his work on the cross, thus becoming the author
and perfecter of our faith.[109]

*Jesus' confession before Pilate and on the cross is the counterpart to his
heavenly confession before the Father*

But now go back to Paul's words in Timothy about Jesus witnessing
a 'good confession' before Pontius Pilate.[110] In that obedient
submission to death at the earthly tribunal, the early church saw
an earthly and historical counterpart to his confession before the
heavenly tribunal. That is why all the Gospels lay such stress upon
the forensic character of the historical judgement and execution of
Jesus. If you were to ask the author of the epistle to the Hebrews
what corresponds in Christ's work to the act of the high priest's
entry into the veil and confession before the throne of God within
the holy of holies, he would answer that it is the confession of Jesus
before Israel and all mankind at the judgement hall of Pilate, his

---

[109] Heb 12.2 KJV/RSV.

[110] I Tim 6.13.

submission to God's judgement in his death on the cross, the rending of the veil of his flesh in an actualised confession in his obedient submission unto judgement. But that earthly and historical event had its counterpart in the entry of Jesus into that very presence of almighty God and his confession to him of our sin, his obedient submission to the Father's judgement on our behalf.

Now let us recall some other words of Jesus, 'every one who acknowledges (*homologēsei*, confesses) me before men, I will also acknowledge (*homologēsō*, confess) before my Father who is in heaven'.[111] That also refers to an earthly confession with a heavenly counterpart. By his death on the cross Christ opened up a new and living way to the Father, and he ever lives before the face of the Father as our advocate and intercessor, as the one who in our name and on our behalf submitted to the divine judgement in actualised confession of our sin, so that on that ground he now confesses us before the face of God as those for whom he died in atoning sacrifice, as those whose names are entered as members of his body.

Christ's confession is our true and only confession

Because that is Christ's confession it is also our confession. We may now take his confession as our own, his answer to God as our answer. His prayer, the Lord's prayer 'forgive us our trespasses', we may take on our lips as our prayer, and in his name go boldly before the throne of grace, for that is what the heavenly tribunal is, the *hilastērion* or mercy seat, sprinkled with the atoning blood of the covenant, a throne of grace, the mercy seat. We go before the presence of God not with our own confession but with Christ's confession as our true and only confession, for that confession of Christ's is the one thing we have to hold on to. It is therefore the confession of our hopes, for all our hope rests upon the obedience of Christ and his vicarious confession before the face of the Father. The confession of the church which answers to the confession before God of the high priest is our sacrifice of praise and thanksgiving to God continually,[112] as the epistle to the Hebrews calls it.

The reconciliation wrought by Christ has been completed once and for all and by its very nature cannot be repeated, but it is given a counterpart in the worship and adoration and confession of the church in the form of eucharistic prayer and praise echoing the heavenly intercession of Christ as we overhear it in John 17.

---

[111] Matt 10.32; Luke 12.8.

[112] See Heb 13.15 KJV.

So far we have been considering this confession objectively as what has been made in Christ on our behalf, but the epistle to the Hebrews also speaks about it subjectively. It is because in Jesus Christ the voice of the judge is identical with the voice of our high priest, because the very voice that condemns us is also the voice that freely forgives us, that Jesus Christ by his atonement *purges* our sinful conscience. The word used here is *katharizein*[113] – often used in the LXX or Greek Old Testament to translate *kipper*, cleanse by atoning.[114] Under the Old Testament liturgy there is a remembrance (*anamnēsis*) of sin in every repeated act of sacrifice, but here in the new covenant there is no remembrance of sin at all, and so the conscience is purged of its guilty consciousness by the sprinkling of the blood of Christ upon it, as it is liturgically expressed. Conscience is strictly our con-science,[115] our *syn-eidēsis* or *knowing-with* God, and when guilt is judged and removed and we are reconciled to God, our conscience with him is altered from enmity to peace. But this purging of a guilty conscience means also the sanctification of the believer; that is to say, the believer is put in a relation of holiness to God, and so is dedicated or consecrated to God as a worshipper. By taking away guilt from their conscience Christ sets the believer free in a relation of rightness to holy God and before him so that they may worship him properly and freely.

Christ's one objective confession is completed in the subjective confession and worship of the church

That fruit of praise and thanksgiving in the confession on the lips of believers answers to the objective confession of the high priest made on their behalf. But this sanctification or consecration is an act done once for all in the atonement on the cross. It cannot be repeated, for we are consecrated in the one act of Christ's vicarious self-consecration. There is no other act of sanctification or consecration than that which has already taken place in Christ Jesus and in which we are freely given to share because it was done on our behalf and for us in Christ. That 'once for all' is sacramentally remembered and celebrated in the thankful celebration of the Lord's supper or eucharist.[116]

---

113 Heb 9.14,22-23, 10.2.

114 Cf. also 1 John 2.2, 4.10, 'expiation, *hilasmos*, for our sins'.

115 From the Latin, *con-scientia*, 'with-knowledge', i.e. *knowledge-with* or *knowing-with*.

116 From the Greek *eucharistein*, 'to give thanks'.

This confession therefore is both objective and subjective – the objective confession has its counterpart in the subjective confession, in the worship and praise of the church, and in its entry into the holy place in the name of Christ its high priest the atonement reaches its appointed end or *telos*. And so the writer of the epistle to the Hebrews speaks not only of confession and purification and sanctification but also of perfection with its double meaning in the New Testament of consecration and completion. This perfection or consecration is at once objective and subjective. It is objective in the sense that we have already noted, that Christ as the author of our faith through the cross and ascension becomes the perfecter of faith. He brings it to its final end or culmination, *telos* or *teleiōsis*. He carries his intercession for mankind, which he began in his compassion and solidarity with them in their sin and weakness, right through to the end in his high priestly entry into the holy presence of God wearing our humanity. But in so doing he brings believers in him to the perfection of glory, believers who are purified and sanctified by his blood as brothers and sisters of Christ Jesus and sons and daughters of God in Christ the Son. Christ's real objective act has its final end *quoad nos* (in regard to us) in that we enter into a new relation with God as his beloved children.

Now this is another way of stating the Pauline doctrine of justification in which the objective deed by which Christ puts us in the right with God involves us in a new human righteousness as we are united to Christ and put on Christ the new man, and so are sons and daughters of God.

(2) The identity of the person of the atoner and the deed of atonement
The uniqueness of the atonement in Christ lies also in the identity of the person of the atoner and the deed of the atonement. Priest and sacrifice in Christ are one. This high priest offers *himself* as sacrifice. In the Old Testament pattern of the liturgy, by contrast, there were two acts, the sacrifice of the victim and the bringing near or offering of its blood to God in expiation, and then in virtue of this and taking with him some of the blood of expiation, the high priest entered through the veil into the holy of holies and made intercession at the mercy seat of God. There God's glory descended, God lifted up the light of his countenance, as it was put, upon Israel and gave it peace. Then the high priest returned with that peace to the people announcing to them the renewal of the covenant in reconciliation with God.

However, in the epistle to the Hebrews, as also in the Johannine writings, Jesus is stated to be both the lamb and the priest, so that here the twofold act in the liturgy of the Old Testament revelation is now one act in the incarnate person of Christ. Once and for all Christ sacrificed *himself* and presented *himself* before God as our sacrifice thus entering into the presence of God as our advocate and mediator to be accepted by him. It is all one indivisible act in one indivisible person. Now the fact that atonement in act is identical with Christ himself, and the fact that Christ is God and man, means that once the act of atonement is made, it is made once for all, and it lives on for ever in the person of the mediator. *Christ Jesus IS the atonement.* This also means that the veil once opened does not close again. There is nothing imperfect about this atonement – guilt is completely expiated and taken away, and we are completely one with God in Christ. Therefore the way into the holy of holies remains wide open and anyone may enter boldly to find grace and help according to their need.

(3) The perfect obedience of Christ, the merciful and faithful high priest

In the act of expiation or atonement, as the epistle to the Hebrews makes clear, the emphasis is laid upon the perfect obedience of Christ who carries to full realisation the oneness of the apostle and high priest. Whatever the act of atonement involving purging of sin and forgiveness may be, it is fulfilled by the obedience of the Son of God in the face of the full contradiction of our sin. To describe that act of atonement or expiation Hebrews used the term *hilaskesthai* of the high priest (the regular translation of *kipper* in the Old Testament to describe the act of high priestly atonement). After speaking of the solidarity of Christ with us and his partaking of our flesh, the author writes, 'Therefore he had to be made like his brethren in every respect, so that he might be a merciful and faithful high priest in the service of God (*hina eleēmōn genētai kai pistos archiereus ta pros ton Theon*), to make expiation for the sins of the people (*eis to hilaskesthai tas hamartias tou laou*). For because he himself has suffered and been tempted, he is able to help those who are tempted.'[117] Here Christ performs the act whereby mankind is delivered from the guilt of sin, and that is the counterpart to the divine act, 'I will be merciful (propitious) to their unrighteousness, *adikiais* (that is reconcile myself to them in and in spite of their unrighteousness) and will remember their sin no more.'[118]

---

[117] Heb 2.17-18.
[118] See Heb 8.12 KJV.

Note that the only other use of the verb *hilaskesthai* in the New Testament is in Luke where the publican praying in the temple says, 'God be merciful (*hilastheti*) to me a sinner.'[119] And Jesus said, 'This man went down to his house justified.' God's act of mercy cancelling guilt and the act of expiation cancelling guilt are one and identical in the death and person of Christ.

(iv) Atonement and redemption – their eschatological setting

This teaching about the atonement as the deed and person of Christ is described as 'redemption', *apolutrōsis*, in the most powerful eschatological setting.[120] Literally, *apolutrōsis* means redeeming by paying a price, and therefore it means emancipation out of bondage and the tyranny of evil. But as we have already seen this redemption is a costly redemption, by the blood of Christ, which far from being paid to the powers of evil robs the powers of evil of their usurped right, and exposes to them that they have no right over humanity, and no right to the price of ransom. Redemption achieves that through expiation of guilt before the law, for it is through their sin that men and women are set under the judgement of the law and forfeit their life. Through redemption by expiation from the judgement of the law, man is also redeemed from the powers of evil which clothe themselves with the power of its accusation and condemnation of the sinner. *Apolutrōsis* (deliverance) is always used in that eschatological sense in the New Testament, and hence carries with it, as the epistle to the Hebrews makes so clear, the annulling of the old order of bondage under law, and so not only leads 'captivity captive'[121] but sets mankind in a new relation of freedom to God. It opens up an entirely new situation in heaven and earth.

The making of a definite past and the creation of an entirely new future

Here we have a very important element in the conception of atonement, that by his cross Jesus Christ *has made a past* – once for all he has put something completely behind him. On one side of the cross there is set the old Adam, the old aeon[122] and all that belongs to them, and they

---

[119] Luke 18.13.

[120] Cf. W. Manson, *Jesus the Messiah*, Hodder & Stoughton, London 1943, p. 150ff, on the essential eschatological element in the mission and impact of the person of Jesus.

[121] Eph 4.8 KJV – cf. RSV.

[122] Gk, *aiōn*, age, era.

will never be resurrected. 'Old things are passed away,' as St Paul put it, but on the other side of the cross, 'all things are become new.'[123] The cross created a past, but only because it creates a new future, or a 'better hope' as the epistle to the Hebrews puts it.[124] That is what Christ has done by his redemption: opened up an eschatological vista for faith in which we are already planted in Christ, and with Christ already enter through the veil into God's presence. It is because Christ ever lives as our redeemer, our surety, our atonement, that our life is set on a wholly and eternally new basis. As such Christ is the head of all things, the head of the new age, the messianic king, to whom the whole of the world to come belongs.[125] That is an eternal kingdom that cannot be shaken, and that is the inheritance in Christ which is freely bestowed upon us. Through Christ the forerunner,[126] the great *podeh-goel*,[127] or mighty kinsman-redeemer, the author and finisher of our faith,[128] we enter already into redemption, tasting already the powers of the age to come,[129] already in anticipation of the great *anapausis*,[130] the final resting place that is the full and blessed enjoyment of the world to come.

---

[123]   2 Cor 5.17 KJV.

[124]   Heb 7.19.

[125]   Eph 1.10,19-23; Col 1.15-20, 2.10; Acts 2.33f.; cf. Rev 1.5,17-19, 11.15f., 17.14, 19.16, 22.13.

[126]   Heb 6.20.

[127]   *Podeh*, 'redeemer', from the root *padah* ; *podeh-goel*, 'kinsman-redeemer'.

[128]   Heb 12.2 KJV, RSV 'pioneer and perfecter'.

[129]   Heb 6.5.

[130]   Gk, rest, refreshment.

Chapter Four

The Atonement in the Teaching of St Paul:
ATONEMENT AS JUSTIFICATION[1]

The emphasis and approach of St Paul in contrast to Hebrews

As we have already had occasion to see, the main difference between the teaching of St Paul on the atonement and that of the author of the epistle to the Hebrews is one of emphasis and approach in which Paul gives the same doctrine from another perspective or angle. In contrast to Hebrews, Paul uses liturgical language from the Old Testament only at crucial points in his doctrine of the atonement, and concentrates on the primary action of God's decisive word for us, the righteous ordinance of grace, the *dikaiōma*. All law and liturgy are understood in terms of that *dikaiōma*. It is when St Paul comes to expound the Christian life and ministry in the witness of believers to the death of Christ that he employs the liturgical language of sacrifice. Liturgy for St Paul is primarily the liturgy of life actualised in flesh and blood. Theology itself belongs to 'rational worship, *logikē latreia*'.[2] In this way the liturgy of the Lord's supper is acted out in the life of the one body that bears about the dying of the Lord Jesus, that the life of the Lord Jesus may be made manifest in our mortal flesh. In other words, here liturgy is the eucharistic life of the new humanity which the church has in Jesus Christ.

---

1   In the original outline of the dogmatics lectures (a two page handout given to students at the start of the course), this and the following two chapters were all part of one chapter entitled *'The Atonement in the teaching of St Paul'*, and under the headings of 'Atonement as justification', 'Atonement as reconciliation', and 'Atonement as redemption' they constituted the three main sections of that extended chapter.

2   Rom 12.1; cf. the KJV 'reasonable service' with the RSV 'spiritual worship' which does not bring out the force of the '*logikē*' (logical, reasonable) as well as the KJV does.

The similarities of doctrine but difference of approach between Paul and Hebrews

Let us note some of the ways in which that similarity of doctrine but difference of approach between Paul and the epistle to the Hebrews comes to light in their teaching on atonement and justification.

(i) In the epistle to the Hebrews the ordinance of grace was expounded over against the liturgical ordinances appointed to bear witness to it. But in St Paul it is expounded in terms of the law appointed to bear witness to it and inculcate it.

(ii) As in Hebrews the liturgical ordinances point beyond themselves to Christ the Word and Son of the Father and are themselves relativised when he comes to fulfil his work, so in Paul's epistles the Mosaic laws are made to point beyond themselves to Christ the Word and Son of the Father, so that they themselves are set aside and Christ is known apart from the law.

(iii) As in Hebrews the exposition concentrates on Christ our high priest, passing beyond the high priesthood of Aaron to the eternal and archetypal priesthood of Christ, so in Paul's teaching the exposition concentrates on our righteousness and life, passing beyond the righteousness of the law and life by the law, to the eternal and personal righteousness of God which in Christ Jesus has been fully actualised in humanity.

(iv) As in Hebrews the ultimate act of atonement is the mystery of the blood of Christ, the mystery of Christ himself who as crucified and risen is our ever living atonement, so in Paul the ultimate mystery of atonement can be described only in terms of 'Christ Jesus whom God set forth to be a propitiation through faith in his blood'[3] and 'If we are saved by his death, how much more shall be saved by his life.'[4]

(v) In Hebrews the new situation is grounded upon the fact that now the voice of righteous judgement and the voice of intercession and forgiveness are one voice, so that the word of forgiveness arises straight out of the heart of divine judgement. Likewise here in St Paul's epistles the gospel tells us that God is just and the justifier of the ungodly, for in the very enactment of God's righteousness and in the complete fulfilment of God's act of righteousness (*dikaiōma*) is complete salvation or justification (*dikaiōma*), and that by sheer grace.

---

[3]   Rom 3.25 KJV.

[4]   See Rom 5.10.

The theme of Romans: the revelation of the saving righteousness of God in the gospel

The main theme of the epistle to the Romans is stated as the revelation of the saving righteousness of God in the gospel.[5] Paul then expounds the negative side of the revelation of the gospel, the shadow side in which the wrath of God is revealed from heaven against all ungodliness and unrighteousness of man who holds the truth in unrighteousness.[6] It is wholly under the light of the revelation of the gospel in its aspect as wrath of God that Paul sets forth the exposure of the sin of Gentile and Jew alike showing that the gospel by its very freeness of grace, unconditioned by human knowledge or righteousness, marks all alike as under sin, so that every mouth may be stopped and all the world become guilty before God. Then in Romans 3 to the end of the epistle, Paul expounds the positive content of the revelation of the gospel as God's righteousness justifying the ungodly.[7] At this point in chapter 3 he expounds the doctrine of the atonement first in terms of *justification* and then a little later in the epistle, after a parenthesis, in terms of *reconciliation*. We shall follow that order, considering atonement as justification in this chapter, and atonement as reconciliation in the next.

1 Atonement as justification – the righteousness of God

(a) The meaning of 'justify' and 'righteousness'[8]

The word used for righteousness in the New Testament is *dikaiosunē* which literally means a life or conduct according to *dikē* meaning custom, justice; *dikē* may also mean a judicial process, or the execution of a sentence, a judgement, and all those meanings play their part in the Pauline usage. But the Pauline usage is governed by its biblical background in the Hebrew and Greek Old Testament.

(i) The Hebrew 'tsedeq' and 'tsedeqah', righteousness

In the Septuagint or Greek Old Testament the verb *dikaioun* usually relates to the Hebrew *tsedeq* or *tsedaqah*. *Tsedeq* in the Old Testament is

---

5   Rom 1.16,17.

6   Rom 1.18 to 3.20.

7   Rom 3.24ff.

8   Apart from the volumes of Kittel (*Theological Dictionary of the New Testament*) which he regularly consulted, Torrance appreciated the biblical studies of C.H. Dodd. Cf. here C.H. Dodd, *The Bible and the Greeks*, Hodder & Stoughton, London 1935, chap. 3, 'Righteousness, Mercy and Truth'.

always related to God and his holy will for man. It refers primarily to God himself and to man in relation to God and his righteousness. God's righteousness is his own, but mankind is given a place within it, to participate in it. The adjective *tsadiq* means primarily 'to be in the right with God', to be related to God's righteousness, and so to be righteous. The verb *tsadaq* in its hiphil or causative form *hitsdiq* means to 'put in the right with God' and so to make righteous. When God puts someone in the right he displays or reveals his own righteousness, and this positive and merciful act is called *tsedaqah*, but this is more or less equivalent to salvation, *yeshuah*.[9] Closely connected with this concept of putting a man or woman in the right with God is the thought of *shalom* or peace. It is peace with God that is the foundation of all peace. This understanding of God's righteousness and his act of putting a person in the right with his righteousness carries a forensic sense;[10] it is an act of judgement which is both saving and condemning. The act of God in *hitsdiq* makes a human being *tsadiq* for it conveys to them God's *tsedeq* by putting them in the right relation with it. The person whom God condemns is called *rasha* (guilty, wicked), but the Hebrew verb *tsadaq* can hardly be used in the sense of condemn (like the Greek *dikaioun*) or the old Scots 'justify', and so it has other verbs connected with it carrying the definite idea of judgement. Thus the Old Testament idea of salvation through righteousness[11] reposes upon the duality of judgement and mercy.

The meaning of the Old Testament *tsedeq* or *tsedaqah* and its cognate words is apparent when we examine its associate expressions and their translation in the Greek Old Testament or LXX.

---

[9]   Cf. Isaiah 46.13, 51.5-6, 56.1. *Tsedaqah* (KJV 'righteousness', RSV 'deliverance') and *yeshuah* ('salvation') are used together and virtually interchangeably in these verses. Cf. similarly Isaiah 61.10, 'he has clothed me with the garments of salvation, he has covered me with the robe of righteousness' and Psalm 98.2 'The Lord has made known his salvation (RSV 'victory'), he has revealed his righteousness (RSV 'vindication') in the sight of the nations'. Note in these verses the feature of Hebrew poetry known as 'parallelism' where the same thought is repeated in a different way so that here *yeshuah* ('salvation') is paralleled and replaced by *tsedaqah* ('righteousness').

[10]   Cf. Isaiah 43.9-26; the root meaning of the English 'forensic' (from the Latin *forensis*, public) is 'related to or involving a court of law'.

[11]   Cf. Hosea 2.19-20 (Hb 21-22) for an example of some of the constellation of words associated with *tsedeqah* and righteousness.

(1) Associates of *tsedeq* particularly in the Psalms and deutero-Isaiah:[12]
hesed (loyal love, mercy), the LXX sometimes translates by *dikaiosunē*
(righteousness),
'emeth (truth), likewise sometimes translated by *dikaiosunē*,
yeshua (salvation), by *dikaiosunē*,
mishpat (judgement), sometimes also translated by *dikaiosunē*.

(2) *Tsedeq* and *tsedaqah* are translated in the Septuagint by *dikaiosunē*
but often by *eleos* or *eleēmosunē* (mercy, pity, compassion). But *hesed*
(steadfast love) is also translated by *eleos* as well as by *dikaiosunē*, and
emeth (truth) is also translated by *eleēmosunē* and *dikaiosunē*.

Thus mercy, truth, righteousness form the positive content of relation
with God in covenant love and faithfulness, and they are the positive
content of salvation.

(ii) The Greek 'dikaiosunē', righteousness

When we come back to the New Testament *dikaiosunē* and its cognates
we find this:

(1) *dikaiosunē* goes back mainly to the Old Testament *tsedeq* and
tsedaqah. In the Septuagint, *tsedeq* is rendered by *dikaiosunē* 81 times,
and *tsedaqah* by *dikaiosunē* 134 times, but *tsedaqah* is the word for
the positive act of righteous mercy, meaning succour, help, and
therefore is often translated as *eleēmosunē*, mercy. This means that
we must take the meaning of *dikaiosunē* to be a positive act of divine
deliverance in mercy and truth, as in the Old Testament expressions.

(2) *dikaioun*[13] in Greek has a double meaning, to do justice to
someone, to judge, condemn, that is, to judge in order to put right
(justify as rectify), but also to deem right (justify as declare right).
In the New Testament *dikaioun* goes back to the Hebrew *hitsdiq*,
put in the right with God, a positive act of grace and to the Hebrew

---

[12] Isaiah 40 – 55.

[13] Cf. T.F. Torrance, *Theology in Reconstruction*, SCM Press, London 1965,
chap. 9, pp. 150-168, 'Justification: its Radical Nature and Place in
Reformed Doctrine and Life', p. 153, 'The Greek word *dikaioun*, like the
Scots word *to justify*, may mean to condemn as well as to vindicate. The
basic meaning, which we find in biblical Greek, is *to put in the right, to put
in the truth*. Thus, if a man is guilty he is put in the right by being
condemned, for that is the truth of the matter; if he is innocent he is put in
the right by being declared guiltless and set free. Justification always
involves a fulfilling of the righteousness, or the enacting of the truth.'

words for judicial acts of judgement, for the Greek can employ one word to translate both aspects as the Hebrew could not. The Greek *dikaiōma, dikaiōsis*[14] are used in this way, but with the sense of salvation uppermost.

(3) *dikaios* (righteous, just) is used in ways that go back to all the senses in the Old Testament, mostly to *hitsdiq*, but contains the ideas of judgement and salvation. Refer to New Testament expressions such as 'faithful and *just* to forgive us our sins, and to cleanse us from all unrighteousness',[15] or '*just* and the justifier (*dikaiounta*) of him which believeth in Jesus',[16] 'him who justifies (*dikaiounta*) the ungodly',[17] but also 'merciful and faithful high priest',[18] where the writer has taken a different word *eleēmōn* to translate the Hebrew.

God's righteousness implicates us in it and becomes event and truth in our midst

There is another aspect of the biblical teaching of God's righteousness that we must look at, though it is not easy to put into precise words. It does not arise out of the various usages of terms but from the way the terms are used and from the contexts in which they are employed. We may recall from our discussion of the Hebrew *dabar*, that when the *event* corresponds to the word, there is *truth*. The word is truth in that it is completely fulfilled in corresponding event. When that word-event is credited as truth it is answered with *amen*.

In the same way both the Old Testament and the New Testament think of God's righteousness. It calls for an answering righteousness in mankind in which God's righteousness fulfils itself. God's righteousness comes to its fulfilment in human confession or acknowledgement of it and in obedience to it. But that is always regarded as the achievement of God's righteousness, not man's. Compare here the notion of sanctification. God sanctifies himself in the midst of his people and that is the sanctification of Israel for

---

[14]   *Dikaiōma*, decree of righteousness, a declaration of something or someone to be *dikaios*, just, right; *dikaiōsis*, the act of pronouncing righteous, justification, acquittal.

[15]   1 John 1.9 KJV.

[16]   Rom 3.26 KJV.

[17]   Rom 4.5.

[18]   Heb 2.17.

they are implicated in God's holiness, drawn into and placed within God's holiness, drawn into and placed within God's hallowing of himself in the midst of his people. That is the meaning, as we saw before, of the opening of the Lord's prayer. 'Hallowed be thy name. Thy kingdom come, thy will be done.' But think again of Psalm 51 and its confession of sin, 'so that thou art justified in thy sentence and blameless in thy judgement . . . thou desirest truth in the inward being'.[19] In the sinner's acknowledgement of God's righteousness, God's righteousness is vindicated.

(b) Three key elements in justification[20]

There are three elements in all this we must note:

(i) God's righteousness is his own supreme righteousness. His act of righteousness sets humanity within the sphere of his divine righteousness and gives them to participate in it.

(ii) This act of God is on God's part both revelation and deed in one, and on man's part knowing and being in one: the enactment and proclamation of God's righteousness requires its acknowledgement and appropriation on the part of humanity. These two sides are inseparable, and both of them, God's part and humanity's part, are fulfilled for us in Jesus Christ. *He is the righteousness of God and the righteousness of humanity* who as such creates and evokes the answer of faith. In his obedience of faith that answers to the divine righteousness, God acknowledges that he has found the full satisfaction of his righteousness. In his faith (*pistis*), God's righteousness actualises itself as truth. In his righteousness, God's righteousness actualises itself in an answering human righteousness and in his faith a human faithfulness answering to his own divine faithfulness.

(iii) That righteousness of Christ is proclaimed to us as the gospel of grace and it is freely bestowed upon us in and through Christ. It is a righteousness in which we are clothed or given to share – or to put it otherwise, a righteousness which becomes the foundation on which we stand for our own life of obedience in the faith.

---

[19] Psalm 51.4,6.

[20] Cf. T.F. Torrance, *Conflict and Agreement*, vol. 2, Lutterworth, London 1960, 'An Aspect of the Biblical Concept of Faith', pp. 74-82, esp. p. 78ff. for the relation between the righteousness and the faithfulness of God.

In the light of that study, we can go on to ask what Paul means by righteousness in the act of atonement, that is, what is atoning justification?

2 Atoning justification – the fulfilment of God's righteousness in truth

The whole gospel of salvation and redemption through atonement is interpreted from the side of God's righteous act of grace, his *dikaiōma*. God is the subject of the action throughout. It is pure act of God, *opus Dei*, work of God, even when from the side of humanity in Jesus Christ. The gospel is thus equivalent to the righteous act of God, the act of divine righteousness that fulfils itself in grace and which does not in any sense need to be placated or propitiated by man, or in any sense need to be made propitious and gracious. The propitiation or expiation is God's own act of grace flowing from his eternal love and mercy. This act of righteousness in grace is the fulfilment of God's truth, of his consistent righteousness and faithfulness against sin. It is thus the fulfilment of his truth. But that is identical with God's grace and pardon and redemption, for God does not burden us with his wrath, but mercifully bears it himself in the passion of his Son who died for us on the cross.

God's righteousness therefore does not need to be toned down, to be softened, to be propitiated or made favourable, as if God had to relax some of his righteous demands in order to have us reconciled to him or to reconcile himself to us. On the contrary, in the very fulfilment of his righteousness, in its absolute and complete fulfilment, we are reconciled to God, translated out of an impossible situation under law, and beyond all possibility or conceivability are made righteous. That is not simply a legal transaction but dynamic concrete reality, and therefore 'apart from law' (*chōris nomou*),[21] an actualisation of righteousness in the flesh and blood, in the concrete reality of Christ Jesus. In him we are given a new humanity and a new human righteousness in the very righteousness of God. The work of justification is no empty word but deed of flesh and blood. As the Word was made flesh in Jesus Christ, so in justification the Word is made flesh in the new humanity which we have in Jesus Christ who was raised for our justification.[22] Justification is thus at once God's word and God's act.

---

[21]   Rom 3.21.

[22]   Rom 4.25.

Justification is at once God's word and God's act

(a) Justification as God's word – 'revealed from faith to faith'

Justification is God's word[23] and Paul speaks of it as the *revelation* of righteousness,[24] the apocalypse of truth. Revelation of righteousness is truth. It is significant that the Hebrew *'emeth*, truth, is sometimes translated in the Greek Testament by *dikaiosunē* and sometimes by *pistis*, faith or faithfulness. Paul seems to have that in mind when he speaks of God's *dikaiosunē* or righteousness in the gospel as 'revealed from faith to faith, from *pistis* to *pistis*',[25] and of that revelation as involving revelation of God's wrath against all ungodliness and unrighteousness of humanity who 'hold down the *truth* in unrighteousness'.[26] Justification is God's *word of truth* and its revelation is truth. This word justification does not have to do simply with righteous living but with righteous *understanding*, for righteousness is God's right or truth as well as his holiness and involves knowing as well as doing, and thus to do righteousness is the same as to do truth. (Compare Jesus' statement, 'you will know the truth and the truth will make you free.'[27]) The revelation of righteousness is the word that puts us in the truth and as such tells us that we are in un-truth. Justification says 'let God be true, but every man a liar',[28] as Paul puts it with reference to Psalm 51. This word of justification which puts us in the truth denies all self-justification and denominates it lying, or un-truth. If God's justification of the ungodly means that no one can boast of their own righteousness, then it also means that no one dares to boast of their own orthodoxy, for to claim orthodoxy is to claim to be in the right, to be in the truth; it is a boasting of the right, whereas in point of fact justification by putting us in the truth, reveals that we are in the wrong, in untruth.

---

[23] Cf. Rom 10.3-17, esp. v. 8.

[24] Rom 1.17f, 3.21f.

[25] Rom 1.17 KJV – cf. below sections 4 (b) on Rom 3.19-22,24, and 5 (a) (iii) on Rom 1.17.

[26] Torrance translation, Rom 1.18 (*tēn alētheian en adikia katechontōn*), cf. KJV.

[27] John 8.32.

[28] Rom 3.4 KJV.

The one revelation of righteousness which uncovers sin and reveals grace

It is important to see that the revelation of God's righteousness is the word of justification which uncovers the truth about Jew and Gentile alike, as in Romans 1.18 – 3.20, and is the same revelation which proclaims the justification of the ungodly by free grace. The whole of Paul's doctrine of atonement rests upon this fact that the word of God that tells us we are pardoned and forgiven is absolutely identical with the word that uncovers our thoughts and judges us. It is that identity of the revelation of wrath and the revelation of justifying righteousness which Paul expounds as a unity from Romans 1.17f. to Romans 3.20f. Therefore to call Romans 1.17f. 'natural revelation', some kind of revelation other than that which Paul is speaking about in the word of justification, is to strike at the very heart of Paul's doctrine of atonement, for it is to divide the revelation of the righteousness of free grace from the revelation of the thoughts and intents of human hearts about God. On the contrary, there is only one revelation, and all that Paul says in Romans 1.17 to 3.20 is in the light of that one revelation of the gospel; even the revelation of God's wrath against all ungodliness and unrighteousness of man is God's revelation and no other. The argument of Wisdom 13[29] to which Paul refers in Romans 1.17f., belongs to the Judaistic division between the mercy and righteousness of God and yet to import that dichotomy (as some people would do without comprehending their unity) into Paul's teaching of Romans 1.17f. by calling it 'natural knowledge' over against the special revelation in Christ, is, as I have said, to strike at the very heart of the atonement, to divide the God of the gospel from the God of judgement, like Marcion![30]

The revelation of righteousness which uncovers the thoughts of human hearts and the revelation of righteousness which reveals the incredible grace of God whereby he justifies the ungodly are one and the same. They are the two sides of the one word of justification, two sides of the activity of the one word made flesh in Jesus Christ. The more the love of God and his righteous will in Jesus Christ penetrate into human hearts the more it uncovers their inmost thoughts, and so in the incarnate life of Christ the Word made flesh we have at once the revelation of the righteousness of God and the revelation of the wrath

---

[29] See the Apocrypha, *The Wisdom of Solomon*, chap. 13.

[30] For Marcion, the God of the Old Testament, the creator God of law and judgement, was different from the New Testament God of love and grace.

of God against all unrighteousness. That is why in an earlier study[31] we considered the significance of what Paul has to say in Romans 1.17f. Justification is the Word made flesh, the word that remains God's word of truth and grace even in the flesh of our sin and ungodliness, where it at once exposes and condemns our sin and untruth in the flesh, and sanctifies our humanity. As such it is at once the justification of God and the justification of the ungodly. It is that word/act of justification which is enacted in our flesh and blood in the obedient life of Christ and on the cross, justification not in revelation or word only but in fact and in power, in completed action. This is the justification which the New Testament calls the 'truth', the word of righteousness actualised in our humanity where the actualisation corresponds obediently and faithfully to the word uttered.

(b) Justification as God's act

Justification is the mighty act of God, eschatological event. It is active righteous intervention in the impossible situation of humanity under the law. It is 'power of God for salvation'.[32] In Jesus Christ, God has intervened decisively in the moral impasse of humanity, doing a deed that humanity could not do itself. That impasse was not simply created by the inability of human beings to fulfil the holy demands of the law and justify themselves before God, but created by the very nature of the (moral) situation of man before God, so that it could not be solved from within itself as demanded by the law. Thus the intervention by God entailed a complete reversal of the moral situation and the setting of it on a wholly new basis. The result was, as Paul put it bluntly, the 'justification of the ungodly', an act in which man, in spite of sin, is put fully in the right with God, and it is such a total and final act that men and women are no longer required to achieve justification by themselves to save themselves before God. They enter into justification through Christ's death, and accept it as a sheer gift of God's grace which is actualised in them as reality and truth.

The one deed and word of justification that exposes our wrong and puts us in the right

Here the deed of justification and the word of justification are seen to be identical. The cross means that the word of God is done into the

---

[31] Cf. T.F. Torrance, *Incarnation*, Paternoster UK & InterVarsity Press USA, Milton Keynes & Downer's Grove, 2008, p. 143f.

[32] Rom 1.16.

flesh and the word and act are one. By putting us in the right with God in the cross, Christ necessarily puts us in ourselves in the wrong and in a way more decisive and complete than otherwise possible. It is supremely from the cross and its gospel of grace that revelation of God's righteousness comes. In the language used earlier, here we have a substitutionary act which does not allow humanity to shelter behind the innocent, but which while it is vicarious deed for humanity, drags them out of their self-imprisonment, out of their hiding place behind the law, and exposes them as utterly guilty before God. Just where justification is total, revelation is equally total in its ruthless exposure of humanity. In the very act of putting us wholly in the right, justification tells us that we in ourselves are wholly in the wrong. In the language of Jesus' parable, even when we have done what it is our duty to do, we have to confess that we are unprofitable servants.[33] Before God we are always in the wrong, just because we are wholly put in the right by sheer grace. That is why the whole of Paul's argument about the sin of Gentile and Jew alike is the corollary of grace.[34] To be put in the right with God by free grace alone shows us that we are completely in the wrong and are unable to right ourselves. To be put in the truth with God, shows us that in ourselves we hold down the truth in unrighteousness and turn it into a lie, and are in untruth.

The radical significance of justification by faith – Christ alone is our righteousness

That is the radical significance of justification by faith. It is not that our faith justifies, for our faith is simply correlative to the justifying Christ, but as such faith involves radical self-denial, repentance (*metanoia*) in which we gladly place ourselves under God's judgement, in which we allow the act of justification to displace us, to dispossess us of our vaunted right and truth, in order that Christ Jesus himself alone may be our right and truth and our righteousness. And so it belongs to our salvation and our great comfort and peace to place ourselves under the total judgement of the cross, that is under God's act of justification, because it is in that justification that we find the right and truth in Christ. That he is our righteousness, is the gospel message, so that its being freely offered to us for our righteousness is the glad tidings of the gospel. That is why repentance is not ascetic love of feeling guilty but the life of joyful self-denial in which we find our righteousness and truth *not in our selves but in Christ alone.*

---

[33]   Luke 17.10.

[34]   Rom 3.21-24.

3 The double problem in justification

This amazing act of justification involves a double problem for God. That is a very anthropomorphic way of putting it, although it is how St Paul appeared to regard it and how can we put it otherwise?

(a) How can God be just and the justifier of the ungodly?

Paul found it difficult to understand why God had apparently allowed sin such a loose reign in the world.[35] Did that mean that sin is not so heinous before God after all, or that God's nature is such that people may assert their own wills over others as they like without interference from God? Surely that would mean that God is not just, not God. But apart from 'winking at'[36] the sins that are past, how can he justify the ungodly,[37] as though the ungodly and the godly were all the same before him? The answer is to be found in the death of Christ where God has wrought a double deed in which he has at last meted out upon sin its complete condemnation, and yet one in which in his grace he justifies man, and so in both God justifies himself.

(b) How can God intensify human sin?

How can God's love do a deed which will so intensify human sin that all the world becomes guilty before God, and guilty of the murder of the Son of God? Surely out of love, God might have prevented mankind from putting Christ to death and so from becoming guilty in a way they could not otherwise have become guilty!?

That, as we have seen, was part of the sharpest agony of our Lord, that by his coming men and women should know sin as never before, and that by the pressure of his love upon them sin should become intensified to an unbelievable extent. And yet that was an essential part of his saving work – the revelation of the righteousness of God against all ungodliness and unrighteousness of humanity. Jesus came not simply bearing a word about divine judgement against man and therefore also against himself as man in his saving work. He was that Word himself. He was the truth of God in the fullness of time, and he came to be the truth uncompromisingly in the midst of sinful contradiction

---

[35] Cf. T.F. Torrance, *The Apocalypse Today* (sermons on Revelation), James Clarke, London 1960, p. 56.

[36] Acts 17.30 KJV, cf. RSV 'overlooked'.

[37] Rom 4.5.

to the truth. He was the right and truth of God, God's very righteousness, asserting himself absolutely in the midst of guilt, and that was necessary to the salvation of mankind. No salvation could be valid behind the back of God's righteousness, apart from the complete vindication of God's holiness or majesty in righteousness and truth. Unless salvation issues out of the very heart of righteousness itself as well as love it could not be divine or real.

(c) *The nature of sin and law*[38]

(i) *Human rebellion and divine judgement – the apparent toleration of sin*

It may help us to remember here the double character of sin as it is revealed in the light of the gospel.[39] On the one hand sin is rebellion against God, but on the other hand sin gains part of its character as sin from the divine resistance to it. If God not oppose sin, there would be no really objective and ultimate difference between sin and righteousness. Thus the divine opposition to sin is a factor in the qualification of humanity as sinful before God, and especially as guilty before him. But, as Paul felt, the disturbing factor seemed to be that God actually withheld his full opposition to sin and allowed it so much freedom that it challenged his righteousness and deity.[40] Yet that was in the very mercy of God, as the cross showed, for the cross reveals that God withheld his final resistance to sin until, in Christ, he was ready to do the deed which would also save us from his wrath. But in the coming of God in Christ, and in the final judgement of sin, the

---

38   For the following, especially the nature of sin and law in a fallen world, the gap between the 'is' and the 'ought', the law as the strength of sin, justification as 'under the law' but 'apart from law', the problem of substitution (how can one person die for others), the backward and forward reference of reconciliation, and the atonement as the redemption of the whole moral order, see T.F. Torrance, 'The Atonement – the Singularity of Christ and the Finality of the Cross: the Atonement and the Moral Order', *Universalism and the Doctrine of Hell* (papers presented at the 1991 Edinburgh Conference on Christian Dogmatics), ed. N.M. de S Cameron, Paternoster, Carlisle (Baker, Grand Rapids) 1992, pp. 225-256, esp. pp. 249-255, 'Atonement and the Moral Order'.

39   Cf. T.F. Torrance, *Incarnation*, chap. 7, 'The Kingdom of Christ and Evil', esp. p. 248ff.

40   See Acts 14.16, 17.30.

breach of sin with God was necessarily revealed to be indeed made absolute by the very act of final judgement. The discontinuity between humanity and God was therefore widened to an abysmal depth in the crucifixion. But that was done deliberately that the last stronghold of sin, death, might be invaded and its power broken once and for all.

(ii) The distance between man and God given a relative validity through law and the withholding of final judgement

A very significant fact we have to consider here is that before the death of Christ the distance between man and God is given an order of relative validity, or established in the extent of its separation from God (compare 'the far country' of Jesus' parables[41]). It was established (a) by the condemnatory law which expresses the divine judgement on sin, although that judgement was not yet fully enacted and inserted into history, and (b) by God's withholding of final judgement against sin, for that means that God withheld from man his immediate presence which, apart from actual atonement, could only mean the destruction of humanity.

The establishment and interim validity of the ethical order

This merciful act of God by which he holds himself at a distance from fallen men and women and yet places them under judgement establishes, as it were, the ethical order in which righteousness has absolute validity and yet in which mankind has relative immunity and freedom. In the language of Genesis, it was in and through the fall of man from God that men and women entered into a moral order in which they could distinguish between good and evil, so that the very tension between the 'is' and the 'ought'[42] indicates their semi-independent relation to the will of God. Thus the moral or ethical order while having absolute and divine sanction, itself belongs to the separation between man and God. That was the situation within which the Old Testament faith was presented. Thus while insisting on the absolute validity of the law, and the idea of separation from sin inherent in the divine holiness, it placed alongside of the law a liturgy of sacrificial expiation in which the holy presence of God is thought of as breaking through to people on the ground of atonement. That divine

---

[41]   Matt 21.33 KJV; Mark 12.1 KJV; Matt 25.14 KJV; cf. Luke 15.13.

[42]   In ethical theory or moral philosophy, the difference between what we actually *are* and what we *ought* to be is known as the tension between the 'is' and the 'ought'.

presence, however, corresponded in its degree of immediateness to the withholding of final judgement, for it was not yet the fullness of time. It is in this relation of law to expiation that we must grasp the Pauline doctrine of the actual deed of atonement.

Old Testament law is suspended revelation of righteousness, not yet fulfilled revelation

In the Old Testament, the *law* is God's revealed will. It is not just ethical law, but the manifestation of God's command in the midst of his chosen people in their covenant relation to him. It is because he has brought them into covenantal relation with himself that here where God gives himself more immediately to his people, that merely legal or ethical relation of fallen man to God is broken through, and humanity is confronted with the revelation of God's righteousness. But even that is not fulfilled revelation – rather is it suspended revelation, for God's word is not yet made flesh, his word has not yet come all the way to man and embodied itself in humanity. Thus even within Israel, as Paul argues in Romans 2, the gospel shows the Jews to be in the same essential relation to God, in spite of the revealed law, as Gentiles who are not related to the Old Testament commandments in the same way. The reason is that even in the case of the law of the Old Testament, mankind holds down the truth in unrighteousness. It is part of human sin in this semi-independent relation between God and humanity maintained by the very giving of the law, that sin seizes upon God's law in order to escape from God's judgement, in order to escape from God. And so the law becomes the strength of sin.

(iii) The use of the law as an abstract buffer against God

Look at it like this. From the point of view of ethics we see that human moral awareness tends to sever its connection with God, its foundation and origin, and to establish itself on an autonomous or semi-autonomous basis. Hence the relation of humanity to God is not direct but rather indirect through the ethical imperative, by inference from it. In ethics, *qua* ethics,[43] the human person does not really enter into private or immediate relationship with God. They relate themselves to God, consciously or subconsciously through duty to their neighbour – that is, they relate themselves to God indirectly through the medium of the universal (for example Kant's universal maxim) and do not relate themselves to God in particular. From the point of view of faith, sin here is seizing the ethical imperative of God,

---

[43]   Lat, '*where* ethics', ie 'ethics as ethics'.

making it an independent authority which is identified with human higher nature, so escaping God and deifying humanity – 'you will be like God'.[44] That is what is so wonderfully and simply described in the opening chapters of Genesis.

The law as the strength of sin[45]

Here then is the fact we have to consider: the law of God which repudiates human sin at the same time holds the world together in law and order and gives it relative stability - but sin takes advantage of that and under the cover of the law exerts itself more and more in independence of God. That is why the New Testament speaks of the law as the strength of sin,[46] for its very opposition to sin gives sin its strength, and by withholding final judgement from the sinner, holds or maintains the sinner in continued being. The great problem here is that the law does not really deal with the root of sin, but on the contrary helps to maintain sin in being before the law. From the sinner's angle, it suits them well that God should deal with them in terms of law, because law is planted between them and God and keeps God at a distance from them. That is why the dialectic of sin always yields the legal outlook, for under the pressure of God the sinner falls back upon formal observance of the law in which as much of the responsibility is thrown upon the law for the rightness or wrongness of action as upon the human person. It is thus that the sinner can yield obedience formally to the law without actually surrendering the citadel of the soul, without committing themselves in really responsible action. Likewise the dialectic of sin produces an impersonal and abstract outlook, for sin refracts the immediacy of truth and exchanges the spirit for the deadness of the letter, exchanges God for an ideal. Humanity as sinful always seeks to put abstract law and thought in place of God and the truth, but in so far as the letter is an abstract of the divine truth it has absolute validity, so that even God does not deny or repudiate it.

(iv) Atonement as the actualisation of truth in the midst of abstract truth

That is what Paul discovers to be the situation of humanity in relation to God's truth and righteousness. It is not something that Paul has himself thought out or attained by wisdom, but something that is

---

[44] Gen 3.5.

[45] Cf. T.F. Torrance, 'The Atonement – The Singularity of Christ...', p. 251.

[46] 1 Cor 15.56, KJV 'strength', RSV 'power'.

directly revealed by the cross of Christ and all that it uncovers of the secret operations of the human heart in holding down the truth in unrighteousness and turning it into a lie, and thus worshipping in its idols, be they of gold and silver or of ethics and moral ideals, the creature rather than the creator.[47] The atoning deed can then be described in terms of the direct actualisation of God's truth in the midst of and in the very teeth of abstract truth, *or* the actualisation of the righteousness of God in the midst of and in the teeth of, the abstract justice which is in point of fact the greatest strength of sin, *or* as the actualisation of God's presence in the form of personal being in Christ in the midst of and in the teeth of religion, for religion becomes the highest form of sin. In St Paul's writings, it is the relation of righteousness to law that is most prominent, but the same point holds good in the whole round of mankind's ethical and religious existence. As we saw, the same point was applied directly by the author of the epistle to the Hebrews to the religious cult of Israel, and it can be applied equally to modern idealistic religion and ethics.

4 Justification and law

The bondage of law

The situation of man that the saving act of God in Christ confronts is bondage, bondage to religion, bondage to law, God's own law and God's own appointed way of worship. In one sense that bondage is a form of *self-imprisonment* because it is the result of sin and because in sin mankind chooses to have the barrier of law flung round them as a sort of protection from the immediate presence of God, and yet it is a very bitter bondage. In another sense it is God himself who imprisons humanity within that bondage, for by the law, in the thought of Paul, humanity is shut up unto sin and disobedience. Man and woman harden their own heart and yet God hardens their heart, for in his judgement of mankind God hands them over to a 'reprobate mind'.[48]

God steps out from behind the law to reveal himself face to face

In that situation, God's mighty saving intervention, God's redemptive action, takes the form of revelation – the *revelation* of God's righteousness. That means that at last God steps out from

---

47   Rom 1.18-25.
48   Rom 1.28 KJV.

behind the law, from behind the veil which Moses wore on his face, from behind the veil of the holy of holies, for God unveils himself immediately. He comes to man and apart from law reveals his righteousness to humanity directly in Jesus Christ, cutting through all distance and abstraction, all law and religion, and sets men and women before him face to face. Here the Word of God is made flesh, in mercy and truth. That saving action Paul calls 'justification', and he speaks of it in a twofold way.

(a) Justification is an act of God 'under the law'

Jesus Christ was 'made under the law' (*hupo nomon*). For Paul, we were 'in bondage under the elements of the world: but when the fullness of the time was come, God sent forth his Son, made of a woman, made under the law, to redeem them that were under the law, that we might receive the adoption of sons.'[49]

This act of salvation under the law was within the validity of the abstract relation between humanity and God which was itself humanity's very bondage. But this law had divine validity although it was always being infringed by sin, and therefore no salvation from the bondage of the law was possible without a full assertion of the validity of the law against sin and evil, that is, in New Testament language, without the fulfilling of the law. But in asserting the validity of the law, God expressed his final *no* against all sin and evil. Here there is no longer suspension of divine judgement, but the absolute fulfilment of God's righteousness, its utter and final revelation against all ungodliness and unrighteousness of man. That is justification, justification fulfilling the law in the judgement of sin on the cross, and in that fulfilment justification passed through the medium of the law and touched men and women personally and directly in the very root of their sins. There was no withholding of God's wrath there, for God declared himself to be absolutely just in negating sin by all the holy majesty and love of Godhead.

Justification can only take place through the complete fulfilment of law and judgement

No act of justification or salvation delivering mankind from the galling bondage of the law could be real to them, or true for them, which did

---

[49]   Gal 4.3-5 KJV. See the footnote in T.F. Torrance, *Space, Time and Resurrection*, Handsel Press, Edinburgh 1976, p. 96, for an explanation of his preference for the KJV '*made* of a woman, *made* under the law' over the RSV '*born…*'.

not carry out in full the condemnation that they encounter in God's word and that therefore echoes in their conscience. That is the forensic[50] element in justification from which we cannot and dare not get away for that would mean God's repudiation of his law for this world. And so Christ entered into our world under law, and submitted to the full bondage of the law, meeting not only the condemning resistance of law to our sin, but now at last the final judgement of God against it. By bearing it in perfect obedience to the Father he was able to set mankind free not only from the bondage of external law but from their own self-imprisonment in the condemnation of their own conscience, for by condemning sin in human flesh and by acquiescing in human existence, in the full verdict of God's judgement against us, he made our judgement of ourselves acquiesce in God's complete judgement.

(b) Justification is an act of God 'apart from law'

Paul writes, 'whatever the law says it speaks to those who are under the law, so that every mouth may be stopped, and all the world may be held accountable to God. For no human being will be justified in his sight by works of the law since through the law comes knowledge of sin. But now the righteousness of God has been manifested apart from law (*chōris nomou*), although the law and the prophets bear witness to it, *even the righteousness of God which is by the faith (i.e. the faithfulness) of Jesus Christ unto all and upon all them that believe . . . being justified freely by his grace through the redemption that is in Christ Jesus*'.[51]

What does Paul mean by 'apart from law'? It cannot mean the denial of law, for Paul asserts on the contrary that the Christian faith establishes the law, and as we have seen, justification asserts to the full the divine validity of God's law, and yet in that very

---

50   Legal or related to law – forensic is the word commonly used to denote the aspect of justification (or atonement) involving law, righteousness in terms of the law and metaphors of the law court.

51   Rom 3.19-22,24. The italicised section of the quotation is the KJV rendering which is closer to the Greek, particularly at the point where Paul speaks of 'the righteousness of God *by (the) faith of* Jesus Christ (*dia pisteōs Iēsou Christou*)', and hence the meaning for Torrance, as indicated by his bracketed parenthesis, is 'the righteousness of God which is by the faithfulness of Jesus Christ'.

establishing of the *right* of the law in God, we are given to look beyond the law to God himself. In so far as the law has become an end in itself, even relatively, a law in itself, it is suspended – suspended in so far as it works wrath and is the strength of sin, suspended as an intermediary between God and man. It is not that the divine demands and commands through the law are set aside or ignored, but that here we look past them in their legalistic or refracted form in the law to God himself the judge. Here God steps out from behind the law and confronts humanity face to face and deals with man and woman personally, directly 'apart from law', *chōris nomou*. He does that on the ground of atonement, on the ground of the complete fulfilment of his righteousness in the cross, so that here the condemnation of the law is no longer in point. 'There is therefore now no condemnation for those who are in Christ Jesus.'[52]

(i) God now deals with us immediately in grace, and no longer through the veil of law

We have also seen a parallel to this in the epistle to the Hebrews, in the setting aside of the liturgical law and the annulling of the old order. With the actual coming of holy God in Christ to deal with our sin, the whole form of God's covenantal relation with humanity is changed. In place of the old covenant founded upon law, or rather administered through law, God has established a new covenant founded upon and ministered by his direct, utterly gracious, and personal dealing with sinners in which he freely grants forgiveness and life. The cross of Christ therefore represents an interruption of the ethical order of the fallen world, and the setting of our life on the wholly new basis of grace. God is not now distant in the far country, one who speaks through intermediaries like prophets and laws. He has come near in the propitiation of Christ. The veil separating holy God from man which the Old Testament represented as woven within and without, without by human sin, within by God's judgement of sin giving it irreparable character, is torn in two from top to bottom and we have free access into the immediate presence of God. God has broken through the barrier of sin and law and religion, and because of the cross he deals with us immediately in grace and no longer on the administrative ground of the law, but wholly on the ground that he gives himself freely to us in spite of our sin which he has already judged. That means a

---

[52]   Rom 8.1.

radical alteration in the whole situation of our human worship and life. We are friends of God and no longer aliens and strangers. We are at peace with God and have God's peace and as Paul says, this is a peace which passes all understanding.[53]

(ii) Justification is 'revelation', a stupendous new act of God

This act of grace in justification which breaks through to us apart from law is spoken of as 'revelation'. We must see clearly that it is revelation, the revealing of a righteousness that could not be known otherwise. It is revelation that is grounded upon its own act as a breakthrough in sheer grace. This new righteousness that forgives and justifies the sinner could not be inferred logically from the abstract order of law or ethics. From that point of view forgiveness is impossible – it is legally speaking immoral or amoral. And if it is a fact, it is a stupendous miracle. From the point of view of ethics it could only take place through what Kierkegaard has called a 'teleological suspension of ethics'. Because it entails this suspension, justification or forgiveness is not something that is demonstrable from any ground in the moral order as such. It only can be acknowledged and believed as a real event that has in the amazing grace of God actually overtaken us. It is a *fait accompli*.

And so Jesus proclaimed that forgiveness, the justification of the ungodly, as the breaking in of the sovereign grace of God among sinners, the kingdom of God actually come and at work among men and women – the kingdom of God come 'near', that is, the kingdom in which God has propitiated himself, drawn near to the sinner, reconciled himself to the sinner, in order to draw the sinner to himself and gather them back into the divine fellowship in righteousness. And so in the Gospels we see it at work in the lives of people like Zacchaeus, Mary Magdalene, Matthew and many others. 'Today salvation has come to this house', said Jesus to Zacchaeus.[54] The word of justification can be understood and revealed only in its actual eventuation and happening as miraculous event. The divine love has taken the field in actual forgiveness and justification even before the cross and the whole initiative rests with God's holy love, which insists on drawing near to the sinner, and precipitating itself upon them.

---

[53]   Phil 4.7.

[54]   Luke 19.9.

(iii) Justification ends all abstraction, without any mitigation of law and judgement

When we try to understand what this justification which forgives and pardons the sinner freely means, we find it does not in any sense mean a mitigation of law or suspension of God's judgement on sin, or any compromising of his holy will even as manifested in law. On the contrary, it carries with it absolute judgement. That is why the experience of forgiveness and justification carries with it such a crushing sense of shame, which is a reflex of the actual deed on the cross, but at the same time and above all there is an unspeakable sense of joy and gratitude, for God's love has broken through the iron bondage of law and guilt and planted us in a new world, and the ground of that world is God's holy love.

Here the will of God is not manifested in refracted form or in the abstract terms of law or ethics or ideas or even goodness, but as *love*. Love cannot be revealed as a general truth, but is actually revealed only in the personal approach of God to man. This is the end of all abstraction in human relations with God, for all detachment, all isolation, all independence of mankind over against God, are excluded – humanity is bound to God in love and perfect peace for God has irrevocably given himself to humanity in perfect love and peace.

(iv) An objective event, of justification and forgiveness, which is ultimately unfathomable

How are we to think of this royal act of grace, the breaking in of the kingdom of God's mercy and pardon, in which justification overtakes us and freely forgives us? St Paul speaks of it in these terms, 'God has made him who knew no sin to be sin for us, that we might be made the righteousness of God in him.'[55] It is an act of substitutionary atonement by which God brings about the expiation of sin, so that we have peace with God. '*Christ died for our sins*'.[56] That is the holy of holies of our Christian faith – the full significance of which is unfathomable mystery. Though our understanding of it cannot in the nature of the case be very definite or pure, it is clear that the action of God was most definite, that a real obstacle of objective character between God and mankind was removed once for all, that an atoning work of objective nature was once and for all accomplished. It could not be accomplished simply by removing or clearing up misunderstanding or by a wave of God's

---

[55] See 2 Cor 5.21 KJV.

[56] 1 Cor 15.3.

hand. It was a deed of desperate anguish even for God, a deed at terrible cost. It was atonement not in word only but in the reality of God's actual relationship with man, and man's relationship with God. Apart from the actual historical death of Christ on the cross, apart from that vicarious sacrifice for us, there is no forgiveness, no justification, no reconciliation, no redemption. Jesus Christ took our place that we might take his place. He did a deed which we could not do, and which is not now required of us. 'Who is to condemn? It is Christ that died.'[57]

5 Justification and the act of atonement

At this point that we must seek to describe as far as we may the act of atonement in relation to justification.

(a) The death of Christ was an expiatory sacrifice

The death of Christ was an expiatory sacrifice in which God judged sin and through which human guilt is completely taken away. In Christ God himself was among men and women judging sin in the flesh, but it was on the cross above all that we find a complete judgement was enacted, and it was there that Jesus Christ stepped forward as the lamb of God to bear our sin and to sacrifice himself under God's holy judgement. We have seen that God withheld full judgement and allowed only such pressure of judgement to bear upon man as he had given in his holy law. That had the effect of holding humanity in sin, and therefore of maintaining in existence a contradiction of God's majesty. Had God simply let man go, disowned mankind altogether, we would have ceased to exist. The dreadful thing for us was that God insisted on holding on to us in spite of our sin, and that fact brought the pressure of God's criticism of sin to burn deeply into our human soul. At last in his mercy and patience, in the fullness of time, God delivered his final condemnation of sin in Jesus Christ who stood under the judgement of God for us. He bore our guilt and was judged as a malefactor, numbered among the transgressors,[58] and in the judgement of Christ, our guilt was expiated and taken away.

---

57   See Rom 8.34 RSV/KJV.
58   Isaiah 53.12 (cf. 9); cf. Luke 23.32f; Mark 15.27; Matt 27.38.

Jesus takes our guilt and judgement on himself, in perfect submission to the divine verdict

That guilt was the barrier between humanity and God, a barrier lent terrible objectivity and irremediable character by the wrath of God. That was the obstacle that had to be removed if there was to be reconciliation between God and humanity. On our part that guilt was irremovable. We were helpless to emancipate ourselves from it. On God's part, guilt had to be judged, judged in finality and completeness in those whom he loved and knew could not survive such judgement. But in Christ Jesus, the judge himself entered into the very heart of our guilty estrangement in order to reconcile us to God in bearing himself the divine wrath. God came in Christ to do from the side of humanity what humanity could not do. So Christ took our place before God and bore our sins on his own body on the tree.[59] He died on our behalf and in that death he offered the perfect submission of humanity to God in holy obedience, and brought to God humanity's perfect acquiescence in the divine judgement. In the words of the 51st Psalm it was an acknowledgement before God of our sin, and of sin as against God only, that God might be justified in his word against us and be supreme in his judgement. But such an acknowledgement of sin was not in word only. It was complete acknowledgement and a complete acquiescence in complete judgement, and so Christ descended into the deepest depths of our guilt and submitted to the complete judgement of God upon it. It was an enacted acknowledgement, an actual acquiescence in actual judgement, and therefore an enduring of death as the final repudiation by God of our sin. It was suffering and death under the divine judgement on our behalf.

(i) An act of God as God and man – enhypostatic *atonement*

It is important to see that all this is an act of God, not only from the side of God, but from the side of humanity. This is not humanity propitiating God. How could humanity either propitiate God or bear God's judgement? How could God, God of all grace and love, allow himself to be propitiated by man, as if he needed to be propitiated before he could be gracious and forgiving? On the contrary, God is himself always *subject* throughout this act of

---

[59] 1 Peter 2.24.

atonement. This is God taking the absolute initiative, not only in justification as the realising of the divine justice against sin, but in stepping into the situation to provide for sacrifice the lamb upon whom his acts of justifying condemnation are actualised. Both in the Old Testament and in the New Testament God is always the prime subject of words to denote atonement, expiation, propitiation. It is God *himself* who expiates sin and guilt, God himself who bears sin and guilt and bears it away, God himself who reconciles himself to mankind and mankind to himself, who endures his own wrath and so in utter grace gives himself in propitiation for man and freely restores man into complete fellowship with himself.

Atonement is act of God, but also real act of real man, enhypostatic in Christ

However, let us be careful here. The act of expiation is certainly act of God, for God judges sin in the death of Christ and removes guilt by judgement – and Paul expresses that by the term justification, the fulfilment of God's righteousness. The Greek *dikaioun*, to justify, means to condemn as well as to make just. But it is also true that justification is an act of man, for when we speak of God as acting from the side of man in Christ, we mean that here Christ's work is as *enhypostatic*[60] as his person, and thus we must go on to stress that Christ's saving work in atonement is equally *enhypostatic*. Christ's humanity was no docetic humanity, nor was his humanity merely instrumental in the hands of God. If this were a pure divine act it would not touch us in our humanity but pass over our head completely.[61] It is important to see that as atoning deed the cross is also human act. Certainly it was wrought for man and not by human initiative, but wrought out of man's life as man's act nevertheless. Here God really became human and translated his divine action into terms of his human action, giving the human action its full place in and with his divine action. It was *enhypostatic atonement*. In other words, the work of atonement was the work of the God-man, wrought for us, in our place, on our behalf, in our stead – a

---

[60]   *Enhypostatic* means that though the humanity of Christ had no independent existence apart from the incarnation of the Word (and was therefore *an-hypostatic* in itself) it did have full human reality *in* the person of the Son: it was *en-hypostatic* in him. See further T.F. Torrance, *Incarnation*, p. 228.

[61]   Cf. F.W. Camfield, *Scottish Journal of Theology*, Vol. 1.3, Dec 1948, p. 292.

work which we could not do, a work so radically substitutionary that it entirely displaces us and all our self-justification requiring from us therefore the most radical self-denial, yet it was a work in which God in Christ acts *as man* as well as God. In this inconceivable union of God and humanity, then, God in Christ took our place and accomplished what we could not do. The infliction and judgement which we could not bear he bore for us. In our place he made 'satisfaction' (to use the language of Anselm) for our sins and for the sins of the whole world.

(ii) Justification is twofold, God in judgement, and man in satisfaction and holiness

That 'satisfaction' Paul calls 'justification' in the twofold sense – (a) of God's just condemnation of sin in which the righteousness of God is revealed and the wrath of God from heaven is revealed against all ungodliness and unrighteousness of humanity,[62] and (b) of God's providing a righteousness from the side of humanity which perfectly and obediently acquiesces in the fulfilment of God's righteous judgement against sin. This is a righteousness with which God is well pleased, a righteousness fulfilled in his beloved Son, God and man in one person.

The atoning death of Christ is justification in that here God is just against sin, justifies himself in the judgement of sin, and it is also justification in that here there is offered to God a righteousness, a holiness, a perfect obedience, completely in accord with God's own righteousness.

In that double deed of the God-man, of God and man in inconceivable union in Christ, atonement is wrought in the life and blood of Christ. It is at once substitutionary *sacrifice* in that life is given for life as Christ stands under the divine judgement obedient unto death, the death of the cross, and substitutionary *oblation* in that here obedience and holiness are offered to God in place of our disobedience and sin. Here we have in one act on the cross, the twofold sacrifice indicated by the Old Testament sin offering and whole burnt offering. It is not merely the death of Christ, his suffering, his blood, his bearing of judgement, that atones or expiates guilt, but along with that and within it all the offering of perfect holiness to God from the side of humanity. Jesus is 'God's beloved Son in whom he is well pleased'.[63]

---

[62] Rom 1.17-18.

[63] Matt 3.17; Mark 1.11; Luke 3.22; cf. Matt 17.5; Mark 9.7; Luke 9.35.

(iii) The double faithfulness of Christ as God and man, the judge and judged

We shall see the full import of that when we come to discuss reconciliation as involving the oneness of God and mankind in mind and will in perfect peace, but here we must think of it as justification from the side of God's faithfulness answered vicariously by justification from the side of man's faithfulness. Justification is that double steadfastness of Christ as God the judge judging sin and as man the judged submitting perfectly to God's holy judgement, and thus it is the twofold justification of God and the justification of the ungodly. Thus in Christ God's righteousness is revealed and actualised from faith, from God's covenant faithfulness, to faith, to answering human faithfulness.[64]

The judgement of the judge takes place within his own person as the one judged

Now before we go on, let us pause to consider the fact that in Christ who is God and man it is God himself the judge, God himself the holy God whose word and will are law, who made himself the judged. He completely identified himself in the incarnation with sinners under his judgement. He took upon himself their human nature in its existence under the divine judgement, in the guilt irreparably attached to it through the divine judgement, so that in himself in his one person he was both the judge and the judged. In that unity of the person and work of Christ, the judgement of the judge could only take place *within his own person* as the one judged, so that judgement was meted out in the form of a determination of the personal being and existence of the incarnate Son. The whole life of this incarnate Son was therefore a life in which, by the incarnation of the judge, the divine judgement was brought to bear upon human flesh and nature, but human flesh and nature in the human nature and flesh of Jesus Christ.

The whole life and existence of Jesus was therefore an existence of the judge and the judged in one person, and because the divine judgement reached out to its ultimate repudiation of sin in death, the whole life of Jesus on earth has death as its ultimate goal and end, for it was in death that the judged was to acquiesce fully and

---

[64]   Cf. Rom 1.17 KJV, 'therein is the righteousness of God revealed from faith to faith (*ek pisteōs eis pistin)'. See further *Conflict and Agreement*, vol. 2, p. 80-82.

finally in that divine judgement. Thus the death of Jesus was an outworking of the incarnation of the judge in our humanity, but it was such an outworking of it, that it was in our human nature that the judge bore his own judgement. It was the full realisation of the holy will of God in our human nature, the full meting out of the divine condemnation against sin, the full outpouring of the divine love into and upon human nature. But in Christ Jesus all that was also gladly suffered and endured for our sakes, so that in him there was achieved in judgement, in complete and final justification, a judgement, a union between God and humanity which death and hell itself could not break or in any way sunder. Nothing could isolate Jesus as man from God, not even the final judgement of God, for Jesus as man was God himself come as man. It is this perfect oneness in the midst of judgement, God's bearing in his own incarnation his own judgement of mankind, that is at once the ground of atonement and also its ultimate end. For it is in that oneness that the fellowship is created and restored between God and humanity and humanity and God, the fellowship which is the goal of all God's merciful work of redemption. Here the doctrine of justification passes over into reconciliation and redemption, so that we shall again pursue this theme later.

(b) The death of Christ the atoning deed of the one for the many

(i) The problem of substitution – how can one die for another and do it justly?[65]

Here we must look more closely at the doctrine of *substitution*, particularly as expounded in Romans 5. From the point of view of the law, substitution is utterly impossible – 'the soul that sins shall die.'[66] That is the only just view of the matter. It is immoral for one person to die for another, or to allow oneself to be put to death for another, thereby at the same time making that person guilty of another's blood. Besides, no one can be a really responsible substitute for another because no one else can really represent another *from within their guilt*. That is why the theology that deals only in forensic terms and speaks only of a purely objective atonement in that sense brings upon itself the suspicion of make-belief, and yet the biblical revelation speaks in the most astonishing terms of this substitutionary act of Christ. 'He who knew no sin

---

[65] Cf. T.F. Torrance, 'The Atonement – The Singularity of Christ...', p. 252.

[66] Ezek 18.4.

became sin for us, that we might be made the righteousness of God in him.'[67] We can only be aghast at this – nor have we any adequate categories in which to construe it. But it is clear that unless something like that did indeed happen, the death of Christ as utterly substitutionary lacked reality or actuality. How are we to understand that? How did Christ enter into our guilt from within and how did he die for us, *the just for the unjust,* and do that *justly?* How can this be justification?

(ii) Only the creator Word can be 'the one for the many'

Paul speaks of this question of the one and the many by contrasting Christ and Adam – not that they are set side by side as parallel figures. We can see the significance of the comparison if we remember that Adam as man[68] was made in the image of God. Man was created by the Word of God, and it is in and from that Word that humanity, as male and female, has true being and true humanity.[69] We have fallen from that estate, but the true secret of our humanity is lodged in the Word. In the incarnation of this Word, Christ became the 'proper man', as Luther called him, the true man, and because that Word made flesh is the creative source and true secret of our humanity, because in him our humanity is lodged, because all mankind consist in him, he is the only one who can really represent all men and women from the innermost centre and depth of human being.[70] He came then, not only as the creator of our race, but as the head of our race, for in him the whole race consists.[71] It was thus that Christ, true God took upon himself our flesh and became true man, and as such made atonement. As such he got at our sin and guilt from within, not simply by wearing our flesh, but as we have seen, by penetrating into the very heart of

---

[67]   See 2 Cor 5.21.

[68]   The Hebrew *adam* is used for man in general (man and woman) and for '*the* man' (*ha-adam*, translated 'man') that God created. Thus, 'Then God said "Let us make man (*adam*) in our image . . . and let *them* have dominion . . . " So God created man (*ha-adam*) in his own image, in the image of God he created *him*; male and female he created *them*. And God blessed *them* . . . ' (Gen 1.26-28).

[69]   John 1.1-4.

[70]   See Athanasius, *On the Incarnation of the Word,* for the same argument.

[71]   Col 1.15-20.

our evil, and within the sinful conditions of our flesh living a life of perfect obedience to God and offering himself without spot to the Father.

(iii) The overcoming of the gap between the 'is' and the 'ought'

Furthermore, here in Christ true God and true man are united in one person – here in Christ, the distance between God and man, and therefore the gap and the tension between the 'is' and the 'ought' within which alone the law as law can operate, are eliminated. Here there is established a relation of union with God apart from law, breaking through the mediation of the law into personal hypostatic union in which the whole will of God for humanity was fulfilled perfectly. Here God steps personally from behind the law and is joined to mankind, certainly under the law, but in a union which is not conditioned by law as such. It is in that union that the substitutionary atonement is made, in the only way and at the only point where substitution could be valid reality. That union of God and humanity in Christ taken into the cross was vindicated by the resurrection. It was such a union that when it passed through the ultimate separation of God and humanity in judgement, death and hell, it remained entire and whole and unbroken. Christ as man could not be trapped in death because he had already passed clean through the chasm between the 'is' and the 'ought' which under final judgement becomes widened to abysmal separation from God in death and hell.

(iv) The resurrection is the ground of justification

Had Christ succumbed to the death of the cross, that would only have indicated that this union of God and man was not real, that it had not actually been achieved, and therefore that the ethical or legal relation, with its gap between the 'is' and the 'ought' and its order of distance from God, still stood valid and therefore that every moral or other objection in regard to it was valid. Had Christ succumbed to the death of the cross, its substitutionary sacrifice would have been the most immoral deed in all the universe, and the only doctrine that could be got out of it would be the pagan idea of humanity placating an angry god by human sacrifice. That is partly why Paul lays such stress upon *the resurrection as the ground of justification*. He speaks of Jesus being 'put to death for our trespasses and raised for our justification',[72] and asks rhetorically, 'who is to condemn? Is it Christ Jesus, who died, yes,

---

[72] Rom 4.25.

who was raised from the dead'?[73] It is because of this resurrection out of the death of the cross that God and humanity have been reconciled in Christ, and therefore that our life has been set on a wholly new basis.

(v) Justification is essentially corporate

The relation between justification and resurrection we shall consider later;[74] but here where we are considering the one and the many and the fact of substitution, it must be pointed out that this means that justification is essentially a *corporate* act. 'In that Christ died, all died.'[75] 'He is the propitiation not for our sins only, but for the sins of the whole world.'[76] As the creator and head of the race in whom all mankind consist, Christ died for all men and women, and the justification involved is total, for all. Because God's act of justification was complete in this one man,[77] because it was total in the body of Christ, justification is to be expressed in terms of the one body of Christ, and is actualised in the individual through incorporation into the one body of Christ.

The modern world with its renaissance view of man completely misunderstands the biblical teaching of justification and sanctification when it shuts its eyes to the essentially corporate nature of the deed of atonement and justification and sanctification.[78] The individual is not left out of sight in the New Testament, but the emphasis is on the corporate union in Christ, and justification is expounded only within that corporate emphasis. In the widest sense and in a very profound sense, Christ's death for all mankind means that all men and women are already involved in God's act of justification – Christ died for them when they were yet sinners,[79] and in that he died, all died,[80] all were condemned and all came under his substitutionary atonement – anything else

---

[73] Rom 8.34.

[74] Chap. 7, 'The Resurrection of Jesus Christ', sections 1 (b) (i) & 2 (a) (i) and (ii).

[75] See 2 Cor 5.14, 'we are convinced that one has died for all; therefore all have died.'

[76] See 1 John 2.2.

[77] Cf. Eph 2.11-22, esp. 15-16; Rom 5.15-21.

[78] Cf. here the Old Catholic theologian E. Gaugler, *'Die Heiligung'*.

[79] Rom 5.8; cf. also 5.6.

[80] 2 Cor 5.14.

completely disintegrates substitutionary atonement and breaks up the wholeness of justification and destroys it. Christ Jesus is himself our wisdom and righteousness and sanctification and redemption.[81] He is our total justification in himself. That corporate justification in Christ, God's righteousness and our righteousness, expresses itself in the church as the one body of Christ, and justification is extended in its actualisation among all humanity through incorporation into Christ by his Spirit,[82] the operation and indwelling of people by the Spirit that is through faith. Thus the complete doctrine of justification is the doctrine of the church, the church of the 'saints' or the *hagioi* in Christ – but we cannot follow out that aspect of it now.

(c) Justification in atonement means rectification and redemption

Justification in the act of atonement means *rectification* – the restoring of a right, the restoring of God's right over mankind as his creatures, and the restoration to men and women of their right as creatures of God, as sons and daughters of the heavenly Father. At an earlier point we saw how the conception of justification passes over into reconciliation. This is the point where it passes over into redemption, in the narrower sense of that word. Here we must think of justification as the eschatological act which translates humanity out of the kingdom of darkness into the kingdom of God's dear Son.

That has both a backward reference and a forward reference. Think once more of the instance of Jesus' healing of the paralytic man as recorded in Mark, where he said to the man, 'My son, your sins are forgiven', and then also 'Rise, take up your pallet and walk'.[83] There we have forgiveness breaking in as a creative act and evidencing itself by its own actuality in healing. So in the cross of Christ and in the resurrection, justification is proclaimed and it comes breaking in upon us as the creative act of God acting upon us radically. It is that creative element that baffles our understanding, as indeed all creation does.

---

[81] 1 Cor 1.30.

[82] See further T.F. Torrance, *Scottish Journal of Theology*, vol. 19.2 (1966), 'The Mission of the Church', esp. the section 'The Church is the Communion of the Spirit', pp. 133-36, where Torrance speaks of the corporate union with Christ in the incarnation as being the same union which is personalised in us through the communion of the Spirit.

[83] Mark 2.1-12.

Here at the cross and in the resurrection of Christ for our justification we are taken back to the original deed of creation and are restored to God's full purpose and glory. Here the eternal purpose of God breaks into the midst and manifests itself in the justification of the ungodly, as regeneration.

(i) The backward reference of justification

(1) The undoing of the past and of guilt

Justification means the reparation of the past, the rectification of the fallen creation. The deed of atonement on the cross has *retroactive effect*, going back to the very beginning. And so Christ in the *Apocalypse*[84] claims to be the first and the last, the alpha and the omega.[85] Here in the cross we do not have mere amnesty, but such a total act of justification that our sins are utterly undone and are done away. At the cross, God puts the clock back. In the language of the prophet, he restores the years that the locust has eaten.[86] He so rectifies us that there is a new creation. That comes out very clearly in the account of the book of destiny in the hands of God sealed with seven seals which, as recorded in the *Apocalypse*,[87] no one in heaven or earth could open, except the lamb of God.[88] He alone has power to open the seals of destiny, to cancel the power of guilt, and to liberate humanity from the determination of a guilty past. Guilt and the irreversibility of time, as we know it in a sinful world, are bound up together inseparably. But in the form of guilt, what is irreversible in the past, and therefore ineradicable, is present, determining human existence under judgement and binding men and women in its tyranny. That applies not simply and not even primarily to individuals before the cross but primarily to the whole adamic race, to our racial past, to the whole of our human existence which, as Paul says, was piling up wrath against itself until the day of judgement.[89] But in the cross, Jesus Christ descended into that awful *sheol* of human existence, into hell

---

[84] The book of Revelation, 'the revelation (*apokalupsis*) of Jesus Christ'; *apokalupsis*, 'uncovering' or 'revelation'.

[85] Rev 1.17, 22.13, cf. 1.8, 21.6.

[86] Joel 2.25.

[87] See further T.F. Torrance, *The Apocalypse Today*, James Clarke, London 1960.

[88] Rev 5.1ff.

[89] Rom 2.5; cf. Matt 23.29-36.

itself, and into that hell as it became hell to the utmost under the final judgement of God on the cross upon our sinful existence. By his atonement, he broke into it and broke it open, leading captivity captive,[90] and now he holds the keys of death and hell in his power.[91]

(2) Contact re-established with creation

It is precisely the suspension of final judgement involved in the law that makes the difference between the Old Testament notion of *sheol* and the New Testament notion of hell. So long as God suspends his final judgement, *sheol* is only *sheol* where believing and unbelieving alike are under the power of death and the *anamnesis* or remembrance of sin. But now that the final judgement is enacted on the cross, now that God has at last poured out his full wrath against sin, *sheol* becomes hell and yet hell and the powers of darkness are robbed of their power and death is robbed of its sting. We are not concerned here with the notion of hell, but we are concerned with the fact that Christ descended into hell. He broke into the kingdom of the irreversibility of time and guilt, and by his complete act of expiation he has undone its power and cancelled guilt and sin. That means that in the atonement on the cross, we have an act of justification that penetrates into the very beginning and sets man back on the basis of God's creative purpose. The cross makes contact with creation. Christ, the second Adam, the last Adam, undoes the work of the first Adam, and heads the race to new and higher glory that far transcends the old.

In a profound sense, as we shall see under redemption, the cross is a cosmic event involving all things and all time. If the giving of God's law both expressed the judgement of God upon evil and yet withheld its final judgement, and so contained evil, establishing a relative order of morality and law that held the creation together and kept it from falling into utter chaos and nothingness, how much more will the full manifestation and enactment of the divine will, with its fulfilment of judgement and justification, mean the establishment of the whole order of creation!?[92] And that is precisely what Paul has in mind when he speaks of the establishing of the

---

[90] Eph 4.8 KJV ('or *led a multitude of captives*' – RSV '*led a host of captives*').

[91] Rev 1.18; cf. 1 Cor 15.54-57.

[92] An implicit allusion to the Pauline 'how much more...?' – cf. Rom 5.10, 11.12,15.

law and of all things under the divine will, and when he also speaks of the recapitulation or summing up and gathering of all things together in Christ the head of all.[93]

(3) The past made to serve the purpose of redemption

At this point however, we are considering only one aspect of that, 'the backward reference of justification'. It is twofold. First, it restores to man the original right of a creature by undoing the past, restoring the years that sin has devoured. Second, it repairs the past in the sense that all the past is now suborned by the cross and made to serve the purpose of God's redemption – that is something beyond all our powers to understand. We see something of how God used the cross, the supreme crime of mankind, for the redemption of mankind, and we cannot but see that by the same cross and the deed of atonement there, God so brings all the past under the sovereignty of his love as to make it yield the peaceable fruits of righteousness, so that he makes all things to work together for good to those that love him.[94] That is God's justification of the past, justification of the ungodly, total justification of the sinner, the total forgiveness of sins.

In Jesus Christ, in his death on the cross, descent into hell, burial in the grave, God has given himself to humanity in its sin and corruption and lost estate, in such a way as to take the course, the punishment, the corruption of sin upon himself, slay the old sinful and perverted adamic existence and bury it, and by penetrating right back into human existence not let it see corruption but raise it out of the grave as a new humanity in the resurrection of Jesus Christ, the first-born of the new creation. In one sense, then, the cross means that God puts human sin completely behind his back – he makes the past forever past, not past in the sense of *anamnesis*[95] and memory, but in the sense that it is utterly forgotten and blotted out even by God for himself, and cannot be resurrected by man or devil. 'Who shall bring any charge against God's elect?'[96] In another sense, God repairs the years that are wasted, and

---

[93]   Eph 1.10 – cf. the RSV/KJV here with the NIV which brings out more fully the force of the Greek *anakephalaiōsasthai*, to gather up together under a head. Cf. also Col 1.15-20.

[94]   Rom 8.28 KJV.

[95]   Remembrance, calling to mind, from the Greek *ana-mimnēskō*, 'again-remind', i.e. 'remember'.

[96]   Rom 8.33.

suborns or bends all that has taken place to minister to the fulfilment of his redemptive purpose, for as the cross is by atonement made to yield the resurrection, so by the cross and by the resurrection God produces new birth out of the old humanity, the new humanity in Jesus Christ, created after the image of God in the righteousness and holiness that derive from the truth.

(ii) The forward reference of justification

This is the point where we think of justification in its forward or future reference, the restoration to mankind of their truth in Jesus Christ. In that Jesus Christ was raised for our justification, men and women are given a new human life and a new human right in Jesus Christ, for 'to all who received him, who believed in his name, he gave power, *exousia*, to become children of God'.[97] That is the Johannine way of stating the Pauline doctrine of the justification of man, for it is the bestowing upon men and women in Christ of a new human righteousness so that they are adopted to be sons and daughters of God, and are given already through justification to participate in the new creation which will be revealed at the *parousia*[98] and in the redemption of the body.

This aspect of justification cannot be fully expounded except in terms of the resurrection of Christ[99] and of the outpouring of the Holy Spirit through whom we are united to Christ and are given to participate already in the new creation, given already a new human righteousness in Christ Jesus through real and substantial union with him in the power of his resurrection. Jesus Christ in his risen humanity is the new man who has inaugurated a new humanity in perfect obedience to the Father, and who by his resurrection has begotten us into this new humanity.[100] Justification has that new humanity with its new divine-human righteousness as its very substance, although that will not be fully apparent until the *parousia*. Two points concern us here particularly.

(1) Justification is participation in the righteousness of Christ

Justification is our participation in the justice, in the righteousness of Jesus Christ the new man, and so it means more than rectification,

---

[97] John 1.12.

[98] Presence, coming, used of the 'final advent' or 'second coming' of Christ.

[99] See further chap. 7 below, 'The Resurrection of Jesus Christ', section 2 (a), *The Resurrection and Justification*.

[100] Cf. 1 Peter 1.3.

more than the restoration to men and women of their human rights as creatures or children of God: it means that we are given to share in the righteousness and the glory of the only begotten Son of God. Justification through atonement means that the Son of God has put himself in our place that we may be put in his place – that is the amazing grace of Christ that he who was rich for our sakes became poor that we through his poverty might become rich.[101] It is in Jesus Christ the new man that we are put in God's place, that is, in Jesus Christ risen from the dead and ascended to the right hand of God the Father. Justification of the ungodly means that Jesus Christ descended into our ungodly estate and that in him we are raised up to be made 'partakers of the divine nature'.[102] That is the substitutionary intervention of God in justification. God has abased himself that we might be exalted. In Christ Jesus, God has burdened himself with the whole of our nature with all its human weakness and shame, unrighteousness and meanness, has made himself responsible for all we are in our sin and guilt. And so he has entered into our damnation and ruin, into the corruption and chaos of our existence, and transformed it all, overcoming sin and guilt, damnation and corruption and death. And in his exaltation of Jesus Christ out of our damnation, in his ascension in full humanity to God's right hand, we the ungodly are given our right, our justification in him, the new man, who justifies us for ever as he stands before the throne of God in our name and on our behalf.

(2) Justification is a completed reality awaiting disclosure

It is important to see that all this is spoken of in the New Testament mainly in the past tense, for this justification is not a process. It is a finished work.[103] In Jesus Christ we have been crucified, have died and have been buried[104] – and so the old age, the power of darkness and the sovereignty of evil are already defeated.[105] In Christ Jesus we have been resurrected, made alive;[106] we are already justified and

---

[101]   2 Cor 8.9.

[102]   2 Peter 1.4.

[103]   Rom 5.9.

[104]   Rom 6.4-6; 2 Cor 5.14.

[105]   Col 1.13, 2.15.

[106]   Col 2.13, 3.1; Eph 2.5-6.

sanctified and redeemed for he has been made our wisdom, righteousness, sanctification and redemption;[107] already we have been reconciled to God;[108] already have peace with God;[109] already our life is hid with Christ in God,[110] and already we have been granted all things necessary for life and godliness that we might have participation in the divine nature.[111] It is only on the ground of this past tense that the New Testament speaks of the present and of the future of humanity, the church and the world. Let it be noted here too that when Paul speaks of the new man, it is the one new man, corporate man, the body of Christ, and the place of the individual is only within that one body.[112]

It is on the ground of justification as a perfection, as a finished work that it has future reference, for the full disclosure of the new righteousness awaits the resurrection of the body. But the new humanity in Christ is given already the breath of the new life. As God breathed into Adam and made him living man, so the Holy Spirit, the very breath of the Father and the Son, is given to the church to breathe into it the breath of the new humanity in Christ.[113] And through that pouring out of the Holy Spirit upon the church, the church is given at once fully real participation in the new man at the right hand of God, and awaits the full manifestation of its new being in the new man at the coming again of Jesus Christ as true man as well as true God. The church is given such a first-fruit and pledge or guarantee (*aparchē* and *arrabōn*),[114] in that future fullness of Christ, that it is already active in the church – although our experience or knowledge of that perfect fullness is limited, that is, is in eschatological arrears.

---

[107] 1 Cor 1.30.

[108] Rom 5.10; 2 Cor 5.18-19.

[109] Rom 5.1; Eph 2.14-17.

[110] Col 3.3.

[111] 2 Peter 1.4.

[112] Cf. Eph 2.11ff.

[113] Torrance's teaching is that God breathed physical breath into Adam and therefore he explicitly rejected the view that God breathed his own Spirit into man. Likewise he rejected the view that the Holy Spirit became the soul of the church. The church, like Adam, remains fully human and therefore fallible.

[114] Rom 8.23 (*aparchē*, first fruits); 2 Cor 5.5 (*arrabōn*, pledge).

*'Imputation' is the concept that holds together the completed reality
and its future disclosure*

It is because the New Testament thinks of justification in this
eschatological relation between the 'It is finished' on the cross[115]
and the 'Behold I make all things new'[116] of the *parousia*, that it
speaks of it in terms of 'reckoning' or as the Reformers interpreted it,
'imputation' or 'reputation'.[117] Imputation describes the perfected work
of grace. It indicates that justification is forensic in the sense that it is
grounded on the once and for all judgement of Jesus Christ on the
cross, but it indicates that what happened there, while complete in its
reality, is yet to be fully disclosed at the advent of Christ. The Pauline
'reckon' (*logizesthe*)[118] or the Reformers *'impute'* is the concept which
holds together those two moments, the forensic and the eschatological,
in one, the once and for all completed work and the full disclosure of it
in the *parousia*, in one. It is because justification is involved in that
tension that we are given the two sacraments of baptism and eucharist,
with baptism enshrining the once and for all corporate act of total
justification in Christ, and the eucharist enshrining our continual
participation in Christ's new humanity until he comes again. Then the
need for both sacraments will be done away and faith and hope will
pass away and *agape-love* only will abide as the eternal being of the
new humanity in righteousness and truth.

---

[115] John 19.30.

[116] Rev 21.5.

[117] For the Reformers, the doctrine of justfication by grace through faith could
be expressed by saying that though we are sinners righteousness is
'imputed' to us, or that we are 'reckoned' or 'reputed' to be righteous. Cf.
the Latin *simul justus et peccator*, '*simul*taneously righteous and sinner', or
at once righteous and sinful.

[118] Rom 6.11 KJV (RSV 'consider'), cf. 4.3ff.,23-24.

Chapter Five

ATONEMENT AS RECONCILIATION

In our consideration of atonement in the thought of Paul, we began in the previous chapter with justification, as Paul himself does in Romans. But though the act of atonement that justifies us is no doubt the basic event of our salvation, it is not an end in itself for in it the legal relation is transcended, in order that we may enter into a deeper and more intimate relation with the Father in which the forensic and condemnatory aspect of the law is removed and we are reconciled to God. It is an action of such a kind that not only is guilt cancelled, but there is wrought out a new relation between God and man, in which man is restored to God as his dear child, as a son or daughter of the heavenly Father. As we saw, that belongs to the fullness of the doctrine of justification, but that is the point where it overlaps with what the New Testament calls reconciliation, the recreating of the bond of union between God and humanity and humanity and God, a bond which is ontological[1] and personal, which involves our human being and knowing. Here atonement means *at-one-ment* in the fullest personal sense and therefore in this chapter we proceed to consider atonement as reconciliation.

1 The New Testament words for reconciliation

The word used for reconciliation between God and man in the New Testament is *katallassō*, with the noun *katallagē* translated once as 'atonement' in the King James Version of the bible but otherwise as 'reconciling' or 'reconciliation', while in the Revised Standard Version *katallagē* is always translated as 'reconciliation'.[2] The root word in Greek is *allassō* meaning to *change*, and also to *exchange*. Thus in Acts, Stephen is accused of speaking against the temple and the law and of saying that Jesus would '*change* the customs Moses gave us (*allaxei ta ethē*)',[3]

---

[1] To do with 'being', involving the nature or essence of something, from the Gk *onta*, what is, reality.

[2] Rom 5.11, 11.15; 2 Cor 5.18,19.

[3] See Acts 6.14.

reminding us very clearly of the thought in Hebrews of what it called *metathesis, change* (of the law) and *athetēsis*, setting aside (of the law or of sin).[4] In Corinthians, Paul says of the resurrection, 'we shall all be *changed (allagēsometha)*'.[5] Likewise in Romans, with reference to passages in the Old Testament,[6] Paul says mankind '*exchanged* the glory (*ēllaxan tēn doxan*) of the immortal God for images resembling mortal man or birds or animals or reptiles.'[7] This notion of change or exchange comes out in the compound expression *antallagma*, 'what shall a man give in *exchange* for his soul?'[8] which goes back to Psalm 49[9] where however the LXX has instead of *antallagma* the word *exilasma* and the Hebrew has *kopher* which is elsewhere translated also by *allagma*.[10]

Katallassō: *reconciliation through substitutionary exchange and expiation*

This helps us to see that the verb *katallassô* refers to reconciliation through a substitutionary exchange and involves expiation. *Katallassō* by itself means to change, exchange, and so to reconcile. The noun *katallagē* refers to the exchange effected by substitution or expiation, that is, atonement or reconciliation through atonement. *Katallassō* is used once in the New Testament of the reconciliation between man and wife,[11] but elsewhere *katallassō* or a stronger form of it, *apokatallassō*,[12] is used only of God's reconciling act, reconciling man or the world to himself.

Now what about the special biblical meaning of reconciliation, that is, what significance did it have for St Paul in the whole tradition of biblical thought and worship? And what contribution

---

[4]   See Heb 7.12, 7.18, 9.26.

[5]   1 Cor 15.51f.

[6]   Psalm 106.20 (105.20, LXX); Jer 2.11.

[7]   Rom 1.23.

[8]   Mark 8.37; Matt 16.26 KJV, RSV 'in return for his life'.

[9]   Psalm 49.7,'Truly no man can ransom himself, or give to God the price (*exilasma*) of his life' (LXX 48.7, Hb 49.8, *kaphro*).

[10] Isaiah 43.3; Amos 5.12; *antallagma*, change, exchange, ransom; *exilasma*, price, equivalent [see the comment on the meaning of *exilasma* by C.H. Dodd, *The Bible and the Greeks*, Hodder & Stoughton, London 1935, p. 92]; *kopher*, the equivalent of a life, ransom; *allagma*, change, exchange, price.

[11] 1 Cor 7.11; cf. Matt 5.24, *diallagēthi*.

[12] Eph 2.16; Col 1.20,22.

to our understanding of it is given by the Old Testament? The verb *katallassō* is used only once in the canonical books of the Greek Old Testament, in Jeremiah, where it means to change thoroughly and does not have a specially religious significance (it is here used of Moab),[13] but the word is used three times in 2 Maccabees[14] of divine reconciliation in much the same sense as it is also used in profane Greek. Thus we do not have an Old Testament Hebrew equivalent to the actual term *katallassō* although it is clear from the cognate expressions such as *allagma* that there lies behind it the Old Testament aspect of atonement by expiation, which is usually rendered by the Greek *hilaskomai*, which we have already glanced at in our discussion of the teaching of the epistle to the Hebrews. But we must now look at it a little more closely in order to get its exact meaning.

(a) The meaning of hilaskesthai, to be merciful or propitious, forgive[15]

Hilaskesthai means to be favourable, or propitious. In profane Greek it is essentially a religious term and is the stock word for expiation, meaning to make propitious, to appease, to effect reconciliation. It is thus a synonym for *areskein*, to make good or make amends.

In biblical Greek, *hilaskesthai* and its derivatives translate several Hebrew words.

(1) The main usage of *hilaskesthai* or *exilaskesthai* is to translate the Hebrew word *kipper*, to atone, cover, blot out, expiate. Here there are two main uses:

a) with God as subject, meaning to be gracious, to forgive, to have mercy, to pardon,

b) with man as subject, meaning to cleanse from sin or defilement with God as remote subject, and indeed with God as remote object, that is, in the sense of 'for God'. In these instances it is always God himself who is the real subject, the ultimate subject, with man acting for him in a liturgical capacity. But God is not the direct object of the verb – except in one instance we shall note.

---

[13] Jer 31.39 LXX, translated as 'broken down' (KJV), or 'broken' (RSV). In the English and Hebrew Old Testament, where the numbering of these chapters in Jeremiah is different from the LXX, the same passage is found at 48.39.

[14] 2 Macc 1.5, 7.33, 8.29.

[15] Cf. here C.H. Dodd, *The Bible and the Greeks*, chap. 5 'Atonement'.

(2) Another usage of *hilaskesthai* translates the Hebrew *salach*[16] forgive (used of God forgiving the individual but more often of God forgiving his people), and another usage (*hilasmos, exhilasmos* or *exilaskein*) renders the Hebrew *hitte* (or the noun *hattat*)[17] meaning to expiate, make a sin-offering, un-sin,[18] un-do sin, purify by sprinkling, but this Hebrew verb is also rendered in Greek by *katharizō* and *rantizō*, cleanse, sprinkle.

(3) Still another usage means to appease - of pagan action on God.

The Septuagint use of hilaskesthai *and* exilaskesthai

In the Septuagint and the New Testament, the verb *hilaskesthai* is not frequent. It is apparently not much liked by the biblical writers of the Old Testament and New Testament.[19] The Septuagint much prefers the stronger term *exilaskesthai* (usually rendering the Hebrew *kaphar*, from the root *kipper*) meaning to nullify, purge or expiate sin (the word is frequently used in this sense of the priest making atonement for the sins of the people[20]) but sometimes with the meaning of to intercede and pray.[21] *Exilaskesthai* and *hilaskesthai* are sometimes used liturgically with a human subject meaning to undo, make atonement or expiation for sin,[22] but not with God as object, except in three passages only.[23] In these three passages, the verb is used of man as subject and God as object of heathen acts of placating or appeasing God and they are used contemptuously. Never once is the verb used in that way of the living God – God cannot be the object of human expiation or propitiation, that is, of appeasement.

Thus in the Septuagint when *hilaskesthai* and its derivatives are used religiously, it is of God as subject, not object (except in those three references to heathen worship), whereas in profane Greek, God is never the subject of the verb *hilaskesthai*. In biblical Greek, the word means to forgive or cancel sin, and so to be gracious toward, or be reconciled to

---

16   Psalm 25.11, 130.4 (LXX numbering 24.11, 129.4), Lam 3.42.

17   2 Chron 29.24; Ezek 43.20,22,23, 44.27, 45.18,19.

18   Cf. Dodd, *op. cit.* p. 84.

19   Psalm 25.11, 65.3, 78.38, 79.9 (LXX 24.11, 64.3, 77.38, 78.9); 2 Kings 5.18, 24.4; 2 Chron 6.30; Lam 3.42; Dan 9.19; Luke 18.13; Heb 2.17.

20   Especially in Leviticus and Numbers, eg. Lev 4.20,26,31,35, 5.6,10,13,16,18 etc; Num 5.8, 6.11, 8.12,19,21, 15.25,28 etc.

21   Psalm 106.30 (LXX 105.30).

22   Num 31.50; Lev 1.4; Heb 2.17.

23   Zech 7.2, 8.22; Mal 1.9.

– there is no occurrence in the Old or the New Testament of the expression *hilaskesthai ton theon* meaning to conciliate God, or placate God, which was a heathen concept.

When we turn to the teaching of St Paul, we find that he avoids the term *hilaskesthai* although he does use the term *hilastērion* with the definite reference to the mercy-seat in the ark of the covenant and an act of God, 'whom God put forward as an expiation (or propitiation), *hilastērion*'.[24] Why does Paul not use *hilaskesthai* which in classical Greek is the normal term for reconciliation through expiation? In profane Greek *hilaskesthai* carries the heathen idea of reconciling God, where God is always the object and never the subject. The Septuagint, as we have seen, does use *hilaskesthai*, (usually rendering *salach*, forgive, or *kipper*), but only of God himself as the subject. But Paul evidently feels that the use of this word compromises the gospel in the Greek world and so he sets it aside in favour of the biblically unusual word, *katallassō*, reconcile, making it quite clear that this is entirely act of God himself, so that there is no possibility of the paganising (or 'pelagianising') of atonement.

Paul's use of katallassō *equivalent to the Old Testament use of* hilaskesthai

We are warranted, therefore, in seeing behind Paul's use of the verb *katallassō*, the Old Testament doctrine of *reconciliation through expiation*, that is, all that *hilaskesthai* in the Septuagint or the epistle to the Hebrews implies, although in the nature of the case we do not have a direct equivalent in Hebrew for *katallassō* as it is not used religiously or theologically in the Old Testament. We have similar features in the New Testament uses of words like *charis* or *agapē* for grace and love which have Old Testament equivalents although new and unusual Greek words are taken to render them (*charis* is unusual in the Septuagint, although frequent in profane Greek, while *agapē* is very new in every sense). As a clear parallel to Paul's use of *katallassō* instead of *hilaskomai*[25] we have the use of Mark's Gospel, 'what can a man give *in return* for his life?'[26] where the Septuagint Greek *exilasma* is struck out from its citation of the Old Testament and the word *antallagma* put in its place for obviously the same reason. This means that we must examine all the more carefully the actual passages in which Paul uses

---

[24]   Rom 3.25.

[25]   The first person form of the infinitive *hilaskesthai*.

[26]   Mark 8.37; Matt 16.26.

the word *katallassō* in order to get his exact meaning. There are three main passages we must look at.

(b) *The meaning of* katallassō, *reconcile*

(i) *Romans 5.8-11: 'reconciled to God'*

Here there is the verb *katallassō* in v.10 (twice) and the noun *katallagē* in v.11. We note a number of things about this whole passage (vv. 1-11).

a) The subject throughout is God, God in the initiative of his love, vv. 5-8. (This is also very clear in the next passage we shall look at in 2 Corinthians 5.14-21)

b) Reconciliation concerns a personal relationship (compare the relation of husband and wife in 1 Corinthians 7.11). There is a personal subject and a personal object. The verb *hilaskomai* can be used of an impersonal object, meaning atoning for sins, but not *katallassō*. It is used only of persons. Reconciliation thus concerns the personal relation between God and man. It is a two sided relationship but in this, the side of man is subordinated to the side of God. It is God himself who forms anew the relation between himself and humanity – the human part is to accept this reinstatement, this reconciliation, and so Paul in Romans speaks of 'receiving atonement or reconciliation (*katallagēn*)'.[27]

c) The reconciliation between God and man is one of peace and love, v. 1 following. The new basis upon which this is set is grace, v. 2.[28] This new relation is in contrast to that of the ungodly, sinners and enemies, vv. 6,8,10. The love of God is poured out in our hearts and the old enmity is gone.

d) Note the parallel between reconciliation and justification: 'being now justified (*dikaiōthentes*) by his blood, we shall be saved from wrath through him' (v. 9) and 'being reconciled (*katallagentes*), we shall be saved by his life' (v. 10).[29] They involve each other.

Reconciliation is just as objective as justification, but in reconciliation the personal relation is in view, envisaging a changed relationship. Reconciliation expresses more the positive side of justification, the new relation and the new humanity (as we shall see in 2 Corinthians 5) but

---

[27] See Rom 5.11 ('atonement' KJV, 'reconciliation' RSV).

[28] Cf. Eph 1.6-7.

[29] Both quotes from the KJV translation which reflects more closely the verbal form of the Greek.

as in justification, this is on the ground of the expiation wrought out in the death of Christ.

(ii) 2 Corinthians 5.14-21: 'God was in Christ reconciling the world to himself'

a) Here too the supreme act is God's. He alone reconciles the world to himself. Although reconciliation is pure act of God, it implies and requires personal response, 'be reconciled', v. 20. It is the part of humanity to receive what is freely offered in the proclamation of reconciliation.

b) Here it is made clear that reconciliation must be thought of in a dual tense. Basically, reconciliation is perfected. 'All this is from God, who through Christ reconciled us to himself', v. 18 - in Romans 5.10 that is likewise stated in the 'aorist' (past) tense.[30] But here Paul also speaks of reconciliation as continually operative. For though 'God was in Christ reconciling . . . and entrusting to us the message of reconciliation', v. 19 (past tense), that perfected reconciliation becomes a word or *logos* of reconciliation through which the perfected reconciliation becomes effective as it is ministered through the ministry, *diakonia*, of the church – and hence the 'be reconciled' of v. 20.

c) This perfected reconciliation involves a complete change in relationship with God and indeed a total change in the whole of our existence. All things become new, for old things have passed away. The result is Christian love, love to Christ and to all humanity, vv. 14-16. Paul does not speak of this as a process, but as completed fact in the finished work of Christ. What goes on is the word of reconciliation. As people receive the word, they enter into this totally new situation which has already been brought about by Christ and which is established once and for all.

d) As in Romans, reconciliation is closely bound up with justification – that is very clear in the Pauline use of *logizesthai*, reckon (which is in Romans 4 used ten times of justification) in v. 19 where Paul says, 'not *reckoning* (*logizomenos*) their transgressions'.[31] And here too, reconciliation like justification is on the ground of expiation, v. 21, 'For our sake he made him to be sin who knew no sin, so that in him we might become the righteousness of God' – that describes the expiatory content of reconciliation, which is substitutionary atonement. That is the

---

[30] Rom 5.10, 'while we were enemies we *were reconciled* (*katēllagēmen*) to God'.

[31] Torrance's rendering – cf. KJV 'not imputing' and RSV 'not counting'.

wondrous exchange at the very heart of the new relation with God. The same fact is expressed in vv. 14 and 15 in other words.

Katallagē, then, denotes the effected salvation which God has wrought by exchange when he took atonement on himself, provided it freely in his love and established a new relationship of peace with the world, so that it is no longer under his wrath, or called to measure up to his demands. The whole world is now faced with the offer of perfected reconciliation, a deed of pure love, and by that it is called to account. Now it is before the judgement seat of Christ himself that we must appear, for judgement is according to the deed of love in Christ.

(iii) Ephesians 2.13-16 and Colossians 1.19-22 – the use of apokatallassō

In these epistles, Paul does not use the word *katallassō* but a more radical and comprehensive compound, *apokatallassō*. The addition of 'apo' seems to have a dual significance. First it makes reconciliation an even stronger expression – it is thorough reconciliation. Second, it suggests powerfully that reconciliation is not just the setting up of a relation of peace that never existed before, but the restoration of a relationship of peace and love that had been destroyed. Thus in the action described by *apokatallassō* there is the closest relation between redemption and creation on the one hand, and the reaching out of reconciliation to all things, *ta panta*, on the other, to the eschatological *plērōma* or fullness. The whole universe comes under reconciliation, angels and all.

Here the absolute subject is God (Col 1.19-20) but because it is God acting in Christ, Christ is also spoken of as the subject of reconciliation. It is an act of pure grace, issuing in the totally new relation to God of all things (Col 1.20). Paul speaks of this in the aorist tense. It is a finished work (Col 1.22; Eph 2.16), resulting in the establishing of peace (Col 1.20; Eph 2.15-17) and the new creation (Eph 2.15). This completed reconciliation of the world to God entails within the world the reconciliation of all things to each other, such as Jews and Gentiles, things visible and invisible etc (Eph 1.10, 2.11-19f.; Col 1.15-20f.). Reconciliation described by *apokatallassō* carries with it the complete unity of all things in Christ in a vast cosmic peace.[32]

---

[32]   Col 1.20; cf. Stig Hanson, *The Unity of the Church in the New Testament*, p. 117ff.

2 The New Testament doctrine of reconciliation

We must now proceed to draw out the biblical teaching about reconciliation and unfold its full content.

(a) Reconciliation as the pure act of God's love

Justification we saw to be the complete fulfilment of the holy will of God, in which God approached mankind directly and personally, putting them in the right with God's own righteousness and truth, and through the expiation of their sin establishing them in that righteousness and truth, thus rectifying their sin-wasted life and restoring them to God as his dear children. From beginning to end, that was considered as the act of the righteousness of God, that is of God being God, being holy in relation to sinful humanity in such a way that he was both just himself and yet justified the ungodly.

Now when we come to consider what the New Testament has to say about reconciliation, we presuppose at its very heart justification through the atoning expiation which effected it. But here we think of the saving act as the complete fulfilment of God's love, in which he freely condescended to be humanity's God and saviour and to effect a restoration of alienated humanity to fellowship and peace with God, thus assuming the fallen creature into union with himself. Both justification and reconciliation involve that two-way relation, in which God acted toward man in such a way as to re-establish man's relation toward himself. In justification, that was an assertion of the holy will of God, and therefore the establishment of men and women within a relation of holiness with God. But in reconciliation we think of that as the pure condescension of God in which he abased himself, identified himself with sinners in their lostness and ruined condition under judgement in order to raise the creature up out of damnation and exalt them to share the life and love of God. Here we have the twofold act of God's pure love in which, while we were yet sinners,[33] he turned himself toward us in utter compassion, and then turned us toward himself in responsive love. Thus if justification stresses the fact that God entered into our human life and within our human condition fulfilled his righteous will, reconciliation stresses the fact that God came down to our estate in order to assume us into fellowship with himself, and to effect such a oneness between the sinner and God, that the sinner is exalted to share with God his own divine life.

---

[33] Rom 5.8,10.

In this first section we must seek to understand that as a pure act of divine love, in which God out of the sheer overflow of his love, without having to be propitiated, poured himself out in love for man. He stooped to save humanity in unconditional grace. He did not even wait for them to show themselves ready to repent. He came when we were yet rebels and sinners out of an absolute will to forgive, and bestow himself upon the sinner. He came therefore both to give himself *to* the sinner and to give himself *for* the sinner in such a way that he might freely and unconditionally give *himself* to the sinner. He came therefore providing himself the expiation in order to remove the obstacle between God and humanity and humanity and God, bearing himself the entire cost of restoring fellowship. Let us think what this means.

'God loved us even when he hated us'

It means in the first place, as Calvin put it, the incomprehensible fact that 'God loved us even when he hated us'.[34] 'God, who is perfect righteousness, cannot love the iniquity which he sees in all. All of us, therefore, have that within which deserves the hatred of God' but 'gratuitous love prompts him to receive us into favour . . . God the Father, by his love, prevents [goes before] and anticipates our reconciliation in Christ. Nay, it is because he first loves us, that he afterwards reconciles us to himself.'[35] Then Calvin quotes Augustine, 'The fact that we were reconciled through Christ's death must not be understood as if his Son reconciled us to him that he might now begin to love those whom he had hated. Rather, we have already been reconciled to him who loves us, with whom we were enemies of account of sin. The apostle will testify whether I am speaking the truth: "God shows his love for us in that while we were yet sinners Christ died for us."[36] Therefore, he loved us even when we practiced enmity toward him and committed wickedness. Thus in a marvellous and divine way he loved us even when he hated us.'[37]

What does this mean but that God out of pure love reconciled himself to humanity – that he drew near, propitiated himself, precipitated himself upon mankind in unconditional love, but did that in such a way as to find the means of expiation, bearing the cost of it in his love and so achieving his end not only in pouring out his love upon the sinner, but in gathering up the sinner again in the communion of his love?

---

[34]   See *Institute of the Christian Religion*, 2.16.4.

[35]   *Institute* 2.16.3 (Beveridge translation).

[36]   Rom 5.8.

[37]   *Institute* 2.16.4 (Battles translation).

The self-giving of God in love to humanity to take our cause upon himself

Now let us consider that act of divine love even more carefully. God's love is his unconditional self-giving to humanity, and therefore it is a giving of himself to humanity for humanity to receive. His love was an act upon humanity and an act to humanity, but withal an act for humanity, in both senses of the word 'for', on behalf of humanity and for the possession of humanity. But this self-giving of God to mankind was the giving to mankind of the holy and loving God, who as holy and loving is unalterably opposed to all that is not holy and not loving. God's self-giving is therefore God's judgement upon mankind, for it is the giving of a love that will not have what is against love, so that the very act of God's self-giving is an act of judgement upon the sin of mankind. But in the very heart of that judgement is the fact that God is opposed to human sin, and therefore he is opposed to human bondage in sin, and opposed to our sinful human refusal of the love of God. The self-giving of God in love to humanity is a self-giving which negates the very barrier of sin which prevents fellowship between humanity and God, and God and humanity. The judgement of sin is in order to remove that sin and its barrier to fellowship with God.

In other words, in pouring out his love upon man, God affirms man as his loved one, and therefore he negates human sin, but he negates human sin only in affirming man as the object of his unconditional love. His *Yes* to men and women contains a *No* to their sin, and his *No* to their sin is part of his unconditional act of love in which he comes to take their part against their sin. God ranges himself on the side of the sinner in opposition to their sin that he may deliver them from their bondage in sin and make them free for fellowship with God. God's love is his unconditional assertion that he is *for* man, on man's side. And therefore it is the love of God that makes humanity's lost and ruined cause God's own cause, so that God stoops to take their cause upon himself in order to emancipate men and women and reconcile them to himself.

The fulfilment of covenant mercy in gathering man into the embrace of divine love

Reconciliation is, then, the great positive enactment of the divine love. It is the fulfilment of the divine love in its out-pouring upon man and its completion in achieving the gathering up or assumption of man into the embrace of divine love. In order to do this the divine love provides out of itself the way of expiation and so of restoration to fellowship with God. We can put that in another way by using the language of the covenant. The out-pouring of God's love upon the sinner corresponds to the covenant will of God, 'I will be your God and Father'. The gratuitous assumption of humanity into fellowship with the divine love, corresponds to the covenant mercy, 'You are my children'. God thus turns himself to humanity, reconciles himself to humanity, in order to turn humanity to himself, in order to reconcile humanity to himself. That covenant will of mercy is fulfilled in the person and life and death and resurrection of Jesus Christ. 'I have given him for a covenant to the people'.[38] Jesus Christ is therefore the incarnate love of God, the incarnation of God's love to humanity, but such an incarnation of that love that it is translated into man, the man Jesus and is now also the love of man toward God. But that carries us on to the second point.

(b) Reconciliation is achieved and completed in the person of the incarnate Son

We saw earlier how justification is achieved and fulfilled in the person of Christ, who is himself the incarnate holy will of God and is yet identified with humanity in its sin under the judgement of that holy will, so that we may say that Jesus Christ is in himself the hypostatic union of the judge and the man judged. Therefore the infliction of the judgement by the judge upon the man judged takes place in the person of the judge himself, for in Christ Jesus the judge is one person with the man judged. Christ was thus God the judge, and yet the sin-bearer who bore our judgement and the penalty for our sin in his own life and death. Similarly, we must think of reconciliation as fulfilled in Christ. He is himself the God of the covenant which we have broken, but he became man by taking upon himself the humanity of the men and women who broke the covenant, and in himself he is not only the turning of God to humanity, but the turning of humanity to God. It is in his own life that Jesus Christ achieves that reconciliation, in which the love of God is poured out upon humanity, God's beloved child. And it is as that beloved child or Son that he lives his life in perfect oneness with God, so achieving the reconciliation of God to humanity, and of humanity to God, all within his own incarnate life and person.

Therefore, just as the New Testament can speak of Christ as our righteousness and as our sanctification, so it can speak of Christ as himself our propitiation, or our expiation in whom we are reconciled to God – Christ is set forth therefore as the *hilastērion* or as *hilasmos*,[39] himself the means through which we are forgiven. That is to

---

[38]   See Isaiah 42.6, 49.8.

say, it is within his own person and life, in his own death, and as Calvin insists, not simply in the passion of his body, but in his *soul*,[40] that reconciliation is wrought out through expiation of sin. Here then we have not only the reconciling of God to humanity and of humanity to God, but the working out of that reconciliation in the inner life and incarnate being of Christ, which is the deepest secret of reconciliation and atonement. (Compare here Paul's phrase about Christ 'justified in the Spirit'.[41])

(i) Reconciliation is the full outworking of the hypostatic union from birth to death

Here again we must say two things. In the first place, reconciliation is the full outworking of the hypostatic union. Reconciliation begins with the birth of Jesus when God and man are brought into real union and it is that real union carried throughout the conditions of our human life in its estrangement from God, in such a way as to restore our human life from its estrangement to fellowship with the Father. Thus the whole life and action of Christ from birth to death constitutes reconciliation. It is ultimately in the death of Christ when he plumbs the deepest depth of our estrangement, in our death, in his suffering the divine judgement upon our sin, that union between God and humanity, begun in the birth of Jesus, and carried throughout his human life, reaches its complete fulfilment. The hypostatic union is inserted into the abysmal chasm of divine judgement upon humanity, and in the heart of that divine judgement the union of God with humanity and humanity with God is established and maintained, and because it is maintained, it survives the ban of God's wrath.[42] This means the resurrection of man out of utter alienation where that alienation is made complete under

---

[39] Rom 3.25, *hilastērion*; 1 John 2.2, *hilasmos* – both translated 'expiation' RSV, 'propitiation' KJV.

[40] *Institute* 2.16.10.

[41] 1 Tim 3.16 KJV, RSV 'vindicated' (or justified), Gk *edikaiôthç en pneumati*.

[42] For Torrance it is important to see that the union between Father and Son, and the hypostatic union between the Son and our humanity remained unbroken even in judgement. It is because the oneness and the bonds of love between Father and Son in our humanity did not snap, but held firm even under the strain of final judgement, that the union begun at Bethlehem is maintained right through death on the cross and issues in the resurrection of Jesus from the dead. Cf. below chap. 7, section 1 (b), under the heading 'The resurrection is the holding firm of the hypostatic union through death and hell'.

the divine judgement, and therefore it is the triumphant restoration of man to fellowship and life with God. We have already studied this reconciliation in the incarnate life of the obedient servant-Son, but here we must think of it particularly in relation to the death of Christ, that is, as hypostatic union fully and finally achieved in Christ and carried through the very depth of our human separation from God and contradiction to God. As such, it is the love of God inserted into our sinful humanity, realising his loving purpose and refusing to be thwarted by the utmost antagonism of evil, so that he loved us to the very end, and emerged triumphant in the resurrection. That is the eternalising of reconciliation with humanity in the life and person of the resurrected Son.

(ii) Reconciliation is the fulfilment of God's assumption of our humanity

Now in the second place, we have to see reconciliation not only as the outworking of the hypostatic union, but as the ultimate fulfilment of God's assumption of our humanity in the incarnation. As we saw earlier, that assumption took the form of the divine condescension and abasement of the Son, when he came down and made himself one with us in our alienation – but that identification of himself with us in our sin, is already our assumption and exaltation to be brothers and sisters of Christ and in him to be sons and daughters of God. That assumption of our fearful and lost condition reaches its supreme point in the cross where the Son freely assumes our damnation and final judgement, freely assumes our God-forsakenness in the *Eli, Eli, lama sabachthani* of death on the cross under judgement. And so he achieves our assumption into oneness with himself, and because that assumption is maintained even in the hell into which the Son descended, it achieves its end in the resurrection of man out of hell and the exaltation of man in Christ to the right hand of God. All that took place *in Christ*, for in him our human nature in and with all its burden of guilt and judgement and corruption has already been assumed, and in such a way through Calvary and Easter that it is actually resurrected out of our estrangement and corruption and exalted to share the eternal life of God himself. That is the meaning of reconciliation, the restoration of men and women in Christ to fellowship with God, and even their exaltation to be partakers of the divine nature, so that they live for ever in the overflow of the eternal life and love of God the Father.

It is then *in the person of Jesus Christ himself, the mediator*, that our reconciliation has already taken place, and as such it remains as enduring and perfected reality available for all in him.

(c) Reconciliation as wonderful exchange

This reconciliation took place through a 'wondrous exchange' (as Calvin called it)[43] in which Christ took our place, that we might have his place. That is what the term 'reconciliation' means, an act of reconciliation effected on the basis of exchange. In the incarnation, the Son of God abased himself, substituted himself in our place, interposed himself between us and God the Father, taking all our shame and curse upon himself, not as a third person, but as one who is God himself, God against whom we had sinned and rebelled, and yet as he who is man identified to the utmost with man's estrangement and disobedience that he might really stand in humanity's place and work out in himself humanity's reconciliation.

In that he thus took our place of sin and shame and death, he freely gives us his place of holiness and glory and life, that we through his poverty might become rich,[44] that we through his being made sin and a curse for us, might be reconciled to God clothed with his righteousness and stand before God in his person.[45] He came in our name, that we in his name might have access to the presence of the Father and be restored to him as his children.

Christ's complete identification with us and intervention in our place

There are two intertwined elements here we must pause to consider, the identification of Christ with us, and his intervention in our place. He so identified himself with us in our sinful state that he met the full assault of our evil and took the full contradiction of our sin upon him, and so he entered also into the conflict between us and God and took that conflict upon himself, bearing it in his own life and heart in order to save us. Therefore he met the full opposition of our enmity to God, and the full opposition of God to our enmity and endured it with joy, refusing to let go of God for our sakes, and refusing to let go of us for God's sake. In laying hold of us as sinners, he judged our sin in himself and reconciled us to God, and in laying hold of God he received his judgement of us upon himself and offered our humanity in himself to the Father.

On the one hand, then, we must say that he abased himself to participate in our alienated life that we might participate in the life of the Son of God. He identified himself with us all in our guilty

---

[43]   *Institute* 4.17.2.

[44]   2 Cor 8.9.

[45]   See 2 Cor 5.21.

estrangement and distance from the Father, that we might be identified with him in his relations with the Father and in him the beloved Son draw near to God, the loving Father. On the other hand, we must say he took our place and did for us what we could not do. He penetrated into the abyss that divides us from God, stood in the gap between God's wrath and human guilt, and by enduring and offering as God and man all that was righteous and true, he destroyed the barrier and effected reconciliation between God and humanity. He was God, standing in our place and bearing the just judgement on our iniquity. He was also man, united with us in our humanity and offering to God in our place what we could not offer, a perfect offering of obedience, faithfulness, thankfulness and praise. He was very God, descending into the depth of our wickedness and laying hold of us in sheer love, and he was very man, receiving and laying hold of God by submitting to the divine judgement and receiving all the self-giving of God in his love which we could not receive and live.

Christ so one with God that what he did God did, and so one with us that what he did we did

In all that, Christ was on the one hand so one with God that what he did, God did, for he was none other than God himself acting thus in our humanity. And therefore there is no other God for us than this God, and no other action of God toward us than this action in which he stood in our place and acted on our behalf. On the other hand, he was so one with us that when he died we died,[46] for he did not die for himself but for us, and he did not die alone, but we died in him as those whom he had bound to himself inseparably by his incarnation. Therefore when he rose again we rose in him and with him,[47] and when he presented himself before the face of the Father, he presented us also before God,[48] so that we are already accepted of God in him once and for all.

Who can understand or plumb the depth of that 'wondrous exchange', that identification and substitution in which he who was rich for our sakes became poor that we through his poverty might become rich, in which he who knew no sin was made sin for us, and died the just for the unjust, that we might be made the righteousness of God in Him. And yet it is that very blessed exchange in identification that lies at the heart of reconciliation, for by it God in Christ has

---

[46]   2 Cor 5.14.

[47]   Eph 2.5-6; Col 3.1.

[48]   Cf. Heb 2.13.

overcome our alienation. In Jesus Christ the mediator,[49] the love of God has forged a union between humanity and God and God and humanity which is as eternal as the being of God himself, for in it God has staked his own divine being and pledged his own eternal life in creating immutably our eternal reconciliation.

(d) Reconciliation as peace with God

Reconciliation in and through the Lord Jesus Christ is the establishment of peace with God. It is the removal of all enmity between God and mankind, and the reinstating of humanity's personal relations with God in love and peace. This is expressed in the powerful New Testament thought that we have *peace with God through the blood of Christ.*[50] Peace is the state of untroubled and undisturbed well-being in the relations between man and God, but a state which is brought about only through the atoning sacrifice of Christ by which the enmity between man and God is removed. Christ is thus the peace-maker, who reconciles to God both those who are near, and those who are afar off.[51] This peace, as we shall see, is both objective, 'peace with God', and subjective, 'peace of God', but whether objective or subjective, it is established through the abolition of deep seated enmity.[52] There is an enmity between humanity and God which is on both sides of that relation, for the variance is on both sides. God is opposed to the sinner in their sin and the sinner is opposed to God, and that enmity must be done away if there is to be peace. Until the enmity is done away and peace is established, there cannot be truly personal relations between them. There are two elements here we must seek to elucidate.

(i) Peace through Christ's bearing the judgement and removing the righteous wrath of God's love

Reconciliation between God and man issues in peace when the wrath of God is removed. That wrath is not removed simply by setting it aside, for that would be the setting of the love of God aside, nay, the setting of God himself aside. The wrath of God can be removed only through the righteous infliction of the divine judgement against our

---

[49] 1 Tim 2.5.

[50] See for example, Col 1.20.

[51] Eph 2.14f.

[52] Col 1.21; Rom 5.10, cf. 8.7 & James 4.4.

sin. Or to use more juridical terms, the wrath of God is removed only when his righteous will has punished sin and judged it. Now it is important to see that we cannot talk here of his mercy as triumphing over his wrath, or of the victory of his love over his judgement – that would be to introduce a schizophrenia into God which is impossible, and to misunderstand the wrath of God and the meaning of the penalty or righteous infliction that is due to sin. Punishment and wrath are terms speaking of the wholly godly resistance of God to sin, the fact that the holy love of God excludes all that is not holy love. Sin must be judged, guilt must be expiated by its judgement and complete condemnation, else God is not God, and God is not love.

But as we have seen, God interposes *himself* between us and his judgement and takes the righteous infliction on sin upon himself, and so provides for its expiation in himself in the sacrifice of Christ. And the sacrifice is to be understood both in a passive and an active sense. That is, it is the sacrifice of Christ in which he offered himself as the lamb of God in a passive sense to suffer judgement in our place, and it is active in the sense that Christ stepped into our place and fulfilled God's holy will for us. We are not at the moment concerned with the latter which we have already discussed fully, but with the former, his passive obedience, in which through the shedding of his blood Christ offered himself in sacrifice, in amen to God's righteous judgement upon our sin, and so accepted our judgement or infliction in our place. In so doing he took into himself and upon himself the righteous wrath of the divine love and freed us from receiving the stroke of the divine condemnation which we could not have endured, for under it we could only have been destroyed.

The will of God's love fully fulfilled and the objective obstacle removed

Christ has thus paid our debt and because he has paid our debt we are freed from it and are emancipated from our burden. But because God has poured out his wrath and executed his final judgement upon our sin in the sacrifice and submission of Christ, he does not re-exact it from us, because he is faithful and just and because our debt and infliction has been fully paid in the sacrifice of his Son.

Who shall then lay anything to our charge?[53] Because of what Christ has done, God has nothing more to say to us in respect of our sin and guilt, for they are put away. It is Christ that died: God cannot and does not and will not go back upon the death of his dear Son, for there is perfect oneness between the Son and the Father and he accepts his

---

[53]   See Rom 8.31,33f.

sacrifice on our behalf as full satisfaction for our sin and guilt, a satisfaction which he accepts because it is offered by himself and borne by himself. Satisfaction means that God has fulfilled the will of his love in taking our judgement on himself and in bearing it in our stead. All that is summed up in the expression that 'through the blood of Christ we have peace with God'.[54] Nothing now stands in between us and holy God righteously calling for his condemnation and judgement. With the removal of the objective obstacle between mankind and God, that is, the double fact of the guilt of humanity and the wrath of God, the conditions for the reinstatement of personal relations of peace between humanity and God are established, and the fulfilment of reconciliation subjectively, as well as objectively, can take place. All we say about that at the moment is that the removal of the enmity means that personal relations, personal communion between God and man and man and God, are restored. Because God has removed the cause of his judgement, nothing can obstruct his love and fellowship. Because Christ has borne our punishment, that now stands behind us and we are free to enter God's love and fellowship.

(ii) The removal of ethical and legal distance by the fulfilment of judgement

But behind all this there is another basic element to be considered. So long as the relations between God and mankind are determined by the distance of ethical or legal relation, so long as God withholds final judgement upon humanity, the action of God upon man is primarily negative, that is of resistance to human rebellion, opposition to human sin, and therefore rejection and disinheritance. Even though God in his compassion and mercy withholds final judgement, nevertheless because God is God, the just and loving one, because he cannot ultimately withhold it, mankind is under the threat of damnation and final judgement. Therefore their own rebellious enmity to God is met by the threat of destruction, of final judgement, of utter rejection. But when in reconciliation God actually takes upon himself the sentence of rejection and bears it instead of mankind, then God takes all his own righteous enmity against sin and absorbs it in himself. As we have seen, that does not mean in the slightest degree a mitigation of the divine judgement, but the very reverse, the complete and entire fulfilment of the divine judgement – and therefore the vicarious act of God in the life and death of Christ is man's complete and total exposure as guilty and a complete and total judgement. The cross is the utter

---

[54] Cf. Rom 5.1,9; Col 1.20.

condemnation of men and women. But when God took that condemnation upon himself, then his action was entirely the positive action of his mercy and will to be on humanity's side, a positive action to accept humanity.

(1) God takes on himself his own rejection of humanity and directs to them only the positive act of acceptance

In the cross of Christ we have humanity's final rejection of God, and in that cross we have God's final rejection of humanity's sin. But in the cross we have behind it all the holy will of God to take upon himself human sin in rejecting God, and to take upon himself his own rejection of humanity, so that he makes the cross the most positive act of the divine love. The cross not only opposes the human will to isolate itself from God and so to reject God, but so takes that rejection, that sinful refusal by humanity upon himself, that God directs toward humanity the amazing act of assumption in which, in pure grace, he gathers men and women in spite of their awful wickedness into fellowship with himself and refuses to let them go.

The cross means that God does not let any positive decision to reject man fall upon man at all, for that positive act of rejection he takes entirely upon himself and directs toward humanity only the positive act of acceptance. Now this positive act of acceptance, of free forgiveness, of gratuitous justification, on the grounds of God's vicarious act and not in the slightest on the ground of human worth, is also the complete condemnation of humanity. It tells men and women that in themselves they have no worth, that they are not accepted at all for what they are in themselves, but are accepted only on the ground of the overflowing love of God poured out unstintingly upon them, and on the ground of the fact that God in his love chooses to take their judgement and rejection upon himself, in order that they may be gathered into the fellowship of the divine life. That if you like is the paradox of the cross: that the divine assumption of our judgement is our most complete judgement, and yet it is in no sense a rejection of humanity, but its very reverse, an entire acceptance of man for Christ's sake, in the blood of Christ.

(2) There is no positive act of rejection of any human being

Let us be clear what this means. It means negatively, that there is no positive act of rejection or judgement extended toward any human being, but only the act of acceptance. It is an act of pure, incredibly loving acceptance, through God's taking upon himself entirely our rejection. Therefore if a sinner is reprobated, if a sinner goes to hell, it is not because God rejected them, for God has only chosen to love them, and has only accepted them in Christ who died for them and on the cross consummated the divine act of love in accepting them and in taking their rejection upon himself. If anyone goes to hell they go to hell, only because, inconceivably, they refuse the positive act of the divine acceptance of them, and refuse to acknowledge that God has taken their rejection of him upon himself, so acknowledging that they deserved to be rejected. Thus we can say, to use the language of reprobation, 'The negative decision of reprobation is the reprobation only of the man who refuses the election of grace, who attempts to isolate himself from it.'[55]

(3) The very nature of the gospel is to bring salvation – 'reprobation is accidental'

The very nature of the gospel, as Calvin constantly expressed it, is to bring salvation, not destruction, and if anyone is reprobated that happens only accidentally *(accidentale)*[56] – how else can we put it? The positive action of God in accepting humanity and taking their rejection upon himself, is the action only of salvation and reconciliation. If therefore any person goes to hell, it is by downright refusal of the perfected work of reconciliation in which God in Christ has already chosen them in pure love and removed enmity between God and man entirely.

Now to get back to the point at which we began. What God has done in the cross for us is positive and fulfilled reconciliation, because in it God has removed the objective enmity between God and humanity, and directs to humanity only the positive act of his divine love and not at all his righteous judgement. It is also positive and fulfilled reconciliation because on the ground of that peace with God, God assumes man freely into fellowship with himself.

Because of the blood of Christ there is no positive decision of God to reject anyone, but only the gracious decision to accept them, and that decision has once and for all been enacted in the cross and resurrection so that nothing in heaven and earth can change it or undo it or reverse it. To reverse it would be to bring Christ back to the cross again, and to

---

[55] F.W. Camfield, *Reformation Old and New*, Lutterworth, London 1947, p. 76.

[56] Lat, *accidentale*, *Commentary on John*, Eng. trans. T.H.L. Parker, ed. T.F. and D.W. Torrance, Oliver and Boyd, Edinburgh 2 vols. 1959 & 1961, vol. 1 (John 1-10): 3.17 (p. 75-6), 9.39 (p. 254); vol. 2 (John 11-21): 12.40 (p. 47), 12.47 (p. 53), 20.23 (p. 208). Cf. T.F. Torrance, *The School of Faith*, James Clarke, London 1959, p. lxxviif.

deny the reality of what he has already done. *That decision is not altered if man refuses it, but if someone goes to hell, they go because they dash themselves in judgement against an unalterable positive act of divine reconciliation that offers to them only the divine love.*[57]

(e) *Reconciliation is objective and subjective*

We must now retrace our steps somewhat and try to understand reconciliation as an act which deals with a variance between God and humanity that is on both sides. If it were simply a matter of enmity on the part of humanity, then that would mean that it was entirely subjective and based on a misunderstanding of God which could be cleared up by a frank disclosure of the real attitude of God. But the plain truth is that in his holiness God is at variance with man, while the fact that he refuses to disown them or cast them off, and insists on holding on to them in spite of their enmity and sin, gives a fateful character to the relation between humanity and God, because it means that God is at variance with humanity in the essential inner relation which constitutes not only their very existence, but the centre of the human person. Though atonement and redemption involve the whole relation between man and God, and not simply something within an existing relation, it is upon this essential and root personal relation that the emphasis is laid in reconciliation.

Atonement must be worked into the mind and heart of man, defeating sin from within

Because sin has to do with the heart of man, with the roots of the human person, an objective atonement as act of God only upon man is not sufficient of itself if they are to be saved. It must be worked through the heart and mind of men and women, until they are brought to acquiesce in the divine judgement on sin and are restored in heart and mind to communion with God. So long as there is any resentment on the part of mankind against the righteousness of God's judgement on sin, which is itself an offence against the love of God, the controversy

---

[57]   For Torrance, faithfulness to the New Testament makes a doctrine of universalism, that all go to heaven, impossible (as it does also a doctrine of limited atonement, that Christ died only for some): see the chapter 'Preaching Jesus Christ', T.F. Torrance, *A Passion for Christ*, Handsel Press, Edinburgh (and PLC Publications, Lenoir) 1999, esp. p. 31 (repr. with a minor addition from pp. 23-30 of T.F. Torrance, *Preaching Christ Today*, Handsel Press, Musselburgh 1994).

between God and mankind cannot be closed. There must be such a reconciliation that God makes himself understood in the midst of it, for that is part of God's reconciling work in defeating sin from within man.

God's personal forgiveness and creation of joint knowing between man and himself

Therefore, God has wrought reconciliation in such a way as to break down the difference in mind and heart between humanity and God, and make understanding (knowing-together, con-science or *syn-eidçsis, con-scientia*[58]) a reality between them, that is, in such a way as to win the human heart to himself. And so God came in unconditional love to pardon and forgive, providing at cost only to himself the means of restoring fellowship, dealing himself with human sin from within human life and dealing with it unconditionally in direct personal action. Because sin is a perversion of a personal relationship, it can be dealt with only personally. A prisoner may be remitted a penalty by the state or made to pay for it in full on grounds that the state may consider just, but whether the prisoner is released or not, they are not really forgiven unless the offended party personally does that. Sin is a personal matter and can be dealt with only personally. Sin against God is supremely personal, and can be forgiven only by a personal act on the part of God which establishes full personal fellowship with man in understanding and confidence and peace and love.

The reconciliation achieved in the person of Christ is at once objective and subjective

If sin is qualified as sin by the personal reaction of God against it, then sin is an objective obstacle that must be taken away. Only God can do that, and only God can remove his wrath from mankind and in that sense reconcile himself to man, and that is what he does in the blood of Christ. But if sin is an act of man going down to the roots of human nature and introducing into the very relation with God which constitutes the human person, a contradiction resulting inevitably in its disintegration (although God in his mercy continues to hold humanity in life), then it is in the inner depth of their personal being that humanity must be reconciled to God and we must be healed of our enmity and contradiction to God. Such a double reconciliation, at once objective and subjective, was achieved in the person and work of Christ, in his incarnation, death, and resurrection. In him whose person

---

[58]   *Suneidēsis* Gk, *conscientia* Lat, literally *with-knowing*, ie. knowing together.

and work are one, we have not only the removal objectively of the obstacle to oneness of mind and will and being between God and humanity, but the removal of it also subjectively from within our human nature and understanding and life. That was achieved in the perfect obedience and love of the Son to the Father, so that Jesus Christ is *himself* our reconciliation objectively and subjectively fulfilled, himself the reconciliation by whom, in whom and through whom we are restored to holy and loving communion with God our heavenly Father.

Now there are several elements here we must single out for fuller examination and discussion.

(i) The restoration of the human mind to truth with God

The breach between man and God which Christ came to heal is an existential breach,[59] an existential relation between man and God which has been so radically altered that mankind has fallen from true humanity, from true human existence. In heart and mind, sinful humanity is no longer positively related to the immediate presence of God, and such relation as God does maintain with humanity, while holding them in existence, acts negatively or critically upon them because of their sin. And so sin which reaches down through the human mind to the roots of human being means a life-severance from God, an existential severance from the truth of God, which, as we have already seen, is truth in the form of personal being.

The breach between humanity's idea of God and the truth of God – the grasping of a lie

Now this enmity of humanity to God brings about a breach between humanity's idea of God and the truth of God or the reality of God, the actual being of God, so that the idea of God which sinful human beings on their part imagine to be the truth, is not substantiated by the reality of God. This idea cannot rest in mid-air, so to speak, and so it becomes attached to such reality as human beings do know, to the world, or to themselves, so that when the mind of the sinner tries to grasp the truth of God, what it does get is a creature, and not the reality of the creator. It grasps a lie, or as Paul said, it holds down the truth in unrighteousness.[60] Here the inner direction of the human mind, as Paul expressed it, is alienated from God: it is turned inward upon the self,

---

59   *Existential*, concerning existence, i.e. a breach in the very nature or roots of human existence as it is in relation to God.

60   See Rom 1.18, (*tēn alētheian en adikia katechontōn*) – cf. the KJV 'hold the truth in unrighteousness'.

so that human beings' idea of God becomes in the most subtle ways the secret deification of themselves, just as the inner direction of their heart is turned in upon themselves in selfishness and their love for others is ultimately a form of their self-love.

The renewal of the human mind from within and below through the incarnation

Here therefore, because the heart and mind of man were turned inward and downward by sin, God became incarnate in order to reconcile man to himself, became man, as Athanasius argued so potently, so as to get at the heart and mind of man from below and from within, and from there to work out reconciliation with God. It was only by such an incarnation that God could get to grips, so to speak, with human understanding, and restore humanity to the original relation, of likeness to God.[61] For some of the Greek Fathers, the renewal of the mind played too predominating a part in our restoration, which tended to thrust the objective question of guilt into the background, but it was right to see it to be an essential part of atoning reconciliation. Reconciliation, however, is not just the clearing up of a misunderstanding, but the eliminating of a lie that has its roots in our nature as fallen and as perverted personal being. Hence the incarnation entailed a physical or ontological union, as well as a Logos-union with man (that is, a union with man in being as well as in word and mind) as the means of reconciliation to God.

(ii) Reconciliation involves subjective as well as objective union with God – 'noetic' and 'ontic' union

The objective union we have already discussed as the insertion of reconciliation in and through the hypostatic union into humanity, into time-relations, into history, but now we must see that to be an insertion into the personal life and understanding of man in Jesus Christ. In other words, we are concerned here with the *enhypostatic* aspect of reconciliation.[62] As we saw earlier, the solidarity of the incarnate Son rests not only upon the assumption of our humanity into oneness with

---

[61] Athanasius, *On the Incarnation of the Word*, §13-16, various editions, e.g. *Nicene and Post-Nicene Fathers*, vol. 4, 'Athanasius', Eerdmans repr, Grand Rapids 1971, pp. 43-45.

[62] The aspect that involves and means the full reality of the personal humanity of Jesus *in* the *person* (*en-hypostasis*) of the eternal Son, and therefore the creation and full reality of our humanity as persons in relation to his person.

himself, but on the interpenetration of Jesus into the lives of people, of men and women through his personal relations, in which he entwined himself more and more with them in their lives, burdens, sins and weaknesses, all in the most acutely personal fashion that led directly to the crucifixion. In Christ, the gulf that separates God from man is bridged not only by the entry of the Son into our human life, and by the obedience to the Father that the Son renders in that life, but by a life in which he personally through compassion and revelation brought his relations with sinners to their completion and then acted for them as their mediator before God. In Christ, then, the gulf between God and humanity, and humanity and God, is so bridged that the bridge enters into the human heart and mind and there is consummated in man's personal life, a union with God that is wrought out throughout the whole historical life of Jesus.

The personal union achieved in the reconciling work of Christ in life and death was then *noetic*[63] as well as *ontic*:[64] it was carried through his conscious personal relations as well as his union in being with God. It is upon the *ontic* relation and within it, that is within the hypostatic union, that the *noetic* or 'knowing' relation has its place. It is this *noetic* relation in personal union that we have now to consider.

The 'noetic' relation between God and man in Christ was twofold

The *noetic* relation was necessarily twofold, for it was the divine Logos uniting himself with our humanity and thus revealing himself within our humanity, but it was also the Logos enabling our humanity to receive his revelation personally, in love and faith and understanding. On the one hand, then, we have to think of this as the condescension of the Word, to enter into our humanity and within our humanity to accommodate himself to us in reconciling revelation. Thus the eternal Word or Son of God veiled his effulgence of glory that our weak eyes might behold him in the meek and lowly Jesus, and in communion with him be raised from seeing him in the form of a servant to seeing him in the glory of the one whose name is above every name. As his poverty means that he stooped down to enter our flesh, that he brought divine omnipotence within the compass of our littleness, frailty and weakness, that he the holy one entered our bondage and curse under the law, so it means that the eternal Word and truth of God entered into the darkness of our ignorance in order to redeem us from the

---

63   To do with the mind or intellect, and therefore involving 'knowing', from the Gk *nous* mind or *noein* to think.

64   To do with 'being', from the Gk *on, ontos*, forms of the verb 'to be'.

power of darkness and ignorance, in order to deliver us from untruth and to make us free for and in the truth of God.

On the other hand, the obverse of this condescension and accommodation on the part of the Word is the teaching of Jesus in which he sought to communicate the truth to people, to men and women as they were able to hear it and to initiate them into the holy mysteries of the kingdom of God. Thus the faithfulness of Jesus to the word of the Father in hearing and receiving it within our frail humanity, and his faithfulness in teaching it and imparting it to those whom he had made his fellows in human weakness, form an essential part of his reconciling work in reinstating mankind in fellowship and communion with the living and true God. The union between man and God in Christ was therefore not just a union in being, else indeed there had been no cross, and the atonement had already been accomplished fully and entirely in the birth of Jesus, in the bare assumption of our human nature into oneness with the Son of God. But of course neither was it a union in Word only apart from the incarnation. It was a union of being through the incarnation in which the Word became flesh, but that union with human being was worked out through the whole personal life and growth of man, worked through the growth of Jesus from infancy to adulthood. It was worked through the mind of man alienated and estranged from God, worked through the whole range of our dark enmity and misunderstanding, even to the ultimate point of God-forsakenness on the cross, where there is on the part of Jesus no misunderstanding and resentment, but entire confidence and trust in the heavenly Father. 'Father, into thy hands I commit my spirit'.[65] (Contrast the view of Albert Schweitzer that Jesus died on the cross with a despairing cry!).

The realising of oneness of mind and heart between man and God in the life of Jesus

Here then reconciliation in the life and death of Jesus was the realising of oneness of mind and heart, of perfect agreement and conformity in faith and love, between man and God, and an insertion of that into the midst of our perverted attitude of heart and mind toward God as well as toward our fellow human beings. That is why the cross represents the culminating point of our reconciliation both objectively and subjectively. It was the *truth of God* asserting itself, or rather himself, uncompromisingly in the midst of human error and sin, pushing the

---

[65]   Luke 23.46; Psalm 31.5.

antipathy of human error and sin to its extreme point where it was exposed and condemned and vanquished. And the cross was at the same time the final act whereby humanity was put in the right and in the truth with God, subjectively as well as objectively.

What we have to try to understand here is that the cross was such an act of reconciliation that through it the truth of God in the form of personal being broke into the ultimate stronghold of human life in its self-isolation from God, in its rejection of God, and in its wilful misunderstanding of him. It restored man to union with God in knowing as well as being, and was the culminating means in the whole movement in the incarnation of healing the breach in human life and understanding between knowing and being.

The hypostatic union brought to fulfilment in the final oneness on the cross

It was because the inner attitude of man to God which is central to the human person had become perverted, that the incarnation meant the invasion of the Word into that perverted inner attitude of our human being in order to heal and straighten it out into perfect obedience toward God the Father. And because perversion of mankind's inner attitude receives objective qualification in the opposition of God to it, the objectivity of that obstacle between God and humanity had to be removed by objective deed, ontological action. But because both are personal realities, the act of reconciliation meant the achievement of oneness of mind between God and humanity in the personal realm, a oneness maintained throughout the whole of the personal life of Jesus. Only when that was carried through to the end was the hypostatic union itself brought to its fulfilment in the personal relations of man to God in Christ. Thus we can say that reconciliation was achieved by the perfect obedience of Christ to the Father in the midst of human sin and guilt, and in the perfect submission of Christ to the Father's will in judgement on our sin and guilt.

From first to last, that was the Word of God in the flesh being utterly true to himself. It was the truth of God asserting himself in the form of personal being in the midst of our disobedient humanity and in the teeth of the enmity of sin. It was the mind of God realising its loving purpose and refusing to be thwarted even by the full antagonism of evil. But on the other hand, it was man in Jesus Christ faithfully obedient to that Word, receiving it and appropriating it and living by it, in utter dependence and trust and confidence and understanding and love. The movement of divine love in assuming humanity into oneness with God is thus met and creatively integrated with a corresponding movement of humanity in yielding to the divine love and accepting the divine grace, in full agreement and obedience to the divine truth. In that double movement in Christ, objective and subjective reconciliation is completed and inserted as a finished reality into the midst of our human existence, and man is restored to the image and likeness of God, in perfect communion with him.

(iii) A comparison with Socrates: Jesus died to achieve union between truth and being

In order to understand something of what this involves, it may help to draw a contrast between the death of Christ and the death of Socrates. Socrates sacrificed himself for the truth, consistent to the last in his view of the truth as separate from physical existence, truth as abstraction from the reality of contingent human being. Death was the natural and logical conclusion of truth as abstraction from life, and so he died for the truth but without any sense of responsibility either for his own being or for that of his wife and friends. It was because truth for him was quite discontinuous with human existence, and indeed with being as such, that he went willingly to death when he might have avoided it. Christ sacrificed himself for the truth for the opposite reason, in order to achieve union between truth and reality, between truth and being. It was in the cross that he and his teaching fully became one in that respect, for the gospel was not in parable only, but in deed. It was by the cross therefore that he became to us truth in the form of being, word of forgiveness that is at the same time actual deed, reconciliation that is identical with our human life.

The establishment of the human mind on the truth of God and the humanising of man

By the healing of the ultimate discontinuity between human life and God, Jesus healed also the chasm between human beings and their own true reality in God, transcending it in a new relation of understanding characterised by at-one-ment in *mind and being* with the truth and reality of God, so that this truth could be grasped by humanity without being abstracted from the reality or the being of God, and therefore without being changed into a lie. Christ died that he might overcome the last abstraction of man from God, and so interpenetrate human being with the truth that men and women might become real both in relation to their own deepest existence in the Word of God and in relation to the existence to which they belong. In other words, reconciliation involved the healing of the breach in the existential relation of mankind to God, the breach or contradiction upon which our sinful and hypocritical human personality was shaped. By the cross man becomes real for the first time, because in

Christ, human existence attains its proper reality in God. The cross is the point at which the dehumanisation of humanity by sin and sin's isolation of humanity is effectively overcome, and the means by which the impersonalisation in human thought and practice is broken down, because here we are set in a new and acutely personal relationship to God, that is, reconciled to God in Jesus Christ.

(f) Reconciliation means 'Immanuel', God with us

We may now return to the point of the previous section, that reconciliation means the establishment of relations of peace between humanity and God. Objectively, that means the peace *with* God which we have through the blood of Christ, but subjectively it also means the peace *of* God which we have in ourselves, in our minds and souls, and in all our relations with the world and with others, as a result of that objective peace with God through Christ. Men and women who are at dispeace with God, are also at cross-purposes with their own existence, and with their fellows and indeed with the world, so that in their deepest existence they are characterised by dispeace and therefore by tension and anxiety. But all that ultimately results from the fundamental fact that they are alienated from God and are at enmity to God in their being and knowing,[66] while because they are estranged from their true being in God, and because their knowing is alienated from its true object in the truth of God,[67] their own human being and knowing are at variance.

If reconciliation is to take place, it must therefore be not only objective, in the removal of the objective obstacle between humanity and God, but be so subjective that it attains its end within the being and knowing of men and women, so that their true being and true knowing are wedded together again in the truth - so that they know the truth and the truth makes them free.[68] Now that reconciliation has been fully accomplished and actualised objectively and subjectively in Jesus Christ, for in him God has turned himself in mercy and reconciliation toward man, and turned man in reconciliation toward himself. It is only *in Christ*, therefore, that truth and being are wholly one for humanity, for in Christ, reconciliation encounters humanity as truth in the form of personal being, and therefore only in knowing Christ are human knowing and being reconciled to one another, so that we are at peace in ourselves, with our own existence.

---

66   Col 1.21.
67   Cf. Rom 1.21; John 17.3.
68   John 8.32.

(i) Reconciliation is not automatic but always personal in its encounter with us

This reconciliation which is objectively and subjectively complete in Christ, and is identical with the living being and presence of Christ, is objective to us, and so encounters us *personally*, that is as other than us asking of us personal relations with it. This reconciliation is truth in the form of personal being and therefore we can only know it and relate ourselves to it personally, so that we cannot in any sense think of reconciliation as automatically effective in its continued operation, but quite the reverse. This is not the place to discuss personal relations with this truth, but this much must be said here. This fulfilled reconciliation encounters me telling me that I am already reconciled to God in Christ, already died for, redeemed and forgiven. It tells me that already the great positive decision of God's reconciling love in my favour has been taken, and it can no more be undone than Jesus Christ can be undone, than the incarnation can be reversed or obliterated, or the cross made as if it had never taken place. Reconciliation tells me therefore that my life has already been set upon the new basis of God's grace, and that I am implicated in it and involved in it for the sole reason that I am a sinner. It was sinners that Christ Jesus came to live and die for, sinners that he came to reconcile to the Father, and the very fact that I am a sinner is, so to say, my title and right to that reconciliation, nay the indication that I am already included in the finished work and already part of Christ, for it was my nature, my humanity, my flesh of sin, that he assumed and made one with himself in his one person.

(ii) God with us means we with God, our adoption into the communion of the divine life

Now let us express that otherwise. What we have in Christ is none other than *Immanuel*, God with us[69], but because that is God with us, in our being, our very bones and flesh and blood, it also means we with God. If we with God is not true, then God with us is not true. *God with us* means that God almighty insists on sharing his divine life with us, on binding himself up with us in the same bundle of existence and being and life, so that we may share with him his divine life. That has been once and for all consummated in Jesus Christ, so that God has for

---

[69] Matt 1.23, '". . . a virgin shall conceive and bear a son, and his name shall be called Emmanuel" (which means God with us)', a quote from Isaiah 7.14 where the Hebrew *Emmanu El* (or *Immanu El*) means literally 'with us – God'.

ever and ever committed himself to us and will no more abandon us than he will abandon himself in Jesus Christ. That fact constitutes the great *palingenesia*,[70] the great change and renewal of all things, the turning point in all creation, in which God has once and for ever bound himself up with his creatures in a reconciliation that is unbreakable and irreversible.

The assurance of God with us – the dawning already of the kingdom and its fellowship

Now that God in Christ Jesus is actually one of us and one with us, everything else is assured. If God is for us and with us, nothing can prevail against us, for in Jesus Christ God has given us everything, and therefore everything freely flows to us out of that incarnation and reconciliation. But this *God with us* means *we with God*. It means that we are already taken up and assumed into fellowship with God, already grafted into the communion of the divine life, and therefore that we are already on the other side of death and judgement, of corruption and hell, already on the side of the resurrection, on the side where God is for us and not against us, that is, within and not without the sphere of the divine love and fellowship. Thus our godlessness and opposition and hostility are removed and replaced by a perfect fellowship with God, for in that fellowship the kingdom of God has already come on earth, and the new day of the resurrection, the eternal day of God's peace, has already dawned.

Because God has thus already united himself to us in the life and death and resurrection of Christ, we can understand the basis of all faith and love to God, for faith and love toward God are grounded upon the solid and eternal basis of what his eternal and incarnate love has accomplished in reconciliation and union with us, but we cannot understand how anyone can fall out of this realm of the divine love. Calvin puts these two points or questions in this way. On the one hand he says, 'we have confidence that we are the children of God, because he, who is the Son of God by nature, hath provided himself a body from our body, flesh from our flesh, bones of our bones, that he might be the same with us.'[71] On the other hand, 'The ungodly, by means of their unbelief, break off and dissolve that relationship of the flesh by

---

[70]   Literally 'rebirth' from the Gk *palin* (again) and *genesis* (birth), hence regeneration, new birth, renewal, Matt 19.28 ('regeneration' KJV, 'new world' RSV); Titus 3.5 ('regeneration' KJV, RSV).

[71]   *Institute* 2.12.2, Allen translation.

which he has allied himself to us, and thus render themselves utter strangers to him by their own fault.'[72]

(g) Reconciliation is cosmic

We must now glance at an aspect of reconciliation which overlaps with redemption and the doctrine of the Spirit. This aspect depends on the nature of the union effected in reconciliation, which we have described as hypostatic union and personal union. There are correspondingly two main elements here we have to note.

(i) The whole creation is involved in reconciliation – a cosmic peace

Because God has become man in Christ, has for ever bound himself up in existence and life with his creation, the whole of creation is involved in reconciliation. No change for the creation could be more momentous than that the creator himself should become a creature, should condescend to enter into it from within and share its created existence and so redeem it. The New Testament thus envisages a *cosmic peace* as the effect of the reconciliation, for all things are involved, and Christ is made the head of all things and in him all things are gathered up being reconciled to God the creator through the cross.[73] Here then we must think of reconciliation as the axis of the divine love thrust through our estranged world which gathers it up into oneness with the divine purpose of love and makes all things revolve round Christ and his cross – literally all things, visible and invisible, things animate and things inanimate, the whole of creation, heaven and earth, are involved in this reconciliation. It is in that reconciled universe that we have our new being in Christ.

(ii) Reconciliation is identical with the living person of Christ

Although the range of reconciliation stretches out in that vast cosmic sweep so that it is as wide as creation, yet at its heart, reconciliation is identical with the living person of Christ, *Immanuel*, God and man in one person. Thus reconciliation once and for all completed lives on and is identical with the personal being and presence of the mediator and surety, the reconciler. It is because reconciliation is identical with the person of Christ, that reconciliation continues to be effective and

---

[72] *Commentary on Psalm 22.22*, Calvin Translation Society 1843, Eerdmans repr., Grand Rapids 1948, p. 379.

[73] Col 1.15-20; Eph 1.10.

operative through the personal presence of Christ and takes the field as communion, as *koinōnia*. The full unfolding of that takes us into the doctrine of the Spirit and the presence of Christ through the Spirit in his church and in the world, but at this point let us note but one thing. Christ is reconciliation *in himself*, but he is that as the Son of God once and for all incarnate in our human and historical existence, so that reconciliation as personal being and as operative through *koinōnia* or communion cannot be divested of historical character or of the time relations which he has assumed in the very work of reconciliation. Hence we must think of the reconciling work of God in the cross, not only as once and for all completed and effected, but as travelling within and through our historical existence, as it were, as continually operative in reconciling intervention within history and all the affairs of humanity, and in the whole cosmos – *Immanuel*, God almighty with us in the midst of history, bearing all its sin and shame in his holy love, for he has already gathered it up upon himself.

The cross and its reconciliation are the ultimate secret of human history

And so we must think of the cross and its reconciliation as the deepest secret and the ultimate secret of all that happens in human history, for it is in and through the cross that now all things are made to cohere and to work together in God's cosmic purpose of reconciliation. Thus the supreme act of the divine judgement in the cross lives on in the person of Christ, the same yesterday, today and for ever,[74] and remains an abiding force determining all history and every crisis in human affairs falls under its action and reflects its meaning - but in the nature of the case, that is to be understood not with observation, but eschatologically, that is apocalyptically. That is what we glimpse in the book of the revelation of Jesus Christ,[75] in which the apocalyptic vision is all focussed ultimately upon the enthroned lamb, and all history and the whole universe is seen as coming under his sovereignty and as yielding at last to the victory of his cross.

Laus Deo – thanks be to God.

---

[74] Heb 13.8.

[75] Rev 1.1, 'The revelation, *apokalupsis*, of Jesus Christ'. See further the author's sermons on Revelation, T.F. Torrance, *Apocalypse Today*, James Clarke, London 1960 – Torrance once commented that prior to preaching the sermons he had read through the book of Revelation each day for twenty-one days in order to immerse himself in it and see it as a whole.

Chapter Six

ATONEMENT AS REDEMPTION

Redemption is used in the New Testament in a general comprehensive sense to speak of the great act of our salvation through justification, expiation and reconciliation in Christ. We have already considered that in the light of the threefold Hebrew root that lies behind it and the three essential aspects of redemption they indicate. But redemption has also a more particular sense in the New Testament, one in which it speaks of God's saving act in Christ as reaching out from grace, *charis*, to glory, *doxa*.[1] That is, here in redemption it is the eschatological and teleological[2] perspective of atonement that is prominent. Atonement is here spoken of as the act of God reaching out to the consummation of his redeeming purposes in the new creation. It is the term which expresses the act of God in bringing justification and reconciliation to their final end or *telos*, and relates the temporal acts of God in the historical Jesus to the eternal reality and fullness of salvation. In other words, by redemption the New Testament tells us that *glorification* is an essential part of our salvation.

The meaning of 'redeem', 'redemption'

We are not going to go over all the Old Testament ground again, but look at the various New Testament terms and their specific meanings.

Lutron, *ransom:* lutrousthai, *redeem*[3]

The basic word is *lutron* which describes the instrument of redemption, the price of our release or emancipation. It is used in profane Greek

---

[1]   Cf. Luke 24.21,26: *lutrousthai*, redeem (v. 21), *doxa*, glory (v. 26).

[2]   Eschatological (or eschatology) from the Gk *eschata* (the last things) and teleological (or teleology) from the Gk *telos* (end) both refer to events at the end of time and history, but in eschatology the emphasis is on the invasion of God into history throwing it into crisis and creating the last events, while in teleology the emphasis is on history reaching forward to its goal at the end of time.

[3]   On *lutron, lutrousthai, luō, apolutrōsis* and their cognates, see further the articles by Procksch and Büchsel in Kittel, *Theological Dictionary of the New Testament*, vol. 4, Eng. trans. Eerdmans, Grand Rapids 1967, pp. 328-356.

for the sum paid for the manumission of a slave, or the redemption of a pledge, or for the release of a prisoner of war, and so comes to mean ransom, compensation, atonement, or means or cost of expiation with reference to the intended result, liberty. For the use of *lutron* in the bible see Mark, the son of man has come 'to give his life as a *ransom* for many',[4] and comments on it in Timothy and Titus.[5]

For the biblical use of words derived from *lutron*, see especially Psalm 49, 'None of them can by any means *redeem* (*lutroutai, lutrōsetai*) his brother nor give to God a *ransom* (*exilasma*) for him; for the *redemption* (*lutrōseōs*) of their soul is precious, and it ceases for ever.'[6] In the New Testament the verb formed from *lutron* (*lutroō*) is found only in the middle voice or in the passive form of the verb. 'But we had hoped that he was the one to redeem (*lutrousthai*) Israel'.[7] Here the word refers to messianic eschatological redemption, which Jesus speaks of as accomplished through his passion. In Titus we have, 'our great God and Saviour Jesus Christ, who gave himself for us to redeem (*lutrōsetai*) us from all iniquity and to purify (*katharisē*) for himself a people of his own (*laon periousion*)',[8] and in Peter, 'You know that you were ransomed (*elutrōthēte*) from the futile ways inherited from your fathers, not with perishable things such as silver and gold, but with the precious blood of Christ, like that of a lamb without blemish or spot.'[9] Compare also Isaiah, 'You were sold for nothing, and you shall be redeemed (*lutrōthēsesthe*) without money.'[10] Here redemption is thought of as carried out through an act of expiation offered to God, and it is a redemption at once out of the bondage of earthly tradition and out of guilt.

Luō, *destroy, release*

The basic verb in Greek is *luō* which means to destroy, set at nought, loosen, release. Thus the word is used in two ways.

1) It is used of breaking a commandment, breaking the sabbath, breaking the scripture, or of breaking down the middle wall or

---

4   Mark 10.45 (Matt 20.28).

5   1 Tim 2.6 (*antilutron*); Tit 2.14 (*lutrōsetai*).

6   Psalm 49.7f. See the LXX, Psalm 48.8-9, for this version of the verse. Cf. Mark 8.37, 10.45; (Matt 16.26, 20.28).

7   Luke 24.21 (middle voice).

8   Titus 2.13-14. Cf. Psalm 130.8 (LXX 129.8, *lutrōsetai*); Exod 19.5 & Deut 14.2 (*laos(n) periousios(n)*; Ezek 37.23 (*kathariō*).

9   1 Pet 1.18-19 (passive).

10   Isaiah 52.3.

partition.[11] A compound, *kataluō*, is used of destroying the temple or the body.[12]

2) It is also used of loosing, from sins for example, as the opposite of binding.[13] We are loosed from our sins,[14] which is the meaning and purpose of redemption,[15] and it is used of the resurrection of Christ Jesus whom God loosed from the pains of death,[16] or of breaking seals and opening a scroll.[17]

These two senses of *luō* are parallel to the twofold dissolve and absolve in Latin and English. Both senses are combined in a passage such as 1 John 3.[18] As used in the New Testament, *luō* involves both the notion of the destruction of evil and liberation from evil. That is precisely what is meant by redemption, which is the work of the Son of God destroying the works of the devil and loosing us from our sins through his blood so as to make us a kingdom of priests unto God.[19]

Lutrōsis, apolutrōsetai, *redemption*

Lutrōsis is found three times in the New Testament[20] where it refers to the twofold deliverance out of oppression and from guilt and its punishment, the deliverance being accomplished through expiation in the sacrifice of Christ, but the eschatological perspective is prominent. *Apolutrōsis* is used with a meaning similar to that found in the cognate expressions we have been examining, but it gathers them all up, with special emphasis upon Christ himself as the agent and content of redemption.

It is significant that the verb *apolutroun* does not occur in the New Testament, while there are highly significant uses of *apolutrōsis*, suggesting that the aspect of atonement called redemption in the New Testament emphasises not the single deed but the far reaching effect of atonement. It does presuppose the great redeeming deed of God in the historical Christ once and for all, but it looks to the full consequences

---

[11] Matt 5.19; John 5.18; John 10.35; Eph 2.14.

[12] Mark 14.58; 2 Cor 5.1, etc.

[13] Matt 16.19, 18.18.

[14] Rev 1.5.

[15] Cf. Exod 6.6-7 (*lutrōsomai*), 19.6.

[16] Acts 2.24.

[17] Rev 5.2.

[18] 1 John 3.8.

[19] 1 John 3.8; Rev 1.5-6; cf. 1 Peter 2.9.

[20] Luke 1.68, 2.38; Heb 9.12.

of that. We have already seen that the New Testament speaks of justification and reconciliation as the completed and finished work of Christ, and that aorist and perfect tenses are used to do that. The act of atonement is complete and final. Looked at from the side of God, the whole work of salvation is accomplished in the Son, but looked at from the human side, from the side of sinners in this fallen world, it is not seen to be completed and fulfilled as yet, not in such a way that the perfect and finished work of reconciliation is fully actualised in us, in our estranged world.

Redemption is the word the New Testament uses to speak of atonement in which God's act, from the point of view of revelation, is still outstanding or future, still to be fully and finally revealed or consummated. We noted in Romans 5[21] that Paul spoke of us as having been justified and having been reconciled, and then added that being justified much more shall we be saved (*sōthēsometha*). The future reference of salvation (*sōtēria*) is prominent in redemption.[22] Our full state of blessedness, or recreation, or liberty, is yet to be revealed with respect to human sight and creation. We still wait for the redemption of the body, the final manifestation of the liberty or glory which awaits the sons and daughters of God who have been justified and reconciled already in the blood of Christ. Redemption tells us that our world is already reconciled and redeemed, so that it is no longer the devil's world, but God's world, Christ's world. But 'we do not yet *see* all things put under his feet'.[23] The church still lives under the cross, as the church militant, and is not yet in the *regnum gloriae*, kingdom of glory. But we are already redeemed for that kingdom and are already sealed for that glorification. The New Testament expresses that by employing the word *apolutrōsis* which by its Greek form stresses the state of redemption as seen from the side of the redeemed.

Apolutrōsis *and* kipper, goel, padah

As we saw earlier,[24] *apolutrōsis* has behind it the threefold Hebrew root, *padah, kipper* and *gaal*.[25] Although *apolutrōsis* is used with these

---

[21]   Rom 5.9-10.

[22]   See the use of *apolutrōsis* in Luke 21.28; Rom 8.23; Eph 4.30; Heb 11.35; and of *sōtēria* in 1 Thess 5.8f.; Rom 13.11; Heb 1.14, 9.28; Phil 1.19, cf. 2.12.

[23]   See Heb 2.8.

[24]   Chap. 2, 'Redemption in the Light of the Old Testament'.

[25]   On *padah, kipper* and *gaal* (or the noun *goel*) here, see further the article by Procksch in Kittel, *op. cit.* pp. 328-335.

in the background, its usage in the New Testament cannot always be schematised in that way. Nevertheless the main ingredients of that Hebrew usage are apparent in New Testament passages and we will look at them in the order *kipper, goel* and *padah*.

1) *Kipper*: redemption by expiation is clear in passages which link redemption with the shedding of blood or the forgiveness of sins or both.[26]

2) *Goel*: other passages, some of them overlapping with the first set, lay stress on the fact that redemption is in the beloved one.[27] Christ himself is the manifestation of the love of God, the incarnate Son of God's love, and as such he stands surety for us. He stands in for us, so that it is *in him* that we have redemption. *He* is made unto us redemption.[28] This thought we get also in the Johannine discourses and in the teaching of Paul, in Romans[8] for example, of the divine *goel* who stands in for us as our advocate and delivers us even from death.[29]

3) *Padah*: redemption is also by the mighty act of God's grace and here it is identified with the breaking in of the kingdom.[30] In this context, redemption from the side of man is the counterpart to the kingdom from the side of God. This redemption is out of suffering and oppression and involves the shaking of the very powers of heaven. It is the mighty eschatological event breaking in already and yet is future.[31]

In these passages, as can be seen from the fact that some of them combine the different emphases, it is difficult to distinguish the three aspects of redemption. The reason is that all three aspects are consummated and transcended in the person of Christ, the saviour, and all instances of *apolutrōsis* with that content gather up the meaning in a fullness unknown in the Old Testament. Christ himself is the content of redemption, Christ the first and the last. He has come for us and our salvation, and he will come again when our salvation in him will be fully unveiled as total redemption. That is to say that *apolutrōsis* in the New Testament is understood in the closest relation to christology and eschatology.

---

[26] Eph 1.7; Col 1.14; Rom 3.24f.; Heb 9.15.

[27] Eph 1.6f.; Col 1.13f.

[28] 1 Cor 1.30.

[29] See Rom 8.34f.; cf. 1 John 2.1-2.

[30] Luke 21.28,31.

[31] Cf. also Col 1.13f.

Peripoiēsis, *possession*

The term *apolutrōsis* is closely associated with another important word, *peripoiēsis*, possession. See Thessalonians 5, where Paul speaks of the hope of salvation, 'For God has not destined us for wrath, but to *obtain salvation (eis peripoiēsis sōtērias)*'.[32] Similarly, 'God chose you from the beginning to be saved, through sanctification by the Spirit and belief in the truth. To this he called you through our gospel, so that you may *obtain the glory (eis peripoiēsin doxēs)* of our Lord Jesus Christ.'[33] In Ephesians, Paul writes, 'In him you also, who have . . . believed in him, were sealed with the promised Holy Spirit, which (who) is the guarantee of your inheritance until we *acquire possession of it (eis apolutrōsin tēs peripoiēseōs)*, to the praise of his glory.'[34]

In 1 Peter we have, 'But you are a chosen race, a royal priesthood, a holy nation, God's *own people (laos eis peripoiēsin,* or 'peculiar people' as the King James Version has it), that you may declare the wonderful deeds of him who called you out of darkness into his marvellous light.'[35]

In Acts, where we have a use of the verb, Paul is speaking to the bishops of Ephesus and he says, 'Take heed to yourselves and to all the flock, in which the Holy Spirit has made you guardians, to feed the church of the Lord which he *obtained* with his own blood (*hēn periepoiēsato dia tou haimatos tou idiou*).'[36]

The meaning in these passages can be summed up by saying that it is in Christ's possession of us, which he gained at the cost of shedding his blood, that we have our redemption. The word *peripoiēsis* has a peculiar double reference: we possess Christ in being possessed by him and that twofold possession or inheritance is our redemption. But this possession in which we are possessed by Christ and so possess him is the church, the 'peculiar' or special people redeemed by the blood of Christ to be his own, so that only in and with the church's redemption are we sealed unto the redemption of the purchased possession.

Now we must go on to unfold the content of this teaching in three main sections.

---

[32] 1 Thess 5.9.

[33] 2 Thess 2.13-14.

[34] Eph 1.13-14.

[35] 1 Pet 2.9.

[36] Acts 20.28.

1 The mighty act of redemption

Redemption is the mighty act of grace delivering us out of the power of darkness into the glorious liberty of the sons and daughters of God. We have already had occasion to discuss this from the aspect of *padah*-redemption out of the authority or power (*exousia*) of darkness, of the law, and of the bondage of sin which finds its strength in the law. It is a deliverance which Christ effected by his holiness and obedience, by his submission to judgement on our behalf, that is through his blood poured out on the cross; but that weakness of Jesus was the mighty act of the kingdom of God, the violence of God's grace, and though we are redeemed by Christ out of tyranny and bondage, the stress is laid upon the new life of liberty in the Spirit into which we are redeemed. That is the special emphasis of the New Testament – the relation of redemption to the Spirit as well as to the blood of Christ. And that is the point we are to consider here.

Redemption and the Spirit

Let us begin by looking at two New Testament passages, first from Matthew, 'if it is by the Spirit of God that I cast out demons, then the kingdom of God has come upon you. Or how can one enter a strong man's house and plunder his goods, unless he first binds the strong man? Then indeed he may plunder his house.'[37] It is in this light that we are to see the incarnate life of Christ leading up to the cross itself and see it as the invasion by the mighty Son of God into the domain of evil in which it had come to exercise its tyranny, in order to break its bonds. But on the other side of the cross we have the resurrection and Pentecost, where we are still concerned with redemption, with the new life in the Spirit and the power of the resurrection into which we are redeemed. Here let us consider some other words of Jesus from Luke, 'When the unclean spirit has gone out of a man, he passes through waterless places seeking rest; and finding none, he says, "I will return to my house from which I came." And when he comes he finds it swept and put in order. Then he goes and brings seven other spirits more evil than himself, and they enter and dwell there; and the last state (*ta eschata*) of that man becomes worse than the first.'[38]

Think of that in contrast to Pentecost when Peter interprets Pentecost in terms of Joel,[39] 'And in the last days (*en eschatais hēmerais*) it shall

---

[37] Matt 12.28-29. Cf. Luke 11.20-22; Mark 3.27.

[38] Luke 11.24-26; Matt 12.43-45.

[39] Joel 2.28f.

be, God declares, that I will pour out my Spirit upon all flesh'.[40] What we have in Pentecost is *ta eschata*, the end or final events of redemption, overtaking the church and filling the church with the Holy Spirit, with the Spirit of Christ. The church is not simply cleansed by the death of Christ (compare the cleansing of the temple), not simply exorcised of unclean spirits, but filled with the Holy Spirit. We recall that after his temptations in the wilderness and his triumph over the devil, Christ came in the power of the Spirit and said 'the Spirit of the Lord is upon me' and cast out demons and preached that the kingdom of God was near.[41] Now after the tribulation of the cross and his triumph over the powers of darkness, Christ comes again in the power of his Spirit to fill all things and to make of the church the temple of his Holy Spirit, so that through the Spirit, the church is given participation in him and in all the benefits of his death and resurrection and ascension. Through the ascension of Christ to reign, through the pouring out of his Spirit, God delivers the church not only from the powers of darkness but translates it into the kingdom of his dear Son. There are several things here to be noted carefully.

(a) The relation of Pentecost to the cross

Here we have the relation of the coming of the Spirit to the death of Christ, of the Spirit of Christ to the blood of Christ. The Spirit is poured out in fullness only after the cross, as a result of Christ's complete victory over the forces of spiritual evil, but that pouring out of the Spirit is itself part of the whole act of redemption. *Pentecost belongs to the atonement,* for the presence of the Spirit is the actualisation amongst us of the new or redeemed life, of the liberty which the sons and daughters of God have in Christ. We shall consider this more fully when we come to consider Pentecost as part of the kingly ministry of Christ, but here let us note that it is Pentecost which is the concept connecting redemption through the Spirit of Christ on the one hand with redemption through the blood of Christ on the other hand.

The atonement is fully completed only in the pouring out of the Spirit by Christ

Through the blood of Christ we are redeemed from the guilt of sin, but through the Spirit of Christ we are redeemed into the life of God. Redemption through the Spirit belongs as much to redemption as

---

40   Acts 2.17f.

41   Luke 4.14-44; Mark 1.14-39; Matt 12.28; Luke 11.20.

redemption through the blood of Christ, so that the atonement is regarded as fully completed and actualised only in the pouring out of the Spirit by the ascended lamb of God. It is through the communion of this Spirit that the church is given to participate in the atonement which Christ had undertaken on its behalf, so that as through his incarnation he incorporated himself into us, so through his Spirit we are incorporated into him, and it is in and through that mutual incorporation that we are redeemed. In the heart of that mutual incorporation there is the hypostatic union carried throughout the life and passion of Christ, through which God reconciles himself to humanity and humanity is reconciled to God.

(b) Redemption is the fulfilment of the covenant

In that mutual incorporation into Christ, through which he lives in us by the Spirit and we live in him we have the final fulfilment of the ancient covenant with Israel, 'I will be your God and you shall be my people.' Thus in the vision of John where he sees a new heaven and new earth, he also hears a voice, 'Behold, the dwelling of God is with men. He will dwell with them, and they shall be his people, and God himself will be with them; he will wipe away every tear from their eyes, and death shall be no more, neither shall there be mourning nor crying nor pain any more, for the former things have passed away.'[42] In the freeing of men and women from the bondage of sin and death into the glorious liberty of the resurrection, into the life of the new creation in which they share the redeemed life of Christ, we see redemption unveiled, God in Christ in the midst of his people. Redemption is thus the fulfilment of the covenant – in the communion of the Spirit.

(c) Redemption is a present possession through the Spirit

Redemption is, through the Spirit, a present possession. Paul can speak of redemption in the context of the present tense, as in Romans, 'Being justified freely through the redemption that is in Christ Jesus, whom God has set forth to be a propitiation through faith in his blood.'[43] Paul can therefore speak of our having redemption, that is, the forgiveness of sins,[44] or Christ himself, for *he* is our redemption.[45] The whole of our

---

[42] Rev 21.3-4; cf. Ezek 37.26-28; Zech 2.10-11.

[43] See Rom 3.24-25 KJV.

[44] Eph 1.7; Col 1.14.

[45] 1 Cor 1.30.

redemption is lodged in him. This is where the term *peripoiēsis* comes in, for we have redemption in Christ only because he has redeemed us to be his possession. We possess him in that he possesses us, but it is through the Spirit that our possession of him is realised, so that our possession of him is the counterpart of his possession of us. Through the Spirit, Christ who is our redemption is present with us, so that we have him dwelling in us, and we possess him, but this Christ is the Christ who has risen and ascended and who will come again, so that our present possession of Christ through the Spirit is one that reaches out to the future. We are therefore said to be sealed by the Spirit 'until the redemption of the purchased possession', sealed for the day of redemption.[46] It is of that, of course, that baptism is the primary sacrament.

(d) The relation of redemption through the Spirit to the body

The Spirit through whom we have redemption in Christ, is directly related to the body – we shall study that later in the doctrine of the Spirit. It will be sufficient here to point out that the New Testament does not speak of our minds or spirits as being the temple of the Spirit, but of our bodies, and of the Spirit as being poured out on all flesh. Therefore the redemption which we have in the present through the Spirit is one that reaches out to the redemption of the body.[47] Paul makes it clear that a bodiless existence is not redemption but shuddering horror, and therefore redemption includes the resurrection of the body.[48] Compare here a passage in Hebrews, 'Women received their dead by resurrection. Some were tortured, refusing to accept release (*tēn apolutrōsin*), that they might rise again to a better life.'[49] That probably refers to the book of Maccabees:[50] Eleazar and the youngest of the seven brothers were offered deliverance (*apolutrōsin*) from death if they denied Judaism, but they refused. That was not their true *apolutrōsis* for their true *apolutrōsis* was a better hope, the resurrection of the body. But the redemption of the body is inseparable from the redemption of all creation, that is from the recreation of the whole world, so that our redemption in body is held back until the *parousia* or second advent of Christ. In the New Testament *apolutrōsis* always carries with it that double sense of present possession and future

---

46   Eph 1.13-14 KJV, 4.30.
47   Rom 8.23.
48   1 Cor 15.35f.; Phil 3.21.
49   Heb 11.35, cf. KJV 'obtain a better resurrection'.
50   2 Maccabees 6 and 7.

inheritance; that is, it is concerned with the relation between grace and glory, of *charis* to *doxa*.[51]

It is not only the kinship which we have with Christ in the body, through his taking our flesh and bone upon himself in the incarnation, but the kinship which we have with him through his giving us his Spirit, that constitutes the *goel*-bond between us and him in virtue of which we are redeemed at last even out of death itself. It is in virtue of this relation that he is our avenger of death, destroying the man-slayer death, and it is in virtue of this that we are redeemed into the life of God and will be redeemed from the bondage of evil and corruption – that is not a redemption from the body but in the body, a redemption of the body from its bondage in corruption and poverty into glory, so that from being this body of humiliation, it becomes a *body of glory*, as Paul puts it.[52]

2 The range of redemption

(a) Who did Christ die for? – the question of 'limited atonement'[53]

The question we have to face here is whether Christ died for every human being, or only for some, those who are finally saved. It is the problem of so-called 'limited atonement'. Three basic questions are raised by this.

(i) Whom did Christ represent in his incarnation and in his death? Did he represent all humanity, or only a chosen few?

(ii) What is the relation between the death of Jesus on the cross and the Father in heaven? Did God himself condescend to take upon himself man's judgement, or did he send someone to represent him and do a work which was rewarded with forgiveness as he saw fit?

(iii) What is the nature of the efficacy of the atoning death of Christ?

---

[51] Cf. Rom 8.17ff.

[52] Phil 3.21, *sōmati tēs doxēs*.

[53] See further T.F. Torrance, 'The Atonement – The Singularity of Christ and the Finality of the Cross: the Atonement and the Moral Order', *Universalism and the Doctrine of Hell* (papers presented at the 1991 Edinburgh Conference on Christian Dogmatics), ed. N.M. de S Cameron, Paternoster, Carlisle (Baker, Grand Rapids) 1992, pp. 225-256. Cf. also here the discussion on the range of the union which Christ effected between himself and human flesh in the incarnation (all humanity or only the elect?), T.F. Torrance, *The School of Faith*, James Clarke, London 1959, pp. cxi-cxii.

Now to look at each of the questions in turn.

(i) Whom did Christ represent in his incarnation and in his death?
This in turn raises two cognate questions.[54]

   (1) What is the relation of the incarnation to the atonement?[55]
If incarnation and atonement cannot be separated, then Christ
represents in his death all whom he represents in his incarnation. If
they can be separated, then even if he represents all humanity in his
incarnation, does he represent in his death only those for whom he
chooses to bear judgement, or only those whom the Father gives him
according to his secret counsel?

*The inseparability of atonement and incarnation and of their range of
representation*
Atonement and incarnation, however, cannot be separated from
one another and therefore the range of representation is the same
in both. In both, all people are involved. In the incarnation Christ,
the eternal Son, took upon himself the nature of man and all who
belong to human nature are involved and are represented, all men
and women without exception, so that for all and each, Jesus Christ
stood in as substitute and advocate in his life and in his death.
Because he is the eternal Word or *Logos* in whom all humanity
cohere, for him to take human nature upon himself means that all
humanity is assumed by his incarnation; all humanity is bound up
with him, he died for all humanity and all humanity died in him.
   At the same time, by the assertion of the union of the incarnation
and atonement, we repudiate the idea that the humanity of Christ was
merely instrumental in the hands of God and the idea that the
atonement on the cross was a merely forensic transaction, the fulfilment
of a legal contract.[56] In the life and death of Christ, there was fulfilled
the one covenant of grace which God out of his free grace made with
all creation, although in redemptive history that assumed the form of

---

[54]   Cf. T.F. Torrance, 'The Atonement – The Singularity of Christ…', esp. pp.
       232-36, 244-45.
[55]   On the nature of the atonement as flowing from the love of God and the
       inseparable relation between the Father and the Son, see T.F. Torrance,
       Scottish Theology, T & T Clark, Edinburgh 1996, chap. 9, 'John McLeod
       Campbell', pp. 287-315, and on the relation between incarnation and
       atonement in particular, see pp. 297ff., 313ff.
[56]   Cf. T.F. Torrance, 'The Atonement – The Singularity of Christ…', pp. 237-39.

an election of one for all. That is, election and substitution combined to be the way in which that covenant was brought to its fulfilment in the midst of fallen humanity. Although it was fulfilled through the particularity of Israel and through the remnant (the church), and at last through the one servant in a unique and utterly vicarious way, it was as such fulfilled for all humanity.

We have to take seriously the teaching of the New Testament that Christ died for all and that he tasted death for every human being. Thus the 'many' (of the son of man giving himself as 'a ransom for many')[57] is interpreted even within the New Testament in terms of 'all'.[58] The other New Testament passages which speak of all, such as for example 'we are convinced that one has died for all; therefore all have died',[59] have likewise to be taken with full seriousness and not whittled down.

(2) What is the relation between the redemptive work of Christ and election?

God's election cannot be separated from Christ and is essentially corporate in him

Whatever we do, we cannot speak of an election or a predestination behind the back of Jesus Christ, and so divide God's saving action in two, into election and into the work of Christ on the cross. God's eternal election is nothing else than God's eternal love incarnate in his beloved Son, so that in him we have election incarnate. God's eternal decree is nothing other than God's eternal Word so that in Christ we have the eternal decree or Word of God made flesh. Election is identical with the life and existence and work of Jesus Christ, and *what he does is election going into action*. Another way of putting this is to say that the covenant and election belong together and are in no way opposed to one another: they are aspects of the one redeeming purpose of God. *Election is essentially corporate* in the covenant and it is that covenant-election that is wholly fulfilled and brought to its completion or *telos*

---

57 Mark 10.45; Matt 20.28.

58 1 Tim 2.4-6; cf. Titus 2.11-14. Cf. Calvin's recognition, with reference to Isaiah 53.12, that the biblical 'many' sometimes denotes 'all', *Commentary on Isaiah*, vol. 4, trans. Rev W. Pringle, Eerdmans repr., Grand Rapids, p. 131, 'It is evident from other passages, and especially from the fifth chapter of the Epistle to the Romans, that "many" sometimes denotes "all"'.

59 2 Cor 5.14.

in the death of Christ the beloved Son, the mediator of the new covenant. Every human being is loved by Christ and all men and women are involved in him, God's elect or beloved Son. God's eternal love is incarnated in him. That love is enacted in the midst of our human existence in his life and death on the cross on our behalf. What Christ is and did is the pouring out of the pure love of God upon all humanity.

(ii) What is the relation between the death of Jesus on the cross, and the Father in heaven?[60]

It is impossible to divide the deity and the humanity of Christ, or Christ from the Father

Now certainly we cannot speak of the Father as being crucified, the old error of so-called patripassianism.[61] At the same time we cannot but speak of God as descending to our condemned state and taking our state upon himself, so that God the judge made himself also the one judged in our place.[62]

The hyper-Calvinist, however, argues in this way, that in Christ's life and especially in his death on the cross, the deity of Christ was in repose. He suffered only in his humanity. On the cross, Christ merited forgiveness sufficient for all mankind. It was sufficient to cover the sins of all, for it was of infinite worth, but it held efficaciously only for those whom the Father had given him. We shall examine later the difference between 'sufficient' and 'efficacious', but here we must look at the relation posed here between Christ in his human nature on the cross and God in heaven. If Christ acted only in his human nature on the cross and God remained utterly apart and utterly transcendent, except that he agreed in will with Christ whom he sent to die, then all that Christ does is not necessarily what God does or accepts. In that case the sacrifice of Christ may be accepted as satisfaction only for the number of the elect that God has previously chosen or determined. But if God himself came among us in Christ his beloved Son and assumed upon himself our whole burden of guilt and judgement, then such an arbitrary view would be impossible. And we must hold the view that it is indeed *God himself* who bears our sins, God

---

[60]   Cf. T.F. Torrance, 'The Atonement – The Singularity of Christ...', pp. 230-39.

[61]   The doctrine that the Father suffered as well as the Son – Lat, *pater*, father, and *patior/passus*, suffer.

[62]   Cf. *op. cit.* p. 234-35.

become man and taking man's place, standing with humanity under the divine judgement, God the judge becoming himself the man judged and bearing his own judgement upon the sin of humanity, so that we cannot divorce the action of Christ on the cross from the action of God. The concept of a limited atonement divides Christ's divinity from his humanity and thus rests upon a basic Nestorian heresy.[63]

Besides how can we think of the judgement on the cross as only a partial judgement upon sin, or of a judgement only upon some sinners, for that is what it is if only some sinners are died for and only some are implicated in Christ and the cross? But what would that mean but a destruction of the whole concept of atonement, for it would mean a partial judgement and not a final *No* of God against sin; it would mean a partial substitution and thus a repudiation of the concept of radical substitution which atonement involves.[64] And it would mean a divorce of the cross from the final judgement, for a judgement upon sin would still have to be poured out. Or to put it in another way: it would mean that outside of Christ there is still a God of wrath who will judge humanity apart from the cross and who apart from the cross is a wrathful God. But that is to divide God from Christ in the most impossible way and to eliminate the whole teaching of the 'wrath of the lamb',[65] namely that God has committed all judgement to the Son.[66]

(iii) What is the nature of the efficacy of the atoning death of Christ on the cross?[67]

The distinction between 'sufficiency' and 'efficacy' in the death of Christ

The scholastic Calvinists make a distinction between the death of Christ as sufficient for the redemption of all humanity, but as

---

[63] Cf. *op. cit.* p. 231,246. Nestorianism is the view that there are two persons, a divine and a human in the one Christ. Although Nestorius himself affirmed the oneness of Christ, his preference for a doctrine of conjunction of divine and human in Christ and a union of will, rather than a hypostatic union of divine and human in one person, was seen as compromising the unity of Christ and was rejected as heretical.

[64] Cf. *op. cit.* p. 245-46.

[65] Rev 6.16.

[66] John 5.22.

[67] Cf. *op. cit.* p. 245-48.

efficacious only for the elect. If that means only that Christ died for all, but that the fruit of his death is the salvation in the end not of all but only of some, then it is understandable, but they usually mean more than this. Thus Wolleb[68] says we must confess that Christ's passion was sufficient to merit the redemption of ten worlds, but if we look to the council of God and intention of Christ, it is false to say that Christ died for all and each. Hence he is said to have died for all sufficiently, but not efficaciously! That is to say, by reason of its worth the merit of Christ was sufficient for all, but by reason of its application it was not efficacious in all, since Christ did not die with the intention that his death should be applied to all.

The concept of irresistible grace and absolute divine causality – does atonement flow from the will or from the nature of God?

Behind this lies a philosophical or metaphysical conception of irresistible grace and of absolute divine causality, such that it could not but be held that all for whom Christ died efficaciously must necessarily be saved. The doctrine of absolute predestination thus appears to supply a notion of causal efficacy to the death of Christ which makes it applicable savingly only to the elect, as otherwise all would be saved. But if we think of an absolute divine causation behind election and or atonement, then how do we preserve the freedom and transcendence of God? With this in mind, Samuel Rutherford and John Brown of Wamphray both dared to say that the atonement reposed upon the arbitrary will of God, that is, upon his *arbitrium* or free-will, upon his transcendent sovereignty. In that way they denied that the atonement flows freely out of the divine nature and yet sought to preserve or safeguard the personal choice or love of God, indeed the nature of God as personal, his lordly freedom, in atonement – but in so doing, they made it *arbitrary*. On

---

[68]　Johannes Wollebius [Wolleb], *Compendium Theologiae Christianae*, 1626, reprinted Amstelodami 1642, LIB I, CAP XVIII.XXIII (1.18.23), p. 104, '*Enimvero si meriti & magnitudinem & dignitatem spectemus, tantam esse fatemur, ut decem mundis redimendis sufficeret: si vero ad Dei consilium ac Christi intentionem respiciamus, falsum est, Christum pro omnibus & singulis mortuum esse. Hinc ab aliis, pro omnibus mortuus esse dicitur sufficienter, sed non efficaciter, i.e. sufficiens esse meritum Christi pro omnibus ratione dignitatis suae, sed non efficax in omnibus ratione applicationis, cum non ea intentione mortuus sit Christus, ut mors eius omnibus applicaretur.*' (Cf. *Reformed Dogmatics*, Eng. trans. ed. J. Beardslee III, OUP, New York 1965, p. 105.)

the other hand, the opposite view, expounded for example in Owen, made the atonement flow out of the nature of God, but if the nature of God is only to love some and not to love others, as we see reflected by the choice of only a few for salvation, then the nature of God is attacked. Be that as it may, if the nature of God is absolute causality and if atonement flows out of that divine nature, then an atoning death for all means the necessary salvation of all.

The 'possibility' of salvation – the alternative of Armininiasm

The alternative to that would be to assert that all that God provided was the possibility of salvation for all in the cross, and that each person has to translate that general possibility into actuality in their own case, but that is to land in Arminianism[69] and to teach that ultimately every one is their own saviour, in so far as they have to co-operate with Christ for their salvation. But if all that has been done in the death of Christ is the creation of the possibility of salvation, then who can be sure of their salvation, since everything depends in the last analysis on human weakness? Hence as against these two possibilities, the hyper-Calvinists settled on the idea that the atonement was only efficacious for those for whom it was intentionally undertaken, and for them alone. They might well assert that God loves all humanity, and even that Christ loves all humanity, but that for them is another thing than to say that Christ died for all humanity. In other words, the action of the cross is divorced from the love of God. Christ's love for all mankind is not translated into action, but if so, can it be said that he loves all mankind, or that he is true love at all? This divorce of the action of Christ from his love really means the dismemberment of Christ, the separation of his person from his work – and that is to destroy the atonement as well as the incarnation.

The rationalism of both universalism and limited atonement

Here we see that man's proud reason insists in pushing through its own partial insight into the death of the cross to its logical conclusion, and so the great mystery of atonement is subjected to the rationalism of human thought. That is just as true of the universalist as it is of

---

[69] Arminius (1560-1609) attempted to hold together in his theology divine sovereignty and human free-will, teaching that Christ died and obtained forgiveness for all, and that God's predestination was based on foreknowledge of whether an individual would freely accept or reject Christ, and persevere in faith or fall away.

those who hold limited atonement for in both cases they have not yet bowed their reason before the cross of Christ.[70]

(b) Positive affirmations on the range of the atonement

What then are we to say positively in answer to the question of 'limited atonement'?

(i) Christ's death for all is an inescapable reality[71]

We must affirm resolutely that Christ died for all humanity – that is a fact that cannot be undone. All men and women were represented by Christ in life and death, in his advocacy and substitution in their place. That is a finished work and not a mere possibility. It is an accomplished reality, for in Christ, in the incarnation and in his death on the cross, God has once and for all poured himself out in love for all mankind, has taken the cause of all mankind therefore upon himself. And that love has once and for all been enacted in the substitutionary work on the cross, and has become fact – nothing can undo it. That means that God has taken the great positive decision for man, the decision of love

---

[70] For Torrance, apprehension of the cross involves a conversion of the reason in which we bow our own reason before the reality and *mystery* of Christ and seek to understand it (as far as we may) out of itself without reducing it to logical schemata of our own making which inevitably break it up into separate elements and distort it. We need to hold together what scripture holds together, refusing to categorise it in ways that distort that wholeness. If we cannot understand how scripture holds together certain things which we find difficult (such as the unconditional love and forgiveness of God for all, the finished work of Christ, the gospel imperative to repent and believe, and the fact that some refuse and are judged by the very gospel that offers them life) then it is not open to us to resolve the tension through a man-made logical schema which emphasises some elements as the expense of others. We need to be crucified with Christ in our natural reason and through the transforming of our mind begin to penetrate into 'the interior logic of scripture' so that we may learn to think as scripture thinks and hold together what it holds together in Christ. Both universalism and limited atonement for Torrance fail to do that. See his discussion on the nature of the systematic element in theology and on faithfulness to the *mystery* of Christ without the imposition of rigid categories of rationalistic understanding, *The School of Faith*, pp. lxff.

[71] See further, *The School of Faith*, pp. cxiii–cxvii.

translated into fact. But because the work and the person of Christ are one, that finished work is identical with the self-giving of God to all humanity which he extends to everyone in the living Christ. God does not withhold himself from any one, but he gives himself to all whether they will or not – even if they will not have him, he gives himself to them, for he has once and for all given himself, and therefore the giving of himself in the cross when opposed by the will of man inevitably opposes that will of man and is its judgement. As we saw, it is the positive will of God in loving humanity that becomes humanity's judgement when they refuse it.

That then is the first thing we have to say, that Christ died for all humanity, and no human being can undo or escape the fact that every one has been died for, and no one can evade, elude or avoid the fact that they are loved by God. Therefore when they do the inconceivable thing in the face of that divine love, namely, refuse it, defy it, turn away from it, that unavoidable self-giving of God is their very judgement. It opposes their refusal of God, it opposes their attempt to elude God, and is therefore their judgement in the very event of refusal. If we think of the incarnation of Christ into our human nature, and therefore of the fact that all men and women have been ingrafted into Christ in that he has made himself brother of all in their flesh and existence, then we may think of human refusal of the atonement, a refusal met by God's opposition of love, as a breaking off of people, like a branch from the vine, and yet that must not be thought of as if it meant the undoing of the fact that Christ died for them.

Objectively, then, we must think of atonement as sufficient and efficacious reality for every human being – it is such sufficient and efficacious reality that it is the rock of offence, the rock of judgement upon which the sinner who refuses the divine love shatters himself or herself and is damned eternally.

(ii) Pentecost is part of atonement

The actualising of the atonement through the Spirit's incorporation of us into Christ

But now we must remember the fact of Pentecost and that the pouring out of the Spirit is one of the mighty acts of redemption and recreation. In other words, the pouring out of the Spirit belongs to atonement. It is atonement actualising itself, really and subjectively within the personal lives of men and women, within their decisions and living actions, and upholding them creatively in their real relation with God. This is not a new event, or some additional event in atonement. As we shall see later on when we come to study it, it is but the one atoning event inserting itself into human lives and actualising itself within them.[72] Or to put it the other way round: if we think of the incarnation and death of Christ as his great work of incorporating himself into our alienated humanity and existence and taking our whole cause upon himself, so that he acts fully and completely for us, then we must think of the baptism of the Spirit as effecting our incorporation into Christ, that is, incorporation into Christ who incorporated himself into us in order to act in our place as our substitute. Thus we think of the communion of the Spirit as our incorporation or participation in Christ our substitute who has already perfectly fulfilled, in our name and in our place, our response to God the Father. Now the New Testament speaks of those who have communion with Christ through the Spirit and so share in his life and death as building together the body of Christ, the *sōma Christou.*

The communion of those incorporated into Christ is the subjectification of atonement

Here the church is the community of believers and their children who are members of Christ not only on the ground that he has incorporated himself into them, but on the ground that they are incorporated into him. Thus the incarnational and redemptional universal range of atonement in Christ has as its counterpart the communion of believers, but this communion of believers reaches out to the ends of the earth and to the ends of the age. It is a *sôma* or body that reaches out to *plērōma* or fullness, and is a provisional anticipation of the cosmic actualisation of redemption which we shall consider later. It is then this subjectification of the perfected reality of atonement which marks out the bounds of the church, the body of Christ, the community of the redeemed in a narrower sense, of those who are sealed for the redemption of the body and the resurrection of the dead. It is this communion of the Spirit which marks out the inner range of redemption. This does not mean that only these are died for efficaciously, but that these are those who accept the decision God has already made on their behalf in Christ's atoning life and death. Through the communion of the Spirit, the work of the mediator is mediated to those in whose name it was undertaken.

---

[72]   Chap. 10, 'The Biblical Witness to Jesus Christ', section 2 (c) & (d).

(iii) The community of the covenant – the church as the middle term

The community of the covenant is reconstituted in Christ for all mankind

However, when we have spoken of these two sides, the objective and the subjective, we have not said enough. There is still a middle term to take into account, the *tertium datur*.[73] The church, the community of the covenant, was already in existence when Christ was born and when he died, and when he did so in a special way for them also. That was included in his death for all mankind, in his one equal love for each and every human being, but it was a fulfilled love that led 'captivity captive'[74] and redeemed Israel. Thus when at Pentecost the Christian church came into being, it was grafted on to the stump of Israel already in being and already in existence. It was out of that stump, as a root out of the dry ground,[75] that Christ was born, or into it that Christ incorporated himself, so that he came not only as man and the son of man, but also as an Israelite gathering up the people of the covenant and the community of the covenant in himself. Thus when he died he made reconciliation for those that are near, Israel, and those that are afar off, the Gentiles, and broke down the middle wall of partition between them, ingrafting the Gentiles into the one commonwealth with Israel.[76] The branches do not bear the root, but the root the branches.[77]

The twofold range of the covenant, universal, yet particular reaching out to the universal

The church was thus not created at Pentecost, but added to and enlarged and extended, and reconstituted in that new covenant in which the economy changes from that of law to that of Spirit, from that of demand to that of grace, from that of the law of Moses to that of the gospel of Jesus; but it is the one covenant of the fatherly love of God and throughout it all the one people of God.[78] And so the New

---

[73] Lat, 'third term', literally 'a third is given'.

[74] Eph 4.8 KJV.

[75] Isaiah 53.2.

[76] Eph 2.11-19.

[77] Rom 11.17-18; cf. John 15.1ff. & Psalm 80.8ff.; also Isaiah 5.1-7 & Ezek 19.10f.

[78] See further chap. 11 below, section 4 (a) 'The oneness or unity of the church'.

Testament can say on the one hand that Christ died for all humanity and yet say that he loved the church and gave himself for her.[79] Here then we must think of a twofold range of the covenant, as universal, and yet as particular reaching out to the universal. And just as we thought of the covenant as operative in the Old Testament through election and substitution of the one for the many, so we must think of the church of the new covenant as operative similarly, as the particular body reaching out to the fullness of redemption in its cosmic range.

The meaning of baptism

The significance of all this we can see if we think for a moment of the meaning of baptism. Is baptism the sacrament of what Christ has done for us in the gospel, or of our faith and decision to accept him as our saviour? It is surely primarily the sacrament of what Christ has done on our behalf when he incorporated himself into our humanity and acted in our place and in our name before God. Then why do we not baptise every one for whom Christ died? If not, are we then to turn round and say, no, we baptise people only on the ground of what they do in their decision of faith, so that baptism then becomes not primarily the sacrament of the obedience of Christ, but of our obedience to him? No, we say that baptism is the sacrament of the fact that God has bound himself to us and bound us to him before ever we bind ourselves to him, and that takes place within the community of the covenant where it is established subjectively as well as objectively. Thus baptism is the sacrament of what Christ has done within the covenant community and is therefore the sacrament of inclusion into the covenant community, and then only secondarily is it the sacrament of the attestation of our faith in Christ as our substitute and saviour.

A threefold ingrafting into Christ

To express all this, Calvin used to speak of a threefold ingrafting into Christ or three degrees of the love of God, to all, to the covenant community and to the individual believer in the decision of faith. And yet that is a somewhat scholastic way of speaking of it. Similarly, Forbes of Corse used to speak of a threefold sanctification in Christ, all in order to do justice to the same point, namely, the middle term between Christ's act on behalf of all humanity and the individual believer, the community of the covenant – and it is that community of the covenant which rests upon the human nature of Jesus and his active obedience for all which we cannot afford to leave out of sight in speaking of the range of redemption.

---

[79]   2 Cor 5.14; 1 Tim 2.6 (cf. Titus 2.11); Eph 5.25.

3 The eschatological perspective of redemption

Here we are concerned with the aspect of the atonement where cosmic reconciliation and future fulfilment of redemption overlap in the fact that the death and resurrection of Christ has set our life back on the basis of creation, and therefore redemption reaches out to the new creation and its ultimate revelation or apocalypse at the *parousia* or final advent of Christ. 'Redemption' is here to be considered 'within the times', between the time of the first advent and the time of the second advent, between the time of Pentecost which is *apolutrōsis*, redemption, and the time of the resurrection which is the *apolutrōsis* of the body. Redemption has already been completed and is yet to be manifested, but between the times it is the mighty acts of God in eschatological operation. Let us examine the Lucan account of 'redemption' where this perspective is clearly given.

(a) Redemption in the gospel of Luke

(i) In the opening of Luke's Gospel, we have the conception of redemption which corresponds to the messianic and eschatological 'year of jubilee', for example, in the *Benedictus* of Zechariah where redemption refers to messianic expectation fulfilled,[80] and in the words of Simeon where the salvation of Israel means also the universalisation of the covenant, 'a light to lighten the Gentiles'.[81]

(ii) Then throughout the Gospel we have an identification of redemption with the breaking in of the kingdom in the life and action of Jesus, and this is especially manifested in his preaching of the gospel to the captives of sin and his healing miracles, for he delivers men and women from the bondage of the power of darkness and corruption. The new creation is already breaking in with power and bringing the liberty of the sons and daughters of God.

(iii) In what is sometimes called 'the little apocalypse'[82] we have a further aspect of redemption. There Jesus speaks of the *parousia* of the kingdom as attended by apocalyptic and cosmic events of fulfilment and judgement. 'Now when these things begin to take place, look up and raise your heads, because your redemption is drawing near ... So also, when you see these things taking place, you know that the

---

[80] Luke 1.68-79.

[81] Luke 2.32 KJV.

[82] Luke 21.5-36; cf. Matt 24, Mark 13.

kingdom of God is near.'[83] Here 'your redemption' (*apolutrōsis humōn*) is identified with the 'kingdom of God' (*basileia tou theou*), where characteristically redemption has its reference to the subjects redeemed, while the kingdom has its reference to the mighty acts of God, the agent of redemption.

(iv) How did the disciples understand this redemption? How did they understand it in their statement in Luke: 'we had hoped', the two disciples said to Jesus on the way to Emmaus, 'that he was the one to redeem Israel'.[84] Then Jesus expounded to them the Old Testament scriptures and showed how Christ had to suffer these things and then enter into his glory. 'Redemption' spans the whole movement from cross to glory. The cross is the breaking in of the kingdom, for the cross is in a real sense the *parousia*, but it reaches out to *doxa*, to glory.[85]

(v) To this theme we find Luke returning again in Acts. What happened as recorded in the gospel is referred to as what Jesus 'began to do and to teach',[86] but now with his ascension and with Pentecost he fulfils what he had begun to do and teach. Thus the church after Pentecost lives in the time of fulfilment, the last days when God pours out the fullness of his Spirit upon the church. Thus the pouring out of the Spirit at Pentecost reaches out to the last day, the final day, when God will judge and renew his creation – and here the prophetic doctrine of the new heaven and the new earth[87] lurks behind the citations made from the Old Testament in interpretation of the redemptive work of Christ. The Spirit is the 'first fruit'[88] of the full harvest, as Paul put it, taking his language from the Jewish festivals or feasts, the feast of firstfruits (also known as the feast of weeks) and the feast of booths or tabernacles, the feast of ingathering.[89] But Paul also thinks of the Spirit as the pledge (or guarantee, *arrabōn*) as well as the first fruit of redemption.[90] It is an inheritance that is made over to us in Christ, freely bequeathed to us, and it is into that inheritance we enter more and more throughout our earthly pilgrimage.

---

[83]   Luke 21.28,31.

[84]   Luke 24.21, *lutrousthai*, redeem.

[85]   Luke 24.26.

[86]   Acts 1.1.

[87]   Isaiah 65.17, 66.22.

[88]   See Rom 8.23.

[89]   Exod 34.22; Deut 16.9-17.

[90]   Eph 1.13-14; 2 Cor 1.22 (KJV 'earnest'); cf. Eph 4.30.

(b) *The whole of creation is involved in redemption*

However this inheritance which we have through the Spirit is inseparable from the inheritance of all God's creation, for the whole creation is involved in redemption. For the benefit of the sons and daughters of God, the actualisation of that redemption in all creation is held in check, so that the gospel can be preached to all nations and all people have time to repent. Until then the physical creation is held in check, and is therefore the prisoner of hope. But as such it is kept also on the tiptoe of expectation – *apokaradokia* – waiting and groaning and travailing for 'the revealing of the sons of God', that is, for the great day of jubilee when redemption and emancipation from all thraldom will be fully actualised in all God's wide creation.[91] Behind all this lies the cosmic reach of the atoning work of Christ, the universal sweep of redemption, involving all things (*ta panta*) visible and invisible, material and spiritual, earthly and heavenly.[92]

Here we must follow the New Testament teaching about the all-comprehensive action of the death of Christ by which 'all things are gathered together in one in Christ, both which are in heaven and which are on earth'.[93] If justification involves the breaking through of God's presence in sheer grace, and so the teleological suspension of the abstract order of a world semi-detached from God, and if reconciliation involves an atonement between man and God living on in the resurrected Christ, now the contemporary of all people and ages, then in God's redeeming purpose the death of Christ is a cosmic event, so that not only human life but the whole of creation has been set *on a wholly new basis*. Thus we must think of the intervention of God in our world as final and as reaching out to the very ends (*eschata*) of the world, so that we can say, 'he is the propitiation not for our sins only but for the sins of the whole world.'[94] That God has dealt with the world *as a whole* is already implied in the absolutely objective character of our salvation, which was wrought apart from our attitude or response to it and while we were yet sinners,[95] but it is also implied in the fact that the atonement is Christ himself. In him, God and humanity have been indissolubly united, and because he lives, the whole of finite

---

[91] Rom 8.19-23.

[92] Eph 1.10; Col 1.16,20.

[93] See Eph 1.10 KJV; cf. Col 1.16-20.

[94] See 1 John 2.2 KJV.

[95] Rom 5.8.

existence suffers a cosmic change, and because he ever lives, that cosmic change is final and cannot be undone. 'He that died dies no more'.[96]

The vast cosmic significance of the cross

The vast cosmic significance of the cross is evident in the Gospels from the very beginning, as for example, in the account of the death of Jesus in a context of cosmic upheaval. The whole of creation was affected, not only the veil of the temple.[97] Just as the whole of creation was affected by man's fall in sin, so here we have in the death of Christ a cosmic reversal on a scale utterly transcending the fall of mankind and the curse of the world. The same thought figures largely in the eighth chapter of Romans where St Paul sets God's redeeming purpose for nature in the context of man's reconciliation with God. Redemption is so vast and comprehensive, involving the whole universe, that the reconciling love of God transcends every dimensional barrier, spiritual or physical, past or present or future. St Paul saw the crucified and risen Christ as the very centre of the universe, he 'who is before all things, and by whom all things consist'.[98] Because atonement has been wrought in the death and resurrection of this same Christ, the whole of reality must be reconstructed round him, so that 'old things are made to pass away, and all things become new'.[99]

The significance of Christ's death is so vast that things in heaven as well as things on earth are affected. St Paul indicates that the spiritual world in which humanity lived had become compromised by the fall and entangled in sin, as for example the whole order of law, which though mediated to humanity by spiritual powers or angels,[100] became the very strength of sin itself.[101] But in the at-one-ment between God and man which entailed a teleological suspension of this spiritual or moral order, the whole of reality became affected – even the spiritual realities. Reconciliation had as much to do with spiritual powers, with things in heaven (for the law had been fulfilled) as with mankind, living under these spiritual powers. That is in line with the whole New Testament teaching, which points forward not only to a new earth, but to a new heaven, that is, to a new relation between the earth and a

---

96   See Rom 6.9 KJV.

97   Matt 27.45,51-54; Mark 15.33,38; Luke 23.44-45.

98   See Col 1.16-17 KJV.

99   See 2 Cor 5.17 KJV.

100   Cf. Acts 7.53; Gal 3.19; Heb 2.2.

101   1 Cor 15.56.

spiritual order far transcending the present one, where humanity is in slavery both to the law and to the elements of the cosmos.[102] The Christian's place as a new creature is in this new world, the kingdom of Christ, where all things are become new. Therefore, says St Paul, 'All things are yours, and you are Christ's, and Christ is God's'.[103] The Christian who lives in Jesus Christ, the centre and sovereign of the universe, is no longer to be mastered by the cosmic elements or by the law or by spiritual powers of any description – 'Do you not know that we are to judge angels?'[104] St Paul asked the Corinthians. As an heir of Christ, the Christian is sovereignly free, because Christ is Lord of all.[105]

Two early church emphases

There are two aspects of this cosmic redemption that were carried on and emphasised in the early church of the second and third centuries. Indeed, they sometimes became the major elements in their conception of the Christian salvation.

(i) By his incarnation and death and resurrection, Christ renewed humanity as a whole.

(ii) By his death and particularly by his resurrection, Christ vanquished the spiritual powers that stalked and ruled the souls of mankind.

Doubtless, these aspects were not held precisely as they were in the New Testament for the element of salvation from guilt tended sometimes to drop out of them, and so salvation tended to be conceived more in metaphysical than in moral terms and the deepest elements in redemption were consequently not grasped. On the other hand, they do represent aspects that later Christianity has tended to neglect and these aspects we must try to restate in the light of the teaching of the New Testament.

(c) Redemption affects all humanity and relates us to the whole of creation

In the cross, Christ dealt with humanity *as a whole*, and therefore when we partake of the saving deed of the cross, we partake of *a universal act* which sets us immediately in a context of cosmic significance. If our

---

[102] Col 2.8-20.

[103] See 1 Cor 3.21,23.

[104] 1 Cor 6.3.

[105] Acts 2.36; Eph 1.20f.; Col 2.10; cf. the teaching of Jesus with reference to 'the Son of man is lord of the Sabbath' (Matt 12.8; Mark 2.28; Luke 6.5), and 'My Father is working still, and I am working' (John 5.17).

own personal atonement lives on in the living Christ who is the very centre of the universe and by whom all things consist, then through our very faith we become participant in the cosmic significance of the cross and are caught up in its vast redeeming purpose. The cross was, so to speak, a world-altar, and it is only at that world-altar that forgiveness is to be attained. We cannot in any sense therefore have that forgiveness without taking into our life and soul a debt to all the world through Jesus Christ. Our faith is rooted in the cross which is essentially correlative to the whole world – therefore our faith must be correlative to the whole world. That is why, Paul said, the cross drove him out into all the world and made him universal property.[106] Because the cross has no boundaries, but reaches out to the very *eschata*, ends, limits of the world, so that nothing is not brought within its significance or action, the Christian believer cannot contain himself or herself under the transcendent impulse of this redeeming love, necessity is laid upon them and they must reach out also to the very ends of the earth.

The cosmic action of the cross, here, carries with it new relations within the cosmos, both in regard to existence in general, and in regard to mankind itself.

(i) Reconciliation with the fabric of the universe

The Christian is, in an important sense, reconciled with the conditions of existence in the world, although because he or she is participant in the redeeming purpose of Christ, they must also find themselves in a relation of tension with the evil fashion of the world. There was a time when the very stars in their courses seemed to fight against them and enslaved them to the elements of the world, but now that humanity is put in the right with God, the law or the general order of the universe is no longer against them. The believer is reconciled in Christ, and Christ is the very centre of the universe, its real principle of consistency and its goal, and therefore their faith transcends the conflicting chaotic conditions of the world in a great bond of peace between them and ultimate reality. We do not yet see all things put under Christ's feet,[107] but the dominating note is of Christ's victory, and through him we are more than conquerors in the world.[108] The cross has cosmic significance in that it claims and suborns the world for its redeeming purpose. Therefore Paul can say, 'all things work together for good to them that

---

[106] Cf. Rom 1.5,14-15, 15.15-29; Col 1.23f.; Eph 3.1f.,7f.

[107] Heb 2.8.

[108] Rom 8.37.

love God',[109] and 'all things are yours, the world, or life, or death'.[110] In the words of James Denney, 'Reconciliation to God is not realised unless it includes reconciliation to the order of God's providence, and to the circumstances of our life as fixed for us by him . . . Not only is God a new God, the world is a new world to the reconciled sinner; he is not at war with the conditions of life – at least he is not at a spiritless, angry, discontented war with them. He knows that if God is for him, no one can be against him and that his very badge as a Christian is that he can overcome the world, combining, as Paul so characteristically combined, much affliction with joy in the Holy Ghost. His faith in providence is an inference from his experience of reconciliation. "He who spared not his own Son, but delivered him up for us all, how shall he not with him also freely give us all things"?'[111]

(ii) Reconciliation between all humanity

For humanity, the redemption of the cross involves at the same time reconciliation of man with fellow man, of all men and women with each other, and particularly of Jew with Gentile, for the middle wall of partition has been broken down and God has made of them one new man in Christ Jesus.[112] The word of the cross is not that all men and women are as a matter of fact at one with one another, but that such at-one-ment is achieved only in desperate and crucial action, through atonement in the death and resurrection of Christ. But because that has been finally achieved in Christ, the cross cuts clean across the divisions and barriers of the fashion of the world and resists them. It entails a judgement upon the old humanity of Babel[113] and the proclamation of a new humanity in Christ Jesus which is necessarily one and universal. That becomes evident in the Christian church, whose function it is *to live out the atonement in the world*, and that means to be in the flesh the bodily instrument of God's crucial intervention. And so the church becomes the sphere in which the great reconciliation, already wrought out in the body of Christ, is being realised among mankind, and the life and action of the church become sacramentally correlative to the life and passion of Christ Jesus.

---

[109] Rom 8.28 KJV.

[110] See 1 Cor 3.21-22.

[111] James Denney, *The Christian Doctrine of Reconciliation*, Hodder & Stoughton, London, 1917, p. 178-9. See also Rom 8.32 KJV.

[112] Eph 2.11-16.

[113] Gen 11.1-9.

Reconciliation must reach out to the ends of the universe

The very life process of the church is the resurgence and expansion of the new creation in Christ, right in the midst of the critical situation brought about by the cross in the world. Here that life process runs parallel to the expansion or the 'catholicising' of the person of Christ from a historical to a cosmic significance which took place at the cross where the redeeming love of God in him was at last universalised and made free to the whole world. It was the death of Christ, so to speak, that emancipated his gospel for the whole world. The cross catholicised or universalised Christ, and so it necessarily universalises or catholicises the believer at the cross and who by the cross becomes joined to Christ and therefore joined to a new universal humanity. Thus the cross introduces into the Christian outlook, the notion of universal expansion or world mission, in which all the barriers of race and language are broken down, and the Christian is constrained to proclaim reconciliation to all and to live it out, for it is by that same motion of universal reconciliation that he and she have themselves been redeemed in the cross. That is why the Christian faith is necessarily missionary, because the word of the cross lodged in its heart is the word of an infinitely expanding redemption that must reach out to the uttermost bounds of the universe, embracing every tongue and tribe and people.[114]

---

[114] Rev 7.9; cf. chap. 11 below, section 4 (c) 'The catholicity of the church'.

Chapter Seven

THE RESURRECTION OF JESUS CHRIST

Author's note: Time did not allow in my dogmatics class for a full account, biblical and dogmatic, of the resurrection, but this was given separately as student handouts and published in the book *Space, Time and Resurrection*.[1]

Editor's note: Although not able for the reasons stated to lecture on the topic, Professor Torrance was able to distribute extensive 'handouts' on the resurrection and ascension to students. These formed the basis for the book just mentioned and with the author's blessing have been incorporated here into his dogmatics lectures for the sake of fullness. As a continuation and an integral part of christology and soteriology, they form an essential part of his dogmatics and without them the lectures would be somewhat truncated. Readers, particularly scholars, may wish to refer to *Space, Time and Resurrection* for the useful footnotes and references to sources which are given in that book.[2]

---

[1]   T.F. Torrance, *Space, Time and Resurrection*, Handsel Press, Edinburgh 1976.

[2]   In the manuscript of his lectures offered for publication, Torrance included on the resurrection only the section entitled '**Introduction – the biblical concept of resurrection**' (the opening section of the student handouts) and prefaced it with the following:

"With the resurrection, the priestly work of Christ merges with his kingly work. The kingdom had already drawn near and had been breaking in with the birth and ministry of Jesus, but with his crucifixion Christ begins to assume his kingly functions, and it is as the mighty king that he rises again from the dead. It is when he ascends to the throne of God that he is enthroned as king and the kingdom of Christ is fully inaugurated. It is as such that he will come again.

In this section of our dogmatics we will be concerned with three chapters.

Section VIII The resurrection of the crucified Christ

Section IX The exaltation of the humiliated one

Section X The coming again of the incarnate one".

[Continues on next page]

Introduction – the biblical concept of resurrection

Resurrection as understood in the bible appears to be without any parallel in the other religions. An idea of resurrection is certainly found very widely in Semitic and Hellenic thought, as in the notion of a dying and rising god, or the divinity immanent in the processes of nature who is reborn with every seasonal change from winter to spring and whose divine life becomes manifest in the resuscitation of nature. Against all this, the scriptures and not least the Old Testament, are sharply opposed. Resurrection has nothing at all to do with any dying or rising god and cosmic rebirth, although, it must be admitted, this heathen notion has so invaded the Christian church that it is constantly reflected in sermons about the springing up of new life as well as in Easter eggs and similar symbols of the dying and rising gods of nature religions. In view of this, the teaching of the Old Testament is peculiarly relevant, for it is just these notions of 'resurrection' that it sweeps aside in the cleansing of thought from heathen influences. This may well be the reason why people whose notions of resurrection have been influenced and infected by the syncretistic ideas that developed in early Mediterranean Christianity have found in the Old Testament so little developed teaching relating to resurrection as they have come to conceive it.

[Note 2 continued:]

There followed a brief abstract of the first two parts of the projected 'Section VIII', ie. **'1 The resurrection and the person of Christ'** and **'2 The resurrection and the atoning work of Christ'**, the full content of which appeared in the student handouts as here published. There was no reference in the abstract to any of the subsequent sections, ie. to **'3 The nature of the resurrection event'**, nor to any of the material in the chapter on the ascension, although clearly the sections mentioned above (**Section IX The exaltation of the humiliated one** and **Section X The coming again of the incarnate one**) can be seen as the chapter in the handouts entitled 'The Ascension of Jesus Christ' and as its final section, 'The ascension and the parousia of Jesus Christ'. The abstract clearly represents an outline draft of material which was later greatly expanded to become the student handouts and which in turn became the basis of the book. While the book contains significant additions to the handouts and an introduction and final chapter, extended references and certain modifications in wording, the bulk of *Space, Time and Resurrection* comes word for word from the handouts.

(a) *The teaching of the Old Testament*

It is only by looking back at the teaching of the Old Testament scriptures from the perspective created by the resurrection of Christ that we are able to discern the positive things they had to contribute to our understanding of the resurrection and we may set these out as follows.

(i) *Restoration through undergirding covenant faithfulness*

Quite basic to everything is the conception of the covenant which embraces the whole of creation but which is peculiarly related to the people of God. God has bound up his people with himself in the same bundle of life, so that his covenant faithfulness undergirds and supports them beyond anything they are capable of in themselves in life or death. The life and existence of Israel, for example, are so tied to the covenant purpose of God in mercy and judgement that they are restored again and again and are given miraculous continuity throughout the changes, chances and disasters of history.

(ii) *Resurrection primarily corporate*

Hence what is dominant in the Old Testament thought is the stress upon the corporate judgement, vindication and restoration of God's people. Any notion of individual resurrection or survival could only be entirely subordinate to that, and in fact largely disappears behind the corporate picture of God and his covenant community. But here it is apparently the concept of restoration through judgement that is the predominating motif, as we can see in passages from Hosea, Jeremiah and Ezekiel for example.[3]

(iii) *The raising up of a promised saviour*

Along with this corporate restoration there is found the promise of a saviour who will be raised up out of the people, such as the shepherd who is to be raised up like David,[4] or even the servant of the Lord.[5] This line of thought in the Old Testament seems to be bound up with the promised messiah who will spring from the seed of David and from the seed of Abraham, for all through the covenanted relation of Israel to God there persists an inner organic continuity in the promised seed which cannot be destroyed and which will be raised up like a root out of the dry ground[6] for the salvation of God's people.

---

[3]   See such passages as Hos 2.16-20ff.; Jer 23, 29.10ff., 31; Ezek 37.

[4]   Ezek 34.23f., 37.24f.

[5]   Isaiah 53.10-12.

[6]   Isaiah 53.2.

(iv) The application of 'goel' to God

We have to add to this the notion of the *goel* applied to God in his relations with Israel. As the Holy One of Israel he stands in as the advocate who makes Israel's cause his own and redeems it out of all its troubles. This applies not only to Israel as a whole but to all God's people within the covenant, as is particularly evident in the Psalms.[7] It is disputed whether these have any bearing upon the development of the thought of the resurrection of God's people, but this dubiety may reflect the 'wrong' concept of resurrection, as well as a failure to understand '*sheol*' (the biblical 'pit' or 'hell')[8] in terms of the suspension of final judgement. Then we have to note the remarkable passage in Job, where the text is certainly rather corrupt, but which nevertheless contains powerfully the idea that God remains the *goel* even in death to those who trust him.[9]

(v) The later concept of a double resurrection

In later strata of the Old Testament, the conception of a double resurrection appears to emerge, resurrection to judgement as well as of the righteous to life,[10] with which perhaps Isaiah 26[11] may be associated. But it is only with the Apocryphal literature, Maccabees, 4th Esdras, and the Apocalypse of Baruch, that the apocalyptic aspect of resurrection arises clearly. It is to this that the epistle to the Hebrews appears to refer in its reference to 'a better resurrection'.[12]

(b) The teaching of the New Testament

In the New Testament the resurrection, understood in realist terms, is a central and quite dominant concept. Basically it is the resurrection of the shepherd son of David[13] and therefore of his people whom he stands in for as redeemer and advocate. Here resurrection is not at all associated with the cyclic processes of cosmic becoming, but is the

---

[7]   See, for example, such Psalms as 16.10f., 49.15, 73.26, and 17.15.

[8]   Although the Old Testament speaks of the soul or life, *nephesh*, going down to '*sheol*' there is no concept of any memory, or of any life, in *sheol*. See, for example, Psalms 6.5, 30.3,9, 88.3-5,10-12.

[9]   Job 19.25.

[10] Dan 12.2.

[11] Isaiah 26.19.

[12] Heb 11.35 KJV (Gk, *kreissonos anastaseōs*).

[13] Acts 13.22ff.; Rom 15.12.

mighty act of God within our humanity and its sin, corruption and death, shattering the powers of evil and death once for all. It is the work of the creator, now himself incarnate and at work in the midst of fallen creation and its estrangement from God the Father. The resurrection takes place in space and time, in physical and historical existence, in the actual resurrection of Jesus of Nazareth who was crucified under Pontius Pilate. It is a creative event within the creation, an abruptly divine act within history, a decisive event completely setting at nought all cyclic processes, putting an end to the futility to which they are shut up but opening and straightening them out in a movement of consummation. Such a resurrection of the incarnate Word of God within the creation which came into being through him is inevitably an event of cosmic and unbelievable magnitude.

The two main words for resurrection, 'anistēmi' and 'egeirō'

The fact of the resurrection altered the whole situation so drastically that quite new modes of thought and speech had to arise to cope with it, so that it is specially important to examine the language which the New Testament employs in order to speak of the resurrection if we are to go on to interpret it in an appropriate way. The New Testament writers employ two main terms to speak of the resurrection, words built up from the verbs *anistēmi* and *egeirō* and sometimes compounded with the prefix *ex*, out of. Both words mean to lift or raise up, which is the common meaning they have in profane Greek. *Anistēmi* is generally used of lifting up from a seat, or rousing from sleep, but also of waking from the dead or coming to life again. *Egeirō* is not used in profane Greek of raising from the dead or of raising the sick, as in the New Testament. Hence this use of *egeirō* is peculiar to the New Testament which would appear, in fact, to prefer *egeirō* to *anistēmi*.

This preference for *egeirō* appears to lay the major stress on the mighty act of God in raising Jesus from the dead. The resurrection is a supernatural or miraculous event, quite inexplicable from the side of human agency or natural process. It is comparable only to the act of God in the creation itself or in the incarnation. The use of *egeirō* in the New Testament to speak of the raising up of the sick is an indication that the miraculous acts of healing are regarded as falling within the orbit of the resurrection, and as belonging to the creative and recreative activity of God in incarnation and resurrection. In these miracles the resurrection is already evidencing itself beforehand in signs and wonders.

Egeirō and *anistēmi* are also used in the New Testament in the middle voice, particularly *anistēmi*, that is, of Christ rising from the dead. Here the emphasis is upon his own victorious activity, his standing up out of the dead, his rising above corruption and mortality, all seen within the orbit of his own sinless life and the regenerating effect of his holiness upon other human life. It is especially important, however, to consider the way in which these terms are used in the New Testament, within the context of the relation between the Old Testament and the New Testament revelation, for it is this that gives peculiar specification to their meaning. Certain Old Testament nuances are allowed to shine through the New Testament usage in a very enlightening manner.

Old Testament nuances behind the New Testament teaching

(i) The raising up and appointing of prophet, king and priest

We note first the Old Testament custom of speaking of the raising up of a prophet, or king or judge or priest, where the ideas of provision and appointment are blended together. The New Testament uses both *egeirō* and *anistēmi* in this connection. Thus when the New Testament speaks of Jesus being raised up, it evidently refers not only to the resurrection of his body from the grave but to his being raised up as the appointed messiah, the anointed prophet, priest, and king. The resurrection implies the installation or enthronement of Jesus in his offices as *Christos*, the anointed one.

(ii) The miraculous raising up of seed out of the barren womb or the dry ground

The peculiar semitism,[14] raising up seed, is also involved in the New Testament accounts of the resurrection of Jesus. He is raised up as a root out of the dry ground,[15] the shoot of the vine, after it had been cut down to the ground. It is a miraculous act, in line with the raising up of seed out of the barren womb, as in the cases of Sarah, Hannah, Elizabeth, etc.[16] This idea also plays its part in the accounts of the virgin birth of Jesus,[17] but here we see already how the birth and resurrection

---

[14]   Semitic or Hebrew expression.

[15]   Isaiah 53.2.

[16]   Gen 17.15-21, 21.1f; 1 Sam 1.1-20; Luke 1.5-37.

[17]   Matt 1.18-25; Luke 1.26ff., 2.4ff. See further T.F. Torrance, *Incarnation*, Paternoster UK & InterVarsity Press USA, Milton Keynes & Downer's Grove, 2008, pp.87ff. 'Christ's Birth into our Humanity'.

of Jesus are linked, for together they constitute, in the understanding of the New Testament, the raising up of the new seed in whom all nations will be blessed,[18] the first-born of the new creation.[19] This means that the whole life of Jesus is to be regarded as downright miracle, the raising up of the saviour and servant out of the dry ground which could not have produced him spontaneously out of itself, the incredible act of God inaugurating a new creation where, from our human side, it was quite unexpected. With the birth and resurrection of Jesus, with Jesus himself, the relation of the world to God has been drastically altered, for everything has been placed on an entirely new basis, the unconditional grace of God.

(iii) The resurrection and full installation of Christ as the Messiah

So far as Christ himself is concerned, then, the notion of the resurrection involves a powerful combination of the concepts of appointment and the raising up of messianic seed, and is related to his birth, baptism, and triumphant life over sin and evil: together they refer to the full installation of the messiah with power and his declaration as God's Son.[20] But as such the resurrection of Christ carries within it the notion of a corporate resurrection. The seed that is raised up is not only Jesus the messiah as an individual but the body of all those who are involved with him in his anointed humanity. In Christ the whole resurrection is already included in a decisive way. The new humanity is already raised up in Christ. He is the corn of wheat which falling into the ground does not come up alone, but with a whole harvest of grain. This concept of our being raised together with Christ and being born anew in him is found not only in St Paul as in Ephesians[21] but also in 1 Peter.[22]

(iv) The universal significance of the resurrection of Jesus

There follows from this the universal aspect of resurrection. The resurrection of Jesus as act of God is a decisive event, a final judgement, which affects the entire state of human existence, the whole situation in which we live and have our being, and as such affects every human being. It is this concentration of universal significance in the

---

[18] Gen 12.1f.

[19] Col 1.15,18.

[20] Rom 1.4, 'declared to be the Son of God with power ... by the resurrection from the dead' KJV.

[21] Eph 2.5-6; cf. Col 3.1f.

[22] 1 Peter 1.3.

resurrection of Jesus that is so very important for the whole of the Christian message. The New Testament does not teach a doctrine of individual resurrection *first*, in the sense that each person is to rise again because they are made of a body and an immortal soul, a resurrection (*anastasis*) because of some interior principle in their creation. The New Testament thinks always of the resurrection of Jesus as the decisive event and of our resurrection as bound up with his.

The resurrection of Jesus carries with it our resurrection as individuals

The general resurrection is thus absolutely dependent on the resurrection of Jesus Christ himself, for it is in his death and resurrection that God has dealt with death and guilt and hell once and for all. He was put to death for our trespasses and was raised for our justification.[23] In the resurrection of Jesus, an objective act of God has been carried out which carries with it our resurrection as individuals. Individual resurrection is applied to us through the preaching of the gospel of the saving judgement of God embodied once and for all in the resurrection of Jesus. Thus believers find that they are already involved once for all in that resurrection, and already included in the objective reality of Jesus Christ risen from the dead. This means that the unbeliever is also affected, for they too will be judged, precisely by this man whom God has raised from the dead[24] and who confronts everyone as the decisive act of judgement or justification freely proclaimed to all.

One final point should be noted about the New Testament teaching, the relation between the resurrection of Jesus Christ and that of the believer, as for example, we find it in Ephesians 2, where it is declared that as Christ was raised from the dead so we also will be raised for we were raised together with him.[25] The parallelism between Christ and the believer is not simply one of similarity. It is that, but more than that. The resurrection of the believer is regarded primarily as the *effect* of the resurrection of Christ, yet not effect in the sense of some new and subsequent event, but effect as something that is *already* involved in the resurrection of Christ. Our resurrection has already taken place and is already fully tied up with the resurrection of Christ, and therefore proceeds from it *more by way of manifestation* of what has already taken place, *than as new effect* resulting from it.

---

[23]   Rom 4.25.

[24]   Acts 17.30-31.

[25]   Eph 2.5-6.

1 The resurrection and the person of Jesus Christ

(a) *The resurrection is inseparable from the person of the incarnate Son*

The teaching of the New Testament makes it clear that we cannot isolate the resurrection from the whole redeeming purpose of God, or from the decisive deed of God in the incarnation of his Son that ran its full course from the birth of Jesus to his crucifixion and triumph over the powers of evil. The resurrection cannot be detached from Christ himself, and considered as a phenomenon on its own to be compared and judged in the light of other phenomena. Rather must it be considered in the light of who Jesus Christ is in his own person, and therefore in the light of his divine and human natures. It was that Christ who rose again from the dead and no other. Nor must it be considered in abstraction from his saving work fulfilled in and through the incarnation when he, the eternal Word and creative source of all life and being outside of God, entered into our mortal and corrupt existence, that was wasting away under the threat of death and judgement,[26] in order to effect the salvation and recreation of the world. Hence a double duality must be kept in view: (i) the duality formed by the union of divine and human natures in the one person of Christ, and (ii) the duality formed by the entry of his life into our mortality, his light into our darkness, his holiness into our corruption. It is because he who lives and acts in this situation is divine and human *in one person*, that all he does in our fallen existence has a dark side and a light side, a side of humiliation and a side of exaltation – the one is the obverse of the other, but as the mediator he has come to overcome our darkness and baseness and to build a bridge in and through himself over which we may pass into the light and glory of God.

The engagement of the Son with our darkness and the attack of evil on his person[27]

We must think of the Son of God as engaging with the forces of darkness immediately he became incarnate, for the whole of his life was a redemptive operation in our human nature where the forces of evil have entrenched themselves and seek to enslave us. He was made one of us in order to submit himself to those forces of evil, in order both to

---

[26] Cf. the stress of Athanasius on this point in his classic, *On the Incarnation of the Word*.

[27] See further T.F. Torrance, *Incarnation*, p. 236ff.

bear and vanquish them in his own human existence and vicariously to provide for us a way of saving obedience and communion with the Father. The incarnation of the Son must be regarded as the entry of the mediator into a situation where the communion between God and man is broken and distorted, where the divisiveness of sin and guilt have affected the very fabric of human existence. Hence the union effected in the incarnate person of the Son inevitably came under attack and strain. The forces of evil thrust against that union, seeking to break it wide open, to divide the human life of the Son on earth from the life of the Father above, to divide the divine and human natures in Christ himself.[28] However, by living the life that he lived in our midst, the life of complete obedience to the Father and of perfect communion with him, the life of absolute holiness in the midst of our sin and corruption, and by living it through the whole course of our human existence from birth to death, Jesus Christ achieved within our creaturely being that union between God and man that constitutes the heart of atonement, thus effecting humanity's salvation and restoration to communion with God the Father.

The life of the Son in our condition means a humiliation and an exaltation, not one after the other, but one as the obverse of the other

We are not to think of the humiliation and exaltation of Christ simply as two events following one after the other, but as both involved in appropriate measure at the same time all through the incarnate life of Christ. The immersion of Christ the eternal Word into our mortal existence is itself also the exaltation of our lowly existence into union and communion with God. The coming of the Son of God into our lost and alienated being constitutes *Immanuel,* God with us,[29] but if God is with us in Christ then in him we are with God. *We with God* is thus the obverse of *God with us.* The exaltation of man is the obverse of the humiliation of the Son of God. It is in that light that we must think of the mutual involution[30] of mortality and immortality, death and life, the crucifixion and the resurrection of Christ. Seen in this way the resurrection is not to be understood merely as something that follows upon the crucifixion but as the other side of it – that is why we really discern the act of God in the crucifixion of Christ when we penetrate through to the other side of it, and see it not only in its dark and terrible side, but also in its light and glorious side. As a matter of fact the New

---

[28]   Cf. *op. cit.* p. 118-19.

[29]   Matt 1.23.

[30]   Mutual involvement or implication, interpenetration.

Testament nowhere presents us with a bare crucifixion, but only with the crucifixion as seen and reported from the perspective of the resurrection where its real secret or significance was disclosed. The whole gospel is seen from the perspective of the resurrection of Jesus Christ in body and it is in his resurrection that he enters into his glory.[31]

(i) 'Christ clothed with his promises'[32]

The integrity of person, word and work in Christ

The New Testament also nowhere presents us with a naked Christ, but only with the Christ who is clothed with his message and robed in his promises.[33] There is no Christ apart from his teaching or his saving acts but only the Christ who confronts us in and through his teaching and healing. Even on the purely human level he confronts us as one who is characterised by an absolutely sincere relation between his person and his word, his word and his deed – for he nowhere meets us a man who ought to have been other than he was or whose actions fell short of his words. But as incarnate Son of God he confronts us as he in whom person and work and word are indissolubly one. It is his own person that he communicates in his words and deeds, while his words and deeds do not only derive from his person but inhere in it. This is why the New Testament nowhere seeks to present Christ to us apart from his *kērygma* or *didachē*,[34] or apart from the mighty acts of healing and forgiving that were wrought by him, but always and only with the Christ who is in himself the secret of his *kērygma* and whose *kērygma* is what it is because of its profound inner relation to his personal being. The Christ who is proclaimed to us in the New Testament, therefore, is the Christ who is clothed with the *kērygma* of his death and resurrection, for they are ontologically and structurally bound up with who he is in himself and in his relation to the Father.

The person of Christ, clothed with his crucifixion and resurrection, is the great paschal mystery of our salvation

Similarly the New Testament does not present us with a message of good Friday and then with a message of Easter, but always and only with the Easter message of Christ the crucified risen again, the lamb

---

[31]   Luke 24.26; John 7.39, 17.1f.; cf. Acts 2.33; Rom 6.9, etc.

[32]   Cf. the section 'Christ clothed with his gospel', T.F. Torrance, *The School of Faith*, James Clarke, London 1959, pp. lxxx-lxxxiii and following.

[33]   Calvin, *Institute of the Christian Religion*, 2.9.3.

[34]   Gk, 'proclamation' and 'teaching'.

'as though it had been slain'[35] but alive for evermore. Think of the way in which this is presented to us in the preaching of Peter in Acts and even more clearly in the first epistle of Peter. The whole course of events in the last weeks of Jesus' life, the passion period, to which the Gospels devote such a high proportion of their account, is regarded as a continuous and structural unity. The early Christians called it the *pascha*[36] in view of the *passover* which was celebrated in Israel at that time and which Christ fulfilled in his own *passion* as the *paschal lamb*. Jesus Christ was regarded as himself constituting the great passover from death to life, from man-in-death to man-in-the-life-of-God, from damnation to salvation, from destruction to new creation. But that *pascha* which he accomplished in himself for our sakes is proclaimed as the great *pascha* which he has accomplished for the church and the world. It is, then, in that profound unity and continuity, ontologically structured in and through the person of Christ as mediator, that the resurrection was understood as forming with the crucifixion the great *paschal mystery* of our salvation.

(ii) The resurrection is not just the completion of our salvation but part of the very being and person of Christ as mediator

We return, then, to the fact that the resurrection is inseparable from the person of the incarnate Son of God who constituted in himself as the mediator the bridge between man and God and between death and life. He condescended in great humiliation to unite himself with us in our weakness, corruption and damned existence, living within it all the life of unsullied purity, truth and holiness in such a way as to atone in life and death for our sin and guilt, overcoming all the estrangement and separation that it involved between man and God, and in such a way therefore as to resurrect in himself our human nature in union and communion with the Father. The resurrection is to be regarded not only as the completion of that saving work but as belonging to *the ontological structure of the mediator himself*, who stood in the gap of the *Eli, Eli, lama sabachthani*,[37] and bestrode it in his own personal existence, supplying for all humanity the living bridge from death to life. As such, of course, the resurrection is also the manifestation of the beloved Son and his installation with power into

---

[35] Rev 5.6.

[36] 'Passover', the LXX translation of the Hebrew *pesach*.

[37] 'My God, my God, why hast thou forsaken me?' Matt 27.46; Mark 15.34; Psalm 22.1.

messianic and mediatorial office. It is the seal that the Father set upon his vicarious life and mission, crowning in a final declaration of power all that he had come to do as incarnate Son of God. The resurrection is the revelation of the Father's acceptance of the life and death of Jesus as full and sufficient sacrifice for the sin of the world and at the same time its finalisation as eternally prevailing mediation between God and humankind.

It is worth recalling at this point the *goel* aspect of redemption which is grounded in the inseparable relation between the redemptive act and the person of the redeemer, that is, the incarnational and ontological aspect of atonement. That is the aspect that comes so clearly and powerfully into the light with the resurrection of Christ as the pledge and surety of our redemption. In him our human life is carried over across the chasm of death and judgement into union with the divine life, so that it is through our sharing in his humanity in death and resurrection that we participate in all the fruits of his atoning work.

Fuller consideration must now be given to two questions: the relation of the resurrection to the *active and passive obedience* of Christ,[38] and the relation of the resurrection to the *virgin birth* of Christ.[39]

(b) The resurrection of Jesus Christ as passive and active

(i) The resurrection as passive – Jesus was raised

In line with his *passive obedience* and submission to the Father's judgement, the resurrection of Christ is to be regarded as the act whereby he was raised from the dead by the Father. Here the emphasis undoubtedly falls upon the fact that in death Jesus submitted completely to our condition in utter weakness and powerlessness. It was real and complete death – our death into which he entered, and where he was so powerless that he had to be raised up by God himself. That was in line with his whole mission, revealed so clearly in the temptations that followed upon his baptism. Son of God though he was, he declined to use his divine power in order to help him in the hunger to which he had been reduced in vicarious fasting and

---

[38]   *Active obedience*, Jesus' fulfilment of the law and positive human righteousness; *passive obedience*, Jesus' suffering the consequences and judgement of sin. For an outline of the mutual importance and inseparability of Jesus' active and passive obedience, see T.F. Torrance, *Incarnation*, pp. 80-82.

[39]   Cf. *op. cit.* 96-97.

penitence, for he had come to appropriate our weakness and meet and overcome all the assaults of evil in our abject condition. The same temptation came with all its force as he hung upon the cross. 'If you are the Son of God, come down from the cross',[40] but he resisted the temptation to use divine power to escape from his vicarious mission and remained still and passive as death overtook him, submitting to the ultimate lot of mankind in the disintegration and finality of death. *Passive resurrection* is the counterpart to that abject passion, and corresponds to the *anhypostatic* aspect of the incarnation[41] and the dramatic aspect of redemption in which we are redeemed by the sheer act of almighty God.

(1) The resurrection as the 'amen' of justification, God's 'satisfaction' in the Son

If the death of Jesus on the cross is to be regarded as the sentence of divine judgement inflicted on him for our sakes and on us in him, the resurrection is to be regarded as the obverse of that, itself also the sentence and judgement of God. Both these aspects are carried in the New Testament notion of *justification*. We recall that the Greek word *dikaioun* means to justify in both senses, to condemn and to vindicate. The resurrection of Christ is thus to be understood in terms of justification by the Father, the justification of Christ following his condemnation in our place, and therefore as carrying the sentence of divine forgiveness and emancipation from the guilt and bondage of sin.

It is of course the positive side of that justifying act that is ascendant here. The resurrection is God's great act of *amen* to the cross. In the crucifixion of Christ we have on the one hand God's judgement on sin and on the other hand Jesus' submission to that judgement in obedience unto death. From God's side the crucifixion is his righteous condemnation of our sin, but from man's side it is Christ's high priestly *amen* to the Father's judgement. But in the resurrection we have the same whole event, not only as God's judgement but as his positive satisfaction in the obedient self-sacrifice of his Son. And here the resurrection is the Father's *amen* to Christ's high priestly self-offering in obedience and sacrifice for sin. If the cross is God's *No* against us in judgement on our sin which Christ endured for our sakes – 'My God, my God, why have you forsaken me?' – the resurrection is God's *Yes* to

---

40   Matt 27.40.

41   The fact that the humanity of Jesus had no independent existence, *apart from* the incarnation of the Word.

us in his affirmation of Jesus as son of man and all that he has done for us in our nature and on our behalf. Hence in the resurrection of Jesus the passion is seen as the same event from God's side.

(2) The proper place of a doctrine of 'satisfaction' in the atonement

This is the point at which a doctrine of *satisfaction* has its proper place in the atonement. Historically, satisfaction has been understood mainly as the fulfilment of a legal requirement in making amendment for wrong and meeting the demands of justice. In the New Testament, satisfaction is the 'good pleasure' of God in the obedient self-offering of the incarnate Son, manifested and expressed in the raising of the Son from the dead and in a refusal to allow him to see corruption. When Jesus submitted to baptism at the hands of John in order 'to fulfil all righteousness'[42] he was greeted with the words of the Father, 'You are my beloved Son in whom I am well pleased'.[43] So here in the resurrection, 'You are my beloved Son, today I have begotten you'[44] is translated into fact, and in him and his resurrection God has made us accepted according to the good pleasure of his will. The atoning sacrifice offered in the life and death of Christ is here acknowledged and affirmed by God, the act of the Son manifested to be the act of God himself. In Pauline language, Christ was raised for our justification.[45] Satisfaction is not the divine satisfaction in death, as compensation for violated law, nor only the satisfaction in the fulfilment of divine righteousness, but the satisfaction of the Father in the Son who has fulfilled the Father's good pleasure in making righteous atonement. Thus in the resurrection the Father owns Christ as his Son and acknowledges his deed in life and death as his own deed.

(ii) The resurrection as active – Jesus rose

(1) Jesus triumphed over the grave by his sinlessness – he had no sin for death to hold him

In line with his *active obedience* as Son on earth offering to his Father in heaven a life of holiness and filial love, the resurrection of Christ is to be regarded as his own act in taking again the life that he had laid down.[46] Here the emphasis falls upon the fact that in death and in

---

[42]   Matt 3.15.

[43]   See Luke 3.22.

[44]   See Psalm 2.7; cf. Isaiah 42.1.

[45]   Rom 4.25.

[46]   John 10.18.

resurrection Christ acted in entire consistency with the way in which he lived his life in unbroken fellowship with the Father and in the perfection of union with him. Although he assumed our fallen and corrupt humanity when he became flesh, he in assuming it sanctified it in himself, and all through his earthly life overcame our sin through his righteousness, our impurity through his purity, condemning sin in our flesh by the sheer holiness of his life within it. That is why death could not hold him even when he entered into and submitted to it, for there was no sin in him which allowed it to subject him to corruption. Death had nothing in him, for he had already passed through its clutches by the perfection of his holiness. Thus by entering into our death as the holy one of God he robbed it of its sting,[47] he took away its power as he accepted the divine judgement in the expiatory sacrifice of his own life, and thus triumphed over the forces of guilt and evil which had made death the last stronghold of their grip over man. He triumphed over the grave through his sheer sinlessness.

(2) The resurrection is the holding firm of the hypostatic union through death and hell

We may also speak of this in terms of the hypostatic union of the divine and human natures in the one person of Christ. That was a living and dynamic union which ran throughout the whole of his life, in which he maintained union and communion with the Father in the steadfastness of the Father toward the Son and in the steadfastness of the Son toward the Father. The resurrection means that this union did not give way but held under the strain imposed not only by the forces that sought to divide Jesus from God, but the strain imposed through the infliction of the righteous judgement of the Father upon our rebellious humanity which Christ had made his own – and it held under the strain imposed by both in the crucifixion: the hypostatic union survived the descent into hell and Christ arose still in unbroken communion with the Father. The resurrection is thus the resurrection of the union forged between man and God in Jesus out of the damned and lost condition of humanity into which Christ entered in order to share their lot and redeem them from doom. Here we are thinking of the resurrection in line with the *enhypostatic* aspect of the incarnation,[48] that is, in the fullness and integrity of his human life and agency in the saving work of God.

---

[47]   1 Cor 15.54f.

[48]   The fact that the humanity of Jesus, with no existence in itself *apart from* the incarnation of the Son, did have real personal existence *in* (*en*) the person (*hypostasis*) of the eternal Son.

(3) Jesus the new Adam who breathes life into others and heads a new creation

Jesus Christ rose again in virtue of his holiness as the second man, the last man, the new Adam who heads the race in the new creation opened up in the resurrection from the dead.[49] As such he rose clothed with the power of the resurrection and is spoken of as life-giving spirit.[50] He was not only an Adam into whom God breathed the breath of life and made a quickened soul, but the Adam with such fullness of life in himself that even as man he breathed quickening spirit into others. He is the resurrected man who has life in himself, and is become in himself the source and fountain of eternal life for others.[51] By living in utter holiness as Son on earth he appropriated for and into our human nature the eternal life of God, and it was by virtue of that 'power of an endless life'[52] that he broke through the bonds of death and the grave. It is that same 'power of an endless life' that now overflows from him to all who are members of his body, and it is therefore out of his fullness that we may all receive.

Since Jesus Christ is himself the resurrection and the life, he is himself also the reconciliation and salvation of humanity – the risen Jesus Christ is the living atonement, atonement in its glorious achievement not only in overcoming the separation of sin, guilt and death, but in consummating union and communion with God in such a way that the divine life overflows freely through him into mankind. Of course if Christ had not risen from the dead, that would have indicated that the atonement had not been achieved, that he had not actually been able to stand in for us and take our place; and then his sacrifice on the cross could have been seen only as a terrible act of final injustice – the atonement would have been a fiasco. However, now that he has risen from the dead, the atonement is shown to have been carried through to its final end. In this accomplishment it is evident that the atonement wrought by Christ and Christ himself its agent cannot be separated from one another – he emerges as the living atonement eternally prevailing in its advocacy before God and eternally prevailing in its perpetuation for man with God.

---

[49]   1 Cor 15.45ff.; cf. Rom 1.4, 5.12ff.; 2 Cor 5.17.

[50]   1 Cor 15.45.

[51]   John 11.25, cf. 5.21f.,26f., 6.35ff.

[52]   Heb 7.16 KJV.

(4) As passive and active the resurrection corresponds to anhypostasia and enhypostasia

As passive and active, then, the resurrection corresponds to *anhypostasia* and *enhypostasia*.[53] It is at once the mighty act of God's pure grace which raises mankind from the dead where they are utterly hopeless and unable to help themselves, but it is that mighty act of God translated into the perfection of a human act which is made to issue freely and fully out of human nature, in which man is made to stand up before God as his beloved Son in whom he is well pleased. Resurrection is atonement in its creative and positive result and achievement, in the re-creation and final affirmation of men and women and children and the assuming of them by grace into union and communion with the life and love of God himself.

(c) The relation of the resurrection to the virgin birth of Christ[54]

It is in the resurrection that we have the unveiling of the mystery of the incarnation: the birth and resurrection of Jesus belong inseparably together and have to be understood in the light of each other. The creation of the world out of nothing means that created existence is made contingent upon the Word and will of God while utterly distinct from him. Therein lies its creaturely contingence and freedom which must be respected. That is why the processes of created existence can be known only by exploring them out of themselves, not by looking at God. It is by looking at God that we know what the creation really is (the contingent creation of God), but by looking at God and his creative relation to the world we are sent back to the world he made and loves in order to explore it out of itself. When the eternal Word by whom all things were made himself became incarnate, he entered within that same contingence and freedom of the creaturely reality, sharing in it to the full, and so may be known only *a posteriori*[55] out of that created order, in Jesus. Such an incarnation of the Son is inevitably a concealing of the divine power, for that power now enters within creaturely reality without abrogating it, in order to operate within it in the fulfilment of the divine will for its healing and re-creation.

---

[53]   For a fuller definition of *anhypostasia* and *enhypostasia* in their complementarity see T.F. Torrance, *Incarnation*, p. 84-5.

[54]   Cf. *op. cit.* p. 96-7.

[55]   By experience, only through empirical investigation, *after* or following on the event, ie. not *a priori*, in terms of reason and first principles, *before* the event and in advance of empirical investigation.

(i) The veiling and the unveiling of God in the life of Jesus

Yet the world into which the Son entered is not merely creaturely – it is the world that has fallen from God and has entered upon a downward, detached and estranged course in which evil and irrationality and enmity to divine grace have embedded themselves in its existence and are at work destroying it. Hence the incarnation of the Son of God means that he is concealed by what is contrary, by the very flesh of sin and the body of death, the fallen existence which he made his own in order to heal and sanctify it. It is not surprising, then, if we are to think of the line from the birth of Jesus to his crucifixion as the line of the hiddenness of God, the line of his activity in penetrating into our estranged existence, in order to get beneath our burden of sin and judgement and to get inside our death. But there is also a line from his birth to his resurrection which is the unveiling of God, a line that becomes fleetingly manifest in the transfiguration[56] as also in the healing miracles and the other manifestations of Jesus' creative power.

If the crucifixion represents the nadir of the hiddenness, the resurrection represents the high point of the revelation of Jesus as the Son of God become man.[57] Just as humiliation and exaltation were involved in one another and were the obverse of each other, so also these two lines of veiling and unveiling mutually involve one another – that is why Jesus revealed himself only slowly and in such a way that his self-disclosure kept pace with the development of his life and the steady march of events to their climax in the cross: one was not allowed to outstrip the other. On top of the final darkness of the *Eli, Eli, lama sabachthani* and burial in the finality of death, came the rending of the tomb and the unveiling of Jesus Christ as the Son of God come to be our saviour. He had come deliberately to share with us our life and death in order to make us share with him his eternal life in God. Since the resurrection is the final unveiling of the secret of Christ, the glorification of God incarnate, it is in the resurrection that the passion becomes lit up and is made articulate: it is transformed into luminous word – the word of the cross as power of God to all who believe.[58]

(ii) Redemption and creation come together in the resurrection

It is in this context of the relation of the resurrection to the cross and the whole life of Jesus that we discern *the secret of him who was born of Mary*: that he was in fact none other than the creator Word of God

---

[56]   Matt 17.1-9; Mark 9.2-9; Luke 9.28-36.

[57]   Rom 1.4; cf. John 20.28.

[58]   Rom 1.16.

come as a creature within the world he had made. In the resurrection of Jesus we see that the saving act of God in the expiation of sin and guilt, in the vanquishing of death and all that destroys the creation, is joined to God's act of creation. Redemption and creation come together in the resurrection. Indeed God's *No* to all evil and its privation of being falls together with his *Yes* in the final affirming of the creation as that which God has made and declared to be good[59] – for that declaration of God about what he had made is now made good through Jesus Christ. Atonement is unveiled to be the positive reaffirmation and re-creation of man. Apart from the resurrection, the *No* of God against our sins and the whole world of evil in which we had become entangled, even his rejection of our guilt, would be in vain – that is why St Paul argues so insistently that if Christ is not risen we are still in our sins.[60] But it is also true that apart from that *No*, the resurrection is no real *Yes*. Apart from God's *No*, in judgement and crucifixion, the resurrection would be only an empty show of wonderful power – it would not have any saving content to it, it would contain no forgiveness. By itself the expiatory death of Christ would mean only judgement, not life, only rejection of guilt – and yet even that could not be carried through apart from the resurrection – but now in the resurrection that act of atonement is seen to be God's great positive work of new creation. Thus the *No* and the *Yes* imply one another, and each is empty without the other. The vast significance of the crucifixion and resurrection emerges only as we see that here *redemption and creation come completely together.*

(iii) The resurrection reveals that the virgin birth was the birth of the almighty Creator-Word

When God created the world, all things were made through his Word.[61] He spoke and it was done. In the resurrection it becomes revealed that Jesus Christ is none other than that almighty Creator-Word of God, but with that disclosure the crucifixion is quite transformed in our understanding, and becomes the way that God's creative activity has taken in the restoration of creation. It is this conjunction of atoning death and re-creation in the resurrection that means that out of the cross there goes forth into the world the creative, saving Word of God almighty, so that all things, visible and invisible, fall under its purpose and sway and are directed to the consummation of all things in the

---

[59]   Gen 1.4,10,18,21,25,31.

[60]   1 Cor 15.17.

[61]   Gen 1; John 1.1-3; cf. Heb 1.1-2.

new heaven and new earth.[62] That is the real meaning of the New Testament *kērygma*, for then the word of the cross is not just a word about the cross but the creator Word and power of God confronting men and women in and through the crucifixion of Christ in such a way as to confront them with the last things and bring upon them the final great acts of the world's renewal and salvation. The resurrection of Jesus Christ from the dead is now in the very forefront of the church's *kērygma*, for it is a stupendous deed, comparable only to the original creation of the universe. Indeed like the incarnation itself, when God himself entered the creation as one of the creatures he had made in order to operate within it, the resurrection transcends it in significance.

This brings up back to the birth of Jesus – the resurrection discloses that the virgin birth was the act and mode of the *creator's* entry into his own creation as man among humanity. Abstracted from the whole field of God's operations in creation and redemption and considered merely in its individual aspect, it can be given meaning only in a relation to other human births where they are all comparable, but seen in the continuum of God's creative-redemptive work it is quite different. Yet it is only when we see that the creator-Word is God, here creatively at work within the midst of the old creation, breaking its continuity in estrangement and beginning a new creation headed by the incarnate Son, that we really penetrate into its inner happening and understand it out of itself as *grace alone* in our midst. It is then seen to be proleptic to the resurrection of the dead and building with it the birth of the new creation, which cannot be understood merely through tracing its connecting lines with the old creation, but only through discerning the transformation of the old order into the new.

(iv) The correspondence of the resurrection to the nature of the person of Christ

Before we can understand more fully the relation of the resurrection to the person of Christ we shall have to examine the specific nature of the resurrection event, but meantime we may gather up the discussion so far by saying that *what Jesus Christ is in his resurrection, he is in himself.* The resurrection was not just an event that happened to Christ, for it corresponded to the kind of person he was in his own being. With the recognition of this complete consistency between the resurrection event and the essence of the resurrected one, comes the full realisation that the whole life of Jesus Christ, together with his resurrection, was the manifestation among mankind in time and history of the ultimate and original and final creative activity of God. Although we may approach

---

[62]   Cf. Col 1.15-20; Eph 1.10.

Christ by meeting him and seeking to understand him in his humanity, as soon as we confront him in the power of his resurrection our understanding of his humanity must be set within the fact of *the whole Christ*, as God manifest in the flesh, the creator in our midst as human creature, come to effect the recreation of human nature from within its existence in space and time. Thus the relation of the resurrection to the person of Christ discloses to us that *it is the whole Jesus Christ who is the content of the resurrection*, for all of his life from birth to resurrection forms an indissoluble unity.

2 The resurrection and the atoning work of Christ

Here we must bear in mind the full content of the doctrine of atonement though we shall be concerned only with the place of the resurrection of Christ within it. We will consider this in relation to justification, reconciliation and redemption, leaving to the last our examination of the nature of the resurrection as an event in space and time.

a) The resurrection and justification

The relation between forgiveness and resurrection

Again and again the New Testament relates the resurrection to the divine act of *forgiveness* which is not just the non-imputation of our sins but a positive act of the divine mercy in which we are reinstated before God as though we had not sinned. Forgiveness here is a stupendous act which only God can do, blotting out what is past, and recreating what has been wasted by sin. As such forgiveness has two sides to it. From the side of God who forgives it is an act in which the forgiver bears the cost and burden of forgiveness. The resurrection reveals that God himself was at work directly in Jesus Christ, making himself responsible for our condition, and fulfilling it by bearing the cost of forgiveness in himself. Forgiveness is not just a word of pardon but a word translated into our existence by crucifixion and resurrection, by judgement and recreation. From the side of those who are forgiven, forgiveness means emancipation from the thraldom of guilt and reaffirmation as God's dear children in Jesus Christ. It means that our status as sinners is rejected and we are freely given the status of people who are pure and holy before God.

The resurrection is forgiveness actualised – the healing of the paralytic

The relation between forgiveness and the resurrection may be seen in the evangelical account of the healing of the paralytic who was let down through the roof into the house in order to be put in touch with Jesus.[63] St Mark, for example, tells us that at first Jesus said to the sick man, 'Son, your sins are forgiven', then anticipating the objection that only God could forgive sins, he added, 'that you may know that the Son of man has power on earth to forgive sins', and then, '*rise*, take up your bed and go home' and we read that immediately the man was made whole. The resurrection term *egeirō* is used here, which reveals that the early church not only understood this incident as falling within the sphere of the power of the resurrection, but understood the relation of the resurrection to the forgiveness of sins after the pattern of these two words of Jesus – the word of miraculous healing demonstrating the divine power in the word of forgiveness, but disclosing at the same time that forgiveness reaches its full reality in the healing and creative work of God upon the whole man. In other words, it is in the resurrection of Jesus Christ that all that God had to say about our forgiveness, and all that Jesus had said about forgiveness, became actualised in the same sphere of reality as that to which we belong. The word of pardon was fully enacted in our existence – that is why, once more, St Paul could say that if Jesus is not risen from the dead, then we are still in our sins, unforgiven and unshriven or unabsolved.

(i) The resurrection is the fulfilment of justification

This is another way of saying that in justification God's *No* and God's *Yes* come together, for the resurrection is the fulfilment of the decisive deed of justification, in rejecting sin and the status of the sinner and in establishing the sinner once more as God's child. Justification is not only a declaratory act, but an actualisation of what is declared. When Christ said to the paralysed man that his sins were forgiven, they *were forgiven* – as the word of healing made clear. It was not that the subsequent word of healing added something to the first word to make it complete, but rather that the full reality of the healing and recreating word spoken in forgiveness was manifested in the physical event of healing that followed the second word. The resurrection tells us that when God declares someone just, that person *is* just. Resurrection means that the Word which God sent on his mission does not return to God void but accomplishes that for which it was sent.[64]

---

63 Mark 2.1-12.
64 Cf. Isaiah 55.10-11.

A purely forensic doctrine of justification bypasses the resurrection, and is empty without an active sharing in Christ's righteousness

When, therefore, the Protestant doctrine of justification is formulated only in terms of forensic 'imputation' of righteousness or the non-imputation of sins in such a way as to avoid saying that to justify is to make righteous, it is the resurrection which is being bypassed. If we think of justification only in the light of the crucifixion as non-imputation of sins because of what Christ has borne for our sakes, then we have mutilated it severely. No doubt we can fill it out with more positive content by relating it to the incarnate life of Christ and to his active obedience, that is, fill it out with his positive divine-human righteousness – and that would be right, for then justification becomes not only the non-imputation of sins but the clothing of the sinner with the righteousness of Christ. Nevertheless, that would still be empty and unreal, merely a judicial transaction, unless the doctrine of justification bears in its heart a relation of real union with Christ.[65] Apart from such a union with him through the power of his Spirit, as Calvin puts it, Christ would remain, as it were, inert or idle.[66] We require an active relation to Christ as our righteousness, an active and an actual sharing in his righteousness. This is possible only through the resurrection – when we approach justification in this light we see that it is a creative event in which our regeneration or renewal is already included within it.

Justification and resurrection stand or fall together

This is a point that must be taken much more seriously today. If justification is only a forensic or judicial act of imputation or non-

---

[65]   Cf. T.F. Torrance, *The School of Faith*, p. cxf, 'it is through participating in Christ that we partake of his benefits, for unless he gives himself to us first, his blessings are not ours. This means that the forensic element in the atoning work of Christ rests upon the basis of his incarnation, upon his person and human life, and therefore that the forensic element in justification reposes for its substance and meaning upon union with Christ. It is through union with him that we enter into the blessing of justification'. For a discussion (in the context of an ecumenical debate with Anglicans) of justification through union with Christ and on Calvin's views, see T.F. Torrance, *Conflict and Agreement in the Church*, vol.1, Lutterworth, London 1959, pp. 63-66. See further, T.F. Torrance, *Theology in Reconstruction*, SCM Press, London 1965, chap. 9, pp. 150-168, 'Justification: Its Radical Nature and Place in Reformed Doctrine and Life'.

[66]   *Institute* 3.1.1.

imputation, then the resurrection is correspondingly an 'event' of the same kind. But if the resurrection is an actual event in the raising of Jesus Christ in the fullness of his humanity from corruption and death, then justification must correspondingly be a creative, regenerating event. A proper doctrine of justification and a proper doctrine of the resurrection hang together – when one is mutilated the other becomes attenuated.

(ii) Questions for the Protestant doctrine of justification

Two questions have to be asked here, particularly about the Protestant doctrine of justification.

(1) Without a real union with the risen Christ here and now is there not a dichotomy between creation and redemption?

Does there not lurk somewhere in the insistence that justification does not mean a making righteous, a Marcionite[67] dichotomy between redemption and creation? But if we take seriously the fact that in Jesus Christ God's *No* to sin and evil and his *Yes* to creation come together, then how can we but expound justification in the unity of redemption and creation? No doubt we must also see this in the eschatological perspective, for there is certainly a time-lag, so far as duration in our space-time is concerned, between the resurrection of Christ the head of the body and of us who are members of his body, yet we cannot without infidelity to the teaching of the New Testament push the fulfilment of the last things wholly into the future. Through the power of the Spirit we have union with the risen Christ here and now and in that union we taste already the powers of the age to come. Thus we are not only delivered by the mighty acts of God in Christ out of the powers of evil and darkness and guilt and death and hell, but we are given to participate in the eternal life of Jesus, victorious over death and corruption, so that in Christ we live on the other side of the cross, on the other side of the power and dominion of sin, on the other side of judgement – already in the new heaven and the new earth, already in the power of the resurrection. Hence the New Testament frequently speaks of our resurrection in Christ in the aorist and perfect tenses[68] and not simply in the future tense, and that must alter the perspective in which we speak of justification.

---

[67] For Marcion, the God of the creation and of the Old Testament is different from the God of redemption and of the New Testament.

[68] Gk past tenses, e.g. 'were raised' or 'rose' (*aorist*), 'have been raised' or 'have risen' (*perfect*).

(2) Without some doctrine of realised justification is there not a dualism between God and the world, and a forgetting of Pentecost?

Does the Protestant rejection of justification as meaning making righteous not imply some form of deistic dualism between God and the world – that is, a situation in which God is not thought of as interacting in any real way with nature or human existence? No doubt there is a kind of suspension between the word of forgiveness and the actualisation of forgiveness in the resurrection of the body, a suspension which the ascension of Christ makes us take seriously, yet once again we cannot forget the fact of Pentecost when the power of the risen Christ was poured out upon the church and indeed upon 'all flesh'. This means that we are not left in history with only a dialectical relation[69] between a 'word of divine pardon' now and a 'word of divine power' that is held over till the last day, but that between the times, here and now through the power of the Spirit, who is God himself present in the immediate energy of his divine being, we are made to participate in the power of the resurrection and God himself is at work creatively in our midst, regenerating, sanctifying and healing. It is this aspect of *realised justification* through the power of the resurrection that we have mediated to us in the sacraments – baptism being here the sacrament of our once and for all justification, and holy communion being the sacrament of our continuous partaking of the power of the risen Lord in anticipation of the new creation and the final resurrection of the body. Every kind of deistic dualism between God and our world is rejected by the resurrection of Christ.

The critical question of bodily resurrection

This raises the question as to how far we are to think of the resurrection as an event in the physical existence of our space and time. The old fashioned deism which one still finds in positivists and humanists rejected the resurrection of Christ in body on the ground that it was not consonant with the way they regarded the relation between God and nature. But one must ask whether there are not other more concealed forms of deism which appear in reinterpretations of the resurrection which detach the dynamic acts of God from any causal (understood in God's unique creative way) relation to physical worldly reality.

---

[69]   A dialectical relation, as the term is used here, is one of close relation between two things in which one impinges on the other but is held apart from it – a dialectical relation between time and eternity, for example, is one in which eternity affects time by continually impinging on it but does not enter into it and so the two are held in close relation but held apart.

Quite evidently, the resurrection has become once again, as in the New Testament and the early church, an issue of supreme importance and one of the most important and distinctive of all Christian doctrines. It may well be that belief in the resurrection as real happening in our human existence, as objective act of God within the space and time of our world, is once again the great dividing line between people in our own day.[70]

(b) The resurrection and reconciliation

Reconciliation between man and God through the initiative of God's grace is finally achieved and consummated in the resurrection where a bond of unity and love is forged in our actual existence which is everlasting and incorruptible. We may think of this in the light of what St Paul has to say in Romans 8.[71] The union of God and man begun in the birth of *Immanuel*[72] reaches throughout the incarnate life and work of Christ and is fully and finally achieved on man's side and on God's side in the crucifixion and resurrection of Jesus Christ. That union of divine love has been inserted into our existence in Christ, and now that it has survived death and judgement in the resurrection, it remains final and complete, which nothing in heaven or earth can or will undo. Two primary aspects of that fall to be considered.

(i) The resurrection is the fulfilment of reconciliation

The resurrection brings the contradiction between God and man to an end. The resurrection of Jesus is the fulfilment of the divine judgement enacted in the crucifixion – and as such is the completed act of God's righteousness. Here we are back again in the relation between the resurrection and justification, but the aspect of that which concerns us here and which overlaps with reconciliation, is the fact that all enmity between man and God has been brought to an end. The relations of holy God with sinful humanity have run their course in such a way that humanity, judged and condemned by God on the cross because of their sin, is by the same God justified and raised up, made to stand before God in complete righteousness and peace as his dear children. That took place in Jesus Christ himself in the whole course of his life from birth to death, but in his resurrection Jesus Christ has carried through to its completion the relations of God and man in such a way there is now

---

[70]   Cf. T.F. Torrance, *Conflict and Agreement*, vol. 1, p. 98f.

[71]   Rom 8.31ff.

[72]   Matt 1.23.

no longer any barrier between God and man – enmity is utterly abolished. Communion with God in the resurrection is restored in the fullest and most positive reconciliation. Atonement without resurrection would not be reconciliation, and without reconciliation atonement would not have reached its proper end in union with the Father, in peace. It is thus the resurrection of our human nature in Christ into communion with the life of God that is the end and goal of atonement.

The fulfilment of the steadfast love of God and the answering trust of the son of man

We may state this in another way. Resurrection means that the steadfastness of the love of God in giving himself to man in spite of judgement and condemnation is a steadfastness that has achieved its end. The resurrection means that God's covenant mercies have triumphed over all the contradictions and separation of evil and their judgement by the holy love of God. God's will of love to give himself unreservedly to man has persisted through the midst of judgement and death and is fully and finally made good in the resurrection.[73] But the resurrection also means that the steadfastness of the son of man is such that it held on its way in utter obedience to the Father in the spirit of holiness in the midst of judgement, death and hell, and in spite of them, so that he raised himself up from the dead in perfect amen to the Father's will, acquiescing in his verdict upon our sin but responding in complete trust and love to the Father. The resurrection is the goal of the steadfast obedience of the son of man in answer to the steadfast love of the Father.

Apart from the resurrection reconciliation would be hollow

God would not have been true to himself had he allowed Jesus to see corruption. Jesus would not have been true to God had he not risen above judgement and therefore out of the grave in complete agreement with the Father for that would have meant that he had failed in his holiness. The amen of the cross was not just an act of infinite resignation on Jesus' part to the Father's will; it was positive and affirmative fulfilment, and the resurrection is the complete amen of the Son to the Father as of the Father to the Son. Resurrection means, therefore, that the work of Christ in life and death, his substitutionary and representative obedience unto death, is perfectly efficacious and sufficient, both from the side of God and from the side of humanity. In summary, the resurrection means that the divine act of reconciliation

---

[73]   Rom 8.32f.,35f.

reaches its completion and end and that apart from the resurrection, reconciliation would prove a hollow fiasco, for separation between humanity and God would have remained in force.

(ii) The fulfilment of Christ's 'I am' – eternal reconciliation

It is in the resurrection that the *I am* of Jesus is made good and fulfilled in act – the *Ego eimi* of God to man, of God in man, and so of man in Christ to God. 'I am the resurrection and the life', said Jesus in the fourth Gospel.[74] In this *I am* of the risen Lord the atonement becomes abiding and enduring fact, and reconciliation becomes eternally valid and eternally living reality between God and humanity. In the *I am* of the resurrection the atonement is not just an act of judgement but *active truth in the form of personal being* – truth as the Lord Christ, atonement as identical with his person in action, reconciliation as the living and everlasting union of God and man in Christ. This is the great message that keeps bursting through the Apocalypse, 'I am he that lives, and was dead, and behold I am alive for evermore'.[75] Reconciliation is identical with the living and personal being of the mediator and as such marches through the ages and is present in the midst of all world affairs and is there meeting us in its final destinies. Through the cross all that was wrought out in the incarnation issues into eternal and prevalent reality, for it is anchored in Jesus Christ in the being of God himself. Thus the resurrection is the final and eternal affirmation and concretion of all that was done for us in the life and death of Jesus Christ, so that *he is our peace*, and *he is our reconciliation*. He is the living atonement or reconciliation in the form of personal being and reality in God.

The implications of this are very far reaching for our understanding of the whole gospel, but we may note several corollaries which can serve to bring out its significance.

(iii) Corollaries of the resurrection

(1) Sonship with Christ – adoption to become children of God

The resurrection carries with it the doctrine of *adoption* or *sonship*. 'By his great mercy we have been born anew to a living hope through the resurrection of Jesus Christ from the dead, and to an inheritance which is imperishable, undefiled, and unfading, kept in heaven for you, who by God's power are guarded through faith (*dia pisteōs*, that is, God's faithfulness which calls for answering faith from us) for a salvation

---

[74]   John 11.25.

[75]   See Rev 1.18 KJV.

ready to be revealed in the last time.'[76] In Pauline language, we are constituted joint-heirs with Christ who is the first-born among many brethren, for we are made to share sonship with Christ the incarnate Son of God.[77] Our human nature is set within the Father-Son relationship of Christ. We share brotherhood with Jesus and so share with him the Fatherhood of God, and in and through him we share in the one Spirit of the living God. We recall the profound and central place this is given in our Lord's high priestly prayer which we are allowed to overhear in John 17, and what a significant part it plays in the epistle to the Hebrews, where we hear of the Son who, having been 'made like his brethren', ascends to the Father as their representative and high priest, presenting them to the Father as sons and daughters consecrated through his own self-offering.[78] In both writings we are told that through the consecrated bonds of our union with Christ we are made to share in the union of the Son with the Father.

The exaltation of man to be a partaker of the life and love of God

It is not surprising that this can be spoken of as the exaltation of man to be a partaker of the life and love that God is, and thereby to be a *partaker of the divine nature* (*theias koinōnoi physeōs*).[79] To think of this clearly we must not divorce our understanding of the resurrection from that of the ascension in which our human nature in Jesus Christ is made to sit down at the right hand of God. But even with the resurrection itself it is made clear that in Jesus Christ man is assumed into the divine life. The relation of Jesus Christ to God is unique for he is God the Son in the unity of the holy Trinity, but the resurrection of our human nature in him implies a reconciliation and a oneness with God which is not identity, yet a real sharing in the union of the incarnate Son with the Father, through a sharing not only in his human nature

---

[76] 1 Peter 1.3-5.

[77] Rom 8.15-17,23,29; Gal 4.4-7.

[78] Heb 1.2, 2.10ff., 4.14ff., 6.4, 7.26f., 10.5ff., etc.

[79] 2 Peter 1.4. See the comment, T.F. Torrance, *The Christian Doctrine of God*, T & T Clark, Edinburgh 1996, p. 95-96 on the possibility of misunderstanding here and the reference to Wolter's suggestion that *theias koinōnoi physeōs* may be translated 'partners of the deity' rather than 'partakers of divine nature'. See also the comment, T.F. Torrance, *The Trinitarian Faith*, T & T Clark, Edinburgh 1988, p. 188f, that the concept of 'deification' or *theopoiēsis* does not mean that we become any less human but that in the incarnation and through the Spirit we are brought into direct and immediate relation to God himself.

but in the life and love of God embodied in him. In him the Godhead dwells bodily[80] and it is out of his incarnate fullness that we receive, but by grace. Let us recall here the threefold distinction in union and communion of which patristic theology used to speak, (a) the *consubstantial communion* between Father and Son in the Holy Spirit who is love, the love that God is; (b) the *hypostatic union* between the divine and human natures in Christ which takes place through the operation of the Holy Spirit who is the love of God; and (c) the *communion* or *koinōnia* of the Spirit who is mediated to us from the Father through the Son and who is the love of God poured into our hearts. It is in virtue of our union with Christ by the power of the Spirit that in and through him we are made to partake of the very love which God himself is, and are thus 'partakers of the divine nature'.

(2) The risen Jesus is the living union of the truth of God and the answering truth of man

It is in the resurrection that we are to understand fully the fact that Jesus Christ is himself the truth – 'I am the truth'. And it is as incarnate Son risen that Jesus Christ remains truth, uncreated truth and created truth in one. He is not simply the eternal Logos of God, but that Logos become flesh, full of grace and truth, not simply Word of God addressed to man, but answering word of man addressed to God in the unity of his one person. We must think likewise of Christ as the truth of God, but truth in such a way that there is in him hypostatic union between the truth of God and the answering truth of man, the truth of the creator and created truth together in the form of his incarnate and personal being. Jesus Christ is the actualisation of the truth of God among us in such a way that it creates its own counterpart in us to itself, truth from the side of God and truth from the side of man in inseparable union. As such Jesus Christ constitutes the bridge between the reality of God and the realities of our world, the connection between the transcendent rationality of God and the created rationalities of this world. He is thus the centre in our midst where the reality and Word of God are translated into human reality and word, and where we human beings may know and speak of God without having to transcend our creaturely forms of thought and speech. It is in and through Jesus Christ therefore that we creatures of space and time may know God the Father, in such a way as to think and speak truly and validly of him, in such a way that the forms of our thought and speech really terminate objectively on God himself in his own ultimate being and reality.

---

[80]   Col 2.9.

The resurrection completion in Jesus' humanity of knowledge of God

Apart from the resurrection we could not say this. If the resurrection did not take place, then not only is there a final disjunction between God's word and God's act, for example in the forgiveness of our sins, but inevitably a final disjunction between our acts of knowing and the reality of God himself, or between our statements about God and their objective reference in God. God is certainly greater that we can ever conceive, so that we cannot but reckon with an infinite discrepancy between our human forms of thought and speech and God himself in his transcendent and ineffable majesty, but the resurrection of the incarnate Son means that God has consummated in Christ such a union between our humanity and himself, and therefore between our human forms of thought and speech as they come to articulation in Christ and himself, that in and through Jesus Christ we may yet know God in his reality beyond ourselves. The whole epistemic function[81] of the incarnation thus comes to its complete fruition in the resurrection of Christ in the fullness of his humanity.

It was for this reason that the early Christians, in their debates with docetic and gnostic thinkers, were so concerned to insist that the Word became *flesh* and that Jesus Christ arose from the dead in the flesh – in the concrete reality of his human and physical existence.[82] Docetic and gnostic thinkers operated with a radical dichotomy between the realm of God and the realm of this world which meant that the forms of thought and speech that we use in this world to speak of God must be treated as merely symbolic, for God in himself is beyond our knowledge. For them we do not know what he is but only know what he is not, as Basilides expressed it. That is to say, our cognition does not rest upon any objective ground in God, and our statements about him do not terminate upon his reality, but are to be regarded as detached expressions in the realm of myth and ritual. In this way of thinking, resurrection is merely the same sort of symbol which we find in the Euripidean play about Alcestis but which does not correspond with reality, although it may play a role in our human dramatic self-understanding and self-expression in face of the mysterious world of what is 'wholly other'.

---

[81] Involving or creating knowledge, from the Gk *epistēmē*, knowledge, i.e. the incarnation's function of restoring knowledge of God as well as the soteriological one of redeeming from sin.

[82] See T.F. Torrance, *Space, Time and Resurrection*, p. 72, for more extended references at this point.

(3) The final pledge of objective knowledge of God in Jesus Christ

The resurrection taken as the New Testament and the early church understood it, however, means that God has established a real bond between his reality and ours in this world. In Jesus Christ he has made his divine reality to intersect and overlap with ours, so that we in Jesus Christ may actually and truly know God and have communion with him without having to take leave of the realm of our own this-worldly existence. The resurrection is therefore our pledge that statements about God in Jesus Christ have an objective reference in God and are not just projections out of the human heart and imagination, objectifying forms of thought in which we fashion a God in terms of the creaturely content of our own ideas.

The discrepancy between the reality of God and this-worldly reality, which is overcome in the resurrection, is to be thought of not simply in terms of the relation between creator and creature, for God continually interacts with what he has made, but rather in terms of the sin and estrangement which have infected both the creature's relation to God and to one another. The creaturely distance of mankind from the creator, and the separation between them and God due to their sinful rebellion and self-imprisonment in guilt, are fully overcome in the incarnation and atonement. That is what is revealed in the resurrection of Jesus Christ from the dead which is itself the final establishment of the bridge between God and humanity on both sides of the chasm that divides them. The resurrection reveals that the disjunction between God and humanity is that which has been created by sin and guilt, a disjunction so great that it could be overcome only by God himself stepping into the breach and bridging the chasm through his own being in the staggering act of incarnation and atonement.

The relations of man with God in being and knowing are healed and fully established

The resurrection reveals here that what divides man from God is not the discrepancy between the finite and the infinite, for God is not limited by human incapacities and weaknesses, although that discrepancy does become a real disjunction for us when it is infected by sin and guilt and enmity. The resurrection demonstrates, here, not only that all division has been removed in atoning reconciliation, but that atoning reconciliation has achieved its end in the new creation in which God and man are brought into such communion with one another that the relations of man with God in being and knowing are healed and fully established. Thus the resurrection of Jesus Christ from the dead sets us in the situation where knowing the truth about God and doing the truth in human existence can be and are valid, for in Jesus Christ a genuine congruence has been established between created truth and the uncreated truth of God.

(c) The resurrection and redemption

(i) The resurrection is the redemption of the whole human being

In its connection with redemption, resurrection is seen to be the redemption of *the whole human being*. Redemption means the emancipation of humanity from bondage and corruption under judgement, restoration from that condition in which human being was menaced and undermined by death and degenerating into nothingness. Mankind's very being has become forfeit and it lapses away from them, crumbling down into the dust, so that their existence is a hovering between being and non-being, between being and rejected being. In that condition they become the prey of the forces of evil and darkness, but redemption is the deliverance of humanity out of all darkness, death and destruction, into light, life and being. When redemption is conceived in terms of resurrection, then we are concerned with the restoration of man in the fullness and integrity of human being, including the emancipation of the body. It is in the resurrection of the man Jesus Christ, the man in whom our nature is assumed and healed, that this kind of redemption is achieved and set forth. Or to put it otherwise, resurrection as redemption means the restoration of men and women *in all the fullness of their humanity*, for it is redemption out of corruption and the lapse toward annihilation into the new being and new life of the new creation. That is why the early church laid such emphasis upon the resurrection of the *flesh*, for it meant the redemption of man's *perishable* form of existence.

The source and heart of this is the redemption of Jesus Christ himself – *his* redemption from the grave, from judgement, damnation and the perdition into which he entered through his identification with us, thereby staking his own being, as it were, and hazarding his own existence, for us and our salvation. What does the resurrection of Jesus Christ mean? As Athanasius used to insist, the resurrection must be understood in accordance with the nature and work of Christ – that is, *kata physin*,[83] in accordance with the nature of the one who rose from the dead. If Jesus Christ rose from the dead, then the 'rose again' must be understood as determined by the nature of the subject of that event, Christ himself. Who is he?

---

[83]   Gk, *according* to the *nature*, or *according* to the *reality* of something.

(ii) The resurrection accords with the nature of the creator-Word made flesh, and is therefore sheer re-creative miracle, shattering the bonds of death

He was the Word of God made flesh, the Word by whom and through whom all things are made that are made, the creator *Logos*.[84] The whole life of Jesus, the Word made flesh,[85] is creative life within our fallen and corrupt existence – it is therefore re-creative. The resurrection of Jesus Christ in body cannot be separated, therefore, from the birth and rising of Jesus in his incarnate actuality out of our mortal and corrupt humanity, when we were dead in trespasses and sins. The very existence of Jesus in history is sheer miracle; his human life in its sinlessness and perfection is itself resurrection, and is in itself the passing of the old into the new. The resurrection of Jesus out of the grave after the crucifixion is thus the same event as the human and historical life of Jesus but now taking place out of the depth of our corruption where corruption is finalised and fixed in death. Or to put it in another way, Jesus is in himself the hypostatic union of the creator and the creature – it is as such that he deliberately allowed himself to be put to death in order to invade the last stronghold of evil, in the finality and ultimateness of its incarceration of us in death, and as such that he broke out of it, shattering the bands of death.

Is the resurrection to be regarded, then, as an interruption of what is called 'the natural order'? Is it an intrusion into the natural processes of this world that passes away? Does it mean some sort of 'infringement of natural law'? The difficulty with a resurrection of that kind is that there is no consistency between it and the nature of the resurrected one, but with the kind of resurrection to which the New Testament bears witness when it speaks of the resurrection of Jesus Christ it is entirely different, for the nature of his resurrection is in full accord with the nature of his person.

The astounding nature of Christ and the consistency of the resurrection with his person

Let us recall how people reacted to his miraculous acts in the Gospel accounts. Who is this man? What kind of person is he? They were utterly astounded at what was going on, and the language that the evangelists use to describe their reactions is the language normally employed to speak of what happens in an earthquake, for they were amazed, stunned, alarmed, bewildered at the nature of the events that took place wherever Jesus went and taught and acted. Yet they were

---

84 Gk, 'word', John 1.1-3.
85 John 1.14 KJV (RSV 'became flesh').

confronted by the fact that in Jesus the person and the deed corresponded perfectly with one another. They were faced with the sheer simplicity and consistency and unity of Jesus, who was transparently in himself the person revealed in his acts, and whose acts were entirely at one with his essential nature as person. Thus the very question they asked, 'Who is he?' was a question prompted by the astounding consistency between person and event. It arose out of consequential thinking, thinking *kat'akolouthian*[86] and *kata physin* to use again the language of Athanasius.

The same thing happened when the astounding events of Easter overtook the world. The actual resurrection of Jesus from the tomb was recognised to be in entire accordance with his nature and person – but that was the stupendous thing about it. This was not just a miracle, not some wonderful event or portent, but something which in all its wonderfulness was not a whit different from the essential nature of the risen one in himself. And what is more, it corresponded to the claim of Jesus, as given in the Johannine literature, '*I am the resurrection and the life*'. '*I am the truth*'.[87] He is in himself the reality of the resurrection and the new life that breaks through and out of death. He is the creator-God among mankind, at work even in the midst of death and corruption and perdition and nothingness.

With the recognition of this utter consistency between the resurrection event and the essence of the resurrected one, came the full realisation that the whole life of Jesus, together with his resurrection, was the manifestation among men and women and on earth and in time of the ultimate and original and final creative activity of God. That is precisely why the resurrection is so baffling to thought and observation.

(iii) A comparison of creation and resurrection – the parallels

(1) Creation can be observed once in being, but not the process or event of creation itself

Let us consider what it means to think of the creation. In natural science we are concerned with the observation of the processes of nature, with

---

[86]   Gk, literally '*following upon, in conformity with*' – *kat'akolouthian* is used by Athanasius of thinking according to the coherent meaning of statements in their reference to reality, or thinking which is consistent with the inner nature of the reality in question. See T.F. Torrance, *Divine Meaning*, T & T Clark, Edinburgh 1995, chap. 8, 'The Hermeneutics of Athanasius', pp. 276, 278ff.

[87]   See John 11.25, 14.6.

the events of the created order, but in the nature of the case we do not and cannot observe the event of creation itself – the process of creating or of being created. Even if creation goes on continuously all the time as some people would have it, on the outer fringes of the universe, millions and millions of light years away, as far as we can send our radio probes, it cannot be observed by any kind of 'observation'. We often speak in natural science of 'observation' metaphorically, of course, when we talk of the kind of detection and discovery we make through the employment of electronic instruments, but that is beside the point. In the nature of the case it is not possible to observe in any way whatsoever those processes through which whatever is created comes into being out of nothing, for then we would have to get behind the creaturely processes in order to observe them – but that is quite impossible and self-contradictory. You can no more observe the very processes by which the observable comes into observation than you can picture how a picture pictures what it pictures, or state in statements how statements are related to what is stated. Yet we make statements about created entities and we observe created processes and explore creaturely events.

(2) Creation and resurrection are not to be thought of as interruptions of the natural order

Thus the idea that creation or resurrection would be the interruption of the natural order is an idea that it is only possible to think on the assumption that the event of creation, or the event of coming into being, is the same sort of event as other events or processes of things that have already come into being. The natural laws by which we bring the connections immanent in nature to expression are all formed *a posteriori*, as *post hoc*[88] features of nature; they cannot be predicted *a priori*[89] or imposed prescriptively upon nature. Natural laws do not apply at all to those processes by which what is nature came into being, but only to those observable processes of a nature that is already in being. Creation itself is something quite different from what can be caught in that kind of formulation. Far from being an interruption of the processes of nature, creation is the manifestation of the creative source of created reality and its immanent order. It is creative activity itself breaking through and manifesting itself within the events of the created world.

---

[88] Lat, *a posteriori*, 'from experience'; *post hoc*, literally 'after this', ie. only after events.

[89] Lat, 'from first principles', by reason alone.

(3) The resurrection can be observed once it has come into being, but it cannot be apprehended within the framework of the old creation

That is the kind of creative happening that we meet in the resurrection. By its very nature it is no more observable than creation as such, yet it is just as factual and real as creation. We cannot observe the creative processes but we may observe the created reality. Nor can we observe the resurrecting processes, but we may observe the resurrected actuality of Jesus Christ – for here too we are concerned with creation, although it is new creation: not creation out of nothing but new creation out of the old order. This brings its further problems, for it means that we cannot apprehend the resurrected reality within the frame of the old order, as if it were not after all a new creation but were continuous with the old creation, comparable to it, and apprehensible entirely within the connections of the old order. It stands to reason that it must be known in accordance with its own nature, out of itself – but this does mean that we have to think through its relations with the whole order of space and time as we have it in our ongoing world. We shall turn to that later.

(iv) The resurrection is the affirmation and restoration of humanity

Meantime let us consider this in relation to the redemptive content of the resurrection, in the consistency between the act and the person of the mediator who rose again from the dead. We recall that the resurrection brings the contradiction between God and man to a final end: here we have not only the rejection of the status of the sinner but the affirmation of man who had sinned as indeed God's own creature, and the making good of God's word in creation that the creature is good,[90] in face of all the sin and evil that have contradicted it. This is the point we have already discussed in the justification of Jesus, and of his being raised for our justification, the fact that in the resurrection God's *Yes* is finalised in and through the *No* of his resistance to all corruption, evil and death. It is in the resurrection, then, that the ultimate content and purpose of atonement and reconciliation come to fruition and to view – in the recreation of humanity in communion with God. This involves the restoration of true creaturehood to man, the affirmation of mankind in the fullness of human existence and reality. *This is the ontological[91] side of redemption, the healing and restoring of being in relation to the creative source of all being.*

---

[90]   Gen 1.4,10,18,21,25,31.

[91]   Involving or relating to 'being', from the Gk *ōn, ontos,* being.

(1) Man is now man, and humanity is now genuine humanity

The resurrection thus means that as applied to man the term *is* now has new meaning, and has meaning in objective depth for us, in a profounder reality than ever we had or were aware of before. As Athenagoras said long ago in the second century, 'If there is no resurrection, human nature could not survive as genuinely human'.[92] The resurrection is the actualisation of human reality, the humanising in Jesus of dehumanised man, the establishing of the fact that man *is* – the end of all *maya* or illusion, and all existentialist philosophies of nothingness, the end of all futility and the void, and of all *mē on* (negated being) and the *mataiotēs* (vanity) bound up with it. Now on the ground of the resurrection and its final rejection of all contradiction between God and humanity, and therefore in its rejection in judgement of all negation of being, we can really believe that humanity *is*, that man is man. Humanity in Christ is the creation God made it to be and may not now cease to be what it is. It is humanity in living communion with the creative source of life. The resurrection of Jesus Christ and of human nature in him is therefore the foundation and source of a profound and radically new Christian humanism.

Thus the resurrection means that the Word which God sent forth in creation, and sent forth in a new way in the incarnation, did not return void[93] but accomplished what it was sent to do.[94] In creation and the affirmation of creation, in recreation and the finalising of creation, the resurrection is the establishing of the creature in a reality that does not crumble away into the dust or degenerate into nothingness or slip into the oblivion of the past. This is a reality that arises and endures, for it is positively and faithfully grounded in its own ultimate source of reality in God.

The resurrection is the affirmation of the reality of creation and creaturely being

This was the point of Athenagoras' statement which we have just cited. It was the point of the early church's unrelenting struggle against all forms of Mandaean and Oriental religion, and all forms of Gnosticism and also of Neoplatonism – against the idea, in whatever form it arose, that man's actuality as man, as creature in a creaturely world, is ephemeral, that human beings must vanish away with all the changes and chances of fleeting time. And so against the view that humanity's

---

[92] See Athenagoras, *The Resurrection of the Dead*, chap. 13f., and especially 15 (p. 157), in *Ante-Nicene Fathers*, vol. 2, Eerdmans repr, Grand Rapids 1967.

[93] Isaiah 55.10-11 (KJV 'void', RSV 'empty').

[94] Cf. Gen 1, 'And God said...', 1.3,6,9,14 etc; John 1.1-3.

existence in space and time is ultimately unreal and but a shadowy evanescent phenomenon, the Christian church asserted with all its strength the resurrection of the body or the resurrection of the flesh, i.e. the resurrection of man in the actuality of human being, as creature of God in space and time. And therein it affirmed the reality of God's creation even for God, as well as the reality of God for the creation. The Christian church is still concerned with this same problem when faced with Buddhism or Hinduism, but also concerned with it, although in a more superficial and less spiritual way, in the teaching of many so called or would be 'avant-garde' theologians for whom the resurrection of Jesus in body, and therefore the resurrection of believers in the body, is strangely abhorrent. Behind all this, however, as the early church saw so clearly in its own day and in its own opponents, is the sheer horror that people of such persuasion have for *the being and action of God himself in space and time.*

The early church emphasis on 'physis' *and thinking according to the real nature of things*

From this point of view the emphasis of the early church upon *physis* (the real nature of things, or simply 'reality'), and upon thinking *kata physin* (according to the nature or reality of things), or what we may call 'cataphysic thinking', is entirely understandable, for it meant thinking in terms of concrete realities or actualities, and the rejection, in the most downright fashion, of the abstract idea that it is impossible to conceive of God's presence and action within human and historical existence. Behind the difficulty which many modern people seem to have with the resurrection lies the same horror of thinking of God in relation to the concrete realities of our world of space and time, the same horror of *physis*, and the same horror of all corporeality and externality in the biblical message.[95] That helps to explain why they fail to understand what the Christian gospel has to say when it speaks about *sōma, sarx, thanatos, zōē, anastasis,* i.e. body, flesh, death, life, resurrection, etc.[96] But to reject this for the thin air of abstract moral judgements or the repetition of existential decisions, or the morbid fascination with self-understanding and subjective states, is in point of fact to take the road of human suicide, the rejection of the sheer humanness of man and all our down to earth existence.

---

[95] See the reference, T.F. Torrance, *The Christian Doctrine of God*, p. 208, to 'what Karl Barth called "a horror of *physis*, of externality, of corporeality"', *Church Dogmatics*, 1/2, Eng. trans. T & T Clark, Edinburgh 1956, p. 130.

[96] Cf. Barth, *loc. cit.*

(2) The empty tomb – resurrection that is not bodily is not resurrection

Since human beings are the concrete reality they are, human resurrection in the nature of the case can only be *bodily resurrection* – any 'resurrection' that is not bodily is simply a contradiction in terms. The New Testament witnesses are indubitably clear,[97] that the resurrection of Jesus is to be understood only in association with his death, for they constitute a unity of the closest kind: if the resurrection is to be thought of as only 'spiritual', the death must be equally so. As death came by *man*, so also by *man* came the resurrection of the dead.[98] The teaching of the New Testament is that the resurrection of Jesus is bodily and historical fact. If the resurrection of Jesus is not bodily and historical fact, then as St Paul saw, the powers of sin and death and non-being remain unconquered and unbroken, and we are yet in our sins in the bondage of death.[99] Everything in the Christian gospel pivots finally upon *the empty tomb* – that Jesus arose in physical body, arose as very man in the fullness and integrity of human nature. And so after Easter there is a history of the risen Jesus who came and went among the disciples, who spoke and ate and drank with them as he willed, in such a way that he could be touched and seen to be no apparition, but above all it was the *personal self-identification of the familiar Jesus* that was the paramount factor: that is the importance and yet the baffling nature of the forty days before Pentecost.[100] Certainly it is of the risen Jesus that the New Testament bears witness, Jesus unveiled in his divine glory, nevertheless in the midst of all that quite indescribable sublimity and light, 'one like unto the Son of man'.[101]

(3) Jesus' life as man before and after the resurrection

Before the resurrection, Jesus, Son of God incarnate, had lived on earth, not 'in the form of God', not snatching at divine power,[102] not calling in 'supernature' to help him out of the weaknesses of our nature which

---

[97] See T.F. Torrance, *Space, Time and Resurrection*, p. 82f. for an amplification of the argument here and additional references.

[98] 1 Cor 15.21.

[99] 1 Cor 15.17f.

[100] Luke 24.13ff.,36ff.; John 20.11ff.,19f.,26f., 21.1ff.; Acts 1.3ff. Cf. Acts 10.39-41; 1 Cor 15.4f.; Matt 28.9,16f.; Mark 16.12f.

[101] Rev 1.13 KJV (RSV 'one like a son of man').

[102] See Phil 2.6f. ('did not count equality with God a thing to be grasped, *ouch harpagmon hēgēsato to einai isa Theō*', v. 6); cf. Matt 4.1f. & Luke 4.1f.

he had made his own, not therefore in the condition of his transcendent glory as eternal Son of God which he had with the Father before the world was, but after the manner of man and in the form and existence of the humble servant he had become in subjection to law. After the resurrection he lived among us on earth after the manner of the exalted Son of God, yet in his nature as man, now victorious and triumphant man, in the midst of history – that is, in the same sphere of reality as that to which we belong, although in this same sphere he lived as new man, man of the new creation, man therefore who could not be confined or held down under the sin-infected and guilt-laden structures of the old creation any more than new wine could be confined within old wineskins.[103]

How are we to understand the reality of Jesus' risen humanity?

As new man he now stands beyond the corrupting processes of this passing age, on the other side of death and perdition, beyond the final judgement, and did so even while he lived amongst men and women after the resurrection, talked with them, communed with them, and as the evangelists report, ate with them to show that he was no ghost but real, physical human being. How are we to understand all this, the life of the risen Jesus in the fullness of the new creation, yet in the fullness of time in the context of real human being? How are we to think of the relation between this new order of being and the order of this world which passes away, between the new humanity inaugurated by Christ in his resurrection and our humanity that continues within ongoing space-time? What is the nature of the resurrection event, and how are we to apprehend it within the conceptualities of which we necessarily partake in a world that still awaits the consummation of all things? In the next section, therefore, having considered here first, the resurrection and the person of Christ, and second, the resurrection and the atoning work of Christ, we move on third, to consider the nature of the resurrection event.[104]

---

[103]   Matt 9.17; Mark 2.22; Luke 5.37-38.

[104]   Rather than have one very large chapter on the resurrection, the following section, '3 The nature of the resurrection event' has been made into a separate chapter as indeed it was also in *Space, Time and Resurrection*.

Chapter Eight

THE NATURE OF THE RESURRECTION EVENT

1 The resurrection is a new type of event

An event in history but one going beyond it into a new creation

The resurrection of Jesus is an event that happens within history in continuity with the living event of the whole historical existence of Jesus, yet as an event of fulfilled redemption the resurrection issues in a new creation beyond the corruptible processes of this world, on the other side of decay and death, and on the other side of judgement, in the fullness of a new world and of a new order of things. How can we think these things together?[1]

The undoing and redemption of the past into a new order of being

We recall that redemption is an act of *anakephalaiōsis*[2] or *recapitulation* with a dual movement. On the one hand, it involves a penetration backwards in time and existence into the roots of human involvement in sin and evil, even into death and hell. We can discern something of the profound implications of that when we think of the descent into hell as a descent into the irreversibility of time and memory and guilt, as a movement that threads regressively along the line of human transgression and fall, undoing the tangled skein of disobedience and rebellion, and breaking the tyranny of guilt-laden existence and time.

---

[1]   [Readers may find some of the first two sections of this chapter (particularly section 2) more demanding as it is more philosophical in tone and may therefore wish to read it quickly initially before going back to study it more thoroughly later – Ed.]

[2]   Gk, from *ana* (again or up) and *kephalē* (head), the act of summing up or gathering up under a head – cf. Eph 1.10, 'to bring all things in heaven and earth together under one head, even Christ' NIV.

On the other hand, recapitulation involves a forward movement, in which the unravelled existence and time of humanity are gathered up and restored in Christ in ontological relation[3] to God. Now the resurrection is that recapitulation in its positive aspect, answering to the descent into death and hell, for it is the healing, lifting up and projection of human being into a new order of things in which its existence before God is finally made good. Think of the Old Testament account of the healing of Naaman the leper as he was baptised in the Jordan, when his flesh was restored to him like the flesh of a little child,[4] or of the prophecy of Joel about the great day of recovery in which God would restore the years that the locust had devoured[5] – the resurrection is like that, the redeeming back of man's life from the wasting power of the destroyer and its restoration it into the fullness of new being.

(a) *The resurrection is a real event in space and time*

Atonement and redemption are empty without resurrection in space and time

The resurrecting of Jesus is to be thought of as the recreating and restoring of man into the same sphere of real being as that to which we human creatures belong, and as such is a historical happening in continuity with the whole historical happening of Jesus, the incarnate Son. If the resurrection is not an event in history, a happening within the same order of reality as we belong to, then atonement and redemption are empty vanities, for they achieve nothing for historical men and women in this world. Unless the atonement through the resurrection breaks into and is real in our historical and physical existence, and continues to be valid as saving power in our earthly and temporal being, it is ultimately a mockery. That is why all docetic[6] conceptions of the risen Christ are quite irrelevant to men and women of flesh and blood and have no message to offer them in their actual existence. It is for this reason that eschatology, with the heart taken out of it in the denial of a genuine resurrection, is meaningless and

---

3 A relation of real *being*, or a connection of real *being* to.

4 2 Kings 5.14.

5 Joel 2.25f.

6 Docetism (from the Gk *dokeō*, appear) was the heresy that Christ only *appeared* to be human. Hence 'docetic' conceptions are ones in which Christ is not fully or really human.

without relevance to the ongoing life of the world. Everything depends on the resurrection of the body, otherwise all we have is a ghost for a saviour.

The resurrection is an event in historical time, which cannot be captured in its framework

Is then, the resurrection an event in historical time or not? Certainly it is an event datable in history, if only by reference to the complex of historical events and agencies within which witness was borne to it; but since the resurrection is a movement of redemption from bondage and subjection to the dark and tyrannous forces of this world, it is something that bursts through the structures and limitations of space and time as we know them where historical, social and human institutions in a fallen world are hopelessly infected by sin and selfishness. If those patterns of our existence, conditioned and determined by sin and guilt, remain rigid and hard, if Christ has not broken through them and opened a way for new being beyond them, he cannot be *our* redeemer, for we cannot be separated from that space-time existence of ours in the world. But if he is the redeemer who does deliver us from the thraldom of sin and guilt, and therefore breaks through the structures determined by them to which we are subjected, then the resurrection event is not something that can be caught within the framework of those structures or interpreted by the secular historian who can only work within it. The methods and canons of credibility with which the secular historian works are strictly appropriate only to the kind of historical happening in a world still schematised to the conditions and determinations of sin and guilt, and therefore are not properly or adequately applicable to the resurrection event that triumphs over them in the redemption of time and history.

(b) The resurrection is a new kind of event in space and time

The resurrection remains continuous live happening that does not decay into the past

The kind of time we have in this passing world is the time of an existence that crumbles away into the dust, time that runs backward into nothingness.[7] Hence the kind of historical happening we have in

---

[7]   See further T.F. Torrance, *Royal Priesthood*, 2nd edition, T & T Clark, Edinburgh 1993, p. 50f., and Brunner, 'The Christian Understanding of Time', *Scottish Journal of Theology*, 4.1 (1951) p. 10.

this world is happening that decays and to that extent is illusory, running away into the darkness and forgetfulness of the past. As happening within this kind of time, and as event within this kind of history, the resurrection, by being what it is, resists and overcomes corruption and decay, and is therefore *a new kind of historical happening* which instead of tumbling down into the grave and oblivion rises out of the death of what is past into continuing being and reality. This is temporal happening that runs not backwards but forwards, and overcomes all illusion and privation[8] or loss of being. This is fully real historical happening, so real that it remains real happening and does not slip away from us, but keeps pace with us, and as we tumble down in decay and lapse into death and the dust of past history outruns us and even comes to meet us out of the future. That is how we are to think of the risen Jesus Christ. He is not dead but alive, more real than any of us. Hence he does not need to be made real for us, because he does not decay or become fixed in the past. He lives on in the present as real live continuous happening, encountering us here and now in the present and waiting for us in the future.

The baffling nature of the resurrection as new historical happening

Because this is historical event emancipated from decay, redeemed from bondage, liberated from the guilty irreversibility of dead time, the resurrection is quite baffling to the historian who considers it in the context of ordinary history. Here we have historical happening within our historical existence and within the same sphere of actuality and reality to which we human beings belong – that is why it is plotted by relation to other historical agents, such as Mary Magdalene, John, Peter and a host of disciples in the primitive church[9] – yet it is historical happening that breaks through the backward movement of time where it becomes fixed in death and decays, and cannot therefore be netted within the frame of the historical as we know it in our interaction with nature and other human agents. Here we have the same kind of continuity and discontinuity that is to be found in the virgin birth of Jesus and which makes it so difficult to grasp. Here, however, we have that new decisive kind of happening in final form which is the incursion of the new creation into our sphere of existence and which at the point of decisive change breaks through its hard and rigid forms in

---

8　　Lat, *privatio*, deprivation.

9　　John 20, 21; Luke 24; 1 Cor 15.5f.

unfettered final disclosure. Hence while the resurrection is an event that happened once for all, it remains *continuous live happening* within history, and must therefore be interpreted as running against the patterned stream of history or the secular framework of our space and time.

The resurrection involves apocalypse and the transformation of the old creation

That is why resurrection by its very nature involves *apocalypse*, both in relation to history and in relation to our understanding of it. What is meant by apocalyptic here is the way in which we must look at history in the light of God's decisive interventions, interpreting it therefore against and counter to the observable patterns of worldly history formed as time flows irreversibly into the past; but in the continuing life of the church apocalypse means that while we live and work on the plane of ongoing world events as the newspapers and history books write of them, we nevertheless live in the power of the resurrection as those who are united to the risen Jesus Christ, and who must not be schematised to the form of the secular world but must be transformed through the renewal of our mind in Christ.[10] We are called constantly to shed the image of the corruptible and put on the image of the new creation,[11] for we are caught up in a movement that runs counter to the regressive flow of corruption and decay and carries us forward into the future to the final and full disclosure of our real being in Christ.[12]

The resurrection means the redemption of space and time and not the end of space and time

So far we have been thinking of the resurrection as an event in space and time and yet as one that breaks redemptively through the framework of space and time as we know it in a fallen world, but it is necessary to see that the resurrection means *the redemption of space and time*, for space and time are not abrogated or transcended. Rather are they healed and restored, just as our being is healed and restored through the resurrection. Of course we cannot separate our being from space and time, for space and time are conditions and functions of created existence and the bearers of its order. The healing and restoring of our being carries with it the

---

[10]   Rom 12.2.

[11]   Eph 4.22-24; Col 3.5-10; cf. 2 Cor 3.18ff.

[12]   Cf. Phil 3.8-21; Col 3.1-4.

healing, the restoring, reorganising and transforming of the space and time in which we now live our lives in relation to one another and to God. Yet immediately we are concerned with space and time, and especially with their resurrection, we are in the midst of eschatology in which our thinking is stretched out beyond us to the ultimate ends of God's purpose in creation and redemption. We cannot think this out adequately apart from consideration of the ascension and final *parousia*[13] of Christ, when he comes to make all things new and when redemption will be fully actualised in the sphere of the body and the whole of created reality – but there are certain major aspects of the redemption of space and time, of time particularly, and of the nature of time and history, that we must consider now.

2 The problem of how we interpret historical events

We have spoken of the kind of time we have on the plane of this fallen world as time that crumbles away into the dust, time as it is implicated in corruption, yet we have also spoken of it as irreversible – time that flows only one way, backwards and down into the dust. While this time is, as it were, alive in the present moment, it decays right away, and suffers from a sort of *rigor mortis*[14], a fixity from which we cannot escape and within which we are incarcerated in our ageing and dying.

(a) Interpreting ordinary historical events

(i) Freedom and necessity in historical events

Let us try to understand this from a merely natural point of view. Think of a historical happening: in taking place it appears as a free happening. Once it takes place, it cannot be undone. Throw a stone through that window and you are engaging in a free act, but once it has taken place, the act cannot be recalled – we cannot turn it backwards as we can a film of the event. Thus once an event has taken place, it becomes 'necessary' – in the sense that it cannot now be other than it is. At this point, however, we are liable to suffer from an illusion, for we tend to think that because it is now a necessary fact, it had to happen. This is the kind of optical illusion we suffer from on the golf course when our

---

13   Gk, 'presence, coming, advent', used specifically of the advent of Christ and especially of the last advent.

14   Lat, stiffness of death.

opponent putts a ball from the other end of the green and it goes right down into the hole – immediately that happens we somehow think it had to happen from the start, but what we have done in a flash is to read the final result back all along the line of the ball's course into the free act behind it. It is through this kind of illusion or indeed delusion that some historians think that historical events are to be interpreted in the same way in which they interpret the events of natural processes as concatenated or linked together through causal necessity.

The distinction between causal necessity and factual necessity

But it is important to distinguish in historical happening between causal necessity and factual necessity, between causal determination of events and the fact that once they happen they cannot be otherwise. An historical event, once it has taken place, is factually necessary for it cannot now be other than it is, but an historical event comes into being through a free happening, by means of spontaneous human agencies. Certainly all historical events are interactions between human agents and nature, as well as interactions between agents and other agents – so that there are elements of causal determination in historical happening that we have to take into account, physical factors relating to the kind of patterns of space and time in which we live and work. But historical events are not by any means merely natural physical processes, for as happenings initiated and bound up with purposeful agents they embody intention which often conflicts with and triumphs over the course of events that nature would take on its own.

(ii) History is the interweaving of natural processes with human intention

It is this interweaving of natural processes and human agencies, of nature and rational intention, that gives history its complicated patterns. The course of events has often quite unforeseen results, for human acts may fail to achieve what would have been expected or may achieve far more than would or could have been anticipated. But in our interpretation of history we must never forget that in the heart of historical events there is free happening which bears the intention in which the true significance of history is to be discerned. Thus while we must appreciate fully the physical factors involved, we must penetrate into the movement of time in the actual happening in order to understand the event in the light of the intentionality and spontaneity embedded in it. The handling of temporal relation has proved very difficult and elusive in the history of thought, for it has so often been assimilated to logical relation and so transposed into something very different. The confusion of temporal with logical connection corresponds here to that between spontaneity and causal determinism in natural science. We can see this error recurring, for example, in notions of predestination where the free *prius*[15] of the divine grace is converted by the scholastic mind into logico-causal relation, while the kind of time-relation with which we operate between natural events is imported into the movements of divine love and activity. It is a form of the same mistake that people make in regard to the resurrection, when they think of its happening only within the logico-causal nexus with which they operate in classical physics.

Historical events need to be interpreted in terms of the human intention behind events

We distinguish, then, in historical happening between logico-causal necessity and factual necessity. This is not to say that the time order of historical events is different from the time order of events in nature, but that the kind of events with which we have to do in history is of a different nature and has a different kind of movement from that which we have in nature. Nevertheless it remains true that as in nature we can appreciate, for instance, the movement of light only by engaging in a movement along with it, only through a mode of kinetic thinking and by renouncing all thought of it from a static viewpoint or from a centre of absolute rest,[16] so here in historical happening we understand it only through a similar kinetic mode of thinking in which we penetrate into the living happening behind the factual necessity and appreciate it as far as possible from within its own movement. But how far can we do that, when time, so to speak, dies on us as it passes from the present moment into the past, and gets all stiffened up in a sort of *rigor mortis*? That is the problem of historians which they seek to overcome by penetrating into the *intentionality* embedded in the historical happening – and it is a problem we cannot escape in historical interpretation of the scriptures or of the historical events they record. But there are two primary factors which we have to take into account theologically.

---

[15]   Lat, 'prior', before, the fact that God loves us *before* we love him.

[16]   That is, as though we ourselves could be at rest, or find a point of absolute rest from which we could think it. There is no such point of absolute rest anywhere in the universe, and we cannot think of the universe, or of anything in it, from a point outside it, as it were. We can only think from inside the universe - that is, by being within and part of the movement of things in the universe, and by thinking of ourselves not statically but dynamically in relation to movements such as light.

(b) Interpreting the resurrection – theological factors

(i) The resurrection needs to be interpreted in accordance with the nature of the person involved

If we interpret historical events not by converting their factual necessity into logico-causal necessity but by penetrating kinetically into their free happening, what is the kind of happening with which we are concerned in the resurrection, for it is the nature of the happening that determines the nature of the historical event once it has happened? And the kind of happening of course is determined by the nature of the subject of the happening. Here we distinguish between the kind of happening we see in natural events, such as the eruption of a volcano, from the kind of happening we have in history, as for example, the stabbing of Julius Caesar. The subjects are different. In one case we have to do only with determinate objects and subjects, in the other case with personal agents and a different kind of subject. Here, however, we have to reckon with the nature of the subject in the incarnation and in the resurrection, for as we have seen, the resurrection is to be understood in consistency with Jesus Christ himself, who is the person who rose from the dead. Here, in fact, we have a divine-human subject, and therefore a unique happening defined by the nature of this unique agent. Other human agents were involved in the life of Jesus, Mary, and Judas, Caiaphas and Pilate, so that we have to interpret the historical Jesus within the kind of historical happening that we find in all other human history, but because we have here a different subject, the Son of God incarnate in human existence in space and time, we have to understand the inner movement of his history in a way appropriate to his nature – that applies to his birth, to the whole of his life, and to his resurrection, for they are all of the same genus and that is why we can speak of the whole historical Jesus from birth to resurrection as sheer miracle or downright resurrection from beginning to end.

The resurrection needs to be interpreted both historically and theologically

Now this means that we cannot interpret the historical happening of the resurrection of Jesus, any more than of his birth and life, without doing it from within the free movement of his life and agency, that is, to use older language (if we divest it of its false psychologising) from within the 'messianic secret' of Jesus. In other words, we can interpret the resurrection only if we interpret it theologically as well as historically. It will not do, however, to interpret it merely 'theologically' as if it could be done apart from history, for that would mythologise and docetise it, and then we would have nothing to interpret. Nor can we interpret it merely historically in the way that we interpret other historical events in human history, only by reference to human agency and natural processes, for that would be tantamount to insisting that all we have here is an ordinary historical happening, and so to rejecting from the start the claim that the agent is the Son of God. Such a procedure would, to say the least, be neither open-minded nor scientific, since it would foreclose the issue completely as to who Jesus Christ is, before we have even considered him in accordance with his nature and self-disclosure. That is one of the false approaches regularly adopted in the quest of the historical Jesus, so that it is not at all surprising that the quest pursued on these lines breaks down time and time again, and is increasingly baffling and bewildering. It could not be otherwise when approached in this way.

Because Jesus is still alive we can penetrate into the historical happening of Jesus' resurrection in a way not possible with any other event

To get back, then, to the point from which we started here, it is incumbent upon us to interpret the resurrection as historical event in accordance with the nature of the agent or subject concerned, and therefore through penetration into the free and living happening of Jesus' life. We can do this because, as we have seen, this is a historical happening not of the kind that fades away from us and crumbles into the dust, but of the kind that remains real and therefore that resists corruption and moves the other way, forward throughout all history to the end-time and to the consummation of all things in the new creation. Jesus remains live and real historical happening, more real and more historical than any other historical event, for this is the only historical event that does not suffer from decay and is not threatened by annihilation and illusion. It is historical event in the fullness of time, and not historical event suffering, as all other historical events do, from the privation or cessation of time. Here time itself is redeemed and recreated and as such is carried forward into the future, for it is not allowed to see the corruption of the grave.

Access into the historical happening of Jesus through the communion of the Spirit

But we can also penetrate inside this historical happening in Jesus because of Pentecost and our union with Christ through the *koinōnia* or communion of the Spirit. It is through the Spirit that we may understand the resurrection in accordance with its own inner and free happening, as the sovereign act of its subject. And that is why, as we saw earlier, the resurrection must be understood *enhypostatically* as well as *anhypostatically*. If it is only understood *anhypostatically*, then it can be interpreted merely in terms of some sort of super-history, touching our history only in a tangential manner and therefore not as really historical. As we have seen, that was the tendency of the early Barth and Brunner, which Barth certainly sloughed off, much as a snake sloughs off its skin, but from which people like Bultmann, Dodd and Niebuhr have failed to free themselves in their eschatology of continual crisis and timeless events.[17]

(ii) The resurrection needs to be interpreted in accordance with its nature as the redemption of time

Resurrection is redemption 'under the law' yet 'apart from law' – within 'nomistic'[18] human existence but out of it

There is this second factor that we have to take into account, for it is the foil, so to speak, of what we have just been considering, the fact that the time-form of the world as we now have it in fallen existence is characterised by *law* – by what the New Testament calls *nomos*. This assumes one form, of course, in natural events, in accordance with their determinate nature and their kind of rationality, but it assumes another form in historical events, and that too must be in accordance with their nature and their kind of rationality. This is the *nomistic form of human existence*[19] that is thrown into sharp relief by justification, that is, the time-form of our fallen existence within which we are fixed in our mortality, and through which we are caught in the irreversibility of guilty deeds and lives which have the force of 'necessity' because once lived or performed they cannot be undone. It is what St Paul called 'the curse of the law'[20] from which we need to be redeemed. Redemption had to take the form of justification 'under the law'

---

[17] See T.F. Torrance, *Incarnation*, Paternoster UK & InterVarsity Press USA, Milton Keynes & Downer's Grove, 2008, p. 293, 309.

[18] 'Nomistic' appears to be a word coined by Torrance to express an important element in his theology.

[19] Existence characterised by constraint under the tyranny of the law (*nomos*) and revealed and highlighted by justification which at once reveals the righteousness of God and uncovers the nature of sin – cf. Rom 1.17 & 18ff.

[20] Gal 3.13.

yet 'apart from law'.[21] Thus 'when the fullness of time was come God sent forth his Son, made of woman, made under the law, to redeem those who were under the law, so that we might receive adoption as sons'.[22] This is precisely the situation with which we are concerned here, as we think of resurrection as the *redemption of time*, for it takes place within the *nomistic* character of our existence, and yet emancipates us from it into a new relation of freedom with God our Father.

In our nomistic existence law prevents lawlessness but imprisons us in our inability to obey it

Man was made for fellowship with God, but when that fellowship was broken by human sin, men and women lapsed into a state in which they were no longer humanity as they ought to be. The moral awareness of humanity, their inescapable sense of obligation, belongs to that condition. Their relation with God became refracted and took the form of ethical or legal relation.[23] In the Old Testament account, a barrier came in between humankind and God – God made known to humankind his divine will but withheld himself from them lest they should be consumed by the divine majesty. The effect of this was to establish man in an ethical or legal order over against God, for the manifestation of the divine will held lawlessness in check, restraining chaos from overwhelming mankind, and at the same time confined them within an order of existence validated by God but within which they were not the people they ought to be. Humanity was thus the prisoner of an ethical or legal order from which they could not extricate themselves, for they could not be what they ought to be or bridge the gap between themselves and God within which the ethical or legal order had its validity. But God in his free grace has come in Jesus Christ to redeem us from our helpless condition under the tyranny and curse of the law, that is, from the 'necessity' or inescapable '*nomistic* form' of our existence, and to lift us up into living fellowship and loving communion with God the Father.

---

[21]   Gal 4.4-5; Rom 3.21.

[22]   Gal 4.4-5 KJV/RSV – see the note, T.F. Torrance, *Space, Time and Resurrection*, Handsel Press, Edinburgh 1976, p. 96, for an explanation of Torrance's preference for the KJV '*made* of woman, *made* under the law' to the RSV '*born* of woman, *born* under the law'.

[23]   See above chap. 4, section 3 (c) following.

The resurrection redeems us from nomistic time into the new time of the new creation

Now the kind of time we are concerned with in historical events is the time of human agents, the time of free happening in the interrelations of human beings, and is therefore time that is inescapably involved with moral and legal experience. That is why the New Testament speaks of the *schema* of this present *aeon* or age as *nomos*, law, for the kind of time we have in our fallen existence is refracted time,[24] time that has broken loose from God, as it were, and yet not time that has been allowed to slip into sheer chaos and nothingness but time that is contained, upheld and overruled by God, within which he works out his redeeming purpose. The kind of time we have in historical events is the time of creation that has fallen from what it ought to be into disorder, and yet is contained through *nomos* from disappearing or vanishing into illusion, but as such it is time in which we are subjected to law, time within which we are all servants.

But when the fullness of time had come the Son of God entered into this existence and this time of ours as a servant under the law; he partook of life within the *nomistic* structure of our time and wrought his redemptive work within it in order to emancipate us from its tyranny. It was in his resurrection that he broke through the *nomistic* form of our existence, rising again no longer in the form of a servant under the law, but in the form of the life-giving new man, entirely and fully human, yet man no longer confined to the kind of limits that are imposed on us in our fallen world by the time-form of law or by the *nomistic* form of time. However, far from this meaning the abrogation of time, it means its redemption. Just as in justification the law was not destroyed but established, so in the resurrection time is not annihilated but recreated, for it is taken up in Christ, sanctified in his human life and transformed in his resurrection as man.

How are we to state this positively? Here we may revert to the doctrine of the hypostatic union of the divine and human natures in the one person of the incarnate Son of God.

3 Positive implications of the resurrection

(a) In the risen Christ, there is a hypostatic union between eternity and new time hidden from us by the ascension

In the risen Christ, in whom hypostatic union between God and man is carried through to its *telos* or end, there is involved a hypostatic

---

[24] Broken time, decaying and sinful, under *nomos* or law but held together by it.

union between eternity and time, eternity and redeemed and sanctified time, and therefore between eternity and new time. The resurrection of the man Jesus and his exaltation to the right hand of the Father mean the taking up of *human time* into God. In Christ the time of human being and life is wedded to eternity. The ascension also means that this time of the new creation in Christ is hidden from us, and, as it were, held back from us until in the mercy of God Jesus Christ comes again to judge and renew all creation. Nevertheless it remains valid that in the risen Christ our human nature in its creaturely and temporal existence is redeemed and renewed and established through being taken up in its affirmed reality into the life of God.

(b) The church lives in two times, the time of this passing world and the time of the new creation

How are we to think of our participation in this new creation and its redeemed time? It is best understood, perhaps, in the perspective of the church as the body of Christ, the body not only of the crucified but of the risen Christ, the body upon which he has poured out his Spirit as he ascended to 'fill all things',[25] the body which, though on earth and within history, is yet made participant in his risen power. The church thus lives, as it were, in two times: it lives in the time of this passing world, that is in the midst of ongoing secular history and world events, the time of decay that flows down into the past and into the ashes of death, but also in the time of the risen saviour and of the new creation that is already a perfected reality in him. This happens through the *koinōnia* of the Spirit, so that the church lives and works and fulfils its mission in the overlap of the two times or two ages, this present aeon[26] that passes away and the new aeon that has already overtaken us in Christ Jesus, the last age or end-time that has telescoped itself into the present and has penetrated the church through the coming of the Spirit.

The church is sent as a servant to live the life of the new creation within the old

Because of its participation in the time of the new creation, the church can continue to live on earth and in history only through being crucified with Christ to the time-form of this world. On the

[25] Eph 4.10.

[26] Gk, *aiōn*, space of time, age, an indefinitely long period.

other hand, because of its union with Christ the church is sent by him to fulfil its mission within the time and history of this world and therefore within its temporal and *nomistic* structures. In other words, though risen with Christ and already a partaker through the Spirit in the new creation, the church is sent like Christ into the world as the servant of the Lord, humbling itself and containing itself in *kenōsis*[27] within the limit and laws of this world in order to proclaim the gospel of reconciliation and to live out reconciliation within the conditions of fallen human existence. As such it is the new wine through which the old wineskins will be burst[28] and the whole framework of the ages will be changed. This is why the New Testament calls the church and its members to 'redeem the time',[29] not to live as those who are dead and asleep, rigid with the fixities of dead time, but to keep vigil[30] as those who are already risen with Christ and wait his coming for their final release like Lazarus from the shrouds of the grave,[31] and yet not like Lazarus freed merely from the shrouds of the grave, but freed from the shackles of the past and all that holds us back from entering into the fullness of our inheritance in the new creation.

(i) The language of apocalyptic, the new seen through the language of the old[32]

In carrying our thinking this far we have already moved into the realm of *apocalyptic*, where we can speak of the new world and the new time only by using language culled from the old world and the old time. That is to say, we are permitted to speak here of the new age only with a prayer for forgiveness, for the very language we use is improper and must pass away with the *nomistic* forms of this world. We are reminded here of the apocalyptic theme of the 'the new song' that is sung on the other side by those who have been redeemed,[33] or 'the new name'[34] which no one knows but

---

27   Gk, self-*emptying*, cf. Phil 2.5-8.

28   Matt 9.17; Mark 2.22; Luke 5.37-38.

29   Eph 5.16 & Col 4.5, *exagorazomenoi ton kairon*, 'redeeming the time' KJV.

30   Matt 24.42–25.13; Rom 13.11-14; 1 Thess 5.1ff.; 1 Pet 1.13f.

31   John 11.1-44.

32   For the following see further T.F. Torrance, *The Apocalypse Today*, James Clarke, London 1960, sermons on the book of Revelation.

33   Rev 5.9f., cf. 15.2f.

34   Rev 2.17.

which is sealed on the foreheads of the redeemed,[35] imprinted with the sign of the cross in their baptismal incorporation into Christ. Thus out of the cross of Christ there breaks in upon the vision of faith something quite indescribable, as indescribable as the majesty of the risen son of man that confronted the apostle as the start of his visions. We can only speak about it in stammering ways, in the fragmented figures of apocalyptic imagery. Let us merely note several features or images used by the New Testament as the reality of the new age is glimpsed shining through the old.

As the old man perishes day by day, so the new man is renewed day by day

The old man perishes day by day, but in Christ the new man is renewed day by day.[36] That is the characteristic of the Christian who is dead and hid with Christ in God, for we are already risen with Christ,[37] and already partake of the power of his resurrection through sharing in his Spirit. That is also the life of the church which in Christ has so partaken of the powers of the age to come that it gets younger and younger with the youth of eternity, or rather with the new time of the new man in whom eternity and redeemed time are united for ever. Think here of the language of Ephesians 5, regarding the nature of the church of Christ as it will be presented to Christ at the end of history, without spot or wrinkle but as a chaste virgin;[38] or think of the vision of Hermas, where he saw the church as a very old lady sitting on a chair – the *ecclēsia presbutera* or old church. Then he looked again and saw that though her body and her hair were old her face was getting younger – the *ecclēsia neotera* or young church. He looked a third time and though her hair was white she had altogether recovered her youth and was young and very joyful and beautiful. Though the church as Hermas saw her, was an old lady with white hair, her flesh was getting younger and younger.[39] 'Now is our salvation nearer' as St Paul used to say, 'than when we first believed'.[40]

---

[35]   Rev 7.3.

[36]   2 Cor 4.16ff.; cf. Rom 6.5f.

[37]   Col 3.1-3.

[38]   Cf. Eph 5.25f.; Rev 19.7f., 21.2,9f.

[39]   *The Pastor of Hermas*, Book First – *Visions*, III.10 (cf. I.2; II.1,4; III.1f,10-13), in *Ante-Nicene Fathers*, Eerdmans repr, Grand Rapids 1967, vol. 2, p. 16 (cf. 10,11,12,13f.,16-17).

[40]   Rom 13.11.

(ii) The millennium time of the already inaugurated kingdom

Let us take the image of the *millennium*.[41] How are we to understand this in the light of the redemption of time? Here we have evidently an apocalyptic figure made up of *'alpha* and *ōmega'*,[42] 1 and 1000, 'the first and the last', which is Christ, 'he who was and is and shall be for ever more', 'he who is and was dead and behold he is alive and has the keys of death and hell'.[43] It is the apocalyptic figure of *the perfect time of the kingdom of Christ,* the sanctified time of the new creation which was inaugurated with the resurrection of Christ the first (*prōtos*), and reaches out to the final advent when he will come again as the last (*eschatos*) to judge and renew the earth, finally to make all things new. The millennium is the time of Christ the new man, and therefore the sabbatical time of the new humanity which in Christ is wedded to the perfection of eternity. It is in this time, millennium time, that the church participates as throughout history it lives in union with the risen Christ through the Spirit.

Millennium time is hidden from sight, but seen by faith and present in the eucharist

This millennium time is hidden from our sight with the ascension of the risen Lord, but it remains, so to speak, *the other side* of the time of this world, for although it has been redeemed by Christ and involved in his vicarious self-sanctification, it still waits for the full actualisation of that redemption in its physical existence. On this side we see the time of human failure and sin, the time of dark and tragic history, the time of wrath, the time of crucifixion, but on the other side, seen only by faith, there is the time of the resurrection or the new age which is, as it were, the silver lining behind the time of secular history. Millennium time will be unveiled with the advent of Christ, for then there will take place the *apocalypse* or unveiling of all that Christ has done throughout history in making the wrath of man to serve him in the eschatological outreach of his kingdom to its consummation in the new creation.

---

[41] See here the exposition on Rev 20 and the 1000 years of the millennium, T.F. Torrance, *The Apocalypse Today*, chap. 15, p. 161ff.

[42] The first and last letters of the Greek alphabet.

[43] See Rev 21.6, 22.13, 1.17-18, cf. 1.8..

Because the church is already participant in that new creation, that is in the millennium time of the resurrection, the kingdom of the risen and ascended and advent Christ already knocks at the door of the church. That happens above all at the holy supper, where the risen Lord is present, in *eucharistic parousia*, and we taste already the powers of the age to come and are given an antepast or foretaste of the great banquet of the kingdom that is to come.[44] As often as we communicate in the sacrament, we participate in the new time of that kingdom. That is why the New Testament thinks of the sacraments as falling within the overlap between the two ages, this present age that passes away and the age that is to come but which in Christ has already telescoped itself into the present and catches us up into it in the communion of the Spirit. Thus as often as the church partakes of holy communion in the *real presence* or *parousia* of Christ it becomes ever anew the body of the risen Lord.

(iii) The need to think christologically, to hold together the two times

But what about *the individual*, and what about the death of the believer? This is where it is impossible for us to think completely together the two times in which we are involved, yet we discern something of how the two 'moments' fall together in our being in Christ. When believers die, they go to be with Christ and are in his immediate presence, participant in him and made like him. That is for each believer the *parousia* of Christ to them. Yet when this is regarded on the plane of history and of the ongoing processes of the fallen world, the death of each believer means that their body is laid to sleep in the earth, waiting until the redemption of the body and the recreation of all things at the final *parousia*. Looked at from the perspective of the new creation there is no gap between the death of the believer and the *parousia* of Christ, but looked at from the perspective of time that decays and crumbles away, there is a lapse in time between them. How do we think these two together? Only by thinking of them exclusively *in Christ*, in the one person of Christ in whom human nature and divine nature are hypostatically united, and in whom our human existence and history are taken up into his divine life. We must think christologically here. But when we relate christology to the time-form of this world what we do see is that the church is sent out in the mission of the everlasting gospel into history, under the sway

---

[44] Matt 22.2f.; cf. Luke 13.29, 14.16f.; Rev 19.7,9

of earthly authorities and powers and within the structures of space and time. It cannot be true and faithful to its Lord if it refuses to live the life of the servant within and under all that, even though it is crucified to the world in Christ and is already risen with him and as such shares his triumphant victory over the powers of the world.

The concept of a 1000 year earthly reign fails to recognise the majesty of the risen Christ

But if we think christologically we have to reject the mythologising of biblical eschatology, that is, reject the objectifying of apocalyptic imagery and the fixation of the kingdom of Christ within the old structures. When Christ comes again it will be with all his unveiled majesty and power, all the manifest glory of the new creation, but if so, as Calvin warns us, it would be an insult to that advent Christ to think of him as dwelling and ruling 1000 years on earth,[45] once more in the form of a servant, even if his reign will be in the glorified form of the chiliast visionaries.[46] Chiliastic or millennarian thinking of this kind fails to realise the nature of the resurrection and the glory and majesty of the risen Lord, or indeed the finished and accomplished nature of the atonement. When Christ comes again, it can only be to make all things new and to reveal what he has already done and is even now working in and under and with all world-events. Then the great unveiling or apocalypse will take place, the judgements of the cross at work throughout history will be brought to their consummation in unveiled finality, and the salvation of Christ that has been proclaimed throughout all history will be brought to its fruition in the unveiled glory of the new creation. It is by the man Jesus that God will finally judge the earth,[47] and by the man Jesus that resurrection and new creation will finally come upon the old creation. Then at last the vast cosmic significance of the incarnation of the Word, of the reconciliation through the sacrifice of Christ and of the resurrection of our human nature in him, will be made clear and manifest to all and we shall know as we are known.[48]

---

[45] *Institute* 3.25.5. For further references see T.F. Torrance, *Kingdom and Church. A Study in the Theology of the Reformation*, Oliver and Boyd, Edinburgh 1956, p. 145.

[46] Gk, *chilias*, a thousand.

[47] Acts 17.31; Rom 2.16; John 5.22.

[48] 1 Cor 13.12 KJV.

(c) The church lives 'between the times' – between resurrection and final advent

Until then, the church and all its members, live *between the times*, between the time of the resurrection and Pentecost, and the time of the final advent; they participate in the time of this ongoing world, yet already participate in the time of the new creation through the Spirit of the risen Christ. If Christ holds back the final unveiling, and keeps us within the overlap of the two ages, still engaged in the humble mission of the servant under the cross, it is in his compassion and patience,[49] for he waits to be merciful and wills to rule over history solely by the word of the cross. It is as enthroned lamb, as mediator and high priest, that he rules from the right hand of God over church and state, over faith and world-happening. In that 'patience' of Christ we have 'the time of the Gentiles',[50] the time of the proclamation of the gospel to all nations,[51] in which the church must live in patience with its Lord, never seeking to force his hand, or to force upon the world the consummation before its time, for then there will be no time for decision, no time for repentance, and no time for change, but only the time of finality. Yet it is because the time of finality presses hard upon us in history, and impinges now upon the church from all sides, that the church finds time running out and knows that at any hour, at such a time as it thinks not,[52] the moment of great reckoning will suddenly come upon mankind.

(d) As in the days of his earthly life Jesus waits for the 'hour' of final consummation

Here we are, as it were, back in the days of Jesus as he pressed toward the cross throughout the three years of his ministry, constrained with the baptism with which he was baptised in the

---

49   This is the biblical concept of *makrothumia* (patience, longsuffering) or *anochē* (forbearance, holding back) which belongs to the covenant mercies of God in the Old and New Testament. See Genesis 8.20ff.; Exod 34.6; Joel 2.13; Psalm 86.15, 103.8, 145.8; Rom 2.4, 3.25, 9.22; 1 Tim 1.16; 2 Peter 3.9,15.

50   See Luke 21.24.

51   Luke 24.47; cf. Acts 1.8; Rom 1.5, 16.26.

52   See Matt 24.42ff. KJV; Luke 12.40ff.; Mark 13.32f.

mission of the cross,[53] yet as crisis after crisis came, he refused to force the issue, waiting for the ripening of God's will in the situation into which he had entered, and only when at last he knew that his 'hour' had come,[54] did he go forward to the passion and the resurrection that transformed everything. The book of Revelation clearly looks at the whole course of history from the resurrection of Christ to his final advent in the light of the course of Christ's own earthly life from his birth at Bethlehem to his crucifixion and resurrection, for it is that incarnate Son of God, crucified and risen for all humanity, who is at work in all history and who reigns over it all. Once again he waits for the 'hour' of final consummation when what took place intensively in Christ himself once and for all in his crucifixion and resurrection, will be actualised extensively in the broad field of creation and history, where the new heaven and the new earth will supervene in the unveiled glory of the triumphant Lord.[55]

The church is commanded to lift up its head in joy, for its 'redemption is drawing near'

Meantime in all its waiting and expectation the church is commanded by its Lord to lift up its head in thanksgiving and joy, for its *'redemption is drawing near'*.[56] The church of the risen Lord has no right to be a prophet of gloom or despair, for this world has been redeemed and sanctified by Christ and he will not let it go. The corruptible clay of our poor earth has been taken up in Jesus, is consecrated through his sacrifice and resurrection, and he will not allow it to sink back into corruption. Hence the whole creation groans and travails waiting for the manifestation of the sons of God, looking forward with eager expectation to the hour of final liberation and renewal in the advent of its risen saviour.[57] The church must learn to take into its mouth the good news of the resurrection and new creation, for that must be its primary note, one of limitless joy and thanksgiving. That is how the church began its mission at Pentecost where the dominant emphasis in all its preaching was the resurrection of the crucified Christ and the

---

53 Luke 12.50.

54 John 13.1.

55 Rev 21.1ff.

56 Luke 21.28

57 Rom 8.19f.

astounding fact that because of Christ the Spirit of God himself was poured out upon men and women. They knew that the last times had overtaken them and that they were caught up in the onward and outward thrust of the resurrection of Christ toward the new creation in which all nations and peoples[58] and all times would be brought to share. The involvement of the church in the suffering of mankind must never be allowed to stifle that supreme note of resurrection triumph or to smother the eschatological joy at the astounding events that have broken into history and pledged for mankind the final day of regeneration.

---

[58]   Rev 7.9.

Chapter Nine

THE ASCENSION AND PAROUSIA OF JESUS CHRIST

The ascension of Jesus Christ

It is with his ascension that Jesus Christ was fully installed in his kingly ministry. His prophetic ministry began with the incarnation: that is the ministry of the Word made flesh, but even there Jesus was born to be king and as he entered his public ministry he stepped forward as the king of the kingdom he proclaimed. His priestly ministry is associated mostly with his passion in which as high priest he offered himself in sacrifice for our sins and holy oblation to the Father, but even in the midst of this ministry he was king, crowned with thorns, but king because of the cross and through the cross. However, it is with his exaltation to the throne of God and his sitting at the right hand of the Father that his kingly ministry properly began. It stretches from the ascension to the final advent, when he will come again as Lord and king of all in open majesty, power and glory. Nevertheless within this kingly ministry we cannot lose sight of the *triplex munus* of Christ, his threefold office as prophet, priest and king. That is the general order in which it is natural to study christology, for it would appear to be the order determined by the mighty salvation events in the course of Jesus' life among us, but as we consider the threefold office within the period inaugurated by the ascension, it is evidently with another order that we have to work – king, priest and prophet. His kingly ministry is supreme from ascension to *parousia*, but within that his ministry as priest and prophet is no less evident than before, for it is brought to fullness in the consummation of his kingship: the priesthood of Christ is a royal priesthood, and the proclamation of Christ is a royal proclamation.

1 The language of ascension

Four main verbs are employed in the New Testament to speak of the ascension of Christ: *anabainein*, to go up or ascend; *kathizein*, to sit down; *analambanein*, to take up; *hupsoun*, to exalt. These words are all used in very ordinary ways in biblical Greek with much the same meaning that attaches to them in extra-biblical literature. But behind the biblical employment of these terms there lies a theological and cultic significance in certain contexts which lends them deeper meaning. That is the specific usage and meaning with which we are concerned here in relation to the ascension or exaltation of Christ to the right hand of the Father.

(a) Anabainō, *go up, ascend*

This term often renders the Hebrew *alah*, to ascend, and in its causative form, to make to ascend or offer. It is a word with a powerful cultic significance. It is used regularly in the Pentateuch[1] of Moses' ascent of Mount Sinai, with the sense of going up to or ascending to the Lord. It came to be a regular term for the ascent to Mount Zion, or to Jerusalem, and for going up to the temple, while within the temple it was used for ascension into the holy of holies. At the same time the word was used for the offering of sacrifice, while the noun, *olah*, may be used as a technical term for the whole burnt offering. It is also found in the enthronement Psalms,[2] with regard to ascent to royal sovereignty, but beyond that there lies the thought of the enthronement of Yahweh himself.[3] It is sometimes used to speak of the ascent of the ark to Jerusalem[4] which appears to carry with it the sacral enthronement of the king. It is language taken from this context of Old Testament thought that we have, for example, in Ephesians 4. The same language of ascent is used also more generally in the Old Testament in various contexts. That is to say, when *anabainō*, meaning to *ascend* is used *religiously* or *theologically* it tends to have a strong royal or priestly significance. It is a cultic term.

This is very apparent in the New Testament scriptures, but it ought to be noted that the cultic nuance of *anabainō* is by no means confined to biblical Greek, for it is regularly used in profane Greek literature of ascent to a temple or a shrine. Such a statement for example as Luke 18, 'two men went up into the temple to pray'[5] is just ordinary Greek.

---

[1]   The five so-called books of Moses (Genesis to Deuteronomy), from the Gk *pente*, five.

[2]   Psalms celebrating the enthronement of the king and through him of Yahweh over Israel and over all the earth.

[3]   Cf. Psalms 2, 24, 68 etc.

[4]   2 Sam 6.12f.; 1 Chron 15.1-16.3.

[5]   Luke 18.10.

But it is particularly in the fourth Gospel that we find the term regularly used in a cultic context, of Jesus going up to Jerusalem, or of his *'anabasis'*, as it is called, to a feast or the temple itself.[6] St Paul uses it in much the same way. In Acts we find it used of the ascent of prayer, for example of the prayer and alms of Cornelius, 'your prayers and your alms have ascended as a memorial before God'.[7]

It is in this way that the term *anabainō* is apparently applied to the ascension of Jesus Christ with distinct theological import.[8] When it is used in these contexts of the ascension it does not shed its cultic nuance, but of course this depends on the significance of the particular context. The main ideas we are concerned with here, then, are:

(1) the ascent of the king, and beyond that, the enthronement of Jahweh, the king of glory;

(2) the ascent to the temple, to the presence of God, for priestly service;

(3) the ascent to God of the whole burnt offering, or more generally of prayer.

Used in these ways the term *ascension* is essentially concerned with the royal priesthood of the crucified, risen and ascended Christ, a priesthood exercised from the right hand of divine power.

(b) Kathizō, *sit*

A study of this term and its employment confirms the applications of *anabainō* we have been discussing. One need only refer to the 110th Psalm which is cited in Acts 2 of the ascension of Christ.[9] It is not surprising that this entered into the full stream of the early Christian tradition and crops up in the later strata of the New Testament as well, as in Ephesians, Hebrews and the Apocalypse.[10] In several of these passages analogical reference to Melchizedek the royal priest is evident.

We recall the fact that in the heart of the holy of holies, to which the priest made his ascent, there was the mercy seat between the cherubim which came to play a role in the prophetic literature, as we see in Isaiah 6.[11] Some passages in the Apocalypse refer directly

---

6   John 2.13, 5.1, 7.8f., 11.55.

7   Acts 10.4.

8   Cf. Acts 2.34; John 3.13, 6.62, 20.17; Eph 4.8-10.

9   Acts 2.34f.

10   Eph 1.20; Heb 1.3, 8.1, 10.12, 12.2; cf. Rev 3.21.

11   Isaiah 6.1f.

or indirectly to this, but there are also passages in the Gospels which bear upon it with reference to the messianic king. It would appear that when the New Testament uses this term in connection with Christ, it is the concept of messianic enthronement that seems to be determinative, that is, his installation in the office of the messianic king in which he dispenses the divine mercy and peace.

(c) Analambanō, *take up*

The use of this term is not so straightforward – compare particularly Mark 16, Acts 1 and 1 Timothy 3.[12] Like the other terms, this is employed, of course, in quite non-theological senses, and with the usual meanings such as lift up, take up, take on board, put on armour for battle, as for example, in Paul's similes. But once again the word is given special significance in certain contexts where it acquires a distinctly cultic nuance, as in the lifting up of the heart in prayer to God. We are familiar with this kind of usage in the Scottish liturgical tradition in which we speak of the 'uplifting' of the offering or the 'lifting' of the cup at holy communion. In the LXX, the Greek translation of the Old Testament, the term is also used of the assumption of Elijah into heaven,[13] and this is given greater frequency in the Apocrypha, with respect to Enoch and Elijah.[14] The noun *analēmpsis* is not found in the Greek Old Testament, but became, apparently, a technical term in the apocryphal literature, for example with reference to the 'assumption' of Moses. In profane Greek the term is used in various ways, of receiving back into the family, of acquisition of knowledge, of assumption into office, of various senses of reception, recovery, recuperation, etc. but it is *not used of death* or of assumption in that sense.

The only time *analēmpsis* is found in the New Testament itself is in Luke 9,[15] where it is translated as receiving up, but where the reference is clearly to the death of Christ. The combination of noun and verb thus indicates that the ascension of Christ to heaven began with his lifting up on the cross. The apocryphal use of assumption has here an evident bearing upon the New Testament use, but the same applies to the cultic use we have noted in the Old Testament.

---

12   Mark 16.19; Acts 1.2,11,22; 1 Tim 3.16.

13   2 Kings 2.9,10,11.

14   Ecclesiasticus 48.9, 49.14; 1 Macc 2.58.

15   Luke 9.51.

(d) Hupsoō, *lift up*

The consideration of this term confirms the meaning found in connection with *analambanō*. *Hupsoun* means to lift up on high, for example in Mary's Magnificat in Luke, 'he has put down the mighty from their thrones, and *exalted* those of low degree',[16] or in a more general sense, 'whoever *exalts* himself will be humbled, and whoever humbles himself will be *exalted*'.[17] But this term also is used technically of the exaltation of Christ from humiliation, for example in Acts,[18] and yet like *analēmpsis* it is used directly of the *death* of Christ, especially in the fourth Gospel.[19] It is thus made clear that the glorification of Christ begins not with his actual ascension or resurrection, but with his crucifixion and indeed with his ascent to Jerusalem and Calvary for sacrifice. Theologically, therefore, this tells us that the unity of crucifixion and ascension means that the sacrifice of Christ also falls within the eternal sphere, within the very presence of God himself, or to use Old Testament language, within the veil of the holy of holies where God's presence dwells and his mercy seat is flanked by the cherubim.

The raising up of Christ begins then, paradoxically, with his crucifixion, and his ascension begins, paradoxically, with his lifting up on the cross. Although the beginning is there, the movement of ascension leads straight to his being lifted up on high to be at the right hand of the Father, where he is exalted to be 'a prince and a saviour'.[20] At the same time we must not forget here the other meaning of the resurrection, which is often used together with ascension and exaltation in these contexts, namely, that of installation in the messianic office, the exaltation of Christ with power as the mighty Son of God. Once again the term *hupsoun* chimes in here, for it also has the meaning of exaltation, or of being raised to an exalted height or *hupsos*, so that the exalted one is clothed with power from on high. This is found in several New Testament passages, but perhaps the meaning comes out most clearly in the language that is used of Melchizedek who is spoken of as 'priest of the most high God',[21] for this is the sense in which it is applied to Christ.[22]

---

16   Luke 1.52.

17   Matt 23.12; Luke 14.11, 18.14; cf. James 4.10; 1 Peter 5.6.

18   Acts 2.33, 5.31.

19   John 3.14, 8.28, 12.32,34.

20   Acts 5.31 KJV.

21   Heb 7.1.

22   For what follows on the threefold office of Christ, see William Milligan, *The Resurrection of our Lord*, 4th edition, Macmillan, London 1894, pp. 136-52; and *The Ascension of our Lord*, 2nd edition, Macmillan, London 1894, pp. 61-226.

To sum up, then, the ascension of Christ in this sense is his exaltation to glory and power but *through the cross*, certainly an exaltation from humiliation to royal majesty, but through crucifixion and sacrifice, for the power and glory of the royal priest is bound up with his self-sacrifice in death and resurrection. It is ultimately in that fusion of resurrection with the ascension in one indivisible exaltation that we are to understand the continuing ministry of Christ in presenting his 'many brethren' ('Here am I, and the children God has given me') along with himself,[23] amidst the sanctities of the new creation and in eternal glorification of the Father. It is as such that he blesses mankind by pouring out upon them his Spirit and fulfilling in them the work of God's reconciling love.[24]

2 The threefold office of Christ in ascension[25]

(a) *The ascension of Christ the king*

The nature of kingship in this context is indicated by the language used of the ascension. Christ ascends as lamb of God and as son of man, an ascension and exaltation to royal power in redemption and creation. It is in the conjunction of grace and omnipotence that Christ ascends to the throne of God in order to fulfil his saving work and fill all things with his sovereign presence and power – yet, as we shall see, the ascension involves the veiling of his divine majesty and power, or the holding back, from our visible and physical contact in space and time, of his unveiled majesty and power. In the language of the Apocalypse, he who has all power in heaven and earth, who alone is able to break open the sealed books of destiny, is the 'lion of the tribe of Judah'; but this figure is identified with the 'lamb as it had been slain'.[26] Even in ascension, the power of Christ is exercised through his sacrifice, through his atoning expiation of guilt, through his priestly mediation before God. It is this very connection (of ascension and priesthood) that we are to understand in the ascension of the son of man, for it is the ascension of representative man in whom all humanity is gathered up and made participant in his self-offering, so that in his

---

23   Rom 8.29; Heb 2.11-13.

24   Acts 2.32-33, 5.30-32.

25   For the role of the Spirit in relation to the threefold office of Christ, see T.F. Torrance, *The School of Faith*, James Clarke, London 1959, pp. ciiiff.

26   Rev 5.5-6ff. KJV.

ascension Christ is installed as head of the new humanity, the prince of the new creation, the king of the kingdom which he has won and established through his incarnate life and passion. The ascension is the enthronement of that Christ at the right hand of the Father in the sovereignty of grace. Henceforth all things are directed from the mercy seat of God, by the enthroned and exalted lamb, who reigns not only over the church but over all creation.

(b) The ascension of Christ the royal priest

We recall that the priestly ministry of Christ is set forth in the New Testament, notably in the epistle to the Hebrews and the Johannine literature, in the light of the Old Testament priestly and liturgical tradition. In this the fundamental priesthood was regarded as that of the word of God to man (which Philo called *ho hiereus logos*, 'the high-priestly logos')[27] with respect to Moses, while the liturgical priesthood, with respect to Aaron, was regarded as bearing witness to that divine word in cultic acts of mediation through oblation and sacrifice.[28] Because the Aaronic priesthood exalted itself beyond the function of witness and obedience to the word of God, arrogating to itself an independent status and clutching at authority or rule through cultic manipulation of the divine will, it was fiercely criticised by the prophets whom God raised up to bring the priestly function back to its true relation to the word of God and in subordination to it. It was in this connection that they called for 'obedience' not 'sacrifice'.[29]

This did not mean a rejection of the divine provision in the cult, but a re-integration of it with the primacy of *torah*,[30] instruction in the word and teaching of God, so that out of the prophetic tradition came the rehabilitation and interpretation of the cultic tradition in the redacted form in which it has been handed down to us in the Pentateuch. But then there developed a tension between a priestly and a scribal tradition which can be characterised as that between legalised liturgy and liturgised law. It was in that context and in the tradition of the cultic

---

[27] See the reference, T.F. Torrance, *Royal Priesthood*, 2nd edition, T & T Clark, Edinburgh 1993, p. 3, to Kittel, *Theological Dictionary of the New Testament*, vol. 3, Eerdmans, Grand Rapids 1966, p. 259.

[28] See also chap. 2 above, section 2 (c) (i) & (ii).

[29] See Amos 5.21-24; Hosea 6.6; Micah 6.6-8; cf. 1 Sam 15.22; Psalm 50.7ff.; 51.6,10,15-19. See also T.F. Torrance, *Royal Priesthood*, p. 3ff.

[30] Hb, direction, instruction, law.

prophets such as the Isaiahs, Jeremiah, Ezekiel, Zechariah, that Jesus engaged in dialogue with the priestly and scribal authorities of the Jews in order to force them back upon true priestly relation to the word of God.[31] He criticised the hardened priestly and scribal traditions and confronted them with the kingdom of God which had 'drawn near' of itself through word and Spirit in direct acts of forgiveness and healing, calling forth the liturgy of praise and thanksgiving from outcast sinners and little children which shamed the priestly and scribal authorities of Israel.

Christ is both apostle and priest in final reality

The New Testament interprets Christ in this situation both as *apostle from God* and as *our high priest*.[32] In Christ both sides of the Old Testament revelation are fulfilled. He himself is the Word of God come down into our midst, and himself the perfect response of man to that word in his obedient self-offering in life and death. Now it is in the ascension of Jesus to the throne of God, or his entry through the veil into the holy of holies, that both aspects come fully and finally together. Here we have priesthood that is no merely symbolic or institutional priesthood of witness to what God has done, for this priesthood is the reality to which the Old Testament priesthood bore witness; it is God's mediatorial action translated into terms of the son of man. Here, therefore, the symbolic and liturgical priesthood of the Aaronic tradition is transcended in a final way. Jesus is not priest in the sense that what he does symbolises or bears liturgical witness to something else, to what God does. No, he *is* Son of God, God *himself* come as priest, priest sent from God, apostle-priest, as well as priest qualified to act for us through his incarnational solidarity with sinners. It is only on that ground that he ascends as priest.

But here we pass from the Aaronic priesthood to priesthood of quite a different order, for he is priest not on the ground of legal ordinance but in a royal and sovereign way on the ground of his own endless life.[33] He is priest in final reality, and his sacrifice actually bears away

---

[31]   Cf. Matt 9.13, where Jesus quotes Hosea 6.6.

[32]   Heb 3.1f. See William Manson who points out that in Judaism the high-priest on the Day of Atonement was recognized as the *shaliach* (the apostle, commissioner) not of man but of God, *The Epistle to the Hebrews*, Hodder and Stoughton, London 1951, p. 54.

[33]   Heb 7.16ff.

our sins and cleanses us from guilt, and takes us into the presence of the Father. He makes a true atonement which no Aaronic priesthood could ever make.[34] This is priesthood that arises out of Christ's Sonship (priesthood in which apostleship from God and priesthood of man are hypostatically united in his own person), royal priesthood – for it is priesthood in which the liturgical witness and the reality witnessed to are one and the same, priesthood in which word and act are identical in his person, and therefore priesthood which is sovereign in its own right. Here liturgical act is identical with kingly act, for what Christ does on our behalf is actually fulfilled with final power, whereas all other priesthood at the very best can only symbolise it or bear witness to it.

The eternal efficacy of Christ's priesthood in heaven

This is what the ascension of Christ means for his priestly ministry: it is the coincidence of grace and power which makes it royal or sovereign priesthood. The resurrection and ascension, however, do not mean that Christ's priestly sacrifice and oblation of himself are over and done with, but rather that in their once and for all completion they are taken up eternally into the life of God, and remain prevalent, efficacious, valid, abidingly real. Christ is spoken of in the epistle to the Hebrews as the forerunner, *prodromos*,[35] or the pioneer, *archēgos*,[36] the one who has gone ahead and broken a way through into the immediate presence of God, who is *our* prince and leader, so that all who are united with him may through the living way which he has prepared in himself enter into the heavenly sanctuary. But Christ is spoken of also as himself the *leitourgos*,[37] the leader of the heavenly worship and chief executive as it were, in the heavenly kingdom. Through 'the power of his endless life'[38] he ever lives to exercise his priestly ministry on our behalf and in the worship that surrounds the throne of the most high. How then are we to think of the work of Christ in his heavenly priesthood?

(i) Christ's endless self-oblation

In the humanity of the ascended Christ there remains for ever before the face of God the Father the one, perfect, sufficient offering for

---

[34] Heb 10.1-22.

[35] Heb 6.20.

[36] Heb 12.2.

[37] Heb 8.2.

[38] See Heb 7.16ff. KJV.

mankind.[39] He presents himself before the Father as the redeemer who has united himself to us and has become our brother. He represents us before the Father as those who are incorporated in him and consecrated and perfected together with him in one for ever.[40] Here we think of the ascension as the act of Christ's self-offering to the Father in which his self-sacrifice on the cross is backed up by his own resurrection and endless life and made an offering to God through the eternal Spirit.[41] The New Testament and patristic understanding of this is evidently an extension of the Old Testament conception of the *minhah*, the thank-offering or tribute which we offer to the king of kings.[42]

(ii) Christ's eternal intercession or advocacy for us

We cannot consider this properly without taking into account the vicarious life of Jesus in obedience and prayer, and the fact that the whole existence of the incarnate Son was both the fulfilled intervention of God among man and the fulfilled response of man toward God, in filial obedience, faith, trust, love, worship, prayer and praise. The very existence of Christ among us, his life, work, crucifixion, resurrection, are all modes of his divine-human intervention or intercession – in Greek, the words for 'intervention' and 'intercession' are the same, *entugchanein*. In the indissoluble fusion of his human life with his divine activity, his vicarious representation of us was backed up by his divine life. We recall how in the incarnation the Son of God staked his own divine being for us by entering into human existence as it had fallen under the judgement of God and the imminent privation of being, in order to redeem us, and how in the resurrection that *goel*-redemption is efficacious over death, so that Jesus Christ remains in himself, in his very union with God the Father, the eternal pledge or surety of our

---

[39] For an understanding of the heart of the eucharist as Christ's vicarious humanity and as his 'uniting us with his self-oblation and self-presentation before the face of the Father', see T.F. Torrance, *Theology in Reconciliation*, Geoffrey Chapman, London 1975, chap. 3, 'The Paschal Mystery of Christ and the Eucharist', pp. 106-38.

[40] Cf. John 17.19.

[41] See Heb 9.14.

[42] See Malachi 1.11-14 (*minhah*, v. 11,13) and references to it in the *Didachç* (*The Teaching of the Twelve Apostles*), chap. 14 (*Ante-Nicene Fathers* [ANF], vol. 7, Eerdmans repr., Grand Rapids 1975, p. 381), and in Irenaeus, *Against Heresies*, Book IV.5 (ANF, vol. 1, Eerdmans repr., Grand Rapids 1975, p. 484).

redemption. It is with that ontological content of his advocacy on our behalf that we are concerned here. It is an advocacy in which his word and person and act are one and indivisible.

Christ is the eternal leader of our intercession and himself our one true prayer[43]

Here is an advocacy in which Christ is the eternal leader of our prayer and intercession, in which he makes himself the true content and sole reality of the worship and prayer of mankind. That is the prayer which (as reported by the evangelist) we overhear at the last supper, in John 17, the prayer we overhear in Gethsemane, the prayer we hear from the cross, the prayer of his whole life, the prayer that is summed up in the words of his own prayer, *Our Father*, which he prayed with us in our flesh and which he puts into our mouth. That is the prayer which Jesus Christ *eternally is* before the face of the Father and in God himself where he ever lives in active intercession and prayer for us. We have to think of this in terms of *substitution* as well as *representation*. If he were only our representative before God, he would represent us in *our* prayer and worship and would be, so to speak, their instrument. But as substitute as well as representative, he acts in our place and offers worship and prayer which we could not offer, yet offers them in such a vicarious way that while made in our stead and on our behalf they are made to issue out of our human nature to the Father as our own worship and prayer to God. We worship the Father not in our own name, nor in the significance of our own prayer and worship, but solely in Christ's name who has so identified himself with us as to make his prayer and worship ours, so really ours that we appear before God with Christ as our one true prayer and our only worship. That identification is so profound that through the Spirit Christ's prayers and intercessions are made to echo in our own,[44] and there is no disentangling of them from our weak and stammering and altogether unworthy acts of devotion.

Christ the mediator of eucharistic worship and prayer

It is in this light that we have to understand eucharistic worship and prayer and are to think of the heart of it all in the Lord's Prayer which we take into our mouths at his command. It is prayer backed up with the pledges of his body and blood which he puts into our hands that

---

[43] See T.F. Torrance, *Theology in Reconciliation*, chap. 4, 'The Mind of Christ in Worship', pp. 139-214.

[44] Rom 8.15-16; Gal 4.6; cf. Rom 8.26-27.

with them we might appear before the Father, for it is his one sufficient and once for all offering of himself for us that is our only sacrifice before God. This is neither a Pelagian[45] offering of the immolated Christ by man nor a Pelagian offering of ourselves in addition to the sacrifice of Christ, but the pleading of a sacrifice which by its very nature is offered on our behalf and in our place and in our stead, so that it is not we but Christ himself who here stands in for us as our mediator and advocate, while we take refuge in his sole sacrifice, finding shelter in his prayer and intercession and not in our own.[46] 'Nothing in my hands I bring, simply to thy cross I cling'.

(iii) Christ's eternal benediction – the blessing of his people in the gift of the Spirit

In his ascension Jesus Christ blessed his people,[47] and fulfilled that blessing in sending down upon us the presence of the Holy Spirit.[48] The language which the New Testament uses to speak of these aspects of Christ's heavenly priesthood is taken from the Old Testament accounts of Melchizedek's blessing of Abraham[49] and the Aaronic blessing of God's people after the completion of the sacrificial liturgy on the day of atonement.[50] We recall the account given of Christ's ascension and of the lifting up of his hands in blessing upon the disciples with the promise of the power of the Spirit.[51] Pentecost is the content and actualisation of that high priestly blessing. He ascended in order to fill all things with his presence and to bestow gifts of the Spirit upon men and women.[52] It is this image of Christ the royal priest that occupies such a central place in the Apocalypse, not least in the opening chapters but also at the end, in the consummation and fulfilment of Christ's blessing in the new Jerusalem that descends from above.[53]

---

[45] Humanly generated – Pelagius believed that we contribute to our own salvation.

[46] See T.F. Torrance, *Conflict and Agreement in the Church*, vol. 2, Lutterworth, London 1960, pp. 148f., 181ff.

[47] Luke 24.49f.

[48] Acts 2.1-33.

[49] Gen 14.18f.

[50] See Num 6.22-27.

[51] Acts 1.1-11; Luke 24.49f.

[52] Eph 4.10f.

[53] Rev 21.2ff.

Christ's blessing of the church in its participation in his royal priesthood

This is, again, an aspect of Christ's royal priestly ministry which is especially relevant to the church's communion in the body and blood of Christ through the Spirit. It is through the church's *koinōnia* with Christ that various gifts are distributed to members of the church which in their manifold character and working together in the one body are made to echo the one priesthood of Christ.[54] Thus the church is also a 'royal priesthood'[55] on earth through the Spirit, but a royal priesthood in a secondary sense, participating in the one priesthood of the ascended king through its *service* of him. The New Testament does not speak of 'a priesthood of all believers' for it no more speaks of the individual as a 'priest' than it speaks of the individual as a 'king'. The priesthood of the church is not constituted through the aggregation of the priestly functions of its individual members, but is only a reflection of the one indivisible priesthood of Christ. Through the Spirit Christ's own priestly ministry is at work in and through the church which is his body.

(c) The ascension of Christ the prophet

Just as the concepts of king and priest are essentially changed when they are applied to Christ, inasmuch as he makes himself their subject and content, so the concept of the prophet is also changed. He is prophet in a unique sense, for he is in himself the Word he proclaims just as he is himself the king of the kingdom and the priest who is identical with the offering he makes. Christ ascended, then, as the Word made flesh, as he who is both Word from God to humanity and word from humanity to God. He is God's own Word translated into human form and reality and returning back to the Father as answering word in perfect fulfilment of his will. It is in that identity of Word of God and word of man that Christ's prophetic ministry is fulfilled.

(i) Christ continues his prophetic ministry through his Spirit in the church

Let us think of this in terms of the end of St Mark's Gospel, 'So then the Lord Jesus, after he had spoken to them, was taken up into heaven, and sat down at the right hand of God. And they went forth and preached everywhere, while the Lord worked with them and confirmed

---

[54] Eph 4.4-16.

[55] 1 Peter 2.9 (cf. 2.5); cf. Exod 19.6 LXX, *'basileion hierateuma*, royal priesthood'.

the message by the signs that attended it.'[56] Here we have a statement about the relation between the church's proclamation of Christ and the activity of Christ himself in that proclamation which is very like that indicated in Paul's words at the end of Romans, 'according to *my gospel* and the preaching of *Jesus Christ*',[57] where the apostolic proclamation of the gospel and Christ's own proclamation are one and the same. That as we have seen is the New Testament conception of the *kērygma*. Primarily it is Christ's own *kērygma*, his self-proclamation, which through the Spirit he allows to be echoed and heard through the preaching of the church, so that their *kērygma* about Jesus Christ is made one with his own *kērygma*. In an important sense that happened once and for all in the fulfilment of the apostolic office, for it was the function of the apostles to translate the self-witness of Christ into witness to Christ, the self-proclamation of Christ into proclamation of Christ by the church, in such a way that it was given extension throughout history as the saving word of God. In and through the preaching and teaching of that word it is Christ himself the incarnate and risen Word who is mightily at work confronting men and women with himself and summoning them to believe and follow him.

The proclamation of Christ to all nations – the Word of God in act and human word

Here, then, we have to think of Christ as the ascended Word – that is, the Word from God to man incarnated in our human existence, made articulate in human word and therefore communicable to people and understandable by them, but he is also the word from humanity to God which in Jesus is directed to the Father. The ascension is not only the bearing of that Word up before the face of the Father, but that Word accepted and honoured by God, that Word fully installed in the divine kingdom, sent back to earth through the Spirit and by means of the church proclaimed to all nations and all ages. Thus the ascended Christ, through the Spirit which he has sent down upon the church to abide with it, continues to exercise his prophetic ministry throughout all history.

It is perhaps in connection with the notion of the *mediator* or *interpres*[58] that we should seek to understand this prophetic ministry, for it is the

---

[56]   Mark 16.19-20.

[57]   See Rom 16.25, 'Now to him who is able to strengthen you according to my gospel, and the preaching of Jesus Christ, according to the revelation of the mystery . . . (*kata to euangeliou mou kai to kērygma Iēsou Christou, kata apokalupsin mystēriou . . .*).

[58]   Lat, broker, interpreter, go-between.

ministry of the word which is not separable from the ministry of reconciliation. It is word of forgiveness now finally actualised by act of God in the cross and resurrection, word that is itself act of God, but it is word in which the historical Jesus Christ and the eternal Word of God are in indissoluble union. That is the kind of word that is mediated to us through the blessing of Christ and the pouring out of his Spirit, a prophetic ministry in which Christ is himself its living, actual and full content, or in which Christ himself ministers to us.

(ii) Christ reigns through his word: the relation between the church's ministry and Christ the head[59]

How are we to think of this ministry as taking place? It takes place in the relation between the church on earth and Christ himself as the relation between the body and the head of the body. The church is the bodily and historical form of Christ's existence on earth through which he lets his word be heard, so that as the church bears witness to him and proclaims the gospel of salvation in his name, he himself through the Spirit is immediately present validating that word as his own and communicating himself to people through it. The church's proclamation of the gospel becomes thus the *sceptre* as Clement of Rome called it, through which the risen and ascended Christ rules over the nations and all history. It is by the word of the gospel that he rules over all things until he comes again to judge and renew his creation.

The ministry of word and sacrament within the church

It is within this 'sacramental relation' between the church as the body of Christ and Christ as the head of the body, in which the church is given '*koinōnia* in the mystery of Christ', that we are to think of the relation between the earthly ministries which arise in the church under the gifts of the ascended Lord and the heavenly ministry of Christ himself. As king and head of the church, Christ has instituted the ministry of word and sacrament within history, whereby he continually nourishes, sustains, orders and governs his people on earth. Within the 'royal priesthood' of the whole church which reflects his own royal priesthood, Jesus Christ has called some to be set apart to this special ministry, to be his ambassadors to teach and preach, and administer

---

[59] On the relation between Christ's own ministry and that of the church, see T.F. Torrance, *Theology in Reconstruction*, SCM Press, London 1965, chap. 11, 'The Foundation of the Church: Union with Christ through the Spirit', pp. 202f., 205f., and esp. 207f. (reprinted from *Scottish Journal of Theology*, 16.2, 1963, and also a student handout).

the sacraments as the seals of their ambassadorial office in his name. This institutional ministry was given its specific form and shape by the apostles in obedience to the commands of Christ himself. Not only did they, therefore, mediate to us the New Testament revelation, in which Christ's own self-witness was translated into the form of witness to Christ and made communicable from person to person in history (which is handed on to us in the canon of the New Testament), but they instituted a historical ministry at the same time, dependent on their own unique ministry, and going out from theirs with the special function of handing on the *kērygma* and *didachē*, the proclamation and teaching of Christ from generation to generation.[60]

(iii) Christ's own ministry in the continuing ministry of the church

But Christ himself is at work in this continuing ministry. Not only did he pour out his Spirit upon the apostles inspiring them for their special task, and not only did he pour out his Spirit in a decisive and once for all way at Pentecost, constituting the people of God into the New Testament church which is the body of Christ, but within that church and its communion of the Spirit he continues to pour out special gifts for ministry, with the promise that as the gospel is proclaimed in his name he will work with the church, confirming their ministry of Christ to others as his own and making it the ministry of himself to mankind. Those who are called and thus endowed with gifts of the Spirit to engage in this ministry, fulfil their office by *serving* Christ who is prophet, priest and king of the church.

In the name of Jesus Christ they expound the holy scriptures, preach Christ crucified and risen, declare the forgiveness of sins and call all people to be reconciled to God, but the Lord himself is immediately present with them in his Spirit, making the preaching of the gospel effectual as word and power of God. In the name of Jesus Christ these ministers lead the worship of God's people, declare the forgiveness of sins, and celebrate baptism and the Lord's supper, but through the power of his Spirit it is Christ himself who confers forgiveness, builds up his church on earth, renews it in the

---

[60]   On the relation between Christ's ministry, the apostolic ministry and the ordained ministry within the church, see further T.F. Torrance, *Conflict and Agreement*, vol. 2, pp. 30-57, 'Consecration and Ordination', esp. p. 38ff., 'Consecration and Ordination of the Ministry in the New Testament'.

power of his resurrection and presents it as his own body to the Father. In the name of Jesus Christ they also have charge over the church on earth, to shepherd it as the flock of Christ, to feed it with the bread of life, to build it up in the unity of the faith, so that by the power of the Holy Spirit, through whom Jesus Christ himself governs the church, it becomes the instrument for the renewal of the world and the extension of his kingdom among all nations.

Although in this way Jesus Christ calls some to be set apart to special office in his church and endows them with the appropriate gifts of the Spirit for its fulfilment, every member of the church which is his body through sacramental incorporation into Christ is engaged in the mission of the gospel, to bear the reproach of Christ, to witness to him as saviour and Lord, to participate in his ministry of reconciliation and to live in the world the new life in him. Thus the mission of the whole church as the body of Christ on earth and in history is called through the Spirit, as it were, into contrapuntal relation to the heavenly ministry of Christ, king, priest and prophet, yet in such a way that the church cannot draw attention to itself, for the patterns of its life and work on earth have their significance entirely and only in directing the world away to the risen and ascended Lord himself.

3 The nature of the ascension event

We are back again here at the same question that we had to face in regard to the event of the resurrection, and certainly it has the same baffling character, especially when it is taken out of the context of the whole movement of the incarnation and the saving acts of God within it. That we cannot take the ascension out of that context is surely one of the lessons to be learned from 'the forty days' between the resurrection and the ascension, for they had nothing to do, as is sometimes alleged, with a progressive spiritualisation or immaterialisation of the body of Christ, but with the training of the disciples through a manifestation of Christ in which the thoughts of suffering and glory, of humiliation and exaltation, were bound up together in his own person in indissoluble union. Nevertheless, while closely tied up with the crucifixion and resurrection in this way, and indeed continuous with them, as is assumed in the epistle to the Hebrews, the ascension must be understood in correlation with the incarnation, as the *anabasis*, the ascent of the Son of God corresponding to his *katabasis*, his descent.

(a) How is the event of the ascension related to space and time?

(i) The question of the 'Calvinist extra'

This is the other pole of the question of the relation of the incarnation to space and time which we looked at in christology and which, as we have seen, gave rise in the sixteenth century to the controversy of the so called *extra Calvinisticum*, 'the Calvinist extra'.[61] Here we look at the same problem but in connection with the ascension. Let us recall the basic question? Did the eternal Son of God, in becoming incarnate, really became man at Bethlehem and so really enter within our existence of space and time? If so, was he incarnate in the babe of Bethlehem in such a way that he left the bosom of the Father or left the throne of the universe? Or are we to say that while he really did become incarnate, flesh of our flesh and bone of our bone, subjecting himself to the conditions and determinations of our existence in space and time, he nevertheless continued to rule the universe as the creator *Logos* by whom all things are made?

Patristic and Reformed theology have always claimed that the eternal *Logos* did enter space and time, not merely as creator but as himself made creature, within the creaturely limits of space and time, and yet did not cease to be what he was eternally in himself, the creator Word in whom and through whom all things consist and by whom all things derive and continue to have their being. This view was rejected by the Lutherans because like the mediaevals but unlike the fathers they operated with *a receptacle view of space as the place containing within its limits that which occupies it*. Hence when Calvin said of Christ that he became man born of the virgin's womb without leaving heaven or the government of the world, he was interpreted by the Lutherans to imply that in the incarnation only *part* of the Word was contained in the babe of Bethlehem or wrapped in the swaddling clothes in the cradle, and that something was left 'outside' (*extra*)[62] – hence the so called 'Calvinist extra'. It was undoubtedly the Lutheran intention to maintain in the fullest possible way real and full incarnation, and that was certainly right.

---

61   See T.F. Torrance, *Incarnation*, Paternoster Press UK & InterVarsity Press USA, Milton Keynes & Downer's Grove, 2008, pp. 216-21, and T.F. Torrance, *Space, Time and Incarnation*, OUP, London 1969, pp. 30f., 49f., for a fuller discussion here.

62   Lat, *extra*, outside.

The difficulties of rejecting the 'Calvinist extra'

Nevertheless, it is clear that a rejection of the 'Calvinist extra' raises very great difficulties, as one can see in a kenotic[63] theory of Christ's *self-emptying*. Quite clearly if one operates with a receptacle view of space, one must think of the *kenōsis* as the emptying of the Son of God into a containing vessel, but this way of thinking creates difficulties that need not be there and which once created need to be solved. The same problem arose in the mediaeval doctrine of the real presence. If a receptacle view of space or place is held, how are we to think of the body of Christ as contained in the host, in every part of it, and in a multitude of hosts at the same time, and how can we think of it as being contained without any relation between the dimensions of the body of Christ and the space of the place that contains him? The usual mediaeval answer was given in the doctrine of transubstantiation in which an artificial distinction was drawn between the substance and the accidents of the elements, their substances being changed into the body and blood of Christ, while the accidents (external appearance or sensible qualities) remained as before. It was basically the same problem that faced the Lutherans and indeed the same kind of answer that was given by them in regard to the question as to how we are to conceive the being of the Son of God as contained in the body of the historical Jesus Christ. The kenotic theories answered by drawing a distinction between the immanent and relative properties of the Son, and claiming either that he shed those that were incompatible with creaturely existence or that their use was restricted in the incarnate state.

The danger of compromising the humanity of Jesus

But in actual fact this way of relating the 'immensity' of God to the finite receptacle – *finitum capax infiniti*[64] – usually meant the extension of the human receptacle to contain the divine, for example in the doctrine of the ubiquity of the body of Christ, which could hardly avoid a form of monophysitism.[65] Another answer, which had already been

---

63   The theory that when Christ became man he *emptied* himself in some sense of his divinity or of some of his divine characteristics, from the Greek, *kenoō*, empty. See Phil 2.7, 'Christ Jesus . . . emptied (*ekenōsen*) himself, taking the form of a servant'.

64   Lat, 'the finite is capable of the infinite'.

65   The doctrine that Christ only had *one nature* (from the Gk *monos* one, and *physis* nature), a divine, ie. the absorption in this case of the human nature into the divine so as to take on its characteristics.

adopted by Luther, was to think of the relation between the divine being and the physical existence of Jesus Christ in space and time as a mathematical point, but that tended to reduce history to a vanishing point. In Lutheran thought it came to imply a radical disjunction between the divine and the human in which there was no interaction between them. This in effect is the same sort of answer as now given by the 'demythologisers' who posit such an infinite difference between the divine being and the creaturely realm of space and time that they are related to one another only tangentially at the point called Jesus, whose historical existence is then only a sort of springboard for a constant leap in existential decision that leaves history behind. The problem is thus 'solved' by the reduction of the historical Jesus to a vanishing point.

The truth in the Lutheran insistence on a real incarnation

The original Lutheran position had its extremely important truth in the insistence that a real and genuine incarnation took place, an incarnation which means that the Word of God is nowhere to be found except in inseparable union with Jesus, the babe of Bethlehem, the real and proper man. But if we press that to mean that in the incarnation the Word was resolved into this Jesus without remainder, so to speak, then insuperable difficulties arise – and solutions such as a metaphysical[66] *kenôsis* or demythologising have to be found. Now of course we cannot say that the eternal *Logos* became flesh in such a way that part of the *Logos* was excluded – that is what the early Lutherans were afraid of, for the *Logos* was totally incarnate – nevertheless he remained wholly himself, the creator and ruler and preserver of the universe of all creaturely reality. He became man without ceasing to be God, and so entered space and time without leaving the throne of God.

(ii) The need to have a 'relational' view of space and time

Our difficulty is that we have to think *both* in accordance with the nature of the *Logos* as eternal Son of God and in accordance with the nature of the human Jesus as creature of space and time. It will not do to think of this in terms of a receptacle view of space and time, nor will it do to cut the knot and think of him only in one way or the other.

---

[66] 'Transcendent' – metaphysics is properly the branch of philosophy which deals with fundamental principles, particularly of being and knowing, but the word is commonly also taken in a looser sense to refer to the abstract or to what is beyond physical reality.

Hence if we are to be faithful to the nature of Christ as very God and very man we have to let that determine our thinking of the incarnational event, and say both that he really and fully became man, human as we are human in space and time, and yet remained God the creator who transcends all creaturely being in space and time. We have to work with a *relational view of space and time*[67] differentially or variationally related to God and to man.[68] Unless we think in this way we cannot really think the incarnation itself without falsifying it.[69] That was the problem of the kenoticists which the demythologisers sought to solve by resolving away the incarnation as an objectifying form of thinking, but at the expense of detaching faith entirely from space and time, from any ground in physical and historical existence.

(1) God exists as God and man exists as man

The question may be easier if we approach it along the line of 'existence'. When we say that God exists, we mean that God exists as God, in accordance with the nature of God, for divine existence is of an utterly unique and transcendent kind. When we say that man exists, the term 'exists' is defined by the subject man, for it is the kind of existence which man has in space and time. Now when we try to think together the existence of the Son of God and the existence of Jesus, son of Mary, in one person, we have to think them in the same way in which we think of the union of divine and human natures in the one person. Similarly we have to think together the relation of God to space and time and the relation of the man Jesus to space and time.

(2) The duality of fallen space-time and redeemed space-time

It is this question that arises again in an acute form when we come to the ascension of Christ, of Jesus who is very Son of God and who

---

[67] In a relational view, space and time are thought of, not as things in themselves, but as inherently *relational* to bodies, forces and events in the universe and as functions of them. See below sections (b) (i) *(1)* to *(3)*.

[68] See the note, T.F. Torrance, *Space, Time and Resurrection*, Handsel Press, Edinburgh 1976, p. 126, and the reference to *Space, Time and Incarnation*, pp. 10-21.

[69] On occasion, Torrance would use a phrase such as 'thinking the incarnation' rather than thinking 'of' or 'about' it, in order to express the immediacy of the relation of our minds and thoughts to reality: for him our thoughts 'terminate on things' and 'we do not just think statements', or think about things through statements, but as he put it, 'we think things through statements'.

ascends from man's place to God's 'place'. In so far as he is man, truly and perfectly man, we must think of the ascension as related to the space and time of creaturely reality. But this involves a duality in itself, between our fallen space-time and redeemed space-time. So far as the companions of Jesus were concerned, that is the disciples as members of this fallen world, living historically on earth, with corruptible natures as part of fallen existence, the ascension of Jesus *from* Peter, James and John and the others must be related to the kind of space and time with which *we* men and women are involved in the ongoing existence of this passing world. But in his own resurrection Jesus had healed and redeemed our creaturely existence from all corruption and privation of being, and every threat of death or nothingness, so that in him space and time were recreated or renewed. We have no adequate language to describe this, and can speak of it only in apocalyptic language, that is in language that breaks down in its very use, but which must break down if it really is to point us to this new reality beyond, which cannot be captured or enclosed in the language of this fallen world.

(iii) The ascension must be thought out in relation to space and time and yet as beyond space and time

Nevertheless the humanity of Jesus, although risen and triumphant over all decay and corruption, was fully and truly human, and indeed more fully and truly human than any other humanity we know, for it was humanity in which all that attacks and undermines creaturely and human being is vanquished. In the risen Jesus therefore, creaturely space and time, far from being dissolved are confirmed in their reality before God. On the one hand then, the ascension must be thought out in relation to the actual relations of space and time. On the other hand however, the ascension must be thought of as an ascension beyond all our notions of space and time, and therefore as something that cannot ultimately be expressed in categories of space and time, or at least cannot be enclosed within categories of this kind. That is why Calvin used to insist that while the ascension was an ascension into the heavens, away from us, yet it was also an ascension beyond the heaven of heavens, beyond anything that can be conceived in terms of earth or heaven.[70]

---

[70] See especially Calvin, *Comm. on Ephesians*, 1.20 (trans. T.H.L. Parker, Oliver and Boyd, Edinburgh 1965, p. 136f.), 4.10 (p. 176f.); *Comm. on Hebrews*, 7.26 (trans. W.B. Johnston, Oliver and Boyd, Edinburgh 1963, p..102), from *Calvin's Commentaries*, ed. D.W. Torrance and T.F. Torrance; *Institute* 2.16.14.

We have heavens that are appropriate to human beings, the sky above the earth, the 'space' beyond the sky, but all these are understood anthropocentrically, for as created realities they are conceivable to human understanding. But God in his own nature cannot be conceived in that way – God utterly transcends the boundaries of space and time, and therefore because he is beyond them he is also everywhere, for the limits of space and time which God transcends are all around us. Hence from this aspect the absence or presence of God cannot be spoken of in categories of space and time, but only when categories of space and time break off and point beyond themselves altogether to what is ineffable and inconceivable in modes of our space and time. Calvin was also right when he said that the biblical writers never thought of the presence of God or of the ascension simply in terms of our space and time or in terms of earth and heaven, for what does the ascension to the right hand of God mean? For Calvin, what else was the right hand of God but the power of God, and 'where' is that but everywhere 'where' God is? What do we mean by 'everywhere where God is', except what is defined by the nature of God himself just as the existence of God is defined by his nature?

(iv) Jesus Christ is the place where God and man meet in space and time

In order to express this more positively, let us turn back to the incarnation for a moment. Jesus Christ, the man Jesus, is the *place* in this physical world of space and time where God and man meet and where they have communion with one another. The temple in the Old Testament was the place where God put his name, where he kept tryst with his covenanted people and where they kept covenant with him. Jesus Christ is that temple of God on earth and among mankind where God has put his name, and where he has appointed us to meet him. It is the place where heaven and earth meet, the place of reconciliation within our historical existence in flesh and blood. Jesus Christ is himself among us God's mercy-seat, God's place in the world where he is really present to us in our place.

As the incarnation is the meeting of man and God in man's place, so the ascension is the meeting of man and God in God's place

Now we have to think of this ascended Jesus Christ as 'in heaven'. In its way, this is the reverse of the incarnation. As in the incarnation we have to think of God the Son becoming man without ceasing to be transcendent God, so in his ascension we have to think of Christ as ascending above all space and time without ceasing to be man or without any diminishment of his physical, historical existence. That is what we mean by saying that Christ is 'in heaven'. But we also mean something more, for the ascension of the incarnate, crucified and risen Jesus Christ inevitably transforms 'heaven': something quite new has been effected in the heavenlies which must alter its material content in our understanding of what heaven is.[71] Whatever else 'heaven' is for us it is the 'place' where Christ is in God. Hence we can speak of Jesus Christ as having a 'heavenly place' far beyond anything we can understand and far beyond our reach. Nevertheless through his Spirit Jesus Christ bestows his presence upon us in the church, so that the church on earth, in the continuing space-time of this world, is the place where God and man are appointed to meet. In the incarnation we have the meeting of man and God in man's place, while in the ascension we have the meeting of man and God in God's place, but through the Spirit these are not separated from one another (they were not spatially related in any case), and our human place on earth and in the space-time of this world is not abrogated, even though we meet with God in God's place. 'Our Father which art in heaven, hallowed be thy name. Thy kingdom come, thy will be done *on earth* as in heaven'.

(b) Two points we have to think together

There are two points here we have to try to think together: (i) in the ascension Jesus Christ ascends from man's place to God's place, (ii) by his ascension Jesus Christ established man in man's place in time and space.

(i) Jesus ascended from man's place to God's place

Jesus Christ has ascended from man's place to God's place, and yet he is in himself the one place in our human and created reality and therefore in the immanent order of time and space where God and man fully meet.

(1) The difficulty of our abstract notions of space, and the need for a new understanding

We have great difficulty in speaking about this because of our abstract notions of space. We are accustomed, for example, to imagining space as something abstract and as something in itself, as though space could

---

[71]   Cf. Karl Rahner, *Sacramentum Mundi*, vol. 5, Burns & Oates, London 1970, p. 333, 'the occurrence of the (his) resurrection created "heaven"…and taken together with the ascension (which fundamentally is an element in the resurrection), is not merely an entry into an already existing heaven.'

exist or be an entity in itself quite apart from the things it 'contains'. Thus we work with a dualism between 'space' and the things thought to be 'in it', and so think it possible to have 'empty' space. But let us remember that as time is to be understood as *time for* something, the time in which we live our life, time for decision, time for repentance, time for action, and the 'time' of God is understood as the time in which God lives his own life, the time which God has in himself for his own eternal will of love, so we must think of space as *room for* something, as place defined in terms of that which occupies it.

Space and time are relational to active agents

This means that we must not abstract the notion of space from that which is located in space – for space concretely considered *is* place, but place not abstracted from purpose or content, and place not without ends or purposeful limits. Space and time must both be conceived in *relational* terms and in accordance with the active principles or forces that move and make room for themselves in such a way that space and time arise in and with them and their movements. That is, space and time should not be conceived in themselves as abstract entities but only *in relation* to active agents and therefore relationally – they are not 'receptacles' apart from bodies or forces, but are functions of events in the universe and forms of their orderly sequence and structure. Space and time are *relational* and *variational* or *differential* concepts defined in accordance with the nature of the force that gives them their field of determination. They are *relational* to the operating forces and therefore *vary* or *differ* in accordance with them as those forces themselves vary or differ.

(2) Man's place is defined by the nature and activity of man, and God's place is defined by the nature and activity of God

In modern thought we also cannot separate space and time but think of space-time in a four dimensional continuum (three of space and one of time) – although there is a difference between them, for, whereas space is three-dimensional, time is one directional or irreversible. But in the nature of the case we cannot separate space from time, or location from time – temporal relation belongs to location. This is another way of saying that we must think of place as well as time in terms of that *for which* they exist or function. This is why we must speak of man's 'place' and God's 'place', but in the nature of the case 'place' is differently defined in each case.

Man's 'place' is defined by the nature and activity of man as the room which mankind makes for itself in human life and movement, and God's 'place' is defined by the nature and activity of God as the room for the life and activity of God as God. Man's space-time is defined in accordance with the field of change and the sequence of coherent structures in which human beings live life, and this way of speaking is appropriate to man as a creature of this physical world – although we would also have to speak about the space-time of human personal, social or mental life in an appropriately differential way.

We do not speak of space-time in relation to God, but we may speak of the 'place' and 'time' of God in terms of his own eternal life and his eternal purpose in the divine love, where he wills his life and love to overflow to us whom he has made to share with him his life and love. 'Time' for God himself can only be defined by the uncreated and creative life of God, and 'place' for God can only be defined by the communion of the persons in the divine life – that is why we speak of the '*perichōresis*' (from *chōra* meaning space or room) or mutual indwelling of the Father, Son and Holy Spirit in the triunity of God.

(3) The ascension is 'bounded' at our end but open at God's end - the reversal of perspective in Byzantine art

When, therefore, we come to speak of the ascension of Christ from man's place to God's place, we make a statement which is delimited and defined or bounded by the nature of man and human space at one end, but a statement which at the other end is 'bounded' by the boundless nature of God, and 'limited' only by the limitless room which God makes for himself in his eternal life and activity. In the nature of the case, statements regarding the ascension are *closed at man's end* (because bounded within the space-time limits of man's existence on earth) but are *infinitely open at God's end*, open to God's own eternal being and the infinite room of his divine life.

Here we discern the immense significance of the intention in Byzantine art where a deliberate reversal of the natural perspective is made in depicting the dais or platform on which the figure of Christ is made to stand, lest it should be enclosed within converging lines, which when 'produced' (extended) meet at a finite point, and which would then depict Christ as 'enclosed' within space.[72] When, as opposed to the customary way of depicting a three dimensional platform in a two dimensional figure (where the lines converge as they go away from us), the lines depicting the dais are made to diverge, against the natural perspective, then when produced they never meet but go out into infinity. At one end of the icon or mosaic the figure of Christ stands in bounded space and time, but at the

---

[72]   Cf. T.F. Torrance, *Space, Time and Incarnation*, p. 18.

other end he transcends all such limitations. He became man without ceasing to be God, and lived within our physical and historical existence without leaving the throne of the universe.

(4) In the ascension Jesus leaves us in the mode of man's presence that he might be with us in the mode of God's presence

Epistemologically,[73] this means that statements about God or Christ must not be such as to enclose them within the finite limits of the conceptualities and determinations of creaturely forms of thought and speech, that is, within the room or space of creaturely comprehension. Here also, then, we must say with Calvin that the ascension is an event which we must speak of on the one hand through its relation with space and time as we know it on earth and in history, within creaturely existence, but on the other hand we must speak of as transcending all that, and as an event infinitely beyond the boundaries of our space and time or anything we could conceive in terms of them.

It is the event in which Christ ascends to God's place and God's place is wherever God is, the place of the omnipresent God, who is as far removed from us as the creator is from the creature, and yet as intimately and indeed infinitely near us as the creator is to the creature to whom he ever gives being through a relation which he maintains of the creature to himself, for he is so present to the creation as to complete its relation as a creature to himself the creator.[74] The ascension of Christ is thus an ascension to fill all things with himself, so that in a real sense he comes again in the ascension. He had to go away in one mode of presence that he might come again in this mode of presence, leaving us in the mode of man's presence to man and returning to us in the mode of God's presence to man, and thus not leaving mankind bereft of himself.[75]

There are two things to note here which we will consider further in due course:

(a) The ascension is the revelation of the *gap* between the time of the new man and the time of the old man, the gap between the resurrection reality of our humanity in Jesus Christ and the corruptible existence which we still wear and in which we are fully implicated.

---

[73] In terms of the nature and meaning of our statements – epistemology is the philosophy of knowledge, its nature and limits.

[74] See further T.F. Torrance, *The Christian Doctrine of God*, T & T Clark, Edinburgh 1996, p. 218.

[75] John 14.18, 'I will not leave you desolate (*orphanous*, orphans); I will come to you.'

(b) The ascension is the exaltation of new man, with a fully and truly human nature, and therefore of man with the 'place' of man, with the 'room' which human beings are given for their human lives, to participation in the divine 'place', the 'place' which God makes by his own life and the 'room' which he has for the fulfilment of his divine love. It is ascension in which our humanity in Christ is taken up into the full communion of Father, Son and Holy Spirit in life and love.

(ii) By his ascension Jesus establishes man in man's place in space and time

(1) The ascension sends us back to the historical Jesus

The withdrawal of Christ from visible and physical contact with us in our space-time existence on earth and in history means that Jesus Christ insists in making contact with us, not first directly and immediately in his risen humanity, but first and foremost through his historical involvement with us in his incarnation and crucifixion. That is to say, by withdrawing himself from our sight, Christ sends us back to the historical Jesus Christ as the *covenanted place* on earth and in time which God has appointed for meeting between man and himself. The ascension means that our relation to the saviour is only possible through the historical Jesus, for the historical Jesus is the *one locus* or place within our human and creaturely existence where God and man are hypostatically united, and where humanity engulfed in sin and immersed in corruption can get across to God on the ground of reconciliation and atonement freely provided by God himself. The ascension thus means that to all eternity God insists on speaking to us through the historical Jesus. Just because it is the historical and risen Jesus who is ascended, what Jesus says to us, the Jesus whom we meet and hear through the witness of the Gospels, is identical with the eternal Word and being of God himself. *Jesus speaks as God and God speaks as Jesus.* Therefore we are sent back to Jesus, for there and there only may we hear God speaking in person, and there and there only at the foot of the cross, where God and humanity meet over the judgement and expiation of sin and guilt may we meet with God face to face and live. Here and here only may we be judged and cleansed and have living communion with him in love through the propitiation of Jesus Christ.

(2) We cannot know God by transcending space and time

Thus the ascension means that we cannot know God by transcending space and time, by leaping beyond the limits of our place on earth, but by encountering God and his saving work within space and time, within our actual physical existence. Hence the ascension is the opposite of all demythologising, for demythologising means that we have to slough off the space-time involvement of the Word and act of God as merely our own projecting and objectifying mode of thought and so demythologising means that we have to try to get to know God in a timeless and spaceless way. The ascension, in contrast, sends us back to the incarnation, to the historical Jesus, and so to a word and act of God inseparably implicated in our space and time. It sends us back to a gospel which is really accessible to frail creatures of earth and history, and a gospel that is relevant to their bodily existence day by day in the structures and coherences of space and time.

(3) We know the risen and ascended Jesus only through the historical and crucified Jesus

All true and proper knowledge of God is thus mediated through the historical Jesus Christ. Now that God has taken *this* way of revealing himself to us in and through the incarnation of his Word in the space-time existence and structure of Jesus Christ, he has set aside all other possibilities for us, no matter how conceivable they were *a priori* by reason. Jesus Christ as the actualisation of the way God has taken towards us thereby becomes the one and only way of approach to God, so that we have to *follow* Jesus exclusively. We derive our knowledge of God *a posteriori*[76] from him who is constituted the way, the truth and the life. There is now no other way to the Father. We cannot and must not try to go behind the back of Jesus Christ, to some kind of *theologia gloriae*, theology of glory, reached by direct speculation of the divine majesty. All contact with the majesty of God as of the glorified Lord is in and through the crucified one. But the obverse of this is, that through the historical and crucified Jesus we really meet with the risen and ascended Lord, we really meet with God in his transcendent glory and majesty – we really are gathered into the communion of the Son with the Father and of the Father with the Son, and really are taken up through the Spirit to share in the divine life and love that have overflowed to us in Jesus Christ.

(4) It is only through the Spirit that Christ can be historically absent and actually present

How are we to think of these two aspects of the ascension together? Clearly this can be done *only through the Spirit*. As it is the pouring out of the Spirit that links the historical Jesus with the ascended Lord, so it is through the communion of the Spirit that we can think these things

---

[76] Lat, *from after* the event, ie. not *a priori* from first principles prior to events, but only after them and in conformity to them, and hence only from Jesus in his actual incarnate life.

together, that is, think of the ascension both as actual historical event in which Christ departed from man's place and as the transcendent event in which he went to God's place. But since God's place is the place where God is, it is through the Spirit that we can think of Christ as historically absent and as actually present. It is through the Spirit that things infinitely disconnected – disconnected by the 'distance' of the ascension – are nevertheless infinitely closely related.[77] Through the Spirit Christ is nearer to us than we are to ourselves, and we who live and dwell on earth are yet made to sit with Christ in heavenly places,[78] partaking of the divine nature in him.

(c) The material implications of the doctrine of the ascension

We must now try to gather together some of the principal points in the material content of the doctrine of the ascension.

(i) The exaltation of man into the life of God

The ascension means the exaltation of man into the life of God and on to the throne of God. In the ascension the son of man, new man in Christ, is given to partake of the divine nature. There we reach the goal of the incarnation, in our great *prodromos* or forerunner[79] at the right hand of God. We are with Jesus beside God, for we are gathered up in him and included in his own presence before the Father.

The preservation of human nature and creaturely being

The staggering thing about this is that the exaltation of human nature into the life of God does not mean the disappearance of man or the swallowing up of human and creaturely being in the infinite ocean of the divine being, but rather that human nature, while remaining creaturely and human, is yet exalted in Christ to share in God's life and glory. This is the ultimate end of creation and redemption revealed in the covenant of grace and fulfilled in Jesus Christ, of which he himself in his ascension is the pledge and first-fruit (*aparchē*)[80] of its fulfilment in us. We ourselves are given a down-payment (*arrabōn*)[81] of that, as it were, in the gift of the Spirit bestowed upon us by the ascended man

---

[77]   See Calvin's discussion in the *Institute* 4.17, especially 4.17.10,12,18,25-33.

[78]   Eph 2.6; cf. Col 3.1.

[79]   Heb 6.20.

[80]   Cf. 1 Cor 15.20,23.

[81]   *Arrabōn*, pledge, down-payment, guarantee, 2 Cor 1.22 & Eph 1.13-14; Rom 8.23, *aparchē*.

from the throne of God, so that through the Spirit we may already have communion in the consummated reality which will be fully actualised in us in the resurrection and redemption of the body.

A warning should be given at this point on the danger of *vertigo* which can quickly overwhelm some people when they think of themselves as being exalted in Christ to partake of the divine nature. One finds a form of this vertigo also in those mystics and pantheists who tend to identify their own ultimate being with the divine being. This would be the exact antithesis of what the Christian gospel teaches, for the exaltation of mankind into sharing the divine life and love, affirms the reality of their humble creaturely being, by making them live out of the transcendence of God in and through Jesus alone. The hypostatic union of the divine and human natures in Jesus preserves the human and creaturely being he took from us, and it is in and through our sharing in that human and creaturely being, sanctified and blessed in him, that we share in the life of God while remaining what we were made to be, human beings and not gods.

(ii) The establishment on the apostolic tradition of a church in history

The ascension means the establishment of a church in history, within space and time on the historical foundation of the apostles and prophets. The ascension finalises the grounding of the church on the historical Jesus Christ, and confirms it on that foundation through the baptism of the Spirit at Pentecost. By withdrawing himself from continuing visible and immediate contact as our contemporary in history, Jesus Christ establishes the people of God within the processes and structured patterns of history as a coherent body. He sends it on an historical mission and determines for it an historical development, since it must live and work in the ongoing sequences and this-worldly forms of life as they develop among the nations and peoples and kingdoms of historical existence.

The establishing of scripture and the basic patterns of church life

Part of this establishing of the church as a fact within the space-time structures of history, is the establishing of holy scripture on the apostolic tradition in its distinction from all other traditions. Another part of it is to be discerned in the development of the church's worship and prayer within space and time out of the basic forms found in the apostolic community, when the self-witness of Christ was translated into witness to Christ and a foundation was laid for continuing patterns of life, worship and prayer in Christ's name. The church's life, worship and prayer can no more be spaceless and timeless than its historical existence can be detached from historical relation to its historical roots in Jesus Christ.

The structures of the church must be essentially 'open' structures

The same applies to the coherent structures of the church's life and mission within space and time, for the church is sent to live as the 'servant of the Lord' within the *nomistic* structures and patterns of creaturely and historical being, yet in such a way that these are made to serve the gospel and are not allowed to restrict or obstruct it. Because of the resurrection and ascension, the coherent and ordered sequences of the church's life and mission are essentially *open structures*, and more like the scaffolding which is necessary for the erection of a building but which is cast away when the building stands complete. Hence we can never identify the patterns of the church's life in worship or ministry with the real inner forms of its being in the love of God, but have to regard them as only temporary forms which will fall away when with the advent of Christ the full reality of the new humanity of the church as the body of Christ will be unveiled.

(iii) The heavenly rule of the ascended Christ is the key to world history

The ascension of Jesus Christ and his session at the right hand of God the Father is the mystery of world history.[82] Our history has been gathered up in Jesus Christ and is taken up with him into the life and rule of God, and in his ascension, it is, as it were, anchored within the veil,[83] by an anchor that will not drag, no matter how fierce and terrible and devastating may be the storms that sweep over the earth and its history. Here we are back again in the theme of the *Apocalypse* which must not be interpreted in the old manner of idealistic Christianity as a flight from history, but precisely the reverse, as the invasion of history by the kingdom of Christ through the everlasting gospel. It is because the kingdom of Christ is operative in and throughout all nations and peoples and all ages that such apocalyptic strife is generated among humanity. Hence to the eyes of faith the great movements of history, even the darkest and most terrible of them, appear as reactions to the real movement within history that takes its cue from the initiative of God's grace and derives from the mighty acts of God in Jesus Christ which are perpetuated in the proclamation of the gospel.[84]

---

[82]   Acts 2.33f.; Eph 1.20f.; cf. 1 Cor 15.24-25; Heb 1.3f.

[83]   Heb 6.19 KJV.

[84]   T.F. Torrance, *The Apocalypse Today*, James Clarke, London 1960, p. 12ff , 45ff , 64ff , 73ff , 95ff , 165ff.

History is to be seen in the light of Christ who makes all things work for his purpose

The obverse of the invasion of the kingdom of Christ and its struggle with the kingdoms of this world is the *millennium-time* of the kingdom of Christ stretching from resurrection to final advent, which is history seen from the point of the triumph of the risen lamb of God[85] who suborns and bends all world events to serve God's saving purpose. He who made the terrible cross to be the supreme instrument for the salvation of mankind, is by the same cross able to make all history serve the ends of God in the new creation. The ascension of Christ is here to be seen as the transcendent act whereby Jesus Christ who is and remains the culminating point of all history is taken up into the consummation of God's kingdom so that he remains the ultimate secret of the history of humanity. Because of the ascension the course of world history is to be regarded in the light of the heavenly session and ministry of the heavenly mediator, for it is what he has done and is and is doing that will prevail until all history is subdued and brought into conformity to his saving will.

Prayer is the link between world history and the intercession of Christ in heaven

So far as the church in history and on earth is concerned, therefore, the great connecting link between world history and the heavenly session of Christ is to be found in *prayer and intercession*. That is why when the New Testament speaks about the relations of church and state it regularly directs the church to prayer as its most important service, for it is in prayer that through the Spirit the heavenly intercessions of the risen and enthroned lamb are made to echo in the intercessions of humanity and the people of God are locked with Christ in the great apocalyptic struggle with the forces of darkness. Because he who rules from the throne of God is the lamb who has been slain, but is alive for evermore and holds the keys of death and hell,[86] the church's engagement in prayer is already a participation in the final victory of the kingdom of Christ. Thus the life, mission, and worship of the church on earth and in history are, as it were, in counterpoint to the victorious paeans of the hosts above who surround the throne of the lamb and worship and glorify God.

---

[85]   Rev 5.6ff.

[86]   Rev 1.18.

4 The resurrection and the ascension

The triumph of light over darkness: is the resurrection body transfused with light?

It should now be clear that the resurrection and the ascension have to be taken closely together, as for example, they are in the epistle to the Hebrews. Think of them in the perspective of Christ's victory over the powers of darkness and over the evil that separates the creation from its creator. Think of the risen and ascended humanity of Christ in the perspective of what the Johannine literature especially has to say in the New Testament about the triumph of light over darkness. Must we not, then, think of the risen and ascended humanity, even in respect of the body, as transfused with light, and as made perfectly transparent? This is not to say that the body of Christ in the resurrection and ascension was transmuted into pure spirit, whatever that may mean, but that the opaqueness and darkness that come from separation from God are utterly overcome and put away. Here redemption makes contact again with the creation in which God turned his back upon the darkness and brought what he had made into the light of life. If the resurrection and ascension bring the work of atoning reconciliation and recreation to their consummation in the humanity of Christ, then here all darkness (our darkness into which Christ descended) is done away, and even the human nature he took from our dark and fallen existence is completely and finally restored to the light of God.[87]

The disciples' fleeting glimpses of Jesus in his resurrection body

We cannot think out all that this means, for it is something we may only glimpse and on which we dare not speculate. But it does help us to understand the nature of the resurrection – for example, the action of Jesus at Emmaus when he vanished out of the sight of the disciples,[88] and the event of the ascension when he withdrew himself from the sight of the world[89] in accordance with his evangelical purpose for all nations, and also those fleeting glimpses of him which he allowed the disciples to have and which they could not capture and fix down in the grasp of mere sense, or in the kind of historiography accommodated to this fallen existence. In addition it does mean, surely, that only when we are redeemed in body ourselves, in the fullness of humanity, when

---

[87] Cf. 2 Cor 4.6.

[88] Luke 24.31.

[89] Acts 1.9.

our eyes are truly and finally pure, that only then will we be able to see Christ in all his risen and transcendent glory. Only, that is, when Christ comes again and transforms us in the whole of our human nature, so that we are resurrected in the wholeness of our humanity, in physical as in spiritual life, will we be able to see him and to know as we are known.[90] When we see him we shall become like him,[91] and when we become like him we shall see him with healed vision and recreated natures.

The idea of the spiritualisation and transparency of the risen and ascended humanity of Christ, through its complete impregnation with divine light, developed in Origenist circles in the early church.[92] Apparently 'the spiritual body' of the resurrection was regarded as an orb of radiant light (this was partly in accordance with the Platonic idea that the essential form of the real was the 'mathematical' sphere) and traces of this idea appear centuries later in Dante, and in the picturesque mythologising of the drama of salvation that is found on the stained glass of many mediaeval cathedrals. In all this there is a failure to observe the proper theological reserve at the boundary of the eschatological; we inevitably fall into error as soon as we transgress the limits set by the word.

(a) 'Spiritual body' means more body and not less body

Two points here deserve our reflection. The resurrection of the body to be a 'spiritual body' no more means that the body is resolved away into spirit than the fact that we are made 'spiritual' men and women in Christ means that our humanity is dissolved away in him. To be spiritual men and women is to be not less man but more fully and truly man. To be a spiritual body is not to be less body but more truly and completely body, for by the Spirit physical existence is redeemed from all that corrupts and undermines it, and from all or any privation and diminishment of being. Hence we must take the *empty tomb* in the gospel reports quite seriously – the body of Jesus Christ was raised, certainly a spiritual body, but it was no less body because it was a body healed and quickened by the Spirit in which all corruption had been overcome. It is *the empty tomb that constitutes the essential empirical correlative in statements about the resurrection of Christ*, the point where

---

[90]   1 Cor 13.12 KJV.

[91]   1 John 3.2.

[92]   See the footnotes to this section in T.F. Torrance, *Space, Time and Resurrection*, p. 140.

the triumph of Christ over the space-time of our fallen world is nevertheless correlated with the space-time of our ongoing existence in this world. We cannot observe or pin down in our grasp the process of resurrecting any more than we can observe or pin down in our grasp the process of creating, but as the created reality is observable, so the resurrected reality was apprehensible to the disciples, apprehensible of course in a mode appropriate to its nature, that is, through the Spirit by faith, by sight as well as faith before the ascension and after by faith,[93] which is the mode of the human reason adapted to divine revelation.

(b) The reality of Christ's resurrection body can only be discerned through the Spirit

There is, however, a deep element of truth in the doctrine of the transparency of the new creation in Christ – its utter lack of all opacity and darkness – which is relevant for our understanding of Christ. So long as we ourselves wait for the resurrection of the body we can only see through a glass darkly, as in an enigma; yet so far as through the Spirit the uncreated light of God already shines upon us in Christ, we may discern the reality of God's ways and works in a deeper and more transparent mode. Theologically this belongs to the content of the doctrine of the Holy Spirit who is sent upon us by the risen and ascended Lord, who creates in us the capacity to discern and understand beyond what we are naturally capable of in ourselves, and who enables us to know the reality of God himself in Christ in such a way as to distinguish it from our own subjective states and conditions. If we say of the risen Jesus Christ that he is spiritually and not carnally discerned, this does not mean that he rose only as spirit and not as body, but that it is only through the power of the Spirit that we are able to apprehend Christ in his actuality as resurrected in the body and thus as the first-fruits of the new *creation* and the first-born of every *creature*.[94] As the early fathers used to express it, when a baby is born it is usually born head first, but when the head is born the whole body follows naturally, for it is the birth of the head that is the most difficult part. Now Christ the head of the body is already resurrected, the first-born of the new creation, and as such he is the pledge and guarantee that we who are incorporated with him as his body will rise with him and be born into the new creation in our physical as well as our spiritual existence.

---

[93]   Cf. John 20.24-31.

[94]   1 Cor 15.23; Col 1.15,18; Rev 1.5; cf. Rom 8.23.

The sacraments are the pledges of participation in Christ's risen humanity

Here we must think of the sacraments with their physical elements as pledges of our participation in that whole reality of the risen humanity in Christ, given for us in the time of our pilgrimage through history until Christ comes again. As surely as the saving work of God was carried out in the physical existence of Jesus Christ, as surely as his body was given and his blood was shed for us, and as surely as he rose again from the dead in his human identity and physical existence, so surely will we be saved in our physical and creaturely being. It is of this that the bread and wine consecrated in the eucharist are pledges, for as surely as in holy communion we eat the bread and drink the wine and they become assimilated into our own physical existence, so surely we who partake of the body and blood of Christ given for us, will rise with him out of the grave into newness of life, attaining at last the redemption of the body in the new creation. No wonder early Christians could speak of the eucharist as 'the medicine of immortality'.[95]

5 The ascension and the *parousia* of Jesus Christ

The one parousia *of Christ*

Christ's parousia *means the coming-and-real-presence of God in the flesh*

Parousia, normally translated as coming or advent, means *coming* and *presence*, the *real presence* of him 'who was, who is, and who is to come'.[96] It is not applied in the New Testament or in the early church in a spiritualised sense, as if it meant a presence in Spirit only. Rather does it refer to a *coming-and-a-presence in the most realistic sense*. This is made clear by its application to the coming of the Son of God in the incarnation – it is the special kind of divine presence in which God is

---

[95] Ignatius, *Epistle to the Ephesians*, chap. 20 (ANF vol. 1, p. 57-58); cf. Serapion, *Euchologion (Sacramentary)*, 1c,17.2 (Eng. trans. *Bishop Sarapion's Prayer-Book*, 2nd edition, SPCK, London 1923, 1c [p. 63], *'a medicine of life'*, and 17 [p. 78], *'a medicine of life and salvation'*) ; cf. Clement of Alexandria, *Exhortation to the heathen (Protreptikos)*, 10 (ANF vol. 2, Eerdmans repr., Grand Rapids 1967, p. 201).

[96] See Rev 1.8; cf. 1.17-18, 22.13.

present in his own being (*ousia*), but in which he has come to us not only as creator but as creature within our creaturely being (*ousia*), for he has entered within the created order to which we belong and is present within its space and time as one of us (*par-ousia*).[97] Moreover the physicality of the incarnation, in which the Word was made flesh and in which Jesus Christ rose again in body, indicates that here we have to do with a presence in which God has bound up the existence and life of his creation with himself. This is not a *parousia* in the flesh which is merely a temporary episode, but a permanent and final presence of God in the flesh. Nor is it a *parousia* which consumes the flesh, but in which the physical being of the creature is established and confirmed through being included in a covenanted relation with the creator actualised in incarnation, resurrection and ascension, as the one *parousia* of the ages. 'Behold I am with you all the days until the consummation of time'. 'I am the first and the last, and the living one; I was dead and behold I am alive unto the ages of the ages (*zōn eimi eis tous aiōnas tōn aiōnōn*)'.[98]

The New Testament understanding of the one parousia *of Christ*

It is significant that the New Testament uses the term *parousia* only in the singular – the plural, *parousiai*, is found only with Justin Martyr, Hippolytus and thereafter, when a distinction is clearly drawn between the *first* and *second parousia* or *advent* of Christ.[99] In the New Testament, however, there is *only one parousia*, which is applied equally to the first advent and the second advent. This indicates the continuity between the first and the second advents and the nature of the coming-and-presence which is envisaged when Jesus Christ comes again to make all things new. Although it will be an advent in glory and power, with all the majesty of God unveiled, it will nevertheless be a *parousia* of essentially the same texture as that of the historical Jesus in the incarnation and the risen Jesus of Easter and the ascension. 'This Jesus will come again', it was said on the day of the ascension, 'in the same way as you have seen him going into heaven'.[100]

---

[97] *Para,* beside; *ousia,* being; *par-ousia,* being-beside, ie. presence.

[98] Matt 28.20; Rev 1.18 (Torrance's literal translations).

[99] See for example Justin Martyr, *Apology*, I.52 (ANF vol. 1, p. 180); *Dialogue with Trypho*, 14, 32, 40, 49 etc (ANF vol. 1, p. 202,210,215,219); Hippolytus, *On Christ and Antichrist*, 44 (ANF vol. 5, Eerdmans repr., Grand Rapids 1971, p. 213).

[100] See Acts 1.11.

(a) The ascension creates an eschatological pause 'in the midst of the parousia'

The distinction and holding apart of 'two advents'

Although there is one whole indivisible *parousia* including the first and the last advent, the ascension has taken place 'in the midst of the parousia' (*en tō metaxu tes parousias autou*), an expression taken from Justin Martyr.[101] The ascension thus introduces, as it were, *an eschatological pause* or interval in the heart of the *parousia* which makes it possible for us to speak of a first advent and a second or final advent of Christ. By withdrawing his bodily presence from sight and from historical contact, the ascended Christ holds apart his first advent from his second advent, distinguishing the first as his advent in great humility and abasement, and pointing ahead to his final advent in great glory and power, when the eschatological pause will be brought to an end and we shall see him as we are seen by him.[102] John Calvin preferred to speak, not so much of the two comings of Christ's kingdom as of the two 'conditions' or 'states' of the kingdom of Christ, for example with reference to the teaching of Christ himself in the 'little apocalypse'.[103]

The kingdom is inaugurated but waits to be manifested

The kingdom of Christ was fully inaugurated with his crucifixion in its condition of humiliation, and with his resurrection in triumph over the forces of darkness and evil and his ascension as the lamb of God to the throne of the Father. That was in the most intense sense the fulfilment of Christ's kingdom. In other words, this is the immediacy and the finality of the kingdom which Christ spoke of as taking place in the lifetime of his hearers,[104] but that same inaugurated kingdom will be openly manifested at the end of time when the veil will be taken away. That is what we traditionally refer to as the 'final advent'

---

[101] *Dialogue with Trypho*, 51 (ANF vol. 1, p. 221, translates the phrase as 'in the interval between his advent').

[102] Cf. 1 John 3.2; 1 Cor 13.12.

[103] *A Harmony of the Gospels*, vol. III, trans. A.W. Morrison, Saint Andrew Press, Edinburgh 1972, Matt 24.30, p. 94 (from *Calvin's Commentaries*, ed. D.W. Torrance and T.F. Torrance). Matt 24 is known as the 'little apocalypse' (as are also the equivalent passages in Mark 13 and Luke 21).

[104] Cf. Matt 10.23, 16.28; Luke 9.27, 10.18; and Matt 26.29; Mark 14.25; Luke 22.16-18.

or simply the *'parousia'* of Christ. Since it is not different from the first advent but is essentially continuous with it, that final *parousia* constantly impinges upon the church in the present so that inevitably it feels and must feel that the final advent is about to dawn. It is in fact already there knocking at the door and waits only for the eschatological moment of its open manifestation when the veil of sense and time of our world will be torn aside. This is all the more inevitable because of the communion of the Spirit, for through the Spirit the church in every age and place is united to the risen and ascended and advent Lord so that it cannot escape the pressure of the consummation of all things upon it.

The time created for proclamation of the gospel

Nevertheless within that tension in which it is called to keep vigil and be alert waiting for the manifestation of Christ,[105] the church lives and works in the time that is established by the ascension for the proclamation of the gospel to all nations and ages.[106] God has established a time in the midst of history in which he waits to be gracious, allowing time and history to run on its course in order that the world may be given time to repent and believe.[107] It is in this connection that many of the parables of Jesus are to be understood, those of the marriage feast,[108] or the parable of the pounds and talents in which, after going on a journey or into a far country and leaving his servants in charge, a king or householder came back for a day of reckoning with his servants.[109] Jesus seems to have clearly envisaged a considerable lapse in time between his first and final advent[110] – and so as far as the church's communion with him was concerned in that long interval, gave them the holy supper that they might eat and drink sacramentally in his presence, proclaiming his death, till he should come again.[111] Thus the ascension must be thought of not only as introducing an eschatological pause in the one *parousia* of Christ but as thereby determining the pattern of mission of the church in history

---

[105]   Mark 13.32-37; Luke 21.34-36; Matt 24.42f.

[106]   Mark 13.10; Matt 24.14, cf. 28.19.

[107]   Cf. 2 Peter 3.9.

[108]   Matt 25.1-13; cf. Luke 12.35ff.

[109]   Matt 25.14-30; Luke 19.12-27; cf. Mark 13.34f.; Luke 12.42-48; Matt 24.45-51.

[110]   Mark 13.1ff.,7-8,30f.; Matt 24.1ff.,6-8,34f.; cf. Acts 1.6-8.

[111]   1 Cor 11.23-26.

and the relation of the church in space and time to himself. The ascension, in fact, constitutes a threefold relation to Christ.

(b) The ascension creates a threefold relation to Christ

(i) Historical relation to the historical Jesus Christ

As we have seen, by withdrawing himself from visible and physical contact with us as our contemporary throughout history, Jesus Christ sends us back by his ascension to the Gospels and to their witness to the historical Jesus Christ. That is the appointed place in which nations and ages may meet with God. But with his ascension Jesus Christ also sent upon the church and indeed upon 'all flesh' his Holy Spirit so that through the Spirit he might be present, really present, but in a different way. In order to think out the relation of the church in history to Christ we must put both these together – *mediate horizontal relation* through history to the historical Jesus Christ and *immediate vertical relation* through the Spirit to the risen and ascended Jesus Christ. It is the former that supplies the material content, while it is the latter that supplies the immediacy of actual encounter. A signal instance of this, and of course a unique instance, was the conversion of Saul of Tarsus. His encounter with the risen Lord and his self-witness on the Damascus road threw him into blindness, and he required the testimony of an historical agent or witness to speak to him of Christ before what he had received by divine revelation came home to him and his eyes were opened.[112] The vertical and the horizontal, the immediate and the mediate relations, intersect and mutually require one another for their fulfilment.

(ii) Sacramental relation to the crucified and risen Jesus Christ

(1) The sacraments are part of space and time but signs of the new creation

Communion with Christ through the Spirit gives the church participation here and now in the mystery of Christ, which takes concrete form in the word and sacrament. The New Testament regards the pouring out of the Spirit upon the church as one of the mighty acts of God in 'the last days', signalising that the end-time had precipitated itself upon the world.[113] As we have seen, this means that the church

---

[112] Acts 9.1-19.

[113] Cf. Acts 2.16ff.; Heb 1.2; 1 John 2.18.

that lives and serves Christ within the time-form of this age, also lives in the new age through being made to participate in him the head of the new creation. The church in history exists in that overlap of the two ages, the overlap, constituted by the ascension, which belongs to the whole of the church's world-mission. The sacraments also belong to that overlap, spanning at once the two ages, the old and the new in which the church lives in the time between the first and second advents. On one side, the sacraments belong very much to earth and its ongoing space and time, as is made clear in the visible, tangible and corruptible elements of this world, the water, bread and wine, that are used. But on the other side, they are signs of the new order which has once and for all broken into our world in Jesus Christ and in which we have constant participation through the Spirit, even though since the ascension that new order is veiled from our sight.

(2) The sacraments are the signs given to accompany the scriptures

With the immediate presence of the Son of God in the incarnation, the authoritative signs of that new order were his miraculous acts of healing and forgiveness taken together, signs that pointed ahead to the crucifixion and resurrection, as the mighty acts of cosmic significance that constituted the ground for all acts of forgiveness and healing in the name of Christ. But with the ascension, the unique revelatory signs associated with the incarnation, and therefore with the apostolic community assimilated to Christ to form the unrepeatable foundation of the church as his body, are no longer prominent, for their unique revelatory function is fulfilled in what came to be handed on as the New Testament, and in their place we are given the holy sacraments to accompany the holy scriptures. Certainly the living Lord continues to heal and forgive sins, but now in ongoing history his healing and forgiving work is normally mediated through the holy sacraments which are given to the historical church to accompany the scriptures and proclamation of the gospel and to seal it in the lives of the faithful. This does not mean that it may not please God throughout history to answer the prayer of his people for direct miraculous healing, but it does mean that with the withdrawal of the resurrected body of Christ from visible and physical contact with us in the world, there is no appointed *programme* of anything like 'faith healing' or miraculous activity of a kindred sort.

The patience of Christ and the holding back of his power

The ascension means that Christ holds back the word of his power, the physical transformation of the creation, until the day when he will return to make all things new,[114] and that meantime he sends the church to live and work in the world in the form of a servant. He calls it to follow his own example on earth, when, as we have seen, in the midst of our hunger in the wilderness he did not call in the miraculous power belonging to him as Son of God in order to make bread out of stones. Although he wrought miracles as signs of the kingdom, as part of his revelation in act and word, he did not call in supernature to help himself, but lived and worked within the nature, weakness and limitations of the creature, to the very end. Even on the cross when the temptation came, 'If you are the Son of God, come down from the cross',[115] he resisted it and suffered patiently – and by his weakness and passion overcame all the powers of darkness.

(3) The sacraments are the 'miraculous signs' of our participation in Christ

But in his lifetime Jesus did institute the sacraments. Taking over baptism from the Baptist he transformed it through submitting to it and made himself its real content. He instituted the holy supper by reconstructing the passover with reference to his own body and blood in the new covenant. Then with his resurrection and ascension, and by the power and presence of the Spirit, these sacraments were constituted the 'miraculous signs' of the church's forgiveness and healing, of its crucifixion and resurrection with Christ, to be used perpetually throughout the course of its historical existence. There are, Calvin once said, two kinds of miracles, one in which a miraculous act takes place in a supernatural form, such as a miracle of healing, and one in which a miraculous event takes place under a natural form.[116] Sacraments are of the second kind, and they are the greater kind of miracle. The two sacraments of the gospel enshrine together the two essential 'moments' of our participation in the new creation, while we are still implicated in the space and time of this passing world. Baptism is the sacrament of our once and for all participation in Christ and may be spoken of as the sacrament of justification, which is not to be repeated. The eucharist is the sacrament of our continuous participation in Christ and may be spoken of as the sacrament of sanctification, which is regularly to be repeated, until Christ comes again. They thus express

---

[114] On the relation of Word to power, see T.F. Torrance, *Conflict and Agreement*, vol. 2, pp. 67-8, 72-4, 159-60.

[115] Matt 27.40.

[116] *Comm. on Isaiah* 7.12 (from *Calvin's Commentaries, Isaiah*, vol. 1, trans. Rev. W. Pringle, Eerdmans repr., Grand Rapids 1958, p. 242).

in their togetherness the core of the ontological and eschatological relation which we have with the crucified, risen and ascended Lord.

(iii) Eschatological relation to the ascended and advent Jesus Christ

(1) Eschatology means the act of God within space and time, and not just at the end

By *eschatological* is meant here what is directed toward the end, or toward the consummation in the final *parousia*, what is related to the *eschaton*, the last word and final act of God in Christ.[117] The word and act of God to which we refer in eschatology, however, must be understood as God's word and act not beyond but *within our world of space and time*, even though it means at the end its transformation. This is quite different from the meaning of 'eschatological' in the thought of Rudolf Bultmann,[118] who speaks of the act of God at the end of the world, where the world ends or ceases. Such a concept of eschatology is in line with Bultmann's radical disjunction between this world and the other world of God, and his rejection of any interaction between God and this world which he holds to be a closed continuum of cause and effect. For him, God's 'acts' are related to this world only in a tangential fashion and are not acts within this cosmos. This is similar to Heidegger's idea of the boundary between being and non-being where we must leap the boundary of being in order to open out the source of being – although how that is possible when it is a leap into nothing is a puzzle. At any rate, that is what Bultmann means by the end of the world, or the boundary of being where we have to take the existentialist leap of decision. But when he speaks of this as eschatological event, it would appear to be the antithesis of what the New Testament means, for in the New Testament eschatology is constituted by the act of the eternal *within* the temporal, by the acts of God within our world of space and time.

(2) The biblical view is teleological as well as eschatological, fulfilling time as well as ending it

On this biblical view, the eschatological acts of God run throughout time to their end at the consummation of time; they are teleological as

---

[117] Cf. the discussion of the eschatology of Jesus and the apostolic age, H.R. Mackintosh, *Immortality and the Future*, Hodder & Stoughton, London 1915, pp. 39ff., 60ff.

[118] For a critique of Bultmann's theology see T.F. Torrance, *Incarnation*, pp. 274-90, 310.

well as eschatological,[119] for they are not just abrupt acts abrogating or terminating time, but rather acts that gather up time in the fulfilling of the divine purpose. In this sense then we may speak of *eschatological* as related to the final act of God but which (in the ongoing world) is still in arrears so far as our experience and understanding of it are concerned, or as related to the ultimate reality of divine fulfilment and completion which will be manifested within our world only at the last day. Yet by eschatology we refer not so much to the *eschaton* (the last event), as to the *eschatos* (the last one), that is, to Christ himself who is the last (*eschatos*) as well as the first (*prōtos*),[120] and who is the last because he is the first, for he who has already come and accomplished his work of salvation in our midst will bring it to its final manifestation and consummation at his coming again.

(3) The parousia *will be the unveiling of the perfected reality of Christ*

Since the ascension, his eschatological operations are veiled from our sight, by the fact that we live within the time-form of this world and communicate with the new creation only through the Spirit in word and sacrament. The final *parousia* of Christ will be more the apocalypse or unveiling of the perfected reality of what Christ has done than the consummating of what till then is an incomplete reality. It will be the unveiling of the finished work of Christ. He will come again in the fullness of his humanity and deity to judge and renew his creation, but that will not be another work in addition to his finished work on the cross or in the resurrection, so much as the gathering together of what the cross and resurrection have already worked throughout the whole of creation and the unveiling of it for all to see, and therefore an unfolding and actualisation of it from our point of view.

(4) The twofold relation in eschatology, between old and new, and present and future

The difficulty about the eschatological relation as set forth in the New Testament is that it involves a twofold relation: (a) *a relation here and now between the old and the new,* as through the Spirit we partake already

---

[119] Eschatological (or eschatology) from the Gk *eschata* (the last things) and teleological (or teleology) from the Gk *telos* (end) both refer to events at the end of time and history, but in *eschatology* the emphasis is on the invasion of God into history throwing it into crisis and creating the last events, while in *teleology* the emphasis is on history reaching forward (in the purpose of God and under his control) to its goal at the end of time.

[120] Rev 1.17, 2.8, 22.13.

of the new creation in the risen Christ; and (b) *a relation between the present (including the past) and the future*, as through the Spirit we are united to the ascended Christ who is still to come again. Because of the ascension, as we have seen, there has been introduced into the midst of the one whole *parousia* of Christ an eschatological pause, so that in all our relations with Christ there is an eschatological reserve or eschatological time-lag. That applies to both relations but in different ways. In the here and now relation to Christ, what stands between us is the *veil of sense*, so that although we communicate with him immediately through the Spirit, he is mediated to us in our sense experience only through the sacramental elements. In the relation between the present and the future, what stands in between us is the *veil of time*, so that although we communicate with him immediately through the Spirit, he is mediated to us only through temporal and spatial acts of sacramental communion with us in the church until he comes. Since through the Spirit we are united to the risen, ascended and advent Christ, he is immediately present to us, and every time we have communion with him we have contact with him in his *parousia*, for the advent Christ impinges upon every moment of our Christian life and work in history. That is why the *parousia* is always and inevitably imminent, and why expectation of it in the New Testament times could never give way to disillusionment but could only be constantly renewed.[121]

The concept of a 'delayed advent'

It is failure to grasp this, and the twofold eschatological relation to Christ which it entails, that has led people to misunderstand the teaching of the New Testament and to invent the idea of a 'delayed advent' which allegedly forced the early church to alter its whole eschatological outlook and to adjust its life and mission accordingly. Apart from the fact that there is little if any evidence in the writings of the early Christians anywhere for any such thorough-going transmutation of their eschatological ideas or expectations, it can hardly be 'got out of' the New Testament without a rather strained and artificial exegesis.[122] This is not to deny that there is a relatively different

---

[121] Cf. Karl Barth, *Church Dogmatics*, 3/2, Eng. trans. T & T Clark, Edinburgh 1960, p. 490f.

[122] See T.F. Torrance, *Space, Time and Resurrection*, p. 153f., for some elaboration of the argument here and for some useful footnotes on this and the next section.

emphasis, and to that extent a change, within the new Testament, for example, between Paul's first letter to the Thessalonians and his letter to the Philippians, but that still falls with the 'all is present, and yet all is future'[123] orientation of the basic outlook of the New Testament. The eschatology of the New Testament is neither simply a 'realised eschatology' nor simply a 'futurist eschatology' but one in which both realised and futurist elements are woven together all the time *in Christ*.

We may now seek to understand this eschatological relation to Christ in its cosmic, corporate and individual aspects.

(c) *The range and reach of eschatology*

(i) *The cosmic range of eschatology*

The whole of creation is gathered up and renewed in Christ

The eschatological relation has the same cosmic range as the incarnation and the atonement. He who was made flesh is the creator *Logos* by whom all things were made and in whom all things are upheld. When he became incarnate, and divine and human natures were united in his one person, his humanity was brought into an ontological relation with all creation. So far as our humanity is concerned this means that all human beings are upheld, whether they know it or not, in their humanity by Jesus Christ the true and proper man, upheld by the fulfilment and establishment of true humanity in his incarnate life, but also through his work in the cross and resurrection in which he overcame the degenerating forces of evil and raised up our human nature out of death and perdition. But the range of Christ's mighty acts in incarnation, reconciliation and resurrection apply to the whole universe of things, visible and invisible. The whole of creation falls within the range of his mighty acts and Lordship as he works out his purpose by bringing redemption together with creation, and actualising the holy will of the Father in everything. Eschatology has here a teleological relation to the whole realm of created existence and leads into the doctrine of 'the new heaven and the new earth'.[124] God does not abandon his creation when he has saved man, for all creation, together with humanity, will be renewed when Christ comes again. Since he is the first-born of the new creation, the head in whom all things, visible and invisible, are reconciled and gathered up, the

---

[123] See H.R. Mackintosh, *Immortality and the Future*, p. 64.

[124] Rev 21.1; 2 Peter 3.13; cf. Isaiah 65.17, 66.22.

resurrection of Christ in *body* becomes the pledge that the whole physical universe will be renewed, for in a fundamental sense it has already been resurrected in Christ. It is understandable, therefore, that for classical Greek theology it was the resurrection, supervening upon the incarnation, that revealed the final cosmic range of God's redeeming purpose.[125]

(ii) The corporate aspect of eschatology

The distance of the ascension and the nearness of the advent

Here we are concerned with the relation between Christ and the church which is his body. The church is not only the body of the crucified and risen Christ, but the body of the ascended and advent Christ, and therefore through its union with him the church is necessarily thrust urgently forward through history to meet its coming Lord. Here we have to take into account what we have already discussed about the church as the body of the risen Christ whose relation to him is determined by the immediate *koinōnia* of the Spirit, but now we must think of the relation of the church to Christ as governed also by the *distance* of the ascension and the *nearness* of the advent. This is the 'eschatological reserve' in the union between Christ and his church, in which the church is sent to carry out its work in the world, in a sense 'on its own', and for which it must give an account to Christ when he comes again. The church is thus given a measure of freedom for its life and operations in the world, for it lives and fulfils its mission within all the ambiguities of history, society, politics and world events.

The church must continually put off the old and put on the new

Although it is already one body with Christ through the Spirit, it is yet to become one body with him, but meantime in the world and history the church is a mixed body, with good and evil, true and false, wheat and tares in its midst.[126] It is still characterised by sin and evil and partakes of the decay and corruption of the world of which it is a part, so that it is not yet what it shall be, and not yet wholly in itself what it is already in Christ. In this eschatological reserve and deep teleological ambiguity the church lives and works under judgement as well as grace, so that it must constantly put off 'the image of the old man' that passes

---

[125] See for example, Athanasius, *De Incarnatione* (*On the Incarnation of the Word*), 29ff.

[126] Matt 13.24-30.

away and put on 'the image of the new man' who is renewed in the likeness of Christ.[127] The New Testament expresses this relation of union and distance between the church and Christ in terms of the twofold figure of the *bride* of Christ and the *body* of Christ – the church waits for the consummation of the mystery of its union with the saviour who when he comes again will present the church to himself, no longer spotted and wrinkled like an ageing lady but 'without spot or wrinkle as a chaste virgin'. This means that the church is constantly summoned to look beyond its historical forms to the fullness and perfection that will be disclosed at the *parousia* and must never identify the structures it acquires and must acquire in the *nomistic* forms of this-worldly historical existence with the essential forms of its new being in Christ himself.

(iii) The individual aspect of eschatology

Servants whose true being is hid with Christ in God

Here we are concerned with the personal union of the believer with Christ. What the New Testament has to say about being *in Christ* and about *Christ in us* may well be primarily corporate, but individuals are certainly given their full and integral place within that corporate union of Christ with his church. Believers find their reality and truth not in themselves but in Jesus Christ risen and ascended and therefore coming again. It does not yet appear what they shall be, but when Christ comes and sees them they will be changed and transformed into his likeness.[128] This implies the resurrection of the body, but in the nature of the case it is an actualisation in the body of the saving acts of Christ only when that takes place within the whole of creation and in the whole body of the redeemed. Hence the individual also lives in the eschatological reserve created by the ascension in the midst of the one whole *parousia* of Christ. They must therefore learn to live and work 'on their own', as it were, for they are sent to occupy themselves with the talents the Lord has given them,[129] and will have to render an account of what they have done with them when Christ comes again to judge the living and the dead.[130]

---

[127] See Col 3.9-10; Eph 4.22-24 – 'put off the *old* man', 'put on the *new* man' KJV (Gk, *palaios/kainos anthrōpos*).

[128] See 1 John 3.2.

[129] Matt 25.14-30; Luke 19.12-27.

[130] Matt 25.31-46; Acts 10.42; 2 Tim 4.1; 1 Peter 4.5.

Like the church individual Christians will not be able to escape the deep ambiguities of this-worldly existence whether in its cultural, social, political or other aspects, and they too will inevitably be a mixture of good and evil, with compromised lives, so that they can only live eschatologically in the judgement and mercy of God, 'putting off the old man' and 'putting on Christ' anew each day, always aware that even when they have done all that it is their duty to do they remain unprofitable servants,[131] summoned to look away from themselves to Christ, remembering that they are dead through the cross of Christ but alive and risen in him. Their true being is hid with Christ in God.[132] The whole focus of their vision and the whole perspective of their life in Christ's name will be directed to the final unveiling of that reality of their new being at the *parousia*, but meantime they live day by day out of the word and sacraments.

Nourished by word and sacrament, until Christ comes again

As people baptised into Christ they are told by God's word that their sins are already forgiven and forgotten by God, that they have been justified once and for all, and that they do not belong to themselves but to Christ who loved them and gave himself for them. As people summoned to the holy table they are commanded by the word of God to live only in such a way that they feed upon Christ, and not in such a way that they feed upon their own activities or live out of their own capital of alleged spirituality. They live from week to week by drawing their life and strength from the bread and wine of the Lord's supper, nourished by the body and blood of Christ, and in the strength of that communion must live and work until Christ comes again. As often as they partake of the eucharist, they partake of the self-consecration of Jesus Christ who sanctified himself for our sakes that we might be sanctified in reality and be presented to the Father as those whom he has redeemed and perfected or consecrated together with himself in one. Here they are called to lift up their hearts to the ascended Jesus, and to look forward to that day when this same Lord Jesus will come again, and when the full reality of their new being in Christ will be unveiled, making scripture and sacrament no longer necessary.

---

[131] Luke 17.10.
[132] Col 3.3.

Chapter Ten

THE BIBLICAL WITNESS TO JESUS CHRIST:

THE COMING OF THE SPIRIT AND THE CREATION OF APOSTOLIC TESTIMONY AND GOSPEL

We now consider the creation of the apostolic and biblical witness to Jesus Christ, and the relation between the coming of the Spirit, knowledge of Christ and the scriptures. In the interim between the first and second coming, the church knows Christ through scripture and sacrament, and is directed forward in eschatological expectation to his coming again. While it is the resurrection and ascension that create the final eschatological perspective of the New Testament, it is the ascension and the sending of the Spirit that creates the apostolic witness to Christ and sends us back to it for knowledge of him through the Spirit. Therefore from the eschatological perspective of the resurrection and ascension, we now consider in more detail the creation of the biblical witness to Jesus Christ, and the relation between the written word and the living Word in the Spirit.[1]

---

[1]   Editor's note – paragraph added to facilitate the connection between the chapters. As mentioned in the editorial introduction to the Christology volume *Incarnation*, this chapter, 'The Biblical Witness to Jesus Christ', was originally the second chapter of *Incarnation*. In that position, it effectively made the introduction rather long and also had some overlap with it in content. At the same time, the Soteriology volume *Atonement* ended with a brief section on the resurrection (an introduction of only five pages) and a thirty page 'addendum' entitled 'Eschatology'. The insertion into the Soteriology volume of Torrance's seventy page student 'handout' on 'Resurrection and Ascension' provided a much fuller account of his thinking on those topics. The insertion here of the 'The Biblical Witness to Jesus Christ' chapter provides an outline of his thinking on the coming of the Spirit, the creation of the apostolic witness and tradition, and the doctrine of scripture.

1 The Apostolate

Here we are concerned with the fact that the self-witness of Jesus Christ is translated into witness to him by human apostles in history. How is that transition from Christ's witness to himself, to human witness to Christ made?[2]

Christ makes the apostolic witness to him his own self-witness

The biblical witnesses testify to Christ in such a way that the power and authority of their witness lie not in their activity of witnessing, but in him to whom they bear witness. Their witness to Christ is such that he takes control of their witness and uses it for himself. The interpretation and doctrine these witnesses bear is not interpretation which they on their part put on Christ, but interpretation he puts on himself, and to which they bear answering witness. Christ clothed with his own meaning, with his own teaching, imposes himself upon the New Testament writers and translates his own self-witness into their personal witness to him. These human witnesses are eye-witnesses of his majesty[3] and immediate hearers of his teaching, and all they have to say is born out of that magisterial self-manifestation of Christ. The apostles apprehended Christ in being apprehended by him.[4] *He* laid hold upon them and declared his name and revealed his glory to them.[5] He gave himself to them in a context of immediate revelation in which he was his own mediator, his own interpreter through his gift of the Holy Spirit to them.[6]

In a real sense our encounter with the living Christ in the witness of the New Testament is like the encounter between the apostles and Christ. The same pattern is discernible in both, but theirs was a unique and foundational encounter, and the revelation with which Christ

---

2   For the nature of revelation in the incarnate life of Christ, his creation through the Spirit of the apostolic and biblical witness to him, the relation between the written word and Christ the living Word, and the function of dogmatic theology see further T.F. Torrance, *Theology in Reconstruction*, SCM Press, London 1965, chap. 8, 'The Place of Christology in Biblical and Dogmatic Theology'.

3   2 Peter 1.16; cf. 1 John 1.1f.

4   John 15.16.

5   Cf. John 17.

6   John 14.26, 15.26, 16.7-15.

clothed himself as he gave himself to be known and understood by the apostles was a final and unrepeatable revelation. The emphasis here is not so much on the persons of the apostles as on their being the eye-witnesses of the resurrection,[7] that is, of the glorified Christ himself, Christ in the unveiled light of his divine manifestation or glory, *doxa*. To understand this let us note several things.

(a) *The Hebrew concept of* 'shaliach' *or authorised representative*

The Hebrew word for apostle is *shaliach* which means a representative or ambassador sent by someone to represent them in some action or communication.[8] 'A man's *shaliach* is as himself',[9] or in other words, when a man sends a *shaliach* to represent him, the *shaliach* is regarded as if he is the man himself, and his word and actions as though they are those of the man himself present in person. The rabbis used to speak of several of the Old Testament prophets as *sheluchim* or *shelichim*, 'apostles', Moses, Elijah and Elisha. They restricted the term to the prophets who not only spoke the word of God, but were obviously authorised by certain miraculous deeds as bearers of the word of God. *Shaliach* referred to the person who speaks for God and acts for God in miraculous signs or *semeia*.[10] There was one other sense in which they used *shaliach*, and that is of the high priest on the great day of atonement, in which he was regarded not as the *shaliach* of Israel but as the *shaliach* of God to Israel, for it was on the day of atonement that the high priest as God's messenger or angel brought to Israel effective pardon and renewal of the covenant in atonement. Here too we have also the combination of word and deed that belonged to the concept of the *shaliach*.

Jesus Christ is the unique 'shaliach' *of God in word and deed*
Now it is supremely in that sense that Christ is *shaliach*: he is the word of God and the deed of God, who not only brings from God his word of pardon, but effectively enacts it. In Jesus Christ the word and deed of God are identical, identical in his person. He *is* the word of God

---

[7] Acts 1.8, 2.32, 3.15, 5.30-32, 10.39-41, 13.30-31.

[8] See the article by Rengstorf on *apostolos/shaliach* in Kittel, *Theological Dictionary of the New Testament*, vol. 1, Eerdmans, Grand Rapids 1964, p. 413-20.

[9] *Op. cit.* p. 415.

[10] Gk, 'signs', the word used, especially in John, of the miracles of Jesus regarded as signs particularly of divine authority.

which he represents, so that his word is not just word about God, but actually *is* God's word, God in his word. His actions not only point to God, but he *is* himself God in action, so that his acts are God's own acts. Christ was sent from the Father not only to forgive sin, but to heal, not only to speak of God's pardon but to enact that pardon in our flesh and blood. It is supremely at the cross that God's word and God's deed in Christ are identical. That is why, as St Paul puts it, Christ is the *logos* of the cross, is the *dynamis* of the cross, i.e. he is the word of the cross, is the power of the cross. In the supreme absolute sense, then, Jesus Christ is the apostle-prophet, the apostle-priest, the Word of God in mighty action, the Word made flesh. In him we have the *self*-manifestation of God and the *self*-giving of God, *objectified and acutely personalised in Jesus Christ*. The whole Word or *Logos* of God is incorporated in him, the *Logos* through whom all things are made, the *Logos* who is himself God's creative action. Jesus Christ is God himself personally in action among mankind in revelation and in reconciliation.

(b) The apostles are the 'sheluchim' or personal representatives of Christ

In the Gospels Jesus sends out the disciples on an apostolic mission (*apostellein, shalach*, send).[11] At this stage in the gospel story they are only once actually called 'apostles',[12] but the verb *apostellein* is used to describe the mission on which they are sent. It is made clear later that this mission is grounded on the mission of the Son from the Father. Christ is the apostle from the Father, but he sends out apostles, first the inner group of twelve disciples,[13] and then a larger group of seventy,[14] to proclaim the word and to heal. On their apostolic mission their word is to be accompanied by *sēmeia*, miraculous signs, apparently after the pattern of the *sheluchim*. Although in reporting the activity of the apostles at that stage the Evangelists hesitate to use the noun 'apostles', later on the word 'apostle' is used in the full sense,

---

[11]   The Greek *apostellein* is the regular translation in the Septuagint for the Hebrew *shalach*, send.

[12]   Mark 6.30; Luke 9.10. Later on in Luke, there are three other instances, 17.5, 22.14, 24.10, and the only other reference is in connection with the calling of the twelve disciples, Matt 10.1-2; Luke 6.13.

[13]   Mark 6.7-13,30; Luke 9.1-6,10; cf. Matt 10.1-5ff.

[14]   Luke 10.1-20.

to describe the authorised ambassadors of the risen Christ, who are sent by him not only to preach the gospel but as those whose word is to be accompanied with following signs, the divinely-given evidences that their word is the mighty word of God in Christ. Hence St Paul defends his position as an apostle by insisting that he too as sent by Christ has the apostolic *sēmeia*.[15]

Christ's recommissioning of the apostles to be his representatives

The disciples, then, are thought of as sent out on a mission with the Hebrew idea of the *sheluchim* in the background, in the sense that as they preached and exercised their function as eye-witnesses of Christ and bearers of his word, the *sēmeia* bore evidence to the fact that it was Christ himself who spoke in and through their *kērygma* or proclamation and acted upon its hearers, upon those who had ears to hear. In all this activity, the persons of the apostles retreated into the background, while in the foreground there was the living, acting word of God, the person of Jesus Christ. The early apostolic mission recorded in the Synoptics was reinforced by the risen Christ, for in his recommissioning of the apostles he breathed on them his Spirit and sent them to do greater works.[16] In their proclamation the word of human beings was to be the very power of God creative of the church. They were sent out not only to preach the word of Christ but to preach a word which would accomplish what it spoke, a word that would not return void.[17] Thus in their proclamation of forgiveness, forgiveness of sins would actually be enacted. 'If you forgive the sins of any, they are forgiven'.[18] That is to say, Jesus Christ gave himself to the apostles through his Spirit, brought them into his own work and sent them out as witnesses to him and fellow-workers with authority to bear his own word, to reflect his own witness in the world, but also to enter into his pain in that witness. It was as that took place that Christ created his church in them and made them his body, his image, his reflection in the world.

How then are we to understand the relation between Christ and the apostolic witnesses, between the word-deed of Christ in his person and work on the cross, and the word-deed of the apostles sent out in the name of Christ to preach and forgive sins? The answer to that question is clearly given in John 20, in the fact that

---

[15] 2 Cor 12.12.

[16] John 20.22, 14.12.

[17] Isaiah 55.10-11.

[18] John 20.23.

in recommissioning the disciples Jesus 'breathed on them and said to them, 'Receive the Holy Spirit. If you forgive the sins of any, they *are* forgiven'.[19]

2 The gift of the Holy Spirit[20]

(a) The Spirit makes the transition from Christ's self-witness to apostolic witness[21]

It is the Holy Spirit who witnesses to Christ, who makes the transition from the self-witness of Christ into the apostolic witness to him and translates the self-witness of Christ into a form in which it enters through the apostles into the stream of history – that is, into the historical Church.

When Jesus breathed the Holy Spirit upon the disciples they knew what that meant, for as John tells us, Jesus had taken pains during the discourses of the last supper when he founded the new covenant, to tell them about his sending of the Spirit, about who the Spirit was and what the sending would mean.

The coming of the Spirit as Christ's 'shaliach' is the coming of Christ

The Holy Spirit is the one sent by Christ, the Apostle-Spirit who represents Christ, who speaks of him but who is in a unique relation of oneness with Christ and with the Father. He is sent by the Father and the Son, by the Father in the name of the Son and in order to

---

[19]   John 20.22-23 (author's italics).

[20]   For further discussion (in the context of Reformed Catechisms) of the relation between Christ and his work and the work of the Spirit, and for an outline of central features in the doctrine of the Spirit and the communion of the Spirit, the doctrine of the church ('Christ and his people are properly One Man – that is the very heart of the doctrine of the church', p. cix-cx), and the church in union with Christ through the communion of the Spirit as reaching out to all humanity and to the new heaven and new earth, see T.F. Torrance, *The School of Faith*, James Clarke, London 1959, pp. xcv-cxxvi. See also T.F. Torrance, 'The Mission of the Church', *Scottish Journal of Theology*, vol. 19.2 (1966), pp. 129-43, and cf. *Theology in Reconstruction*, chap. 14, 'Come, Creator Spirit, for the Renewal of Worship and Witness', pp. 240-258.

[21]   Cf. 'The Mission of the Church', pp. 130ff., the section 'The Sending of the Spirit and the Mission of the Apostles'.

reveal the Son.[22] The Son declares in his prayer immediately after the supper[23] that he has manifested his name[24] to the disciples, and it is in that name[25] that the Spirit is sent to the disciples, not only to reveal Christ to them but so to gather them into abiding union with Christ that he will be their constant companion and friend and support. Thus the Spirit is also called by Jesus the paraclete (*paraklētos*),[26] the advocate, whom Christ sends to support and assist the apostles, who will act on their side and on their behalf, so maintaining them in relation with Christ that they will not be left like abandoned orphans (*orphanous*)[27] without protection and care in their faith and discipleship. Through this Apostle-Advocate-Spirit the relation of communion and knowledge and mission between Christ and the Father is projected between the disciples and Christ himself. '*As the Father hath sent me,*

---

[22] Cf. John 14.16,26, 15.26, 16.7-15.

[23] See John 17, 'the great high-priestly prayer' of Jesus.

[24] There appears to be a difference between Torrance's text here in which Christ speaks of manifesting his name to the disciples and of the Spirit being sent in his name ('The Son declares...that has manifested *his* name to the disciples, and it is in *that* name that the Spirit is sent') and John's Gospel where the name that Christ speaks of manifesting is the Father's (17.6) while it is in Christ's name that the Spirit is sent (14.26). In his *The Christian Doctrine of God* (T & T Clark, Edinburgh 1996), Torrance speaks of 'the oneness between the "I am" of Yahweh and the "I am" of Jesus' (p. 121, 164), of Jesus as 'the incarnate "I am" of God' (p. 160) and of 'the self naming of God as "I am" (being) taken up in the "I am" of the Lord Jesus Christ' (p. 104). The oneness of the Father and the Son, and their mutual indwelling, mean that the one 'I am' of God applies to both Father and Son, and this means that in manifesting the 'I am' of the Father, Jesus is also manifesting the 'I am' of the Son. Manifesting the name of the Father as *his* Father inevitably means manifesting his own name as the Son of the Father. The oneness of the Father and the Son means not only that manifesting the name of the Father means manifesting the name of the Son, but that the Spirit is sent by the Father and the Son (cf. John 14.26,16 & 15.26, 16.7). See further, *The Christian Doctrine of God*, esp. chaps. 5 and 6 – Ed.

[25] John 14.26.

[26] Literally, *paraklētos* means *someone called to one's aid* in a judicial cause, and hence an *advocate, pleader, intercessor,* translated 'counsellor' RSV and 'comforter' KJV, John 14.16,26, 15.26, 16.7; cf. 1 John 2.1.

[27] John 14.18, 'I will not leave you desolate (*orphanous*); I will come to you.'

even *so* send I you. And when he had said this, he breathed on them the Holy Spirit.'[28] And so John records the words of Jesus, 'But the *paraclete* whom the Father will send in my name, he shall teach you all things, and bring to your remembrance all that I have said to you.'[29] 'Do not be afraid . . . I will come to you.'[30] In the strict sense it is the Holy Spirit who is Christ's *shaliach* or apostolic plenipotentiary (envoy invested with full authority), and even the Holy Spirit is *shaliach* in such a way that he does not draw attention to himself or speak of his own person, but speaks only of Christ,[31] so that through the Spirit it is Christ himself in person who returns to speak his own word with quickening power.

(b) Through the Spirit the apostolic witness becomes the foundation of the church

The inner meaning then of the apostolic witness is that through the gift of the Spirit the apostolate is given to echo and reflect Christ's self-witness in the world, and thus through the Spirit-relation with Christ the apostolate is given to be the foundation of the church, the body of Christ in history through which Christ makes his own image to appear, his own voice to echo, his own witness to be effectively operative among mankind. Only the Holy Spirit has that unique *shaliach* relation to Christ in that he only is the *personal* representative of Christ and is inseparable from him, though also distinct in person. But it is the sending of this *shaliach-Spirit* upon the disciples that makes them apostles, so that in all their witness to Christ and representation of him, their word and deed in his name will be made real and effective through the power and presence of the Spirit, and be honoured by Christ himself as his own word and deed.

Through the Spirit Christ is present himself in the apostolic 'kērygma' – the relation between word and Spirit

We may define the relation of the apostles to Christ as twofold: (a) it is a relation through the Apostle-Spirit sent upon them in the name of Christ, and (b) it is a relation characterised by their abiding in Christ's word and keeping His commandments. And so St John tells us that between the announcement of the coming of the *shaliach*-Spirit and the designation and empowerment of the apostles as witnesses of him,

---

[28]   See John 20.21-22.

[29]   See John 14.26.

[30]   See John 14.27-28.

[31]   John 16.13-15, cf. 15.26, 14.26.

Christ discourses on the relation of abiding in his word and love and keeping his commandments.[32] It is that relation between word and Spirit which lies at the heart of the apostolic *kērygma* as authoritative proclamation of the word and acts of Christ. Through the power and presence of the Spirit, it is Christ himself who in the apostolic *kērygma* personally and actually proclaims himself, makes his word effective for salvation and bestows himself in all his grace and love upon humanity. The supremely distinctive thing about the apostolic *kērygma*, therefore, is that it not only enshrines Christ's own *kērygma* of himself, not only contains witness to Christ based on the great events of his life and work, but has for its content nothing less than *Jesus Christ* the living Lord.

It is this fact that makes the apostolic *kērygma* and *didachē* entirely different from any other proclamation or teaching, Jewish or Hellenic, that its content is the person of the living Christ, who in that *kērygma* and teaching is dynamically present as the Lord of it, controlling it, using it directly as his very own. It is because *the content of the apostolic kērygma is the living Christ himself*, that their *kērygma* is identical with Jesus Christ's own *kērygma*, in which he proclaimed himself and through which he confronted men and women with his own person, so that the apostolic *kērygma* is an extension of Christ's own *kērygma*. It is not only the resurrection of Christ but the bestowal of Christ's Spirit upon the apostles that makes that a reality.

Through the Spirit of truth, the disciples are fully instructed and empowered in Christ

The doctrine of the Spirit tells us, then, that Christ comes to act as his own interpreter. He sends his own Spirit who is his 'other self', as it were, his apostle, his advocate who personally represents him and so acts toward the disciples that they are fully instructed and empowered in Christ as Christ himself would have them instructed and empowered and their witness to him filled and filled out with his own self-witness. This Spirit is the Spirit of truth who comes to reveal Christ to them, to set in order before them all that Christ had himself communicated to them, so that through the Spirit they might know Christ fully and appropriate him in truth, in a way they could not before. Hitherto in his ministry Christ had revealed himself to the disciples 'as they were able to hear',[33] and in such a way that revelation by word kept pace step by step with revelation by his life and acts in a successive and progressive communication.

---

[32]　John 15.7-10.

[33]　Mark 4.33.

(c) The Spirit could only come to reveal Christ after the resurrection and ascension[34]

However, until the final great acts took place, Christ could not, in the nature of the case, reveal himself fully to them, for his unique revelation was not by word in abstraction from his life and work, but was revelation all through by the word made flesh, and until the final great acts of crucifixion, resurrection and ascension took place, the disciples were unable either to truly read the Old Testament scriptures or take in in their proper light what Christ had himself taught them about the Old Testament scriptures and about himself. And so even up to the crucifixion Jesus said to the disciples, 'I have yet many things to say to you, but you cannot bear them now. When the Spirit of truth comes, he will guide you into all the truth; for he will not speak on his own authority, but whatever he hears he will speak, and he will declare to you the things that are to come. He will glorify me, for he will take what is mine and declare it to you.'[35]

(i) The bringing of the apostles to understanding

It was therefore only after resurrection, ascension and Pentecost that the disciples were finally brought to understanding. It was only after his resurrection when Christ breathed his Spirit upon them, opening their eyes in the light of his crucifixion and resurrection, enabling them now through the Spirit to apprehend the astounding events that had taken place, and it was only after Pentecost when the Spirit was sent upon them in fullness after Christ had opened the kingdom of heaven for them by his ascension, that the apostles were able at last fully to take in, assimilate and understand all that Christ had taught them by word and by deed. Consider, for example, the transformation that took place in Peter,[36] or to put it the other way round again, what happened when Jesus Christ returned to the disciples clothed in his Spirit, the Spirit of truth. Jesus gave himself to be known and appropriated by them in his own Spirit, in his own truth, in his own light and glory, and so gave himself to be, as the living Jesus, himself the living dynamic content of this *kērygma*.

---

[34]   Cf. H.J. Wotherspoon, *What Happened at Pentecost*, T & T Clark, Edinburgh 1937, a book Torrance used to refer to with appreciation.

[35]   John 16.12-14.

[36]   Cf. Luke 22.54-62 (Matt 26.69f.; Mark 14.66f.; John 18.15f.); Acts 2.14ff., 3.12ff., 4.8ff., etc.

It is from that perspective that all the Gospels were written. It was to the understanding and teaching of this *word* that the apostles gave themselves daily immediately after Pentecost, so fulfilling their function as the earthen vessels specially chosen and trained by Christ and then specially endowed by his Spirit to understand and assimilate his teaching and his actions that they might bear it forth as *word* and *kērygma* creative of the church. It was thus, as we read in the Acts of the Apostles, that the word increased and multiplied, so that through their apostolic word, Jesus Christ himself fulfilled what he had begun to teach and do when he was on earth.[37] That was what Paul himself called the fulfilment of the word of the mystery of Christ in the midst of the church.[38]

(1) The coming of the Spirit is essential to revelation, enabling the disciples to receive him

Let us put it this way. In his birth, life and ministry, death and resurrection, Jesus Christ was the objective revelation of God. In him the Word became flesh through the Spirit: the Word objectified himself in human form, and that objective revelation in the incarnation was final and complete in Christ. The Spirit of truth had not one iota to add to that revelation. Thus in the incarnation the whole objective reconciliation was wrought out and the whole objective revelation was given. All that was wrought out through the Spirit from the birth of Jesus to his resurrection, but in its full dimension of depth it is actualised as revelation and reconciliation within the church only when and as the Holy Spirit supervened upon the objective work of Christ in the incarnation, making it to shine in its own reality and truth, and enabling the apostles to receive it and so to become the realisation of Christ's own self-witness in the world. That is why Jesus said he would come back to the disciples when the Spirit of truth came and abide with the disciples, have communion with them and make them one with himself.[39] The Spirit of truth who is sent in the name of Christ is absolutely essential to the fact of Christ as the revelation of God, for it is through his will that the objective revelation in the historical church is subjectively established in the apostles and given subjective character in them as revelation received and understood and thus as communicable and transmissible.

---

[37]   Acts 12.24, 6.7, 2.41f., cf. 4.29f., 8.4f., etc.

[38]   Cf. Eph 3.9-10; Col 1.25-27.

[39]   John 14.16ff.

(2) Revelation could only be partial until the coming of the Interpreter

Now we see why, or partly why, Jesus hesitated to reveal himself directly to the disciples at first, and only did it gradually and with increasing readiness as he neared the cross, the hour of his glorification, for *unless we have along with Christ his own interpreter, the Spirit of truth, we cannot apprehend Christ,* or really receive him so that his objective revelation becomes a subjective reality in our midst. The whole fact of Christ is not only the fact of the objective revelation, but the glorified Christ of the Spirit's illumination. Thus the whole Christ who becomes the object of the church's faith is the Christ of history who died and rose again, but that very same Christ glorified with the glory which the Son of God had before the world began, interpreted and revealed by the Holy Spirit. The Christ who is the whole fact of faith is not simply the Christ known according to the flesh, *kata sarka,* but the Christ known in the Spirit, *kata pneuma,* the Christ who is not only the object of faith but also the subject and agent even in faith's knowledge of him. He is the objectively known historical Jesus Christ of flesh and blood now dwelling in the midst of the church and clothed with his own Spirit.

(ii) The Christ who is known through the Spirit is the same historical Jesus himself acting and speaking to his people

That Christ who was known on earth had to depart in his mode of being before Pentecost, the mode of physical presence, in order that he might be present in the mode of universal presence, the mode of being in and through which he could be known and interpreted. The Christ who dwells in the church, the mind of Christ, known only through the mind of the Spirit, is no mere transcendental Christ, not a Christ-idea, not a timeless Christ-event, but none other than the historical Jesus Christ who comes in this other mode of being through the Spirit, the Spirit who is as himself, and through whom it is Christ himself who acts and speaks. In the incarnation of the Son of God the Word became flesh, but now through the Spirit that same Word, resurrected in the flesh of Jesus, addresses us personally and livingly as Word of God, and it is through the Word and Spirit that Christ holds communion with his church and communicates himself to the world.

(iii) The twofold act of revelation is now completed by Christ in the apostolic mind

We are not to think, therefore, of the revelation of Christ as ending with the cross or with the resurrection and ascension – in one sense it did, materially and objectively, that is, so far as its material or factual content was concerned – but in a profound sense it was only with the ascension and Pentecost that revelation achieved its own end, as revelation to those to whom it was communicated, when it was Jesus Christ himself, not simply his words or teaching about him, but Christ 'clothed with his gospel',[40] as Calvin expressed it, that became its full content. Thus St Luke speaks of his gospel as giving us what Jesus *began* to do and teach,[41] and the author of Hebrews speaks of the word of salvation which 'at the first *began* to be spoken by the Lord, and was confirmed to us by those who heard him'.[42] After Pentecost, as the Spirit supervened upon the church and lit up for the apostles the objective revelation of the historical Christ, Jesus Christ disclosed himself in greater fullness to the apostles, and it is that Christ in the fullness of his self-disclosure, the Christ 'after the Spirit',[43] who is the object of the church's faith. He ascended to fill all things and to fulfil his own revelation and reconciliation in the church as his body.

Through the Spirit, therefore, the revelation of Christ becomes revelation within the mind of the church. It does not become revelation for the first time, for it already is revelation, but as revelation it now enters into the understanding of the church, is actually received, and is unfolded in the mind of the church through the mind of the Spirit. It may help us here to glance at the biblical concept of *revelation* or *unveiling*. In the Old Testament idiom revelation is a twofold act. It is the uncovering of God, but it is also the uncovering of the ear of man. In the New Testament it is manifestation, the unveiling of God, but it is also the taking away of the veil from our darkness and blindness. Real and full revelation is an act of God that is met by an act of man, but the act of man meeting it is one which is inspired and created by the act of God's self-unveiling. It is not only the revelation of the face of God in Jesus Christ, but the realisation of that revelation within the enlightened intellectual and spiritual understanding of the Church.

---

[40] *Institute*, 2.9.3.

[41] Acts 1.1.

[42] See Heb 2.3 KJV.

[43] Or, 'according to the Spirit', the Christ known in the light of the Spirit, as opposed to the 'Christ after the flesh' of 2 Cor 5.16, i.e. the Christ known only with the eyes of the flesh – the Greek *kata pneuma* and *kata sarka* is regularly translated 'after the spirit' and 'after the flesh' by the KJV, while the RSV has 'according to the spirit' and 'according to the flesh' Cf. Rom 8.4,5; Gal 4.29.

Hence it is not only an objective revelation but a subjective revelation, not simply an objective and historical unfolding of God's word but a subjective unfolding of it in faith.

(iv) Pentecost could only take place after the completion of atonement and reconciliation

Because this is so, the subjective unfolding of revelation within the mind and understanding of the apostles had to wait until the work of atonement and reconciliation had been completed. For how could unreconciled man, alienated and estranged man, receive revelation? How could humanity, whose fallen existence is marked by such a deep cleavage between being and knowing, between what they are and what they were made to be, receive the divine revelation? Once the breach between humanity and God had been healed on the cross, once the kingdom of heaven had been opened to all believers, through Christ's atonement, resurrection and exaltation to the right-hand of God by which he opened up a way for us to approach God, then the way was open for God to pour his Spirit upon man, and for man through the same Spirit to draw near to God in Christ. With the enmity of the human mind done away and the veil of darkness it entailed torn aside, the way was open for humanity to enter into that intimate communion with God within which alone real revelation could be fulfilled, not only from the side of the giving God, but from the side of receiving humanity, not only from the side of grace but from the side of faith. That is what happened when Christ's great work of atonement and reconciliation was completed and he ascended to open the kingdom of heaven to all who should believe in him. Then he himself through the gift of his Spirit completed his self-disclosure within the apostolic mind and understanding, within the apostolic obedience and life.

(d) Pentecost is not a new revelation but the final unfolding of the one revelation of Christ

What then do we have after Pentecost? Not any new revelation, not any new interpretation put upon the objective facts, but an actual unfolding within the apostolic mind and understanding of the one objective revelation Christ had already given them when on earth. That full unfolding of the mind of Christ within the mind of the apostolic church was the completion of his incarnational revelation through the Holy Spirit, not completion in the sense that the apostles had to add anything to it, or to work creatively upon it, but in the sense that the one revelation mediated through the historical life, teaching, death and resurrection of Christ, now shone out in all its own divine glory and truth within the mind of the New Testament church. Thus revelation completed its own movement in the inspired perception and apprehension and witness of it by the apostles, and upon that foundation the faith of the church in Jesus Christ was built once and for all. It was through the Spirit that the apostles received the revelation of Christ, and through the Spirit that Christ created and established the church in them. In that the apostolic church received his revelation, faithfully echoed and reflected it in its witness and life, it became Christ's body, his earthly historical form of existence, his image among humanity. That is, it became the foundation of the whole historical church in Christ.

3 The apostolic gospel

(a) The revelation of Christ was grounded and earthed in the apostolic gospel[44]

We have already noted that the disciples were brought into special relation to Christ as apostles, special witnesses carefully instructed, specially commissioned, authorised and empowered so that their preaching of Christ was not in word only but in power, a *kērygma* confirmed with signs or *sēmeia*. These apostles as a body were the chosen instruments through whom the objective revelation of Christ became once and for all subjective revelation within the church on earth, and that happening, the subjectivising of the objective revelation, was the actual grounding of the church on earth in the apostolic witness. The apostles formed the definite medium in flesh and blood, where the unfolding of the mind of Christ was faithfully acknowledged and obediently answered, where, so to speak, the revelation of Christ through the Spirit became earthed. The apostles constituted the actual place where the revelation of Christ became rooted in humanity, in the mind and language of the church. Thus the apostolate formed the human end, the receiving end, of the incarnational revelation. It was not a new revelation but the same revelation, objectively given in Christ, but now through the Spirit, subjectively taking shape in the mind of the church in authoritative and final form. Because this is the one revelation of Christ, the apostolate, expressly formed and created by

---

[44] Cf. the section 'Christ clothed with his gospel', *The School of Faith*, pp. lxxx-lxxxiii.

Christ for this purpose as the human end of revelation, belongs to the once and for all nature of the incarnation, and is caught up in its finality and authority, so that in this its primary sense *the apostolate is unrepeatable*, like the particularity of Jesus, or the particularity of the New Testament revelation.

The unrepeatable event of Christ becomes eschatological event in human testimony

Here in the apostolate composed of disciples who are chosen and sent out as eyewitnesses of the resurrection of Christ, the original unrepeatable event of revelation takes form as human testimony or word empowered by the Holy Spirit. When the apostles proclaimed Christ, then through their acting as mere stewards or earthen vessels, or as ambassadors speaking Christ's word in Christ's stead, the amazing thing happened: the crucified and risen Christ miraculously encountered men and women. His incarnation, death and resurrection confronted them as the mighty acts of God, so that they knew that they stood face to face with the last things, the final acts of God upon which their destiny depended. This proclamation of Christ was itself eschatological event, charged with the urgency of the decisive intervention of God for humanity's salvation, charged with all the fatefulness of the final judgement, but bearing above all the incredible good tidings that once and for all God's own Son had given his own life in vicarious sacrifice for the world's reconciliation, and that having finished that work he was here and now through this proclamation of that gospel gathering the undeserving children of humanity into the fold of his love. That is the apostolic gospel. That is what Paul, profoundly conscious of his divinely appointed task as an apostle to the Gentiles calls, 'my gospel'.[45]

(b) The apostolic gospel is Christ's full and final revelation of himself

The unique enshrining of the mind of Christ in the apostolic gospel

Now of course we cannot forget that the whole church is given the Spirit, and that all believers in a real sense may have the mind of Christ, for they are all indwelt by the Spirit who conveys Christ to them – but we must note carefully the fact that this only takes place through the word of the New Testament, through the apostolic testimony to Jesus Christ. Therefore we have to distinguish sharply between our having

---

[45] Rom 2.16, 16.25; 2 Tim 2.8.

the mind of Christ in the church from age to age, and the apostolic gospel as in a unique sense enshrining the mind of Christ. That is of course the doctrine of the canon of holy scripture in which the church acknowledged the apostolic testimony to be unique and apart, different from the continuous tradition of the church dependent upon the apostolic tradition. There is no doubt that the apostolate was a special instrument chosen by Christ and used by him to give full and final form to his revelation, a specially fashioned vessel through which he could pour himself out to the world for its obedient and faithful receiving.

The apostles are the specially inspired witness to the one revelation of Christ

We see that already in the disciples whom Jesus chose to form one body with himself in a most intimate way. With them he ate the last supper as those who were to be with him watching and praying with him in the terrible hour of his agony in Gethsemane, and to them after Calvary he was to return in the fullness of his revelation in order finally to commission them as his representatives in the founding and launching of his church. Thus the disciples became more than disciple-learners; they were apostolic delegates sent out to teach in the name of Christ, having the keys of the kingdom, which means the keys of the knowledge of Christ as well as the authority to bind and loose in the apostolic *kērygma*. They are sent out as a specially inspired medium, a college of apostles whose joint knowing of Christ and witnessing to him becomes one revelation of him through their faithfulness to the one *kērygma* of Christ and under the power of the one Spirit of truth.

The apostolic word joined to Christ by the Spirit to become word of Christ

Thus the apostolic proclamation of Christ through the Spirit is joined to the incarnate, risen and ascended Word, so that the apostolic word is word of Christ, and through the apostolic message and gospel Christ himself is at work in personal self-revelation and in active fulfilment of his reconciliation once and for all wrought out in his obedient life and death on the cross.[46] Through the apostolic gospel and through their preached or written word which we have in the New Testament, Christ has unfolded his own mind in self-interpretation, and thus here we have the full out-pouring of his Spirit, the final revelation in the light of which all else is to be apprehended and comprehended. That is all carried out through human thoughts, conceptions and categories drawn from the long ordeal of Israel's training under the impact of

---

[46] Cf. 2 Cor 5.11-20, 4.1ff.

God's word in the past but remoulded in the incarnation and unfolded in the apostolate. In the apostolic gospel, then, Jesus Christ has completed the final revelation of himself to humanity in such a way that they may appropriate him and have faith in him, may believe in the fact of Christ and actually know him in whom they believe.

(c) The Gospels and Epistles together make up the apostolic gospel and neither can be interpreted apart from the other

Now there is something important here that we must take note of. Christian faith does not go back to the Gospels only but to the apostolic gospel, for the gospels themselves are part of the tradition of the apostolic gospel – far less is Christian doctrine to be grounded upon our reconstructions of the very words, the *ipsissima verba* of Jesus, all-important as they ultimately are, but upon the whole apostolic gospel within which alone we can apprehend the *ipsissima verba* of Jesus. The doctrine of the church is not founded upon this or that selection which we may want to make or try to make out of the apostolic tradition, but upon the apostolic gospel as a whole, which means Gospels and Epistles, for it is both of these together which are inspired to convey to us the one Jesus Christ, the Christ who comes to us in the power and glory of his resurrection, the Christ who shines in his own light through the Spirit of truth, the whole Christ mediated to us through the apostolic mind, the whole New Testament Christ. This apostolic gospel is grounded upon and derived wholly from the *kērygma* of Jesus, and so Paul claims an identity between his gospel and Jesus' own *kērygma*.[47] Hence also it is this apostolic gospel enshrining the *kērygma* of Jesus, which gives the New Testament its remarkable unity in spite of the wide diversity in witnesses and perspectives.

Thus neither the so-called Christ of the Gospels nor the Christ of the Epistles can be understood and interpreted without the other. The Christ of the Epistles is not just some apostolic interpretation of Jesus added to the original gospel, but essentially the Christ himself, the consummated Christ who has fully revealed himself as he could not before his glorification and the sending down of his Spirit. Though the Gospels themselves are written from the perspective of the apostolic gospel, they inevitably lay great stress upon the objective revelation and we have in them all the elements of the revelation we have in the Epistles. But it is in the Epistles especially that we are given clearly and fully, on the basis of the objective revelation enshrined in the

---

47   Rom 16.25.

Gospels, what Jesus revealed in life and deed as well as by word, and what could only be revealed after his great deeds had been accomplished in his crucifixion, resurrection and ascension.

The unfolding of a Christian view of the finished work of Christ

There can be no question, therefore, of allowing any wedge to be driven between the Christ of the Gospels and the Christ of the Epistles, or any appeal to the Christ of the Gospels against the Epistles of Paul or Peter or John. Both together, in the light of each other, form the whole apostolic gospel of the one Christ Jesus, because the one Christ Jesus is not only the teacher, the healer, the master, but the crucified, risen and ascended Son of God whose word and deed are inseparable in his divine person and who has now fully revealed himself through the Spirit in the apostolic mind and gospel. Thus in the witness of the Gospels and of the Epistles together forming a unity, we find the full unfolding of the mind of Christ in regard to his person and work. The point of view of the apostles is the point of view which Christ means us to have of him, for their point of view as the human end of the incarnational revelation is the point of view of those who have come into saving contact with Christ. In them we have the Christian view of Christ, a view given in a way and in a fullness Christ himself could not give while on earth, for this is given not only in the light of his finished work but in the light of the revelation of the Spirit. That revelation came with the mighty act of his ascension, the opening of the kingdom of heaven to believers and the actualisation of salvation in the life and understanding of the apostolic foundation of the church and that is the perspective which must guide our doctrine of Christ from beginning to end.

4 The apostolic tradition and the New Testament[48]

(a) The apostolic tradition is given permanent form in the New Testament

In the apostolic witness the self-witness of Christ was given a form in which it passed into history as the apostolic gospel or apostolic *kērygma* given continuation or succession beyond the apostles themselves. But because it is already a final gospel become part of the New Testament

---

[48] Cf. *Theology in Reconstruction*, chap. 8, section 2, 'The Apostolic Foundation of the Church', pp. 134-40.

revelation, it is given succession in such a form that it ever remains identical with itself through its historical transmission. 'I received from the Lord what I also delivered to you . . . I preached to you the gospel, which you received . . . For I delivered to you as of first importance what I also received'.[49] These words of St Paul from 1 Corinthians make it very clear how the apostles themselves regarded the gospel or the *kērygma*, and precisely how it was handed on and how it was received through the apostolic tradition or *paradosis*.[50] That tradition assumed form and shape in written word and in the sacramental ordinances, as we see from these very passages from 1 Corinthians, but even in the tradition of the sacramental ordinances, the ordinances are themselves handed on as ordered by the apostolic word, so that it is the tradition of the word that is of primary importance. It is that tradition of the word in written form that we have in the New Testament writings, and which may therefore be called the deposit of the apostolic tradition.

Some of the New Testament was written directly by the apostles themselves, some by Paul as an apostle 'born out of due time',[51] some by fellow-workers of the apostles under their apostolic inspiration and authority, but it is the apostolic tradition of Christ's own *kērygma* that gives the whole its unity as the one gospel of the Lord, now handed on in a permanent historical form accessible to all generations until the final advent of Christ. As written word, the New Testament revelation assumes form in our human language and thought and as such is the counterpart on earth to the incarnate Word risen and ascended to the right hand of God. Thus the whole of the New Testament forms on earth and in history the *lalia*, the speech, of Christ who is himself the *Logos*, the Word in his own person.[52] By reason of their apostolic authority, by reason of their power as God's special revelation and word, these documents of the New Testament canon have imposed themselves on the mind and conscience of the church as no others have done, as the specially formed and selected means whereby Jesus Christ the Lord continues to speak, testifying to the mighty acts

---

[49]   1 Cor 11.23, 15.1,3.

[50]   Gk, 'handing down'.

[51]   1 Cor 15.8 KJV.

[52]   See John 8.43, KJV, 'Why do you not understand my speech (*lalian*)? because you cannot hear my word (*logon*).' Cf. T.F. Torrance, *Theological Science*, OUP, London 1969, p. 150-1, on *logos* and *lalia*, and also p. 148-9. Cf. also T.F. Torrance, *Conflict and Agreement*, vol. 2, Lutterworth, London 1960, p. 62-63.

whereby he has redeemed the world and offers himself to men and women as saviour and Lord.

Apostolic scripture is so conjoined to the divine Word as to be the written word of God to man

The scriptures are of course human documents, but they are so conjoined through the Spirit to the divine Word as to be the written word of God to man, deposited through the apostles as the treasure of the church out of which it lives and according to which it orders its life throughout the generations. In and through the scriptures the church continues to hear God speaking to it, and acknowledges therefore that they are holy scriptures and the authoritative word of God. As human testimony to God's Word, the scriptures are to be distinguished from the Word of God, but not separated from it, for God has through his Spirit graciously elected and formed scripture as the means whereby he continues through the Spirit to declare his mind to the church and to call the church into union and communion with himself.

The scriptures as written human documents are of course the product of the apostolic church, but both the church and the scriptures are the product of the gospel of Christ himself creating and shaping the message of the gospel in the mind of the apostolic church. It is through church and scripture, apostolic church and apostolic scripture, that Christ now conveys himself to men and women everywhere, and through both that Jesus Christ is known and believed. Apostolic church and apostolic scripture are inseparable, for it is through both together that Christ's salvation is conveyed. It has thus become part of the church's faith that the apostolate and the New Testament form together the one indivisible organ appointed by Christ in a final way to convey his own revelation to humanity.

The New Testament acknowledged as the authentic apostolic tradition

When the church in the early centuries came to acknowledge the canon of the New Testament, that is, came to be obedient to the self-imposition of these scriptures upon the mind and conscience of the church as the only *holy* scriptures, it thereby also acknowledged that the apostolic tradition had curtailed itself in that self-sufficient form recorded in the New Testament, and that all later tradition in the church was to be judged and measured by the unique and primary and foundational tradition of the apostles enshrined in the New Testament. In that tradition alone was the content identical with Christ the Lord, so that apostolic tradition became *supreme over all other tradition*. Or to put it the other way round, when all other tradition submits itself to the living apostolic tradition, it is thereby submitting itself to the living Lord himself. It is therefore to that tradition alone that we go to seek Christ, to the tradition that is identical with the holy scriptures of the apostolic church, that is, of the New Testament. It is there that we find Christ, not only the historical Christ, but the historical Christ clothed with his own gospel, who steps out of the pages of the New Testament and livingly encounters us as our Lord, the crucified and risen saviour, as our God.

(b) *The relation between the Word made flesh and the written word*[53]

All this brings us to enquire more precisely, what is the relation between the Word made flesh in Jesus Christ and the written word in the holy scriptures? That raises the whole question of the doctrine of holy scripture, which can be answered only by inquiry into the doctrine of Christ and into the relation the Word bore to the flesh he assumed at the incarnation. Thus the answer to the problem of the mystery of holy scripture is determined by our answer to the mystery of the incarnation itself. We may say several things at this point, without working out all their implications.

(i) *The relation of the written word to the living Word is like that of the flesh to the incarnate Word*

If the relation of the *Logos* to the *flesh* it assumed is the primary relation in theology, here in the doctrine of holy scripture we can only state the relation between the Word of God and the word of man in a way analogous to that primary and unique relation. If the flesh assumed by the *Logos* was flesh of our fallen humanity, sanctified in the very act of its assumption by the Word, then here we must say that the Word of God has assumed our fallen human speech into union with itself and sanctified it in that assumption so as to make it holy speech, holy scripture.

(ii) *The relation of the written word to the living Word is unlike that of the flesh to the incarnate Word*

The relation here between our fallen human speech, our fallen modes of thought and the Word of God, while analogically alike, is also analogically unlike, and therefore not identical with the hypostatic union in Christ. It is like it and yet unlike it, parallel to it only and on quite a different level. In Jesus Christ there was a hypostatic and

---

[53]   Cf. the striking and revealing passage on the relation between the Word made flesh and the written word of scripture, *Theology in Reconstruction*, pp. 138-40.

personal union between his deity and his humanity. In him there were two natures in one person, and all his words and actions were words and actions of that one person and within that hypostatic union. Here in the written word of the holy scriptures there is no such personal union, but that which is human is used and sanctified in its use by God as an instrument which remains *outside* his own person, although its character reflects the pattern of the hypostatic union.

The sacramental and eschatological relation between the written and the incarnate Word – election and judgement

We may speak here of the relation between the incarnate Word and our human language as eschatological and sacramental in nature. It is eschatological because the relation of our imperfect and fallen speech to the crucified and risen Lord implies judgement as well as election. It implies election because Jesus Christ chose and chooses to use this New Testament language as his own holy instrument of communication, and therefore he shaped and formed it to that end. But it also implies judgement because we confess that our speech is an imperfect servant, and its imperfection comes under the judgement of the perfection to which it bears witness and in which it shares. Now we see through a glass darkly in the holy scripture, and only in part, but then we shall see face to face and when we do see face to face, the need for scripture will pass away.[54] Scripture must therefore be understood and used in that eschatological perspective as the word of God in written form reaching out to the last Word, the *eschatos Logos*, which comes to meet us in Jesus Christ.

The sacramental participation of scripture in the whole divine-human Word of Christ

Until then, this relation between the written word and the incarnate Word in holy scripture is also sacramental, for through the operation of the Holy Spirit the words and signs employed in holy scripture are given to share in the obedience of the humanity of Christ to the will and mind of the Father, so that the written word in scripture shares in and is moulded by the covenanted obedience of Jesus Christ who is not only Word of God to man but perfectly obedient word of man to God. The whole Word of God incarnate is not simply the eternal Word

---

[54]   1 Cor 13.12 – see the footnote, T.F. Torrance, *Royal Priesthood*, 2nd edition, T & T Clark, Edinburgh 1993, p. 3 where Torrance sees in Paul's language a reference to the unique knowledge by Moses of God 'face to face', Num 12.7-8; Exod 33.11 (cf. 33.18-23); Deut 34.10.

of God communicated to man, but also the faithful reception and understanding of it, and the perfect response to it, all included in the one Jesus Christ.[55] It is in that whole divine-human Word, in the Word directed from God to man and in the obedient word of man in response to God, that holy scripture is given to share through the communion of the Spirit. In this sacramental participation of the written word in the obedience of Jesus Christ on the one hand, the language of the written word points away like a sign to the thing signified, but on the other hand the knowledge of the thing signified is not given except through the sign, that is through the written word. The relation between outward word and inner content, between sign and thing signified, must be thought out after the pattern of the hypostatic union in terms of the Chalcedonian[56] *without separation* and *without confusion* (*inseparabiliter* and *inconfuse*).[57]

(iii) The communication of properties between the written and the incarnate Word

The guiding analogy of the relation between the divine and human natures of Christ

In this case we must also speak of a *communicatio idiomatum* (communication of properties) between the written word and the incarnate Word in the holy scripture, but this must be governed by the way we are to think of the *communicatio idiomatum* between the divine

---

55   The whole theme of the 'bi-polarity in revelation', as Torrance calls it, and of the inseparability of revelation and reconciliation in the person of Christ is central to his theology – revelation involves not only God revealing but man receiving revelation, not only an act of God in Christ revealing but an act of man in Christ understanding, and neither are possible apart from the reconciliation in Christ of man to God. See *Theology in Reconstruction*, pp. 129-34.

56   The Council of Chalcedon, 451 AD – see T.F. Torrance, *Incarnation*, Paternoster UK & InterVarsity Press USA, Milton Keynes & Downer's Grove, 2008, pp. 83,197,200 for the Chalcedonian statement and its theology.

57   Two of the four adjectives used by Chalcedon to describe the union of two natures in the one person of Christ, *without confusion, change, division, or separation.* Applied to the scriptures, this means that there is to be no *confusion* between the written word and the divine-human Word, but nor any *separation* either (just as there is also to be no changing of one into the other, nor any division between them) – Ed.

and human natures in Christ himself.[58] In Christ we think of the eternal Son of God condescending in his grace to assume human nature and existence into oneness with his divine nature and existence, so that in and through that amazing act of humiliation in which the Word of God comes to us in the form of human word obedient to the will of God, we must think of the human word as exalted and sanctified in the divine. In the amazing grace of God this does not mean a humanising of the divine Word nor a deification of the human word, but the will of the divine Word to assume human form without ceasing to be divine, and therefore the will also of the divine to assume the human word into union with itself without in any way annulling its human nature.

If that is the way in which we are to think of the *communicatio idiomatum* in Christ Jesus himself, it will be in appropriately analogical fashion that we must think of the relation between the incarnate Word and the written word in the scriptures, except that here the written word is not assumed into one person with the divine Word, but is given to share in its human nature in the obedient humanity of Christ, so that it is *through the mediatorship of Christ alone* that we are to think of the human word in the scriptures as being endowed with the properties of the divine Word itself. At no point therefore can we regard the human word in holy scripture as limiting or enclosing the divine Word, and therefore as having such power over it that it can confer and cause the divine Word *ex opere operato*,[59] that is, out of the reading or understanding of the human word as such. In his sovereign freedom Jesus Christ uses the human word of holy scripture not because he is bound to it, but because he binds us to himself by it. He uses the human word and assumes it into instrumental union with his own divine Word in such a way that he always remains Lord of it, and in such a way that our hearing and understanding of him through this human word in the scripture is entirely dependent upon his grace and upon the sovereign freedom of his Spirit. In technical language, the communication of properties (*communicatio idiomatum*) in a doctrine of holy scripture has to be understood as a communication of actions (*communicatio operationum*).[60]

(iv) The basic text is the obedient humanity of Jesus Christ

---

[58] See *Incarnation*, p. 209f.,223f.,225f. – cf. p.221f.

[59] Lat, literally, '*by the work worked*', ie. by itself, simply by the performance of the work.

[60] See *Incarnation*, p. 224,226 – cf. p. 221f.

By way of summing up this whole section on the apostolic tradition and holy scripture, let me put it all in another way. When theology turns to the holy scriptures and in exegetical and theological interpretation seeks to articulate the content of the word of God, how does it handle the text of the New Testament scriptures? The New Testament text is the glass or the window in and through which we look at the basic text which underlies all the New Testament writings, all the apostolic tradition which they enshrine. That basic text is the text which the apostles themselves 'read', studied, interpreted, and expounded directly – their text was a living text, the words and deeds and life of Jesus Christ all woven into one seamless pattern, in which word, deed, life are inseparable in the person of Jesus Christ. *The basic text is the obedient humanity of Jesus Christ alone.*

The New Testament is the inspired secondary text

That basic text is given a secondary form in the apostolic witness in the New Testament, so that when we look at that witness we look *through* it to the basic text in the obedient humanity of Jesus Christ, and we look *through* it in such a way as not to confound the secondary form of the text with the primary reality. In the secondary form we do have an analogy to a holy sacrament, an analogy to the primary form of the self-witness of Christ in the whole of his obedient life, but the secondary form (and the written text created by it) is also revelation, for it is in and through it that the primary text is given to us objectively, and given to us to be received subjectively through the Spirit. The secondary form of the text is the creation by the majesty of Christ, in the power of his Holy Spirit, in the obedient and faithful reception of it in the apostolic witness, so that the secondary form is the inspired means which Christ still uses to confront us with the basic text of revelation in his own humanity. When theology reads and studies the text of the New Testament in this way, in faithful obedience and correspondence to the mind of Christ revealed in his humanity, then theology is engaging in its true task of bringing the mind and life of the church into conformity with Jesus Christ the Lord.[61]

---

[61]   On the task of theology in the church see *Theology in Reconstruction*, chap. 8, 'The Place of Christology in Biblical and Dogmatic Theology', pp. 128-49, esp. pp. 146-47f.

Chapter Eleven

THE ONE CHURCH OF GOD IN JESUS CHRIST

Editor's note: As with chapters 7-9 above, the material in this chapter was not part of Torrance's lectures on Christology and Soteriology or of the manuscript offered for publication, but was given to students in the form of duplicated 'handouts' and included here provides readers with his theology of the church. The two parts, A and B, represent the contents of two different handouts, the first handout in part and the second in full, as detailed in the introductory footnotes to each section. The two parts are different in style, the first part 'The Foundation of the Church' more discursive and fluent, while the second 'The Doctrine of the Church' is denser in content, less discursive and more succinct in style, and represents a careful and considered account of the doctrine and theology of the church with particular reference to the Apostles' Creed.

---

¹   This section is an abridged version of a duplicated student handout (23 pages) entitled 'The One Church of God'. The handout was 'part of an essay written for the Faith and Order "Commission on Christ and His Church", of the *World Council of Churches.*' The first two sections of the handout were published in the *Scottish Journal of Theology (SJT)*, vol. 16.2 (1963), pp. 113-31, under the title 'The Foundation of the Church' and subsequently reprinted in *Theology in Reconstruction* 1965. The third and final section 'The Sending of the Spirit and the Mission of the Apostles' appears to have been published only in the *Scottish Journal of Theology*, vol. 19.2 (1966), pp. 129-43, under the title 'The Mission of the Church'. Considerable overlap between some sections of 'The One Church of God', particularly section 3 ('The Mission of the Church'), with parts of the previous chapter here 'The Biblical Witness to Jesus Christ' and with the handout 'The Doctrine of the Church', which forms part B of this chapter, means that there has been considerable abridgement. As with section B below, the biblical references, explanatory footnotes and unnumbered headings have been added for the convenience of the reader.

A THE FOUNDATION OF THE CHURCH[1]

The church is grounded and rooted in the eternal purpose of God in Christ

The church is grounded in the being and life of God, rooted in the eternal purpose[2] of the Father to send his Son Jesus Christ to be the head and saviour of all things. Its mystery and destiny, hidden from the foundation of the world,[3] is revealed and fulfilled in the incarnation of the Son of God and in his glorious work of redemption, for in Jesus Christ the church as the redeemed people of God is the crown of creation, living in praise and gratitude to the creator and reflecting with all things, visible and invisible, the glory of the eternal God.

The three forms of the church: preparatory, new in Christ and eternal in the new creation

The church was formed in history as God called and entered into communion with his people. In and through them he embodied and worked out by mighty acts of grace the purpose of love which he brought at last to its fulfilment in Jesus Christ. While there is only one people and church of God throughout all ages from the beginning of creation to the end, there are three stages or phases of its life. It took *a preparatory form before the incarnation* when in the covenant mercies of the Father one people was called and separated out as the instrument through which all peoples were to be blessed; it was given *a new form in Jesus Christ* who gathered up and reconstructed the one people of God in himself, pouring out his Spirit upon broken and divided humanity that through his atoning life and death and resurrection all humanity might be reconciled to God and to one another, sharing equally in the life and love of the Father as the new undivided race; but it is yet to take on its *final and eternal form when Christ comes again* to judge and renew his creation, for then the church which now lives in the condition of humiliation and in the ambiguous forms of this age, will be manifested as the new creation without spot or wrinkle,[4] eternally serving and sharing in the glory of God.

The mission of the church to proclaim by word and life the reconciling love of God

As the Son was sent by the Father to be the saviour of the world, so the church lives its divinely given life in history as the servant of Christ

---

[2]   Eph 1.5,9-11, 3.11.

[3]   1 Peter 1.20; Eph 3.9, cf. 1.4f., 3.4f.

[4]   Eph 5.25-27; Rev 21.1f.,9f.

sent out by him[5] to proclaim the gospel of God's love to the whole world and to be in itself as the reconciled people of God, the provisional form of the new creation.[6] It is therefore the mission of the church to bring to all nations and races the message of hope and by the witness of its word and life to summon them to the obedience of the gospel,[7] that the love of God in Jesus Christ may be poured out upon them by the Spirit, breaking down all barriers, healing all divisions and gathering them together as one universal flock to meet the coming of the great shepherd,[8] the one Lord and saviour of all.[9]

1 The people of God under the old covenant[10]

The earthly beginning of the church in Adam

The church had its earthly beginning in Adam for then it began to subsist in the human society formed by God for immediate communion with himself. But in Adam the whole church fell through disobedience, and its immediate relation with God was broken and interrupted by the barrier of sin and guilt.[11] It fell not as a divine institution but in its constituent members, and therefore the church upheld by the eternal will of God took on at once a new form under his saving acts in history.

---

[5]   John 20.21.

[6]   Cf. T.F. Torrance, 'The Mission of the Church', (*SJT* vol. 19.2), p. 138, on the church as the instrument for the extension of the kingdom of Christ, 'What has been fulfilled intensively in the church through the operation of the Spirit must be fulfilled extensively in all mankind and all creation. As such the church is to be regarded as the new humanity within the world, the provisional manifestation of the new creation within the old.' The church here is the beginning at Pentecost of 'an ever-widening movement of universalisation. What took place intensively in Jesus Christ, within the limits of his particular historical life, then began to take place extensively, reaching out to all humanity in all ages in a movement as expansive as the ascension of Christ to fill all things.' (*Op. cit.* p. 132).

[7]   Cf. Rom 1.5.

[8]   John 10.14-16; Heb 13.20.

[9]   2 Pet 1.11, 2.20, 3.2,18; cf. 2 Cor 5.14; 1 Tim 2.3-6, 4.10.

[10]   On this section, see further T.F. Torrance, *Incarnation*, Paternoster UK & InterVarsity Press USA, Milton Keynes & Downer's Grove, 2008, chap. 2, 'The Incarnation', section 1 'The incarnation and the old Israel', pp. 36-56.

[11]   Gen 3; Rom 5.12-19; 1 Cor 15.21-22.

The calling of the church with Abraham and its establishment at Sinai

In spite of their sin God did not give up his people but maintained with them a covenant of grace, in which he allied himself with his creatures as their God and saviour, committing himself to them in paternal kindness and taking them into communion with himself as his dear children. From generation to generation he sought to reveal himself to his people as they were able to apprehend him and called them by his word to a life of obedience and faith and righteousness. In the fulfilment of this purpose for the whole human race God chose one people[12] from among the others to be the medium of his revelation, the special sphere of his redemptive acts leading throughout history to the fulfilment of his promise of salvation. Thus while the covenant of grace embraced all men and women, it was when God called Abraham and specifically promised him 'I will be a God to you and to your seed after you',[13] that the church began to be separated out from the nations and brought into definite form as the appointed sphere in history of God's revealing and redeeming activity through which all nations and all creation would be blessed. But it was with the redemption of Israel out of the bondage of Egypt[14] and its establishment before God as a holy people in the ratification of the covenant at Sinai[15] that Israel stood forth as the *ecclesia* or church of God.

Israel constituted as prophet of God bearing his oracles and the promise of the Messiah

Thus Israel came to be constituted God's prophet among the peoples of the earth, his servant entrusted with the oracles of God and the promises of the Messiah,[16] equipped with ordinances[17] to train it in the ways of righteousness and truth and faith. While the ordinances were temporary, belonging only to the preparatory economy of the divine covenant, the oracles and promises pressed forward throughout the whole history of Israel to their fulfilment, the incarnation of the Word in Jesus Christ and the establishment of his messianic kingdom through a redemption that would embrace all races and nations in a new covenant of the Spirit and in one universal people of God.[18]

---

12   Gen 12.1-3f. (cf. 18.18), 15.1-6f., 17.1ff.

13   Cf. Gen 17.1ff.

14   Exod chaps. 1 – 14.

15   Exod chaps. 19 – 40, esp. 19 – 20, 24, 31 – 34, 40.

16   Rom 3.2, 9.4-5.

17   Exod 18.20 KJV; Lev 18.4-5; 2 Kings 17.34,37; 2 Chron 33.8.

18   Jer 31.31-34; Ezek 36.22-28; Joel 2.28-29; Isaiah 42.6, 49.6; Eph 2.11-3.6.

Israel the preparatory form of the church waiting for fulfilment

When the Christian church came to refer to itself as the *ecclesia*[19] it was claiming continuity with the *qahal* or the people of God under the old covenant, but in so doing it clearly regarded the people before the incarnation as the church under the economy of the old covenant. It was the *ecclesia* or *qahal* that arose and existed through election, that was actively engaged in God's purpose of revelation and salvation, that was caught up in the mighty events in which God intervened redemptively in history, and that became involved in the forward thrust of the covenant toward final and ultimate fulfilment. It was the church of God in its preparatory form in the tension and struggle of expectation, unable to be yet what it was destined to be when incarnation and reconciliation were fulfilled. Only with the consummation of the mediation between God and man in Jesus Christ,[20] could the people of God under the old covenant fully become church in its permanent form in the body of Christ. Nevertheless it was that one church in the process of formation, waiting for its new birth in the resurrection and in its universalisation at Pentecost, while the mode and structure of its existence in the redemptive movement of God's grace in Old Testament history were determinative of the Christian church, built upon the foundation of the prophets as well as the apostles.[21]

(a) Israel the chosen people of God

Israel was *the chosen people of God*, elected not for its own sake but for God's sake, in the fulfilment of his revealing and redemptive purpose. It was church, therefore, not in the merely sociological or political sense of *ecclesia*; it was society formed by divine not by human convocation or calling. It was church as act of God, as the community called into being by the Word of God and constituted through union and communion with him. Yet by being separated out as a covenant-community with an ordered life of its own, Israel was also established

---

[19]   Gk, literally 'called out', ie. the people 'called out', the church (used in the New Testament for both the local community of Christians and the whole body of Christ). *Ecclesia* is the regular translation in the Greek Old Testament for the Hebrew *qahal*, the assembly, community, congregation of Israel.

[20]   1 Tim 2.5.

[21]   Eph 2.20.

as a nation among the peoples of the earth. Thus there arose and persisted through the history of Israel a struggle between Israel and its Lord, between its 'ethnic'[22] aspirations to be a *nation* like the other nations of the earth and its 'laic' calling to be a *people* in covenant-communion with God. It was this conflict that plunged Israel into its long ordeal of suffering. Precisely because it was the bearer of divine revelation it could not be a secular *nation* like the others, and because it was elected for the fulfilment of God's redeeming purpose it had to be the holy *people* exercising a vicarious mission through which the whole human race was to be transformed.

(b) Israel the servant of the Lord

Israel was called to be the *servant of the Lord*,[23] the one people within the Adamic race set apart for vicarious[24] mission in the redemption of the many. Through the cult Israel had been taught that the covenant could be fulfilled only through an obedient response or sacrifice provided by God himself from within the covenant, but through the prophets Israel learned that such an obedient response had to be translated into its very existence and life and made to issue out of it. The election of the one for the many called for the election within the one people of a servant chosen of the Lord[25] who would fulfil in his own body and soul the covenant will of God for his people, and fulfil the covenanted obedience of the people to God's will. This righteous servant would mediate the covenant by bearing the sins of the people in himself and being cut off out of the land of the living for the sake of God's people, so that they might be pardoned and healed and restored to fellowship with God.[26] The covenant thus mediated would be transformed to extend far beyond the bounds of Israel, for all nations would come at last under its light and salvation and share in the fellowship it bestowed between God and man.[27]

---

[22] 'Ethnic' from the Greek *ethnos*, nation; 'laic' from the Greek *laos*, people. On Israel as *ethnos* and *laos*, see *Incarnation*, p. 48,51, and on Israel's ordeal of suffering, see p. 41ff., 46ff.

[23] Psalm 136.22; Isaiah 41.8, 42.19, 43.10, 44.1-2,21; 45.4, 48.20; Jer 30.10, 46.27-28; Ezek 28.25, 37.25.

[24] From the Latin *vicarius*, 'acting in the place of another'.

[25] See the 'servant songs' of Isaiah, 42.1-7, 49.1-6, 50.4-10, 52.13-53.12 (cf. 61.1-2).

[26] Isaiah 53.4-12.

[27] Isaiah 42.6, 49.6; cf. 2.1-3 & Micah 4.1-2.

(c) Israel the bearer of the Messiah

Israel was called to be *the bearer of the Messiah*, the mother from whom the new race should spring. And so to the end of time it remains true that 'salvation is of the Jews'.[28] It is not only that Israel was called to be the bearer of the promises of God and therefore to be the messenger of hope, but that throughout her long history in her concrete existence in the flesh, Israel always bore within her the seed of the messianic saviour and of the messianic race. Throughout all its ordeal of suffering, it was not least that organic union of Israel with Christ that constituted it church and preserved it from extinction, so that when at last it gave birth to the Messiah, its whole historical life was gathered up in him and together with the church of the Gentiles it was constituted one new man,[29] the Israel of God,[30] the universal body of Christ.

The transition to the new covenant only through the death and resurrection of the Messiah

But the transition from the people of the old covenant to the people of the new covenant was only through the death and resurrection of the Messiah. Even though it was church of God, the holy people bearing the presence of God in its midst, Israel was concluded under sin with the Gentiles,[31] in the solidarity of the whole adamic race, in the one equal grace of God freely extended to all mankind. By condescending to be made flesh of our flesh in Israel,[32] the holy Son of God incorporated himself into the continuity of sinful human existence, taking on himself our body of sin under the curse of the law and the judgment of God, and even our body of death,[33] that through his death and resurrection there might take place the death

---

[28] John 4.22 KJV (RSV 'from the Jews').

[29] Eph 2.15.

[30] Gal 6.16.

[31] Gal 3.22 & Rom 11.32 (KJV 'concluded', RSV 'consigned').

[32] A reference to Gen 2.23-24, where Adam recognises that he and the woman God made share the very same flesh, and to Eph 5.25-32, where Paul sees in the incarnation the same oneness of flesh existing between Christ and the church as exists between man and woman, indeed where Paul thinks of the 'one flesh' of man and woman as a pointer to the mystery, in the union of Christ and the church, of the even deeper oneness of Christ and our flesh.

[33] Rom 6.6 KJV; Gal 3.13; Rom 2.1ff., 7.24.

of the old man and the resurrection of the new,[34] the destruction of the temple and the raising of it again,[35] the cutting of Israel down to the very root and the springing up of the new shoot, the vine of truth.[36] Thus in the dying and rising of the body of Christ, the old was translated into the new and the new was grafted into the continuity of the old.

The Christian church now grafted on to Israel and part of the race of Abraham

The Christian church must not forget that it has no independent existence, for through Christ it is grafted on to the trunk of Israel,[37] nor must it imagine that God has cast off his ancient people or that the promises made to Israel as a people of divine election and institution have only a spiritualised fulfilment.[38] As God's first-born son[39] Israel too has part in the resurrected body of the Messiah, and grafted into it[40] together with the Gentiles and sharing its riches,[41] forms the one commonwealth of the people of God.[42] All members of the church are of the race of Abraham, and there is no messianic race but Israel.

---

[34]   Rom 6.1ff.; Col 3.9-10 & Eph 4.22-24 KJV.

[35]   John 2.19-22.

[36]   Isaiah 6.13, 11.1f., 53.2; John 15.1f. (cf. Psalm 80.8ff., Isaiah 5.1-7).

[37]   Rom 11.16ff.

[38]   Rom 11.1f.,11f.,15f.,18f.,23f.,29f.

[39]   Exod 4.22.

[40]   The reference here is to Rom 11.23, the power of God 'to graft them in again', Paul's argument that if some of the branches of Israel were broken off for the grafting in of the Gentiles, the branches broken off could be grafted 'in again...and so all Israel will be saved', Rom 11.11-26.

[41]   Rom 11.11-12, cf. vv. 15,25-26 – the continuing centrality of the Jews for Torrance (the church does not replace Israel but is grafted into its root) is fundamental to his theology and in his lectures he used to point to Paul's argument that if the sin of Israel means salvation and 'riches for the Gentiles' (11.11-12) and 'if their rejection means the reconciliation of the world, what will their acceptance mean but life from the dead?' (11.15), or as Torrance used to paraphrase it, 'if Israel's rejection means the reconciliation of the world, their acceptance would be an event so momentous that it means the resurrection of the dead?'

[42]   Eph 2.12ff.

2 Jesus Christ and his messianic community

The coming of the kingdom of God in Jesus

From the very start of his public ministry Jesus came proclaiming the gospel of the kingdom of God and saying, 'The time is fulfilled, and the kingdom of God is at hand; repent and believe in the gospel,' and then set about at once calling people to himself in his mission to gather and redeem the people of God.[43] With his advent and presence, the transcendent kingdom of God that had so long been the object of longing and prophecy had arrived and was active among men, women and children for their salvation. In the whole historico-redemptive activity of God in Israel, the kingdom of God and the people of God were essentially correlative and inter-related conceptions, or rather two different aspects of the one rule of God grounded in creation and made good in redemption. It was to be fulfilled through the saving acts of God in Israel but on fulfilment it would inevitably transcend the boundaries of Israel and take form as the universal kingship of God over all his creation.

The kingdom and the people of God concentrated in and around the Messiah

That kingdom was to be ushered in with the coming of the Messiah, the anointed king, through whom it would be grounded on earth in the redeeming and raising up of a people who would enter into the kingdom as its constituent members and be themselves the instrument through which the kingdom would extend its rule over the ends of the earth. Small though its beginning was, grouped immediately round the person of the Messiah, it would grow and spread until all nations were brought under its rule.[44] 'Fear not little flock; for it is your Father's good pleasure to give you the kingdom.'[45] That is the context in which Jesus Christ and his messianic community are presented to us in the scriptures – the kingdom and the people of God alike are concentrated in him, while the life and mission of the church, the people of the new covenant, are rooted in his sending as the Son from the Father and take their form and shape from his incarnate ministry on earth.

---

[43] Mark 1.14-20.

[44] Cf. Luke 13.18-21 (Matt 13.31-33; Mark 4.30-32).

[45] Luke 12.32.

The nature and mission of Jesus as Messiah determine the form and structure of the church

It was the kind of person Jesus was and the kind of mission he undertook which determined and gave form and structure to the messianic kingdom and messianic people. The church inhered in his very being as the incarnate Son, was rooted in his humanity as the historical Jesus, and grew out of the fulfilment of his ministry in the flesh. As the church of the new covenant, it arose out of the indivisible union of the Messiah and the people of God he came to redeem and raise up; it grew out of the concrete way in which he lived his divine life within their human existence thereby transforming their whole way of life; it took shape and form in every act that he performed and it derived its essential structure from the way in which he fulfilled his ministry on their behalf. This change in the people of God, the new birth or foundation of the church in the Messianic era, had two phases, one before and leading up to the crucifixion, and one after and arising out of the resurrection.[46] Like the grain of wheat it had to be planted in the ground and had to die before it could spring up and bear abundant fruit.[47]

(a) The rooting of the church in the person and ministry of the historical Jesus.

Right from the start of his public ministry Jesus set about restoring the people of God by gathering followers or disciples round himself and building them up as the nucleus of the messianic community in whose midst the kingdom of God was actively at work.[48] This messianic office he fulfilled personally, not by mighty impersonal deeds, but by direct personal and individual ministry on his part. Hence we have the three arduous years of his personal ministry, in lowly, patient service; in preaching the kingdom and summoning all to repentance,[49] in seeking and saving the lost,[50] in healing the sick and forgiving sins,[51] in teaching

---

[46]   Cf. T.F. Torrance, *Incarnation*, pp. 156-60, the section 'The building up of the messianic community and the creation of the church'.

[47]   John 12.24; cf. 1 Cor 15.36f.; Matt 13.23 (Mark 4.8; Luke 8.8); John 15.5f.

[48]   Mark 1.16-20, 2.14, 3.13-19 (Matt 4.18-22, 9.9, 10.1-4; Luke 5.1-11,27, 6.12-16; cf. John 1.35-43).

[49]   Matt 4.23f.; Luke 5.32.

[50]   Luke 15, 19.10.

[51]   Mark 1.30f., 2.1-12 (Matt 9.2-8; Luke 5.18-26).

all who had ears to hear[52] and feeding them with the bread of life,[53] in transforming their lives and communicating to them a new righteousness, in instituting in their midst the final law of God[54] and moulding them into a structured community with its authoritative centre in himself.

(i) The essential and constitutive nature of Jesus' human and individual ministry

The direct word and action of Jesus himself was essential in all this. As we have traditionally failed to see that the historical ministry of Jesus, his teaching and praying, his living and obeying, his miracles and parables, are an integral part of his atonement, so we have failed to pay sufficient attention to the essential and constitutive nature of his personal and individual ministry in its fulfilment of the special office laid upon him by divine authority for the building of the church of God among his followers. The only comparison possible is with Moses. It was with divine authority that Moses delivered and reconstituted Israel, instituted the covenant at Sinai, promulgated its laws and installed people in office in the covenanted community.[55] Moses' authority was supreme in Israel.[56] But in Jesus there is not only a new Moses,[57] but the Messiah himself, the Son of Man endowed with authority on earth to forgive sins[58] and utter final commandments. Jesus fulfilled his office with an authority greater than that of Moses or than any to which the scribes and pharisees appealed. It was the immediate authority of the Father which had been laid on him. He did nothing by himself, but acted only in accordance with the will and mission and word of the Father who sent him,[59] and therefore he resorted to prayer before all the major acts of his ministry.[60] What he had to do and did was to found the new Israel and inaugurate the new covenant.

---

[52] Mark 1.21-22,27,39, 2.2,13, 4.1f.,23f., 6.2,6,34, 8.31, 9.31, 10.1, 11.17-18, 12.35,38, 14.49.

[53] John 6.25-59 (cf. 6.63,68).

[54] Matt 5.17-48; cf. Matt 22.34-40 (Mark 12.28-34; Luke 10.25-28); John 13.34-35, 16.12f.

[55] See Exodus, Leviticus, Numbers, Deuteronomy.

[56] Cf. Deut 34.10; John 5.46.

[57] Cf. Deut 18.15,18.

[58] Mark 2.10 (Matt 9.6; Luke 5.24).

[59] John 5.19,30.

[60] Luke 3.21, (5.16), 6.12, 9.18,28f., (11.1), 22.41f.

(ii) The basis of the new Israel in the incorporation of the disciples into his messianic mission,

He laid the basis for the new Israel when out of the people prepared for the Messiah and out of the band of those he had called to be his disciples, he chose twelve to be with him to be the inner nucleus of his church.[61] It was a tremendous act for it meant that the longed-for age of salvation had come when the tribes would no longer be scattered but be gathered into one. Hence he formed and instituted them into one body with himself, calling them to take up his cross and deny themselves, that they might have their centre of unity not in themselves but in him.[62] He initiated them into his messianic secret, incorporated them into his messianic mission, sending them out to exercise his own ministry in preaching and healing, granting them to be baptised with his baptism and to drink the cup which he was to drink, and even to watch and pray with him at the last in the garden of Gethsemane.[63]

(iii) The indissoluble bond of Messiah and people in the inauguration of the new covenant

As long before Elijah had gathered together twelve stones representing the twelve tribes of Israel to build an altar for sacrifice, Jesus gathered twelve living stones, such as Peter the rock, and built them round himself the lamb of God to be offered in sacrifice.[64] They were the 'many' inhering in the 'one'. They had one name in the Son of Man who came to give his life a ransom for the many.[65] In the indissoluble bond between *the one* and *the many*, the Messiah and the people, the nucleus of the church received its fundamental shape and form, and together the little flock went up to Jerusalem where it was to be given the kingdom.[66] Then there took place the last supper where Jesus inaugurated the new covenant in his body and blood, renewed the consecration of the disciples in himself, and in covenantal action appointed to them a

---

[61]   Matt 10.1-4 (Mark 3.14-19; Luke 6.12-16).

[62]   Matt 16.24f. (Mark 8.34f.; Luke 9.23f).

[63]   Mark 8.27ff. (Matt 16.13ff.; Luke 9.18ff.); Mark 6.7-13 (Matt 10.1,5ff.; Luke 9.1ff.); Mark 10.38-39 (cf. Matt 20.22-23); Mark 14.32ff. (Matt 26.36ff.; cf. Luke 22.39ff.).

[64]   1 Kings 18.30-39; Matt 16.18; John 1.36.

[65]   Rom 5.15-19; Mark 10.45 (Matt 20.28).

[66]   Luke 12.32.

kingdom making them a royal priesthood to sit with him at last on twelve thrones in his kingdom.[67]

(iv) The death and resurrection of the Messiah inaugurating the new economy

Then came the crucifixion, the scattering of the disciples, the laying of the axe to the root of Israel, the destruction of the temple, the death of the Messiah.[68] In the ultimate hour he was left alone, dying in lonely substitution on the cross, the one for many.[69] But in his death, the many who inhered in him died too,[70] and indeed the whole body of sin, the whole company of sinners into which he incorporated himself to make their guilt and their judgment his own, that through his death he might destroy the body of sin,[71] redeem them from the power of guilt and death, and through his resurrection raise them up as the new Israel, the new humanity, the church of the new covenant, the one universal people of God. The death and resurrection of the Messiah brought the old economy in God's household to an end and inaugurated a new economy through union with himself in his risen body.

(b) The rebirth of the church in the body and Spirit of the risen Jesus

The church did not come into being with the resurrection or with the pouring out of the Spirit at Pentecost. That was not its birth but its new birth, not its beginning but its transformation into the body of the risen Lord quickened and filled with his Spirit. Jesus Christ had already gathered and built up the nucleus of the church round himself, but because he loved it he gave himself for it, that he might cleanse it and change it through the mystery of union with himself in death and resurrection.[72] The form he had given it through his ministry was necessarily of a provisional character before the crucifixion and

---

[67] Matt 26.20-28 (Mark 14.22-24); John 13.5ff., 15.3, 17.19; Luke 22.28-30 KJV 'I appoint unto you a kingdom', RSV 'I appoint [a kingdom] for you' (cf. Matt 19.28); cf. 1 Peter 2.4-9.

[68] Mark 14.27 (Matt 26.31); Luke 3.9 (Matt 3.10); John 2.19-22; Matt 27.37ff. (Mark 15.25ff.; Luke 23.38ff.; John 19.19ff.).

[69] John 16.32.

[70] 2 Cor 5.14.

[71] Rom 6.6 (KJV 'body of sin', RSV 'sinful body'); cf. Rom 7.24, 'body of death'.

[72] Eph 5.25f.; Rom 6.6ff.; cf. Eph 2.5f.; Col 3.1f.

resurrection. He had prepared it for this hour, and therefore far from rejecting it he reaffirmed it, reconstituted it, and recommissioned it, giving it to participate in him now on the ground of his atoning work in a depth and fullness which was not possible before.

(i) The pouring out of the Spirit to breathe quickening life into the church

The body had already been prepared, the people and the structure he had given them remained, but the body was broken and humbled to the dust – it needed to be quickened by the breath or Spirit of God.[73] That had already happened to Jesus himself, the head of the body, for God had not allowed him to see corruption but had raised him bodily from the dead to be the new life-giving Adam, the head of the new race.[74] Now first upon the apostolic nucleus he breathed his quickening breath and then poured the Spirit out in fullness upon the whole church, and so the body prepared for Christ arose and lived.[75] The Christian church was born, the one body of Christ incorporating the faithful of all ages before and after the incarnation.[76]

(ii) The church rooted in Christ to participate in his life and his messianic mission and ministry

The Church has no independent existence or any life or power of its own, apart from what is unceasingly communicated to it through its union and communion with Christ[77] who dwells in it by the power of the Spirit,[78] filling it with the eternal life and love of God himself.[79] It is

---

[73] Cf. Ezek 37.

[74] 1 Cor 15.20; Col 1.18, 2.19 (Eph 1.22-23, 4.15, 5.23); Acts 2.31f., 13.34-37; 1Cor 15.45 (cf. Rom 5.12-21; Col 1.18-20).

[75] John 20.22; Acts 2.

[76] Cf. Eph 2.11-3.11; Heb 11 esp. vv. 39-40, 12 esp. v. 1f.,22f.

[77] Eph 2.20-22, 4.15-16; Col 2.6-7; John 15.1-5.

[78] John 14.16-20; Eph 2.21-22; 1 Cor 3.16-17; 1 John 3.24, 4.13

[79] John 5.21,26, 6.32-35ff.,57f., 10.30,38, 11.25 – cf. 8.58; 1 John 1.1-3, 2.24-25, 4.8,12,15-16; Col 1.15-19 esp. v. 19, 2.9f. (cf. Eph 3.19, 1.23, 4.4-6, 2.18,22). While it is clearly based on the kind of texts cited, Torrance's trinitarian theology of the church here comes from putting such texts alongside others and interpreting them together. When for example John 14.12-18 (*Jesus leaving the disciples and the Spirit coming to be with them, yet Jesus not leaving them desolate but himself coming to them*) is put together with John 14.23 (*the Father and the Son together coming to make their home with someone*), with John 14.26 (*the Father sending the Spirit in the name* [continued opposite]

quickened and born of the Spirit;[80] it is filled and directed by the Spirit,[81] but in order that the church may be rooted in Jesus Christ,[82] grounded in his incarnate being and mission, and in order that it may be determined in its inner and outer life through participation in his life and ministry.

This means that through the Spirit the structure and functions of the messianic community which Jesus had gathered about him in the days of his ministry in the flesh continued to be determinative for the life and functions of the church after the resurrection and the ascension. Jesus and his disciples shared in one messianic mission and Jesus and his disciples formed one messianic body.

Jesus' initiation, consecration and then recommissioning of the disciples into his mission

Before the crucifixion Jesus took care to initiate his disciples into the same ministry as he was exercising, incorporating first the twelve[83] and then the seventy[84] into his own mission by sending them out to minister in the name of the Messiah as he the Messiah had been sent to minister in the name of the Father.[85] The disciples were permitted to baptise, to go forth as his representatives bearing the *kērygma* of the kingdom on their lips and with authority to heal and forgive sins in his name; at the last supper the twelve were solemnly washed and

---

of Jesus to remind the disciples of all he had said), with John 15.1-11 (*the need for the disciples to abide in union with Christ*), with John 15.26 (*Jesus sending the Spirit from the Father to bear witness of him [Jesus]*) and with John 16.13-16 (*the Spirit coming to guide the disciples into the truth, because all that the Father has Jesus' has and the Spirit takes what Jesus has [or says] and declares it to them*) – when all of that is put together, together with the wider raft of scriptural texts, and interpreted in the light of the inner connections or 'inner logic' of scripture as a whole then a trinitarian structure of understanding begins to emerge in theology, articulating and making explicit the theological understanding which the text or various texts of scripture can be said to imply.

80   Cf. John 3.1-14; 1 Cor 15.45 & 2 Cor 3.3,17-18; Rom 8.11.

81   Acts 2.4, 4.31, 9.17 & Eph 5.18; Rom 8.4 & Gal 5.16,18,25; Acts 6.10, 8.29, 10.19, 11.28, 16.7 etc.

82   Col 2.7; cf. Eph 3.17.

83   Luke 9.1-6 (Mark 6.7-13; Matt 10.1ff.).

84   Luke 10.1-20.

85   Cf. Luke 10.16; John 20.21.

consecrated as his servants and prepared for office. Jesus commanded them at the supper to continue to fulfil this ministry until he returned[86] and prayed for them in distinction from the rest in the fulfilment of their special office;[87] after the resurrection he forgave their failure and recommissioned them as his representatives, sending them out to follow his example in shepherding and feeding the flock, to be teachers and heralds of the kingdom, making disciples of all nations.[88]

Jesus' intention to leave a ministry patterned on his and based on the apostles and Pentecost

The records make it clear that Jesus intended to leave behind a community with a structure and form and leadership, a community with a ministry shaped on the pattern of his own, and that while all were called to be disciples and to engage in a ministry of witness to him, some were given special responsibilities and a special commission of pastoral care over his flock, endowed with an authoritative office to act in his name. The constituent elements of the church were all there, but now with the commissioning of the disciples as *apostles* and the pouring out of the *Spirit* at Pentecost, the church was given by its risen Lord the permanent form which he intended it to take throughout history until he came again.

(iii) The presence of Father, Son and Spirit in the ministry of Christ and in that of the church[89]

Just as when the Father sent the Son, the Father himself was at work in his ministry,[90] so when Christ sent the apostles he was present in their ministry.[91] Thus the ministry of the apostolic church is Christ's own personal ministry within the place of the church. Christ did not act instead of the Father, but Father, Son and Holy

---

[86] John 13.1-35.

[87] John 17.6-19.

[88] John 20.19-23, 21.15-19; Matt 28.18-20; cf. Acts 1.1-8.

[89] Paragraph added from T.F. Torrance, 'The Mission of the Church', (*SJT* vol. 19.2), pp. 131-32 (p. 15 of the student handout 'The One Church of God').

[90] See the theme in John's Gospel of the inseparability of the Father and the Son and their mutual co-inherence and co-working, esp. 3.34-35, 5.17,36-38, 8.18-19,29, 10.30,36-38, 11.42, 17.1-11,17,21-26.

[91] Cf. Acts 2.47, 3.12,16, 4.29-31, 9.15, 10.44-48, 11.15-18, 13.2 etc; 2 Cor 5.20, 6.1.

Spirit were present and acting in him; likewise the apostolic church does not act instead of Christ, for he is present in the church, and though distinct from its ministry acts in and through it, making it his own.

(iv) Christ the only absolute and proper minister of the church before God

The important point here is to discern both the rooting of the apostolic ministry in the ministry of Jesus, and to discern the difference which comes about when the self-ministry of Jesus is translated into ministry in his name. It is the vicarious mediation of Jesus which is of fundamental importance here and explains why the early church worshipped the Father and ministered only in the name of Christ, and why they regarded Christ in the absolute and proper sense as the only minister of the church before God,[92] the only one who was appointed and anointed (*Christos*) for office in the kingdom of God, the only one endowed with all authority in heaven and earth,[93] the supreme householder[94] in God's kingdom who at the end would hand over everything to the Father.[95]

The ministry of the apostles and the church shares in the one ministry of Christ in his body

Grounded upon the apostles and determined by their ministry, the ministry of the church is both like and unlike the ministry of the historical Jesus. It is rooted in it and patterned after it, and in a real sense shares in it. But it is a ministry of redeemed sinners, whereas his ministry is that of the redeemer. This essential and fundamental translation in the form of the ministry (from Jesus' self-witness to the church's witness to him) was carried out by the apostles, so that all true Christian ministry is ever after determined at its root by the special function of the apostles in their immediate relation to Jesus' ministry on the one hand and to the historical church of forgiven sinners and its mission in the world on the other hand. As there is only one Christ and only one body, so there is only one ministry, that of Christ in his

---

[92] See further T.F. Torrance, *Theology in Reconciliation*, Geoffrey Chapman, London 1975, chap. 4, 'The Mind of Christ in Worship: The Problem of Apollinarianism in the Liturgy', pp. 139-214, and the concluding summary of the chapter, p. 208ff.

[93] Matt 28.18.

[94] Heb 2.2-6.

[95] 1 Cor 15.24; see the important comment, T.F. Torrance, *The Trinitarian Faith*, T & T Clark, Edinburgh 1988, p. 274, on the patristic insertion into the creed of the phrase 'whose kingdom shall have no end'.

body.[96] But Christ shares in it in his utterly unique way, as vicarious redeemer and Lord; the church shares in it in an utterly different way, as the redeemed people who as servants and heralds point away from themselves to Christ alone.

B THE DOCTRINE OF THE CHURCH[97]

The church is part of the creed and an essential part of faith in the gospel

In the Apostles' Creed the church is given a place within the articles of belief under faith in the Holy Spirit, and is bracketed together with the forgiveness of sins, the resurrection of the body and the life everlasting. The doctrine of the church belongs to the doctrines of saving faith. It does not belong to the periphery of the faith, to some marginal area which is not important and where differences of opinion do not matter very much. On the contrary, it is essentially evangelical doctrine, inseparably bound up with faith in the holy Trinity and with the saving operation of Christ through the Holy Spirit.

---

[96] Eph 4.4-12; Col 2.19; cf. the whole depiction of Christ as high priest in Hebrews, Heb 2.11f.,17, 3.1, 4.14-5.10, 6.20, 7.15-8.6 (8.1-2, 'we have such a high priest, one who is seated at the right hand of the throne of the Majesty in heaven, a minister, *leitourgos*, in the sanctuary and the true tent'), 9.11f.,24ff. to 10.21f.; cf. also 13.20.

[97] 'The Doctrine of the Church' is the text of a 'handout' given by Torrance to students at New College. Although it is his main dogmatics course, the lectures on Christology and Soteriology to all second year students, which forms the basis of his books *Incarnation* and *Atonement*, Torrance did lecture on the Church, Ministry and Sacraments to third year honours students. Some of his handouts here, usually lectures prepared for events and publications outside New College but made available to his students, did appear in print, notably 'The Foundation of the Church: Union with Christ through the Spirit' in *Theology in Reconstruction* 1965, and 'The One Baptism Common to Christ and his Church' and 'The Paschal Mystery of Christ and the Eucharist' in *Theology in Reconciliation* 1975. Much of his thinking on these topics also appeared in the two volumes of *Conflict and Agreement* 1959 & 1960, in *Royal Priesthood* 1955 (2nd edn. 1993) and in the yearly *Reports of the Commission on Baptism*, 1955 – 1961, for the General Assembly of the Church of Scotland. Apart from limited sections which overlap with

[continued opposite]

The church is thus a part of the gospel and an object of faith. The church is not indeed an independent object of faith, because considered in itself alone it is nothing, but it is included within faith in the one God, the one Mediator, and the one Spirit. Correspondingly, there is only one church, which bears within it the heavenly treasure of forgiveness of sins and communion in the divine life, and outside of which there is no ordinary possibility of salvation.

1 The church is the work of the three divine persons

The church derives from the eternal purpose of God to create humankind and to share with them the life and love which he has within himself as Father, Son and Holy Spirit. It is rooted in the incarnation of the Son of God, for in him the love of God has overflowed into the world and embodied itself in our humanity, and it is maintained through the operation of the Spirit who unites it in body and spirit to Christ and in him makes it participate in the divine nature. Thus the church owes its existence solely to the grace of God and lives only through the faithfulness of the Father, Son and Holy Spirit.

The grounding of the church in a threefold communion

In Jesus Christ the church knows that the communion of the Spirit which constitutes and quickens its life in history derives from its union with Jesus Christ, and in him and through him from the eternal communion in God. Thus the mystery of the church's being is grounded

---

and are recognisably similar to material published elsewhere, 'The Doctrine of the Church' would appear to have been produced purely for students and never to have been published as such although it clearly represents a topic of major importance in Torrance's thinking. Its insertion in this volume complements the chapter in *The Trinitarian Faith* on the patristic understanding of the church. Together with section A above, 'The Foundation of the Church', it helps to fill out his published material on the doctrine of the church, making his theology of the church more widely accessible and therefore helping to present a fuller and more comprehensive picture of his whole dogmatics.

Although Torrance's language here recognisably abounds in biblical phrases, allusions and references, often running several together in the same sentence, there are no explicit biblical references in the text and only occasionally a direct quote. Biblical references have therefore all been added as have the explanatory footnotes and unnumbered headings for the convenience of the reader.

in a threefold communion. Antecedent to all is the eternal communion of the Father, Son and Holy Spirit, that is, the love that God is eternally in himself, the *consubstantial communion* of the Father and the Son in the Holy Spirit. That love of God has been poured out for us and embodied in Jesus Christ, the beloved Son, in whom by the operation of the holy Spirit divine nature and human nature were uniquely and *hypostatically united in one person*. It is that same love mediated by the atonement that is poured out by the Spirit within the church, for through the *communion of the Spirit* the church partakes of the oneness of the Father and the Son in Jesus Christ, and is constituted in itself the community of love on earth in whose midst God himself dwells.[98] Because God is love, the pouring out of his love upon man is the pouring out of the divine life.[99] The participation of the church in that divine life, which it is given through the communion of the Spirit, is its supernatural life, which it lives from age to age only as it is grounded in the measureless love of God[100]. Thus the *communion of the Father, Son and Holy Spirit* has wonderfully overflowed into our humanity in the incarnation, taking unique form in the *hypostatic union* and reconciliation wrought out in Jesus Christ, and through the *communion of the Spirit* flows over from him into history in the life and mission of the church. As such the church is the work of the three divine persons.

(a) *The church is the universal family of God the Father sharing sonship with the Son*

The church is the universal family of God the Father sharing brotherhood with Jesus Christ and therefore sharing with him sonship to the Father.[101] In Jesus Christ, his only begotten Son, God has fulfilled his covenant of grace in which he gives himself to us as our heavenly Father and adopts us as his dear children. This church is the one household of God in heaven and earth in which all barriers and divisions are abolished and proscribed, and all men and women are equally sons and daughters of the heavenly Father, sharing together

---

[98] 1 John 4.12-16; cf. John 13.34-35, 14.21-23, 15.9-10; 1 Cor 13; Eph 3.17-19, 4.15-16, 5.1-2; Col 2.2, 3.14.

[99] See the emphasis in both the Gospel and letter of John on Jesus as the life and love of God manifested for our eternal life and salvation, e.g. 1 John 1.1-2, 4.7-12, 5.11-12.

[100] Cf. Eph 3.19; 2.4-7.

[101] Cf. Eph 3.14-15; Gal 3.26, 4.4-7; 1 Cor 1.9; Rom 8.29; 2 Cor 6.18.

in the inheritance of Jesus Christ his beloved Son.[102] This church is the holy people of God, the building not made with hands, the habitation of God among humanity, consecrated to his worship and glory and devoted with all creation to show forth his praises in adoration and thanksgiving for ever.[103]

(b) *The church is the community of the reconciled, finding its life in union with Jesus Christ*

The church is the community of the reconciled, redeemed through the blood of Christ, for in him God has abolished the enmity and sin that estranged us from him and has given us the Spirit of true love. Through union with Jesus Christ the church shares in his life and in all that he has done for mankind. Through his birth its members have a new birth and are made members of the new humanity. Through his obedient life and death their sins are forgiven and they are clothed with a new righteousness. Through his resurrection and triumph over the powers of darkness they are freed from the dominion of evil and are made one body with him. Through his ascension the kingdom of heaven is opened to all believers and the church waits for his coming again to fulfil in all humanity the new creation which he has already begun in it. Thus the church finds its life and being not in itself but in Jesus Christ alone, for not only is he the head of the church but he includes the church within his own fullness.

(c) *The church is the communion of saints living in communion with God through the Holy Spirit*

The church is the communion of saints, the whole company of the redeemed in heaven and earth,[104] living in communion with God through the Holy Spirit. The church is the temple of the Spirit, the royal priesthood, where prayer is made, where worship and thanksgiving and spiritual sacrifices are continually offered, the sanctuary of God on earth where Christ dwells through his Spirit and which he unites with the sanctuary of God in the heavens.[105] As such it is the community of men and women filled with the presence of the

---

[102] Eph 2.19; Gal 3.26-29.

[103] 1 Peter 2.4-9; 2 Cor 5.1 (cf. Heb 11.10,16, 12.28, 13.14-15); Eph 2.22 (KJV 'habitation', RSV 'dwelling place'); Psalm 9.14, 79.13 & Isaiah 43.21 KJV.

[104] Cf. Eph 3.18; Heb 11.39-12.1, 12.22-23.

[105] 1 Cor 3.16-17, 6.19; 1 Peter 2.5,9; John 14.17-23; Heb 7.26ff., 9.11f.,24, 10.19f.

Spirit, partaking of the plenitude or fullness of the blessings and riches of God, and therefore sent out in the power of the Spirit to live out the divine life and love among humankind as the bodily instrument and image of Christ in the world and the one comprehensive communion of the Spirit.

The church is thus the work of the three persons of the holy Trinity, comprising all who are baptised in the name of the Father, the Son and the Holy Spirit and live in faith and obedience to him. There is one body and one Spirit, one Lord and one faith, one God and Father of all who is above all, and through all, and in us all.[106]

2 The church is the body of Christ

The twofold meaning of the 'body of Christ' – the whole Christ and the body of the head

The New Testament uses the expression 'body of Christ' in two ways. On the one hand it is used in a comprehensive sense to speak of *the whole Christ who includes the church* within his own fullness, the new man in whom the new race is concentrated, the true vine that includes the branches.[107] In this sense Christ is the church, for he embodied himself in our humanity and as such gathers our humanity in himself into oneness with God. He identified himself with us, and on that ground claims us as his own, lays hold of us and assumes us into union and communion with him, so that the church finds its essential life and being only in him. Christ is the church, but it cannot be said that the church is Christ, for Christ is infinitely more than the church although in his grace he will not be without it. Hence on the other hand, the New Testament uses the expression the body of Christ to relate the church to him in such a way that it is distinguished from him as *the body of which he is the head,*[108] as the servant of which he is the Lord, and yet as his friend[109] and partner upon which he freely bestows his own royal inheritance as the Son of God.

That the church is the body of Christ means that it participates in him, draws its life and nature from him, sharing in all he has done for it and sharing in his very life as the incarnate Son of the Father.

---

[106]   Eph 4.4-6; cf. 1 Cor 8.6.

[107]   Cf. Eph 2.15; Rom 5.12ff.; 1 Cor 15.45f.; Col 1.18f.; John 15.1f.

[108]   Col 1.18, 2.19; Eph 4.15-16.

[109]   Cf. John 15.15.

Everything that the church is as church it owes to Christ and derives from his grace, so that everything that it does or says or thinks must be in the name of Christ and to his honour and glory alone. It is only through participating and sharing in Christ that the church is to be regarded as his body, as his image and likeness among mankind, as the expression of his love and truth, as the reflection of his humility and glory, as the instrument of his gospel, as the earthen vessel[110] that holds his heavenly treasure and holds it forth for all humanity to share freely. Only on the ground of this participation in Christ is the church a community of believers, a communion of love, a fellowship of reconciliation on earth.

The scriptures use many names and images with which to speak of the church, all of which have to be taken into account, for they all modify and qualify one another in a rich complex of meaning. It is only as we let the other analogies and images play their part in opening up and enriching the concept of the body that it can serve its purpose in declaring the nature of the church. But this analogy is of especial importance for it is the most central and the most deeply christological of them all. It refers us directly to Christ himself as the head and saviour of the body. That is apparent in our Lord's words at the inauguration of the new covenant in his body and blood.[111] It is that holy covenant that binds the people of God so closely together with Christ that he makes them his own body, giving them to feed upon him, to eat his body and drink his blood, and to have union and communion with him.[112]

The whole life and essence of the church is to be found in Christ alone

The term body of Christ directs us at once to Christ himself, laying the emphasis not on the body but on Christ. Thus it does not focus attention on the church as an entity in itself or as something that exists for its own sake, but upon the church as the immediate property of Christ which he has made his very own and gathered into the most intimate relation with himself. It reminds us that the church is only the body of which he is the head, and is therefore to be subject to him in everything. Jesus Christ alone is the essence of the church. It is only in Christ that the church is church, only in him that it coheres and has its principle of being and unity,[113] and only in and through him does it have its

---

[110] Cf. 2 Cor 4.7.

[111] Matt 26.26-28; Mark 14.22-24; cf. Luke 22.15-19.

[112] Cf. John 6.35ff., 15.1ff.

[113] Cf. Col 1.15-20, 2.6-7,19; Eph 1.22-23, 4.15-16.

function and mission in the gospel. Because the christological reference is paramount, at no point in all our thinking and understanding of the church can we allow anything in the church to obscure Christ himself, to stand in his way or set him aside, or to subordinate him to another interest or end, even momentarily. From first to last Christ is, and must be, all in all.[114]

The relation of the church as body to Christ as head and Lord is determined by the incarnation, the atonement, and Pentecost.

The church's relation to Christ determined by incarnation, atonement and Pentecost

(a) The church is rooted in the incarnate Son – it is the church of the Word made flesh

In the incarnation God's eternal decision to give himself to man in all his freedom and love, and his eternal election of man for fellowship with himself, have become actualised in our midst. That eternal decision or election is the Word of God that has become flesh in Jesus Christ, so that he is himself the reality of the relationship which God has established between himself and mankind, and the life which he lived in the flesh is the effectuation and realisation of the fellowship of mankind with God.[115]

That eternal Word had already come to Israel calling it out of the world as the people entrusted with the oracles of God,[116] as the chosen community in which God communicated himself through his word and summoned man to fellowship with himself. It was the community waiting for fulfilment. With the incarnation of the Word, that divine communication and fellowship were fulfilled in Jesus Christ, for in him the life of God broke into the life of mankind and consummated in its midst, in and around Jesus Christ, a holy fellowship of men and women in communion with God. In him the church is grounded in the eternal purpose of love or divine election that has invaded the world and has been actualised in the beloved Son. This election is essentially corporate in nature and operates in history through the encounter of men and women with the Word made flesh and through their incorporation into him. Thus the Christian church arose rooted in the incarnate life of the Son of

---

[114] Cf. Col 3.11.

[115] See further T.F. Torrance, *Incarnation*, pp. 178-80.

[116] Rom 3.2; cf. Acts 7.38.

God and spread out from him as the community sharing in his revelation and his love. It was initiated into the inner fellowship of the Father and the Son and the Son and the Father, and incorporated into the mission of the saving love of God toward all humanity. It was the community which Jesus bound to himself as his own body, upon which he breathed his divine breath and to which he committed the Word of divine revelation, giving it unity with himself in Spirit and truth.

The church is rooted in Christ's being as individual and corporate, particular and universal

As the body of Christ, the church is the community of believers that inheres in him and coheres round him, in and through which he continues to be known, and in and through which he continues to function in the world. But it is rooted in him and grows out from him as he whose being is both individual and corporate, is particular and yet universal. It is the community in which Jesus Christ is personally present, meeting and addressing each individual and asking of them the personal response of faith and love.[117] It is the sphere of communion with God mediated through personal relations with Christ, in which each member is equally the object of the divine love and equally free to converse and commune with

---

[117] Cf. T.F. Torrance, 'The Mission of the Church', pp. 134-5, where Torrance speaks of the work of the Spirit in the encounter between Jesus as a particular man and each human person, 'It is through this relation in the Spirit that union with Christ is actualised as a concrete reality within the conditions of human life...On the one hand, this is a union between Christ and the church as a whole as a body...On the other hand, this is a union between Christ and each believer. In the incarnation the Son of God became one particular and individual man, for that was the way in which he entered into relation with all humankind in the flesh. Hence in the new economy of the covenant determined by the incarnation, the relations of God with each man and woman are relations through this one man, Jesus. That is to say, the relationship of God with every human being is acutely personalised through personal and historical relation to Jesus. It belongs to the work of the Spirit to function in correlation with this particular man, and so to operate in and through encounter between him and every human person...It is in that encounter that each human being may through the Spirit share in the faith and obedience of Christ, and live personally the life of faith and obedience to him.   *[continued on next page]*

him. But it is the community in which God gives himself to each only as he gives himself to all, and in which he loves each only with the love in which he has bound all to himself. It is such a community of faith and love that in it no one can hear God's word or believe by themselves, for each requires the service of the other, and no one can live unto themselves for each is bound to the need of their brothers and sisters, and all find their life only in him who loved them and gave himself for them and made them his own.[118]

(b) The church is grounded in the atonement – it is the body of the crucified and risen Christ

It is impossible to pass directly from the incarnation of the Word to the church, for the cross comes in between. In other words, the union between God and man in Christ in which the church is rooted could only be consummated through the expiation of sin and the removal of enmity. It was into fallen flesh that the Son of God incorporated himself; it was with sinners in their alienation from God that he identified himself in his incarnation. Hence the will of God to establish fellowship with men and women had to take the form of atonement and reconciliation. The union of God and humanity which the incarnation involved actually intensified the state of enmity between humanity and God. By uniting God to man the judgement of God was brought to bear upon mankind as never before; by uniting man to God man

---

[continued] It is because Christ is himself 'the one and the many', the one who includes the many, and the many who includes each one, that he encounters men and women always and only in this twofold way, within the corporate community of the many, and within the life of each person. It is in that togetherness that the gospel is communicated and received in and through the communion of the Spirit, so that private and corporate communion in the Spirit belong inseparably together and are mutually dependent within the fellowship of the church. It is a corporate communion of mutual participation through the Spirit in Christ and his graces, and a personal communion which each may have with Christ within the corporate communion.' Cf. here T.F. Torrance, *Incarnation*, pp. 228-32 on *Anhypostasis* and *Enhypostasis*, particularly the section 'The *anhypostatic* union and solidarity of Christ with all humanity, and the *enhypostatic* encounter with people in personal relation', p. 231, (cf. also the following section 'The *anhypostatic* assumption of fallen humanity, and the *enhypostatic* purity of Jesus and personal responsibility for sinners').

[118] Gal 2.20; Eph 5.2, cf. 5.25.

was brought under the divine judgement as never before. Therefore the incarnation led straight to the crucifixion of Jesus. He loved the church and gave himself for it; he the just stood in the place of the unjust under the judgement of God and died in taking its place, that the church which had no justification before God might be pardoned and made to stand before God just and holy in him.

The church's relation to Christ determined by substitution, atonement and incorporation

That is the substitutionary relation that determines the way in which the church as body is related to Christ the saviour of the body and head of the church. There atonement and incorporation belong together, but incorporation into Christ is on the ground of the atonement. He who knew no sin was made sin for us that we might be made the righteousness of God in him.[119] Though he was rich, yet for our sakes he became poor that we through his poverty might become rich.[120] He took our place that we might take his place before God. Thus when Christ presents the church to the Father as his own body[121] it is on the ground that he took its place and gave himself in sacrifice on its behalf. Hence as the body of Christ the church is the place where that substitution is actualised within history, for only as it lets Christ take its place, only as it yields place to Christ, is it his body. That relationship between the church and Christ is deeply enshrined in both sacraments of the gospel, baptism being the sacrament of substitution and of justification in Christ, holy communion the sacrament in which the church takes shelter in the sacrifice of Christ as its only plea before God, and continues to deny itself, taking up Christ's cross until he come.

The other side of the crucifixion of Christ, however, is the resurrection in which he has triumphed over all that separates and divides from God, and therefore the obverse of the crucifixion of the church with Christ is its resurrection in him to stand before the Father, cleansed and renewed and clothed with divine righteousness and filled with the divine life. United with Christ in his death, it is raised with him in the power of his resurrection,[122] so that ever afterwards the church is the body of Christ because it is united, in all its believers, to the risen body of its saviour.

---

[119] 2 Cor 5.21.

[120] 2 Cor 8.9.

[121] Cf. Heb 10.10,12-14, cf. 2.13.

[122] Rom 6.4f.

(c) *The church is united to Christ through the communion of the Spirit – it is the body of the ascended Lord, the head of all things visible and invisible*[123]

The church is also rooted and grounded in Christ by being incorporated into him through his Word and Spirit. It is called into fellowship with him and united to him by the baptism of the Spirit, so that its members are made to share in Christ's obedient life and are assimilated to his new humanity. Thus the incorporation of Christ into our humanity, his becoming one body with us sinners in order to reconcile us to God, has as its correlative[124] the incorporation of the church into him as the body of those who through faith in his word and the communion of the Spirit become partakers of him and of all that he has done on our behalf.[125] This incorporation into Christ can be regarded on the one hand as the subjective actualisation in us through the Spirit of the objective revelation and reconciliation fulfilled in the incarnation and atonement. Yet this is not something in addition to the finished work of Christ, but rather that same work effectively operative in the church. On the other hand this incorporation into Christ through the Spirit is to be regarded as our participation in the new covenant in him. In his own life and death, in his own body and blood, Jesus Christ has fulfilled once and for all the holy will of God toward man, and fulfilled for all humanity their true relation toward God. He fulfilled the covenant as God's act of saving grace, but fulfilled it also as mankind's response to God's grace in laying hold of God and in receiving from God the gift of the Spirit. Thus in pouring out upon the church the same Spirit which was poured out without measure upon himself,[126] Christ assimilates the church into the new covenant in his body and blood and makes it the heir of all its riches and promises.

---

[123] See further T.F. Torrance, 'The Mission of the Church', pp. 132-36, the sections on *The Sending of the Spirit* and on *The Church is the Communion of the Spirit*.

[124] Corresponding movement; *correlative*, corresponding, complementary, reciprocal.

[125] Cf. 'The Mission of the Church', p. 133, 'The communion of the Spirit has to be understood as correlative to the union of God and man wrought out in the incarnation, life and work of Jesus Christ.'

[126] John 1.32-33, 3.34; cf. 7.37-39, 15.26, 16.7, 20.22; Acts 2.33; cf. Luke 3.16,21-22, 4.1,14,18-19; Acts 1.4ff., 2.1ff.

Hence the participation of the church in Christ does not add anything to the perfection of what he has already accomplished, but it is a sharing through the Spirit in the whole self-offering of Christ to the Father, a sharing in the power of his resurrection and an assimilation to his divine-human life.

(i) The twofold incorporation, of incarnation and the baptism of the Spirit, is the basis of the church as the body of Christ

It is this twofold incorporation through the incarnation and through the baptism of the Spirit that gives us the doctrine of the church as the body of Christ. That the church is the body of Christ refers first to the fact that he has embodied himself in our humanity and through his atoning life and death made himself one body with us, and it refers secondly to our embodiment in him through union and communion with him.[127] Between his embodiment of himself in us and our embodiment in him there is the atoning work of Christ on the cross and the pouring out of the Spirit at Pentecost. The church is not therefore the extension of the incarnation or the prolongation of Christ in the world. It is the body of sinners with which he has identified himself and which he has graciously assumed into unity with himself as the earthly and historical form of his existence. He has united it to himself in his new covenant, pouring into it his own Spirit and divine life and refusing to be separated from it. He will not divorce his church. He will not break his covenant. Even if the church becomes unfaithful, he will remain faithful, and will bring it at last to perfect purity and holiness, presenting it to himself as a chaste virgin.[128]

Body and bride, united to and yet still distanced from Christ

The fact that the New Testament speaks of the church both as the body and as the bride of Christ makes clear that while it is united and affianced or betrothed to him, its union is yet to be consummated.[129]

---

[127] Cf. Torrance, *loc. cit.* 'There are not two unions, the one which Christ has with us which he established in his incarnation, and another which we have with him through the Spirit or through faith. There is only one union which Christ has created between himself and us and us and himself, and in which we participate through the Spirit which he has given us. The church can thus be spoken of as the corporate union we have with Christ through the communion of the Spirit.'

[128] Cf. Eph 5.25-32.

[129] Eph 5.25-32; Rev 19.7f., 21.2f.,9f., 22.17.

The distance between Christ and his church is made clear in the ascension, for it was only when he had ascended as the Lord and head of the church that he poured out his Spirit upon it and dwelt within it as his body on earth. The oneness and the difference, the likeness and unlikeness between Christ and his church cannot be confused without grave error. In all its union with Christ, the church remains distinct from him and must never be confounded with him. The church must never try to usurp his place and give itself out to be another Christ (*alter Christus*), and so stand between people and Christ, arrogating to itself what belongs to Christ alone. The church is only the body of Christ and remains other than he even in its union with him, for he alone is the saviour and head of the body, the Lord and husband of the church.[130]

(ii) Similarity and dissimilarity between the hypostatic union in Christ and the church's union with him

Because the church is united to Christ and brought into conformity to him through the Spirit, its relation to Christ is both like and unlike the relation between his deity and his humanity. In Jesus Christ divine nature and human nature are united in such a way that they cannot be separated from one another or be confused with one another, but are united within the one divine person of the Son.[131] In the relation between Christ and his church, the divine-human nature of Christ and the human nature of the church are likewise united in such a way that they are neither to be separated nor to be confused, but they are not hypostatically united within one person. The hypostatic union in Christ himself is utterly unique and unrepeatable. The union between Christ and his church is a union between the one person of the Son of God and the whole company of creaturely persons whom he has gathered and incorporated into himself as his body, but within that body the individual persons remain human and distinct. Although they participate in the human nature of Christ and share in his divine life and love, they are not made gods, and although they are compacted together into one indivisible body they remain differentiated in their individuality. In the communion of the Spirit, the unity and multiplicity of the people of God is maintained, and far from being swallowed up in deity they are all affirmed and loved and upheld in their creaturehood.

---

[130] Eph 5.23.

[131] For a fuller statement of the nature and significance of the 'hypostatic union', the union of divine and human natures in the one person (*hypostasis*) of the eternal Son, see T.F. Torrance, *Incarnation*, p. 83, 199f., 206ff.

The difference between Christ's sinless union with fallen humanity and the church's union with him

In its union with Christ, the church is also unlike him in that its union with him is one between sinners and their saviour. In the hypostatic union on the other hand, while the Son of God incorporated himself into our fallen flesh in the incarnation and took to himself a body from our corrupted and alienated humanity, he healed and sanctified it in the very act of his assumption, condemning sin in the flesh[132] by his holiness and living out from beginning to end a perfectly sinless life. But the church is a body of sinners forgiven and redeemed by Christ. Although the church is sanctified and consecrated in Christ and his self-consecration on its behalf, its constituent members remain sinners constantly in need of his pardon and healing and sanctifying, and therefore until he comes again they must be ever renewed in their membership of his body through participation in his body and blood, individually and corporately. Thus it is in holy communion that the church ever becomes what Christ in his grace has made it, when he loved it and gave himself for it and adopted it as his own body.

The church is at once holy as part of Christ and stands with sinners needing forgiveness

When we speak of the church as the body of Christ meaning the whole Christ, head and members, we must speak of it as sinless and perfectly holy, for then we speak of the church in its concentration in Christ himself. But when we speak of the church as the body of Christ meaning the body of sinners with which he identified himself in life and death, so that through the crucifixion of the body of sin he might raise it a glorious body[133] clothed with his own holiness and purity, then we speak of the church as constantly in need of forgiveness and constantly directed away from itself to find in Christ alone its justification and its sanctification. Yet it is this very body, constituted out of sinful men and women, that Christ appropriates as his very own and brings into such union and communion with himself that, in spite of sin, he dwells within it and heals and hallows it and makes it the instrument of his saving love among all nations. This church cannot dissociate itself from the sinners that make up its membership or reckon itself untarnished by their sin and error and so separate itself from them. The church does not stand on the side of the redeemer who died and rose again for all, but stands on the side of those for whom Christ died, who

---

[132] Rom 8.4.

[133] Rom 6.6 KJV, cf. 8.10; Phil 3.21.

come under the total judgement of the cross and are called to deny themselves and take up the cross and follow Christ. Hence far from standing aloof from the world, the church can only stand with it in the solidarity of the sin in which it is concluded and judged by the grace and justification of God. Only then can it proclaim and minister to it the saving love of God in the good news of the gospel that Jesus Christ himself was made sin for us that we might be made the righteousness of God in him.[134]

(iii) The triangular relation of the church on earth to the historical, ascended and advent Christ

As the body of Christ on earth the church has a triangular relation to Christ: to the historical and crucified Christ, to the risen and ascended Christ, and to the advent Christ who comes to judge and renew his creation. By withdrawing himself in his ascension from visible and tangible contact, Jesus Christ sends the church back to the apostolic witness to the historical and crucified Jesus, for there it finds its root in the life and work of the messiah and its basic structure in the messianic community which he gathered and built around himself. By pouring out his Spirit upon the church Jesus Christ makes it partake of the power of his resurrection, transforming it into a spiritual body filled with his own presence and making it the place among humanity where his saving acts continue to operate effectively for all who hear and believe in the gospel. By ascending and waiting in mercy, Jesus Christ has established the church in history in order that it may fulfil the mission of reconciliation on which he has sent it, but because he to whom it is united will come again in judgement and renewal, the church is continually called to repentance looking to the judgement which will begin at the house of God,[135] continually renewed by the power of the Spirit and partaking already in time of the eternal life which it will receive in fullness in the new creation. Meantime the church lives and works between the times, between the time of Christ's first advent in grace and humiliation and his final advent in glory and power. Through the Spirit it is not only established once and for all upon the finished work of Christ, it is not only stretched out in hope and eager expectation waiting for the coming and manifestation of the kingdom, but it lives in communion with its Lord from age to age and serves the purpose of his mercy in which he waits to bring all things to their consummation.

---

[134]   2 Cor 5.21.

[135]   1 Peter 4.17.

3 The life and mission of the church

The being of the church in Christ and its nature as love

The term communion or *koinōnia* applied to the church refers primarily to our participation through the Spirit in Jesus Christ and therefore in the holy Trinity, but it refers secondarily to the communion or fellowship which we have with one another on that basis. It is a joint or conjoint participation in Christ and therefore a corporate fellowship in him which we have on earth. Through the Spirit the *being* of the church is grounded in the being of Christ – that is the ontological[136] basis or *esse*[137] of the church. But through the Spirit the *nature* of the church derives from the love of God in Christ poured out upon the church. The very nature of the church is therefore *agapē*[138] which it is the life of the church to express. The being and the nature of the church are inseparable, but whereas the *being* of the church refers to its ontological rooting in the incarnate Son, the *nature* of the church refers to the life of the church in which it grows up into Christ in love and which it manifests in love toward the world.[139]

The church's being and nature in Christ are inseparable from its mission of love

The being and nature of the church are equally inseparable from its *mission*, that is, its sending by Christ on the mission of the love of God, just as the sending of Christ by the Father is inseparable from his being and nature as the incarnate Son. As the Father loves the Son, so the Son loves the church;[140] as the Son was sent by the Father, so the church is sent by the Son.[141] Since the being and nature and the mission of the church interpenetrate each other in the concrete life of the church, we can never think of the being and nature of the church statically, but always in terms of the divine act, the divine movement of love from God to man, and from man to God and man to fellow man in a gathering of the life of men and women into communion with the life of God.

---

[136] To do with 'being', involving the nature or essence of something, from the Gk *onta*, what is, reality – hence, fundamental, essential, grounded on being or reality.

[137] Lat, *to be*, hence 'very being'.

[138] Gk, love.

[139] Eph 4.15-16; Col 2.6-7, cf. 1.17-19.

[140] John 3.35, 13.34-35, 15.9f., 17.26.

[141] John 20.21.

This double, active communion is what is involved in the designation of the church as 'the body of Christ' – that is, not the exclusive company of the privileged, but the company of men and women bound into one body with Christ and so filled with his Spirit and love that it becomes an ever widening communion in which the church presses out in expansion toward a fullness in the love of God in all its height and depth and length and breadth which more and more assimilates to itself men and women from the ends of the earth.[142]

(a) The church is a communion of love

The Spirit is God in his freedom to be present to creation in the overflow of the divine love

The Spirit of God is God in his freedom to be present to his creation and to realise its relation to himself, giving it true being and life.[143] In sending his Spirit upon the church Jesus Christ is free to be present to it, not from without and above it, but from below and within it, in order to realise its true relation to himself. Through the Spirit he not only meets the church and adopts is as his own body but dwells within it, giving it life and adapting it for communion with God. In this way he creates out of the church a community within humanity where the love of God is poured out freely by the Holy Spirit, and where men and women, in their life on earth and within the social cohesions of human nature, are given to share together in the overflow of the divine life in love.

The life of the church is indwelling the love of God in Christ

God is love, so that the church that dwells in love, dwells in God and God in it.[144] By making the church the dwelling place of the Father and the Son, the Spirit makes the church participate in the concrete embodiment of the love of God in the incarnate Son.[145] It is in that indwelling and love that the church has its essential life. Love in the church is precisely its participation in the humanity of Jesus Christ for he is the love of God poured out for mankind. In him it is rooted and

---

[142] Cf. Eph 3.8f.,17-19, 4.13f.

[143] See T.F. Torrance, *The Christian Doctrine of God*, T & T Clark, Edinburgh 1996, p. 60, 218; cf. T.F. Torrance, *The Trinitarian Faith*, T & T Clark, Edinburgh 1988, pp. 227-29, for sources of this understanding in the Greek fathers.

[144] 1 John 4.8f.,12f.,16.

[145] John 14.23 and see the whole context, 14.15 to 16.15.

grounded in love, and in him it becomes itself a communion of love through which the life of God flows out in love toward every human being. As he is, so are we in this world.[146]

Christ's life of servant love the pattern for the church

In Jesus Christ the form that the love of God took was the form of a servant who poured out his life for mankind, but the form that God's love took in him is the pattern for the communion of love in the church.[147] What he has done to us we are to do to one another, each serving the other in love,[148] each spending our life in the service of the love of God toward all. Jesus Christ poured out his life in ransom for the many for he was the redeemer who made atonement for the sins of the world, and he is the only mediator between man and God.[149] The church is sent by him to live out its divinely given life among men and women and by love to bring them into the fellowship of healing and peace with God. But it follows in the steps of Christ the servant of God, not in order to be a co-redeemer with him, but to identify itself with the world in its sin and guilt, to bear it up in prayer and intercession before God and in sympathy and compassion born of the overflowing love of God to spend itself in the service of the gospel, until all humanity are confronted with the saviour and all nations and people are brought within the active reign of Christ.

The church can only fulfil its mission by being a fellowship of reconciliation

In order to fulfil that mission the church must be in itself a communion of love, a fellowship of reconciliation – it must live out in its own life the reconciling love of God which brought it into existence and determines its innermost being. The church can be such a fellowship only as it lives from out of its centre in Christ, for in him God has established a place in the midst of the world where all division and hostility are overcome and where the mutual relations between man and God, and man and fellow man disrupted by sin are restored. It is through the common participation of all members in this centre that the church is restored to its true life of mutual sharing and love. Participation in Christ carries with it participation in one another, and our common reconciliation with Christ carries with it reconciliation with one another. That is the communion of love

---

[146] 1 John 4.17.

[147] Phil 2.1-8.

[148] Gal 5.13; cf. John 13.15,34, 15.12.

[149] Mark 10.45 (Matt 20.28); 1 John 2.2; 1 Tim 2.5.

maintained by the Spirit, within which the Father and Son dwell, and by means of which the kingdom of God's love is extended over all the world.

(b) The church is the community informed with the mind of Christ

By its very nature the church is not self-centred but Christ-centred, for it is the community of those who have been redeemed from sin and self-will to live and act only in the name of Christ. It is the community of those who die with Christ and rise again to be new creatures, who are crucified to their old selfish ways of thinking and acting and are transformed in Christ so that they no longer live unto themselves but unto him.[150] That transformation in our inner self in which we learn to think from a centre in God rather than from a centre in ourselves is the basic reorientation that takes place in the church of Jesus Christ. Christian discipleship is the disciplined habit of thinking and acting *in Christ*, for he is the one place where we may really worship God and believe in him as our Father.[151]

Reconciliaton and transformation in mind

Because the church is united to Jesus Christ in spirit as in body, it must not only live out in its bodily existence the reconciling love that was embodied in Jesus Christ, but it must let the mind that was in Christ be in its mind, in order that the whole understanding of the church may be transformed and renewed in him,[152] and in order that the whole structure of its thought may be determined by his truth. In other words the church must be reconciled in the depths of its conscience, in that joint-knowing (*con-scientia*) which its members have together with God in Christ and with one another in Christ. This is the theological task of the church which takes place under the critical and creative operation of the Spirit as the church listens to God's word and seeks to be obedient to it in all its knowing and thinking of the truth.

Theology primarily the function of the church – learning the mind of Christ with others

Theology is not primarily the function of individuals but of the church, for Christian thinking is essentially joint-thinking, thinking-in-fellowship, in which we share with one another and learn from one

---

[150]   Rom 6.3ff.; Gal 2.20; 2 Cor 5.15.

[151]   Cf. John 4.20-26.

[152]   Phil 2.5 KJV; Rom 12.2.

another in Christ, and refuse to run off on private byways of our own. Christian thinking is essentially ecumenical thinking in which we submit ourselves to the teaching and criticism of others that we may learn more and more of Christ through them and with them seek to let the one mind that is in Christ be in our mind.[153]

To have the mind of Christ is to be ready at all times to understand the other person's point of view, to regard them in Christ, to listen to what Christ has to say to us through them, and to rethink our own views in the light of what we thus learn. The Christian way of thinking is always open to the thinking of other Christians, and is always ready to repent, to revise and reconstruct its own ways in order to become more and more conformable to Christ. The Christian way of thinking seeks to make the conscience of the other person one's own while sharing one's own conscience with the other, that in a common knowing of the one Christ we may have a common mind and a common conscience in him. The individual that takes their own private road, without regard to the conscience of others, is essentially a fanatic if not a heretic, and the 'church' that entrenches itself behind its own self-centred position without regard to the convictions of other Christians is fundamentally fanatical or sectarian.

The discipline of theology – bringing the church's understanding under the word of God that it may be conformed to Christ[154]

In and with the Christian thinking of its members, the church as a whole must constantly engage in the discipline of theology in which it brings its teaching and preaching and worship to the criticism of God's word in order that through repentant self-denial it may be conformed in mind and understanding to the mind of Christ. It must concern itself with the integrated and orderly unfolding of the content of the Word of God according to the Word's own essential norms as they operate effectively and creatively within the mind of the historical church. The church that is built upon the apostles and prophets continues to be the church of Christ as it continues in the apostolic tradition of obedience to Jesus Christ. It is by constant listening to the Word of God speaking through the holy scriptures delivered to the

---

[153] Phil 2.5 KJV.

[154] See further here T.F. Torrance, *Theology in Reconstruction*, SCM Press, London 1965, chap. 8, 'The Place of Christology in Biblical and Dogmatic Theology', esp. p. 140f., 145ff. For a summary of Torrance's understanding of the nature and purpose of theology and dogmatics see T.F. Torrance, *Incarnation*, pp. xxiii-xxix.

church by the apostles, by being drawn into, and by continuing within, the sphere of the apostolic community in which the risen and ascended Lord fulfils his own revelation and reconciliation among men and women, by submitting in the obedience of faith[155] to the same revelation and reconciliation, that the church continues to be ever the same, 'identical with itself', in its sole foundation in Christ. Then it lives throughout all the changes of history and all temporal succession in such a way as not to be conformed to this world, but to be transformed by the renewing of its mind[156] and so conformed to Christ. It is within that movement of growth and change, continuity and identity, that the church is charged with maintaining doctrinal purity, with the discipline of assimilating all its thinking and speaking to the mind of Christ, that it may continue to be built up in him as a habitation or dwelling place of God, and may continue to grow up in him as the body of which he is the head and so stand before the world as the pillar of truth.[157]

(c) The church is sent out into the world as the servant and herald of Christ

The church that is united to Christ in love and truth[158] is sent out by him into the world to be his image in human society, to express and hold him forth before all, and so to be the medium of his own self-communication and self-revelation to mankind.

When Jesus Christ ascended to the throne of God he entered upon his universal kingdom, filling all things with his presence through the Spirit.[159] But in uniting to himself the church on earth as his earthly and historical form of existence, he endowed it with the keys of the kingdom[160] and made it his bodily instrument in the service of the gospel, that in and through the church acting in his name, he himself might be present in its midst fulfilling his own ministry of reconciliation to all humanity. In the days of his flesh, he had already laid the foundations of the church in the disciples whom he gathered around him and by

---

155   Rom 1.5; cf. 2 Cor 10.5 KJV.

156   Rom 12.2.

157   Eph 2.20-22, 4.15-16; Col 1.18, 2.19; 1 Tim 3.15.

158   In addition to the Johannine emphasis on 'life' and 'love' (as on 'light') see also that on 'truth' in the Gospel and all three letters of John, e.g. John 8.32, 14.6, 15.26, 16.13f., 17.19; 1 John 1.6,8, 2.4,8,21, 3.18 etc.

159   Cf. Eph 4.10.

160   Matt 16.19.

incorporating them into his own messianic mission as heralds and apostles he gave their ministry a shape and a structure patterned on his own. After his resurrection he recommissioned the apostles in his service. As the Father had sent him so he sent them, breathing on them his Spirit and saying, 'If you forgive the sins of any, they are forgiven; if you retain the sins of any, they are retained.'[161] Having himself received all power in heaven and earth, he sent them into all the world with a commission to preach and teach in his name and poured out his Spirit upon the whole church that all its members might exercise a ministry of witness and reconciliation according to the gifts which he sent down upon them.[162]

The church's ministry as body is correlative to Christ's ministry as head[163]

Because Jesus Christ is pleased in this way to use the church as his body and to use it in his ministry of reconciliation, we must think of the ministry of the church as correlative to the ministry of Christ and yet as quite different from his. The ministry of the church is the function of the body appropriate to it as the body of which he is the head, but the ministry of Christ is the unique ministry of the saviour.[164] He exercises his ministry as king and Lord over the church. The church exercises its ministry as herald and servant in obedience to him. Yet the kind of service that the church performs as the body of Christ is not that of an impersonal instrument or a mere institution controlled by him, but the service of love freely and thankfully yielded to the saviour.

The servant pointing to Christ and not to itself

It is in the fulfilment of this ministry that the church learns to find its life more and more not in itself but beyond itself in Jesus Christ, the ascended head of the church. Thus the mission or function of the church is not to be understood as the operation of its own immanent processes, but as the service of Christ and his saving purpose for all. The church fulfils its ministry not by calling attention to itself but by pointing away from itself to the fullness of Christ. Indeed the whole life and mission of the church is inseparably bound up with its function in serving the gospel of Christ, so that its edification in history, its growth through

---

[161] John 20.21-23.

[162] Matt 28.18f.; Acts 2.33; Eph 4.7f.; cf. Rom 12.6f.; 1Cor 12.4ff.

[163] On the relation of the church's ministry to that of Christ, see T.F. Torrance, *Royal Priesthood*, 2nd edition, T & T Clark, Edinburgh 1993, p. 35ff.

[164] *Op. cit.* p. 35,37.

the ages, and all its ministry, are oriented toward the fullness of God's purpose of love that awaits its revelation in the advent of Christ.

In this perspective nothing could be worse than for the church to call attention to itself, to proclaim itself as if it were the salvation of humanity. To put itself in the place of Christ is doubtless the temptation of the church in all ages, but to yield to that temptation would be the greatest sin that could be committed in the church. Certainly the church must stand over against the world as the community in which the Spirit of Christ is at work for the saving and renewing of the world, and it cannot help but call attention to itself in that respect, but if so it can only manifest itself as the provisional form which the new creation assumes here and now in the ambiguities of history, as it presses forward to and waits for the revelation of its fullness in the *parousia* of its Lord. Thus far from regarding itself as an end in itself on earth, the church regards itself as the instrument of the ascended king and head of the church for the extension of his kingdom. It regards itself solely as the servant of the Lord engaged by him in the work of his vineyard. The last thing it can do is to usurp the vineyard for itself, and so reject the rightful heir when he returns from the far country.[165] Everything that the church has and is, is held in trust in the service of the ascended and advent Lord. Thus the whole life of the church on earth is a fellowship of action in the service of the gospel, while all that concerns its edification and growth in history is subordinated to this end – the proclamation of the Lordship of Christ and the praise of the glory of God.

4 The attributes of the church

'I believe in one, holy, catholic, and apostolic church'[166]

The attributes of the church are first and foremost attributes of Christ himself

The unity, holiness, catholicity, and apostolicity of the church are the four **notes** affirmed by the creed in distinguishing the church of Christ throughout the centuries. They do not denote independent qualities inhering in the church, but are affirmations of the nature of the church as it participates in Jesus Christ and are strictly discernible only to faith. The **marks** of the church, the word of God purely preached, the sacraments of the gospel rightly administered, and godly discipline,

---

[165] Matt 21.33ff.; Mark 12.1ff.; Luke 20.9ff.

[166] Cf. the exposition of this section of the Nicene-Constaninopolitan Creed in T.F. Torrance, *The Trinitarian Faith*, p. 279ff.

indicate where the true church is to be found; they do not define it or describe it but point to it. The **notes** of the church, however, describe the essential properties of the church which it derives from its foundation in Jesus Christ. *They are first of all attributes of Christ himself, but attributes in which the church shares through its union and communion with him.* Therefore in the unity, holiness, catholicity, and apostolicity of the church it is the image and face of Christ himself that comes to view and is discerned and affirmed by faith.

(a) The oneness or unity of the church

(i) The oneness of the church goes back through union with Christ to the triune oneness of God

The oneness of the church derives ultimately from the triunity of God. Because there is only one God and Father of all, there has been and is and will be only one people of God in all ages from the beginning of the world to its end.[167] It is not a oneness that derives from the people themselves but a oneness that derives from the life of God above. As in God himself there is one holy fellowship of love, so there is only one holy fellowship of love in the church, the counterpart on earth to the unity in God of Father, Son and Holy Spirit.

The church participates in that oneness through union with Jesus Christ, for as he and the Father are one so he has consecrated the church into oneness with himself in God.[168] It is because Christ is one, one in whom the fullness of the Godhead dwells bodily, that the church which is his body is one.[169] Its principle and centre of unity do not lie in itself but in him, and therefore it is a unity which is given to it by him and in which it participates freely through union and communion with him.

The church includes an infinite multitude of people in all ages and comprises a diversity as wide as the creation itself, yet it is essentially one in Jesus Christ who is the only mediator between God and man and who reconciles and gathers up all things in himself.[170] He alone constitutes and organises the many members of the church into unity, giving the church in its many members to participate in his one and unique relation to the Father through the Holy Spirit, and maintaining it and securing it in that unity by including it within the one body of which he is the head.

---

[167] Eph 4.4-6; cf. 1 Cor 8.6, 12.4f.,12-13; Eph 2.11-3.19; cf. Heb 11.39-12.2, 12.22-24, 13.14.

[168] Cf. John 17.11,19-23.

[169] Cf. 1 Cor 1.13; Col 1.19, 2.9; Eph 2.14-16, 4.3ff.

[170] Rev 7.9; 1 Tim 4.4f.; Col 1.20; Eph 1.10.

(ii) The oneness of the church is grounded in the incarnation and atonement

This oneness of the church is grounded in the incarnation and in the atonement. In Jesus Christ the one Word of God, by whom all men and women were made and in whom all men and women cohere, became flesh[171] and incorporates into himself all who believe, compacting them together into one universal body. It is a oneness which he has formed and created out of broken and divided humanity, a oneness which derives from his expiatory and reconciling work in overcoming all division between God and man, and between man and fellow man. Thus the oneness of the church among its members derives from the oneness of the church with God wrought out in atonement through the blood of Christ. The very existence of the church is grounded in the overcoming of division, in the abolishing of the disunity between mankind and God and the overcoming of the enmity of sin[172] and the separation of guilt. Just because the unity of the church is rooted and grounded in the incarnate and atoning work of Christ, it can no more be destroyed than the incarnation and atonement can be undone or God go back upon the death of his dear Son. But for the same reason, for the people of God to live in disunity, for the church to allow the divisions of the world to penetrate back into its life, is to live in disagreement with its own existence, to call in question its reconciliation and to act a lie against the atonement.

A divided church is something so terrible that it reaches back behind the church to its constitutive relation to God, to its faith in Jesus Christ himself. Is Christ divided?[173] As there is only one Christ and one atonement, so there can be only one church united in Christ. Therefore a disunited church is an attack upon Christ himself and a direct contradiction of his atonement.

The reconciliation demanded and renewed through participation in holy communion[174]

It is particularly at the table of the Lord that disunity and division in the church is so scandalous. The discipline of the Lord teaches us that because the holy supper witnesses to our unity in Christ, we must first be reconciled with our brother and sister before we

---

[171] John 1.1f.,14; 1 Cor 8.6; Col 1.16f.; Heb 1.2f.

[172] Cf. Rom 8.7 & Eph 2.15-16 KJV (RSV hostility); James 4.4.

[173] 1 Cor 1.13.

[174] Paragraph abridged and added from T.F. Torrance, 'The Mission of the Church', p. 143.

bring our gift to the altar,[175] but it also teaches us that it is here above all that we are renewed in our reconciliation with our Lord, and therefore that it is by this renewal that we can be reconciled to one another. The oneness of churches in Christ therefore demands both a resolve before communion to seek reconciliation with one another and a resolve in and through communion to work out together a unity that is as actual in the body, in outward discipline and polity, as our joint participation in the holy sacrament. 'Let this mind be in you, which was also in Christ Jesus'.[176] That is what actually takes place when we communicate in the body and blood of Christ in the holy supper and resolve to be obedient, like him, even unto the death of the cross.[177]

(iii) The oneness of the church derives likewise from the one Spirit of God

The oneness of the church derives also from the one Spirit of God through whom it is united to Christ. The Spirit is the principle of multiplicity as well as unity, but he is the principle of unity in the heart and wealth of all multiplicity.[178] Therefore when he came upon the church at Pentecost binding the people of God together in one, it was the antithesis of Babel,[179] the dividing and confounding of the people gathered to glorify their own name, for at Pentecost the ancient promises and prophecies of the healing and restoration and reunion of God's people are fulfilled as they call upon the name of God and are saved, as they are given one heart and one mind and one voice in their praise and thanksgiving to God for Jesus Christ his Son.[180] Because he sheds abroad the love of God in the hearts of the people of God,[181] he heals their dissensions and restores them to fellowship and unity with one another in God. Therefore the continuance of division in the church cannot but grieve and quench the Spirit in its midst,[182] cripple and weaken the church and destroy the roots of its communion with the life and love of God.

---

[175] Matt 5.23-24.

[176] Phil 2.5 KJV.

[177] Phil 2.8 KJV.

[178] 1 Cor 12.4ff.; Eph 2.18f., 4.3f.

[179] Gen 11.1-9.

[180] Acts 2.44f., 4.12,24f.,32.

[181] Rom 5.5 KJV.

[182] Eph 4.30f.; cf. 4.3 & 1 Thess 5.19.

(iv) The unity of the church is both bodily and spiritual

Because the church is united to Christ in body and in Spirit its unity is both bodily and spiritual. It cannot have a unity in the Spirit without working it out in its physical existence in the flesh and in the concrete relations of human society and life.[183] Its unity is not built up from the flesh, it is not made with hands and is not constructed out of the visible organisation of the church. Therefore its centre and source of unity do not lie in some visible and tangible principle that can be manipulated by human agency. It is a unity that is given to it by God, that is supernaturally created within it by the Holy Spirit, that is begotten of its unity with Jesus Christ, but for that very reason it is a unity that involves bodily and visible oneness. The church is not the body of the Spirit, but through the Spirit the body of the incarnate and risen Son of God. It is the unity of the church as a spiritual body, living out in its flesh and blood existence its unity with Christ and its obedience to his atoning reconciliation. It behaves and acts in space and time in such a way that the order and unity of its physical and temporal life are in worthy agreement with the gospel by which it lives.

(v) The unity of the church on earth and in heaven

Because the church is united to Christ through the communion of the Spirit, there is no division between the church triumphant and the church militant, between the church invisible, hid with Christ in God, and the church visible on earth for it is the visible church on earth that is hid with Christ in God.[184] Death is swallowed up and destroyed in Christ's death and resurrection[185] so that there is only one communion of saints in heaven and earth. There are not two churches, the one earthly and historical, the other supernatural and spiritual, the one visible and tangible and the other mystical. There is only one body which has an earthly and historical form within this world, but a heavenly form within the new world of God. And it is in that one all-inclusive communion that the church lives and works on earth and worships the Father in heaven.

---

[183] Cf. the argument of 1 Corinthians that the life of Christ must be lived out by the church in unity and in the ordering of its bodily life in the Spirit, e.g. chap. 6.19-20.

[184] Col 3.1, 'For you have died, and your life is hid with Christ in God.'

[185] 1 Cor 15.1ff.,54.

(b) The holiness of the church

God's hallowing of himself in the midst of his people

In its ultimate sense, the holiness of the church is its relation to God, its participation in the fellowship of the divine being and life and truth. 'You shall be holy, for I the LORD your God am holy'.[186] The Israel of the Old Testament was a holy people *because God hallowed or sanctified himself in its midst*. By bestowing upon it his own presence he brought it within the sphere of his own holiness. Thus the very term 'holy' carries with it the notion of the church as the sphere among humanity of God's hallowing. It is therefore with the incarnation of the Son of God, the presence of the Holy One of God in the midst of our humanity,[187] that the church came into being as the community around Christ, participating in his self-sanctification as he lived out in its midst his holy life, expiating sin and restoring human nature in himself to communion with God.

(i) The 'holiness' of the church is its participation in the unique holiness of God

Holy church refers to a unique relation to God, in which as one and holy (the *Una Sancta*)[188] the church is drawn into the holiness of God himself, into the fellowship of the holy Trinity, partaking of that fellowship through the Holy Spirit. *Holy* church refers to the ontological[189] grounding of the being of the church in the self-impartation and self-revelation of God to it, thus sharing with it his own holy life and informing and purifying its mind with his divine truth.

As such the church is distinguished from the world. Although it is in the midst of the world, the church as holy or godly stands out in the world as the people living within the world that is God's world and clothed with divine gifts and qualities. That distinguishes the church from all other communities and bodies in the world. The church as holy is not a natural community like any of the other fellowships or social entities among the peoples of history. Holy church means that the church is church through God alone, having

---

[186] Lev 19.2, 20.7-8, 20.26, cf. 11.44-45.

[187] Isaiah 12.6, 30.15, 41.14, 43.3,14,15, 48.17 etc; Ezek 39.7; Hosea 11.9; Mark 1.24; Acts 3.14.

[188] Lat, *una*, one; *sancta*, holy.

[189] Concerning the very nature of things in their inner reality.

its own unique ground and its own unique end in God. Hence however much the church in history and on earth may be conditioned by involvement in this or that society, nation or race, the church stands out against all that as distinct, in holy relation to holy God through the Holy Spirit. As such and over against all worldly and cosmic entities, the church has its own essential life, its own essential form and order, its own inner law and being.

(ii) The holiness of the church is its sharing in the self-sanctification of Christ

The holiness of the church is derived from God through Jesus Christ, through his self-sanctification or self-consecration in life and death on our behalf. He sanctified himself in the human nature that he took from us, that we might be sanctified through the Word and truth of God incarnated in him.[190] In the person of Christ himself there took place a holy union between divine nature and human nature. In him God humbled himself to enter into our estranged existence and unite himself to us, but in that movement of grace in the atoning life and death and resurrection of Jesus Christ he has exalted our human nature into union with his own divine life. That took place uniquely in Jesus Christ, for he only is the Holy One of God. He only has divine nature, but through union with him in his human nature, hallowed and sanctified by the truth of God, the church is marvellously made a partaker of divine nature.[191] Hence the holiness of the church is the holiness of Christ in which it shares by grace, being anointed with his anointing, sanctified with his sanctification, and so sharing in his holy relation to the Father through the Holy Spirit.

(iii) The holiness of the church is its participation through the Spirit in Christ's holiness

This holiness is actualised in the church through the communion of the Holy Spirit. He only is the Spirit of holiness, he only the Spirit of truth;[192] and therefore it is only through his presence and power in the church that it partakes of the holiness of Jesus Christ. Since the holiness of the church is its participation through the Spirit in Christ's act of self-consecration for the church, then that is the

---

[190]   John 17.17-19 (KJV 'sanctify'; RSV 'consecrate'); cf. Heb 2.11-17, 10.10.

[191]   2 Peter 1.4.

[192]   Rom 1.4; John 14.17, 16.13.

only holiness, the only hallowing of the church that there is. That is the holiness which was actualised in the church when it was baptised with the Holy Spirit at Pentecost and the union of the church with Christ was fulfilled from the side of the church as well as from the side of Christ.

The church is not holy because its members are holy or live virtuous lives, but because through his presence in the Holy Spirit Christ continues to hallow himself in the midst of the church, hallowing the church as his body and the body as his church. Thus the true holiness of the members is not different from this but a participation in it, a participation in the holiness of Christ the head of the church and in the holiness of the church as the body hallowed by Christ. Participation in this holiness however involves for the members of the church a life of holiness, just as it involves a life *in Christ*, of faith relying upon his faithfulness, of love that lives from the overflow of his love, of truth that comes from the leading of the Spirit. Because the church is the body of Christ in which he dwells, the temple of the Holy Spirit in which God is present,[193] its members live the very life of Christ through the Holy Spirit, partaking of and living out the holy life of God. Therefore their personal holiness, and all the qualities of the divine life and love found in their lives, are the fruits of the Holy Spirit.[194]

(1) The holiness and sanctification of the church is already complete in Christ

Because the holiness of the church is its participation through the Spirit in the self-sanctification of Christ that has already been completed, the church is holy in a once and for all sense. Just as justification is not something that is to be repeated for it has taken place once and for all, so the sanctification of the church is already complete in Christ[195] and is the enduring reality into which it is unrepeatably initiated in baptism and in which it is continually participant in holy communion. In Christ the holiness of the church in unshakeable and incorruptible. In him it is sinless and perfect, without spot or wrinkle, for it is clothed with his righteousness and sanctified with his holiness in truth. The church cannot fail in regard to its holiness because that holiness comes from the head of the church and is not a holiness which comes or accrues from its members.

---

[193] 1 Cor 3.16-17, 6.19.

[194] Cf. Gal 5.22f.

[195] Cf. 1 Cor 1.30.

*(2) The church has no holiness in itself and must continually die and
rise with Christ*

Because the church finds its holiness in Christ, it knows that it does
not derive it from itself and is not a source of holiness in itself. In itself
it is the company of sinners which Christ loved, with which he
identified himself in our body of sin and death[196] and for which he
gave himself in sacrifice on the cross. The church knows itself in Christ
to be that body which he took from our fallen and sinful humanity
and presented to the Father for judgement and healing in his own self-
offering for the sin of the world. Although in Christ the church is
already raised from the dead as his body, and through the power of
the Holy Spirit is already participant in the new creation, yet so long
as we wait on earth for the redemption of the body[197] and the
resurrection of the dead, the church knows, as often as it partakes of
the body and blood of Christ, that it is such a body that it must ever be
crucified with him in order that it may live with him his divine life
and bear in itself the life of the risen and glorified Lord.

Until Christ comes again the church constantly needs the cleansing
of Christ and the fire of divine judgement. It is the very fact of the
church's holiness in Christ, the reality that in Christ the church is
already justified and sanctified for ever,[198] that reminds the church that
so long as it lives in this world that passes away, and partakes of its
sinful patterns and forms,[199] it is involved in error and wrong. Therefore
it lives in such a way that its participation in divine holiness is the
condemnation of sin in its flesh;[200] it lives bearing about in its body the
dying of the Lord Jesus Christ that the life of Jesus may be manifest
even in its mortal flesh;[201] and therefore from day to day and from age
to age, until Christ comes again, it must live by putting off the old
nature with its corruption and sin, and putting on the new nature[202]
with which it is clothed through the baptism of the Spirit uniting it to
the risen and glorious body of Jesus Christ.[203]

---

[196]   Rom 6.6 KJV, 7.24

[197]   Rom 8.23.

[198]   Rom 5.9,16f.; Heb 10.10,14; 1 Cor 1.30.

[199]   Cf. 1 Cor 7.31.

[200]   Cf. Rom 8.3f.

[201]   2 Cor 4.10-11 KJV (RSV 'carrying in the body the death of Jesus . . . ').

[202]   Eph 4.22-24f.; Col 3.9-10f.

[203]   Cf. Rom 6.3-5; Col 2.12; Phil 2.9f.,21.

Regarded merely in itself the church on earth can err, can fail, can become heretical, can be weak and sickly. Yet the church cannot be regarded merely in itself, for its true life is in Christ who has bound it to himself in a holy and everlasting covenant, in which he sanctifies it with his holiness, establishes it in his truth, maintains it as his very own body and will present it at last to himself in all the perfection and purity of the divine life which he imparts to it.

(c) *The catholicity of the church*

(i) *The catholicity of the church is its participation in the fullness and universality of God*

The catholicity of the church is its participation in the immensity of God, in the plenitude and fullness of the divine life in Christ, and in the universality of the Holy Spirit. It is the counterpart in the life of the church in space and time to the whole fullness of God. The catholicity of the church describes, therefore, the fullness of the church in all its height and depth and length and breadth, in the height of holiness and depth of truth, in the length of its history and the breadth of its expansion in the world. The catholicity of the church is its universal mission and unity coterminous[204] on earth only with the boundaries of creation, but deriving from the universal love of God.[205]

In its earliest use 'catholic' referred to the faith and orientation of the church in the universal redemption of Christ for all humanity alike,[206] as opposed to an esoteric *gnosis* or secret knowledge for the few 'spirituals'. Hence it described the traditional apostolic church as opposed to the heretical sects who limited the atonement and rejected its universal range. Thus it came to denote an essential element in the church, the universality of the gospel of reconciliation deriving from the foundation of the apostolic church in Jesus Christ, and the expanding life and mission of the church through all peoples and ages in unity and fellowship with that foundation.

(ii) *The identity, continuity and universality of the church in all the world and in all ages*

Hence the catholicity of the church refers to the identity, continuity and universality of the church throughout all the world and throughout

---

[204] Co-extensive, having the same boundaries.

[205] Cf. Paul's understanding of the church in Ephesians, e.g. 1.19-23, 3.9-10,17-19.

[206] Cf. T.F. Torrance, *The Trinitarian Faith*, pp. 282-5.

all ages. The one holy catholic church has an essential character in virtue of which it is everywhere the same and is everywhere to be acknowledged in this sameness. Jesus Christ, the head of the church, is the same, yesterday, today and for ever.[207] The church which is his body participates in his sameness. Because the church is the same in all ages, in all peoples, and in all forms, it is catholic. In so far as the church in this or that age evinces and preserves this sameness, this identity, it is the church of Jesus Christ, the same yesterday, today and for ever.

Thus 'catholic' is the designation of the church as true over against a false, so-called church. The false church is that which chooses to go its own way, in departure from the sameness of the catholic church, that is, a 'heretical' church.[208] The church that insists on being heretical and manifests itself in independence as having a being other than the same identical being of the one apostolic church is apostate, that is, fallen from grace. Against heretical sects and apostate communities, the catholicity of the church refers to its cohesion in the truth, which in its holiness in Christ binds the church to the one universal Lord and his gospel and distinguishes the church from the world and all who deny the sole lordship of Christ. The church is catholic or it is not church. To be the one holy church of Christ is to be catholic for catholic means that the church is always 'identical with itself' in its sole foundation in Christ, in the sole foundation of the apostles and prophets laid in Christ.[209]

(iii) The universal mission of redemption reaching out to incorporate all humanity[210]

Because the church is filled with the one universal Spirit of divine love, it is caught up in the universal movement of that love that ceaselessly flows from God through Jesus Christ out into all the world. Hence the church is also catholic in that it is incorporated in

---

[207] Heb 13.8.

[208] *Heretical, heresy*, from the Gk *haireisthai* (to choose), *hairesis* (choice), referred originally to those who *choose* to go their own way in opposition to the orthodox and catholic belief of all the saints.

[209] Eph 2.20.

[210] See further here the section *The Church is the Kingdom of Christ*, T.F. Torrance, 'The Mission of the Church', pp. 138-40, on the church as the instrument through which Christ in his kingly reign reaches out through the Spirit to all for whom he lived and died and to all creation.

the universal mission of redemption and is essentially missionary.[211] This is a movement that is limitless and universal, reaching out in all directions, geographically to the ends of the earth, socially through all racial, cultural, economic and political forms, historically through all the changing movements and circumstances and events from age to age. It continues and persists through it all because it is the dynamic movement of God's Spirit of love and it overcomes all barriers and breaks through all boundaries because it is the Spirit of reconciliation which brings all people in all ages into the one universal family of God the Father.

(iv) Catholicity in understanding the fullness of Christ

Behind this catholicity of extension in the mission of the church there is catholicity of depth in the grounding of the church's life and understanding in the fullness and comprehensiveness of Jesus Christ and the holy Trinity.[212] This is the fullness of the church, the wholeness of the one body of Christ as over against its individual members. Catholic means that Christians are first members of Christ and therefore of the body of Christ the church, and as such and only as such are they individual Christians in their own sphere and duty and private existence. It is this catholicity in depth that is manifest in the eucharist, which is the Lord's supper as distinct from a private supper. The true eucharist is catholic because it is the Lord's and not the private possession of a particular church.

---

[211] Cf. *op. cit.* pp. 138-39, 'At its heart lies hidden the mystery of the union between Christ and his church which presses out toward universal fullness. Because Christ the head has ascended to fill all things, the church as the body of Christ cannot but be the complement of that fullness. It is the church's participation in Christ through the one universal Spirit of God that makes it so . . . The church does not possess the mystery in and for itself. It shares in it, but the whole creation shares in it, so that the frontiers of the church are open toward all those outside and toward the full consummation of the purposes of God for all things. Thus the range of the church's life and existence is co-extensive with the range of God's Spirit in all his operations, and co-extensive with the range of Christ's kingdom. It is this relation to the Spirit and kingdom of Christ, and therefore to the fullness of creation and of all God's purposes for it, that catholicises or universalises the church and makes it reach out to the fullness of him who fills all in all.'

[212] Eph 4.13ff.; cf. 1.16-23, 2.9-19; Col 1.9-20,26f., 2.2f.,9-10,19.

Christian faith primarily the faith of the one body – the mind of Christ unfolded in the Spirit

Similarly the Christian faith is not primarily the faith which is common to members of the church in their fellowship or association together, but the faith of the one body of Christ as it is rooted in and implicated in Christ himself. The Christian faith is therefore primarily the faith of the one body and as such is confessed by the individual members of the body. The Christian faith is not the aggregrate, or the lowest or highest common denominator, of the faith of the individual members. Catholic dogma is thus the unitary unfolding of the one mind of Christ in the one body of Christ through the one Spirit of Christ – a unitary understanding governed by the one Spirit and reaching back to the unity of faith in the fullness of Christ. As such catholic dogma is opposed to individual opinion. Individual opinions in the church should be determined by obedience to Christ the head of the church, and in so far as that happens, they are catholic opinions, but they are reached only through the mutual relations of members in the one body in which each is subordinate to the other and each serves the other in their conjoint or shared participation in the truth as it is in Jesus Christ.

(v) The church known only through faith and catholicised only by Christ

It is this church, which is rooted and grounded in the holiness and truth of God in Jesus Christ and extends throughout all the world under the impulse of the one universal Spirit of divine love, which is the catholic church. It is known not by historical inspection and is measured not by outward and worldly standards, but through faith in the holy Trinity. The church cannot make itself catholic any more than it can make itself holy or unify itself in the midst of the world's divisions. The church believes and is obedient, and the Christ in whom it believes and whom it obeys is the one who catholicises the church, makes it his own one habitation, makes it the pillar and ground of truth, makes it the rock against which the gates of hell cannot prevail.[213]

(d) The apostolicity of the church

Apostolicity the determining factor behind the attributes of the church

The apostolicity of the church is the grounding of the one holy catholic church in Christ through the New Testament revelation. Apostolicity

---

[213] Eph 2.22 KJV (RSV 'dwelling place'); 1 Tim 3.15 KJV (RSV 'pillar and bulwark'); Matt 16.18 KJV (RSV 'powers of death' – Gk, *pulai hadou*, gates of Hades).

thus supplies the criterion by which we may determine how far we have to do with the true church as one, holy and catholic. The church that is not apostolic is not catholic, for if it is not apostolic today, then it is not identical with the church founded on the apostles. It has changed its identity and ceased to be catholic. Apostolicity governs the attributes of unity and holiness in the same way, for there is only one foundation laid by Christ in the apostles,[214] and there is only one sanctification by the truth conveyed to us through the apostolic tradition of the gospel. It is thus within the sphere of the apostolic revelation and mission deriving directly from Christ that the church as one, holy and catholic has its truth and reality from age to age. Apostolic church refers to the whole continuity of the one holy catholic church with Christ who through the apostles founded the church on himself.

Apostolic church and apostolic sucession means continuity in word and deed with Christ

Just as in the incarnation word and deed are inseparable in the revelation and reconciliation of Christ, so in the foundation of the church upon the apostles in Christ the word and deed of Christ are inseparable. This means that the apostolic church is one which remains in continuity with Christ in word and deed, in truth and obedience to the truth, in teaching and ordinances. It was the orderly and responsible transmission of the apostolic teaching and ordinances, through regularly and carefully ordained ministers within the apostolic foundation and commission, that attested[215] or evidenced the faithful transmission of the apostolic faith and attested faithful obedience to that faith. Thus apostolic succession came to include the concept of a continuity in the ministry of the apostolic faith and apostolic ordinances. But the concept of apostolic succession referred to the continuity of the whole body of the church in word and deed with Christ, and it was only within that, that ministerial succession in obedience to the church founded once and for all on the apostles had its proper meaning and place.

(i) Apostolic means the church created in the apostolic sending of Christ from the Father and the apostles from Christ

'Apostolic church' means the church that is created in the apostolic mission of Christ from the Father and of the apostles from Christ. The

---

[214] 1 Cor 3.10-11.

[215] *Attest*, demonstrate, make clear, evidence.

sending of the apostles by Christ is correlative to the sending of Christ by the Father. As the Father endowed Christ with the Holy Spirit without measure in sending him on his mission as redeemer, so Christ breathed his Spirit upon the apostles in sending them out on the mission of the gospel in proclaiming reconciliation to all.[216] The sending of the apostles by Christ is thus an empirical counterpart to the sending of the Holy Spirit upon the church by the Father in the name of the Son.[217] In that sense the apostolic foundation of the church is correlative to the baptism of the Spirit at Pentecost.

The church's double relation to Christ: founded historically on the apostles and supernaturally through the Spirit

The church on earth is thus founded historically upon the apostles, but founded supernaturally by the pouring out of the Spirit. Hence the church ever afterwards has that double relation to Christ, *historically* through the apostles and *supernaturally* through the Holy Spirit. These two missions of the apostles and of the Holy Spirit are not to be regarded in dialectical relation[218] to one another, but as grounded together in the new covenant which Christ established in his body and blood and fulfilled within the church in the communion of the Spirit. The place of the apostles in that covenant was their special relation to the incarnate Word and to the Spirit in which they were constituted the foundation of the new Israel, the people of God filled with his Spirit and incorporated into Christ as his body. Through the apostolate Jesus Christ gave his church its basic form and structure deriving from himself and his messianic mission; this was a structure both in the knowledge and understanding of his divine revelation and a structure in the redeemed life and obedience of his people.

The outward and inward form of the covenant and apostolic succession in which all participate[219]

The bond of the covenant remains steadfast and sure and nothing can prevail against it. It is that covenanted faithfulness of God in

---

[216] Cf. John 1.32f., 3.34, 20.21f.

[217] John 14.26; Acts 1.4f.

[218] I.e. as contrasting opposites; *dialectic*, the interplay between opposing concepts, e.g. time and eternity.

[219] On the sacraments as the outward form of the covenant, the communion of the Spirit as the inward form, and the whole substance of the new covenant in its outer and inner form as Jesus Christ himself, see T.F. Torrance, 'The Mission of the Church', p. 136.

Christ which undergirds the whole foundation of the church and the whole of its continuity throughout all the changes and chances of history. But as part of the covenant and as the fulfilment of the promise of the covenant, God bestowed upon his church the Holy Spirit through whom the church founded upon the apostles is given communion with Christ immediately and supernaturally, as well as mediately and historically through the apostles. The outward form that this covenant continues to take in the life of the apostolic church is found in the holy sacraments, the pledges of God's faithfulness in Christ, the signs and seals of his fulfilled promises. The inward form which the covenant continues to take is the communion of the Spirit through which the apostolic church shares in the life and love of the Father and of the Son and of the Holy Spirit.[220] It is that communion in the very life and love of God, that continuity through communion of the redeemed life of the church in Christ, that is the inner substance and heart of the apostolic succession or continuity in the apostolically founded church. Hence all members participate through baptism in the apostolic succession and all are called to take part in the ministry of the gospel.

(ii) Apostolic means grounded on the unrepeatable foundation of the apostles

'Apostolic church' means that in the apostolate the church is grounded on an unrepeatable foundation. There can be no more laying of foundations,[221] any more than there can be other incarnations or other crucifixions of Christ. Because in this primary and foundational sense the apostolate is unrepeatable, it cannot be extended in time on the stage of this world. It is not the initial stage of a continuous process, but the perpetually persisting foundation of the church. In this sense there can be no talk of apostolic succession for the apostolate cannot be transmitted.

---

[220] Cf. *op. cit.* p. 138 where Torrance also speaks of baptism as the 'outer frontier' and holy communion as the 'inner frontier' of the church and where he says, 'Holy communion is the sacrament of the church's feeding upon Christ in his body and blood until he comes again, in which it continually receives into itself the indwelling presence, is renewed as his body, and through union with him is lifted up to participate in the heavenly worship of the whole communion of saints in heaven and earth in eucharistic oblation and adoration and praise.'

[221] Cf. 1 Cor 3.11.

Apostolic means following the apostles in both doctrine and ordinances

There is, however, another sense in which we must speak of apostolic church, as the church that continues to follow the apostles. In this sense we may legitimately speak of an apostolic succession. That does not mean that new apostles arise from generation to generation in the seat of the apostles, continuing their inspiration and exercising their judicial authority in divine revelation over the church. But it does means that in the continued mission of the church going out from the apostles into history, the church is given a continued ministry, dependent on that of the apostles, through which the church in history continues to be schooled in the apostolic gospel, and continues to be obedient to it as it is transmitted through the apostolic tradition of the New Testament.

It is the church which through that ministry is led and guided into obedience to the apostolic witness and teaching that is the apostolic church. This church continues to be apostolic when it moves out into history shaped and moulded by the apostolic tradition in both doctrine and in ordinances,[222] and so continues to proclaim the apostolic *kērygma*[223] and to be ordered in its life by the apostolic commands. The church has not only been grafted into Christ through the apostles, but given form and order and structure through their wise masterbuilding.[224] It was built up and compacted together by them after the pattern of their own incorporation into the messianic ministry of Christ, and as such it multiplies and increases and is extended throughout history.

Thus apostolic succession means that the church as the living body apostolically begotten through the incorruptible word of God[225] continues in being in history, in reliance upon the covenant promises of Christ. This church continues to be apostolic in that it continues throughout its history from age to age to be discipled in the apostolic tradition, to be ordered, shaped and determined by the apostolic obedience to Christ and his gospel. It is therefore a succession, through the Spirit, in obedience, in mission, a succession in service, a succession in faith and in doctrine.

---

[222] Authoritative direction and decrees on church practices or usage.

[223] Message and proclamation of Christ, from the Greek, *kērygma* proclamation, preaching.

[224] 1 Cor 3.10f.

[225] Cf. 1 Peter 1.23ff.

The threefold apostolic foundation: canon of scripture, rule of faith, and apostolic ministry

Through the unique ministry of the apostles in laying its foundations, the historical church has been equipped with oracles, ordinances and ministry. These are (1) *the Canon of Holy Scripture*, (2) *the Rule of Faith*, that is the canonical[226] structure of doctrine and worship, and (3) *the Apostolic Ministry*. All three belong together and are not to be torn apart from one another. Thus we cannot separate the doctrine of Scripture from the doctrine of the apostolate and so from the apostolic foundation of the church. Nor can we separate it from the rise of the Rule of Faith, for it was through the Rule of Faith that Canonical Scriptures were set apart and others were rejected, and so apostolic tradition was sharply differentiated as normative and authoritative from all other tradition. Again, it was the regular and responsible devolvement of the Ministry from the apostles, in obedience to the apostolic commands and in the apostolic tradition, that attested and secured the faithful keeping and handing on of the apostolic Scriptures and Rule of Faith. The Canon of Holy Scripture occupies the supreme place, but it is not to be separated theologically or historically from its relation to the Rule of Faith and the Apostolic Ministry.

The inseparable intertwining of apostolic ministry with apostolic scripture and the rule of faith

All these three factors are inseparably intertwined: they belong together and one must not be isolated from the other. That applies above all to the Apostolic Ministry and its continuity in the life and mission of the church. Thus if the ministerial succession is separated from continuous subordination to the apostolic word in the Holy Scriptures and from sound doctrine as attested in the Rule of Faith, it is a false succession, no matter how historically unbroken the links may be. However, it is also true that even if ministerial succession is broken here and there historically but is knit into the togetherness of the other apostolic gifts, then its defects are more than amply made up in the coherent succession of the whole apostolic tradition, because underlying it all is the covenant faithfulness of Jesus Christ who continues to send his Spirit upon the church and through his own presence in it continues to make it his own body and to fulfil his own ministry in and through it.

---

[226] Authoritatively prescribed, orthodox, from the Gk *kanōn*, standard.

The Apostolic Ministry in the history of the church is the orderly passing on of ministerial responsibility and authority from generation to generation, in reliance upon the command and promise of Christ given to the apostles in the foundation of the church. The sign of the laying on of the hands of the presbytery[227] was given by the apostles to be used in attesting and making evident the faithful transmission of the *kērygma* and *didachē*[228] of Christ, and to attest and affirm the reliance of the church and its Ministry upon the faithfulness of Christ who remains true to his promises and fulfils them in spite of our weakness and sinfulness. But this continuity is only the sign of the real thing, namely, the redeemed life of the people of God which they receive from Christ through his Word and Spirit. The laying on of hands is not instituted as a saving ordinance, but is the apostolically appointed sign which appropriately attests the continuity of the church in the authentic Ministry of Word and Sacraments and in the Rule of Faith, all under the authority of the Apostolic revelation handed on to us in the New Testament. It is this apostolic authority that attaches to and governs the necessity of historical succession in the church's Ministry from age to age. But because it is apostolic authority that is paramount, what is paramount is obedience to the Word of God in the Holy Scriptures and to the doctrinal content of the Word unfolded according to the Rule of Faith.

(iii) Apostolic means scripture as the source and norm of the church's life

In its most concrete sense 'apostolic' refers directly to the holy scriptures as the source and norm of the church's continued

---

[227] *Presbyteriou*, 1 Tim 4.14; cf. 2 Tim 2.6. In the Presbyterian tradition, oversight is exercised by a 'corporate episcopate' or corporate bishop, the presbytery, while in the 'historic episcopate' oversight is exercised by an individual bishop (Gk, *episcopos*, overseer, superintendent, bishop). For an outline of biblical principles governing a doctrine of the episcopate and an understanding of the concept of the 'corporate episcopate' see T.F. Torrance, *Royal Priesthood*, chap. 5, 'The Corporate Episcopate', pp. 88-108; and on 'the difference between the *presbyter in the Church of Scotland* and *presbyter in the Church of England*' and the question of their interrelation, see p. 104ff.

[228] Gk, *proclamation* (of Christ) and *teaching*.

existence throughout history. The apostolic church is the church that lives by the New Testament as its canon[229] of life and faith. This church continues to be begotten from age to age in the apostolic tradition on the ground of exegetical study of the holy scriptures and continues to be built up by their teaching.[230] It is this fact that gives the church its form, that continues to shape and order the church as the body of Christ. By listening to the apostolic witness, by the study of the New Testament and by the obedience of faith to its revelation, the church lives throughout the changes and chances of history and throughout all temporal succession in such a way as not to be conformed to this world but to be transformed by the renewing of its mind and so conformed to Jesus Christ.[231]

Because it is the apostolic scriptures that give the church its form, the form of Christ, through sharing in the pattern of his obedience as the servant-Son,[232] apostolic scripture is the criterion of the church's continual being as the true, holy, catholic church. Jesus Christ is himself the true vine which includes the branches, and because he is the truth his word cleanses the church, purges the branches and sanctifies the church through the truth.[233] This word, found in the holy scriptures, is the norm for the church's teaching and life. It is the critical criterion because it is the creative norm. Any church that fails to conform to the truth of the apostolic scriptures, which refuses to be reformed and cleansed and purged by the word of truth mediated through the apostles, thereby declares that it is not the one holy catholic church. It calls in question its own apostolicity and therefore its catholicity, for it loosens its moorings in the foundation of the church laid in Christ Jesus. The church which has the promise that the gates of hell will not prevail against it is the apostolic church. To be the one, holy, catholic church means that through all the changes of history until the final advent

---

[229] Gk, *kanōn*, rule, standard, norm.

[230] See the pastoral instruction in 1 & 2 Timothy and Titus on the ordering of the church through sound doctrine in accordance with the gospel of Christ, e.g. 1 Tim 1.3f.,10, 2.3-7, 3.15 – 4.16, 6.3; 2 Tim 1.10-14, 2.1,15, 3.14 – 4.5; Titus 1.1-3,9,13, 2.1,5,10-15.

[231] Rom 12.2, cf. 8.29.

[232] Cf. Phil 2.5f.; John 13.14f.

[233] Cf. John 15.1f., 14.6, 15.3, 7.31-32, 17.17-19.

of Christ, the church remains what it is, 'identical with itself' and faithful to its identity in maintaining the teaching of the apostles as delivered to us by the holy scriptures. It does not alter its nature by changing its foundation, by subtracting from it, or by adding to it anything other than what has already been laid down in the holy scriptures. Therein lies the concrete apostolicity of the church.

Chapter Twelve

JESUS CHRIST THE FIRST AND THE LAST: THE ESCHATOLOGICAL PERSPECTIVE OF THE GOSPEL

1 New Testament eschatology and its indispensable place in the church[1][2]

(a) The historical weakness of eschatology in the church

The *kērygma* of the New Testament is eschatological through and through, *yet only* three periods appear to stand out in the history of the church as rich in eschatology,[3] the first century, the age of the Reformation and the present day. No period has ever been without its

---

[1] Following the transfer to *Incarnation* (for the reasons stated in the editorial introduction there) of the main text of the 'Eschatology Addendum' from this volume, and in order to preserve the full eschatological emphasis of his thought here, the following portions have been retained as an abridged version of the less technical passages of Torrance's addendum, the full text of which can be read in the appendix to *Incarnation*, Paternoster Press UK & InterVarsity Press USA, Milton Keynes & Downer's Grove, 2008, pp. 297-344. A few words in italics have been added here to help make connections between passages (or retained as such if italicised in the 'Addendum').

[2] On the nature and place of eschatology in the church and the crucial issue of the humanity of the risen Christ, see T.F. Torrance, *Royal Priesthood*, 2nd edition, T & T Clark, Edinburgh 1993, chap. III, 'The Time of the Church, pp. 43-62.

[3] From the Greek, *eschatos*, last, the doctrine of the last things at the end of history or 'the last days', regarded in the New Testament as having already begun with the coming of Christ and therefore imparting an urgent eschatological orientation to the essential structure of Christian faith and doctrine.

eschatology, but as a general rule theologians have been content to give only the last chapters of their works to eschatology, as if it were a mere addendum to faith and not the 'fibre of the living strand'.[4] The great question that must force itself upon us immediately is this: Why was it that the church failed so early to grasp and absorb into her whole life and thought the eschatological teaching of the New Testament? And why was it that after the Reformation the Lutheran, Reformed, and Anglican churches largely lost the eschatological note in spite of the fact that their hymns and liturgies are resonant with it?

Why also was it that when the church came to formulate her teaching about such doctrines as death and judgement, the life everlasting and the return of Christ, she tended to append it to the end of dogmatics rather uncertainly, failing to grasp these doctrines aright in themselves, and failing to take up the New Testament stress upon eschatology as integral to the very heart of the gospel and to every doctrine of the faith.

Whatever be the final answer or answers we must give to these questions, it seems clear that the deepest significance of the best biblical scholarship of our day is that it is wrestling with precisely this problem, with the result that the new biblical scholarship is producing an understanding of the bible unparalleled in the history of the church since the first century. No one can read the volumes of Kittel's *Theological Dictionary of the New Testament* without being profoundly impressed with the fact that scholars from all sides and of many varieties have this in common that their *biblical* studies have forced them back into an exposition of the faith that bears something of the eschatological cast that characterises all the scriptures. Undoubtedly the renewed understanding of the Old Testament and its relation to the thought of the New Testament has a great deal to do with this, which would seem to justify the historian in the judgement that whenever the church has been tempted to tear Christianity from its God-given roots in Hebraic soil it has destroyed something so essential that its effects bear strange fruit for centuries afterwards.

(b) The nature and roots of New Testament eschatology

(i) The prophetic view of the kingdom of God

The Christian view of the kingdom of God and the last things undoubtedly goes back to roots in the Old Testament and particularly

---

[4]   Cf. H.R. Mackintosh, *Immortality and the Future*, Hodder & Stoughton, London 1915, p. 107f. (quote p. 108).

to the double consciousness in the Hebrew mind of the kingdom as bound up with creation and yet as the pure act of God. In the world of history and trouble the reality of that kingdom can be imaged forth only dimly, but the Old Testament prophets are mastered with the consciousness that it will be fully realised in the same sphere of reality in which people daily live and suffer, for God is the Lord of all the earth who will not forego his purpose in creation. At the same time they are equally conscious that though the kingdom is imaged in the pattern that has been given to Israelite society and history, it is not something that will arise out of history but will supervene upon it until it breaks out into apocalyptic vision. But the Old Testament apocalyptic eschatology is still rooted and grounded in history, and speaks proleptically in anticipation of the kingdom as a state in time. No doubt it is bound up with a transcendent community, but it is one that will be realised only in cosmic circumstances perfected by the word of God when creation and kingdom come together. That duality which holds together in unshakeable unity the redeemed community and a redeemed earth, carrying with it the seeds of the Christian doctrine of the resurrection of the body, lies at the heart of the New Testament eschatology and it is there that its most decisive expression is found.

(ii)) The Old Testament emphasis on the future has now been shifted to the present

In the Old Testament the kingdom of God was revealed at certain decisive points in the history of Israel, but because its domain stretched necessarily over the whole creation it reached beyond Israel, and because the world was a world in estrangement from God, it could be manifest only as a mystery behind it and yet impinging upon history. In the New Testament the kingdom is regarded as having broken into time and is overtaking men and women in Jesus Christ, but because it comes into the particularity of history its universal domain is as yet hidden from the eyes of humanity. It confronts them not first extensively in its universality, but intensively in decisive encounter. This means that though the kingdom of God is present among mankind it is nevertheless known only in a continuation of the double consciousness of the Old Testament where the kingdom is seen as bound up with creation and yet as the pure act of God. But the whole emphasis has been shifted. In the Old Testament the main accent lay upon the future; in the New Testament the main accent lies upon the present, but here the accent on the present has no meaning apart from the future when the kingdom of God now realised intensively in temporal and historical encounter, *in Christ and his encounter with people,* will be realised extensively in a new heaven and a new earth.[5]

(iii) The New Testament kingdom is both present and future

It is precisely the tension between those two stresses which is at the root of what we call today the eschatological element in the New Testament. The kingdom is both future and present. The Christian's relation to salvation is both a having and hoping. 'The hour is coming,' said Jesus, 'and now is'.[6] It is that double significance which makes *parousia* such a difficult thought, for the New Testament teaching about the *parousia* alternates between a future advent and a realised presence here and now. Thus in the fourteenth chapter of the fourth Gospel, particularly as seen in the light of the first epistle of John, the advent presence of Christ undoubtedly refers both to his presence through the Spirit and to his presence on the last day, and that doubleness is very apparent in the Johannine teaching about judgement.

On the lips of Jesus himself, as we see in the Synoptics, the emphasis is upon the presence of the kingdom in his own person, and as he himself was then present in the flesh the accent fell largely upon the present, though there are undoubted references, as several recent scholars have demonstrated (notably Stauffer, Kümmel, Michaelis and Cullmann),[7] to a future coming not to be wholly identified with resurrection, ascension and Pentecost. After the ascension, however, from the angle of the redeemed sinner to whom Jesus is no longer

---

[5]   Cf. T.F. Torrance, 'The Mission of the Church', *Scottish Journal of Theology,* vol. 19.2 (1966), p. 132, where Torrance speaks about what has taken place 'intensively' in Jesus now taking place 'extensively' in humanity and creation, 'Thus at Pentecost the Christian church was fully called into being, as the life of the Father, Son and Holy Spirit, mediated to the world in Jesus Christ, broke forth into the lives of men and women in an ever widening movement of universalisation. What took place intensively in Jesus Christ, within the limits of his particular historical life, then began to take place extensively, reaching out to all humanity [men] in all ages in a movement as expansive as the ascension of Christ to fill all things.'

[6]   John 5.25.

[7]   The indications are that this was written in the early 1950s. See the more extended footnote in the main 'Addendum', *Incarnation,* pp. 297-344, and the similarities (referred to in footnotes below) between passages here and Torrance's paper 'Eschatology and the Eucharist' of 1952, reprinted in T.F. Torrance, *Conflict and Agreement,* vol. 2, Lutterworth, London 1960, pp. 154-202.

present according to the flesh, the emphasis necessarily falls as much upon the advent hope as upon communion in the real presence here and now, while the intense personal nearness of the risen Christ impresses itself inevitably upon faith as always imminent. That means that redeemed sinners can only think of their reconciliation with Christ eschatologically, but also that they cannot think of the advent in purely futurist terms. That is why the New Testament constantly thinks of the *parousia* in terms of epiphany,[8] for the relation between the *today* and the *eschaton* is much more a tension between the hidden and the manifest, the veiled and the unveiled, than between dates in calendar time. What is still in the future is the full unveiling of a reality, but the reality itself is fully present here and now.

(iv) The prophetic view of a kingdom hidden until the time of its fulfilment

The prophets also taught, as we have had occasion to see, that the presence of the kingdom in a fallen world must mean that it comes as a hidden kingdom, at least until the apocalyptic moment when it is fully revealed in a new heaven and a new earth. That is surely the thought of the New Testament which it holds all the more decidedly just because the *eschaton* has entered time. No doubt it cannot be discerned by observation in the passing fashion of this fallen world, but it necessarily entails within the world the creation of a new community through which the kingdom is actual in conditions of time. That is indeed the mystery of the kingdom, but unlike the messianic remnant of the Old Testament which had not yet received the promise, this community is actual in the fullness of time, rooted and grounded in the incarnation, a community that has foundations. But though its builder and maker is God[9] and just because it is actual in time, it partakes also of the contradictions and conflicts of history with another law in its members warring against the law of God.[10] In spite of being in the likeness of sinful flesh[11] the new community is indeed the body of Christ, the mystery through which the unveiling of the righteousness of God takes place in the world in the preaching of the Gospel, but therefore also the unveiling of the wrath of God as the redeeming purpose of divine love in effective conflict with the forces of evil.[12]

---

8   Sudden revelation, manifestation of deity, from the Greek *epiphaniea*, an appearing.

9   Cf. Heb 11.10.

10   Cf. Rom 7.23.

11   Cf. Rom 8.3.

12   Eph 1.22-23, 3.9-4.16; Rom 1.16-18ff.

(c) The coming of the kingdom in Jesus but the holding apart of final judgement

In the earthly ministry of Jesus, when the word was broadcast to all and sundry, the *eschaton* confronted people in the person of Christ standing in their very midst as the mystery of the kingdom, the *eschatos*,[13] invading the realm of their choices and decisions, throwing them into ferment and crisis, and (as C.H. Dodd has described so well) acting selectively upon them so that their reaction to it is itself the divine judgement. That inevitably happens when the kingdom of God comes into the midst, for the king takes charge of the situation and his word acts upon people whether they will or no, giving their own choices and decisions an essential form *vis à vis* the kingdom. Nevertheless this breaking in of the last judgement is veiled in the form of the parable and presented as it were obliquely in order both to bring men and women face to face with the last things in crucial decision and yet to leave them room for decision, which could not happen if the *eschaton* were wholly realised, as C.H. Dodd would have it, and the time-element were eliminated. And so the fourth Gospel puts very clearly the whole Synoptic teaching of the parables when Jesus says, 'I judge you not, but the word that I have spoken to you, that shall judge you at the last day.'[14] That final judgement confronts people here and now, but its full action is delayed until the last day. Had the *eschaton* encountered men and women in its unveiled openness they would have been damned on the spot without room or freedom for the decision of faith – that is why Jesus held apart the prophetic and the apocalyptic views of the kingdom.[15]

The mystery of evil

However, just because room and time are given for reaction, the terrible possibility is allowed for the reaction of evil in its final and intense contradiction to the kingdom of God. That is what the New Testament calls 'the mystery of iniquity',[16] which is also unveiled through the preaching of the gospel and will be unveiled fully at the last day and be destroyed. But just as in the earthly ministry of Jesus, that mystery

---

[13] *Eschaton*, the last event, the end (Gk, neuter); *eschatos*, the last one (Gk, masculine).

[14] See John 12.47,48.

[15] Cf. Reinhold Niebuhr, *The Nature and Destiny of Man*, Nisbet, London 1943, Gifford Lectures vol. II, p. 49.

[16] Cf. 2 Thess 2.7.

of iniquity was provoked out of its mystery and pressed by the finger of God to the point of ultimate decision in the terrible conflict that issued in the cross, so the church as the body of Christ, proclaiming the same word of the kingdom in order that all may repent and believe the gospel, also provokes such a reaction of evil in the conflicts of history that there is also an eschatological fulfilment of evil culminating in the last judgement. The tares and the wheat grow side by side[17] and so as Niebuhr has said, history is 'the story of an ever-increasing cosmos creating ever-increasing possibilities of chaos.'[18]

The church must remain an eschatological community, proclaiming the new creation

Throughout this the accent must undoubtedly fall upon the triumphant certainty of the finished work of Christ, for Christ is already the new man in whom all things are become new and in whom we have proleptically even now the consummation of the divine purpose of creation. Just because that is complete already we cannot think in terms of an extension of the incarnation, but only of an eschatological 'reiteration' of the incarnation (including the death and resurrection), which is the doctrine enshrined in the sacrament of holy communion. The proclamation of this new humanity is the most explosive force in the world not only because it is proleptic to the final judgement of holy love and proleptic to the new heaven and new earth, but because in it the last things actually confront people creatively here and now in time. It is therefore only as an eschatological *community*[19] that the church can really carry out her divine mission in the world, to confront all humanity with the crucial word of the gospel and so penetrate every aspect of human life with the power of the resurrection, intensively as well as extensively. The great missionary task of the church lies therefore both in the evangelisation of the world and in being the instrument by which the dynamic word of this gospel intervenes in

---

[17] Matt 13.24-30.

[18] Reinhold Niebuhr, *An Interpretation of Christian Ethics,* SCM Press, London, 1936, p. 108.

[19] The Torrance text here has 'magnitude' – cf. here section (b) above, first paragraph, where Torrance speaks of Old Testament eschatology as being bound up with a *'transcendent community'*. Cf. also section 3 (b) (v) below where Torrance speaks of 'the church in history as the *eschatological community,* the community that reaches out beyond this present age into the age to come' (*Conflict and Agreement in the Church,* vol. 1, Lutterworth, London 1959, p. 312).

every form of human existence and action, social, national and international. Without the creation of such thorough going fermentation in the world, the church will not be in a position to proclaim the gospel in any way proportionate to her great passion, nor will she have the power to alter the face of present human society so as to make it by the very power of God an instrument in the furtherance of his redeeming purposes.

(d) *The reign of Christ and the kingdom of God – the biblical tension of present and future*

Oscar Cullmann draws a distinction between the kingdom of God and the reign of Christ.[20] The kingdom of God has come decisively among humanity in Christ even if it remains essentially a future reality. The reign of Christ however has already begun and continues through the church, being actualised in the word of the gospel reaching out to the whole world, so that all worldly powers and authorities are made to function only within the lordship of Christ. This means that we are really living in the last times, for the reign of Christ is essentially proleptic to the kingdom of God which will be established at the end of this present age. The conception of *the kingdom of God* carries with it the element of judgement upon this present evil world whose form and fashion must pass away.[21] Apart from final judgement history becomes meaningless, but with the final judgement it is given the teleological[22] end of the conflicts of history. In the conception of *the kingdom of Christ*,[23] by contrast, the essential oneness of God's purpose in creation and redemption is maintained, inasmuch as in Christ there is a new creation,[24] carried through history into the kingdom of God where it entails the eschatological judgement of all history.

---

[20] O. Cullman, *Christ and Time*, 3rd (revised) edition, SCM Press, London 1962, p. 151f., 208.

[21] 1 Cor 7.31 (RSV 'form', KJV 'fashion').

[22] From the Greek *telos*, end, teleological refers to history or events in terms of their end or purpose. Whereas in eschatology the emphasis is on the invasion of God into history throwing it into crisis and creating the last events, in teleology the emphasis is on history reaching forward to its goal at the end of time.

[23] Torrance is here using the terms 'kingdom of Christ' and 'reign of Christ' interchangeably.

[24] 2 Cor 5.17; cf. Gal 6.15; Rom 8.21f.

The new creation is as yet a hidden creation, hidden with Christ in God,[25] but always on the point of becoming manifest. Until then the church lives in the eschatological tension between the first coming of the kingdom and the final coming, and carries out her task as the crucified body in the realm where sin and the flesh are still found and where the subordinate powers still try to break free from the lordship of Christ. Nevertheless the church lives in the Spirit on the day of the Lord, that is to say, on the victory side of the kingdom, and the song in her mouth is the triumphant chant of Psalm 2, 'Why do the nations conspire, and the peoples plot in vain? . . . I have set my king on Zion, my holy hill . . . Ask of me, and I will make the nations your heritage, and the ends of the earth your possession.'[26]

(e) The concept of time in the New Testament and the nature of the eschatological tension

There seems little doubt that the New Testament gives us teaching on eschatology without committing itself to any specific conception of time. It is usually content to express the truth in terms of limited or limitless duration. On the analogy of the doctrine of the Trinity, however, where a formed doctrine is not given either, it may be that the eschatological teaching of the New Testament requires definite clarification in our theology. If so must we not go on to form a time-concept on the analogy of the incarnation? Must we not say with Karl Barth that because the Word has become flesh it has also become time?[27]

(i) The tension between old time as we know it and the new time of the new creation

And must we not say further, that we have to do with that new time here and now even in the midst of old time? That would mean that the eschatological tension is to be thought of as between new time in the new creation, and old time as we still know it in the continuation of

---

[25] Col 3.3.

[26] Psalm 2.1,6,8.

[27] *Kirchliche Dogmatik* (*KD*) 1/2, Verlag der Evangelischen Buchhandlung Zollikon (EBZ), 1938, p. 55 [Eng. trans. (ET), *Church Dogmatics* (*CD*) 1/2, T & T Clark, Edinburgh 1956, p. 50]; see *KD* 2/1, EBZ 1940, p. 66-7 [ET, *CD* 2/1, T & T Clark, Edinburgh 1957, p. 61-2]; and *KD* 3/2, Evangelischer Verlag A.G. Zollikon (EVZ), Zurich 1948, p. 524ff. [ET, *CD* 3/2, T & T Clark, Edinburgh 1960, p. 437ff.] [English refs. added – Ed].

this fallen world. That would also mean that new time is as yet concealed under the form and fashion of old time, or (shall we say?) under the likeness of sinful time.

To work out this relation carefully we must undoubtedly go back to its ground in the incarnation, for in the person of Jesus Christ, in his God-manhood, we have consummated already the union of the eternal and the temporal.[28] And may we not think of that helpfully in terms of the great Chalcedonian doctrine of the hypostatic union? Just as in Christ God and man are united in such a way that there is neither fusion on the one hand nor yet separation on the other, a union without any diminishing of the completeness or perfection of deity or of humanity, so here too we may think of there having taken place in the incarnation, as it were, a sort of hypostatic union between the eternal and the temporal in the form of new time. And just as Christ for ever lives our mediator and our atonement, in whom all things cohere and in whom all things in heaven and earth will be brought back to the fullness of God, so we must think here of a union between the eternal kingdom of God and the new creation, indeed a union between the eternal and time made new in Christ Jesus, and of that as an abiding union even in the heart of our world's estrangement.

But here we must go a step beyond Chalcedon, and remembering that the captain of our salvation was made perfect through suffering, carry the hypostatic union in our thought through the cross to its perfection in the resurrection. We must think therefore of the union between the kingdom of God and new time as having in Christ entered into the heart of our alienation from God, into the heart of the conflicts of history. Then there in the teeth of all the contradictions of sin and all the 'abstractions'[29] of fallen time, we must think of the union between the kingdom and new time in Christ as having perfected itself through the cross and resurrection into the abiding triumph of a perfection in God, which both consummates the original purposes of creation and crowns it with glory.

(ii) The twofold nature of the eschatological tension, between eternity and time, and between new time and old time

Now we are able to see that the eschatological tension is really twofold. It is the union achieved in the tension between the eternal

---

28   Cf. *Conflict and Agreement*, vol. 2, p. 171f.

29   In T.E. Hulme's sense of the word.

and the temporal, and also in the tension between the holy and sinful. The central fact in this for eschatology is this: that the union of the eternal and the temporal, or as we have spoken of it earlier, the bringing together of the apocalyptic and prophetic views of the kingdom, in the conditions of our humanity and our history inevitably creates a new tension, that between the new creation and the fallen world. Because it is the first-fruits of the new creation, the entry at Bethlehem of an abiding union between God and man and its perfection in the cross and resurrection inevitably entails conflict in the conditions of time and history. That is why, although we must say that the kingdom of God has come already and come in power, we must also say that the conflict continues in time just because the new creation is here and now breaking up the old, until the hour when the veil of sense and time in the fallen world is torn aside, and the kingdom of God comes at last with observation in the new heaven and the new earth.

(iii) Apocalypse is the unveiling of the hidden reality of the new creation in Jesus Christ

Apocalypse in its deepest sense is the unveiling of Jesus Christ,[30] who has come into our world and history as the suffering servant or the lamb of God, the transcendent Son of God. At his death and resurrection the veil of the temple was torn aside[31] and men and women beheld the glory of the only begotten of the Father full of grace and truth.[32] In Jesus Christ we think of the kingdom of God as having entered our world, as veiled behind history, behind the forms and fashions of this age, so that we are unable to see it directly, just as people were unable to discern the Christ behind the likeness of the sinful flesh of our fallen humanity except by revelation or apocalypse. The pattern of that kingdom cannot be discerned by the inspection of the course of history. But in the Spirit on the day of the Lord[33] it is possible for faith to see proleptically, if only under the shadow of God's hand, something of the glory of God that passes

---

[30] Rev 1.1, *Apokalupsis Iēsou Christou*, 'The revelation of Jesus Christ', (*apokaluptein*, to reveal, uncover). See T.F. Torrance, *The Apocalypse Today* (Sermons on Revelation), James Clarke, London 1960, p. 12ff.

[31] Matt 27.51; Mark 15.38; Luke 23.45; cf. Exod 26.31-35; Heb 10.19f.

[32] John 1.14 KJV.

[33] Rev 1.10.

through history.[34] Apocalypse therefore is the unveiling to faith of history already invaded and conquered by the lamb of God.[35] Apocalypse is the unveiling to faith of the new creation as yet hidden from our eyes behind the ugly shapes of sinful history, but a new creation already consummated and waiting for eschatological unfolding or fulfilment in the advent presence of Christ. No doubt we are unable to trace the lineaments of the kingdom of God in history, but it is nevertheless a fact that even now God governs and orders the course of the world so as to make all things to work together for good,[36] and even the wrath of man to praise him.[37]

(iv) The key to history is the lamb of God who must reign until his enemies are under his feet

The key of the ages, the clue to history, is Christ crucified, the lamb of God. It is the person who in faith has seen the veiling and unveiling of Jesus Christ who can penetrate apocalyptically behind the guilt and wrath of history and see the veiling and unveiling of God's kingdom in it all. And yet even the children of faith will be surprised at the last day, as our Lord taught in a parable.[38] The achievements of the church in time are not what they appear, for even when she has done what she ought to do she must confess that she is an unprofitable servant.[39] The kingdom of God is concealed even behind the temporal forms and fashions of the church, all of which must pass away at the final judgement. Only God can fulfil the purpose of history. The new Jerusalem comes down from above.[40] God has already put everything under the feet of Christ, but Christ must reign nevertheless until all his enemies are put under his feet.[41] We do not see that as yet, but we do see Jesus already crowned with glory and honour and wait for the fulfilment of his reign.[42] That is the faith and hope of the church.

---

[34] Cf. Exod 33.18-23, the story of Moses being allowed to glimpse from behind the glory of God as he passed by.

[35] *The Apocalypse Today, ibid.*

[36] Rom 8.28 KJV.

[37] Psalm 76.10 KJV.

[38] Matt 25.31f.

[39] See Luke 17.10.

[40] Rev 21.2.

[41] 1 Cor 15.27,25.

[42] Torrance's text here has simply, ' . . . but we do see Jesus (Heb 2.8-9).'

2 The sacraments and eschatology

(a) *Between the times, the sacraments of baptism and holy communion*[43]

Between the times, faith and hope are confirmed and nourished by the two sacraments of the Word made flesh, baptism and holy communion, which are essentially signs belonging to the fullness of time, that is to say, filled with the complete incarnate presence of the Son of God, who gives himself to us in forgiveness and reconciliation through the cross and the resurrection. That is communicated in baptism, on the one hand, in a once and for all sense, and here the wholeness of Christ and the completeness of our salvation are particularly enshrined. In baptism we have to do with the new creation, the perfect body of Christ into which we become incorporated. In holy communion, on the other hand, we have to do with the continuance of that new creation and its breaking in as enduring event in conditions of time, with the church as the bodying forth in this fallen world of communion with Christ.

(i) *The correspondence of the sacraments to the twofold tension of Christian eschatology*

These two sacraments correspond to the twofold tension of Christian eschatology.[44] The doubleness of the eschatological tension of the *parousia* as both a presence and a coming, as something once for all and yet as the showing forth of that tension until the Lord come, is enshrined in both of them. But the emphasis upon the once and for all union of God and man, of the eternal and the temporal falls most heavily upon the sacrament of baptism, while in the eucharist or sacrament of holy communion we have the emphasis mostly upon continual participation and renewal in that complete event throughout all the contradictions and abstractions of fallen time. If in the sacrament of baptism there is enshrined the faith that once for all we have been put in the right with God through Jesus Christ, in the sacrament of holy communion we have the unshakeable conviction that in the

---

[43] For a much fuller account of baptism and the eucharist and their relation to eschatology see *Conflict and Agreement*, vol. 2, pp. 93-202. See also T.F. Torrance, *Theology in Reconciliation*, Geoffrey Chapman, London 1975, chap. 2 'The One Baptism Common to Christ and his Church' pp. 82-105, and chap. 3 'The Paschal Mystery of Christ and the Eucharist' pp. 106-38.

[44] Cf. *Conflict and Agreement*, vol. 2, p. 163ff.

presence of Christ we are in the wrong and we need constantly to receive communion in his body and blood for 'he who has washed does not need to wash, except for his feet'.[45] If at baptism we think of our union with Christ as *opus dei*, work of God which takes place in and for its own sake, at communion we think of the same union inserted into our flesh and blood, into time and history as by faith we partake of Christ's flesh and blood. If at baptism we think of our having died and risen with Christ, born anew in him as new creatures so that old things are passed away and all things are become new,[46] at holy communion we think of that creation not only as a *datum*, a given, but as a *dandum*, that is as a given which must ever be given from moment to moment in the conditions of our passing and sinful world, so that every time we communicate is eschatological time (*kairos*) until we drink it new in the kingdom.

Unquestionably therefore, the two sacraments are given to us to enshrine the double consciousness of the New Testament eschatological faith and hope, to enable us to hold in the grasp of our faith and hope the *parousia* as both a real presence here and now and yet as an advent presence still to come. At the same time both sacraments make it quite clear that the kingdom of God is amongst us not in word only with suspended action, not in Spirit only, but in deed and in power, as real act in time, as word-deed enacted in our flesh and blood and inserted into history. But precisely because it is both, it is both an abiding reality and also an eschatologically reiterated event until Christ comes.[47]

(ii) Baptism is the primary eschatological act, whose reality in Christ waits to be fully revealed

Baptism is the primary eschatological act of the gospel through which we are ingrafted into the wholeness of Christ.[48] Something absolutely decisive is wrought in baptism. Baptism in the name of Jesus, in the name of the holy Trinity, means that Christians are delivered from the power of darkness and translated into the

---

45 John 13.10 KJV/RSV.

46 Rom 6.3f; 2 Cor 5.17.

47 The following paragraphs (with the exception of the first sentence), down to the end of the paragraph headed 'The eucharist spans past and future . . .', have been added from *Conflict and Agreement*, vol. 2, 'Eschatology and the Eucharist', pp. 167-171. [Headings added]

48 *Op. cit.* p. 165.

kingdom of the Son of God. A radical change has taken place which can only be described in terms of a complete change of lordship. The Christian is no longer under the domination of the law or the elements of this world, but is dead to sin and alive to God through the lordship of the Spirit, so that old things are passed away and all things are become new. Outwardly baptism is no doubt incorporation into the earthly church, initiation into the operational sphere of the salvation-event, and outwardly the church on earth knows itself to be embroiled in the relativities of history and the sin of mankind, but behind and beyond all that, baptism has a dimension in depth which is its eschatological mystery: 'You are dead and your life is hid with Christ in God.'[49] The really significant event in baptism is a hidden event; it recedes from sight in the ascension of Christ and waits to be revealed fully at the last day.

(iii) The provision of the eucharist for the renewal of faith and recurring confirmation of baptism

However, the Lord has not simply left his church stricken with anguish and awe at the foot of the cross, or standing looking up into heaven from Galilee.[50] He has provided for the renewal and maintenance of its life and faith – in the eucharist. Through continual communion in the body and blood of the saviour, the church finds that baptism is given its complement and recurring confirmation. After the baptism of John, Jesus had called twelve disciples and formed them round himself into one body, the reconstituted Israel of God. They were pledged to drink his cup and be baptized with his baptism, but the mystery of the kingdom, the new Israel incorporate in the messianic saviour, baffled them. They understood indeed that they were called to cast in their lot unreservedly with Jesus and to share his life, but in the crucial moment they found themselves standing not with Jesus but with the crowd of sinners who were crucifying him and for whom he was dying. They had all forsaken him and fled.[51] At the last the messiah was left unutterably alone under the judgement of God upon the world's sin. He was their Lord and master. He was their

---

[49]   See Col 3.3.

[50]   Cf. Acts 1.11.

[51]   For this and what immediately follows see W. Manson, *Scottish Journal of Theology* 1950, vol. 3.1, 'The Norm of the Christian Life in the Synoptic Gospels', pp. 38ff.; and *The Way of the Cross*, Hodder & Stoughton, 1958.

representative and their very life, but in the agony of substitution he was unutterably alone, the lamb whom God had himself provided for sacrifice.[52] The disciples could only stand afar off in sin and shame and fear, broken-hearted that the bonds between him and them were utterly severed.

The last supper designed to form an unbreakable union with Christ cemented on the cross

Then they remembered the last supper. That was why he had designed it, for he meant them to remember. And they realized that within that awful separation and in spite of it he had effectuated his oneness with them in a way that nothing could break, for he had given them in the supper a sacramental counterpart to his atoning death. And then they knew that their baptismal incorporation into one body with their Lord had come to its stark reality in the sacrificial death and its sacramental counterpart. They understood how in that wonderful last supper Jesus 'had definitely consecrated them for inheritance in the kingdom of God as those who, despite their brokenness so soon to be made visible, formed one body with himself. He had given their lives a sacramental dependence on his own.'[53] In the Lord's supper and in the enactment on the cross the mystery of their baptismal incorporation into Christ, and into the Israel of God, actually became materialized in flesh and blood.

The meaning of Jesus' parables and teaching, shepherding and feeding the people

After the resurrection and ascension the disciples understood why, again and again, Jesus had gathered the lost sheep of the house of Israel, the cultically unclean and those debarred from the temple liturgy of sacrifice. Although it scandalized the priests he deliberately broke down the barriers erected by the cultus and enacted in their midst a sign of the messianic meal, when many would come from the east and the west and sit down with Abraham, Isaac and Jacob in the kingdom of heaven.[54] That eschatological meal was not an eating and drinking

---

[52] Gen 22.8; cf. Cullmann, *Christ and Time*, pp. 107ff. [The reference here appears to be to *Christus und die Zeit*, pp. 107ff. (*Christ and Time*, 3rd edition, pp. 121ff.) – Ed.]

[53] W. Manson, *op.cit.* (*SJT*), p. 39.

[54] Matt 8.11; cf. E. Lohmeyer, *Kultus und Evangelium*, Kommissionsverlag Vandenhoeck & Ruprecht, Göttingen 1942, pp. 36f., 80, and 90f.

between holy priests and holy people, but the marriage-supper of the lamb,[55] who because he had come to bear their sin, gathered the poor and the outcast, the weary and the heavy laden, the publicans and sinners, and fed them with the bread of life and gave them living water to drink.[56] The disciples remembered also the parables of the prodigal son and his feasting in the father's house, of the bridegroom and the wedding-feast, and of the final judgement which would discover those who had given or not given food to the hungry and drink to the thirsty,[57] and they understood their bearing upon the Lord's supper as the great eschatological meal of the kingdom of God through which that very kingdom is realized here and now, as far as it may be in the conditions of this passing world. The disciples recalled, too, those Galilean meals of fellowship with Jesus, the miraculous feeding of the multitudes by the great shepherd of the sheep, and the equally wonderful words he spoke about manna and water, about his flesh and blood, and the life-giving Spirit,[58] and they knew that what had been parable and sign and miracle had then at last materialized in the Easter breaking of bread.[59]

(iv) Standing in the new creation and sharing the power of Christ's resurrection

They saw in his death and resurrection such fulfilment of the Old Testament oracles as gave their teaching creative reinterpretation and threw a flood of light upon the mystery of the cross. In that Jesus had died for them and risen again, he had inaugurated a new covenant within which they could sit down together and eat bread and drink wine, assured that they were one with their Lord, given to partake of his sacrifice, to share in the power of his resurrection and to be bound up with him in the same bundle of life.[60] The ends of the earth had already come upon them, for by this sacramental meal they tasted its powers and were given to stand with Christ on the other side of the judgement, in the new creation. The incredible mystery of baptism

---

55 Rev 19.9.

56 Matt 11.28, 9.10f.; John 6.35ff., 7.37f.

57 Luke 15.11-32; Matt 22.1-10 (cf. Luke 14.15-24); Matt 25.31-46.

58 Matt 14.13-21 (Mark 6.32-44; Luke 9.10-17); Matt 15.32-38 (Mark 8.1-9); John 6, 7.37f.

59 Cf. Luke 24.30-35; John 21.13; Luke 22.15-18 (Matt 26.29; Mark 14.25).

60 1 Sam 25.29 KJV.

was become a visible reality, and the disciples continued in the breaking of bread to commune with their Lord and to proclaim his death as the power of God unto salvation.

The converging of the passover and covenant meals of the Old Testament and the messianic meals of Sinai and Galilee

In order to unfold more fully the significance of the eucharist we must return to the event of the upper room. The apostolic records of that night make it clear that they saw converging in the institution of the supper both the pascal[61] and covenantal meals of the Old Testament[62] and the messianic meals of the wilderness of Sinai and the hills of Galilee.[63] It was charged through and through with eschatological significance. At the beginning of the meal Jesus must have followed the Jewish custom of passing round a cup of wine in token of thanksgiving to God; but before that was done, a piece of bread and a cup of wine were set aside for the messiah in case he should suddenly come to his own in the midst of the feast. Then at the end of the meal charged with pascal and covenantal significance, Jesus took the bread and wine set aside for the messiah and said, 'This is my body.[64] This is my blood which is shed for you.' By breaking the bread and giving it to the disciples, by passing round the cup, he associated them with his sacrifice, giving their existence in relation to himself a new form in the kingdom of God, indeed constituting them as the church concorporate with himself. When

---

[61]　Passover, adjective from *pascha*, Greek for 'passover' (Hebrew *pesach*), Exod 12.1-27.

[62]　Cf. chap.1 below, section 2 (a) (i) *(2)* & (ii).

[63]　Torrance is interpreting the feeding of the manna in Sinai as a messianic foretaste – cf. John 6 and Jesus' comparison of himself as the true manna from heaven, 6.31-35,48-51.

[64]　Torrance customarily spoke of 'This is my body which is broken for you' (the variant reading of 1 Cor 11.24), a reference to the fact that Christ's body though not literally broken, was broken on the cross in the sense of dying for us. Following an observation, however, by D.W. Torrance, that for Jewish Christians it is important that Christ's body was not broken on the cross but remained whole as a perfect and unblemished offering (cf. the passover lamb not a bone of which was to be broken [Exod 12.46; Num 9.12; cf. John 19.36] and the offering of sacrifices 'without blemish' [Exod 29.1; Lev 1.3, 3.1f, 4.3 etc]), Torrance was happy to agree to the use of the shorter synoptic wording.

the apostolic church looked back upon that last supper they recalled that Jesus had bidden them do this repeatedly in remembrance of him, proclaiming thus his death till he should come again to drink it anew with them in the kingdom of God. St John records, too, that the original supper was set in the context of our Lord's high-priestly prayer in which he consecrated himself and interceded for his church.[65]

The eucharist spans past and future, joining the church to the death and advent of Christ

There is a great deal here which we must discuss in order to elucidate its theological structure. We may begin by noting the two fundamental moments within which the eucharist has its place: 'the night on which he was betrayed' and the 'till he come', as St Paul puts them. The eucharist is therefore at once bound to history and related to the advent of Christ at the end of history. It reaches into the past, to the death of Christ, and sets it in the present as reality operative here and now in the church. On the other hand, the eucharist reaches out beyond the present into the future and becomes the means whereby the church in the present is brought under the power of the advent of Christ. The eucharist thus belongs to the very nature of the church, rooting and grounding it in the historical Christ and his saving acts, and also bringing to the church its own ultimate reality from beyond history. By the eucharist that ultimate reality stands not only at the end of time but impinges creatively upon the church throughout history, for it is both the *prōton* and the *eschaton*[66] of its existence. Through the eucharist the church becomes, so to speak, the great arch that spans history, supported by only two pillars, the cross which stands on this side of time, and the coming of Christ in power which stands at the end of history.[67] From age to age the church is grounded upon these two supports by the eucharist, so that its very being is bound up with the essential unity of the two events, the perfected event of the death and resurrection of Christ, and the future event of the *parousia*. It is because the church receives its being ever anew, through the eucharist, as the new creation which is yet to be

---

[65] John 17, known as Jesus' high-priestly prayer.

[66] Gk, *first* and *last*.

[67] Karl Heim, *Jesus the World's Perfecter*, Eng. trans. Oliver & Boyd, Edinburgh 1959, chap. 16, p. 153.

revealed at the parousia, that it lives in dynamic tension here and now on the very frontiers of eternity.[68]

In view of this teaching from the sacraments there are several things that must be said about the eschatological relation when the union with God in Christ is inserted into history.

(b) The sacraments and the eschatological relation[69]

(i) The eschatological relation is not an easy one – the sacraments' twin emphasis

The eschatological relation is not easy. Just as it became fact and reality for us once and for all only through the desperate passion of the cross, so we can follow Christ only by bearing the cross daily. 'I have been crucified with Christ; it is no longer I who live, but Christ who lives in me; and the life which I now live in the flesh I live by the faith of the Son of God, who loved me and gave himself for me'.[70] While on the one hand we are given the real presence of the whole Christ, yet on the other hand that is to be realised in sacramental obedience enacted into our daily life. It is a reconciliation, as we have seen, thrust into a world that continues in its estrangement from and contradiction to God, and that is why in addition to the sacrament of baptism we have the eucharist. We are taught by this that while in new time we are complete in Christ Jesus, yet in the conflicts and abstractions of fallen time we are unable to realise that wholeness, but must nevertheless reckon that we are dead to the old life and created again in the new. That means that while in faith we are a new creation yet we are unable as yet to join body and soul, the invisible and the visible, the material and the spiritual, etc,[71] in any closer union than is given to us in the tensions of the cross through holy communion. The two sides are joined together only in the death and resurrection of Christ.

To try to evade that tension is to deny that although we are redeemed, we wait for the redemption of the purchased possession.

---

[68] End of quotation from *Conflict and Agreement*, vol. 2, pp. 167-171.

[69] For what follows cf. *Conflict and Agreement*, vol. 2, pp. 172-175.

[70] Gal 2.20 RSV/KJV.

[71] This would be appear to be an earlier way of expressing things. Torrance's later thought appears to be expressed in more integrative terms, although clearly with the same tension between the new and the old. Cf. T.F. Torrance, *The Mediation of Christ*, new edition, T & T Clark, Edinburgh 1992, pp. 15-17 – Ed.

It is to deny the eschatology of the eucharist: 'For as often as you eat this bread and drink the cup, *you proclaim the Lord's death until he comes.'*[72] However, although the tension between the invisible and the visible, the new and the old, cannot be resolved in time as we know it, it remains the function of the church in the world to carry the union already perfected in Christ into all the conditions of time, and how the church is constrained until it is accomplished![73] The church has therefore the sacrament set at the heart of her worship in order that she may indeed be the suffering servant in the world, although no doubt she will pray desperately, 'Father if it be possible let this cup pass from me'. But let it be quite clear that unless the church that communicates in the body and blood of our Lord is prepared to throw herself into the heart of the world's trouble, however costly that may be, and act out there the communion which is her very life, she does not take up the cross and follow her Lord. It is thus that 'the kingdom of God presses in and men of determined purpose lay impatient hands upon it'.[74] The church can do that because she knows her Lord in the power of his resurrection.

(ii) The eucharist points to an eschatological fullness still to be unveiled

The perfect union of God and man that has broken into time in the virgin birth, inserted itself into history at the cross, and yet is not the prisoner of fallen time because of the resurrection, entails a new creation that travels through old time inasmuch as Christ Jesus lives on. Although we must communicate again and again in the ever given presence of Christ in the sacrament of holy communion, we cannot forget the reality of baptism, that since the church is incorporated once and for all into Christ there is a sense in which faith feeds uninterruptedly upon the flesh and blood of Christ (John 6) and as such has eternal life abiding in her (John 15). That is the reality which churches can strive to grasp in a doctrine of apostolic succession construed as temporal and historical continuity. But the danger is that when so construed it can fail to realise the important eschatological element in the eucharist in which the church, every time she communicates, receives the judgement of the cross upon

---

[72] 1 Cor 11.26 (Torrance's italics).

[73] Cf. Luke 12.50.

[74] Matt 11.12, W. Manson's translation, *Jesus the Messiah*, Hodder & Stoughton, London 1943, p. 65; cf. Luke 16.16.

the forms and fashions of this passing world, even upon the orders of the church so far as they partake of the forms and fashions of this world. And that judgement in the death of Christ must be shown forth until he comes.[75]

The church must continually transcend herself and her forms in the new creation

Nevertheless, behind it all there is the ever-living continuity of Christ himself, the new creation. And it is precisely because there is that continuity travelling through and under the visible and historical continuities that the latter are disrupted, and inevitably break up, for the axe is already laid to the root of the tree.[76] Whenever the church denies that eschatological element in the eucharist it becomes a human church for then it denies that the church transcends herself in the new creation, and tries to perpetuate in faith an un-crucified Christ who has not really made all things new in the power of the resurrection. It is precisely because the church lives on in the power of the resurrection that she must refuse to be imprisoned in the wrappings of human systems and decisions. Because she is already a resurrected body the church cannot claim, without arresting repentance[77] and quenching the Holy Spirit, that in this fallen world historical succession is of the *esse*, the very nature of the church.[78] Nevertheless, we have in the sacraments, in the union between the visible and the invisible, the material and the spiritual, eschatological pointers to the fact that the complete union which we possess in faith here and now will be unveiled finally in a new heaven and new earth, when not only in faith but in the fullness of sight there will be perfect union between the visible and the invisible, material and spiritual, sense and faith.[79] Apart from that consummation the sacrament of communion has no final meaning, for that consummation is the fulfilled joy of triumph. 'Be of good cheer. I have overcome the world.'[80]

---

[75] On the eschatological element in the eucharist, and the implication that there can be no final validity in any church structure or historical continuity, see *Conflict and Agreement*, vol. 1, p. 174f., 196ff.

[76] Matt 3.10; Luke 3.9.

[77] Cf. Visser t'Hooft, *The Kingship of Christ*, SCM Press, London 1948, p. 69f.

[78] *Esse*, Lat 'to be', the very nature of something.

[79] See the note above, (section (g) (i)), suggesting that in Torrance's later thought this would be expressed in more integrative terms.

[80] John 16.33.

(iii) The wholeness of Christ is a matter of eschatological expectation and not of temporal repetition

We walk by faith and not by sight, until Christ returns and we see him as he is

It is apparent, therefore, that the wholeness of Christ given to us in the sacraments can be thought of only in terms of eschatological expectation and eschatological reiteration, *not* temporal repetition[81] (*as if* the particularity of the incarnation *could be perpetuated* as extension in fallen time,[82] as though Jesus Christ had not risen again). That is the way in which the continuity of the new creation and of new time is manifest in the midst of old time. It could not be otherwise. The New Testament Gospels, in their accounts of the transfiguration and the resurrection appearances, teach us that the transfigured and risen Christ cannot be perpetuated in the institutions and conditions of this passing world. He inevitably vanishes out of our sight. We cannot anticipate the second advent: of that hour not even the son of man knew.[83] Without any doubt whatsoever his real presence is with us, and yet he is still to come. Christ does not communicate himself to us here and now as he will at the second advent, nevertheless his presence is as fully real as it will be then. In the repeated communicating in the body and blood of Christ in the sacrament, the continual feeding of faith upon Christ (John 6) is crowned with vision, but because Christ is wholly identical with himself, and the new creation is a new creation and cannot be identified with this present evil world, it is a Christ who vanishes out of our sight again and again, for as yet we walk by faith not by sight.[84] It is, however, because faith is nourished and crowned with vision in the sacrament again and again, the vision of the transcendent Christ – the alpha and the omega, the beginning and the end who cannot be expressed in terms of this fallen world[85] – that apocalyptic images are an inner necessity for faith. It is faith reaching forward in eager expectation of sight because it is faith that has already seen invisibly the risen saviour. And faith knows that day will come when Jesus

---

[81]   Cf. the footnote, *Conflict and Agreement*, vol. 2, p. 72.

[82]   The original reads, ' . . . Temporal repetition in whatever form is the attempt to perpetuate the particularity of the incarnation as extension in fallen time'.

[83]   See Mark 13.32.

[84]   2 Cor 5.7.

[85]   See Rev 1.13ff.

Christ, the incarnate Son of God, will return and the veil will be torn aside and we shall see him as he is and become like him.[86]

3 Christ the first and the last, the hope of the world[87]

(a) *The differences between apostolic eschatology, Greek idealism and Jewish eschatology*

We may begin here by trying to see the contrast between the eschatology of the apostolic Church and Greek idealism on the one hand and then between apostolic and Jewish eschatology on the other hand.

(i) *The contrast between the eschatology of the apostolic Church and Greek idealism*

Greek thought is not characterized by eschatology, but by a concern for an ideal world, a world of ideas. In classical Platonism,[88] to be sure, the ideal world was not conceived in the modern subjectivist sense but rather in a most real way; nevertheless it was concerned with a world of ideas and not of actions.

Hebrew and Greek: the difference of language

It is worthwhile pausing here to contrast the two languages, Hebrew and Greek, for they appear to reflect the two contrasted outlooks. No doubt Greek was originally as concerned with the verb as Hebrew, but it certainly came to be more concerned with substantives and abstract

---

86 1 John 3.2.

87 'A lecture delivered in Edinburgh, October, 1953, in a post-graduate course on the history of eschatology.' With the addition of headings, and some minor omissions or editing such as the incorporation of inclusive language, the lecture 'Christ the First and the Last' has been reprinted from T.F. Torrance, *Conflict and Agreement*, vol. 1, Lutterworth, London 1959, pp. 304-15. Functioning as a kind of epilogue here, it gathers up and expresses the essential eschatological outlook of Torrance's theology, complementing and amplifying some of the points already expressed more compactly in the eschatology 'addendum' section of this chapter – Ed.

88 The philosophy of Plato, 5th – 4th century B.C, a philosophy concerned with a transcendent, objective and ideal world containing the eternal forms of goodness, truth and beauty which are only imperfectly realised in this world and of which this world is a pale shadow.

conceptions and adjectival relations. Hebrew on the other hand never seems to have grown out of its early verbal emphasis, for its nouns and adjectives are ad-verbial in form and character. The fundamental relation is verbal and therefore, as Martin Buber has taught us, it is action that is primary in Hebrew thought, and that means the kind of action that takes place between persons.

(1) The general contrast between the Hebrew concern with dynamic action and the Greek concern with abstract conceptions and logical relations

Now doubtless this contrast cannot be wholly maintained when we examine linguistic details between the two languages, but for all that it remains true that the Greek language belonged to a way of life and involved a whole web of meaning basically different from that of the Hebrew language. It was not accidental, for example, that it was out of Greek that formal logic emerged; for Greek is much concerned with abstract conceptions and their formal logical relations, but not much with dynamic action. Indeed formal logic eliminates the active verb and translates propositions into forms of the verb 'to be' and that in the present tense. Hebrew language and thought, by contrast, were not concerned with abstract conceptions and their logical relations but with action and personal relation. Thus Hebrew thought about God is not concerned with ideas such as his infinitude, omnipotence, omnipresence, omniscience and the like. These are essentially Greek ideas derived from finite existence and abstractly raised, as it were, to the nth degree and then posited as attributes of the infinite. That whole way of thinking was foreign to the Hebrews, although they had expressions corresponding to those just mentioned, but they were conceived rather as the properties of God in action in creation and history and among humanity. He is the living God and we know him not as we know ideas but as we know people in love and meeting.

Perhaps the difference between the two ways of thinking and speaking comes out most clearly when one takes the vivid dramatic sentences of the Hebrew, with its images and daring analogies and intense activity, and translates them into Greek which, beautiful and accurate as it is, robs the Hebrew of its dramatic imagery and tones down its activism and tends to substitute, in the place of its dynamic temporal movement, static relation between ideas and conceptions. And yet it was the Greeks who taught us how to write history and not the Hebrews – this is where the contrast tends to cut across any schematized comparison between them; but after all the Hebrews were concerned to speak of the acts of God in history and the Greeks were not, and ultimately it is Hebrew and not Greek thought that takes time seriously.

The mutual contribution of Hebrew, Greek and Latin

I do not for a moment mean that we can do without Greek, or even Latin, for in the divine providence it was when Hebrew thought came to be translated into Greek that the great doctrines of Christ and the Trinity began to emerge into something like clarity or at least to be given clear statement. On the other hand theology cannot rest content with purely Greek, and certainly not with purely Latin, formulations: that is, partly at any rate, the meaning of the Reformation. The theology that gained so much from the precision and clarity of Greek and Latin had to be reminted in the Hebraic world of thought in order to regain its dynamic and living character, and so biblical studies and biblical theology have ever since played a fundamental role in the churches of the Reformation.[89]

(2) Differences in the conception of election – personal categories and abstract determinism

Let us consider for a moment the Hebraic conception of election, a most intensely personal choice by God of a personal community, a choice that was actively being fulfilled in the history of that community. But when we translate that loving election of the living God into the abstract categories of Greek and Latin thought, it is very difficult indeed to avoid determinism, for the whole notion of election is translated into terms of logical relation; but logical relation means necessary relation, and necessary relation means deterministic predestination. Hebrew thought in Judaism shows the same tendencies when it enters the world of European thought – and yet is not the reason for that precisely what lies behind Greek thought and played such a prominent and at times such a disastrous role in the fathers, namely the concept of 'the immutability of God'?[90] A God who is so conceived is a prisoner in his abstract deity and is not free to enter into active relations with people, and in that respect is far more Greek than Semitic and certainly

---

[89] Cf. T.F. Torrance, *Theology in Reconstruction*, SCM Press, London 1965, p. 14f., on the different contributions of Greek, Roman and Hebrew culture to the modern world.

[90] On the immutability and impassibility of God see further T.F. Torrance, *The Christian Doctrine of God*, T & T Clark, Edinburgh 1996, chap. 9, 'The Unchangeableness of God', esp. pp. 239-40, 246-54; cf. T.F. Torrance, *The Trinitarian Faith*, T & T Clark, Edinburgh 1988, p. 184ff. for a discussion of the impassibility of God in a patristic context and how it is to be understood.

far removed from the living active God of the Old Testament and God the Son who became incarnate in Jesus Christ. It is ultimately the doctrine of God that stands behind the great contrasts in eschatology.

(3) The difference between the Hebrew 'eternal end' which enters time and history, and the Greek timeless and 'ideal end'

But to return to an earlier point, Hebrew thought is concerned not with logical, timeless relation but with action and with time, or rather with God acting in time, God acting among men and women in history. Therefore the end of God's action is also an historical end as well as an eternal end. It must be concerned with an eternal end, for it is the action of the eternal God; but it is the action of the eternal God in time and history, an action that reaches throughout history to future fulfilment and perfection. Greek thought, on the other hand, is ideal, and reaches out not to an historical end but to an ideal end, a timeless end. There is therefore a vast difference between the Greek notion of end and the biblical notion of end, and the biblical notion of end is precisely the core of the gospel. If the end is ideal, no matter how much someone strives to realize it, that is, to be what they ought to be, the end is still ideal and beyond their attainment. But in the Christian gospel this end has broken into the present and is even now operative in the world. Because that final end has already entered history, the whole of Christian thought and action can no longer be construed in terms of idealism but in realistic terms of history and time, in terms of a new creation, a new heaven and a new earth.

A further characteristic of biblical eschatology is that the divine action which intervenes in the lives of men and women in history, bodies itself forth concretely in human history, embodies itself in humanity. Hence the place of the messianic community in the heart of biblical eschatology. The action of the living God is intensely personal as well as historical, and creates a community of persons as the sphere of divine operation in the world. That is the significance of Israel – but more and more that divine action becomes acutely personalised as it presses toward the incarnation and reaches its end and fulfilment in Jesus Christ in the fullness of time.

(ii) The contrast between Christian eschatology and late Judaistic eschatology – the telescoping together of the two ages of Judaism

It is here in this fulfilment in Jesus Christ that we come to see the contrast between Christian eschatology and Jewish eschatology – by Jewish eschatology I mean the late Judaistic eschatology which diverged somewhat from the prophetic teaching of the Old Testament.

The characteristic way in which Judaism stated its view was through the contrast between the two ages or realms, between the present age (*aiōn houtos*) and the future age (*aiōn mellōn*). This present age, the historical cosmos as we know it day by day, will pass away and it will be replaced by a new age entailing a new heaven and a new earth, and entailing a community which is both continuous with the old in lineage and yet radically new. But the second of these ages follows hard upon the heels of the first, so that as long as we are still in this present age which passes away, the new age is entirely future. The Christian gospel, however, is synonymous with the exciting news that the future age has already come upon us, telescoping itself, as it were, into the present age. This present age still goes on; history continues in the same old way, but the whole framework is altered, for the final goal of history has come into the midst of time and is now lodged in the very heart of it. That is the eschatological significance of the incarnation, and that is what Jesus preached. 'Repent! for the kingdom of God is at hand; it has come upon you.'[91] In Jesus the king of the kingdom, the judge of all the ages, is actively present among humanity.

The turning point between the old age and the new and the dawning of the new age

But with the death and resurrection of Jesus Christ, the apostles came, as Jesus predicted, to a deeper realization of what had happened and was still happening. In the death of Jesus Christ the final judgement of the world had precipitated itself into the present; the final, ultimate conflict between God and evil had taken place on the cross.[92] That was the great decisive point in the ages, the turning point between the old age and the new age. With the resurrection of Jesus from the dead the apostles realized that not only had the decisive event taken place, but the new age had already dawned; the new creation was already revealed in its transcendent perfection and glory in the risen man, Jesus – the first-fruits of the resurrection, the new Adam, the last Adam, the earnest and pledge of our inheritance.[93]

Apostolic eschatology was therefore breathless with excitement and wonder, for the ends of the world had come upon mankind, and the final victory of God over the forces of evil lay behind. The apostolic

---

[91]   See Mark 1.15; Matt 4.17.

[92]   John 12.31-32, 16.8-11; cf. Acts 17.30-31; Rom 1.18ff.; Luke 3.7ff.

[93]   Acts 2.17ff.; 1 Cor 10.11; 2 Cor 5.17; 1 Cor 15.20ff.,45ff.; Eph 1.13-14 (cf. 2 Cor 1.22, 5.5; Rom 8.23).

age is on the resurrection side of the cross, advancing into the promised land.

With Pentecost, the outpouring in fullness of the Holy Spirit, the apostles realized that not only was Jesus himself the beginning of the new creation, but by participating in the Holy Spirit the apostles themselves were already participating in the powers of the age to come[94] and were already living in the new age. The new community was inaugurated in the church and as such it advanced into history increasing and growing and expanding; beginning with the nucleus of the twelve disciples and the one hundred and twenty on the day of Pentecost, it reached out in ever widening dimensions under the command and promise of the Lord which directed them to the ends of the earth and the ends of the age.[95]

(b) The main features of apostolic eschatology

But now to be more precise, let us try to summarize the main features of this eschatology in several sections.

(i) The basic fact of the person of Christ, the risen Lord ascended to kingly rule

The basic fact is the person of Jesus Christ, the risen Lord ascended to kingly rule over all in heaven and earth. The resurrection and ascension mean the completion of his work and include the certainty of his advent in glory. At the heart of the apostolic eschatology, therefore, lies the emphasis upon the present lordship of Christ, a lordship asserted by his death and resurrection over all principalities and powers and all dominions.[96] The assertion of that sovereignty is an accomplished fact in the complete triumph of the cross and resurrection, and therefore the kingdom has already come with power in the very first generation of the followers of Jesus Christ. The full unveiling of that triumph is still awaited, when Christ will make an open show of his power and exhibit the spoils of his victory.

(ii) The one parousia of Christ, from incarnation to final advent in glory

Eschatology concerns the *parousia* of Jesus Christ the king of the kingdom. That *parousia* comprises his birth, life, death, resurrection,

---

94   Heb 6.4-5.

95   Acts 1.15,8; Matt 28.18f.

96   Acts 2.33-36; Eph 1.20f.; Col 2.9-10,15, cf. 1.15-20; Eph 1.10, 4.10.

ascension and second advent as one extended event, the great inclusive event of *Immanuel*, God with us. From the aspect of ongoing history, however, the *parousia* is both the decisive intervention of the kingdom in time, in the incarnation of the Son of God in Jesus Christ, and also the final advent in glory. The link between the two advents is the *parousia* of Christ through the Spirit, the abiding *parousia*. It is this trinitarian understanding of *parousia* that is of the very essence of eschatology in the apostolic age, as we see with particular clarity in the Apocalypse: Christ the *prōtos* or first, the Alpha who was, Christ the *eschatos* or last, the Omega who is to come, but also the Christ who is here and now in the midst of his church on earth.[97] It was not till the middle of the second century that the church started to speak of two advents of Christ and so to use the word *parousia* in the plural – at least I am not aware of any earlier use of it. The *parousia* is strictly one inclusive coming-and-presence operating with different modes of revelation.

(iii) The two great moments of the death-and-resurrection of Christ, and the final apocalypse in glory

The two great moments in the eschatological economy are the death and resurrection of Christ, and the final apocalypse of his glory. It was in the incarnation, death and resurrection of Christ that the perfect work of redemption was accomplished. The work of the kingdom in Jesus Christ was final, once for all. To that finality belongs the outpouring of the Spirit at Pentecost, the New Testament revelation, and the constitution of the apostolate and so the foundation of the church. That final deed in Christ was also regarded as having cosmic import and cosmic effect, the significance no doubt of the witness recorded as to the cosmic disturbances when Jesus died on the cross.[98] The cross was the great *kairos*, moment or time, when the sovereignty of God struck into the heart of the world, and it is still by that cross that he draws the whole world into the sphere of his redeeming operation. All history is now placed under the power of the cross, while in the resurrection the new age already dawned overlaps this present age, the age of ongoing empirical history. The full manifestation or unveiling of the new age, the perfection of Christ's work of redemption and its full power, are yet to be revealed in the final *kairos* when Jesus Christ will come again in glory. Then this present age, the cosmos as it

---

97   Rev 1.17-18, 21.6, 22.13.

98   Matt 27.45,51-54 (Mark 15.33,38; Luke 23.44-45).

is now constituted, the world in its present conditions with all its forms and patterns suited to human selfishness and sin, will pass away, and the new age, the new creation, will stand revealed. Meantime all that happens on earth and in time, within or without the church, is conditioned proleptically by the coming of Jesus Christ as judge and saviour.

(iv) Between the moments, the ascension and the presence of Christ through the Spirit

Between those two eschatological moments or *kairoi*, the first advent and the second advent, the *parousia* refers to the abiding presence of Jesus Christ. He is the *prōtos* who was, the *eschatos* who will be, but he is also *Egō eimi* the "I am", the '*ho ōn*', "he who is".[99] It is here that we must see the place of the ascension in apostolic eschatology. The ascension means on the one hand that Christ has ascended to the throne of God almighty, and from there rules over all things and fills all things; it means on the other hand the pouring out of his Spirit in fullness upon the church on earth[100] – so that while he is above, the Lord of the ages, king of the aeons, yet he is present in the midst of his people on earth and in history.

How is the *parousia* of Christ here and now connected with the *parousia* of his kingdom in the fullness of glory? Clearly, Jesus Christ has withdrawn himself from sight, from ongoing empirical history, withdrawn himself from contemporaneous contact within history for reasons of mercy. Full manifestation of the risen Lord now in all his glory and majesty would mean the immediate end of this age, the end of the world, the final judgement – and so Jesus gave only fleeting glimpses of that glory to his disciples after his resurrection, sufficient to show them that he had risen indeed, in body and in the fullness of his humanity.[101]

(1) The ascended Lord can be known only through the historical Jesus

Moreover, by withdrawing himself from sight the ascended Lord sends the church back to the historical Jesus, to the gospel story of the incarnation, public ministry, death and resurrection as the only *locus* or place where he may be contacted. If Jesus had continued to be with

---

[99] Rev 1.18.

[100] Acts 2.33-36; Eph 4.8ff.

[101] Matt 28.9-10,17f.; Luke 24.13-31,36ff.; John 20.14-18,19-23,26-29, 21.1-23; Acts 1.3,6-9.

his church all through history as the visible contemporary of every generation, the cross would have been relegated into the past and treated as a passing episode, and not as the fact of final and supreme and central import. The whole historical life and revelation of Jesus would have lost much of its significance. But he has veiled his present glory, so that if we would find him we must go back to the historical Jesus. That is the only place where we may meet him, but there we make contact with him through the cross at the point where the final act of God regarding sin has been accomplished. There is no other road to the *parousia* of the risen Jesus, the Lord of glory, except through the Jesus of humiliation, the Jesus of Bethlehem and Judaea and Galilee and Calvary.

(2) The ascended Lord is known in the historical Jesus, but only through the Spirit,

But even when we turn to the historical Jesus we can no longer make contact with him as the disciples did before his crucifixion and resurrection. We must seek to contact him, therefore, not after the flesh but after the Spirit. We go back to the historical Jesus, to the gospel story, but there it is with the risen and ascended Lord that we make contact. We look back at the historical Jesus from the perspective of the resurrection and we encounter the risen Christ in his abiding *parousia*. We find that *parousia* only as the Jesus of history is transfigured before us; that is partly the significance of the way in which the fourth Gospel presents Christ, but it is clearly the import of the Johannine presentation of Christ in the opening chapter of the Apocalypse: the familiar figure of Jesus clothed with his transcendent majesty and glory, and yet for all that still the same Jesus.[102]

(3) Between the times Jesus is known through historical witness, by word and Spirit

The ascension means, therefore, that we who live between the times, between the first advent of Christ and his second advent, can only encounter the risen Lord if we go back to the first advent, to Jesus as he was; that is, if we go back to the historical witness, to the word of the gospel. But on the other hand, the ascension means that we who live between the times have the gift of the Spirit, and yet we have that gift only as we go back to the historical Jesus, for the Spirit is sent not to speak of himself but to take of the historical Jesus, the life and words, the death and resurrection of the historical Jesus, and to reveal them

---

[102] Rev 1.12ff.

to us in their full significance and reality.[103] Thus between the two advents of Christ, eschatology is concerned with the double movement: the thrusting of the word of the gospel into history by the witness of the church, but as that word of the gospel is proclaimed in all the world, it is Christ the lamb of God who by his Spirit reigns over all things, making all things to serve his purpose of redeeming love. That means that eschatology and world-mission belong together, as Jesus made clear in his final commands to the apostles before he ascended. In other words, eschatology is concerned with the relation between the word and the Spirit, whether that be within the fellowship of the church in word and sacrament, or in the witness of the church unto the ends of the earth that Jesus is Lord and saviour, or in the disturbance and upheaval caused among the nations by the proclamation of the gospel, that is, apocalyptic tension and conflict.

(v) The church as the eschatological community reaching out to the age to come

We come now to the church in history as the eschatological community, the community that reaches out beyond this present age into the age to come and derives its life from there, even though it still participates in the ongoing history of this present age. The church lives in the midst of that eschatological tension, but that tension is itself dual – this is the difficult thing about the eschatology of the New Testament, but its very heart. The tension is twofold: (1) tension between the new and the old here and now, and (2) tension between the present and the future.

(1) The tension between the new and the old – hope and the expectation of Christ's coming

The tension between the new and the old is created by present participation through the Spirit (in word and sacrament) in the new creation. Therefore the church, already in the new creation and tasting its powers, inevitably feels that the thinnest veil of sense and time divides it from the full experience of the new. The new is absolutely near through the Spirit, and its impact on the old means even now the break up of the old. The tense awareness of the new age, of fellowship in the power of the resurrection here and now carries with it the imminence to faith of the epiphany of Christ, his final unveiling in glory. That eschatological expectation, the hope of Christ's appearing

---

[103] John 14.26, 16.13-15.

just round the corner, so to speak, is essential to faith in Jesus Christ, for he is there already present waiting to unveil his majesty. That is why the writers of the New Testament are acutely aware of the pressure of the *parousia* upon them, the knocking of the advent Christ already on the door.[104]

(2) The tension between the present and the future – faith is inherently eschatological

But faith exists not only in hope in the epiphany of Christ; it is bound up with the veiling of Christ, with the ascension, and here we come back to the other reason for the ascension or the purposed withdrawal of Christ from sight. Faith can exist only where there is a gap, an eschatological reserve, between the present and the future, between actual participation in the kingdom here and now and the future manifestation of its glory.[105] Let us consider it like this. If Jesus had manifested his full divine glory on earth so that men and women were confronted face to face with the ultimate majesty of God, then they would have been damned on the spot; they would have been face to face with the final judgement. But the veiling of his ultimate glory meant that Jesus was giving people a chance to repent; he was holding them at arm's length away, so to speak, giving them time to repent, room for decision. He came veiling his glory, yet revealing himself obliquely, so as to give people enough light to believe but not enough finally to blind them or judge them. That is why he refused to give a compelling demonstration of himself, but sought to evoke faith. Faith is not sight, but faith answers to revelation that is yet only in part, for faith exists in the gap between partial and final manifestation. Faith is, therefore, essentially eschatological in its inner nature.

Now the ascension means that Jesus Christ has withdrawn himself from sight and history in order to allow the whole world time for repentance.[106] He holds back the final unveiling of his glory and majesty, holds back the final judgement when there will be no time to repent, and when, as the Apocalypse puts it, the person that is filthy will be filthy still.[107] That gap between the times is the eschatological time when this present age is already interpenetrated by the age to come,

---

[104]   Rev 3.20.

[105]   Cf. 2 Cor 5.6-8; 1 Peter 1.5ff.; 1 John 3.2; John 20.29-31; Heb 11.1-12.2; Eph 3.17.

[106]   2 Peter 3.4f.,9,15; cf. Rom 2.4, 3.25.

[107]   See Rev 22.11.

but it is time when the new age in all its glory is as yet veiled from sight, in order to leave room to preach the gospel and give all opportunity for repentance and faith. Thus the world-mission of the church is part of God's grace, for it is God's grace alone that keeps back the dissolution of this age.

(vi) The church must live by being transformed in Christ and therefore in tension with the forms of this world

We have seen that it is the church's participation through the Spirit in the new age that involves it in that situation of eschatological tension, but now we must see that the involvement of the church in this present age gives particular form to that tension. The real life of the church lies in its participation in the resurrection, in the new creation, and so in its detachment from the forms of this present evil age.

Therefore the church is warned in the New Testament against systematization or schematization to the patterns of this cosmos; for it lives through being transformed and renewed in Christ[108] and it must not live in disagreement with its essential nature. That contrast is also of the essence of eschatology. In Pauline language it is the contrast between law and Spirit, between works and grace.[109] The form of this present world is law, but the essential character of the church's life is freedom in the Spirit.[110] The epistle to the Galatians, therefore, from this point of view, is the most eschatological of all Paul's epistles. Christian freedom in the Spirit is grounded in justification – by grace and not by works – therefore we are made free from the law of works. God's grace has set our life on a wholly new basis in which love and gratitude operate on the ground of what Christ has completed in his death and resurrection on our behalf. In Johannine language this is the contrast between death and eternal life, between darkness and light, between the lie and the truth; and here too, one must say, from this perspective, the first epistle of John is a thoroughly eschatological piece of writing. In the language of the Apocalypse, this is the clash between the perfect kingdom of God and the kingdoms of this age, between the perfect pattern of the new creation and the bestial and brutal images thrown up out of the sea of the nations in defiance of God's love and grace.[111]

---

[108] Cf. Rom 12.2.

[109] Rom 7 – 8; Gal 2.26-5.25; Eph 2.5ff.; Phil 3.3-9; 2 Cor 3.

[110] Gal 4 – 5; Rom 6.1-8.17; 2 Cor 3.17.

[111] Rev 13.1ff.

(vii) The suffering servant with the song of indescribable joy and triumph in Jesus Christ

The church that is launched into this situation in history is the suffering servant, the church under the cross, and to all outward appearances the weak and helpless, the despised and downtrodden church, but it is also the church of the victorious king. The shout of a king is in its midst! A new song is in its mouth, the song of final and complete triumph, a song of indescribable joy and confidence in Jesus Christ. The apostles of this church were essentially the ambassadors of the king of kings, sent into all the world as heralds of the new era, already inaugurated, and soon to be revealed. They were eye witnesses of the resurrection,[112] of the fact that the last day had already dawned, and they were heralds of its coming in power. That is why the *kērygma* of the New Testament is eschatological through and through, because it is exultant with the glad news of the kingdom.

---

[112] Acts 1.22, 2.32, 3.13, 5.32, 10.41; cf. Luke 1.2; 2 Peter 1.16.

Epilogue:

THE RECONCILIATION OF MIND

A Theological Meditation upon the Teaching of St Paul[1]

In Christ all the fullness of God was pleased to dwell, and through him to reconcile to himself all things, whether on earth or in heaven, making peace by the blood of his cross. And you, who once were estranged and hostile in mind, doing evil deeds, he has now reconciled in his body of flesh by his death, in order to present you holy and blameless and irreproachable before him.

Colossians 1.19-22

I appeal to you therefore brethren, by the mercies of God, to present your bodies as a living sacrifice, holy and acceptable unto God, which is your spiritual worship. Do not be conformed to this world but be transformed by the renewal of your mind, that you may prove what is the will of God, what is good and acceptable and perfect.

Romans 12.1-2

Alienation in mind – the difficulty of the 'unbaptised reason' of ancient and modern culture

In these statements, St Paul stressed the fact that we are alienated or estranged in our minds, and indeed are hostile in mind to God. This is

---

[1]   Reprinted, with the addition of headings, by kind permission from *Theology in the Service of the Church: Essays in Honor of Thomas W. Gillespie*, ed. Wallace M. Alston Jr., pp. 196-204 (© 2000 Wm B. Eerdmans Publishing Company, Grand Rapids, Michigan – all rights reserved). Torrance's essay here encapsulates a number of themes central to his lectures and theology, in particular the rationality of faith in Jesus Christ, the profound transformation necessary in the unbaptised human reason in order to know the truth of God in Christ, and the need for the church to attempt to evangelise the very foundations of human thought and culture so that the gospel may be better able to take root in them. As an epilogue it also helps to give a more personal glimpse into the nature, challenge and task of theology as he saw it.

a basic New Testament conception which was deeply resented by the rational culture of the ancient classical world of Greece and Rome, and which the rational culture of the medieval world and the rational, philosophical, and scientific culture of our modern world have found very difficult to accept. This applies not least to 'evangelical Christianity' today, which on the whole still seems to work with what may be called an 'unbaptised reason', for it does not seem to have thought through sufficiently the transformation of human reason in the light of the Word made flesh in Jesus Christ. Hence the *mind* of the church and the *mind* of society are not inwardly formed by the gospel – they remain basically unevangelised. The reason for this is that we have not taken seriously this New Testament emphasis that the mind of man is alienated at its very root. It is in the human mind that sin is entrenched, and so it is right there, the gospel tells us, that we require to be cleansed by the blood of Christ and to be healed and reconciled to God.

The reality of mind in the human person

According to the teaching of the bible, man has been created in mind as well as body out of nothing. We must not forget that a creaturely human mind has 'being'. This is a fact which, interestingly, our neurologists, brain-scientists and psychiatrists have been coming to recognise. Some of them speak of the mind as constituting a 'fifth dimension', and others refer to the 'ontology of mind'. The mind is ontologically real – it has being. What they do not often recognise, however, is that it is deep in this mental being that our humanity is twisted and distorted, and indeed, to use Old Testament language echoed here by St Paul, is 'desperately wicked'.[2] We do not find in St Paul, any more than in the Old Testament, any body/soul or body/mind dualism, for as James Denney used to express it, a human person is the body of their soul and the soul of their body, or the body of their mind and the mind of their body, a unitary whole. It is as such that man has fallen and become alienated from God, and as such needs to be redeemed.

The need for healing in the ontological depths of our human mind and being

Now the mind of a human being constitutes what the Greeks called the *hēgemonikon* or the governing principle, for it is the mind that governs or directs our behaviour as human beings. Thus where modern

---

[2]   Jer 17.9

people tend to refer to the will as the determining factor in human behaviour, the Greek fathers traced everything back to the mind. It is a mistake to think that because they laid this emphasis upon the mind as the governing element in human nature they were not interested in the will and did not therefore stress the freedom of the will as modern people do. The Greek fathers realised, however, as perhaps few people do today that although we may have freewill, we are not at all free to escape from our self-will. That is why they put their finger on the twisted state of affairs in the depths of the human mind. It is in the heart of our mental reality which governs and controls all our thinking and culture that we have become estranged from the truth and hostile to God. And it is right there, in the ontological depths of the human mind, that we desperately need to be redeemed and healed.

Apollinarianism: the replacement of human mind by divine mind in Jesus

As I have indicated, the rational culture of the ancient classical world found this very difficult to accept, so that inevitably difficult problems arose whenever the gospel began to take root and find expression in Greek life and thought. Thus we find cropping up fairly early within the church an insidious heresy that came to be known as 'Apollinarianism'. It took its name from Apollinaris, a very clever theologian, who refused to believe that in his incarnation, the Son of God took upon himself our alienated, twisted mind because it was in that mind that sin had become rooted and entrenched. If Jesus had taken our alienated mind upon himself, so argued Apollinaris, he must have been a sinner, in fact an original sinner. And so he held that the Son of God became incarnate in our human existence in such a way that in Jesus, the human mind was displaced by the divine mind. It was therefore some sort of neutral humanity that the Son of God assumed, and not the actual humanity in which we sinners all share.

The agonising struggle of Jesus in his atoning reconciliation of the human mind to God

However, the fathers of the church found this conception of the incarnation to be evangelically and soteriologically deficient. If at that point, in the heart of our mental being, we are not redeemed and cleansed by the blood of Christ then we are not really saved at all. If in the fundamental controlling principle of our human mind, we are untouched by the incarnation and the atonement, then we are no better off than the pagan Greeks. And so the Christian church insisted that we must take very seriously the fact that in the incarnation, the holy Son of God assumed our fallen, enslaved human nature, our twisted, distorted, bent mind, *but* that in assuming it right from the very beginning, our Lord converted it, healed it, and sanctified it in himself. In taking from us our fallen human nature upon himself, instead of sinning in it as we all do, Jesus condemned sin in our carnal mind,[3] and was himself wholly without sin.[4] And so by living out a life of perfect holiness and purity in his mind, he sanctified and healed our human mind in the whole course of his incarnate and redemptive life from his birth to his crucifixion. He carried our mind into the very depths of his agonising and atoning struggle on the cross – he descended into the hell of the utmost wickedness and dereliction of the human mind under the judgment of God, in order to lay hold upon the very root of our sin and to redeem us from its stranglehold upon us. Yes, it was not only our actual sins, but it was original sin and original guilt that the Son of God took upon himself in incarnation and atonement, in order to heal, convert, and sanctify the human mind in himself and reconcile it to God.

Irenaeus: Jesus' assumption and conversion of leprous humanity and diseased mind

There is extant a fragment of a second-century theologian, Irenaeus, which I like to think of in this connection. In it there seems to be a suggestion that the incarnation may be understood in the light of the incident recorded in the gospel when Jesus touched a leper, and, instead of becoming leprous himself, he healed the leper.[5] In the western world today one hardly ever comes across a leper. I used to pass a leper colony when I went to school every day as a boy in China. That was long ago, but I have never forgotten the horrible emaciation of face and hand and limb in leprous flesh. If I sense what Irenaeus had in mind in that tantalising fragment, it was that Jesus had taken what Irenaeus spoke of as our leprous humanity upon himself, but that instead of becoming a leper himself, he healed and transformed our 'leprous' human nature

---

3   Cf. Rom 8.3-4ff.

4   2 Cor 5.24; Heb 4.15.

5   Mark 1.40-42.

and restored it to be like the flesh of a newborn child.[6] But let us not forget that it was our diseased *mind* that our Lord assumed for our sakes. In assuming it, however, far from sinning himself or being estranged and alienated from the Father, even when he penetrated into the fearful depths of our alienation – 'My God, my God, why have you forsaken me?'[7] – he converted it from the very bottom of our disobedient human being, from the roots of our estranged mental existence, into perfect oneness with the mind of God – 'Father, into thy hands I commit my spirit.'[8] In the epistle to the Colossians, as in the epistle to the Ephesians, St Paul thought of that atoning reconciliation as embracing heaven as well as earth, for all things invisible as well as visible need to be cleansed by the blood of Christ and reconciled to God and even be renewed in 'the spirit of our mind'.[9] Reconciliation in Christ applies to the invisible mental life of human being!

The patristic principle that what Jesus did not assume in his incarnation has not been saved

It was in order to conserve this biblical teaching that great patristic theologians in the early church enunciated as a fundamental principle, *'The unassumed is the unhealed'* (Gregory of Nazianzus), or *'What Christ has not assumed has not been saved'* (Cyril of Alexandria). They reckoned that the church would be soteriologically and evangelically deficient if it refused to take seriously that Christ took our fallen mind upon himself in order to redeem and save it. That is a truth which I first learned from my beloved Edinburgh teacher, H.R. Mackintosh, who had himself been profoundly influenced by the christology of these Greek fathers. But it was only when I studied Karl Barth's account of this doctrine that its truth broke in upon my mind in a quite unforgettable way. I refer to that section in the *Church Dogmatics* 1.2 where Barth expounded the mystery of the virgin birth.[10] Overwhelmed by the immense significance of what our Lord had done all for our

---

[6]   Cf. 2 Kings 5.14 (5.1-14).

[7]   Mark 15.34 (Matt 27.46).

[8]   Luke 23.46.

[9]   Cf. Col 1.15-20; Eph 1.9-10, 4.23 ('the spirit of your mind', tō pneumati tou noos humōn).

[10]   Karl Barth, *Church Dogmatics*, 1/2, Eng. trans. T & T Clark, Edinburgh 1956, pp. 172-202.

sakes and in our place, I fell to the ground on my knees trembling in awe and wonder at the sheer miracle of God's grace in the birth, life, and passion of Jesus – the miracle that foul, wicked, depraved humanity twisted in upon itself, had been appropriated from us by the Son of God, and been cleansed, changed, redeemed, and sanctified in him.

Karl Barth and the evangelisation of human reason through the gospel

There we have to do with the inner heart of evangelical theology – the transforming of the human mind in such a way that it is no longer conformed to the patterns of this world but brought through renewal into conformity to Christ, through the communion of our mind with the mind of God in him, and its assimilation to the holiness and truth of God incarnate in Jesus. That is far from being easy, but it is something which fidelity to the gospel will not allow us to avoid. It was because Karl Barth, for example, took this so seriously that he spent so much of his life thinking out in the light of God's self-revelation in Christ what the renewal of the human mind means, and what knowledge of the truth as it is in Jesus implies for the transformation of reason, intelligibility, and objectivity in Christian theology. Karl Barth was above all an evangelical theologian who spent his life in evangelising the human reason, whereas the great majority of Protestant and Roman Catholic theologians still operate, I am afraid, with an unregenerated and unbaptised reason, and thus avoid the agonising experience of working out conformity to Christ in the ontological depths of their minds.

The restructuring of human hands for the piano

Sometimes the inner conflict in which people find themselves can be very sharp, as I learned as soon as I began to teach Christian theology, so that I regularly made a point of alerting students to what was involved. I used to tell them about a friend of mine who went up to Basel to study music when I went there to study theology with Karl Barth. In those years before the war, there were two of the world's greatest musicians in Basel, Adolf Busch and Rudolf Serkin – it was with the latter that my friend Edgar wanted to take piano lessons. Serkin looked at his hands and asked how old he was. When he said that he was twenty-seven, Serkin shook his head and told him that he was too old for him to take on, and declined to enrol him. But Edgar hung about and when Serkin found that he had an unusually keen 'understanding for music', he sent him to a friend in Salzburg who gave him exercises for six months on end, until the muscular functioning of his hands was transformed. I recall his talking to me afterwards about the drawn-out pain and agony of that experience. But it had been worth it, for when the muscles in his hands had been sufficiently restructured, Serkin at last took him on – and in due course Edgar became a distinguished musician, and indeed a composer, himself.

The restructuring of the human mind in theology through the truth of the gospel

In recounting that story to my young students I used to say to them, 'Something similar may well happen to you in these classes, for as you let the truth of the gospel have its way with you, you will find the very shape and structure of your mind beginning to change.' That is indeed what the gospel is about, a *metanoia*, a radical repentant rethinking of everything before the face of Jesus Christ. No better account of theological method has been given than that which Jesus gave to his disciples when he said: 'If any man would come after me, let him deny himself and take up his cross and follow me.'[11] That is what repentant rethinking means: you cannot separate evangelical theology from that profound experience of the radical changing and transforming of your mind that comes through dying and rising with Christ.

The struggle between the structure of our natural reason and the mind of Christ

There often came a point in my classes when I felt that the students wanted to throw their books at me, as the inner struggle between the gospel and the frame of mind they brought to it became intense. Let us make no mistake about it: divine revelation conflicts sharply with the structure of our natural reason, with the secular patterns of thought that have already become established in our minds through the twist of our ingrained mental alienation from God. We cannot become true theologians without the agonising experience of profound change in the mental structure of our innermost being.

'Let this mind be in you (*touto phroneite*)' as St Paul wrote to the Philippians, 'which was also in Christ Jesus'.[12] The early Greek fathers

---

[11] Mark 8.34

[12] Phil 2.5 KJV.

gave a great deal of thought to that injunction. They cultivated what they called 'the apostolic mind' (*phronēma apostolikon*), for it was only through the mind of the apostles embodied in the holy scriptures that the church could be imbued with the mind of Christ (*phronēma Christou*) himself. That is precisely what a faithful theology is about, the assimilation of the mind of the church to the self-revelation of the Father through the Son and in the Spirit.

Conformity to the mind of Christ: theology and the evangelisation of human mind and culture

Thus a regular question raised by Christian theologians, concealed behind all the great debates in the early centuries, was whether they were really thinking *worthily* of God in accordance with the mind of Christ Jesus as it has been imprinted by the Holy Spirit in the apostolic foundation of the church and expressed in the apostolic scriptures. All through those early centuries as the gospel was carried from end to end of the Mediterranean world, Christian theology played a major role in the evangelising of nation after nation, for it was only as the mind and culture of people were brought into conformity to the mind of Christ that the church could put down permanent roots in the soil of humanity. As in the New Testament, preaching and teaching (*kērygma* and *didachē*) were always interwoven with each other, so in the remarkable growth and expansion of the church after New Testament times, theological and evangelising activity always functioned inseparably together. By its intrinsic nature an evangelical theology is an evangelising theology, for it is concerned with the winning and transforming of the human mind through conformity to the mind of Christ Jesus – not simply the minds of individual human beings but the mind of human society and culture in which individual human beings exist.

The challenge of evangelising society and its roots as well as individuals

What does this have to say to us today about what we call 'evangelical Christianity'? We have been concerned with evangelising men, women and children as individual human beings, calling for repentance and personal decision for Christ as Lord and saviour, and rightly so. But have we been concerned with the evangelising of the *mind* of the society in which these people live? If not, how can a Christian church put down roots in an unevangelised society and remain genuinely

Christian? I believe this is where evangelical Christianity today has failed terribly. By and large, as far as I can see, even the mind of the church, let alone the mind of society, is still secular in that it shares the mind of the secular society within which it exists. We have Christian people, but do we really have a *Christian* church? We have people who profess to believe in Christ as Lord and saviour, but do we have a church that is so imbued with the mind of Christ that its members individually and as a community think *instinctively* in a Christian way?

The need and importance of developing a theological instinct

I have been wonderfully blessed with a mother and a wife who have a profoundly Christian, and indeed a remarkably theological, *instinct.* My mother had little academic training in theology, but her life and her understanding were so tuned in to the mind of Christ that she knew at once where the truth lay and was quick to discern any deviation from it. This is also very true of my dear wife, who is imbued with an unerring *theological instinct*, evident again and again in her reaction to ideas put forward by preachers or teachers. At the end of the day that was the test I used to put to my students, as I read their essays and examinations or listened to them in the chapel.[13] 'Has this person a genuinely theological instinct or not? Is his or her thinking spontaneously and naturally governed by the mind of Christ?' That is much more important than being theologically learned, much more important than being able to offer a formal academic account of some doctrine or historic debate in the church. What really counts in the end is whether a person's mind is radically transformed by Christ and so spiritually attuned to the mind of Christ, that he or she thinks instinctively from the depths of their mental being in a way worthy of God.

Thinking in accordance with the nature of God: theology and not mythology

As Athanasius used to insist, we must learn to think strictly 'in accordance with the nature' (*kata physin*) of God the Father as he is made known to us through the Son and in the Holy Spirit, that is, in an essentially godly way (*eusebōs*). To think like that from a centre in God himself, in accordance with his essential nature revealed in the incarnate Son, is, he claimed, what *theologia* strictly is. If any one does

---

[13] The daily prayers in New College chapel led by a student or member of staff after morning lectures and before lunch.

not think in that way, but thinks from a centre in oneself, governed by the devising of one's own reason, then one is bound to think of him in an unworthy or irreligious way (*asebōs*) – which Athanasius designated *mythologia*. Either you think from out of a mind centred in God through union with the mind of the Lord Jesus, or you think from out of a mind centred in yourself, alienated from God and inwardly hostile to the truth incarnate in the Lord Jesus, that is, in a way that is finally governed by the unregenerate and unbaptised reason.

The transformation of the mind in theology is impossible without daily prayer through Christ

The transformation of the human mind and its renewal through assimilation to the mind of Christ is something that has to go on throughout the whole of our life – it is a never-ending discipleship in repentant rethinking as we take up the cross and follow Christ. That is why we cannot be theologians without incessant prayer in offering ourselves daily to God through the reconciling and atoning mediation of Christ; and that is also why we cannot be evangelists without being theologians whose minds are constantly schooled in obedience to Christ. It is after all with our minds that we worship God and it is only with our minds that we can preach the gospel and evangelise the world. Is that not, in part at least, what St Paul was concerned with in the two verses from the twelfth chapter of his epistle to the Romans, 'I appeal to you therefore, brethren, by the mercies of God, to present your bodies a living sacrifice, holy and acceptable to God, which is your spiritual worship (*logikē latreia*). [By *logikē latreia*, however, St Paul meant not just spiritual but *rational* worship.] Do not be conformed to this world but be transformed by the renewal of your mind, that you may prove what is the will of God, what is good and acceptable and perfect.'[14]

The interrelation of mind, body and worship in the development of a theological instinct

Notice the distinctive way in which St Paul interrelated the renewing of the mind with the offering of the body as a living sacrifice and with rational worship. It is not with disembodied minds that we have to do here, but with the created unity of mind and body in which the human self is constituted. While stress may be laid upon the transformation

---

[14]   Rom 12.1-2.

of the mind and its assimilation to Christ, it is the whole human self that is involved. The transformation the apostle called for is so deep that it evokes out of the rational self an instinctive judgment about what is good, acceptable and perfect before God. That is to say, in the way I have been expressing it, we are called to be transformed in such a profound way that there develops within the depths of our rational being a *theological instinct* in virtue of which we are able to make true theological judgments. Without such a theological instinct we are little more than people with secular minds loosely clothed with a Christian profession. A genuine *theological instinct* of the kind St Paul has in view cannot be gained apart from a constant self-offering in rational worship to God, for it is through that inner relation between prayer and the transforming renewal of our minds, that we may be so tuned in to God that we fulfil our service in the rational way acceptable to him.

Tuning in to the mind of God incarnate in Jesus so that the gospel may transform society

In his scientific autobiography, Werner Heisenberg tells us that again and again when the mathematics of quantum theory proved to be as difficult as they were intricate, he would go away for three or four weeks at a time to play the piano or the violin in order, as he put it, to tune in to the 'Central Order' – the name he used in that context for God. When his whole being was tuned in to that Central Order he would come back to find his mathematical equations working out more easily. It is something similar that happens in theological activity. Through study of the holy scriptures, through meditation and prayer we tune in to the mind of God incarnate in Jesus Christ, the source of all rationality until our own minds, healed, renewed, and sanctified in him, are instinct with his truth – then it is that we may preach and teach the gospel, and find it transforming the lives and minds of people and the society to which they belong.

BRIEF GUIDE TO FURTHER READING

Since Torrance has written so much and in so many fields, there are numerous points in his writings where the content of the lectures can be profitably followed up. The following is a brief guide to the further reading which is closest to his lectures in subject matter, style and general accessibility. Much of it has already been referred to with original publication details and is also referenced in the general index to *Incarnation* and *Atonement* under 'Torrance T.F. (writings)'. Comments about books are intended for those new to theology and not yet familiar with the more technical theological and philosophical concepts used in some of the books.

It is fortuitous that the publication of these lectures coincides with the publication of *Participatio,* the online journal of the T.F. Torrance Theological Fellowship (TFT TF). The first issue of this, which is devoted to reminiscences and theological appreciation of T.F. Torrance and his legacy, appeared this summer. The journal and the TFT TF website are extremely useful online rfesources. The website includes various links and the first chapter of Elmer Colyer's *How to Read T.F. Torrance*, originally published by InterVarsity Press, Downers Grove 2001 (the first chapter is a valuable biography of 'TFT' and guide to his publications). Access to both the journal and the website is free: *http://www.tftorrance.org/journal.php*

The availability of several of Torrance's publications is currently a problem. Some are sadly out of print (o/p). Some are 'print on demand' (p/d) but very expensive. While books in general are increasingly becoming accessible online and while many of Torrance's publications are available in libraries or for sale online, it is fortunate that many of them (indicated in the lists below by an asterisk and 'W&S') have been republished by Wipf and Stock Publishers, Eugene, Oregon. Torrance's many articles in the *Scottish Journal of Theology* (characterised in general by a simpler style of writing and a wide variety of topics) can also be accessed online up to 2002 (quarterly from 1948) through the Cambridge University Press.

Writings closest in content and readability to the lectures

Books:

The Mediation of Christ (highly recommended as the single book closest in theme to the lectures – new edition 1992 with an extra chapter, 120 page paperback, o/p in UK, available from Helmers and Howard, Colorado Springs, USA).

Conflict and Agreement in the Church *W&S (vol. 1, problems of ecumenical dialogue, nature and mission of the church, oneness and disunity, Israel and the incarnation; vol. 2, the meaning of order, consecration and ordination, baptism and its meaning, a doctrine of the eucharist and eschatology – an excellent introduction to Torrance on the wide ranging topics of gospel, church, ministry and sacraments).

The School of Faith *W&S (Catechisms of the Reformed Church – Torrance's own very readable 100 page introduction recommended by him as preparatory reading for the dogmatics lectures).

Theology in Reconstruction *W&S (although in places the most challenging of the books in this section, the Prologue, the major sections 'Through Jesus Christ' & 'And in the Holy Spirit', and the Epilogue are particularly recommended, while the section 'Knowledge of God' and the chapter on 'The Roman Doctrine of Grace' are more technical and philosophical).

Articles or shorter books and sermons:

Chapter: 'John McLeod Campbell' in *Scottish Theology* (Torrance's penetrating analysis of McLeod Campbell's theology of incarnation and atonement and Christ's substitutionary bearing of sin understood in terms of the unbroken relation of the Son to the Father – 25 pages, T & T Clark, p/d).

Chapter: 'The Atonement – The Singularity of Christ and the Finality of the Cross: The Atonement and the Moral Order' in *Universalism and the Doctrine of Hell* (a lucid, trenchant account of the singularity and finality of Christ, the inseparability of incarnation and atonement in the person of Christ and the redemption of the moral order – 30 pages, o/p)

Appreciation: 'Hugh Ross Mackintosh: Theologian of the Cross' by T.F. Torrance in *The Person of Jesus Christ*, new edition, ed. T.F. Torrance, T & T Clark 2000 (94pp. pb.), first published in the *Scottish Bulletin of Evangelical Theology*, 1987, pp. 160-73 (Torrance recommended the book 'as one of the really great works in Christian Dogmatics'. His appreciation of his teacher H.R. Mackintosh and his theology is remarkable not only for the insight into the shaping of Torrance's own theology by him but for the way in which almost everything that Torrance says about Mackintosh and his dogmatics lectures could also be applied to his own – 24 pages, o/p).

A Passion for Christ (extracts compiled for pastors and lay people from the theology of the three Torrance brothers with the first two chapters by 'TF' and a concluding biography of the brothers, o/p in UK, available from Presbyterian Layman Publications, Lenoir, USA).

Preaching Christ Today (booklet – preaching the gospel in the context of a modern scientific culture, o/p).

When Christ Comes and Comes Again *W&S (sermons selected to help show the inter-relation between theology and evangelism).

The Apocalypse Today (sermons on the book of Revelation, now available from Lutterworth Press).

Books with more numerous scholarly-biblical references, using more theological and philosophical language

The Trinitarian Faith (an exposition of the Nicene Creed especially as understood by the great theologians of the early church – one of Torrance's major and most significant books, T & T Clark, p/d).

Royal Priesthood, 1993 edition (the priesthood of Christ and the church and a theology of ordained ministry in the context of ecumenical dialogue, with a wealth of biblical discussion and references, T & T Clark, p/d).

The Doctrine of Jesus Christ *W&S (Torrance's earliest course of lectures, aged 25, given at Auburn Seminary, New York – numerous overlaps, but also much material here not in the New College lectures).

Theology in Reconciliation *W&S (major chapters, some of them more technical, on ecumenism, baptism, the eucharist, the mind of Christ in worship, Athanasius and the church in an era of scientific change).

God and Rationality (one of the best introductions to Torrance's understanding of the nature of reason in faith, theology and science – readers unfamiliar at first with some of the language and concepts involved are encouraged just to keep reading! OUP, p/d).

Books with greater challenge and complexity of thought

The Christian Doctrine of God, One Being Three Persons (the last of the major works published in Torrance's lifetime – a book of considerable complexity and immense depth on the whole doctrine of God as three persons in one being, written despite its profundity with lucidity and eloquence; available from T & T Clark).

Theological Science (one of Torrance's most important books – lucid and fluent but a challenging read given its depth and extensive use of philosophical and theological concepts, o/p).

Biographies

T.F. Torrance, Alister McGrath, T & T Clark, Edinburgh 1999 (excellent biography with the focus on Torrance's intellectual development, an extended introduction to his thought on theology and science, and a complete bibliography of his writings which is immensely useful; likely to become p/d).

The Promise of Trinitarian Theology: Theologians in Dialogue with T.F. Torrance, ed. Elmer Colyer, Rowman and Littlefield, Lanham & Boulder & New York & Oxford 2001 (contains a biography of his brother by D.W. Torrance, together with several essays on aspects of his theology by leading exponents, together with a response from Torrance himself). Available from the Publisher.

As mentioned above, Colyer's *How to Read T.F. Torrance* (now available from W&S) also contains a biography, and *A Passion for Christ* contains a brief biography of all three Torrances.

Torrance's theology undoubtedly involves an element of strenuous intellectual exercise, but it was also for him worship and prayer, as seen in the brief prayer with which he opened each lecture and which always summed it up succinctly. Despite being incomplete two such prayers, taken down in a student's lecture notes, illustrate the point.

Lecture on the mediation of Christ:

> '*O God, our Father, we thank you that you have not left this world to tumble down into dust, but in Jesus Christ your Son you have raised it up . . . taken our cause . . . through Jesus Christ's birth, life, death, resurrection and endless life . . .*'

Lecture on the nature of scripture:

> '*Receive us, O God, as we bow our minds before you . . . give us your light, for only with your light can we understand your holy scriptures and through them come to know you . . .*'

GLOSSARY OF THEOLOGICAL TERMS

As most theological, philosophical or non-English terms are defined in the text, the glossary contains only the most important or those most useful for reference. The definitions given follow the meanings used in the text and where possible have been taken or adapted from the text. Asterisks after a word indicate it as a separate glossary entry.

Accommodation – associated with Calvin, the term refers to God's 'coming down' to meet us at our level and make himself known in human language and in ways the human mind can understand.

Active and passive obedience – active obedience refers to Jesus' active fulfilment of the will and law of God and his life of positive human righteousness, while passive obedience refers to his suffering the consequences and judgement of sin.

Adoptionism – the theory that Jesus was born human but adopted to be the Son of God.

Anabaptist (literally 're-baptising') – a term generally referring to movements of the 16th century which rejected infant baptism and advocated the baptism (or rebaptism) of believers able to decide for themselves.

Anamnēsis – in worship remembering the great events of salvation (such as the Lord's supper) in such as way that they are not just past events, but living and present events in which we participate (Gk, 'remembrance', calling to mind again, re-calling).

Anhypostasis **and** *enhypostasis* – *anhypostasis* refers to the fact that the humanity of Jesus had no independent reality of its own apart from the incarnation of the Son, while *enhypostasis* refers to the fact that the humanity of Jesus did have real personal being *in* the person of the Son as a result of the incarnation (Gk, *an-hypostasis*, literally 'not-person', i.e. with no personal being except in the Son; *en-hypostasis*, literally 'in-person' or 'person-in [the person of the Son]', i.e. having real personal existence *in* the person of the Son).

Apocalyptic – the new creation in Jesus Christ (hidden at present from human sight and beyond human understanding) as glimpsed fragmentarily in terms of the language and images drawn from the old creation (Gk, *apokalupsis*, apocalypse, the unveiling of Jesus Christ in the book of Revelation).

Apollinarianism (Apollinarius c.310 - c.390) – the teaching that in the incarnation the eternal Word took the place of the human spirit or mind (*nous*). This was condemned at Constantinople in 381 on the ground that it impaired the perfect humanity of Christ because it meant Jesus did not have a normal human mind. See Councils.

A posteriori – from experience, through empirical investigation (Lat, 'from after', hence following events, according to experience, i.e. obedient to reality). See *A priori*.

Apostle – an authorised representative ('*shaliach*'), someone specially trained, commissioned and authorised by Christ to represent him in word and deed as though he was himself there in person (from the Gk *apostellein*, Heb *shalach*, send). See Dogma.

A priori – from first principles, by reason alone, independent of experience (Lat, 'from the first', i.e. *before* events and in advance of empirical investigation). See *A posteriori*.

Arianism (Arius c.250 - c.336) – the belief, condemned at Nicaea in 325, that Jesus was not of the same being as God and therefore not God but the highest of creatures, created by God for a mediatory and creative role. See Councils.

Arminianism (Arminius 1560 - 1609) – a system of doctrine which attempts to hold together divine sovereignty and human free-will (as a capacity to choose), teaching that Christ died and obtained forgiveness for all, and that God's predestination is based on foreknowledge of human decision to accept or reject salvation, of whether an individual would freely accept or reject Christ and persevere in faith or fall away.

Atonement – the divine work of covering and putting away sin, thus creating 'at-one-ment' between God and man. The term is especially used of Christ's work of salvation which culminated in his death and divine-human self-offering and sacrifice on the cross. See also Incarnation, Christology, Soteriology, Justification, Reconciliation, Redemption.

(For Torrance, several elements are all involved in atonement, penal-substitution*, representation, expiation* and propitiation*, satisfaction*, active* and passive obedience* and forensic* elements, all held together in the action of God and man in the one person of Christ. For Torrance, however, the penal-substitutionary, satisfaction and forensic elements of the atonement need to be interpreted not in the 'detached and purely forensic categories of the Latin west', but in the 'New Testament terms of the intimacy of the Father-Son relation, in which the Son submits himself to the Father's judgement and is answered through the Father's good pleasure').

Catholic – universal, the term used to describe the identity, continuity and universality of the one church in scope and outreach throughout all the world and throughout all ages. In its earliest use 'catholic' referred to the universality of the gospel and of the church in its universal mission as opposed to the heretical sects who limited* the atonement and rejected its universal range.

Christian Dogmatics – the church's orderly understanding of scripture and articulation of doctrine in the light of Christ, and their coherence in him.

Christology – the doctrine of Christ, particularly of the person of Christ, truly God and truly man, one person in two natures. For Torrance, christology and soteriology are inseparable as it is the person of Christ atoning who makes atonement.* See Councils and Soteriology.

Communicatio idiomatum – communication of properties, used for the mutual transference of qualities between the divine and human natures of Christ, the fact that the properties special to the divine or human nature may be applied to or predicated to the other through their sharing in the one person of Christ (Lat, *communicatio* communication, *idiomata* properties, from the Gk, *idioma* special property, i.e. one 'peculiar to' the deity or humanity of Christ).

Contingency – the fact that the universe is not necessary and does not have to be the way it is, but is 'contingent' on the freedom of God to create it and might have been otherwise.

Councils – the great ecumenical councils were formal gatherings of bishops of the whole church assembled together to take key decisions on doctrine and creed. The most important councils, listed together with their central affirmations, were:

(i) *The Council of Nicaea* in AD 325 affirmed that Jesus Christ is truly God, of one being (*homoousios**) with the Father, in an affirmation of faith against the Arians.*

(ii) *The Council of Constantinople* in AD 381 affirmed that Jesus Christ was perfectly man, against the Apollinarians* whose teaching impaired the perfect humanity of Christ.

(iii) *The Council of Ephesus* in AD 431 affirmed that Jesus Christ is one person, against the Nestorians* who divided Christ into two persons.

(iv) *The Council of Chalcedon* in AD 451 affirmed that in Jesus Christ there are two distinct natures in one person, and that in the one person of Christ they were hypostatically united 'unconfusedly, unchangeably, indivisibly, inseparably' ('without confusion, change, division or separation'). The first two adverbs specifically targeted the Eutychians* and Monophysites*, while the last two targeted the Nestorians*. See Hypostatic Union, *Hypostasis*.

(v) *The Council of Constantinople* in AD 680 asserted that Jesus Christ possessed a human will as well as a divine will, against the Monothelites* who asserted that in Jesus Christ there was only one single will.

Covenant – an unconditional agreement between two parties (as opposed to a 'contract', an agreement based on mutual conditions), used in the bible principally for the unconditional promise of God to his people, 'I will be your God and you shall be my people', which was fulfilled from both sides in the 'new covenant' in Jesus.

Creatio ex nihilo – 'creation out of nothing'.

Day of atonement – the pivotal event in the Old Testament calendar, when once a year and wearing the garments engraven with the names of the 12 tribes of Israel, the high priest entered the 'holy of holies' in the temple with the blood of sacrifice, to confess the sins of Israel, to renew the covenant and receive forgiveness for Israel.

Decalogue – the 'ten commandments' (from *deka logoi*, 'ten words', the Greek translation of the Hebrew equivalent).

Deism – the view of God as the creator who, having brought the universe into being, leaves it to run according to natural law.

Docetism – the theory that while Jesus was God, he only *appeared* to be human (from the Gk, *dokeō*, to seem or appear). Generally, any theory which denies the full reality of Jesus' humanity.

Dogma – the church's authoritative formulation of doctrine in accordance with apostolic teaching. See Apostle.

Dogmatics – see Christian Dogmatics.

Doxological – giving praise or glory to God (from the Gk, *doxos*, glory).

Dualism – any theory or way of thinking which so rigidly separates entities which should be seen in relation to each other (e.g. God and creation, body and soul), that they are held artificially apart and can no longer be properly understood in relation.

Dyophysitism – the view that after the incarnation Christ had two natures, divine and human (from the Gk, '*duo*' two, and '*physis*' nature).

Ebionism – the view that Jesus was not God but an ordinary man, adopted to become Son of God.

Enhypostasis – see *Anhypostasis* and *enhypostasis*.

Exegesis – the interpretation of biblical texts.

Epistemology – the philosophy of knowledge, its nature, methods, sources and limits.

Eschatology – the doctrine of 'the last things' or end of history, 'the last days', regarded in the New Testament as having already begun with the coming of Christ and his resurrection. The certainty of the resurrection, as the first fruits of a new creation already begun, means that Christ's second coming is thought of as imminent, not simply in terms of time, but in terms of his nearness through the Spirit continually breaking into history and imparting an urgent orientation to Christian faith. Both *eschatology* (or *eschatological*, from the Gk, *eschata*, the last things) and *teleology* (or *teleological*, from the Gk, *telos*, end) refer to events at the end of time and history, but in eschatology the emphasis is on the invasion of God into history throwing it into crisis and creating the last events, while in teleology the emphasis is on history reaching forward to its goal at the end of time. See Teleology.

Eschaton – the end, the last word and final act of God in Christ. The eschaton is the end of history, but not an event beyond it but within it, which means its transformation into the new creation.

Eutychianism (Eutyches c.378 - 454) – a doctrine of 'two natures before the incarnation and one after'. This was condemned at Chalcedon in 451 on the ground that it implied Christ's human nature was no longer the same as ours but had been swallowed up by his divinity. See Councils.

Existentialism – the philosophy which emphasises personal *existence*, courageous decision and living in the present moment. (*Existential* – concerning existence, to do with the nature of human life, or affecting the roots of human existence).

Expiation – appeasement, making propitious, the effecting of reconciliation. See Propitiation.

Forensic – legal or related to law. Forensic is the word commonly used to denote the aspect of justification* (or atonement*) involving law and metaphors of the law court, righteousness in terms of the law and the fulfilment of its requirements. The root meaning of the English 'forensic' (Lat, *forensis*, public) is 'related to or involving a court of law'.

Gnosticism – the belief in a secret, higher spiritual realm of knowledge (Gk, *gnōsis*) to which an enlightened person could gradually attain in order to reach God and be liberated from the material realm.

Hermeneutics – the art or science of interpretation, especially of scripture.

Homoousion – the term used of Jesus' identity of being with the Father and adopted at the Council of Nicaea in 325 (from the Gk, *homo-ousios*, 'same-being' or 'of one being' with…'). See Councils.

Hypostatic union – the doctrine, first formally adopted at Chalcedon in 451, of the union of God and man in Jesus, two distinct natures, divine and human, in one person (*hypostasis*). See Councils, *Hypostasis*.

Hypostasis – a term with two distinct meanings, originally objective or substantial reality (from the Gk, *hypo-stasis*, standing under; the Lat, *sub-stantia*, substance) but then used to denote the unique reality or 'personal subsistence' of the three 'persons' in the one being of God. From the time of the Council of Constantinople in 381, the formula 'three *hypostaseis* in one *ousia*', 'three persons in one being', became the orthodox doctrine of the Trinity. See Councils, Hypostatic Union.

Idealism – a philosophy of knowledge which generally emphasises ideas and the contribution of the human mind to knowledge. In a stronger form, idealism emphasises the 'necessary truths of reason' at the expense of the 'accidental truths of history'.

Incarnation – God's becoming man (from the Lat, *in carne*, in flesh), when the eternal Son of God became true man in one person. Understood in the light of the patristic emphasis on Jesus Christ assuming 'fallen flesh' in the incarnation (but without sin), the union of God and man in the incarnation (hypostatic union*) can be seen as the beginning of the atonement brought to a climax on the cross. See Christology, Councils, Atonement.

Justification – atonement* as the act of God declaring and making humanity righteous in Christ through the incarnate life, death and resurrection of Jesus (Gk, *dikaiōma*, decree of righteousness, a declaration of something or someone to be *dikaios*, just, right; *dikaiōsis*, the act of pronouncing righteous, justification, acquittal).

Kenotic theory – the theory (in various forms), particularly in Lutheran theology, that when Christ became man he *emptied* himself in some sense of his divinity or of some of his divine characteristics, such as omniscience and omnipotence in order to become human with limited knowledge and power (from the Gk, *kenoō*, empty, Phil 2.7; *kenōsis*, emptying).

Kērygma – the New Testament proclamation of Christ (from the Gk, *kērygma*, proclamation, preaching), in which the apostolic proclamation, that Jesus is the Christ, was inseparable both from what Jesus was and did in history and from his own self-proclamation in the apostolic *kērygma* by the Spirit.

Koinōnia – primarily, communion and participation through the Spirit in the mystery (*mystērion*) of Christ, the union of God and man in him; secondarily, the fellowship which is the church, the communion which exists between members of the body of Christ on the ground of their participation in him (Gk, communion, fellowship).

Limited atonement – the belief that Jesus did not die for all humanity but only for the elect.

Marcionism (Marcion died c.160) – the belief in the incompatibility of the Old Testament God, the creator God of law and judgement, with the New Testament God of love and grace. For Marcion, the Demiurge (Gk, *dēmiourgos*, 'craftsman'), the God of creation and the Old Testament is an inferior God, different from the supreme God of redemption and the New Testament.

Metanoia – literally 'change of mind', Gk *meta-noia*, translated 'repentance', not simply or primarily repentance for sin but a deeper and more radical change in one's way of thinking (which includes sorrow for sin), reorientating one's life and being in a whole new direction.

Mishna – Heb, 'instruction'. Traditionally dated in its compilation to the early centuries of the Christian era, the Mishna is the collection of

Jewish oral law and teaching, regarded as given to Moses at the same time as the written law and accepted along with the Talmud (a wider compilation containing the Mishna and commentary on it) as authoritative in Judaism, and secondary only to the scriptures in influence and importance.

Monophysitism – the view that there is only one nature (divine) in Christ not two (divine and human), [from the Gk, *'monos'* one, and *'physis'* nature]. Condemned at Chalcedon in 451. See Councils.

Monothelitism – the view that Christ only has 'one will' (a divine will) and not two (a divine and a human), [from the Gk, *monos* one, and *thelein* 'to will']. Condemned at Constantinople in 680. See Councils.

Moral influence theory – a theory of the atonement,* associated mostly with Abelard (1079-1142), which emphasises the power of the cross, as a demonstration of the love of God, to evoke the response of repentance and love.

Nestorianism – the theory of a conjunction of two persons, divine and human, in Christ. Although Nestorius (died c.451) did affirm the oneness of Christ, his teaching of a conjunction of divine and human in Christ and a union of will, rather than a hypostatic union* of divine and human in one person, was seen as compromising the unity of Christ and was condemned at the Council of Ephesus in 431. See Councils.

Objective – based on the object, true to reality, adjective used to describe the faithfulness of disciplines or human thought to the nature of reality. See Subjective.

Ontological – to do with 'being', involving the nature of things in their being or inner reality and essence, hence real, essential, grounded on reality. An ontological relation is a connection or relation of real *being* to something, one grounded on being and reality, or simply 'real'.

Ontology – literally, the science or study of 'being' (from the Gk, *ōn, onta*, being, what is, reality).

Pascal (lamb/sacrifice) – passover (lamb/sacrifice), adjective from *pascha*, Gk for 'passover', (Heb *pesach*).

Passive obedience – see Active and passive obedience of Jesus.

Passover – one of the two most important religious feasts or events in the Old Testament, celebrating the 'passover' and exodus, i.e. the evening sacrifice and eating of the 'passover lamb', the angel of death's 'passing over' the houses of Israel and their deliverance by morning out of slavery in Egypt (Exodus chapter 12).

Patripassianism – the doctrine that the Father suffered on the cross as well as the Son (from the Lat, *pater*, father, and *patior/passus*, suffer).

Patristic theology – the theology of the early church 'fathers' (from the Gk, *patēr*, father).

Parousia – normally used of the 'second coming', the final or last advent of Christ, *parousia* more accurately refers to the first and second advents as one whole coming-and-real-presence of Christ in the flesh (from the Gk, *parousia*, 'presence, coming').

Pelagianism (Pelagius c.354 - 415) – the belief in human capacity and freedom to co-operate with divine grace for salvation.

Penal substitution theory – the belief that in his death Christ suffered the penalty for our breaking of the law and died as a substitute in our place (*penal*, involving penalty or legal punishment, from the Lat, *poena*, punishment, penalty, compensation). See Atonement.

Pentateuch – the first five books of the bible, the so-called 'five books of Moses', Genesis to Deuteronomy (from the Gk, *pente*, five).

Perichōresis – the mutual indwelling and communion of persons, Father, Son and Holy Spirit, in the one God. See Trinity.

Predestination – at root the priority of the love of God, the fact that the election or choice by God of humanity is prior to their choice of him. For Torrance, election and predestination is to be thought of not primarily in terms of individuals, but first and foremost in terms of Christ; Jesus Christ in time is identical with and *is* the eternal election of God in eternity moving into time and becoming flesh. He is the elect one, the chosen one in whom the Father is well pleased, so that the election of people 'in Christ' is the only proper starting point for understanding their election (one that leads neither to limited atonement* or to universalism*).

Propitiation – appeasement, rendering favourable, atonement by sacrifice, expiation. *Expiation** refers to the atoning act through which reconciliation is effected, while *propitiation* refers to the personal healing and personal reconciliation effected. Propitiation in the bible is initiated and carried through by God, both from the side of God toward man and from the side of man toward God. (Gk, *hilastērion* and *hilasmos*, both translated 'expiation' RSV and 'propitiation' KJV).

Ransom theory – associated with the *Christus victor* concept (Lat, Christ the victor), ransom theory saw the atonement* and death of Christ as a ransom paid to liberate humanity. In the eyes of Origen and many of the Latin Fathers, the ransom was paid to the devil who held humanity captive because of sin.

Recapitulation – the theory associated with Irenaeus (c.130 - c.200) that Jesus in his human life summed up the human race and its history. He undid its sin and disobedience by his obedience and gathered it up as a new humanity under his headship as the new Adam.

Reconciliation – atonement* as the personal reconciling of God and humanity in the person of Christ through the wonderful exchange he worked out in his divine and human life, exchanging our sin for his righteousness, our corruption and death for his life.

Redemption – literally 'buying back', the reclaiming of creation by God: atonement* seen in its far reaching effects as the final liberation of physical existence out of death and decay to become the resurrection body of the new creation.

Reformed – name used for the branch of the Reformation which, in distinction to the Lutheran, was generally Calvinist in doctrine and organisation.

Repentance – change of thinking. The root meaning of repentance (from the Gk, *meta-noia*, 'change of mind') is the radical change of mind required by the gospel, resulting in a complete reorientation of life. See *Metanoia*.

Sabellianism – a form of *modalism*, that Father, Son and Spirit are not eternal persons in God himself but *modes* or ways that he successively reveals himself.

Satisfaction theory – associated with Anselm of Canterbury (c.1033 - 1109), the theory interprets the incarnation* and atonement* in terms of satisfaction, as God becoming man in order to pay the satisfaction due by man to God.

Septuagint – the Greek translation of the Old Testament, also known as the LXX, the Roman numerals for 70 since it was translated by '70 scholars' (the actual number was 72).

Socinianism (Socinus 1539 - 1564) – a unitarian* theology which teaches that Christ is not divine, but a mortal man begotten through the Holy Spirit and then re-begotten in the resurrection to be immortal. Though not an atoning sacrifice, his death was accepted as a ground for forgiveness and was important for its revelation of the love of God.

Soteriology – the doctrine of salvation, especially of the work of Christ (Gk, *sōtēr*, saviour). The doctrine of Christ is traditionally thought of in terms of his 'person' (christology) and his 'work' (soteriology) but each is only to be understood in the light of the other. See Christology, Incarnation, Atonement, Justification, Reconciliation, Redemption.

Subjective – term used for thought based on human opinion, on the views of the thinker or human subject, and not based on the object. See Objective.

Suffering servant – the figure in the prophecies of Isaiah (particularly in chapter 53) who would suffer for the sins of the people, the one for the many in order to justify the many.

Teleology – the doctrine of the end of history or the interpretation of history in terms of its end, purpose or goal (from the Gk, *telos*, end). See Eschatology.

Torah – Heb, law, direction or instruction in the law, used of the priests giving '*torah*' or instruction in the law of God and commonly used of the whole Mosaic law embodied in the Pentateuch.*

Total depravity – the doctrine of the constitutive change introduced by sin into the whole being of humanity, such that every part of the human person, body, mind and soul is affected.

Trinity – the central doctrine of the Christian faith that the one God exists in three eternal persons. See *Hypostasis*.

Triplex munus – term used for the 'threefold office' of Christ as 'king, priest and prophet' (Lat, *triplex munus*, threefold office – *duplex munus*, twofold office, king and priest-prophet).

Unitarianism – the belief in the unity and unipersonality of God which denies the doctrines of the Trinity* and the divinity of Christ.

Universalism – the belief in universal salvation, that in the end all will be saved.

Vicarious humanity of Christ – term referring to the fact that Christ in his humanity stands in our place and represents us, so that what is true of his humanity is true of us, and that what he did in his (our) humanity is ours (Lat, *vicarius*, 'acting in the place of another').

GENERAL INDEX

A

Aaron 19, 20, 63, 72, 74, 98, 271
Abel 84
Abelard 54, 58
Abraham 10, 12, 28, 74, 203, 276, 344
Adam 126, 217, 343
adoption 229
anamnēsis 92
Anglican theology 55
anhypostasia 54, 76, 218, 253
Anselm 57, 123
apocalypse 411
apocalyptic 257, 286
  meaning of 247
Apocrypha 204
Apollinarianism 70, 439
apolutrōsis. See also lutron
apostle/apostolic, meaning of 318, 399
apostles 352, 357
Apostles' Creed 341, 358
apostolate 315f., 430
  nature of 329
apostolic gospel 329, 331. *See also* Gospels and Epistles
apostolic succession 393, 398
Aquinas 57, 59
ark 266
Arminianism 187
ascension 265, 281. *See also* Christ: ascension of
  and space and time 256, 282, 287
  time for repentance 434-5
Athanasius 126, 161, 235, 312, 445
Athenagoras 239
atonement 1ff.
  and incarnation 182
  and justification 97-136
  and satisfaction 215
  as propitiation 22
  as reconciliation 137-70
  as redemption 171-200

INDEX OF BIBLICAL REFERENCES